CADOGANguides

THE DORDOGNE, LOT & BORDEAUX

'Intensely rural, a land of small traditional family farms, overflowing with the good things of the earth, southwest France serves hearty dishes so delicious that eating and drinking are two of the most compelling reasons to visit.'

Dana Facaros & Michael Pauls

About the Guide

The **full-colour introduction** gives the authors' overview of the region, together with suggested **itineraries** and a regional **'where to go' map** and **feature** to help you plan your trip.

Illuminating and entertaining **cultural chapters** on local history, food and drink, and other topics give you a rich flavour of the region.

Travel covers the basics of **getting there** and **getting around**, plus entry formalities. The **Practical A–Z** deals with all the **essential information** and **contact details** that you may need, including a section for disabled travellers.

The **regional chapters** are arranged in a loose touring order, with plenty of public transport and driving information. The authors' top **'Don't Miss'** (1) **sights** are highlighted at the start of each chapter and there is also a useful **colour touring atlas** at the back that covers the whole region.

A **language and pronunciation guide**, a **glossary** of cultural terms and a comprehensive **index** can be found at the end of the book.

Although everything we list in this guide is **personally recommended**, our authors inevitably have their own favourite places to eat and stay. Whenever you see this **Authors' Choice** ★ icon beside a listing, you will know that it is a little bit out of the ordinary.

Hotel Price Guide

Luxury	€€€€€	€230 and above
Expensive	€€€€	€150–230
Moderate	€€€	€100–150
Inexpensive	€€	€60–100
Budget	€	€60 and under

Restaurant Price Guide

Very expensive	over €60
Expensive	€30–60
Moderate	€15–30
Inexpensive	under €15

About the Authors

Dana Facaros and Michael Pauls have lived all over Europe and written more than 40 books for Cadogan Guides. They currently live in an old presbytère near the Lot.

6th Edition Published 2007

INTRODUCING THE DORDOGNE, LOT & BORDEAUX

01

above: Château de Beynac, p.173; Place du Marché, Sarlat, p.162

If southwest France could croon a tune, it would have to be that old Inkspots' hit, 'I don't want to set the world on fire, I just want to be the one you love.' Endowed with the soft, gentle beauty of vine-clad river valleys and oak forests and chestnut, the region presents no overwhelming itinerary of high cultural shrines that demand your awe and homage. But, like all true lovers, it magically opens your eyes to the grace and charm in little things, in everyday life. Of course the southwest has its place in the macrocosm as well – there are a thousand proud châteaux and as many medieval villages, the world's foremost wine region and its very first art, the long secret cave paintings of Lascaux, Font-de-Gaume, Pech-Merle and a score of others.

In general, apart from Bordeaux and Toulouse, nothing much has happened here since the Hundred Years' War. Out of history, out of mind, this region retains something that most of the industrialized world has lost in its mad rush towards modernity. If you talk to an old farmer, he may mention *eime*, the Occitan word for soul similar to the Catalan *seny* – the intangible spirit of the nation, its good sense, its spirit of measure and moderation. The southwest may be the land of mystical troubadours, but it is also the land of France's most reasonable thinkers, of Montaigne, Fénelon, La Boétie and Montesquieu.

For if nothing else, southwest France is a fine place to hear yourself think. The great wine helps, of course, and the delicious regional cuisine puts your digestion in harmony with the universe. The pace of life is slow, and there's time to contemplate that old

above: Bucolic scene near Rocamadour, p.143

opposite: Relaxing spot near Bergerac, p.183

stone farm on the next hill, blending into the environment naturally and effortlessly. The wall by your chair is covered with eglantine and honeysuckle; the fragrance, the warm sun and the blackbird trilling away just beyond the garden make you delightfully drowsy, and once again all plans and outings are postponed. You can't put it off forever, of course – there's a full whack of sights and surprises for you in this book – but the true purpose of this corner of the world is in teaching us all to pause and regain a bit of perspective. Or, as in the words of Montaigne:

The value of life lies, not in the length of days, but in the use we make of them; a man may live long, yet live very little. Satisfaction in life depends not on the number of your years, but on your will.

Where to Go

This book covers the Aquitaine Basin, a great bay in the ocean millions of years ago, now divided into the *départements* of the Dordogne, Gironde, Lot, Lot-et-Garonne and Tarn-et-Garonne. This is river country *par excellence* – once the Dordogne, Lot, Tarn and Garonne plunge from their sources in the Pyrenees and Massif Central and carve out their steep gorges, we pick them up where they put on their watery brakes to weave gracefully down to the broad estuary of the Gironde and the Atlantic.

If you're driving down from Britain, chances are you'll pass through the verdant valleys and woodlands of the northern *département* of the Dordogne, or **Northern Périgord**, a lush land dotted with fairytale castles and domed Romanesque churches, culminating in the astonishing St-Front in the handsome town of Périgueux. You then delve into the misty past along the enchanting **Vézère Valley**, still within the Dordogne, with caves and shelters that hold the densest concentration of prehistoric art on the planet, including the sublime Grotte de Lascaux.

Next comes the **valley of the Dordogne river**, first descending from Argentat to Domme, passing by way of some of the busiest tourist attractions in the southwest – the immense chasm and underground river at Padirac, the medieval pilgrimage town of Rocamadour, and the beautiful Renaissance town of Sarlat. Then you follow the river past the first vineyards, from Bergerac (also home to the national tobacco museum) to lovely St-Emilion and Montaigne's château, ending up at the mighty citadel of Blaye.

Bordeaux with all its 18th-century frippery and fine museums is followed by its *département*, the **Gironde**. This is home not only to France's most celebrated vineyards and its rarefied wine châteaux (Mouton, Lafite, Yquem, Margaux), but also to long beaches of silver sand, deep pine forests, the busy bird sanctuary at Le Teich, the enormous sand dune at Pilat and the grand old seaside resort and oyster haven of Arcachon.

above: Medieval carving, Figeac, p.297; Château Périgord, pp.77–112; Vineyards, Lot, pp.285–342

right: Oyster shack, Arcachon, p.276

opposite: Albas and the Lot river, p.330

Backtracking east, you head down the wild limestone plateaux and the river Lot in the region of **Quercy**, wiggling dramatically under cliffs, castles, picturesque old villages such as St-Cirq-Lapopie and the medieval city of Cahors, with its landmark triple-towered Pont Valentré. The Lot flows next into the *département* **Lot-et-Garonne**, a rolling land of orchards dotted with charming medieval new towns, or *bastides*, as well as French prune capitals Villeneuve and Agen and more picture-postcard castles at Bonaguil, Duras and Nérac.

South from here is rural **Tarn-et-Garonne**, a *département* decorated with hundreds of dovecotes and the delightful brick city of Montauban, not to mention the great abbey of Moissac, one of Romanesque Europe's finest works. Last of all comes **Toulouse**, the dynamic, cosmopolitan 'Ville Rose' of the southwest, boasting a clutch of medieval masterpieces, worthy museums, charming brick streets and squares, and the best shopping and nightlife in this book.

Chapter Divisions

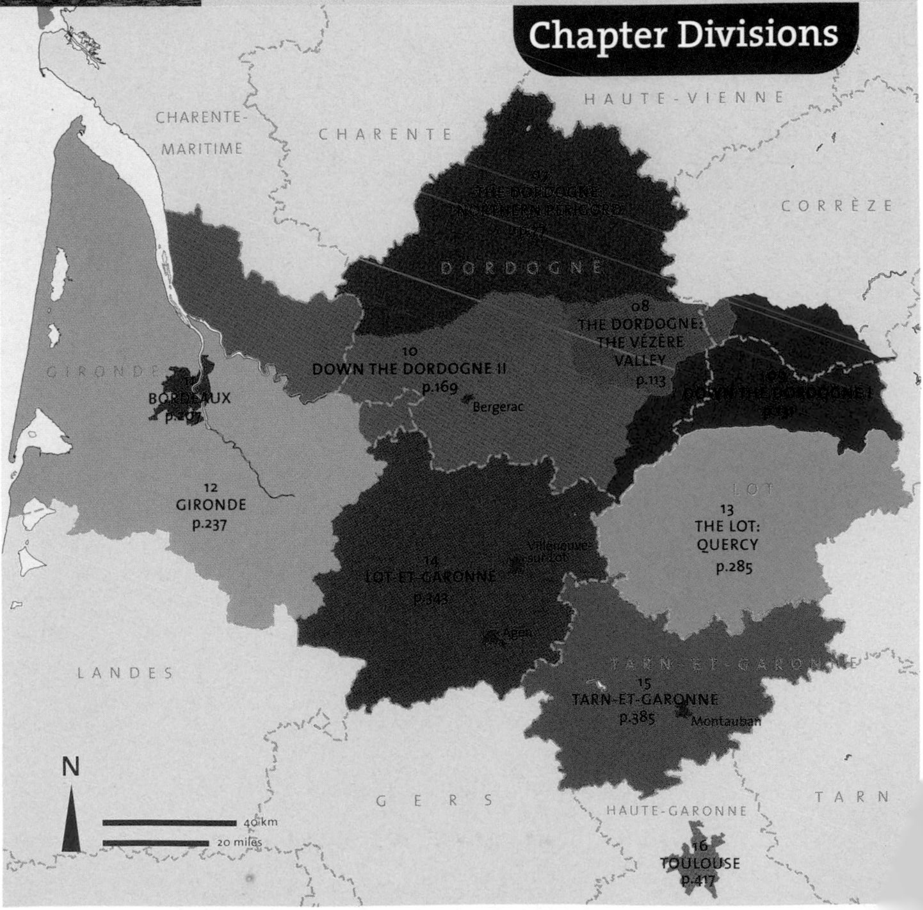

Watery Delights

There are many *départements* in France named after their rivers, but the Dordogne, Lot and Tarn and their tributaries are among the country's most beautiful, flowing serenely past medieval villages and castles and forests before merging with one of France's four great rivers, the 'Laughing' Garonne, and the Atlantic Ocean. In the old days these blue ribbons were the *autoroutes* of the region; in many places locks are now being built and other obstacles removed, creating new possibilities for anyone hankering to play Huck Finn *à la française*, in the slow lane. The Atlantic shore of the area, the northern Côte d'Argent, has some choice bits as well: the magnificent lighthouse of Cordouan, Arcachon Bay with its oysters, and the Moby Dick of sand dunes, the Dune de Pilat.

above: The Lot river valley near Albas, p.330

right: Le Roque-Gageac, p.170

Green Spaces

Many people who come here love the open spaces best of all – few places in Europe offer such beguiling landscapes with so few people to fill them. There are the moments of drama, for sure – the lofty cliffs and limestone plateaux along the Dordogne and Lot rivers, and the gorges of the Aveyron – but much of this region is rolling and green, peaceful and bucolic. In some of the most luscious corners, such as the Parc Naturel Régional du Périgord-Limousin, the Limargue, the Boriane, the *bastide* country and the northern Tarn-et-Garonne, you can often drive through mile upon mile of oak forests, fields of sunflowers or seas of vines without seeing a soul – beyond a hawk circling high above.

City Lights

It's not all sunflowers and duck fat – two of France's most dynamic cities, Toulouse and Bordeaux, are edgy troves of urbanity. Toulouse, *la Ville Rose*, once the capital of powerful counts who ruled much of the southwest, is the home of Airbus, hi-tech firms, a major university and some splendid mansions and excellent museums. Its rival, aristocratic Bordeaux, medieval capital of the Duchy of Aquitaine, has so preserved its 18th-century appearance that it's been used as a film set, masquerading as Paris. After a few decades of doldrums, it's been cleaned up and is back on track in a big way, as symbolized by its swish new trams.

from top: Sunflowers, Padirac, pp.141–3; Tram, Bordeaux, pp.207–36; Pont Neuf, Toulouse, p.439; Quartier St-Pierre, Bordeaux, pp.225–6

left: Galiot's giant pigeonnier, Lot, p.294

To Market, to Market

Outdoor markets in the southwest are a barrage of colour, scent and sound, but they're also social occasions, bringing together rural residents for their weekly chinwag. Many have been going strong on the same day of the week in the same place since the Middle Ages, when feudal lords granted towns their much sought after market privilege. Some are dedicated to food and wine, others are *biologique* (organic) farmers' markets, others are full-blown *foires* where you can stock up not only food but everything from double-glazing to underpants. Others, still more specialized, only happen in autumn and winter, such as the truffle market of Lalbenque or the *marchés au gras* ('Fat Markets' – fattened ducks and geese) of Périgueux.

clockwise from top: Pastries, Bordeaux, pp.207–36; Prayssac market, p.330; Antiques market, Domme, pp.165–7

opposite: Wine shop, St- Emilion, pp.193–9; Wine Château, Gironde, pp.237–84

Red Wine Country

Thank goodness red wine is good for you – southwest France makes more of the stuff than any place on Earth. In spite of New World competition, Bordeaux is still the world's biggest and most prestigious wine region, and it's not about to relinquish its crown without a fight – 2005 has already been heralded as the vintage of a lifetime. Yet the fabulous and daunting mosaic of Bordeaux appellations is only part of the tale: follow the wine roads upriver to Bergerac, Cahors, Buzet, Pécharmant and others, all of which would be more famous if they weren't overshadowed by their kingly neighbour and which are just waiting to be discovered – at a fraction of the price of a Bordeaux *grand cru*.

clockwise from top: Wine festival fireworks, Bordeaux, p.50; Musical Celebration, Lot-et-Garonne, pp.344–84; Gay Pride, Toulouse, pp.417–50

Let's Dance

Pound that accordion, blast that sax, and tango the night away – the French love to party, and know how to throw a shindig with just enough organization to make for a great time. A typical village fête in the southwest means three days of funfair rides, markets (including the ever-popular *vide greniers* or 'attic emptiers' – like car-boot sales), competitions and exhibitions (bicycle races, boules, art exhibitions), and music and dance, culminating in fireworks. And that's just the start – high-profile events include the Bordeaux wine festival, the Médoc marathon and Jazz Montauban, and there are music festivals of all kinds, flower shows, nocturnal street markets, outdoor cinema, bonfires and folklore celebrations. In fact, in July and August it's hard to stay in – there's something going on every day of the week.

above: St-Sernin, Toulouse, pp.432-4

below: Rocamadour, pp.143–8; Pont Valentré, Cahors p.319

Itineraries

The Best of the Middle Ages in Fifteen Days

Days 1–2 Begin in Toulouse, which had its own school of Romanesque sculpture; visit its core medieval neighbourhoods and churches – Les Jacobins, St-Sernin, St-Etienne and the art in the Musée des Augustins.

Day 3 Drive an hour north to Moissac to visit the sublime portal and cloister of its abbey. Then head up the Garonne to visit Le Mas-d'Agenais, a lovely *village perché*, La Réole, with the oldest Hôtel de Ville in France, and medieval St-Macaire.

Days 4–5 Stop in Rions, the little 'Carcassonne of the Gironde', and check in at Bordeaux. Visit (among other things) St Michel, the Grande Cloche gate, the cathedral, and St-Seurin.

Day 6 Drive west into Entre-Deux-Mers to Créon and the ruined Abbaye de la Sauve-Majeure, then carry on to Blasimon to see its church and rare fortified medieval mill, and to beautiful St-Emilion, famous for its monumental Eglise Monolithe.

Days 7–8 Head up the Dordogne to Beaumont-de-Périgord, St-Avit and Cadouin, all with lovely old churches (the latter abbey is home to 'Christ's turban'). Then drive north to Périgueux to see its fabled multi-domed cathedral of St-Front and the pretty medieval objects in the Musée du Périgord. Make a jaunt north to see the fairytale castle at Jumilhac.

Days 9–10 Return to the Dordogne river to visit the mighty castles at Beynac and Castelnaud (home to the museum of medieval warfare), the pretty village of La Roque-Gageac and the lofty *bastide* of Domme, and Ste-Marie at Souilliac, famed for its delightful Romanesque reliefs.

Day 11 Carry on east to Carennac, Martel ('City of Seven Towers') and the Château de Castelnau, one of the greatest military castles of France, then proceed to Beaulieu-sur-Dordogne with its excellent *Last Judgement*.

Day 12 Head south to Rocamadour via the enchanting villages of Loubressac and Autoire. In the late afternoon, drive down to Figeac.

Day 13 Explore Figeac's cosy medieval lanes, then drive down the enchanting Célé river, taking in picturesque Espagnac-Ste-Eulalie, the abbey of Marcilhac-sur-Célé, and St-Cirq-Lapopie hanging from a cliff.

Day 14 Hop just west to Cahors to see the famous medieval bridge, the Pont Valentré, the cathedral and the old quarter. After lunch, venture southeast to the pretty medieval villages in the Gorges of the Aveyron.

Day 15 Head down to Montauban, the prototype *bastide*, then return to Toulouse.

A Week's Exploring with Kids

Day 1 Visit the spaceships in the Cité de l'Espace in Toulouse, then take the *autoroute* north to Rocamadour.

Day 2 Ride the gondolas in the magical Gouffre de Padirac in the morning; after lunch, watch eagles soar over Rocamadour's Rocher des Aigles.

Day 3 Meet the macaques and Barbary apes in the Forêt des Singes; in the afternoon, continue the animal theme by visiting the wolves and other European species at Gramat's Parc Animalier.

Day 4 Kayak down the Dordogne.

Day 5 Drive down to Le Bugue to watch the artisans at work in the Village du Bournat, then admire the huge sturgeon in the Aquarium du Périgord Noir.

Day 6 Drive east to Arcachon for a day of scrambling along the beach and up and down the Dune du Pilat.

Day 7 For a grand finale, spend a day at southwest France's biggest amusement park, Agen's Parc Walibi.

A Palaeolithic Week in the Dordogne and Lot

Before you come, be sure to book tours to those caves that only take limited number of visitors (see the websites in the revelevant chapters).

Day 1 Explore Bordeaux's Musée d'Aquitaine then drive east to Montignac.

Day 2 In Montignac, take the tour of Lascaux II, then see the Gisement du Regourdou (site of a Neanderthal bear cult) just above it and the Centre of Prehistoric Art at Le Thot.

Day 3 Drive down the Vézère river to Rouffignac and take the train into the Cave of a Hundred Mammoths. Downriver, take a look at some places where people lived in Palaeolothic times – Castel-Merle, Roque St-Christophe and La Madeleine.

Days 4–5 Spend the day in Les Eyzies-de-Tayac, visiting the National Museum of Prehistoric Art, Abri Pataud, Grotte de Font-de-Gaume and Grotte des Combarelles, Abri du Cap Blanc and Gisement Laugerie Haute. On the last afternoon, drive southeast to Gordon.

Day 6 Head into the Grottes de Cougnac, then continue southeast to Cabrerets or St-Cirq-Lapopie.

Day 7 Admire the spotted horses in the Grotte du Pech-Merle, then return to Bordeaux.

from the top: Peregrine falcon, Château Les Milandes, pp.173–4; Dune du Pilat, p.278; Prehistoric art, Lascaux, pp.118–19

CONTENTS

01 Introducing the Dordogne and the Lot 1
Where to Go 6
Itineraries 15

02 History 19

03 Topics 31
Microtourism 32
Bertran de Born 33
Market Values 35
Dances with Bears 36
Art Begins Here 38
Goose Lore and Livers 40
The Architecture of Springtime 41

04 Food and Drink 45
The Cuisine of the Southwest 46
Drinks 49
Restaurant Basic 52
Menu Decoder 52

05 Planning 57
When to Go 58
Tourist Information 59
Embassies and Consulates 60
Entry Formalities 60
Disabled Travellers 60
Insurance and EHIC Cards 61
Money 61
Getting There 62
By Air 62
By Train 63
By Coach 64
By Car 64
Getting Around 64
By Air 64
By Train 65
By Bus 66
By Car 66
By Bicycle 66
By *Roulotte* 67
On Foot 67
Where to Stay 67
Specialist Tour and Self-Catering Operators 70

06 Practical A–Z 71
Conversion Tables 72
Crime and the Police 73
Eating Out 73
Electricity 73
Health and Emergencies 73
Internet 73
National Holidays 74
Opening Hours 74
Post Offices 74
Sports and Activities 74
Telephones 76
Time 76
Tipping 76
Toilets 76

The Guide

07 The Dordogne: Northern Périgord 77
Arriving from the North: Périgord Vert 79
Brantôme and Bordeilles 83
Northeast Perigord 87
Up the Côle, to St-Jean-de-Côle and Thiviers 87
Down the Isle and Auvézère 89
Périgueux 93
The Cité 98
Around Périgueux 102
West to Aubeterre-sur-Dronne and its Eglise Monolithique 106
The Fôret de la Double 109
The Lower Isle Valley 110

08 The Dordogne: the Vézère Valley 113
The Northern Vézère 115
Downriver from Montignac to Les Eyzies 121
Les Eyzies-de-Tayac 126
To Le Bugue-sur-Vézère 130

09 Down the Dordogne I 133
Dordogne Quercynois 136
Padirac and Rocamadour 141
Carennac to Lacave 148
Into the Dordogne 154
Souillac 154
Souillac to Sarlat 157
Sarlat-la-Canéda 159
The Plâteau of Périgord Noir 165
Domme: the 'Acropolis of Périgord' 165

10 Down the Dordogne II 169
The Central Dordogne: Beynac to Bergerac 170
St-Cyprien to Cadouin 175
Back along the Dordogne 180
Bergerac 183
Around Bergerac 187
West of Bergerac to St-Emilion 190
St-Emilion 193
The Libournais 199
Libourne 199
North of Libourne 200
West of Libourne 201
The Haute-Gironde 203

11 Bordeaux 207
History 210
Ste-Croix and St-Michel 218
Musée d'Aquitaine 219
Cathédrale St-André 220
Musée des Beaux-Arts 221
St-Seurin 224
Quartier St-Pierre 225
The Golden Triangle 226
Esplanade des Quinconces and Around 228
The Chartrons 230
Pessac 232

12 The Gironde 237
Southeast of Bordeaux 239
Entre-Deux-Mers 239
Along the Valley of the Garonne 245
South of the Garonne: the Graves and the Bazadais 250
North of Bordeaux: the Gironde Estuary and Médoc 260
The Côte d'Argent 269
Around Pointe de Grave 269
Côte d'Argent: The Lakes 273
Arcachon and its Bassin 275

13 The Lot: Quercy 285
Between the Dordogne and Lot Rivers: the Causse de Gramat 288
Figeac 297
The Célé Valley 302
Down the Lot to Cahors 306
South of the Lot: Truffles and the Causse de Limogne 312
Cahors 313
South of the River Lot: Quercy Blanc 323
Down the Lot: Cahors to Touzac 326
Puy-l'Evêque to Touzac 332
North of the Lot: La Bouriane 335
Gourdon 336

14 Lot-et-Garonne 343
Fumel and the Château de Bonaguil 346
Bastide Country 348
Down the Lot: from Fumel to Villeneuve-sur-Lot 353
The Prune Kingdom: Villeneuve to Aiguillon 358
The *Pays des Serres* 361
Agen 364
The Néraçais 369
Nérac 369
Bastides, Castles and a Famous Mill 372
Western Lot-et-Garonne 375
Down the Garonne Valley 375
Marmande 378
Along the Dourdêze and Dropt, and the Pays du Duras 380

15 Tarn-et-Garonne 385
Northeast Approaches: Down the Bonnette and Aveyron Valleys 388
In the Gorges of the Aveyron: Lagupié to St-Antonin-Noble-Val 390
Further Down the Aveyron, to Caussade 391
Montauban 395
Around Montauban 402
Moissac 403
North of Moissac 410
The Lomagne 411
Heading West 411
South Towards Toulouse 413

16 Toulouse 417
History 420
Place du Capitole 429
From Place du Capitole to the Basilica of St-Sernin 431
Around Place St-Sernin and the Quartier Arnaud-Bernard 434
Les Jacobins 435
West of Les Jacobins 436
Pastel Palaces and Violets of Gold 437
Along the Garonne 439
The Quartier du Jardin 440
From Place du Salin to the Musée des Augustins 440
North of the Musée des Augustins 443
Toulouse's Left Bank 443
Le Mirail, Toulouse's Shadow Utopia 444
On the Outskirts of Toulouse 445

Reference

17 Glossary 451
18 Language 453

Maps and Plans

The Dordogne and the Lot *inside front cover*
Chapter Divisions 7
Périgord 78
Périgord Vert 80
Northeast Périgord 88
Périgueux 94–95
West of Périgueux 104
The Vézère Valley 114
Down the Dordogne I 134–35
Down the Dordogne II 170–71
Central Dordogne 173
Bergerac 185
West of Bergerac 190
Bordeaux 208–09
Gironde 238
Southeast of Bordeaux 240
Gironde Estuary 262
Bassin d'Arcachon 275
The Lot: Quercy 286–87
Between the Dordogne and Lot Rivers 289
Cahors 314
Quercy Blanc 324
Down the Lot and La Bouriane 326
Lot-et-Garonne 344–45
Tarn-et-Garonne 386–87
Montauban 396
Moissac Abbey Cloister 406
Toulouse 418–19
Colour Touring Maps and Wine Regions *end of guide*

19 Index 456

History

400,000–600 BC 20
600 BC–AD 507 21
507–1000 22
1000–1271 23
1271–1453 25
1453–1594 26
1594–1789 27
1789–1940 28
1940 to the Present 29

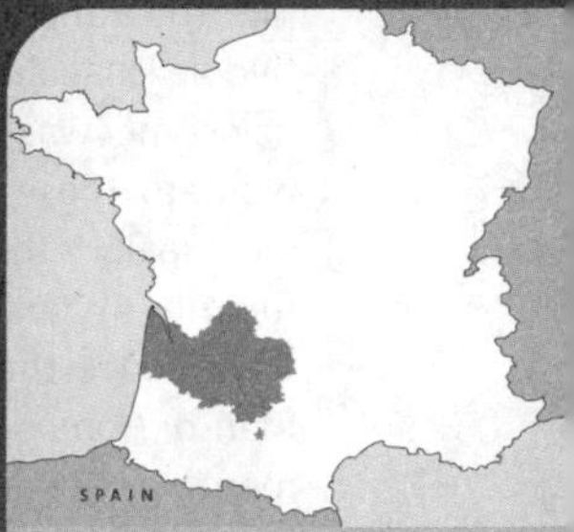

02

400,000–600 BC

An extremely precocious start is made, and humanity's first summer art course held

Europeans tend to think of 'early man' as some low-browed troglodyte living in Africa or the Middle East. But the roots of humanity are as deep in Europe as anywhere – going back a million years in some places. Destiny chose this particular corner of France to be the scene of some of the earliest and most significant developments in culture and art. A mere 400,000 years ago, somebody was poking around Périgord and other parts of the southwest, laboriously making flint tools and managing to get a fire lit. The crossing from the Lower to the Middle Palaeolithic occurred in this area approximately 75,000 years ago; the newcomer was **Neanderthal man** (presumably accompanied by Neanderthal woman). These come across as thick-skulled brutes in most accounts, but they were really rather clever, inventing better tools and techniques, and developing the first rituals and burials: the elements of the 'Mousterian culture' in the southwest. The Neanderthals get pushed off the stage about 40–35,000 BC) by **Cro-Magnon man**, or *Homo sapiens sapiens* – us, more or less; books on Cro-Magnon man usually mention with a touch of whimsy that if one of them got on the bus today in a business suit, nobody would notice.

The creations of the Cro-Magnon (named after the hamlet in Périgord where their bones were first discovered) are varied enough for scholars to define distinct **Upper Palaeolithic** cultures. The Perigordian and Aurignacian (35–20,000 BC) left jewellery, finely crafted spear points, and the world's first painting and sculpture (*see* p.39). In the Solutrean culture (20–15,000 BC), people brought their stone tools – axes, spear points, arrowheads, knives, and even sewing needles – to a point of perfection. The Upper Palaeolithic reached its height with the Magdalenian culture (15,000–9000 BC), with the beautiful paintings found in the caves at Lascaux and elsewhere. This period was the slow end of an ice age, and it is possible that the people who created Magdalenian art gradually migrated northwards, following the herds of reindeer and other animals that they hunted. The **Mesolithic** cultures that followed them (9000–4000 BC) did not paint, nor do much of anything else that was interesting.

Neolithic culture reached the area about 4000 BC, by either migrations or transmission of ideas – a lot of ideas: better tools, the first pottery, sedentary agricultural life, the domestication of animals and a complex religion. The Neolithic peoples made Europe's first great civilization and were its first builders. Their dolmens, menhirs, stone circles and tumuli are common all along the continent's coasts, but the Lot and the Dordogne have the greatest inland concentration of them anywhere. The Neolithic age was peaceful, probably matriarchal; people lived in unfortified villages, and evidence of warfare is singularly lacking. Lost so far back in time, hard facts are few, and Neolithic culture leaves us with a tangle of fascinating riddles: the purposes of their megalithic monuments and their siting of them, their considerable achievements in astronomy, and above all the vision of an extremely sophisticated culture, living in close harmony with nature and living well, without metals or technology.

This world lasted for more than three millennia in many areas. But the unity of Neolithic civilization was broken c. 2000 BC, with the arrival of new peoples such as the metalworking Artenac civilization, around Bordeaux. Over the next millennium and a half the picture grows increasingly confused, as ever more peoples and cultures pass through. The first to have a name, courtesy of later Roman writers, are the **Aquitanii**; they arrived in the 7th century BC (or much earlier, according to some opinions), and they may have been related to the various tribes of Celts who followed them.

600 BC–AD 507

Celts and the Romans first bash swords, and later clink glasses

In the 6th–4th centuries BC, new waves of **Celtic** peoples slowly spread over what came to be called **Gaul**. The Romans, when they arrived, found the area inhabited by a number of Gaulish tribes and wrote down their names: the Petrocorii north of the Duranus, or Dordogne, and south of it the Eleuteti and the fierce Cadurcii, who gave their name to Divona Cadurcorum (Cahors) on the Oltis, or Lot. In what is now the lower Lot-et-Garonne lived the Nitiobroges; while the plains around Toulouse were home to the Tolosates and Volcae Tectosages. The region around Bordeaux was occupied by the Biturges Vibiscii, who called themselves the 'Kings of the World'. A culturally complex people who nevertheless preferred pretty jewellery to the less mobile trappings of civilization – such as temples and cities – the Celts, or Gauls, did settle a number of small towns, or *oppida*, which often served as trading stations. Even in this remote age, the 'Gallic isthmus' between the Atlantic and Mediterranean was a busy trade route; tin from Cornwall went one way, and back the other came imports from the Greek world, including wine, of which the Gauls were very fond.

Rome's conquest of Gaul was hardly an overnight affair. Julius Caesar, who arrived in 59 BC, gets credit for the job, but Roman influence in the south at least was already strong – a Roman garrison was installed at Tolosa (Toulouse) around the middle of the 2nd century BC. Caesar's invasion came in response to revolts among Gauls who already found Roman control a little too heavy for their tastes. Burdigala (Bordeaux) was captured in 56 BC by Caesar's political partner Crassus, a wealthy magnate who, like Caesar, had bought a command because conquest was not only the path to power but also the only business more profitable to a Roman than city land speculation. The last great effort of the Gaulish nation and its leader, Vercingetorix, ended in total defeat at Gergovia in the Auvergne. The last Gaulish redoubt to fall, Uxellodunum, was somewhere in the Lot or perhaps Périgord (as with Gergovia, scholars are still arguing today over just where Uxellodunum was). The southwest, from the Loire to the Pyrenees, was organized into the Roman province of Aquitania.

Under direct Roman rule, southern Gaul became completely integrated into the Mediterranean economy. The new rulers apportioned out much of the land to Roman investors and veterans of the legions. Among the many new crops they introduced to the area was the grape, and soon the new Gallo-Roman Aquitania was not only meeting its own considerable demand for wine but exporting it to Italy. Some of the *oppida* grew into towns – Tolosa, Burdigala and Divona Cadurcorum among many others; others naturally declined and died, and their ruins can be seen at such places as Mursens and Luzech, in the Lot. Mines and quarries were exploited, and many towns made a good living on manufactures, especially ceramics. By the 1st century AD, the larger towns were looking quite opulent, with forums, temples, public baths and amphitheatres imitating the cities of Italy.

Despite all this, life in Aquitania would not have looked so rosy to the average person. As elsewhere in the western Empire, Roman Gaul was a profoundly sick society, a pyramid with a few fantastically wealthy land-owning families at the top, their estates tilled by vast armies of slaves. In the last centuries of the Empire, things got progressively worse. The small middle class in the towns was ground into poverty, as taxes rose and trade declined. Like the equally small class of free farmers, the middle class found itself gradually pushed into serfdom by debt. Not surprisingly, at the end of the Empire large areas of the country were controlled or at least threatened by the *bagaudae* – guerrilla bands out to destroy the system, especially strong in Aquitania.

The **Germanic** raids of the mid 3rd century were an omen of troubles to come. In 256 the Franks and the Alemanni broke through the Rhine frontier. For two decades they roamed over Gaul almost at will. Though the legions eventually recovered and drove them out, things would never be the same. The towns suffered most, including Tolosa and Vesunna (Périgueux), which contracted after the invasions to a fraction of their former size, huddling inside circuits of hastily built walls. By this time the elite had already given up on urban life, and in the 4th century their sumptuous villas grew into cities in themselves; well-defended and self-supporting, these were the centres of what economic life remained in the last days. The fatal invasions came after 407; both **Vandals** and **Visigoths** passed through the region, and after 420 it found itself part of the new Visigothic kingdom, with its capital at Tolosa. Barbarian Franks replaced the barbarian Goths in 507, after the Battle of Vouillé, but this meant little to a part of Gaul that had effectively dropped out of history altogether.

507–1000

In which Aquitania is frankly demoralized

Christianity had come to the region in the 4th century, as it was being established everywhere as the state religion of the Empire. The first recorded bishops are at Burdigala, in 314. The Church strengthened its power in the 6th century under the newly Christianized **Franks**. The Frankish Merovingian kings held only a tenuous control over most of Gaul, and only brought their army down to meet a foreign invasion, or when tribute was slow in coming; the day-to-day government was usually in the hands of landowners and their younger brothers in the Church. One bright light in the Dark Ages was Cahors. Controlled by a long line of powerful bishops beginning with the legendary Didier, the city survived and somehow prospered through the troubles; Cahors's aqueduct and baths were even restored in the grim 7th century.

Under the Merovingians, Frankish and Roman landowners gradually fused through intermarriage into a new ruling class much like the old one. Over generations their villas began to metamorphose into castles, while the landowners themselves gradually made their logical transformation into feudal barons. The Merovingians created the duchy of **Aquitaine** in the 7th century; for seven centuries the largely independent dukes would be in control of all the western coast from Poitou to the Pyrenees. In this poor backwater, they weren't always up to the task. The **Arabs** roared through from Spain in the early 700s, seizing Bordeaux and dominating the area until Charles Martel beat them at Poitiers in 732. Soon afterwards, the Frankish kingdom under its new **Carolingian** dynasty – headed by Charles's son Pepin the Short – tried to seize the duchy, while the duke, Waiofer, sheltered refugee lords who had been dispossessed by the Carolingians and led the southern resistance to the ambitious new power descending from the north. The result was a bloody war of three decades; Aquitaine was not completely brought under control until 774.

Pepin's son **Charlemagne** found a compromise solution: raising the duchy of Aquitaine into a kingdom, the first 'king' of which was his son Louis; this title lasted only until 877. The height of Frankish power under the Carolingians was a peaceful time for most of France, though it was shortlived. Charlemagne was still warm in his grave when his empire started to disintegrate, and the western shores suffered the visits of the worst barbarians ever: the Normans, or **Vikings**. In 848 they sacked Bordeaux, and all century their regular raids brought terror and destruction to the river valleys as far as Toulouse. The bits and shards of Roman civilization that had survived this long now finally faded out. Many people in the 9th century, looking forward to the millennium, were convinced that the end of the world was at hand, when in fact the ground was only being swept clean for something new and better.

1000–1271

The southwest creates a civilization, and the French and English come down to make nuisances of themselves

If the 9th century was the low point for the southwest and many other parts of Europe, the sudden strong impulse of cultural achievement and economic power that followed – the dawning of the **Middle Ages** – is all the more surprising. The Vikings' settling down in Normandy marked an end to foreign invasions, and in a period of relative tranquillity (marked by constant but not-too-serious feudal warfare) the feudal system in the southwest reached its perfection. The crazy quilt of *comtés*, *vicomtés*, *sénéchaussées* and *duchés*, interspersed with huge areas where local barons were free to do what they liked within the limits of their feudal oaths, made for a finely balanced anarchy that somehow managed to permit a rapid rebirth of towns, trade, wealth and culture.

In the brilliant 12th century, great abbey complexes appeared under the patronage of local rulers, and new stone churches in the Romanesque style were underway in every town and village – the biggest one in Europe, **St-Sernin**, went up under the wealthy and enlightened counts of Toulouse, the strongest lords of the southwest, who tended all to be named Raymond. Along the coast lived their near-equals, the dukes of Aquitaine; all these were Guillaumes, and the list included **Guillaume IX** (1086–1127), who besides his capable political leadership was one of the first of the troubadours, heralding the rebirth of poetry in Europe. That poetry was written in Occitan, the *langue d'oc*, and it was the pride of an **Occitan** nation, stretching from the Atlantic to the Alps, that was just beginning to become aware of itself when it was overwhelmed by invaders from the north.

Guillaume had a granddaughter, a beautiful and wilful woman whose life would be the stuff of romances, and whose career would change history: **Eleanor of Aquitaine**. She was sole heir to the rich duchy, and when she married Louis VII in 1137, the French crowed for having plucked the biggest feudal plum. Eleanor did her best with the cold, pious Louis, even accompanying him on a crusade. Her manifest discontent led inevitably to a divorce, in 1152, and two years later she found a more convivial marriage with Louis' mortal enemy: **Henry Plantagenet**, Duke of Anjou, soon to be Henry II, King of England. With Eleanor came the land, and for the next three centuries Aquitaine was a possession of the English crown. The Plantagenets, in constant need of cash, introduced an intelligent, well-organized administration; if the tax burden was high, the resources were there to pay it. The English proved good rulers, usually sympathetic to local concerns, and they gained a high degree of loyalty from the people of Aquitaine. (One sour note at the beginning came with the depredations of Henry and Eleanor's sons – worst of all Richard the Lionheart, a fellow who gets off all too easily in history and legend. Richard battled and pillaged across the region more to line his pockets than to solidify English rule, and in Aquitaine, as elsewhere, he gained a well-deserved reputation as a bloody-minded thug.) Under English control, Bordeaux grew into a city of 30,000 with a new prosperity based on wine; at the height of the trade with England, in 1308, Aquitaine exported almost as much of the stuff as it does today.

Toulouse, under its counts, grew even bigger and richer than Bordeaux, though the city that might have been a natural capital of an Occitan nation instead itself became a victim of imperialism from the north. The French would have made their play for Toulouse in any case, but in the early 1200s fortune provided them with a cause: the presence of the **Cathars**. This heretical sect, which came from the Balkans by way of north Italy, found a perfect haven in the sophisticated, tolerant atmosphere of the Toulousain and Languedoc. In 1209, a sordid deal between Pope Innocent III and the French king Philippe-Auguste paved the way for the **Albigensian crusade**, supposedly directed against the heretics but in reality a naked grab at the lands of the counts of Toulouse. The troops were provided from Paris, a force under the cruel, lucky and always victorious **Simon de Montfort**; this army plundered its way through Quercy and the Agenais before the main event, the total subjection of the south. This was clinched by De Montfort's victory at the Battle of Muret, near Toulouse, in 1213; resistance continued, though, giving King Louis VIII an excuse to bring down another army to finish the job in 1226.

In 1271, the French Crown inherited Toulouse by a forced marriage; long before that, fiefs and offices had been handed out to northerners, and the **Inquisition** was introduced, not only to incinerate the few surviving Cathars but to ensure that the free culture that made heresy possible would be extinguished forever.

1271–1453

The French and the English continue their quarrels and mischief

Despite the vicious way in which the French had gone about their conquest, with plenty of bloody massacres *pour encourager les autres*, recovery was rapid. The surest sign of the continuing economic boom was the founding everywhere of *bastides*, planned new towns, usually built on lands that had gone back to forest or swamp during the late Empire and Dark Ages; the first of these was Montauban, a creation of Count Alphonse-Jourdain in 1144. *Bastides* had their political aspect too. More than a score were founded by Alphonse de Poitiers, the first French count of Toulouse, King Louis' brother and the man in charge of establishing French control over the new conquests. The English in response founded scores of their own *bastides* in Aquitaine.

The vigour of society in these times can be read on any map today; hundreds of town and village names show their origins in the 11th–13th centuries: *bastides* are often named *Villeneuve* or *Villefranche* – free towns with their own charter. Many other names end in *-artigues* or *-essart* – words that denoted reclaimed land, a constant necessity in times when the population was increasing rapidly. A village that grew up around a castle is often named *Castelnau*, and the various places called *Sauveterre* began as *sauvetés* – church foundations that at least in theory were 'safe', exempt from feudal warfare and pillage. The older towns also continued to thrive, notably Cahors, which attracted a number of Italian banking families who fled the disruptions of the Albigensian crusade. The little city on the Lot soon grew into a major financial centre with its own university, and even supplied a pope, John XXII.

England and France, now the only two powers in the region, battled fitfully for a century after the marriage of Eleanor and Henry II, until Louis IX (St Louis) agreed to the **Treaty of Paris** in 1259, formally ceding Périgord and Quercy to the English. From then on the two parties suspiciously eyed one another, in an uneasy truce that occasionally broke out into open hostilities; the French occupied Bordeaux for a decade, until a revolt of the Bordelais threw them out in 1303.

But for all the politeness that was generally shown by both sides, it was a situation that could not last. In an age when nation-states were dawning, feudal logic no longer worked: as dukes of Guyenne (from the English mispronunciation of Aquitaine), the English kings owed homage to the kings of France – a fine position to be in whenever the two nations' interests were in conflict. The inevitable final showdown began with a quarrel over Guyenne in 1337, and went into the books as the **Hundred Years' War**.

The first decades of the war saw Aquitaine as the major battlefield, without major results until the arrival of Edward of Woodstock, son of Edward III, in 1355. The **Black Prince**, as he came to be known, ended the war's first round decisively with the Battle of Poitiers (1356), capturing King Jean II among many others. Now in undisputed control of the southwest, England declared its lands a principality free of any claims of French allegiance; the Black Prince ruled it from Bordeaux until his death in 1376.

The next round went to the French, under Bertrand du Guesclin, who recaptured Quercy and most of Périgord by 1369. As the war dragged on, the exhausted combatants found it increasingly difficult to maintain control of events. Both sides hired **mercenary** companies; these got out of hand, and, combined with the other desperados that were shaken loose from society by constant warfare and disruption, they formed the *routiers* ('highwaymen'), armed bands loyal to nothing but their own profit that reduced much of the southwest to anarchy. Coming on the heels of the Black Death (1348–50), which reduced the population by a third in many areas, it caused a time of troubles the region had not known since the days of the Normans.

In the early 1400s, it seemed that France was coming apart once and for all. The English regained all they had lost, and even took Paris in 1420, a time that coincides with the worst ravages of the *routiers* in the southwest. Thanks to **Joan of Arc**, of course, the French soon recovered and prevailed. They blockaded Bordeaux in 1451, and two years later the climactic Battle of Castillon, near Bordeaux, put an end to the wars and to England's continental empire forever.

1453–1594

The lobotomized southwest starts arguing with itself over religion

The French moved quickly to consolidate their new possessions. Bordeaux got a big new fortress to watch the citizens, and a *parlement* to scrutinize their morals and political opinions; the city's wine trade with England was ended by royal decree, sending it – along with most of Aquitaine – into economic decline. For both Aquitaine and the Toulousain, French rule meant not only impoverishment but also the enforced death of cultures that had been among the most promising of the Middle Ages. The 1539 decree of Villars-Cotterets mandated the French language in law and government, the first step along the road to the eradication of the *langue d'oc*, which would not be completed until our own time. Before the French came, the south had its own traditions of literature, architecture and art; under a new rigid authoritarianism, directed from Paris, all this withered away quickly. Southwesterners, when able to build, sculpt or write at all, found themselves forced to ape the fashions imported by their governors from the north, and over the generations it became a habit.

The French grip was strong, and, with political opposition impossible, the following wave of southern rebelliousness came in the form of religious dissent. **Protestantism** first seeped into the southwest from Calvin's Geneva, and it found its most attentive audience among the industrious middle classes and some of the more enlightened courts. The first Protestant communities appeared in Ste-Foy-la-Grande and Agen about 1532. Soon after, the court at Nérac of the **Albrets**, a powerful noble family of the Agenais, became a centre of humanistic learning and religious heresy (Calvin came to visit). This happened in the reign of the learned Marguerite d'Albret – or rather Marguerite of Navarre, for this ambitious family had, with French help, worked its way to the kingship of that small and woebegone Pyrenean realm.

Protestantism swept across the south, bringing the good news that there was more to life than abject submission to Rome and Paris. With the spirit of the time, civil war was inevitable – the **Wars of Religion**. The conflict gathered steam from 1560, with the massacre of Protestants in Cahors, and the expulsion of Toulouse's Protestant community two years later. Atrocities went both ways; in Gourdon it was the Protestants who were doing the slaughtering. Towns and regions chose sides. Cahors, with its powerful bishops, remained steadfastly Catholic and fought a continuous battle with Protestant Montauban and Figeac; Protestant Bergerac stomped on Catholic Périgueux as early and as often as possible. The religious rebels found a firm pillar of support in Jeanne d'Albret, daughter of Marguerite and a grisly bigot for the new cause, as Protestant and Catholic armies recaptured the spirit of the Hundred Years' War, prowling the region and looking for enemy towns and souls to burn.

In much of the rest of France it was the same story; now, however, for the first time, the southwest stepped up to centre-stage in France's history, thanks to the Albrets and Jeanne's son Henri, who by a complicated set of circumstances just happened to be heir to the French throne. Henri of Navarre was a good Protestant and a hardy warrior; among other things, he sacked Cahors in 1580 with more bloodshed than was really necessary. In two decades of campaigning to win his rightful crown, the Protestant lands of the southwest were his solid base. In the end, though, Henri's good sense and goodwill made him the man to put an end to the Wars of Religion – by the conversion of convenience that finally made him acceptable to the Catholics controlling Paris. As **Henri IV**, he ruled well, proclaiming religious tolerance with the **Edict of Nantes** (1598), and earned a secure place for himself as a national hero in the southwest, particularly in his native Gascony.

1594–1789

In which the French try to make everyone miserable, and the southwest fights back and loses

With religious troubles out of the way, the southwest was free to return its thoughts to the joys of rule from Paris. Riots and popular revolts had been common enough in the 1500s, usually over oppressive taxes such as the *gabelle*, or salt tax. In the sympathetic Henri's reign, the first of a century-long series of peasant uprisings occurred. The movement of the '***Croquants***', in Périgord and Quercy, was more directed at the grasping nobles and their high rents. In 1594 the *Croquants* formed a peasant army in Périgord; the barons organized and beat them, and punished the survivors with memorable ferocity. Henri's successors in Paris heaped more woes on the common folk: more taxes, more forced labour, and lots of revenue agents and troops to enforce them. The early 17th century would have been rough enough without them. High rents and prices, combined with bad harvests, recurring outbreaks of plague (1629 and 1652) and a climate of hatred and everyday violence, the heritage of the religious wars, made further revolts inevitable. In Toulouse, in 1629, things were so bad that even the royal governor, Montmorency, joined the rebels, and Louis XIII had to lead a big army down from Paris to crush them.

From 1637 to 1642 the *Croquants* were back in business again. This time they nearly captured Périgueux, though once again the arms of the king and the nobles had the last say. This was the last revolt on a large scale, though smaller outbreaks were regular features of rural life up until the Revolution. For the nobles, times were never better, as witnessed by the large number of great châteaux built in this period. At the same time, a lot of the old-style castles were disappearing – pulled down on the orders of Louis XIII's minister Cardinal Richelieu, who didn't want any strong places that could shelter resistance to the national state. If the countryside was in despair, the two large cities weren't doing too badly. Bordeaux found a new prosperity in the late 17th and 18th centuries, based not only on wine but also on the slave trade with the Americas; the city grew enough to become the third-largest in France. Toulouse in the 16th century was still enjoying a modest boom from the manufacture of *pastel*, dyer's woad, and the building by local initiative of the Canal du Midi in Languedoc (inaugurated in 1681) made the city the centre of a new trade route that crossed the French isthmus. The *pastel* business dwindled in the face of foreign competition, however, and despite its natural advantages, Toulouse generally continued its long slide into cultural and economic torpor.

For most of the region, hard times continued through the 1700s. Bordeaux could find no better way to profit from the New World than through the slave trade, but the Americas offered many poor Aquitains a way out: tens of thousands emigrated to Canada and the West Indies. Most of the Protestants had already gone to Prussia and elsewhere, after Louis XIV revoked the Edict of Nantes in 1685. For those who remained, the century was a drowsy era, at least when the peasants weren't revolting. *Intendants* (administrators) from Paris ran everything and made a few lasting contributions, notably an excellent network of roads (usually embellished with pretty rows of plane trees, still seen in many places today). The *intendants* also dressed up Bordeaux, remodelling the city into a grandiose provincial copy of Paris.

1789–1940

In which the southwest helps make a revolution, regrets it and takes a long nap

In 1789 there were no people in France more cheerfully assiduous than the southwesterners in smashing up churches and châteaux, finding and burning the tax records and rent rolls. But at the same time, at the National Assembly in Paris, Bordeaux's merchants, and southwesterners in general, were providing most of the voices of moderation and good sense. Their faction, the **Girondists**, stood for liberal reforms and political decentralization. When the radical, Paris-dominated **Jacobin** faction gained control in 1792, the Terror began; the Girondists and their federalist hopes became its first victims. A 1793 federalist counter-revolt in the southwest failed, largely because Toulouse and Montauban wouldn't have anything to do with it; stoutly conservative areas like the Lot were against the Revolution from the start.

The Lot, ironically, loved Napoleon and contributed more than any part of France to his *Grande Armée*, including fine soldiers such as Joachim Murat, the son of a village innkeeper, who ended up King of Naples. Jean-Baptiste Bessières of Prayssac, who was in charge of the occupation of Moscow, briefly claimed the title of Duke of Istria. At the end, though, southwesterners were as tired of Napoleon as anybody else. The Duke of Wellington marched through in 1814, on his way up from Spain. When he arrived at Toulouse, the people hailed him as a liberator.

If the Revolution had been a disappointment, nothing in the century that followed it would be any improvement. Paris-appointed prefects replaced Paris-appointed *intendants*, and the old regional distinctions and boundaries were destroyed in favour of homogeneous *départements*, but through all the 19th-century shifts of the Gallic banana republic/monarchy/empire, no one lifted a hand to help the southwest; nor did the region ever show much energy of its own. Aquitaine and the Toulousain had become the most sluggish and listless of all French provincial backwaters, and anyone with any spunk or talent was off to Paris as soon as he could manage it.

The railway arrived in Bordeaux in 1850; seven years later the line from there to Toulouse and the Mediterranean was finished. Instead of catalysing trade and industry, however, this merely made it easier to leave, and easier for imported goods to flow in and ruin the already hard-pressed southwestern farmers and manufacturers. The farmers tried their hardest, introducing useful new crops such as tobacco and types of corn, and they managed just barely to survive the 1868 **phylloxera** epidemic that killed off nearly all of their vineyards, but prices stayed low and business stayed bad. And all across the southwest, the villages began to dwindle.

Undoubtedly the biggest event of the last century was one that happened elsewhere – the **First World War**. Of the millions who died pointlessly for the glory of France, the southwest contributed more than its share. Many towns and villages lost a third of, or even half of, their young men; in every one you will see a pathetic war memorial or plaque in the church to remind you of France's greatest catastrophe since the Black Death. Between the war and rural abandonment, the southwest declined in population by almost 25% from 1850 to 1950; in some parts of the Lot and other *départements*, the figure was as high as 60%.

1940 to the Present

A Nazi interlude, followed by the unexpected return of the English

Though the **Second World War** was less costly and destructive, it was still a miserable and dangerous time for the people of the southwest, however far removed they were from the actual fighting. From the beginning, the Germans seized a strip along the entire Atlantic coast. The 'border' between the occupied zone and Vichy-controlled territory was heavily patrolled, and locals needed special papers to cross it – plenty of people were killed trying to visit their cousins, or sneaking produce over the line to the nearby village market. Deportation of men to forced labour in Germany was a terrible burden, and not all who went ever returned. Another strain, particularly in Périgord, was supporting the wave of refugees from Belgium and northern France who had come down in 1940, but this one the people handled ungrudgingly.

The **Résistance** was not much of a force until 1943, but from then on it operated effectively in the lonely *causses* of Quercy and Périgord, where one of its leaders was the writer and future culture minister André Malraux. In retaliation for their acts of sabotage, the Germans sent the SS *Das Reich* division on a tour of the southwest in May 1944; these distinguished themselves with wholesale massacres of civilians at Mussidan, in Périgord, Frayssinet-le-Gélat and Montpezat-de-Quercy. Liberation came for most of the southwest in August 1944; Bordeaux's story was much like that of Paris. Colonel Kühnemann, the German commander, was in civilian life a wine merchant with many friends in the city. He had orders to blow up nearly everything on his way out, along with all the bridges as far as Agen, but instead he spent a delicate week dodging the Nazi spooks while successfully negotiating with the Resistance for a peaceful exit. Some German units, trapped at Royan and Verdon on the Gironde, held out almost to the end of the war.

Since the war, the big news has been the unexpected awakening of **Toulouse**. With considerable assistance from the government planners, the city followed up its early prominence in aviation by becoming France's forward-looking City of the Air, home of Airbus and the French space agency, a manufacturer of satellites and supersonic airliners. Striving to become the European 'technopole' of the 21st century, Toulouse has also fixed up its historic centre, which is now sitting well-scrubbed, pink and pretty in its location on the Garonne. Bordeaux, meanwhile, is still Bordeaux, and oddly proud of it.

Large numbers of refugees from the Spanish Civil War, and a wave of *pieds noirs* (French settlers in Algeria, forced out in 1962) have settled in the southwest, adding a touch of diversity not only to the population but to the cuisine – if there's a dinner on at a village festival, school pageant or whatever, it's likely to be paella or couscous. The British invasion of the Dordogne began in the 1960s, when people found out that lovely country homes in that delightful region could be had for a song. That particular song is ended, but the *département* today has one of France's largest British expat colonies. There is also a sizeable British population in Haute-Garonne, Gironde, Lot and Lot-et-Garonne. The Consulate at Bordeaux estimated in 2000 that there were about 25,000 British people living in southwest France – a town's worth. The locals joke that the English are trying to buy back what they lost in the Hundred Years' War; so far, though, relations are generally good.

Politically, the only major change of the post-war era was the Socialist government's 1981 **decentralization** plan, creating the regions of Aquitaine and Midi-Pyrénées. So far the regions have only limited powers, but as the first reverse in seven centuries of Parisian centralism, it brings at least a hope that the southwest may some day finally regain some degree of control over its destiny.

Topics

Microtourism 32
Bertran de Born 33
Market Values 35
Dances with Bears 36
Art Begins Here 38
Goose Lore and Livers 40
The Architecture of Springtime 41

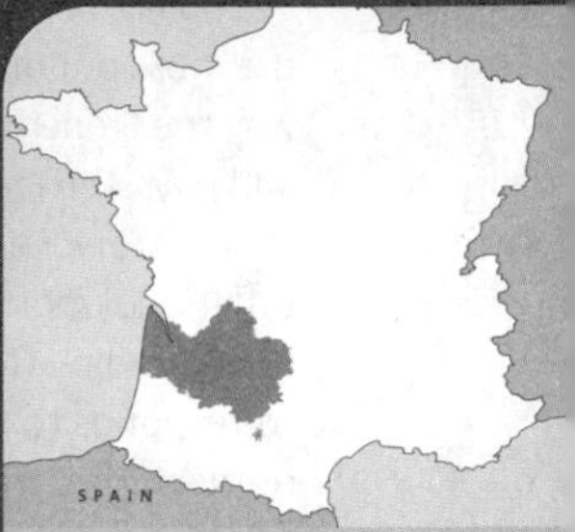

03

Microtourism

We don't have any Eiffel Towers or Chartres Cathedrals to offer you in this book. Famous, familiar sights are rare in the southwest, and anyone who wants great art will have to look for it in unlikely places such as Moissac or Souillac, or in the Palaeolithic caves of Périgord. But the hordes of visitors and expats that prowl this part of France hardly feel the lack. Most of them seem content with the area's wealth of pretty villages and châteaux, along with the wine, fresh air and *confits de canard*, and they might spend a slow weekend in the big towns for a look at a church or a museum.

People who do spend a lot of time down here really need never be bored. Getting the most out of any part of rural France requires learning to look at the country the way the French do – on a small scale. Connoisseurs of every particularity of village and *pays*, the French are passionately interested in the detail of traditional life and local history. For example, painstaking cartographers have compiled maps showing traditional roof styles in France: where they are high-pitched or shallow, and where the boundary is between slate and canal tiles (except in Périgord, this roughly corresponds to the boundary between the *langue d'oïl* and *langue d'oc* – it's all connected). Other maps display the types of construction used for *pigeonniers*, or dovecotes, notable features of the landscape in the southwest. In some areas they are round, in others square and set on stone pillars, or attached to the house.

Get locals talking about these subjects and they'll go on for hours, explaining how in some areas only nobles were allowed to keep pigeons, which went out every day and ate all the peasants' grain and so caused the Revolution, which allowed everyone to keep pigeons, and farmers let the poo pile up for their daughters' dowries, but later they planted groves of poplars when a girl was born, because the trees would mature just in time for her marriage, by which time chemical fertilizers had made pigeon droppings less valuable than firewood... You get the idea. And by the way, you've probably noticed how the poplars are always planted in orderly quincunxes, but scholars are divided on whether this fashion, invented by King Cyrus of Persia, came into France in the Middle Ages or in the time of Louis XIV...

If you want to play too, the first thing to do is pick up the *Cartes IGN: Série Bleue* map for the area that interests you. Drawn on a scale of 1:25,000, these are the equivalent of the Ordnance Survey or US Geodetic Survey maps. You'll find them in any good newsagent or bookshop; hunters and mushroom-lovers probably account for much of the demand. From the first glance, you'll get a feeling for the traditional life and the slowly evolving fabric of your area: the villages and hamlets, each with its patch of cleared farmland, like islands in the vast green of the forests, along with the works that kept life going: sawmills, remains of old watermills, *pigeonniers*, sandpits and quarries, sources and fountains.

The map will show you some surprises, even if you think you already know the area well. Naturally it will help you find the nearest swimming hole, and some nice places for a walk in the woods, but there will be other surprises too: maybe a dolmen or menhir, a collection of *gariottes* or a fortified tower, or a medieval chapel in an unlikely place that may turn out, like one we found, to have seven devils frescoed on the walls inside. Ruins, by the score, are generally marked on the map without further detail, so take pot luck; ruins can mean anything from bits of a Roman aqueduct to a *routiers*' stronghold that was destroyed in the Hundred Years' War, or a barn abandoned by a farmer who moved to the city when phylloxera hit.

Once you get to know the country and its history better, you'll be able to read these maps like a detective. That village surrounded by a circuit of roadside crosses must have been a *sauveté* of the Church in the 1100s; the crosses marked the limits within which knights were forbidden to bash each other or molest the peasants. Crosses of all kinds grow thick along the roadsides of the southwest. Around Toulouse, people used to believe the Cathars made them first, but in fact many are simply the latest incarnation of markers that go back to Neolithic times (only 200 years ago, a bishop of Cahors was demolishing menhirs and replacing them with crosses, because country people would not stop worshipping secretly at the sites).

Not least among the virtues of rural France is modesty. This doesn't mean a lack of pride in one's region – on the contrary, nearly everyone here is convinced that their particular corner is Paradise on Earth – but rather modesty as an outlook, as a way of life. As historian Emmanuel Le Roy Ladurie has noted, France is the country where bars are called *Au Petit Bonheur* or *Au Petit Profit*. Ladurie and others have developed an equally modest and original way of looking at the past. 'Microhistory', studying a single place and time in the minutest detail, not only flushes out unwarranted generalities and clichés but adds real depth to our understanding. And a little understanding is all the southwest and its people ask of the visitor. Deeply in love with their country, they are concerned that we learn to appreciate it as they do. With understanding, the *petits bonheurs* and sweet surprises begin to add up, secret doors into a part of France where the roots of life are rich and deep.

Bertran de Born

East of Périgueux is the Château de Hautefort, replacement of the impregnable 12th-century citadel of the war-loving troubadour Bertran de Born (c. 1140–1214). Bertran's career makes mincemeat of the Hollywood stereotype of troubadours as long-haired, love-lorn wimps. Though capable of writing delightfully about love, he liked nothing better than stirring up trouble through his battle songs and sirventes, the topical, satirical songs of the troubadours: 'I want great barons always/to be angry with one another,' wrote Bertran; and elsewhere: 'Peace does not comfort me/I am in accord with war/Nor do I hold or believe/Any other religion.' The minor nobility of Aquitaine listened to his sirventes, and agreed; feudal anarchy between overlords offered their only chance for independence and profit. But what assured Bertran's fame is the striking vividness and power of his poetry, capable of enchanting such diverse spirits as St Francis of Assisi, who sang his songs as a wayward youth, and Ezra Pound, who translated many of them so well.

In his day, Bertran was feared by all for his biting satire, so much so that he was blamed for the death of the Young King, Henry Court-Mantel, Henry II's heir and the older brother of Richard the Lionheart. The chroniclers tell the story: Bertran through 'ruse and felony' had kicked out Hautefort's co-owner, his own brother Constantine. Constantine appealed to Richard the Governor of Aquitaine as his overlord for justice. Bertran resolved to seek aid in other quarters, and wrote a series of sirventes taunting his friend the Young King, whom Bertran knew was sick with jealousy of Richard; the Lionheart already ruled Aquitaine and attracted great renown and money for his exploits, while his older brother chafed with little to do (and a small allowance) while waiting to inherit the throne of England. To every noble court Bertran sent songs of a 'lord of little land' and commented that 'It ill beseems a crowned king to live upon a dole and spend but a Norman carter's tax'. Bertran's satires had their doleful effect in spring 1183, when a general uprising against Richard's tyranny broke out across Aquitaine. The Young King joined the rebels, at first reluctantly, and then wholeheartedly when Henry II came down in person to aid Richard. The Young King was now fighting not only his brother but his father, and he raised money for his mercenaries by plundering; after a raid on the holy shrine of Rocamadour, he sickened along the road, and died at Martel.

Grief-stricken, old King Henry blamed Bertran for his son's death, and sent Richard and Alfonso II of Aragon to besiege Hautefort. Bertran scorched the earth before the enemy, so they'd have nothing to eat. But when Alfonso asked him as an old friend for sustenance, Bertran offered the Aragonese armies 10 days' worth of food for the promise that they would not attack the weakened south wall of Hautefort. Of course that was precisely where the Aragonese unchivalrously began their attack, and Bertran surrendered at once, to spare further damage to his beloved castle.

Bertran was carted off before King Henry, who received him in a towering rage, and determined to have him put to the sword. Then he said: 'Bertran, Bertran, once you said that you never needed more than half your wits. Surely now you need them all!' 'My lord, what I said is true,' Bertran replied in tears. 'Although since the day of the death of your son, the beautiful and valiant Young King, I have lost all my wits, judgment, and mind.' His grief so moved the king that he fainted, and when he recovered he wept and said: 'Ah Bertran, unhappy Bertran, it was only right that you have lost your wits in losing my son, for he loved you more than any other man in the world. And I, for love of him, return to you your liberty, goods, and castle. And I will add 500 marks to rebuild the south wall of your castle. Thanks to this letter from my son Richard, I know of your worthy conduct in the siege of Hautefort. It is as much for your noble acts as a soldier as for your celebrated talents as a troubadour that you have earned today my clemency.'

If Bertran had used his grief to get out of a tight jam, it was sincere – his famous *planh* (lament) for the Young King is a masterpiece of Occitan literature. But the experience hardly cooled Bertran's heels; out of Hautefort the volley of sirventes continued, now lampooning King Alfonso II for playing Bertran false, now egging Richard to battle with verses as vivid as Villon's:

If both kings are bold and fearless,
we'll soon see fields strewn with bits
of helmets, shields, swords and saddlebows,
and bodies split open from head to foot,
and horses wandering about aimlessly,
and lances protruding from ribs and chests,
and joy and tears, and grief and happiness.
The loss will be great, but the gain yet greater.

As the translator Ezra Pound commented, 'This kind of thing was much more impressive before 1914 than it has been since 1920.' Yet for all his love of war, Bertran died in a monastery, from where Dante sent him straight to Hell to wander about as a headless trunk, holding his severed head aloft as a lantern. The head explains to Dante: 'Know that I am Bertran de Born, who gave evil counsel to the Young King and made father and son rebel against one another... Because I parted those who were joined, I carry my brain parted from its roots in this trunk.'

Market Values

The old vans and lorries will start wheezing in some time after eight, unloading prunes and geese and greens and oysters in the morning fog while the children are passing through on their way to school. The stallholders in French village markets aren't the sort of people to knock themselves out coming at dawn. That's the whole point. The Friday morning market here has probably taken place since the Middle Ages, and today it is a symbol of liberty, and a refuge for everyone from the clock-driven, bureaucrat-infested life of the cities. Free men and women come and go when they damn well please: there are no receipts, and no VAT that can't be avoided; no advertising, no special discount offers, no Styrofoam and no barcodes; just real food, scents, colours and conviviality. European legislation to try and keep fresh food on markets refrigerated has hardly been adopted with vigour, in this country where they like their cheese running off the plate. Perhaps this is that Free Market they're always chattering about in the newspapers.

The village market is the reliable country calendar of France, and all of us down here measure the seasons by the asparagus, spring onions, raspberries, wild strawberries, melons, *cèpes* and chestnuts that rise and pass across its firmament, each at its appointed time. It is also the best way to check on the state of the land. Even vendors who are middlemen, and didn't grow the stuff themselves, are willing to discuss the relative merits and demerits of their produce, with a long discourse on the weather responsible for them if they're not too busy. Farmers who bring in chickens will recount their life stories, and tell you to which special fate in the kitchen they think each of them best suited. If you're not in the mood for such discussions, and even if you're not intending to buy anything, you'll come to the market just the same, for the sensual assault that makes it the climax of the week. Best are the fish stands – glistening rainbow trout, pink *rougets* and prawns, inscrutable sea urchins and lithe purple Art Nouveau squids (and a *tielle*, a little Languedocien fish pie, to take home for lunch). Next door are flats of spring flowers, ready for planting, and across the way the green spectrum of the vegetable stand has been arranged with a master's eye for the maximum effect of colour. There's a touch of colour in the market people too, the rosy flush that comes from spending most of their time outdoors.

The French aren't averse to noise. One thing that distinguishes many villages is the vintage air-raid horns that bellow out from atop the *mairie* to mark midday (when the market closes), as if to say '*Bon appétit*!' If they go off unexpectedly, flattening delicate sensibilities for miles around, it's probably to announce a fire;

French villages depend on volunteer firemen, that doughty crew that comes roaring up to your house with lights and sirens ablaze just before Christmas with their calendars (if you give them a donation for the calendar, they'll come to your fire). And every village with an alert *syndicat d'initiative* has wired itself for sound, providing a little canned music to regale shoppers at the market in the busy seasons. You may get accordion music, lukewarm rock, or morose Parisian crooners; in Prayssac, the girls at the SI have grown fond of a tape of Ella Fitzgerald with Chick Webb's band. They play it all the time, and under the plane trees at nine o'clock, in a French village market, everyone seems to think it hits just right.

The music isn't the only eclectic element. In our market, a solemn Dutchman with dirt under his fingernails sells his organic bok choy and Chinese cabbage, Jerusalem artichokes and spiky African melons. Lots of Dutchmen, passionate gardeners from a space-starved country, come down here for a little tranquillity and a little good earth. An Englishman who grew up here provides sweetcorn in late summer – the best you can get in Europe; the seed came from Pennsylvania. Even some of the French have gone exotic. The space cadet at the natural foods stand will sell you popcorn, Canadian wild rice, bulgar or fat-free nacho chips, and just around the corner a lady with a smile like the first sunny day in April is frying Vietnamese *nems* and samosas. Near the *librairie*, next to the fellow who's cooking a gigantic paella in a metre-wide pan, there's the pick-up truck selling live trout in the tank.

All this may seem a bit disconcerting, if you're given to fantasies about finding a bit of 'unspoiled' rural heaven in deepest France. If that's what you really want, try the Gers or the Aude, fine *départements* both. But the flagrant cosmopolitanism of many of our village markets has done no harm to their more traditional aspects. One can still pick up live geese, or rabbits and chicks in wooden cages, and farm wives still set up folding tables to sell carefully braided strings of garlic and onions, homemade walnut cakes or delicate-looking but potent discs of *cabécou*. Unless a comet collides with the Earth, you can bet that five centuries from now they'll still be doing it (though maybe by then the list of traditional southwestern specialities will include sweetcorn and *nems*). Once, on a chilly, drizzling day in early autumn, we saw a thoroughly miserable old farmer, staring blankly out from under a flowered umbrella. A shrewish pinchpenny wife had undoubtedly chased him out in the rain to sell the one treasure he had brought, a sinister-looking courgette the size of a steam boiler, precariously balanced on a wooden box with a sign: *€1/kilo*. Five centuries from now, he'll probably still be there too.

Dances with Bears

Onward the kindred Bears, with footsteps rude,
Dance round the pole, pursuing and pursued.

Erasmus Darwin (grandfather of Charles), in *Economy of Vegetation*

Have you ever wondered why it is that children respond so viscerally to teddy bears? One possible reason is pure atavism: way back in the Middle Palaeolithic or Mousterian culture (*c.* 120,000–35,000 BC) bears often occupied the same caves and shelters as our ancestors, and perhaps not always as dangerous rivals. In the

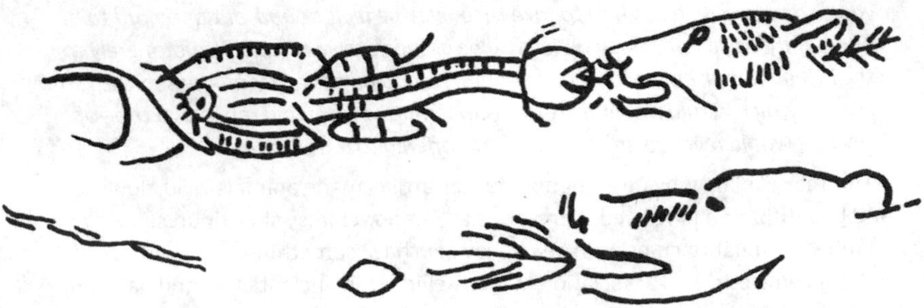

Grotta della Basura on the Italian Riviera, the chamber dubbed the 'Corridor of the Imprints' has fossilized footprints suggesting that bears and people once danced together; in another room a large quantity of bear bones were discovered. And in the 1950s, just above Lascaux at Régourdou, a ritual bear graveyard was discovered; each dead bear had been given 'gifts' of dead animals (*see* p.119).

In the vivid mural art of the Upper Palaeolithic in southwest France, bears (like people) are rarely portrayed among the bison, horses, aurochs and other favourite animal subjects: there's a fine one engraved in the Grotte de Bara-Bahau in Le Bugue (in a cave where bears lived for tens of thousands of years) and another at Lascaux, hidden in the body of the bull, as if it were part of a kids' find-the-hidden-picture game. Other drawings and engravings are accompanied by bear clawmarks. Most suggestive of all are the carvings on staffs found at La Madeleine (Dordogne) and at Massat (Ariège). Few other Palaeolithic works are as explicitly, and mysteriously, sexual: these staffs are the basis for the idea that some of the mysterious symbols in cave art represent male and female principles. Old Eskimo statuettes, from a culture technologically similar to the Upper Palaeolithic, show an intimacy with bears that is shocking by the nursery standards of Christopher Robin and Pooh Bear.

The evidence suggests that our ancestors' relationships with bears were limited to hunting cultures, as in the bear cults that survived into historical times. These were discovered by travellers and scholars in northernmost Japan (the Ainu people) or Siberia, where bears were not only a main source of food and clothing, but were also regarded as the representatives of gods. According to legend, the Ainu descended from the son of a woman and a bear. Ainu hunters apologized profusely when they slew one, and set up bear skulls (where the animal's spirit resides) in a place of honour. When a bear cub was captured, it would be suckled by an Ainu woman and raised with her children until it became dangerous; then for two or three years it would be put in a cage and pampered with delicacies, in preparation for a Bear Festival. Then the bear would be given a huge last meal in a great show of sorrow, as the Ainu apologized and carefully explained to the bear the reasons for sending it to its mountain ancestors. Then it would be ritually strangled and eaten. In commenting on the Ainu in *The Golden Bough*, James Frazer wrote:

...the sharp line of demarcation which we draw between mankind and the lower animals does not exist for the savage. To him many of the other animals appear as his equals or even his superiors, not merely in brute force but intelligence; and if

choice or necessity leads him to take their lives, he feels bound, out of regard to his own safety, to do it in a way which will be as inoffensive as possible not merely to the living animal, but to its departed spirit and to all the other animals of the same species, which would resent an affront upon one of their kind much as a tribe of savages would revenge an injury or insult offered to a tribesman.

This may explain why Cro-Magnon hunter-artists made animals vivid, flowing and beautiful, and portrayed themselves as inferior, clumsy stick figures.

Prehistoric relationships with bears may also have something to do with that 'relic of some primeval association of ideas' evident in ancient India and Babylon, in the Book of Job, in Hesiod and Homer and native North American Indian tribes, which have all identified the circumpolar constellation as a bear – the Great Bear, or Ursa Major, which is pursued or watched over by the bright star Arcturus (from the Greek word for bear-keeper). And hence the word for Arctic and Arthur – the early English designated King Arthur's home there in the heavens, and some speculate that the circle, once known as 'Arthur's Wain', described by the stars was the origin of the Round Table. The common English name for the constellation, Charles's Wain, derives from the medieval legendary association of Charlemagne and Arthur.

Which brings us back to southwest France where the Great Bear in the sky is now called a casserole, where Charlemagne took his licks at Roncesvalles, and where along the coast of the Landes there are legends of King Arthur galloping to the hunt at night, legends unlike any in Brittany, where one might guess they were common. It is equally fitting that Heinrich Heine's Atta Troll, the last great literary Bruin (before Winnie-the-Pooh, anyway), roved the same land that has preserved our earliest known representations of bears.

Art Begins Here

Art is art. Everything else is everything else.

Ad Reinhardt

Two-thirds of the 115 or so prehistoric decorated caves known in the world are in southwest France. No one will ever know if Upper Palaeolithic art was once as common everywhere, or if the natives of Lot and Dordogne valleys were especially inspired or gifted between 30,000 and 10,000 BC, or if it is only by accident that conditions here were ideal for the preservation of their art – warm valleys with caves rich in sedimentary deposits that, often thanks to rockslides or other accidents, were long blocked off from light and air.

Created by a people so antediluvian that they are almost impossible to imagine, the works are very difficult to look at as pieces of art in themselves and not as brief, mysterious encounters with another world. Or as P. M. Grand wrote in *Prehistoric Art*: 'The glamour of the sacred is particularly strong in our epoch, which has almost lost sight of the sources of the supernatural. Not to be deceived by this glamour is a major requirement in any investigation of cultures that present to us vastly more questions than answers.' The fact that there may well have been a ritualistic or supernatural motivation behind the drawings and paintings takes nothing away from their aesthetic value; art has always willingly served religion. Forget, too, the

Hollywood view of hairy, grunting brutes dragging Raquel Welch around by the hair when they aren't punching dinosaurs; these people were our intellectual equals, with a keen eye for observations, a capacity for abstract or symbolic expression, and imaginative innovations that would take later artists until the 20th century to duplicate. 'This is the infancy of art, not an art of infancy' as the saying goes.

Prehistory itself is a very recent field. Until the 19th century, Upper Palaeolithic artefacts (tools, decorated throwing sticks, carvings in bone or stone, staffs, 'Venuses') were called 'thunderstones', to be dismissed somehow as the 'accompaniments of lightning'. In 1859, the discovery of tools in the same strata as the bones of extinct animals convinced scientists of their great antiquity and led to an increased interest in the field – further fuelled by the publication of Darwin's *On the Origin of Species* the same year. The idea that a stone-tool culture was also capable of the lofty, 'noble' art of painting was much more difficult for many intellectuals. When the first extraordinary murals were discovered in the cave of Altamira in northern Spain in 1879, all but a tiny handful of scholars sincerely believed they were a hoax.

The Doubting Thomases began to change their minds in 1895, with the discovery of the Grotte de La Mouthe in the Dordogne, where along with the paintings and wall incisions a prehistoric lantern was found. A 23-year-old priest named Henri Breuil was invited to trace the drawings, beginning the career of a man now known as 'the father of prehistory'. Once Breuil and his fellow pioneer Denis Peyrony knew what to look for, important discoveries followed quickly; in 1901, the men found the reliefs and paintings in Les Combarelles and Font-de-Gaume, both near Les Eyzies. Local children, enthused by the finds in their villages, began to seriously explore the countryside. In 1922 they discovered Pech-Merle in the Lot, in 1940 Lascaux, so magnificent and beautiful that there's the temptation to stand Breuil's description of the cave as 'the Sistine Chapel of prehistoric art' on its head, and say that the Sistine Chapel is the Lascaux of Renaissance art.

One of the many intriguing things about the painted and engraved caves decorated some 16,000 years ago is that they achieve so many of the aims of art in the last half of the 20th century onwards – they suggest far more than they actually show and invite the viewer to participate actively in their meaning; they make admirable use of their environment and the palette that nature presents (bulges in the stone wall give animals a three-dimensional feel, the shadows suggest water, a protrusion becomes the muzzle of a horse); they are not bound as compositions into the artificial rigours of a canvas, much less to any sensation of up and down or north or south. A cave is a natural installation and a natural sanctuary, and it's a shame that Matisse or Joan Miró never had a good crack at one. Most of all, they combine their formal perfection with a function and meaning that, even if the exact nature of it may never be discovered, leaves a powerful and poignant impression even after thousands of years. Nothing means as much or will ever be as immediately close to us as the animal world was to these first artists. The only composition that the 20th century produced that comes close to the powerful impact of Lascaux is Picasso's *Guernica*, a work about new technological advances in death and horror.

Goose Lore and Livers

In the southwest the national bird of France, the strutting cockerel, seems far removed, a symbol rarely seen outside the backyard coop. Instead, visitors are confronted everywhere by giant plywood geese, beckoning clients into tiny shops selling foie gras and *confits*.

Although it would be heresy to say so in the southwest, the national dish, *confits d'oie*, may have originated in medieval Venice, where one staple was *bigoli con sugo di oca conservato* (fat buckwheat spaghetti with a goose *confit* sauce). In fact, for centuries Périgord pâté was made not of goose but of partridges stuffed with truffles and chicken livers. In 1726 the partridges got a break when a certain Close de Strasbourg discovered that goose liver with truffles tasted much finer, and the bigger the liver the better. It had already been noted (by the legendary Egyptian savant Imhotep, in 4700 BC) that pigeons that stuffed themselves silly on corn developed swollen, delicious livers, and the concept was extrapolated to geese and ducks (which are much more amenable to *gavage*, or force-feeding). After spending the life of Riley wandering at will in meadows and walnut groves, the geese are fed a three-week adjustment diet of flour, corn, and meat before being enclosed in autumn for three weeks of *gavage* three times a day – traditionally women's work – each bird downing between 30 and 40kg of corn to create the perfect creamy pink liver weighing up to 1.4kg, mostly in preparation for the Christmas holidays and the New Year, when half of France's foie gras is consumed. Foie gras was also a hit abroad; one of Talleyrand's secret weapons of diplomacy was his chef, who softened up ambassadors and heads of state with pâté de foie gras and a glass of golden Monbazillac.

To many foreigners (and not a few French citizens as well), *gavage* seems the height of barbarism. They wince at the postcards of geese being force-fed by crafty old women stroking a goose neck with one hand while holding a funnel of corn down its throat with the other; they are horrified that many farms invite visitors to watch, and that many geese willingly waddle over for their corn tipple (they look happier than battery chickens, at any rate). During the Occupation, the Nazis with their delicate sensibilities found the practice offensive and banned *gavage*, with the curious result of making foie gras a proud symbol of the Resistance. In an effort to make *gavage* more humane (but mostly to save the intensive labour involved) attempts have been made to adjust the thymus gland in geese and ducks to make them naturally piggy, but up until now biologically engineered *auto-gavage* has had limited success.

The goose that lays the southwest's golden egg faces an even greater challenge in the form of importers from Romania, Israel and beyond, who are flooding the market with phoney foie gras, or foie gras incorporating all kinds of fillers – counterfeits that threaten to undermine both the traditional producers and confidence in the product. It's bad enough that such things happen in Paris, but down here, in the sanctuaries of traditional foie gras, such cheating is blasphemy. Yet anyone passing through the region can't help but notice the disparity between the amount of foie gras on offer and the actual number of geese and ducks. These days connoisseurs and restaurateurs have to know their sources personally.

But the strange attachment of the area to its fowl fetish goes back centuries before anyone thought to tamper with goose livers. The Basques tell of a race of lovely but goose-footed fairies, the laminak, and Toulouse was the home of the famous Visigothic queen Ranachilde, wife of Theodoric II, *la reine pédauque or pé d'aouco*, the goose-foot queen who could swim better than walk and had aqueducts built in Toulouse so she could paddle from her palace to the city. Her story inspired others, like those of Berthe, mother of Charlemagne (d. 783), who was said to have webbed or at least very large feet, and another goosey Berthe, the wife of King Robert the Pious. This couple was excommunicated for a consanguineous marriage, and their incestuous relationship is said to have produced a goose-headed child.

One of the Berthes, at any rate, was customarily represented as a rather domestic queen, telling children tales by her spinning wheel (French tales customarily begin with 'In the time when good Queen Berthe spun...'). Andrew Lang in his researches located the first reference to Mother Goose, la *Mère l'Oye*, in a 1650 book called *La Muse Historique*, predating Charles Perrault's 1697 *Contes de ma Mère l'Oye*; in English the first reference to Mother Goose appeared in a fairytale book printed in London in 1729. Perhaps most mysterious of all are the Cagots, a vanished people who lived in the Pyrenees and were said to be albinos, or dwarfs or lepers; in the Middle Ages they were renowned as excellent architects and carpenters, though they were forced to live apart and wear a goose foot around their necks.

The Architecture of Springtime

So it was as though the world had shaken herself and cast off her old age, and were clothing herself everywhere in a white garment of churches.

Ralph Glaber, 11th-century English chronicler

On a typically rainy autumn afternoon we saw an old farmer trudging in the mud alongside the road, so we stopped to give him a lift. It turned out he wasn't a farmer at all, despite the beret, overalls and rough-cut walking stick. He was a retired Swiss teacher who had decided to spend the rest of his life walking around Europe, looking at Romanesque churches. That made for some good conversation along the way; we compared notes on buildings in Apulia and the Abruzzo, and Templar chapels along the pilgrimage routes in Old Castile. We told him about one unknown church in a tiny nearby village, one with horseshoe arches derived from Muslim Spain and a Celtic spiral carved over the door. He knew about it already.

Such a devotion may seem eccentric, but this fellow was hardly alone. The Romanesque is a bug that bites unexpectedly; no other art and architecture in the West has the same inexplicable capacity to enchant. At first sight, especially if you've been indoctrinated in school, you might think that the products of modern Europe's first artistic urge are mere 'primitives', the first child steps on the way to the Gothic and Renaissance. A closer look reveals an immensely sophisticated art that seems to have sprung, fully formed, out of nothing at the dawn of the Middle Ages. In fact the ideas of Romanesque had been around for a while, breaking out occasionally in unexpected places such as Armenia, or Asturias in northern Spain. Only in the huge economic upsurge of the 11th.century did anyone in Europe really have a chance to build. When they got the chance, they built for the ages, solidly and in good stone. At first sight their works may seem heavy, with the little light that filters through the narrow windows in the afternoon. Not until the late 12th century, with the new Gothic advances, would the technology appear to allow those windows to get bigger. But let your eyes adjust to the shadows for a minute, and you'll see wonders.

'Romanesque', for such a momentous and varied movement in architecture, is as misleading a term as 'Gothic'. Among the few things it has in common with ancient Rome are the use of round arches and a habit of using the basilican plan for churches; large projects, of which the southwest can offer only a few survivors, such as St-Sernin in Toulouse or Ste-Croix in Bordeaux, also often attempt to recapture the monumentality of the Roman manner. But Romanesque has nothing to do with the classical Orders of ancient buildings; rather it depends on a new system of sacred geometry, which probably began with Hagia Sophia in 6th-century Constantinople and gradually spread across both Europe and the Muslim world. Anyone with a mathematical bent will enjoy looking over the churches or their plans; every point in the ground plans and elevations can be proved with a compass and straightedge, the same way the master masons designed them.

In the springtime of the medieval world, nearly every large region of western Europe developed its own distinctive style. Freedom and fancy were in the air in the 11th and 12th centuries; standards were high and rules few. Provence had its stiff, heavy buildings and octagonal cupolas; the Catalans built similarly, and accentuated their works with elegant towers and brilliant sculpture, while the Auvergne contributed unique patterned façades perhaps inspired by the caliphate of Andalucía. The basic element in Aquitaine is the *clocher-mur*, a west front that rises above the roofline to make a wide belfry, providing a memorable façade and saving the great expense of building a separate tower. There are some eccentricities, such as the cave-churches of St-Emilion and Aubeterre-sur-Dronne, cut out of the rock, while Périgord also came up with the most exotic flower of all Romanesque styles, impressive churches with shallow Byzantine domes – an idea brought back from Syria and Palestine after the First Crusade. Many others in Périgord are fortified churches, a testimony to the roughhouse feudal warfare there, though aesthetics may suffer a bit.

Along with the architecture goes its sculptural decoration – the first great age of sculpture since classical Greece. Early medieval society found the resources not only to raise all these buildings but to decorate their portals and columns with a wealth of sculpted detail, even in some village churches. The southwest contributed more than its share, including the most accomplished workshop, the 'School of Toulouse' that created the vibrant, flowing reliefs on the portals of Moissac and Souillac; many consider Moissac's to be the greatest masterpiece of all medieval sculpture.

And what have the French done with this heritage? The Parisian conquest of the Midi and other lands currently French ensured a calculated devaluation of their art and culture. From the Renaissance Italians, the French first learned a rationale for contempt for their greatest buildings, and set off on a path of slavish imitation of the Romans and a submission to academies and rules – a disaster that plagues the national culture to this day. In the philistine 17th and 18th centuries, the tastemakers in the academies considered anything medieval the artistic equivalent of *patois*, especially if it came from the early centuries when the provinces, not Paris, were the vanguard. They spoilt the interiors of thousands of churches, plastering them over with gaudy Baroque frippery and gilded knick-knacks (most of that has been cleared away in the last few decades). There was more to the world of the Romanesque than the Enlightenment ever dreamt of in its philosophy, and in the first days of the Revolution uncomprehending mobs gleefully smashed some of the finest medieval sculpture. Casualties included the School of Toulouse's cloisters of St-Sernin and St-Etienne; you can see the surviving fragments in the Musée des Augustins. After the Revolution, scores of churches and monasteries saw duty as barns, warehouses and barracks; many more were simply torn down for their stone.

When the first attempts at restoration were made, the result was often just as unfortunate – the classic example in all France being Paul Abadie's supremely arrogant job on St-Front in Périgueux, in which more was wrecked than restored, while the building was changed out of all recognition. France, surprisingly one of the most backward nations of Europe in historic preservation, has only got its act together in the last few decades. Even in the 1920s, entire cloisters were being sold off or destroyed – a lot of the southwest's best sculpture was purchased for John D. Rockefeller and moved to his Cloisters Museum in Manhattan.

Wandering among the fragments of the early Middle Ages one often feels like an archaeologist exploring the enigmatic survivals of a lost civilization. It *is* a lost civilization; we know as little about the inspirations and motivations of early medieval artists as about classical antiquity or the Egyptians. The architecture speaks for itself – an inexhaustible vernacular of simple arches, barrel vaulting, pilasters and apses recombined in 1,000 different ways. The sculpture is more of a problem; its imagery often reflects concepts that have nothing to do with orthodox religion, or indeed with Christianity at all. Why is the prophet Isaiah dancing at Souillac, and what made the seemingly obscure episode of Daniel in the lions' den the most copied and most significant image in the sculpture of the southwest and Languedoc? And what about the mermaids? In scores of churches around the region, and across Europe, images of mermaids appear in hidden places, sometimes cradling babies, sometimes alone, spreading their forked tails in an unseemly way – any fan of the Romanesque is sure to be reminded of the capital of this strangeness, Italy's Monte Sant'Angelo, where coiled serpents whisper ancient secrets into the mermaids' ears.

The sculpture is the key, though you'll always have to look carefully to find it. When you visit a Romanesque church, even a simple one in a village, scrutinize every corner, inside and out. The great themes of the Life of Christ and the Apocalypse are portrayed for all to see on the portals, but the esoteric bits are in places you wouldn't expect, perhaps to hide them from the casual eye, perhaps in their pride to force us to look all around, and so come to appreciate the work as a whole as they did. The faces are everywhere, especially on the *modillons*, or corbel-stones around the roofline: hundreds of faces, grimacing, smiling, interspersed with monsters, cats, dogs, boars, unicorns and all the other inhabitants of the medieval imagination. There may be a giant with a club, a dim memory of ancient

Hercules, or a fine lady in a small boat (her name is Phaedria, and she symbolizes Desire). On the capitals inside, hunters and lovers, lions and kings stare down at you. The meaning, and even the identity of the characters, is often lost to us, though if you could go back to the 1100s a troubadour poet, or a street singer, or a monk with a little Latin, might have explained them all. But you can't, and unless you're willing to cut yourself a walking stick and spend the rest of your life at it, travelling and reading and looking, you'll never know.

Food and Drink

The Cuisine of the Southwest 46
Périgord and Quercy 46
The Bordelais 48
Markets, Picnic Food and Snacks 48
Drinks 49
Wine 50
Restaurant Basics 52
Menu Reader 52

04

When the French talk about abandoning the charms of nouvelle cuisine for good old country cooking, or *cuisine du terroir*, southwest France is often the first *terroir* that springs to mind. Intensely rural, a land of small traditional family farms, overflowing with the good things of the earth, it serves hearty dishes so delicious that eating and drinking are two of the most compelling reasons to visit. Indeed, everyone is so pleased with the local fare that it can be hard to find a restaurant that serves anything else.

The Cuisine of the Southwest

Périgord and Quercy

For all the talk of tradition, the dishes that bring hungry Parisians down here en masse only date as popular fare from the 19th century; before then, local barons were so rapacious that the peasants' diet was based on red cabbage, chestnuts, turnips and fruit, plus fish if they lived near the river; hunting was a privilege of the nobility. These days, perhaps to make up for the past, meat is liable to appear in every course except dessert. The otherwise calorie- and cholesterol-conscious can take courage from recent studies showing that the basic southwest diet, with all its duck and goose fat ('*sans beurre et sans reproche*', as the great gastronome Curnonsky described it), garlic and red wine, is actually good for you and your heart; heart disease is half the rate that it is in the United States. Many natives live well into their nineties.

The best place in which to tuck into a traditional meal is a *ferme-auberge*, or farm restaurant, where most of what you eat has been raised on the spot. A typical meal in a *ferme-auberge* or a good traditional restaurant may start with an apéritif, a kir (maybe with *vin de Cahors* instead of white wine) or a *fénelon* (a delightful cocktail of walnut liqueur, cassis and red wine). Then comes the *tourain* (or *tourin*), an onion and garlic soup cooked in a broth with duck or goose fat and lard, ladled over slices of country bread and cheese. The proper way to finish up the dregs is *faire chabrot*: pour in a dash of red wine, swish it around, and drink it directly from the bowl.

The next dish is generally a pâté, often of duck or goose, or *rillons* (the meat that's left over after preparation of foie gras and *confits*, mixed with a bit of fat to make a smooth paste) or foie gras, the enlarged liver of either a goose or duck (*see* pp.40–41), perhaps studded with a 'black diamond' – a bit of truffle that it doesn't really need but that jacks the price up even further. Foie gras usually comes prepared in a terrine or half-cooked (*mi-cuit*) in a frying pan, served with thin slices of toast and a chilled glass of sweet white Sauternes, Loupiac, or Monbazillac. Goose is finer and more delicate; duck is tastier (and cheaper). Other popular starters include a salad of *gésiers*, or gizzards, cooked and sliced with lettuce, walnuts and croutons, or a plate of *charcuterie*. In the spring, asparagus often makes an appearance, and sometimes in Périgord you'll see *boutons de scorsonères* – flowers of black salsify – cooked in omelettes. For an autumn delicacy, try an omelette with fresh *cèpes* (boletus mushrooms) or fragrant black truffles. In autumn and winter, Lalbenque in the Lot hosts one of the biggest truffle markets in France, but don't expect to find any bargains.

Main courses often feature yet more duck in the form of *confits*. These are the southwest's traditional way of keeping meat: thighs, legs, or wings are cooked and then potted in their own fat, and reheated when it's time to eat. *Magrets* (or *maigrets*), a relatively new cut of meat on the market, are steak-like fillets of duck breast, simply grilled and served with a very light cream sauce with parsley and garlic, or a fruit sauce. *Cou d'oie*, goose neck stuffed with a truffled minced pork and foie gras, and *demoiselles*, carcasses of fattened ducks grilled on a wood fire, are traditional rural favourites that occasionally make it on to pricey restaurant menus. The duck or goose fat that preserves the *confits* is the essential ingredient for preparing *pommes de terre sarladaise* – sliced potatoes sautéed in fat, with garlic and parsley, and *cèpes* in the autumn. It's a combination that lifts the humble spud to culinary heaven (they used to put truffles in them too, back when truffles were still affordable). Another main destination for *confits* is cassoulet, a dish that reaches its epiphany in Toulouse (*see* p.448).

Poultry – free-range Gascon chickens with black feet, or guinea fowl, capon, pheasant and pigeon – is always delicious, occasionally served in a fricassée, in a *ballottine* (a galantine of rolled poultry and stuffing) or *alicuit*, a traditional Gascon ragout of poultry giblets (even testicles), wings, potatoes, carrots and onions. Occasionally on the menus of *fermes-auberges* you'll see a *mique*, a dumpling of maize flour cooked in bouillon that was long a staple in old Quercy and Périgord.

Game dishes appear in season – venison, pheasant, boar and *marcassin* (young boar, served in a *civet* or red wine stew). Beef dishes are fairly rare, outside of *tournedos* – fillet of beef with a rich sauce of foie gras and truffles – in Périgord. Lamb, especially *agneau de causse*, grazed on Quercy's limestone plateaux, is very popular but is often served too rare for many Anglo-Saxon tastes. Pork appears in sausages – the omnipresent fat *saucisse de Toulouse*, or thinner chipolatas and spicy merguez – a contribution of the southwest's Spanish immigrants. *Andouillettes* are chitterling sausages; much rarer are pinkish *anguettes*, made with turkey's blood, unappetizing to look at but much appreciated fried in goose fat, with a spoonful of vinegar, garlic, and nutmeg. In the Lot-et-Garonne, pork is often cooked with prunes and wine in a delicious sweet and savoury combination. Trout, pike (*brochet*, often prepared as *quenelles*, or cakes), and *écrevisse* (crayfish), *sandre* (pike-perch), *alose* (shad) and salmon are the principal fish on the menu, and increasingly you'll see sturgeon, which is delicious smoked.

The classic salad is made of curly lettuce and walnuts, seasoned with walnut oil, and forms the perfect accompaniment to the famous goats' cheese of the region, little roundlets of AOC Rocamadour or *cabécou*. The Lot also produces a *bleu des Causses*, similar to Roquefort, while the larger weekday markets offer a variety of sheeps' and cows' milk cheeses produced on family farms.

The locals love their sweets, and in some restaurants the desserts are the stars of the show. Traditional specialities often involve walnuts (*tarte aux noix*, walnut tart; *gâteau aux noix*, walnut cake, sometimes coated with bitter chocolate) or prunes (in a *tourtière*, marinated in Armagnac and orange-blossom water and topped with layers of paper-thin pastry called *pastis*, of one part butter to four parts flour). A *flognarde* is a *clafoutis* (batter cake) with pieces of apples, pears or plums; light crispy *échaudés* are flavoured with aniseed liqueurs, *vieille prune* (old prune) or *eau de noix* (made with green walnuts). A *toureau* is a Sunday or holiday bread-like cake in a ring served as a dessert, flavoured with orange-blossom water, lemon, oranges, rum, vanilla and Grand Marnier, with home-made jam (leftovers are good toasted). Fresh strawberries in season appear in a wide variety of desserts; melons, *pêches de vigne* (peaches grown between vines, now rare), apricots or cherries in Armagnac round off a meal in style.

The Bordelais

Cross over into the Bordelais and menus take on a whole new cast of ingredients, beginning with the oysters of Arcachon, traditionally served on the half-shell with buttered bread and little grilled sausages called *crépinettes*. Mussels, *coques* (cockles) and *praires* (clams) are other tasty local shellfish; from the Gironde estuary come *pibales* (tiny baby elvers fried in oil), shrimp, shad (especially as *alose à l'oseille*, stuffed with sorrel and grilled over vine cuttings, which helps dissolve its fine bones), eels, salmon, salmon trout and, perhaps a bit shocking to the uninitiated, lamprey, a dish so prized that the canons of St-Seurin in Bordeaux gave up all their rights to property in the city in 1170 in exchange for 12 good fat lampreys a year (*see* p.217).

If garlic is the totem elsewhere in the Midi, shallots are just as essential to the Bordelais: *à la bordelaise* means topped with a *hachis* of parsley and shallots (but, confusingly, it can also mean accompanied with *cèpes*, or red wine sauce). Chopped shallots attain a kind of epiphany when served on grilled steaks – the famous *entrecôte à la bordelaise* (*see* p.258). Much passion is reserved for *cèpes*, and hunting them in the autumn, especially on someone else's property, can lead to slit tyres, dog bites and gunshots. There are two kinds: the true *cèpe bordelais* (*cèpe de chêne*) and the less tasty *cèpe des pins*. Asparagus, both green and white, is one of the joys of spring in the region.

A speciality revived since 1985 is milk-fed lamb, or *agneau de Pauillac*, which holds pride of place among meat dishes along with the beef from Bazas and capons from Grignols; in the autumn, wood pigeon is a favourite dish, although few would countenance the way they are caught – netted a flock at a time. Amongst the sweets, look for *compote de vigneron*, apples melted in red Bordeaux; in the big city itself, try a *canelé*, a delicious pastry made according to a recipe invented by people living around the port of Bordeaux from the remains of flour left in the holds of ships after the main cargo had been unloaded, then adopted and made popular by the nuns of the Annonciade in the 16th century.

Markets, Picnic Food and Snacks

In most villages, market day is the big event of the week, and rightfully so. Brimful of fresh farm produce, and often just as brimful with local characters, they are fun to visit on their own, and become even more interesting if you're cooking or gathering the ingredients for a picnic. In the larger cities they take place every day, while smaller towns and villages have markets just one day a week, which double as social occasions for the locals. Most markets finish up around noon. In summer keep your ear open for the newly popular *marchés gourmands* – once a week in the evening in pretty rural settings, villagers set up tables and various producers set up stands selling soup, salads, potatoes, main courses, and desserts and wine, which you can pick and choose from to make up your own meal, often for only a few euros.

Other good sources for picnic food are the *charcuteries* or *traiteurs*, both of whom sell prepared dishes that are sold by weight in cartons or tubs (as do larger supermarkets). Cities are snack-food wonderlands, with outdoor counters selling pastries, crêpes, pizza slices, *frites*, and a wide variety of fillings stuffed into long thin crispy baguettes.

Drinks

Cafés serve drinks, but they are also a home away from home, places in which to read the papers, play cards, meet friends and just unwind, sit back and watch the world go by. Prices are listed on the *tarif des consommations*: note that they are based on whether you're served at the bar (*au comptoir*), at a table (*dans la salle*) or outside (*à la terrasse*).

French **coffee** is strong and black but lacklustre next to the aromatic brews of Italy or Spain. If you order *un café* you'll get a small black espresso; if you want milk, order *un crème*. If you want more than a few drops of caffeine, ask them to make it *grand*. For **decaffeinated**, the word is *déca*; in summer try a *frappé* (iced coffee). The French only order *café au lait* (a small coffee topped off with lots of hot milk) when they stop in for **breakfast**. There are baskets of croissants and pastries, and some bars will make you a baguette with butter, jam or honey. If you want to go native, try the Frenchman's Breakfast of Champions: a *pastis* or two, and five non-filter Gauloises. *Chocolat chaud* (**hot chocolate**) is usually good; if you order *thé* (**tea**), you'll get an ordinary bag; an *infusion* or *tisane* is a **herbal tea** – *camomille*, *menthe* (mint), *tilleul* (lime or linden blossom) or *verveine* (verbena). These are kind to the all-precious *foie*, or liver, after you've over-indulged at the table.

Mineral water (*eau minérale*) is available in both sparkling (*gazeuse*) and still (*non-gazeuse* or *plate*) versions; if you feel run-down, Badoit has lots of peppy magnesium in it. Apart from bottled **fruit juices** (*jus de fruits*), some bars also serve freshly squeezed lemon and orange with a jug of water (*citron pressé* or *orange pressée*). The French are also very fond of fruit syrups – red *grenadine* and ghastly green *diabolo menthe*.

Beer (*bière*) in most bars and cafés is run-of-the-mill big brands from Alsace, Germany and Belgium. Draught (*à la pression*) is cheaper than bottled beer. Nearly all resorts have bars or pubs offering wider selections of draughts, lagers and bottles. Smarter bars and cafés in the cities sell cocktails – even mojitos are starting to breech the mighty walls of southwest traditions.

The strong spirit of the Midi comes in a liquid form called ***pastis***, which was first made popular in Marseilles as a plague remedy; its name comes from the Latin *passe-sitis*, or thirst quencher. A pale yellow 90° nectar flavoured with aniseed, vanilla and cinnamon, *pastis* is drunk as an apéritif before lunch and in rounds after work. The three major brands, Ricard, Pernod and Pastis 51, all taste slightly different; most people drink their '*pastaga*' with lots of water and ice (*glaçons*).

Wine

One of the greatest pleasures of travelling in southwest France lies in discovering new wines and drinking them for a fraction of what you'd pay at home. Buying wine direct from the producers, the *vignerons*, is half the fun and will save you money as well. In the text we've included a few addresses for each wine to get you started, but do ask locally as well. And don't pass up a *fête du vin* – buying a glass and tasting your way around the stands is a quick way to hone in on the ones you like best. Because the joy (and now the despair – *see* box opposite) of France is that no two estates are alike.

The wine region of Bordeaux, the largest in the world, covers 117,000 hectares in the *département* of the Gironde, and produces more than 500 million litres a year – enough to launch a battleship. Nearly all of this area is AOC (*appellation d'origine contrôlée*): divided into 57 different *appellations*, including some of the most prestigious in France – Pomerol, Sauternes, Saint-Emilion, Pauillac, Margaux – encompassing about 3,500 red and white *crus*. Each *cru*, or growth, results from a unique combination of the soil, climate, location, vine and grower's skill. A *premier cru* or *grand cru* is the top of the top: a Château Lafite, Latour, d'Yquem or Ausone that you have to own several oil wells to afford on a regular basis. But even wines that aren't designated as *crus* are now better than ever, thanks to the introduction of new techniques and care.

Similar improvements have been made to other AOC wines of the southwest – Côtes de Duras, Buzet, Cahors, Bergerac and the sweet white wine of Monbazillac. Many were famous in the Middle Ages, and even preferred to Bordeaux wines, but because they were upriver they were for centuries denied access to northern markets – by the Bordelais, of course. If you like to visit wineries or *chais* (a Gascon word for the buildings where the wine is stored in oak barrels, before being bottled and laid in the *cave*, or cellar), those of the Haut Pays tend to be friendly and easy to get into without booking – for a look around and a tasting, often with the proprietor.

Make sure that you don't neglect wines bearing less exalted labels, especially those labelled VDQS (*vin de qualité supérieure*) or *vin de pays* (which are guaranteed to originate in a certain region: Côtes de Quercy and Vin du Tsar are worth a try), with *vin ordinaire* (or *vin de table*) at the bottom, which may not send you to seventh heaven, but at least it's cheap.

If you're buying direct from the producer, you'll be offered glasses to taste from various bottles, each older than the previous one, until you are feeling quite jolly and ready to buy the last (and most expensive) vintage.

A good many producers (especially in the Haut Pays; it seldom happens in Bordeaux) sell loose wine. This is often good AOC stuff that you can take home and bottle yourself (or just drink, as the case may be). You will need to invest in an inexpensive *cubivin*, a plastic flexible container with a tap housed in a cardboard box; it collapses as you use it and preserves the wine for a few weeks. *Cubivins* come in various sizes, up to 33 litres; if they're not available in the vineyards, they can tell you where to get one.

The French Revolution, Part II

In hindsight, the first warning shot came in 1976, when the British wine-shop owner Stephen Spurrier held a blind tasting in his Paris premises, pitting eight of France's most prestigious wines against a dozen of California's finest. French experts were shocked when the two top-ranked wines were American.

At the time, the French wine world shrugged a great Gallic shrug; it was a fluke for the colonial upstarts. When memories of the famous tasting niggled, they reminded themselves that aristocratic Bordeaux and Burgundy, after all, had the bloodlines and the prestige, backed by long tradition and strict laws a century old (*see* p. 241). Besides, the newcomers were obviously amateurs in understanding the mystique of the *terroir*, the combination of soil and drainage and climate and position that made each vineyard different and wine-making such an art. The *terroir* also assured that only serious connoisseurs knew differences and vintages among the 10,000 producers in the Bordelais alone.

In the meantime, while France ate cake in the spirit of Marie Antoinette, a host of other countries prepared to assault its position as the top wine exporter in the world. Not hidebound by French regulations (and the French sense of superiority), wine-makers in the Americas, Australia, Spain, New Zealand and South Africa began to plant and experiment and, most of all, to improve, often by doing things that were forbidden to the French with their AOC rules, such as irrigating vineyards and adding woodchips to counteract astringency. Like good capitalists, the New World wine-makers sold their product by brands, according to the grape variety. They standardized their wine so that every year it tasted the same, in order that the buyer knew exactly what to expect.

Meanwhile, the French were drinking less wine every year (average per capita consumption today is half what it was in the 1960s), while the new growth markets in the UK and USA were demanding better quality. And the new imbibers had different habits and different tastes; unlike the French, who think wine (preferably dry) belongs only on the dinner table, people elsewhere were quaffing it in bars, and sought a fruitier, sweeter non-tannic wine that the New World wineries supplied. Classic Bordeaux may be great with classic French cuisine,but worldwide food tastes were changing to more exotic, sweet and spicier foods. The upstarts go better with a Thai curry. Even before the surge of the euro, many were cheaper, too.

The *Académie* has yet to approve it, but you can hear a new word in French wine circles: *parkerization*, for the effects on the industry wrought by Robert Parker, highly respected US wine critic and author of the bible of Bordeaux. Parker didn't give a hoot about reputations, price, *terroir* or tradition, and to his mind many a prestigious château was sitting on its past laurels. Some innovative growers saw which way the wind was blowing and began experimenting to create new, more fashionable wines in their garages – hence *garagistes*. Some bottles go for €100 or more (prices are sometimes kept high by limited production).

Still, it has to be said that the extent of Bordeaux's dramatic fall from grace, in spite of the warning signs (and in spite of recent excellent years), has put France in a state of shock. In 2003 (a hot, potentially powerfully great year in Bordeaux) French wine exports worldwide fell, for the first time, behind California, Australia and Chile, and no wine sales have fallen faster than those of Bordeaux, down another 10 per cent between 2003 and 2004. While the very elite first growth châteaux (constituting only 5 per cent of Bordeaux production) command ever higher prices, a thousand small producers hover on the edge of bankruptcy. Even domestic consumption dropped by 5 per cent in 2004, although much of this was due to stricter drink driving laws. But to add insult to injury, even the French are drinking more imported wines.

Confusion reigns. An initial step has been to allow AOC wines to mention the grape variety on the label to level the playing field. Parker suggests letting *vignerons* experiment with grenache and other forbidden varieties. There may be a plain old Bordeaux Cabernet Sauvignon or Merlot before you know it. One *garagiste*, Jean-Luc Thunevin of Château Valandraud, even wants to sell great wines in *hypermarchés*!

Remember, the French know a thing or two about revolutions, too.

Restaurant Basics

Restaurants generally serve between 12 and 2 and in the evening from 7 to 9pm, with later summer hours. In the southwest people tend to arrive early, to have a better choice of dishes, and to get a crack at the specials – turn up at 1 for lunch or 8 for dinner and your choice may be limited. All post menus outside the door so you'll know what to expect; if prices aren't listed, you can bet it's not because they're a bargain. Most restaurants have a choice of set-price menus. If you have the appetite to eat the biggest meal of the day at noon, you'll spend a lot less money – the best way to experience the finer gourmet temples if you're on a budget. Eating *à la carte* will always be much more expensive; in most average spots no one ever does it.

Menus sometimes include the house wine (*vin compris*), which is usually quite drinkable; in *fermes-auberges* as often as not the bottles or carafes will just keep reappearing until you pass out. If you choose a better wine anywhere, expect a big mark-up. If service is included it will say *service compris* or *s.c.*, if not *service non compris* or *s.n.c.* Some restaurants offer a set-price gourmet *menu dégustation* – a selection of chef's specialities, which can be a great treat. At the other end of the scale is the *plat du jour* (daily special) and the no-choice *formule*, popular in cafés.

A full French meal may begin with an apéritif, hors d'œuvres, a starter or two, followed by the main course, cheese, dessert, coffee and chocolates, and perhaps a *digestif* to finish things off. If you order a salad it may come before or after but never with your main course. For everyday eating, most people condense this feast to a starter, main course, and cheese or dessert. **Vegetarians** often have a hard time in the southwest, but most establishments will try to accommodate you somehow.

When looking for a restaurant, homing in on the one place crowded with locals is as sound a policy in France as anywhere. Don't overlook hotel restaurants, some of which are absolutely top-notch. To avoid disappointment, be sure to call ahead to reserve a table, especially in the summer.

French Menu Reader

Starters and Soups (*Hors-d'œuvre et Soupes*)

amuse-gueule appetizer(s)
assiette assortie plate of mixed cold hors d'œuvre
bisque shellfish soup
bouchées mini vol-au-vents
bouillon broth
charcuterie mixed cold meats: salami, ham, etc.
consommé clear soup
potage thick vegetable soup
velouté thick smooth soup, often fish or chicken

Fish and Shellfish (*Poissons et Coquillages*)

aiglefin little haddock
anchois anchovies
anguille eel
barbue brill
baudroie anglerfish
belon flat oyster
beurre blanc sauce of shallots and wine vinegar whisked with butter
bigorneau winkle
blanchailles whitebait
brème bream
brochet pike
bulot whelk
cabillaud cod
calmar squid
carrelet plaice
colin hake
coque cockle
coquillages shellfish
coquilles St-Jacques scallops
crabe crab
crevettes grises shrimps
crevettes roses prawns
daurade sea bream
écrevisse freshwater crayfish
éperlan smelt

escabèche fried fish, marinated and served cold
escargots snails
espadon swordfish
esturgeon sturgeon
flétan halibut
friture deep-fried fish
fruits de mer seafood
gambas giant prawn
gigot de mer a large fish cooked whole
grondin red gurnard
hareng herring
homard Atlantic (Norway) lobster
huîtres oysters
lamproie lamprey
langouste spiny Mediterranean lobster
langoustines small Norway lobsters
limande lemon sole
lotte monkfish
loup (de mer) sea bass
maquereau mackerel
matelote d'anguilles eels in a wine sauce
merlan whiting
morue salt cod
moules mussels
omble chevalier char
palourdes clams
petit gris little grey snail
poulpe octopus
praires small clams
raie skate
rouget red mullet
St-Pierre John Dory
sandre zander or pike-perch
saumon salmon
sole (meunière) sole (with butter, lemon and parsley)
tellines tiny clams
thon tuna
truite trout
truite saumonée salmon trout

Meat and Poultry (*Viandes et Volailles*)

agneau (pré-salé) lamb (grazed in fields by the sea)
aloyau sirloin
andouillette chitterling (tripe) sausage
autruche ostrich
biftek beefsteak
blanc breast or white meat
blanquette stew of white meat, thickened with egg yolk
bœuf beef
boudin blanc sausage of white meat
boudin noir black pudding
brochette meat (or fish) on a skewer
caille quail
canard, caneton duck, duckling
carré crown roast
cassoulet haricot bean stew with sausage, duck, goose, etc.
cervelle brains
chapon capon
chateaubriand porterhouse steak
cheval horsemeat
chevreau kid
chevreuil venison
chorizo spicy Spanish sausage
civet meat stew, in wine and blood sauce
cœur heart
confit meat cooked and preserved in its own fat
contre-filet sirloin steak
côte, côtelette chop, cutlet
cou d'oie farci goose neck stuffed with pork, foie gras, truffles
crépinette small sausage
cuisse thigh or leg
cuisses de grenouilles frogs' legs
dinde, dindon turkey
entrecôte ribsteak
épaule shoulder
estouffade a meat stew marinated, fried and then braised
faisan pheasant
faux-filet sirloin
foie liver
foie gras goose liver
frais de veau veal testicles
fricadelle meatball
géline de touraine rare black hen of the region
gésier gizzard
gibier game
gigot leg of lamb
grillade grilled meat, often a mixed grill
jambon ham
jarret knuckle
langue tongue
lapereau young rabbit
lapin rabbit
lard (lardons) bacon (diced bacon)
lièvre hare
maigret/magret (de canard) breast (of duck)
manchons duck or goose wings
marcassin young wild boar
merguez spicy red sausage
mouton mutton
museau muzzle
navarin lamb stew with root vegetables
noix de veau (agneau) topside of veal (lamb)
oie goose
os bone
perdreau, perdrix partridge
petit salé salt pork
pieds trotters
pintade guinea fowl
plat-de-côtes short ribs or rib chops
porc pork

pot au feu meat and vegetables cooked in stock
poulet chicken
poussin baby chicken
quenelle poached dumplings made of fish, fowl or meat
queue de bœuf oxtail
rillons pork pieces cooked in their fat, a speciality from Touraine
ris (de veau) sweetbreads (veal)
rognons kidneys
rosbif roast beef
rôti roast
sanglier wild boar
saucisse sausage
saucisson salami-like sausage
selle (d'agneau) saddle (of lamb)
steak tartare raw minced beef, often topped with a raw egg yolk
suprême de volaille fillet of chicken breast and wing
tournedos thick round slices of beef fillet
travers de porc spare ribs
tripes tripe
veau veal
venaison venison

Vegetables, Herbs, etc. (*Légumes, Herbes, etc.*)

ail garlic
aneth dill
anis aniseed
artichaut artichoke
asperges asparagus
aubergine aubergine (eggplant)
avocat avocado
basilic basil
betterave beetroot
blette Swiss chard
cannelle cinnamon
céleri celery
céleri-rave celeriac
cèpes ceps, wild boletus mushrooms
champignons mushrooms
chanterelles wild yellow mushrooms
chicorée curly endive
chou cabbage
choucroute sauerkraut
chou-fleur cauliflower
choux de Bruxelles Brussels sprouts
ciboulette chives
citrouille pumpkin
clou de girofle clove
concombre cucumber
cornichons gherkins
cresson watercress
échalote shallot
endive chicory (endive)
épinards spinach
estragon tarragon
fenouil fennel
fève broad (fava) bean
flageolet white bean
fleurs de courgette courgette flowers
frites chips (French fries)
galipette large round mushroom
genièvre juniper
gingembre ginger
haricots beans
haricots blancs white beans
haricots rouges kidney beans
haricots verts green (French) beans
jardinière mixed diced garden vegetables
laitue lettuce
laurier bay leaf
lentilles lentils
macédoine diced vegetables
maïs (épis de) sweetcorn (on the cob)
marjolaine marjoram
menthe mint
mesclun mixed-leaf salad
morilles morel mushrooms
moutarde mustard
navet turnip
oignons onions
oseille sorrel
panais parsnip
persil parsley
petits pois small green peas
pied bleu wood blewit (type of mushroom)
piment pimento
pissenlits dandelion greens
pleurote type of mushroom
poireaux leeks
pois chiches chickpeas (garbanzo beans)
pois mange-tout sugar peas, mangetout
poivron sweet pepper (capsicum)
pomme de terre potato
potiron pumpkin
primeurs young vegetables
radis radish
riz rice
romarin rosemary
roquette rocket
safran saffron
salade verte green salad
salsifis salsify
sarriette savory
sarrasin buckwheat
sauge sage
seigle rye
serpolet wild thyme
thym thyme
truffes truffles

Fruit and Nuts (*Fruits et Noix*)

abricot apricot
amande almond
ananas pineapple

banane banana
bigarreau black cherry
brugnon nectarine
cacahouète peanut
cassis blackcurrant
cerise cherry
citron lemon
citron vert lime
coco (noix de) coconut
coing quince
datte date
figue fig
figue de Barbarie prickly pear
fraise (des bois) (wild) strawberry
framboise raspberry
fruit de la passion passion fruit
grenade pomegranate
griotte morello cherry
groseille redcurrant
lavande lavender
mandarine tangerine
mangue mango
marron chestnut
mirabelle mirabelle plum
mûre mulberry
mûre sauvage blackberry
myrtille bilberry
noisette hazelnut
noix walnut
noix de cajou cashew
pamplemousse grapefruit
pastèque watermelon
pêche (blanche) (white) peach
pignon pine nut
plstache pistachio
poire pear
pomme apple
prune plum
pruneau prune
raisin grape
raisin sec raisin
reine-claude greengage plum

Desserts

Bavarois mousse or custard in a mould
bombe ice-cream dessert in a round mould
bonbon sweet/candy
brioche light sweet yeast bread
charlotte sponge fingers and custard cream dessert
chausson turnover
clafoutis baked batter pudding with fruit
compote stewed fruit
corbeille de fruits basket of fruit
coupe ice cream: a scoop or in a cup
crème anglaise egg custard
crème caramel vanilla custard with caramel sauce
crème Chantilly sweet whipped cream
crème fraîche slightly sour cream
crème pâtissière thick pastry cream filling made with eggs
crémets fresh cream cheese, normally from Anjou and mixed with fresh cream and sugar
gâteau cake
gaufre waffle
génoise rich sponge cake
glace ice cream
macaron macaroon
madeleine small sponge cake
miel honey
mignardise same as petits fours
œufs à la neige floating islands/meringue on a bed of custard
pain d'épice gingerbread
parfait frozen mousse
petits fours sweetmeats; tiny cakes and pastries
profiteroles cream-filled choux pastry balls covered with chocolate
sablé shortbread
savarin a filled cake, shaped like a ring
tarte, tartelette tart, little tart
truffe chocolate truffle
yaourt yoghurt

Cheese (*Fromage*)

chèvre goat's cheese
doux mild
fromage (plateau de) cheese (board)
fromage blanc yoghurty cream cheese
fromage de brebis ewe's milk cheese
fromage frais a bit like sour cream
fromage sec general name for solid cheeses
fort strong

Cooking Terms and Sauces

bien cuit well-done (steak)
à point medium (steak)
saignant rare (steak)
bleu very rare (steak)

aigre-doux sweet and sour
à l'anglaise boiled
à la bordelaise cooked in wine, bone marrow and diced vegetables
à la châtelaine with chestnut purée and artichoke hearts
à la diable in a spicy mustard sauce
à la périgourdine in a truffle and foie gras sauce
à la provençale cooked with tomatoes, garlic and olive oil
au feu de bois cooked over a wood fire
au four baked
barquette pastry boat
beignet fritter
broche roasted on a spit
chasseur cooked with mushrooms and shallots in white wine

émincé thinly sliced
en croûte cooked in a pastry crust
en papillote baked in buttered paper
épices spices
flambé set aflame with alcohol
frais, fraîche fresh, cold
frappé with crushed ice
frit fried
galantine cooked food served in cold jelly
galette savoury pancake
garni with vegetables
(***au) gratin*** topped with melted cheese and breadcrumbs
grillé grilled
haché minced (ground)
hollandaise a sauce of egg yolks, butter and vinegar
marmite casserole
médaillon round piece
mijoté simmered
mornay cheese sauce
pané breaded
pâte brisée shortcrust pastry
pâte à chou choux pastry
pâte feuilletée flaky or puff pastry
paupiette rolled, filled slices of fish or meat
piquant spicy hot
poché poached
salé salted, spicy
sanglant rare (steak)
sucré sweet
timbale pie cooked in a dome-shaped mould
à la vapeur steamed

Drinks (Boissons)

bière (pression) beer (draught)
bouteille (demi) bottle (half)
brut very dry
café coffee
café au lait white coffee
café express espresso coffee
café filtre filter coffee
chocolat chaud hot chocolate
citron pressé freshly squeezed lemon with sugar and jug of water
demi a third of a litre
doux sweet (wine)
eau water
...***gazeuse*** sparkling
...***minérale*** mineral
...***plate*** still
eau-de-vie brandy
eau potable drinking water
glaçon ice cube
infusion/tisane herbal tea
jus juice
lait milk
moelleux semi-dry
orange pressée freshly squeezed orange with sugar and a jug of water
pichet pitcher
sec dry
thé tea
verre glass
vin (blanc, mousseux, rosé, rouge) (white, sparkling, rosé, red) wine

Planning Your Trip

When to Go 58
Climate 58
Festivals 58
Calendar of Events 58
Tourist Information 59
Embassies and Consulates 60
Entry Formalities 60
Disabled Travellers 60
Insurance and EHIC Cards 61
Money 61
Getting There 62
By Air 62
By Train 63
By Coach 64
By Car 64
Getting Around 64
By Air 64
By Train 65
By Bus 66
By Car 66
By Bicycle 66
By Roulotte 67
On Foot 67
Where to Stay 67
Specialist Tour and Self-Catering Operators 70

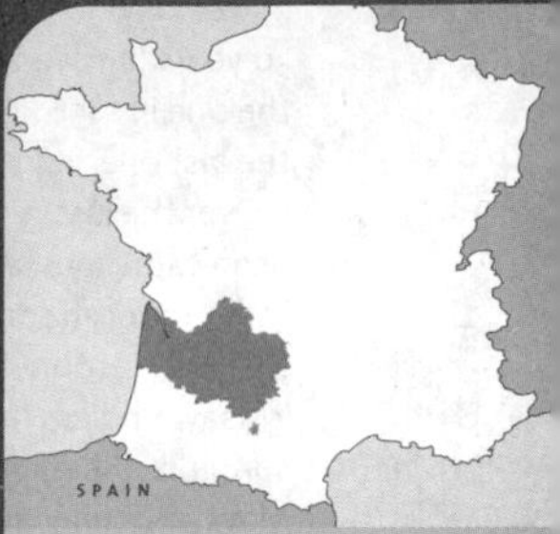

05

When to Go

Climate

The Aquitaine Basin, shielded from intemperate Continental influences by the Massif Central, has a fairly balmy, humid Atlantic climate, with long hot **summers** broken by heavy thunderstorms.

Early **spring** and late **autumn** usually get the most rainfall – and it can rain for weeks at a time. **Winters** are fairly mild, with only 20–40 days of frost a year, although every 30 years (on average) killer frosts descend: the one in 1956 killed off 95% of the vines; the last one, in 1985, massacred the mimosas.

Over the last 15 years or so the weather has been capricious: after five years of drought that produced some of the greatest wine of the 20th century, the autumns of 1992 and '93 saw endless rain and floods, followed by springlike Januarys and Februarys, and soggy Mays and Junes. In 1996 summer never came; in 1997 April and May were as hot as July, June was as cold and rainy as November, August to October was dry, warm and altogether perfect. December 1999 saw some of the strongest and most destructive storms in France's recent history, then 2003 produced a summer of relentless, unforgiving heat.

Unless you're coming to learn about preparing foie gras, winter can be bleak: hotels, restaurants and sights close, and it's often cloudy all day. The first crocuses often show up in January, but nothing really opens until the first tourist rush of the year – Palm Sunday and Easter week. May and June, usually warm and not too crowded, are among the best times to visit.

Hot July, August and early September are French school holidays; the southwest is invaded by Parisians and other French as well as thousands of Dutch, German and British holidaymakers. Towns and attractions are crowded, prices rise, and there are scores of village fêtes, fairs, concerts and races.

The region often looks its best in early October, when the tourists have gone and everyone is concentrating on the *vendanges*; November and December can be dismal, but wild mushrooms, truffles, walnuts and game dishes offer some consolation.

Average Maximum Temperatures in °C/°F

	Jan	April	July	Oct
Cahors	11/52	17/63	26/79	20/68
Périgueux	10/50	17/63	25/77	18/65
Agen	9/48	17/63	25/77	18/65

Festivals

The French know how to throw a party, and in the southwest the number of *fêtes* has increased exponentially over the past decade. Every village celebrates at least once a year: up go the fairylights and flags, the big tables and folding chairs for the feast, and a platform for the band in the main *place* – larger towns can afford both a *bal musette* (accordion waltzes, tangos and French songs) for the grown-ups and a local rock band for the kids.

There is invariably plenty of animation (everything from a local merchant chattering on a microphone to jumping motorbikes, or dogs pulling sledges on wheels). In larger villages, a travelling funfair and/or circus pulls into town for the small fry; there may even be fireworks if the *mairie* has some money to blow. *See* also box, below.

National Holidays

See p.74.

Calendar of Events

February/March

Thurs before Mardi Gras *Fête des Bœufs Gras*, Bazas

Mardi Gras Périgueux

March/April

Late March/early April *Mascarade de Soufflets*, Nontron (even-numbered years)

May

1 Traditional rural fair near St-Aulaye in Forêt de la Double; also Fête de St-Sicaire, Brantôme

Dates vary Flower and strawberry festival, Marmande

2nd weekend *Floralies* excellent flower show, St-Jean-de-Côle

Late May *Alors Chante*, four-day festival of French song, Montauban

Late May Amateur theatre festival, Cahors

Sat late May Great wine festival in Albas (Lot)

June

Pentecost Mon *La Ringueta*, traditional games and sports, even-numbered years, Sarlat

Mid-month *Les Epicuriales*, two-week celebration of food, Bordeaux

23 St John's Day bonfires, homage to the bull and week of events, Bazas

July

Late June–early July *Bordeaux Fête le Vin* (even-numbered years)

Dates vary International folklore festival, one week, Montignac

Dates vary *Féria de Toulouse* at Fenouillet, with a Spanish ambience and *corridas*.

1st Sun *La Félibrée*, Occitan folk festivities, floats, music and theatre, in a Périgord town (run by Lo Bornat dau Périgord, 13 Rue Kléber, Périgueux); huge antiques fair, Belvès

Mid-month Blues festival, Cahors; *Festival de la Voix*, Moissac.

14 Bastille Day celebrations at Arcachon; regattas on Dordogne, Bergerac; fireworks all over.

3rd weekend *Fête de la Madeleine*, festival, wine and funfair at Duras; *Festival de Jazz de Souillac.*

Mid-July Jazz festival, Montauban

Late-July–mid-Aug *Festival du Haut Quercy*, St-Céré and the Lot

End July Entre-Deux-Mers wine festival, Sauveterre-de-Guyenne

Dates vary Theatre festival, Sarlat; *Festival des Nuits Atypiques*, four days of world music in Langon; *Art Lyrique*, opera and recitals in St-Céré and Château de Castelnau, Bretenoux

End July Jazz festival, Andernos

August

Early August Theatre and music festival, Bonaguil

1–15 *Festival International du Mime Mimos*, one world's biggest bashes for mimes, Périgueux (attend at your own risk)

Mid-month Music and arts festival, Assier; medieval festival, Monflanquin; fleamarket (*brocante*), Duras; sea festival, Arcachon; and *Fête de la Presqu'île*, Claouey

Aug/Sept Arts festival, Uzeste and Villandraut

September

8 Pilgrimage at Rocamadour

Early–mid-Sept *Piano aux Jacobins*, piano music festival, Toulouse

3rd Sun *Fête du Chasselas*, Moissac; beginning of *vendanges*, St-Emilion

Third weekend *Journées du patrimoine*, private historical monuments open their doors

Late Sept–mid-Oct *Toulouse Les Orgues*, festival of organ music, Toulouse

Last Sun *Fête de la Montgolfière*, Rocamadour: hot-air balloon festival

Various dates *Festival Occitania*, Toulouse: Occitan culture showcase

November

All month Cinema festival, Sarlat

1 Traditional week-long All Saints' fair, La Réole

11 16th-century turkey fair, Varaignes

December

All month *Marchés au gras* in most towns

Tuesdays *Marchés aux truffes*, 2pm, Lalbenque

End of month Christmas music festival, Uzeste

Tourist Information

Check the list of events (*see* above) to help you decide where to be and when, and then book your accommodation early.

If you're visiting one area, write ahead to local tourist offices (*syndicats d'initiative* or *offices du tourisme*) listed in the text for maps and lists of accommodation in their areas, or see their websites. Or contact one of the agencies in the UK or USA (*see* p.70).

The main tourist office in France is the **Maison de la France**, 20 Av de l'Opéra, 75041 Paris, **t** 01 42 96 70 00, *www.franceguide.com*.

French Tourist Offices Abroad

UK: 178 Piccadilly, London W1J 9AL, **t** 09068 244 123, *www.franceguide.com*.

Ireland: 10 Suffolk St, Dublin 1, **t** (01) 635 1008

USA: 16th Floor, 444 Madison Av, NY 10022, **t** 212 838 7800; 676 N. Michigan Av, Chicago, IL 60611, **t** (312) 751 7800, 9454 Wilshire Bd, Suite 715, Beverly Hills, CA 90212, **t** (310) 271 6695.

Canada: 1981 Avenue McGill College, Suite 490, Montréal, Québec, **t** (514) 288 4264.

Australia: Level 20, 25 Bligh Street, Sydney, NSW 2000, **t** (02) 9231 5244.

Useful Web Addresses

There are excellent websites that provide information on the area. In addition to the French government tourist office (*see* p.59), try *www.tourisme.fr* or *www.france.com*.

Embassies and Consulates

Foreign Embassies in France

UK: 353 Boulevard du Président Wilson, 33073 Bordeaux, Cedex, **t** 05 57 22 21 10 (consulate).

Ireland: 4 Rue Rude, 75116 Paris, **t** 01 44 17 67 00 (embassy).

USA: 25 Allée Jean Jaurès, 31000 Toulouse, **t** 05 34 41 36 50 (consulate).

Canada: 35 Avenue Montaigne, 75008 Paris, **t** 01 44 43 29 00 (embassy).

Australia: 4 Rue Jean-Rey, 75724 Paris, **t** 01 40 59 33 00 (embassy).

New Zealand: 7 Rue Léonard-de-Vinci, 75116 Paris, **t** 01 45 01 43 43 (embassy).

French Embassies Abroad

UK: 58 Knightsbridge, London SW1X 7JT, **t** (020) 7073 1000, *www.ambafrance-uk.org*; 21 Cromwell Rd, London SW7 2EN, **t** (020) 7073 1200, *www.consulfrance-londres.org* (*for visas*); 11 Randolph Crescent, Edinburgh EH3 7TT, **t** (0131) 225 7954, *www.consulfrance-edimbourg.org*.

Ireland: 36 Ailesbury Rd, Ballsbridge, Dublin 4, **t** (01) 277 5000, *www.ambafrance.ie*.

USA: 4101 Reservoir Rd NW, Washington, DC 20007-2185, **t** (202) 944 6195, *www.ambafrance-us.org*
205 North Michigan Avenue, Suite 3700, Chicago, IL 60601, **t** (312) 327 5200, *www.consulfrance-chicago.org*

10990 Wilshire Bd, Suite 300, Los Angeles, CA 90024, **t** (310) 235 3200, *www.consulfrance-losangeles.org*

934 Fifth Av, New York, NY 10021, **t** (212) 606 3600, *www.consulfrance-newyork.org*.

There are also French consulates in Atlanta, Boston, Houston, Miami, New Orleans and San Francisco.

Australia: 6 Perth Av, Yarralumla ACT 2600, **t** (02) 6216 0100; Level 26, St Martins Tower, 31 Market St, Sydney NSW 2000, **t** (02) 9261 5779 , *www.ambafrance-au.org*.

Entry Formalities

Passports and Visas

EU citizens do not need visas in order to enter France. **US and Canadian nationals** do not need visas for stays of up to 90 days, but everyone else still does. Apply at your nearest French consulate: the most convenient is the *visa de circulation*, allowing for multiple stays of three months over a five-year period. If you are a **non-EU citizen** and intend on staying longer, you need a *visa de long séjour* and eventually a *carte de séjour*. You need to apply for an extended visa at home – a complicated procedure requiring proof of income, etc. For further details, see the French government site *http://vosdroits.service-public.fr*.

Customs

EU nationals over the age of 17 can now import a limitless amount of goods for their personal use. Arrivals from non-EU countries have to pass through French customs.

Duty-free allowances have now been abolished within the EU. For travellers entering the EU from outside, the duty-free limits are 1 litre of spirits or 2 litres of liquors (port, sherry or champagne), plus 2 litres of wine, 200 cigarettes and 50 grams of perfume. Much larger quantities – up to 10 litres of spirits, 90 litres of wine, 110 litres of beer and 3,200 cigarettes – bought locally and provided you are travelling between EU countries, can be taken through customs if you can prove that they are for private consumption only and taxes have been paid in the country of purchase.

Residents of the USA may each take home US$400-worth of foreign goods without attracting duty, including the tobacco and alcohol allowance. Canadians can bring home $300 worth of goods in a year, plus their tobacco and alcohol allowances.

Disabled Travellers

When it comes to providing access for all, France is not exactly in the vanguard of nations; many Americans who come here are appalled. But things are beginning to change, especially in newer buildings. Contact the **Comité National Français de Liaison pour**

Disability Organizations

In the UK

Holiday Care Service, t 0845 124 9974, *www.holidaycare.org.uk*. Travel information, accessible accommodation and care holidays.

RADAR (Royal Association for Disability and Rehabilitation), **t** (020) 7250 3222, *www.radar.org.uk*. Publications for every stage of a holiday: planning, transport and accommodation.

Royal National Institute of the Blind, **t** (020) 7388 1266, *www.rnib.org.uk*. The RNIB Holiday service offers information on a range of issues for the blind and visually impaired and will answer any queries.

Royal National Institute for the Deaf (RNID), 19–23 Featherstone Street, London EC1Y 8SL, Infoline **t** 0808 808 0123, textphone **t** 0808 808 9000, *informationline@rnid.org.uk*, *www.rnid.org.uk*. Call their information line for help and advice.

In the USA and Canada

American Foundation for the Blind, **t** (212) 502 7600, *www.afb.org*. An excellent information source for visually impaired travellers.

Mobility International USA, **t** (541) 343 1284, *www.miusa.org*. Practical advice and info.

SATH (Society for Accessible Travel and Hospitality), **t** (212) 447 7284, *www.sath.org*. Advice on all aspects of travel for the disabled.

Access-Able, *www.access-able.com*. A website with access information.

In Australia

Disability Information and Resource Centre, **t** 8236 0555, *www.dircsa.org.au*.

la Réadaptation des Handicapés, 236 bis Rue de Tolbiac, 75013 Paris, **t** 01 53 80 66 66, for access information. Hotels with facilities for disabled people are listed in Michelin's Red Guide to France. Also contact Gîtes de France (main office) for a leaflet on holiday accommodation: **Maison des Gîtes de France**, 59 Rue St-Lazare, 75439 Paris, Cedex 09, **t** 01 49 70 75 75, *www.gites-de-france.fr*.

Insurance and EHIC Cards

Citizens of the EU should bring along their **European Health Insurance Card** (EHIC), which can allow for free or low-cost medical treatment; apply online at *www.ehic.org.uk*, or pick up a form from a post office. The card gives access to state-provided care only, so you should also have **insurance** to cover the gap – as the French do. This might be included on your credit card if you used that to pay for your holiday. If not, consider a travel insurance policy covering theft and losses and offering a 10% medical refund; check to see if it covers extra expenses if you get bogged down in airport or train strikes. Accidents resulting from sports are rarely covered by ordinary insurance. Canadians should check if they are covered in France by their provincial health cover; Americans and others should check their individual policies.

Money

The **euro** is divided into 100 **cents**. There are seven banknotes, in denominations of 5, 10, 20, 50, 100, 200 and 500, and eight coins, in denominations of 1 and 2 euros, and 1, 2, 5, 10, 20 and 50 cents.

Traveller's cheques are the safest way of carrying money, but the wide acceptance of **credit and debit cards** and presence of **ATMs** (*distributeurs de billets*) even in small towns, makes cards the readiest method. Visa (Carte Bleue) is the most widely accepted credit card; American Express is often not accepted. Smaller hotels and restaurants and bed and breakfasts may not accept cards at all. Under the Cirrus system, withdrawals in euros can be made from bank and post office ATMs using your PIN. The specific cards accepted are marked on each machine, and most give instructions in English. Card companies may charge a fee for cash advances, but rates are often better than those at banks.

In the event of **lost or stolen credit cards**, call the following emergency numbers:

American Express, Paris, **t** 01 47 77 79 28; Bordeaux, **t** 05 56 00 63 36.

Barclaycard, **t** (00 44) 1604 230 230 (UK).

Visa, Paris, **t** 0800 901179, US **t** 1 410 581 9994.

Exchange rates vary, and most banks and *bureaux de change* take a commission of varying proportions. *Bureaux de change* that do nothing but exchange money, hotels and train stations usually have the worst rates or take the heftiest commissions.

For **bank opening hours**, *see* p.74.

Getting There

By Air

From the UK and Ireland

The international airports in the region are at **Bordeaux** and **Toulouse**; both have direct connections with London Gatwick on British Airways and Dublin with Aer Lingus. There's also a sweet little airport at **Bergerac**.

You can find cheap – often absurdly cheap – no-frills deals with **easyJet** (London Gatwick and Bristol to Toulouse; Luton to Bordeaux); **BMI Baby** (Birmingham, East Midlands and Manchester to Bordeaux); **Flybe** (Birmingham, Bristol, Exeter, Leeds and Southampton to Bergerac; Bristol, Norwich and Southampton to Bordeaux; Birmingham and Bristol to Toulouse) and **Ryanair** (London Stansted, East Midlands and Liverpool to Bergerac).

For airline contact details, *see* below. Destinations keep changing, so check their websites to see what's new. Bear in mind that scheduled British airlines' flights may be cheaper at some times of year.

Airline Carriers

UK and Ireland

Aer Lingus, Dublin, **t** 0818 36 5000, *www.aerlingus.ie*.

Air France, UK **t** 0870 142 4343, France **t** 0820 820 820, *www.airfrance.co.uk*.

BMI Baby, UK **t** 0871 224 0224, France **t** 0890 710 081, *www.bmibaby.com*.

British Airways, UK **t** 0870 850 9850, France **t** 0825 825 400, *www.ba.com*

easyJet, UK **t** 0871 244 2366, *www.easyjet.com*.

Flybe, UK **t** 0871 700 0535, *www.flybe.com*.

Ryanair, UK **t** 0871 246 0000, Ireland **t** 0818 303030, *www.ryanair.com*.

USA and Canada

Air Canada, Canada/USA **t** 888 247 2262, *www.aircanada.ca*.

Air France, USA **t** 800 237 2747, *www.airfrance.us*; **Canada t** 800 667 2747.

Air-Transat, **t** (1877) 872 6728, *www.airtransat.com*.

American Airlines, **t** 800 433 7300, *www.aa.com*.

British Airways, USA/Canada **t** 800 247 9297.

Delta, **t** 800 221 1212, *www.delta.com*.

KLM, USA represented by North West Airlines, **t** 800-225 2525, *www.nwa.com*.

Lufthansa, USA **t** 800 645 3880, Canada **t** 800 563 5954, *www.lufthansa.com*

Charters, Discounts and Special Deals

UK and Ireland

Budget Travel, 134 Lower Baggot St, Dublin 2, **t** (01) 631 1100, *www.budgettravel.ie*.

Trailfinders, 194 Kensington High St, London W8 7RG, **t** 0845 050 5940, *www.trailfinders.com*.

United Travel, Stillorgan Bowl, Stillorgan, Co. Dublin, **t** (01) 215 9300, *www.unitedtravel.ie*.

For bargain deals try websites such as *www.cheapflights.co.uk*, *www.expedia.co.uk*, *www.whichbudget.com* and *www.lastminute.com*.

USA and Canada

Air Brokers International, USA **t** 800 883 3273, *www.airbrokers.com*.

Last Minute Travel Club, Canada **t** (416) 449 5400, *www.lastminuteclub.com*.

www.traveldiscounts.com, PO Box 3396, Carmel-by-the-Sea, California, **t** (408) 813 1111.

Student Discounts

Students with ID cards can get reductions on flights, trains and admission fees. Agencies specializing in student and youth travel can help apply for the cards, as well as filling you in on the best deals. The International Students' Identity Card (ISIC), for full-time students in the present academic year, is widely recognized; student travel offices sell them.

Europe Student Travel, 6 Campden St, London W8 7EP, **t** (020) 7727 7647. This is for students and non-students.

STA Travel, *www.statravel.co.uk*. London: 117 Euston Rd, NW1 2SX, **t** 0870 166 2603, and Sherfield Building, Imperial College, SW7 2AZ, **t** 0870 166 2609; Bristol **t** 0870 166 2590; Leeds **t** 0870 168 6878; Manchester **t** 0870 166 2622; Oxford **t** (01865) 262300; Cambridge **t** 0870 166 2591 and many other branches in UK; in **USA**, New York City **t** (212) 627 3111, *www.statravel.com*; in Australia, Sydney **t** 02 9212 1255, *www.statravel.com.au*.

Travel Cuts, 187 College St, Toronto, Ontario M5T 1P7, **t** (416) 979 2406, *www.travelcuts.com*. The largest student travel specialist in Canada, with branches in most provinces. In the USA, call **t** 1-800-592-2887 (*www.travelcuts.com/us*).

Whatever way you fly, you can usually save money by purchasing your ticket a few weeks in advance. It can be even cheaper to Toulouse if you don't mind driving an hour or so from Carcassonne or Limoges (both reached by Ryanair from London Stansted, East Midlands and Liverpool). It may work out cheaper to fly to **Paris** and get a domestic flight from there.

A useful website directory for all budget flights in Europe is *www.whichbudget.com* which explains all the options – enabling you to find flights within Continental Europe too – and links to the airline websites.

From North America

The only direct flights to southwest France are from Montreal on Air-Transat, which in summer flies direct to Bordeaux and Toulouse. Otherwise, your best bet is to find a cheap flight to a European hub (KLM, by way of Detroit and Amsterdam, is often the cheapest to Toulouse, for instance, or by Lufthansa to Munich and then on to Toulouse) and continue from there.

Air France (*www.airfrance.us*) also has summer flights from various US airports to the southwest.

By Train

This is quite pleasant, if sometimes more expensive than the plane, if you do it the nice way, using **Eurostar** for the London–Paris leg. No matter how you do it, though, you'll have to change trains in Paris (either by metro or taxi), from the Gare du Nord to the Gare Montparnasse or Gare d'Austerlitz (*see* below).

The fastest trains between Paris and the southwest are the high-speed **TGVs** (*trains à grande vitesse*), with an average speed of 270/kmh: the journey from Paris' Gare Montparnasse on the TGV Atlantique to Bordeaux takes 3hrs (for Périgueux, get off at Libourne for a connecting train) then continues to Toulouse by way of Agen and Montauban in slightly less than 5hrs. There are also direct trains to Périgueux from Paris Austerlitz, taking around 5hrs. Costs are a tad higher on TGVs; all require **seat reservations**, which you can make when you buy your ticket or at the station before departure.

Another pleasant way of getting there is aboard an overnight **sleeper** (these slow trains for the southwest depart from the Gare d'Austerlitz in Paris; Paris–Toulouse takes roughly 7hrs).

Under 26s are eligible for a 30% discount on fares if they have an ISIC or other student ID card (*see* opposite), and there are also discounts if you're 60 or over, available from major travel agents. If you plan on making several long train journeys throughout France, there are a variety of **rail passes** (*see* **Rail Europe**; addresses in box below). The **EuroDomino** pass entitles those resident in Europe for at least 6 months to unlimited rail travel in France for 3–8 days in a month, while the **Inter-Rail** pass (again, for those resident in Europe for at at least 6 months),

Booking Train Tickets, Prices and Schedules

The main French railways site, *www.sncf.fr*, is available in French and English. You can book tickets online and have them sent to addresses outside France.

Note that the German railways' website *www.bahn.de* has a useful journey planner for all Europe (in German).

Also check out the independent train travel website *www.seat61.com*.

In the UK

Rail Europe UK, 178 Piccadilly, London W1, **t** 08708 371371, *www.raileurope.co.uk*. This handles bookings for all services, including Eurostar and Motorail, sells rail passes and acts for other continental rail companies.

Eurostar, Waterloo Station, 12 Lower Rd, London SE1 8SE, **t** 08705 186186, *www.eurostar.com*. Note that Eurostar tickets can be bought in conjunction with tickets for onward travel to selected destinations. You can also get information and tickets at Waterloo International terminal, Ashford international terminal and main rail stations.

In the USA

Rail Europe USA and Canada: **t** 877 257 2887 (USA), or **t** 800 361 RAIL (Canada), *www.raileurope.com*.

TravelMatrix LLC, 711 Daily Drive, Suite 106, Camarillo, CA 93010, **t** (805) 482 8210.

In Australia

Eden Travel, Shop 526, Royal Arcade, 255 Pitt St, Sydney, **t** (61) 292 664 8302.

offers 16 days' unlimited travel in France, Belgium, the Netherlands and Luxembourg. Both include 50% discounted fares on some cross-Channel ferries plus reduced fares on Eurostar but not travel on UK trains.

Passes for **North Americans** include the **France Railpass** – 4 days' unlimited travel throughout the country in any one month plus special rates on Eurostar and an option to purchase 6 extra days if required. There's an equivalent **France Youth Pass** for under-26s. The **France Rail 'n' Drive pass**, valid for one month, gives 2 days' unlimited first-class rail travel in France and 2 days' car rental.

Also for non-Europeans only, the **Eurail Pass** allows unlimited first-class travel through 18 European countries for 15, 21, 30, 60 or 90 days; it saves the hassle of buying numerous tickets but will only pay for itself if you use it a lot. The 15-day **Eurail Pass Youth** for under-26s is for second-class travel only. The **Eurail Pass Flexi** allows first-class travel for any 10 days or 15 days in a 2-month period. All fares include discounted fares on Eurostar plus free or discounted travel on selected ferries, lake steamers, boats and buses.

By Coach

One of the cheapest means of reaching southwest France, all costs included, may be by coach: a standard London–Toulouse return is £89. It takes ages (20–25hrs), but once on you don't have to deal with luggage 'til you're there (you don't change). **National Express/ Eurolines** has up to four journeys a week all year to Toulouse and Bordeaux, plus up to three journeys a week to Brive, Souillac, Cahors and Montauban April–Oct.

National Express/Eurolines, Victoria Coach Station, London SW1, **t** 08705 808080, *www.nationalexpress.com/eurolines.*

By Car

Although the Dover–Calais ferries are the most frequent and cheapest, it means going through or around Paris on the *périphérique*, a task best tackled either side of rush hour. To avoid it and save money on the *autoroutes*, sail instead from Portsmouth, Poole or Plymouth to Caen, Le Havre or Cherbourg; descend by way of the N158/N138 to Le Mans and Tours, and continue on the N10 to Poitiers, from where you can branch off for Bordeaux, via Angoulême, or Cahors, via Limoges. Another Bordeaux alternative is the *autoroute* A10 from Tours. It's a long day all told, but not difficult, especially if you nap on the ferry; **Brittany Ferries** is the main line. If you're visiting the west end of the region, you could sail to St-Malo (from Portsmouth) or Roscoff (from Cork or Plymouth) and take in Rennes, Nantes, La Rochelle and Saintes, picking up the A10 there towards Bordeaux.

Eurotunnel transports cars on purpose-built carriers through the Channel Tunnel between Folkestone and Calais. It is cheaper to book in advance, although it is possible to just turn up and wait – you will be put on a standby list and given space on a first-come, first-served basis. There are four departures an hour at peak times. Flexible (Flexiplus) return tickets, which allow you to turn up when you want, cost £199; standard fares are less, especially at unsociable hours. The fare is for the car only, regardless of the number of passengers. Check in is at least 25mins but no more than 2hrs before departure. Wheelchair users must inform Eurotunnel staff of their needs when booking. The British terminal is off junction 11a of the M20, the French one off junction 13 of the A16. The journey lasts 35mins.

Drivers with a valid licence from an EU country, Canada, the USA or Australia don't need an **international driving licence**. A car entering France must have registration and insurance papers. If you're coming from the UK or Ireland, the dip of the **headlights** must be adjusted to the right. Carrying a warning triangle is advisable; it should be placed 50m behind the car if you have a breakdown.

Brittany Ferries, **t** 08709 076103, *www.brittany-ferries.com.*

Eurotunnel, **t** 08705 353535, *www.eurotunnel.com.*

Getting Around

By Air

The deregulation of the French skies has made for competitive fares, especially if you don't mind flying early or late. **Air France's Navette** flies every 30mins or so from Paris

Orly or Charles de Gaulle to Toulouse for as little as €60, depending on when you go. Arch-rival **Air Lib** has up to 9 flights each weekday from Orly Sud to Toulouse.

Airlinair links Aurillac, Béziers, Brive, La Rochelle, Lyon and other cities in France.

Air France, t 0820 820 820, *www.airfrance.com.*

Air Lib, t 0825 09 09 09, *www.air-liberte.fr.*

Airlinair, t 01 45 12 17 17 (booking **t** 0820 820820), *www.airlinair.com.*

By Train

For information and reservations on the French National Railways (SNCF), contact the stations direct, or visit the website at *www.sncf.com*. From the UK, contact the Rail Europe Travel Centre (*see* box, p.63).

Southwest France has a decent network of trains, although many of the smaller lines have only two or three connections a day, making it rather difficult to see much of the country by rail; in places SNCF buses have taken over former train routes. **Fares**, if not a bargain, are still reasonable, and there are a wide range of **discounts** available, especially if you begin your journey at an off-peak time, known as a *période bleue* – basically Mon noon–Fri noon, Sat all day, Sun until noon (but not on major holidays or in the summer holidays); generally these blue periods shrink at anything that might be considered a peak time. Busy days are now all white (*périodes blanches*). In response to complaints about the complexity of the old system, the SNCF has tried to simplify its discounts, but they're still confusing ; *see* below for a guide, or see if you can fathom the SNCF booklet *Le Guide du Voyageur* or website *www. voyages-sncf.com*.

Short-distance regional trains are often basic, but long-distance *Trains Corails* can be delightful when not too crowded. They have snack trolleys and bar/cafeteria cars (the food isn't bad, but it's rather expensive; most stations sell cheaper packed lunches), and some offer play areas for small children.

All tickets must be stamped in the orange machines by the door to the tracks that say *Compostez votre billet* (this dates the ticket to keep you from re-using it). Any time you interrupt a journey until another day, you have to re-*compost* your ticket.

In the current security climate, you're unlikely to be able to use the mechanical lockers (*consignes automatiques*) in stations.

Discount Rail Fares

Découverte discounts are free but are only available on tickets booked in advance. The annual *cartes* must be paid for. Ask about extra perks with the *cartes*, such as Avis car hire, hotel discounts, and discounts on Corsica ferries and travel to other European countries.

Découverte Séjour Return journeys of at least 200km, comprising one night's stay-over at the weekend, entitle you to a 25% discount if you depart during a *période bleue*.

Découverte à Deux If two people (related or not) make a return trip together, including a one-night minimum stay-over at the weekend, they are eligible for a 25% discount on first or second class for journeys begun in blue periods.

Carte Enfant+ This card is issued in the name of a child under 12, costs €65 and allows the child and up to 4 people who travel with them up to a 50% discount on TGVs and other trains. It is valid for one year and entitles you to a discount on Avis car hire. Travel is free for under-4s.

Découverte Enfant+ A 25% discount for one child under 12 accompanied by up to 4 people.

Carte 12–25 Young people 12–25, travelling frequently, can purchase this card for €49; it's good for a year and gives a 25–50% discount on all trains and 25% reduction on Avis car hire.

Découverte 12–25 Young people are eligible for a 25% discount if they buy their ticket in advance and begin travel in a *période bleue*.

Carte Sénior People over 60 can purchase this for €53. Valid for a year, it entitles you to 25–50% discounts on travel, plus 25% when travelling by train abroad if the railway adheres to Rail Plus, and a 25% discount on Avis car hire and Mercure hotels, among other offers.

Senior Découverte Eligibility for 25% off the journey for those over 60, travelling in *périodes bleues*, plus a discount on Avis car hire.

Grand Voyageur A €30 card valid for 3 years for those travelling at least twice a month, and offering various services to make travel easier.

Carte Escapades A card for 26–29-year-olds, costing €85 a year, giving 25–40% reduction on travel covering at least 200km (return) and a stayover at the weekend, plus a 20% reduction on Avis car hire.

By Bus

Do not count on seeing any part of rural France by public transport. The bus network is barely adequate between major cities and towns (places often already well served by rail) and rotten in rural areas, where more remote villages are linked to civilization only once a week or not at all. Buses are run either by the SNCF (replacing discontinued rail routes) or private firms. Rail passes are valid on SNCF buses and generally coincide with train schedules. Private bus firms tend to be a bit more expensive than trains; some towns have a *gare routière* (coach station), usually near the train station, while in others the buses stop at bars or any other place that catches their fancy. Stops are hardly ever marked (although in some areas there are bus stops everywhere, yet hardly any buses).

By Car

Unless you stick to major towns, cycle or walk, a car is the only way to see much of southwest France. This has its drawbacks: hire costs, quite expensive petrol (about €1.30 a litre for regular unleaded at the time of writing), and a relatively high accident rate – double that of the UK and much higher than the USA. Recent government crackdowns have improved driving standards, but it's still true that French logic and clarity often break down completely on the asphalt. Go slow and be careful, especially on country lanes and anywhere in the half-hour before lunch or dinner, when hunger pangs or haste or too many apéritifs can make for risky driving.

Roads are generally excellently maintained, but anything less than a *départmentale* route (D-road) may be uncomfortably narrow. **Petrol stations** are rare in rural areas (where they're often connected to supermarkets) and closed on Sunday afternoons and often Monday mornings too, and at lunchtimes. The automated out-of-hours pumps still don't accept foreign credit/debit cards, even with PINs. Nearly all serve *super* (leaded), *sans plomb* (unleaded) and *gasoil* (diesel); the latter, though still cheapest, is catching up in price. The French have one admirably civilized custom: if oncoming drivers unaccountably flash their headlights at you, it means the *gendarmes* are lurking up the way.

France used to have a rule of giving **priority to the right** at intersections. This has largely disappeared, though there may still be some, usually in towns, where it applies – these are usually marked. Watch out for the *Cédez le passage* (Give way) signs and be careful. Generally, as you'd expect, give priority to the main road, and to the left on roundabouts. If you are new to France, think of every junction and roundabout as a new, perilous experience. Watch out for Byzantine **street parking** rules (do as the natives do, and be especially careful about village centres on market days).

Look into air and holiday package deals to save on **hiring a car**; budget airlines usually have deals with car-hire companies and you can book cars online at the same time as booking your flights. Note also that the national rail company has an agreement with Avis whereby travellers can book a hire car from stations; see *www.voyages-sncf.com*. Or try **ADA**, **t** 0825 169 169 (in France) or **t** (33) 1 55 46 19 99, *www.ada.fr*, which has cars from €55 a day up to 200km, less if you reserve at least two weeks ahead and for longer hire periods.

Speed limits are 130km/80mph on the *autoroutes* (motorways); 110km/69mph on dual carriageways (divided highways); 90km/55mph on other roads; 50km/30mph in 'urbanized areas': as soon as you pass a white sign with a town's name on it and until you pass another sign with the name barred. Fines for speeding, payable on the spot, begin at about €90 but rise rapidly depending on circumstances, place and speed, and can be astronomical if you flunk the **breathalyser** (more than an *apéro* and a couple of small glasses of wine may take you over).

If you wind up in an **accident**, you must fill out and sign a statement (*constat à l'amiable*). If your French isn't sufficient, wait until you find someone to translate. It's wise to arrange **breakdown cover** in advance from a firm such as **Europ Assistance**, **t** 0870 737 5720, *www.europ-assistance.co.uk*, but on motorways you must use the emergency phones or call the police, **t** 17.

By Bicycle

A plethora of tiny rural roads and lack of strenuous mountains make the Dordogne and Lot valleys ideal for cycling holidays.

A number of companies (*see* p.70) will arrange all the hotels along your route and carry your suitcase for you.

French drivers, not always courteous to fellow motorists, usually give cyclists a wide berth; yet, on any given summer day, half the patients in a French hospital are there from accidents on two-wheeled transport. Wear a helmet. Maps and info are available from the **Fédération Française de Cyclotourisme**, **t** 01 56 20 88 88 21, *www.ffct.org*; in Britain information on cycle touring in France is available from the **Cyclists Touring Club**, **t** 0870 873 0060, *www.ctc.org.uk*.

Air France and British Airways carry bikes free from Britain. From the USA, Canada or Australia most airlines carry them if boxed and included in your total baggage weight; call first to check. Most French trains carry bikes for free, in luggage racks on TGVs and in the wide areas in Corail coaches if they can be folded or wrapped, with wheels removed, in special covers available from sport shops such as Decathlon. Otherwise, trains with a bicycle symbol on the timetable should let you stash your cycle in the luggage van. SNCF can transport your bike to any location in France for about €49, within three days.

You can **hire bikes** of varying quality (most 10-speed) at some SNCF stations and in main towns and tourist centres. Hiring from a station means you can drop it off at another, as long as you specify where when you hire it. Rates run at around €10 a day. Private firms have mountain bikes and better-quality touring bikes for hire by the week.

By *Roulotte*

Several places hire out horse-drawn wooden caravans, or *roulottes*, that sleep up to four people – a leisurely way to explore country lanes. In the Dordogne, you can hire them in Quinsac to visit the Brantôme area: in July and August a week costs €700, in low season prices are as low as €475 a week, or €210 for a weekend. Book through the **Comité Départemental du Tourisme Dordogne-Périgord**, **t** 05 53 35 50 00. In the Lot, you can hire *roulottes*, each with a capacity for four adults and a child, from **Castel** at the château in Aynac, **t** 05 65 11 08 02; or from **Roulottes du Quercy** at Sérignac, **t** 05 65 31 96 44.

On Foot

A network of long-distance paths, ***Grandes Randonnées*** (GRs; marked by red and white signs, or splodges of red and white paint; at path junctions, an 'X' denotes this is not the right one to take), take in some of the most beautiful scenery in southwest France. Each GR is described in a ***Topoguide***, with maps and details about campsites, *refuges* and *rando-étapes* (inexpensive shelters) and so on, available in area bookshops and larger tourist offices, or from **Fédération Française de la Randonnée Pédestre**, 14 Rue Riquet, 75019 Paris, **t** 01 44 89 93 93, *www.ffrp.asso.fr*.

Among the most scenic are the GR36/6, the Traversée du Périgord, from Angoulême down the Vézère valley to Cahors; the GR65 Sentier de St-Jacques Cahors–Roncevaux (the southern bit covered in the *Cadogan Guide to Gascony and the Pyrenees*); and the GR8, which follows the Atlantic coast from Pointe de Grave to the Lac de Cazaux. Besides the GRs, each *département* has local networks of walking paths through their most scenic regions (including day and half-day *Petites Randonnées*, or PRs); local tourist offices can tell you which maps and guides you need, and there are often leaflets for each walk.

Where to Stay

Hotels

Like most countries in Europe, the French tourist authorities grade hotels by facilities (not by charm or location), with stars from four to one, and there are some cheap but adequate places undignified by any stars (their owners probably never bothered filling out a form for the authorities; their prices are usually the same as those of one-stars).

Almost every establishment has a wide range of rooms and prices – a very useful and logical way of doing things. In some hotels, every room has its own personality, and the difference between them in quality and price can be huge: a large room with antique furniture, a TV or a balcony over the sea and a full bathroom can be more than twice as much as a poky back room in the same hotel, overlooking a car park, no antique furniture, and the loo in the corridor. Some proprietors drag out a sort of menu for you to choose

Hotel Price Ranges

Note that prices listed here and elsewhere in this book are for a double room in high season.

luxury	€€€€€	€230+
very expensive	€€€€	€150–230
expensive	€€€	€100–150
moderate	€€	€60–100
inexpensive	€	-€60

what price and facilities you would like. Most two-star rooms have an ensuite shower and WC; most one-stars have a choice of rooms with or without. The price-range box above will give you an idea of what prices to expect.

Single rooms, relatively rare in France, are usually two-thirds the price of a double; rarely will a hotelier give you a discount if only doubles are available (as each room has its own price). On the other hand, if there are three or four of you, booking triples or quads or adding extra beds to a double room is usually cheaper than staying in two rooms.

Breakfast (usually coffee, a croissant, bread and jam for €5–12) is nearly always optional in French hotels: you'll do as well for less in a nearby bar. As usual, rates rise during the holidays and in summer, when many hotels with restaurants require that you take half-board (*demi-pension* – breakfast and a set lunch or dinner). Many hotel have superb restaurants, which we've described in the text; non-guests are welcome. At worst hotel-restaurant food will be boring, and it can be monotonous eating in the same place every night when there are lots of tempting restaurants around. But don't be put off by obligatory dining. It's traditional – French hoteliers think of themselves as innkeepers, in the old-fashioned way. In the off-season, board requirements vanish into thin air.

Your holiday will be much sweeter if you book ahead, especially from May to October. July and August are the only really impossible months; otherwise it usually isn't too hard to find something. Phoning a day or two ahead is always a good policy, although beware that hotels will usually only confirm a room if you give them your credit card number, and may charge your for the room (or take a percentage of the room rate) if you cancel at short notice (terms differ, so check).

Tourist offices have lists of accommodation in their given areas or even *départements*; many will even call around and book a room for you on the spot for free or a nominal fee.

There are **chain hotels** (Climat, Formule 1, etc.) in most cities, but they're generally dreary and geared to business travellers, so you won't often find them in this book. Don't confuse chains with umbrella organizations such as Logis de France (*www.logis-de-france.fr*), Relais du Silence (*www.silencehotel.com*) or the prestigious Relais et Châteaux (*www.relaischateaux.fr*) that promote and guarantee the quality of independent hotels and their restaurants. Their Internet sites provide useful information on the hotels and offer online booking. Many are recommended in the text. Larger tourist offices usually stock their booklets, or you can pick them up before you leave from the French National Tourist Office. You could also have a look at *www.chateauxandcountry.com* for castles.

Bed and Breakfast

In rural areas, there are plenty of rooms in private homes or on farms: look for *chambres d'hôte*, often listed separately from hotels with the gîtes in tourist office brochures (*see* below). Some are connected to *ferme-auberge* restaurants, others to wine estates or a château; average prices are in the €40–60 for a double with breakfast, and payment is often in cash only. Local tourist offices can provide you with a list.

Gîtes de France and Other Self-catering Accommodation

Southwest France has a vast range of self-catering accommodation, from inexpensive farm cottages to history-laden châteaux and fancy villas. The **Fédération Nationale des Gîtes de France** (*www.gitesdefrance.fr*) is a French state service offering inexpensive accommodation by the week in rural areas. Lists with photos for each *département* are available from the French National Tourist office, from most local tourist offices, or in the UK from the official rep: **Gîtes de France**, 178 Piccadilly, London W1J 9AL, **t** 09068 244 123. Prices for gîtes range from about €230 to €770 a week, depending very much on the time of year, location and facilities; nearly always you have to to begin your stay on a Saturday. Many *départements* also have a second (usually less expensive) listing of gîtes in a guide called *Clé Vacances* (*www.clevacances.com*).

The Sunday papers are full of options, and, increasingly, the Internet, which allows you to get in direct contact with the owners. Or try one of the firms listed on p.70. The accommodation they offer will nearly always be more comfortable and costly than a gîte, but the discounts holiday firms offer on the ferries, plane tickets, or car rentals can make up for the price difference.

Youth Hostels

Most cities have youth hostels (*auberges de jeunesse*) with simple dorm accommodation and breakfast for people of any age for about €15 a night. Most offer kitchen facilities as well, or inexpensive meals. They are the best deal for people travelling on their own; for people travelling together a one-star hotel can be as cheap. Most are in ungodly locations – in the suburbs where the last bus goes by at 7pm, or in the country miles from transport. In summer the only way to be sure of a room is to arrive early in the day. Most require a Hostelling International (HI) membership card; you can usually buy these on the spot, although the regulations say you should buy them in your home country.

For more info on youth hostels in France, contact the **Fédération Unie des Auberges de Jeunesse** (**t** 01 48 04 70 40, *www.fuaj.org*).

UK: HI International Youth Hostel Federation, 2nd Floor, Gate House, Fretherne Rd, Welwyn Garden City, Herts AL8 6RD, **t** (01707) 324170, *www.hihostels.com*. Also contact YHA, Trevelyan House, Dimple Rd, Matlock, Derbyshire DE4 3YH, **t** 0870 770 8868, *www.yha.org.uk*.

USA: Hostelling International USA, 8401 Colesville Rd, Suite 600, Silver Spring MD 20910, **t** (301) 495 1240, *www.hiayh.org*.

Canada: Hostelling International Canada, 75 Nicholas St, Ottawa, ON K1N 7B9, **t** (613) 235 2595, *www.hihostels.ca*.

Australia: AYHA, 11 Rawson Place, opposite Central Station, Sydney, 2000 NSW, **t** (02) 9218 9000, *www.yha.com.au*.

There are also some private hostels. An alternative in cities are single-sex dorms for young workers, *foyers de jeunes travailleurs et de jeunes travailleuses*; these let individual rooms, when available, for slightly higher rates than youth hostels.

Gîtes d'Etape and *Refuges*

A *gîte d'étape* is a simple shelter with bunk beds and a rudimentary kitchen, set up by a village along a GR walking path (*see* p.67) or scenic bike route. Lists are available for each *département*; detailed maps mark them too. In the mountains similar rough shelters along GR paths are called *refuges*, most of them open summer only. Both charge around €15.

Camping

Camping is a very popular way to travel, especially among the French, and there's at least one campsite in every town and village – often an inexpensive, no-frills one run by the town itself (*camping municipal*). Other sites are graded with stars like hotels, from four to one: at the top, expect lots of trees and grass, hot showers, a pool or beach, sports facilities, and a grocery, bar and/or restaurant, and prices rather similar to one-star hotels.

Camping on **farms** is big in the southwest, and is usually less expensive than organized sites. If you want to camp wild, ask the landowner first, or risk a furious farmer, his furious dog and perhaps even the police.

Tourist offices have lists of sites in their regions, and there are lists on *départmentale* websites (*see* the relevant chapters of this book). If you're planning to move around a lot, the *Guide Officiel Camping/Caravaning* is sold in most French bookshops. You can also find comprehensive listings on the website *www.campingfrance.com*.

Houseboats

You can spend a week or half-week in summer on a wide variety of houseboats on the river Lot and the Canal Latéral à la Garonne. You don't need a boat licence to drive one, and **Safaraid**, **t** 05 65 35 98 88, *www.canoe-dordogne.com*, hires out canoes and kayaks to make your cruise complete.

Other firms from which it's possible to hire houseboats are listed throughout this guide.

Specialist Tour Operators

If you want to combine a holiday with study or a special interest, contact the **Cultural Department of the French Embassy**, 23 Cromwell Rd, London SW7, **t** (020) 7073 1300, or at 4101 Reservoir Road, NW Washington 20007, **t** (202) 944 6400. The Internet is also a rich source of information on specialized theme visits: *www.tourisme.fr* for instance, has a list of unusual ways of seeing the country.

In France

Crown Blue Line, Le Grand Bassin, BP1201, 11492 Castelnaudary, France, **t** (00 33) 4 68 94 52 72, *www.crownblueline.com*. Self-drive boating holidays cruising along the waterways of the Lot, Garonne and Canal du Midi

In the UK

ATG Oxford, 69–71 Banbury Rd, Oxford OX2 6PJ, **t** (01865) 315 678, *www.atg-oxford.co.uk*. Walking holidays in the Dordogne and Lot.

Arblaster & Clarke, Clarke House, Farnham Rd, West Liss, Hampshire GU33 6JQ, **t** (01730) 893344, *www.arblasterandclarke.com*. Wine tours of Bordeaux.

Blakes Holiday Boating, Spring Mill, Earby, Barnoldswick, Lancs BB94 OAA, **t** 0870 220 2498, *www.blakes.co.uk*. Self-drive boating holidays along the waterways of the Lot.

Cycling For Softies, 2–4 Birch Polygon, Rusholme, Manchester M14 5HX, **t** (0161) 248 8282, *www.cycling-for-softies.co.uk*. Easy cycling tours in the Dordogne.

Headwater Holidays, The Old School House, Chester Rd, Castle, Northwich, Cheshire CW8 1LE, **t** (01606) 720033, *www.headwater.com*. Cycling, walking and canoeing in the Dordogne and Lot.

Hooked on Cycling, 5 Redmill Court, East Whitburn, West Lothian, Scotland EH47 0PL, **t** (01501) 744727, *www.hookedoncycling.co.uk*. Serious cycling holidays in the Dordogne and Lot.

Inntravel, near Castle Howard, York, YO60 7JU, **t** (01653) 617949, *www.inntravel.co.uk*. Independent walking and cycling holidays through the Dordogne valley and to Rocamadour, and cycling in the Lot.

Sherpa Expeditions, 131a Heston Rd, Hounslow, Middlesex TW5 ORF, **t** (020) 8577 2717, *www.sherpa-walking-holidays.co.uk*. Walking and cycling holidays in the Dordogne.

In the USA

Du Vine Adventures, 124 Holland St, Suite 2, Somerville, MA 02144, USA, **t** (617) 776 4441, *www.duvine.com/bordeauxhotels.html*. Tours and holidays focusing on châteaux and wine.

Self-catering Operators

In the UK

Allez France, **t** 0845 330 2056, *www.allezfrance.com*. Everything from cottages to châteaux.

Bonnes Vacances, **t** 08707 607071, *www.bvdirect.co.uk*. Villas, cottages and apartments.

Bowhills, **t** 0870 235 2727, *www.bowhills.co.uk*. Farmhouses, cottages and villas in the Dordogne and Lot.

Dominique's Villas, **t** (020) 7738 8772, *www.dominiquesvillas.co.uk*. Large villas and châteaux with pools in the whole region.

France Direct, **t** (020) 7407 2724, *www.francedirect.co.uk*. A large selection of cottages and villas you book directly with the owners.

French Affair, **t** (020) 7381 8519, *www.frenchaffair.com*. Houses and villas.

French Life Holidays Ltd, **t** 0870 336 2877, *www.frenchlife.co.uk*. Various self-catering options in the Dordogne and the Lot.

Holiday in France, **t** (01225) 310 623, *www.holidayinfrance.co.uk*. Cottages, farmhouses and châteaux.

Inghams/Just France, **t** (020) 8780 4480, *www.justfrance.co.uk*. Villas, cottages, apartments, farmhouses and châteaux, many with pools.

Something Special Holidays, **t** (01279) 642820, *www.somethingspecial.co.uk*. Dordogne villas.

VFB Holidays, **t** (01242) 240340, *www.vfbholidays.co.uk*. Gîtes, cottages and flats.

In the USA

At Home Abroad, **t** (212) 421 9165, *www.athomeabroadinc.com*

Drawbridge To Europe, **t** (888) 268 1148, *www.drawbridgetoeurope.com*

Hideaways International, **t** (603) 430 4433, *www.hideaways.com*

Just France, **t** (610) 407 9633, *www.justfrance.com*. Villas, cottages and apartments.

Villas International, **t** (415) 499 9490, *www.villasintl.com*.

Practical A–Z

Conversion Tables 72
Crime and the Police 73
Eating Out 73
Electricity 73
Health and Emergencies 73
Internet 73
National Holidays 74
Opening Hours 74
Post Offices 74
Sports and Activities 74
Telephones 76
Time 76
Tipping 76
Toilets 76

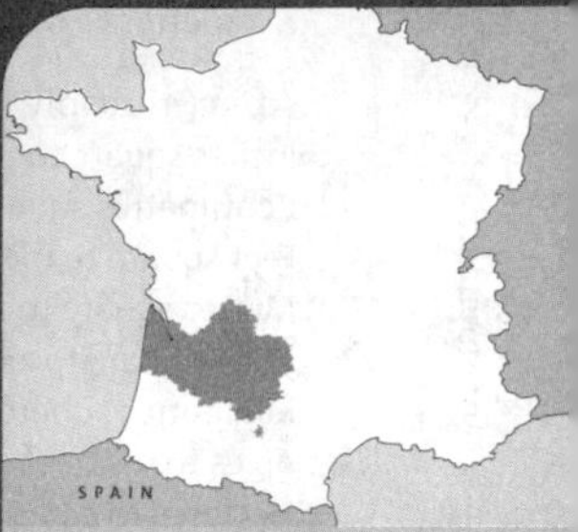

06

Imperial–Metric Conversions

Length (multiply by)
Inches to centimetres: 2.54
Centimetres to inches: 0.39
Feet to metres: 0.3
Metres to feet: 3.28
Yards to metres: 0.91
Metres to yards: 1.1
Miles to kilometres: 1.61
Kilometres to miles: 0.62

Area (multiply by)
Inches square to centimetres square: 6.45
Centimetres square to inches square: 0.15
Feet square to metres square: 0.09
Metres square to feet square: 10.76
Miles square to kilometres square: 2.59
Kilometres square to miles square: 0.39
Acres to hectares: 0.40
Hectares to acres: 2.47

Weight (multiply by)
Ounces to grams: 28.35
Grammes to ounces: 0.035
Pounds to kilograms: 0.45
Kilograms to pounds: 2.2
Stone to kilograms: 6.35
Kilograms to stone: 0.16
Tons (UK) to kilograms: 1,016
Kilograms to tons (UK): 0.0009
1 UK ton (2,240lbs) = 1.12 US tonnes (2,000lbs)

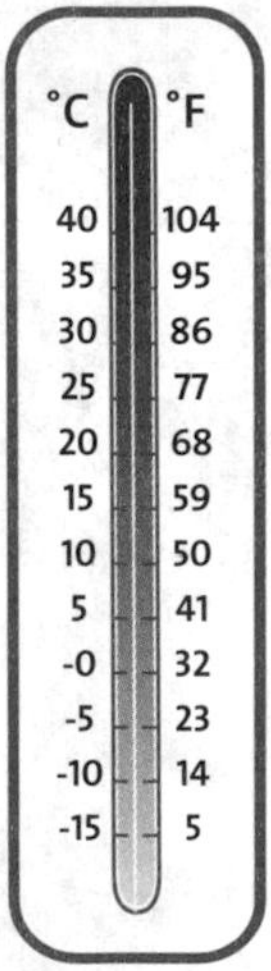

Volume (multiply by)
Pints (UK) to litres: 0.57
Litres to pints (UK): 1.76
Quarts (UK) to litres: 1.13
Litres to quarts (UK): 0.88
Gallons (UK) to litres: 4.55
Litres to gallons (UK): 0.22
1 UK pint/quart/gallon = 1.2 US pints/quarts/gallons

Temperature
Celsius to Fahrenheit: multiply by 1.8 then add 32

Fahrenheit to Celsius: subtract 32 then multiply by 0.55

Italy Information

Time Differences
Country: + 1hr GMT; + 6hrs EST

Daylight saving from last weekend in March to end of October

Dialling Codes
Note: omit first zero of area code

France country code 33

To France from: UK, Ireland, New Zealand 00 / USA, Canada 011 / Australia 0011; then dial 33 and the full number including the initial zero

From France to: UK 00 44; Ireland 00 353; USA, Canada 001; Australia 00 61; New Zealand 00 64; then the number without the initial zero

Directory enquiries: 118 000; **International directory enquiries**: 00 33 12 + country code

Emergency Numbers
Police and car breakdown: 17
Ambulance: 15
Fire: 117

Embassy/Consulate Numbers in France
UK: 05 57 22 21 10; **Ireland** 01 44 17 67 00;
USA: 05 34 41 36 50; **Canada** 01 44 43 29 00;
Australia 01 40 59 33 00;
New Zealand 01 45 01 43 43

Shoe Sizes

Europe	UK	USA
35	2½ / 3	4
36	3 / 3½	4½ / 5
37	4	5½ / 6
38	5	6½
39	5½ / 6	7 / 7½
40	6 / 6½	8 / 8½
41	7	9 / 9½
42	8	9½ / 10
43	9	10½
44	9½ / 10	11
45	10½	12
46	11	12½ / 13

Women's Clothing

Europe	UK	USA
32	6	2
34	8	4
36	10	6
38	12	8
40	14	10
42	16	12
44	18	14

Crime and the Police

Southwest France isn't exactly a high crime area. Isolated holiday homes get burgled, as anywhere else; cars are occasionally broken into or stolen. Generally the police are more annoying than the crooks, especially the mobile *douane* or customs officers; these can turn up anywhere in the interior, and they have nothing better to do than arbitrarily stop cars from outside their *département* and give them the once-over.

Report **thefts** to the nearest *gendarmerie* – not an enjoyable task but the reward is the bit of paper you need for an **insurance** claim. If your **passport** is stolen, contact the police and your nearest consulate (*see* p.60) for emergency travel documents. By law, the police in France can stop anyone anywhere and demand **ID**; in practice, they only tend to do it to harass minorities, the homeless and scruffy hippy types. If they really don't like the look of you, they can salt you away for a long time without any reason.

The **drug** situation is the same in France as anywhere in the West: soft and hard drugs are widely available, and the police only make an issue of victimless crime when it suits them (your being a foreigner just may rouse them to action). Smuggling any amount of cannabis into the country can mean a prison term, and there's not much your consulate can or will do about it.

Eating Out

The French tend to eat quite early, often at 12 or 12.30 for **lunch**, and generally between 7 and 9pm in the evening, with slightly later summer hours for **dinner**. Brasseries and cafés are flexible and open long hours, but restaurants don't often like serving late. Most restaurants recommended in this book offer a choice of set-price menus, and these are the prices we provide to give a rough idea of cost. Most places post their menus outside the door so you know what to expect. If service is included it will say *service compris* or *s.c.*; if not, *service non compris*, or *s.n.c.*

For more on eating in the Dordogne and the Lot, including specialities, wines and a menu decoder, *see* **Food and Drink** pp.45–56.

Restaurant Price Categories

Restaurants are split into four categories, based on prices for a three-course meal per person, without wine; *à la carte* is normally more expensive:

very expensive	€€€€	€60 or more
expensive	€€€	€30–60
moderate	€€	€15–30
inexpensive	€	less than €15

Electricity

The electric current in France is 220 volts. British and Irish visitors with appliances from home will need two-pin European plug adaptors (readily available in supermarkets if you don't bring one), and North Americans with 110v equipment will normally need a voltage transformer as well.

Health and Emergencies

Ambulance (SAMU) **t** 15
Police t 17
Fire t 18

The local **hospital** (*hôpital*) is the place to go in an emergency (*urgence*). Doctors take turns going on duty at night and on holidays, even in rural areas: pharmacies will know who to contact. Or telephone the local **SOS Médecins** – if you don't have access to a phone directory or Minitel, dial directory assistance, **t** 118 000. To be on the safe side, always carry a phonecard (*see* p.76).

If it's not an emergency, **pharmacies** have addresses of local doctors (including those who speak English), or the nearest outpatient clinic (*services des consultations externes*). Pharmacists are trained to administer first aid, and also dispense free advice for minor problems. In cities pharmacies open at night on a rota basis; addresses are posted in their windows and the local newspaper. You can ring the doorbell of most rural pharmacies after hours and rouse the pharmacist on duty.

For information on **EHIC** cards and health **insurance**, *see* p.61.

Internet

The old saying that it doesn't pay to be first certainly applies to France with its national computer system, the Minitel, which was distributed to every phone subscriber in the 1980s. Next to the Internet it seems a Neanderthal, but its presence considerably slowed French interest in the Internet. This is changing fast; most cities and towns now have **cybercafés** (the tourist office will give you a list), and most **hotels** have their own websites with online booking.

Opening Hours

Most **shops** with the exception of larger supermarkets close on Sunday and nearly as many on Monday, or at least in the afternoon. In some towns Sunday morning is when people go to the market. Nearly all shop close from noon until 2pm or 3pm, except for the larger supermarkets, which tend to stay open all day; in fact, lunchtime is often the calmest and best time to shop.

Generally, **markets** (daily in the cities, weekly in villages) are a morning-only affair, although clothes, flea and antique markets can run into the afternoon, and there are special night markets in some places.

Banks are generally open 8.30–12.30 and 1.30–5; they close on Sundays, and most close on Saturdays or Mondays as well. Exchange rates vary, and nearly all take a commission of varying proportions. It's always a good bet to purchase some euros before you go, especially if you arrive during the weekend.

Museums, with a few exceptions, close for lunch, and often on Mondays or Tuesdays, and sometimes for all of November or the entire winter. Most close on national holidays. Hours change with the season: longer summer hours begin in May or June and last through September – usually. Some change their hours every month. We've done our best to include them in the text, but don't be surprised if they're not exactly right. Most give discounts if you have a student ID card, or are an EU citizen under 18 or over 65 years of age; most charge admission of €1.50–4.50.

For **post offices**, see below.

Churches may open all day, or be closed all day and only open for mass. Sometimes notes on the door direct you to pick up the key from the town hall (*mairie*) or priest's house (*presbytère*). If not, ask at the nearest house – they may have it. There are often entry fees for cloisters, crypts and special chapels.

National Holidays

Banks, shops and businesses close on national holidays; some museums also close, but most restaurants stay open. These holidays are:

1 January
Easter Sunday
Easter Monday
1 May
8 May (VE Day)
Ascension Day
Pentecost and the following Monday
14 July (Bastille Day)
15 August (Assumption)
1 November (All Saints')
11 November (First World War Armistice)
Christmas Day

Post Offices

Known as PTTs or *bureaux de poste*, post offices are easily discernible by their sign – a blue bird on a yellow background. You can receive letters *poste restante* at any post office; the postal codes in this book should help your mail get there in a timely fashion. To collect it, bring ID; you may have to pay a small fee. You can purchase stamps in *tabacs* (tobacconists) as well as post offices.

Post offices are open in the cities Monday to Friday 8am–7pm, and Saturdays 8am until 12. In villages, offices may not open until 9am and may close for lunch, and shut at 4.30 or 5.

Sports and Activities

All the *départements* publish booklets on the wheres, whens and hows of the sports available in their little realms, and local tourist offices are also extremely helpful.

Aerial Sports

Cliffs and updraughts in the Dordogne and Lot are ideal for **hang-gliding** (*parapente*) and ULMs, both practised year-round.

You can learn to **parachute**: lessons for beginners (from age 15), jumps and gear are available from the Aérodrome de Lalbenque in the Lot (south of Cahors), **t** 05 65 21 00 54; the latter can also take you up in a glider.

Look down on the scenery from a **hot-air balloon** (*montgolfière*) from Rocamadour,

t 06 79 24 28 21, or float above the Château de Hautefort (**t** 06 87 33 86 66, *www.perigord-montgolfiere.com*).

Another possibility is going up with a pilot in a small three- or four-seater **plane** from the many local airfields around the southwest; rates are a lot lower than you might expect.

Bicycling

Mountain bikes (*VTT* in French) are very popular in the southwest, and there are many places where you can hire them to take off along the specially marked GR hiking and riding paths. *See* **Getting Around**, pp.66–67.

Canoeing and Kayaking

Every year, more miles of the southwest's beautiful network of rivers are open to navigation. The Dordogne, the Vézère, the Dronne, the Lot and the Célé are favourites, and operators hire out canoes or kayaks by the week or half-day. You can plan excursions of several days, with returns to base by bus, through UK operators or easily enough in France: tourist offices have lists.

Caves

Speleology, potholing, spelunking – whatever you want to call it, it's very popular, especially in the pocked limestone hills and mountains of the Causse de Gramat in the Lot. For details and keys contact M. Andreau at the **Comité Départemental de Spéléologie**, Mairie de Labastide-Murat, via its website *http://cds46.free.fr*.

Fishing

You can fish in the sea without a permit, as long as your catch is intended for local consumption. Freshwater fishing (extremely popular in this region of rivers and lakes) requires an easily obtained permit from a local club – a *carte vacance* is good for two weeks, between June and September; tourist offices can tell you where to find them. Often the only outdoor vending machine in a town sells worms and other bait.

Ocean-fishing excursions (for tuna and more) are organized by the day and half-day, arranged in advance; Arcachon's tourist office (*see* p.283) has numbers.

Gambling

The only **casinos** in this book are in Arcachon, Lacanau and Soulac-sur-Mer, or you can do as the locals do and play for a side of beef, a lamb or VCR in a **Loto**, in a local café or municipal *salle des fêtes*. Loto is just like bingo, and some of the numbers have names: 11 is *las cambas de ma grand* (my grandma's legs) and 75, the number of the *département* of Paris, is *los envaïssurs* (the invaders). Everybody plays the horses at the local bar with the **PMU** (off-track betting) outlet.

Golf

New courses are opening all the time. You'll find some at Périgueux, Bergerac, Belvès, Le Bugue and Sarlat, in the Dordogne; Arcachon, St-Loubès, Lacanau-Océan and Bordeaux (three courses), in the Gironde; Agen, Villeneuve-sur-Lot and Barbaste in the Lot-et-Garonne; Sauveterre (near Castelnau-Montratier), St-Céré and Lachapelle-Auzac (near Souillac) in the Lot; and at Toulouse.

Horse-riding

Each tourist office has a list of *centres hippiques* or *équestres* that hire out horses. Most offer group excursions, although if you prove yourself an experienced rider you can head off on your own. Each *département* offers treks year-round, at weekends or during the week, with vans organized to take your luggage ahead and overnight stabling of your horse. The Dordogne has 850km of riding trails; the Lot has 1,500km.

Dordogne: Comité Départementale du Tourisme , 25 Rue Wilson, BP 2063, 24002 Périgueux, **t** 05 53 35 50 24.

Lot: Association de Tourisme Equestre du Lot, BP 103, 46002 Cahors, CEDEX 9, **t** 05 65 35 80 82.

Pétanque

Pétanque is an essential ingredient of the south of France, and even the smallest village has a rough, hard court under the plane trees for practitioners – nearly all male, though women are welcome to join in. It's similar to *boules*: the object is to get your metal ball closest to the marker (*bouchon/cochonnet*). Tournaments are frequent and well attended.

Rugby

Since 1900, rugby, perfectly adapted to the Gascon temperament and physique, has been the national sport of southwest France, and the cradle of most of the players on the national team (although movements to change one of the Six Nations from France to Occitania have so far fallen flat).

Bordeaux, Toulouse and its neighbour Colomiers are among the top teams in France; in some places, especially towards Toulouse, they play heretical 'Cathar rugby' – 13 to a side instead of 15. There's a women's version without tackling called *barette*.

Walking

See 'Getting Around On Foot', p.67.

Telephones

UK and Irish **mobile phones** work in France if they have a roaming facility; check with your service provider. If you're going to be in France a while and using your mobile a lot, and as long as your mobile is not locked to a UK network, avoid high charges (outgoing and incoming) by temporarily replacing your UK SIM card with an international one (sold, for example, at *www.0044.co.uk*). or by buying a pay-as-you-go phone from a large supermarket or communications shop.

Nearly all **public telephones** have switched over from coins to *télécartes*, which you can purchase at any post office or newsstand at €7.41 for 50 *unités* or €14.74 for 120 *unités*. The easiest way to **reverse charges** is to spend a few euros ringing the number and giving your number in France (always posted by public phones). For **directory enquiries**, dial **t** 118 000, or see *www.pagesjaunes.com* (the French *Yellow Pages* online) or try your luck and patience on the free, slow, inefficient Minitel electronic directory in post offices.

The French have eliminated area codes, giving everyone a 10-digit telephone number.

If you're ringing France from abroad, the **international dialling code** is 33, then drop the first '0' of the number.

For international calls from France, dial 00, wait for the change in the dial tone, then dial the **country code** (UK 44; US and Canada 1; Ireland 353; Australia 61; New Zealand 64), then the local code (minus the 0 for UK numbers) and number.

Time

France is one hour ahead of UK time and six hours ahead of North American EST. French summer time runs from the last Sunday in March to the last Sunday in October; clocks change on those days.

Tipping

Many people leave a tip if they're happy with their meal and the service; if you eat *à la carte*, you might add a gratuity of around 10% (service is included in the price of set menus; *see* p.52 and p.73).

Toilets

The hole-in-the-ground lavatory is still surprisingly common in France. Bars and cafés normally don't mind you using their facilities, but it's polite to make a small purchase at the same time.

If you're driving, it makes sense to head for the nearest (free) service station facilities, and it's wise to keep a stock of emergency toilet paper with you at all times. There are some public toilets for which you have to pay, either to get into – those funky, modern oval-shaped street facilities – or to get out of, when there's a caretaker (you should leave them a small tip).

The Dordogne: Northern Périgord

Périgord, the old region more or less synonymous with the départment *of the Dordogne, is at once the gateway to greater southwest France and a region with a strong character of its own. Cross its frontiers from the north and simple words such as* vin *and* pain *turn into* vaing *and* pang*, the menu fills up with dishes based on duck, goat's cheese and walnuts; there's a warmth in the air and in the colour of the very stones. To this add Périgord's unique qualities, its truffles, troubadours and love of medieval domes, its lush green colour and forests, carved by a dozen rivers of exceptional beauty, and you have a countryside as Arcadian as an eclogue.*

07

Don't miss

1. France's most romantic roofs
   Château de Jumilhac p.89
2. The Little Venice of the Dronne
   Brantôme p.83
3. Arcadian landscapes
   Parc Naturel Régional du Périgord-Limousin p.79
4. Old Curiosity Shop churches
   Aubeterre-sur-Dronne p.107
5. Prehistoric and natural art
   Grotte de Villars p.85

See map overleaf

Périgord

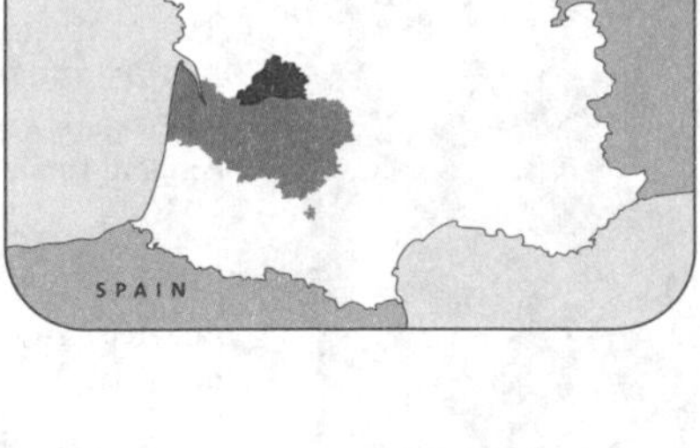

p.171
p.114

Don't miss

1 Château de Jumilhac p.89
2 Brantôme p.83
3 Parc Naturel Régional du Périgord-Limousin p.79
4 Aubeterre-sur-Dronne p.107
5 Grotte de Villars p.85

Petra si ingratis,
cor amicis,
hostibus ensis.
Haec tria si
fueris Petra-
cor-ensis eris.

(A stone to the unpleasant, a heart to the friendly, and iron to the enemy. If you're all three, then you're a Périgourdin.)
Popular saying

'The nearest thing to Paradise this side of Greece' is how Henry Miller described Périgord. Ironically, this Paradise is the result of long centuries of war and poverty and neglect. So is much of the architecture that so delights visitors today – nearly 1,000 castles and fortified churches, and medieval villages with black-stone (*lauze*) roofs and farmhouses no one ever had the wherewithal to improve. If Périgord could make a wise guy from Brooklyn go sloppy, there must indeed be something to it. In fact, so many people agree with Miller that the likes of neo-fascist Jean-Marie Le Pen can complain that what the English couldn't conquer in the Hundred Years' War, they've been buying up like crazy in the last few decades. Périgord fulfils a communal dream for a comfortable place, a simpler, rural world of beauty and pleasure. These days the main danger it faces is that of any place that has kept its integrity: of tourism destroying precisely the 'real, authentic' thing it seeks.

The name Périgord comes from the Gaulish nation known as the *Petrocorii* ('the four tribes'), who according to Caesar sent 6,000 troops to aid Vercingetorix in his final defeat against Rome. From the days of the Vikings to the end of the 16th century, it was governed by vicious counts. Under them, Périgord was subdivided into four baronies (Mareuil, Bourdeilles, Beynac and Biron), which survived until the Revolution, when they were combined to form a single *département*, the third largest in France, renamed after its biggest river, the Dordogne. This first chapter covers the northern section, commonly called Green Périgord (after the trees) and White Périgord (after the stones); later chapters take in the great valley of the Dordogne – most of Black Périgord (after either its truffles or the deep shadows cast by its oaks) and the Purple Périgord – purple, that is, after its wine. For a quick guide to the area, *see www.perigord.tm.fr* or *www.dordogne-perigord.com*.

Arriving from the North: Périgord Vert

3 Parc Naturel Régional du Périgord-Limousin

It was Jules Verne who dubbed northern Périgord, where deep forests, shady rivers and green limestone hills remain luscious even in midsummer, 'Green'. The region that's contained in the triangle formed by the three towns of Périgueux, Angoulême and Limoges is now protected as part of the **Parc Naturel Régional du Périgord-Limousin**. The charter that established the Parc in March 1998 stated the government's aim of developing opportunities and wealth for the local population while preserving the area's natural heritage and culture. If you're driving down to the southwest, you may find you have no desire to go any further.

Getting around the Périgord Vert

Several **bus** lines cross this area. One, run by CFTA (**t** 05 55 17 91 19), links Angoulême, Mareuil, Brantôme and Périgueux three times a week. Another, also run by CFTA, runs between Ribérac and Périgueux three times a day in the week. The website *www.cfta.co.fr* is useful for keeping up to date with local timetables.

Mareuil-sur-Belle and its Château

Château de Mareuil
t 05 53 60 74 13; open April–June and Sept–early Oct Mon and Wed–Sat 10.15–12 and 2–5.15, Sun 2–5.15; July and Aug Mon–Sat 10–12.15 and 2–6.15, Sun 2–6.15; early Oct–mid-Nov Wed–Sun 2–5; Dec–mid-Mar Sun 2–5, but times change regularly so come mid-morning or afternoon to be on safe side

If you take the A10 motorway or N10 south to Poitiers, continue south through Angoulême and aim southeast for Périgord, you'll enter the *département* of the Dordogne by way of the ancient fief of the barons of Mareuil. These had their seat at the 15th-century **Château de Mareuil**, confidently built on a plain and defended by moats filled by the waters of the Belle; inside is a Flamboyant Gothic chapel, the dungeons, and Louis XV furniture.

Mareuil was also the home to troubadour Arnaud de Mareuil, son of a castle workman. Arnaud fell deeply in love with the lovely Countess Adélaïde of Béziers but kept his passion secret by hiring a *jongleur* to sing his love songs. Eventually one of Arnaud's lyrics gave him away, but rather than scorn her humble-born troubadour, the countess gave him many gifts – until King Alfonso of Aragón, himself a troubadour and lover of Adélaïde, made her send Arnaud packing. Dante sent him even further, to Purgatory, though his only

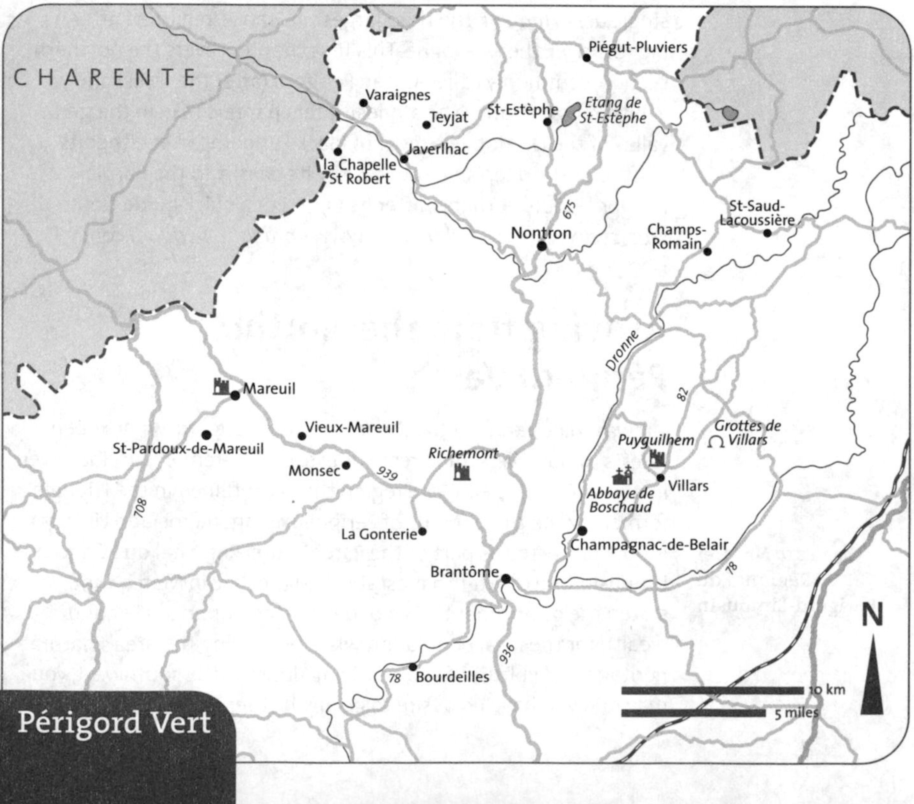

sin was to be admired. His poetry, so celebrated in his day, is nearly impossible to translate, 'the result of a technique honed to the point where all signs of effort vanish, where the words, sounds and rhythms flow past with a mellifluous ease, resulting in a poetry of extraordinarily gentle and delicate beauty' (Anthony Bonner).

Have your first look at Périgord's domed Romanesque churches near Mareuil: just south, **St-Pardoux-de-Mareuil** has a sombre one with an impressive belltower, while the fortified church at **Vieux-Mareuil** to the east has three domes crowning the length of its nave.

Nontron

High on its promontory, Nontron (in Celtic, 'valley of ash trees') began as a Gaulish ***oppidum*** over the river Bandiat. It won't take long to exhaust its charms: there are a few picturesque medieval streets in the lower town, and in the upper town an 18th-century château in Place Fort. Since the 15th century Nontron has been famous for its knives with boxwood handles, in various sizes – the smallest can be folded into a hazelnut shell. You can see and buy them at the **Coutellerie Nontronnaise**, and watch them being made at the workshop in Place Paul Bert. There is also a knife festival in August; ask at the tourist office. These days, however, the town makes a better living making neckties and porcelain for Hermès of Paris; examples are exhibited and can be bought at the shop on Route de Piégut, a few minutes north of the tourist office.

Coutellerie Nontronnaise
*33 Rue Carnot, **t** 05 53 60 33 76; open July and Aug Mon 10–12 and 2–6, Tues–Sat 9.15–12 and 2–7, Sun 10.30–12.30; rest of year Tues–Sat 9.15–12 and 2–7; **workshop t** 05 53 56 01 55; open Mon–Fri 9–12 and 1.30–6 plus Sun July and Aug, but call first*

Espace Paul Bert
*Place Paul Bert, **t** 05 53 60 74 17*

In recent years Nontron has been establishing itself as a centre for the arts under the banner of the Pôle Expérimental Métiers d'Art (*http://poleexperimentalmetiersda.typepad.com*). Throughout the year exhibitions are hosted by the **Espace Paul Bert**, which also has a boutique, and other venues in the area. There are also displays of contemporary art at the Jardin des Arts behind the castle.

In even-numbered years, in late March or early April, Nontron is invaded by *souffla-culs* ('whistle-arses'), participants in a hysterical 13th-century custom. Dressed in nightshirts and nightcaps, they march through the streets, squatting here and there to blow their whistles up the nightshirt of the person in front while chanting: 'We are all children of one family; our father was a whistle-maker. No, you're not going to see the colour of my gaiters. No, you're not going to see the colour of my stockings.' The procession ends with the judgement and fiery death of a dummy symbolizing Carnival.

Around Nontron, on the Limousin Frontier

More peculiarities, especially geological, await in the countryside to the north of Nontron, off the D675: eroded formations such as the Roc Poperdu 3km north, and, another 5km north, the huge **Roc Branlant**, said to rock when touched. It's above a stream with a picturesque spill of granite boulders, the 'Devil's Chaplet'. Get here by way of the Etang de St-Estèphe, a wooded lake with a sandy beach – a favourite retreat in summer. Further north, the striking, cylindrical 21m **Donjon de Piégut** stands isolated on a spur, a last memory of the castle wrecked by Richard the Lionheart in 1199.

A bit further north, where the tip of Périgord is wedged between the Charente and Limousin, you could make a detour to medieval **Bussière-Badil** to see its beautiful, fortified 12th-century church of St-Michel, a hotchpotch of local Romanesque styles: Limousin in the octagonal belltower and the flat pendentives under the dome; Charente in the animal and foliage sculptures on the arches of the porch; Périgourdin in the capitals and dome. The whitewashed interior is as impressive as a basilica's, though the nave is curiously misaligned with the apse, and the walls and columns aren't exactly plumb straight – hence the buttresses added later to keep the thing from falling over. In summer it's a lovely setting for concerts.

Atelier-Musée des Tisserands et de la Charentaise
t 05 53 56 35 76; open April–June, Sept and Oct Mon and Wed–Sat 2–5; July and Aug Mon and Wed–Sat 10–12 and 2.30–6.30 and Sun 10–12; school hols outside summer Mon and Wed–Sat 10–12 and 2–5 and Sun 10–12; Nov–Mar by reservation

Grotte de la Mairie
open by appointment with Font-de-Gaume, t 05 53 06 86 00

Moulin de Pinard
t 05 53 60 56 13; open June–Sept daily 3–6, or by appointment

West of Nontron is **Varaignes**, which won an award for its restorations, especially of its 13th–16th-century château (minus its magnificent Flamboyant portal, sold in the 1920s to an American). The château now houses the **Atelier-Musée des Tisserands et de la Charentaise**, where you can learn about the local weaving and textile industries, in particular how to make thick and comfy *charentaises* slippers. Ask about visits to local slipper-makers, textile producers and mills, and the old royal marine cannon works. In **Teyjat**, the **Grotte de la Mairie** has prehistoric engravings of animals from the late Magdalenian, discovered in 1889, only a few years after findings of the first Cro-Magnon skeletons at Les Eyzies.

South of Varaignes, the 12th-century church at **La Chapelle St Robert** is, like Bussière's, a mix of styles, with a dome and lovely belltower; inside, the apse is supported by sculpted capitals. In nearby **Javerlhac**, the older inhabitants keep their ancestral Occitan alive. There is a 13th-century abbey church, a 1400s château with a tubby tower, and the Versailles of all *pigeonniers*, with niches for 1,500 birds. Between Javerlhac and Nontron, near Bourdeix, is a restored medieval watermill, the **Moulin de Pinard**.

Market Days in the Périgord Vert

Nontron: Saturday.
Mareuil: Tuesday.

Where to Stay and Eat in the Périgord Vert

ⓘ Mareuil ›
12 Rue Pierre Degail, t 05 53 60 99 85 (summer only)

Vieux-Mareuil ✉ 24340

*****Auberge de L'Etang Bleu, t** 05 53 60 92 63, *www.perigord-hotel.com* (€). A hotel overlooking the local swimming hole – a blue lagoon in the woods that can sometimes become very crowded – with its own restaurant (€€€–€€). *Closed Sun eve and Mon out of season.*

Monsec ✉ 24340

****Beauséjour**, just south of Vieux-Mareuil on D939, **t** 05 53 60 92 45 (€). A Logis de France hotel that, despite its position on a main road, offers a range of comfy rooms and includes a good restaurant (€€–€) that can get very busy, serving southwest food such as duck breast with honey and raspberry vinegar. You can dine on the terrace overlooking the garden. *Closed Fri eve and Sat Oct–Easter and Christmas period.*

La Gonterie ✉ 24310

Le Coudert, south on D939, **t** 05 53 05 75 30 (€). A charming, very friendly, ivy-covered *chambres d'hôte* with three bedrooms, two with antique furniture and huge bathrooms. The flower-crammed garden has a wild edge to it. Evening meals (€€) are available by prior arrangement except Sunday evenings and public holidays. *Closed Jan.*

Nontron ✉ 24300

***Hostellerie St-Jacques**, St-Saud-La Coussière (✉ 24470), towards Limoges, **t** 05 53 56 97 21, *hostellerie.st.jacques@wanadoo.fr* (€€–€). A charming hotel with a garden, heated pool and tennis court, and a good restaurant (€€€–€€). *Closed mid-Nov–mid-Feb and Sun eve, Mon and Tues mid-Sept–mid-June.*

****Grand Hôtel Pélisson**, 3 Place Agard, **t** 05 53 56 11 22 (€). A traditional hotel in the centre, with rooms equipped for the disabled, an inner courtyard and pool and the best restaurant (€€€–€€) in Nontron, serving excellent, filling food; note the certificate from Napoleon III dated 1867, proclaiming the inn the official provider of foie gras to the imperial table. *Closed Sun eve Oct–May.*

Champs Romain ✉ 24470

Château Le Verdoyer, near St Saud-Lacoussière, **t** 05 53 56 94 64, *www.verdoyer.fr* (€€). Five rooms and an apartment in a castle, and a good campsite (€) where you can pitch a tent or rent a mobile home or a bungalow. You can swim and play tennis, football and mini-golf. There is a restaurant (€€€–€€), as well as a less expensive bistro/snack bar and a bar. *Closed mid-Oct–Easter; restaurant also lunch and Wed.*

Varaignes ✉ 24300

Auberge du Vieux Château, **t** 05 53 56 31 31 (€€–€). A restored barn in the town centre, offering a good selection of reasonable menus featuring classic and regional dishes. *Closed Sun eve and Mon, plus part of winter (call for details).*

ⓘ **Nontron >**
1 Avenue du Général Leclerc, **t** *05 53 56 25 50*

★ **Hostellerie St-Jacques >**

ⓘ **Varaignes >>**
Château Communal, **t** *05 53 56 35 76*

Brantôme and Bourdeilles

Brantôme

Brantôme

The main roads from Mareuil and Nontron lead south to Brantôme, a charming town of medieval and Renaissance houses built on an island in the river Dronne. Inhabited since Gaulish times, it has an abbey founded by Charlemagne in 769; he endowed it with the relics of St Sicaire, a slave of Herod who converted to Christianity after participating in the Massacre of the Innocents. Sacked by the Normans in the 11th century, the abbey was rebuilt beside the river against a steep bank. During the Hundred Years' War it was defended by the barons of Bourdeilles, and it survived the Wars of Religion thanks to one of their descendants, Pierre de Bourdeilles (1540–1614), abbé of Brantôme, known in French literature simply as Brantôme.

Brantôme became abbot aged 22 and used the abbey's revenues to finance his escapades as a soldier of fortune and lover of court ladies: he accompanied Mary Stuart to Scotland, visited Morocco, Portugal and Venice, and planned an expedition to Peru, only to be frustrated by the Wars of Religion. He rendered a genuine service to his abbey by keeping the Huguenots at bay, diplomatically appealing to the Protestant leader – an old companion-in-arms from his army days. But he was never content in his role as a churchman, and when Henri III vetoed a promotion, he decided to go to Spain and fight against France, only to be gravely injured falling off his horse. Prevented from committing treason, he spent the rest of his life convalescing while writing gossipy, spicy accounts of the people of his time, especially the *Vies des hommes illustres et des grands capitaines* and scandalous *Vies des dames galantes* – so true he left instructions for his heirs to wait 50 years before publishing them, to make sure all his subjects were dead. He is remembered in town with a bust, overlooking the pool of the Fontaine Médicis.

The Abbey

Abbaye de Brantôme
t 05 53 05 80 52; open (inc museum) April–June and Sept Wed–Mon 10–12.30 and 2–6; July and Aug daily 10–7; Feb, Mar and Oct–Dec Wed–Mon 10–12 and 2–5; adm

A charming 16th-century dogleg bridge with a Renaissance pavilion, built by a dreamy abbot to watch the reflections in the river water, crosses from the island town to the white pile of this abbey. The 11th-century church, after suffering a string of bad luck and reconstructions, was given the *coup de grâce* when it was handed over to the 19th-century architect-restorer Paul Abadie, who was never one to preserve when he could rebuild. Only the detached belltower (the oldest in France), with its Merovingian base, pyramid roof and complex tiers of windows and arches from the 11th century, attests to the abbey's former grandeur (ask at the tourist office about guided tours in July and August). The church lost its dome in the 13th century, when the Angevins remodelled it; after the Abadie treatment, only a bas-relief of the *Massacre of the Innocents* under the porch and a carved capital, used as a font, survived from the original church. Of the cloister, rebuilt in the 16th century, only one gallery remains. The best bits are the curious *grottes et fontaines sacrées* in the cliff behind the abbey – caves, quarries, shelters, the fountain of St Sicaire, once a pilgrimage site, and the striking *Grotte du Jugement Dernier*, where the 15th-century monks carved striking reliefs of the *Last Judgement* and *Crucifixion*.

The abbey has a **museum** of paintings by Fernand Desmoulin, born in Nontron in the 1830s, a friend of Zola and follower of spiritualist Allan Kardec. In this world Desmoulin was known for his portraits of greats such as Victor Hugo; in the beyond, painting in darkness with the aid of a medium, he produced strange works in a totally different style. The abbey also houses the town's administrative and cultural services, including a library and exhibition rooms.

The Town

Musée Rêve et Miniatures
8 Rue Puyjoli, t 05 53 05 80 52; ask about opening hrs at tourist office; adm

Besides strolling through the streets and perhaps visiting the **Musée Rêve et Miniatures**, where a meticulous collector has assembled historic interiors for Lilliputians, you can have a look at the ivy-covered **Peyrelevade dolmen**, 1km east of Brantôme on the road to Thiviers – the best-preserved of many megalithic monuments in the area, even if it's supported by a crutch of blocks.

Around Brântome: Richemont, Château de Puyguilhem and Villars

Château de Richemont
t 05 53 05 72 81; open mid-July–late Aug daily 10–6; adm

From 1564 to 1568 Brantôme built his **Château de Richemont** to the northwest, in St-Crépin de Richemont. He wrote most of his works here, and declared in his will that his family was never to sell it but to keep it in his memory. So they have, and you can see the great man's bedroom and the chapel where he lies buried under the epitaph he composed.

Château de Puyguilhem
t 05 53 05 65 65 (Mon–Fri), t 05 53 54 82 18 (Sat and Sun); open April–June Tues–Sun 10–12.30 and 2–6; July and Aug daily 9–7; Feb, Mar and Sept–mid-Dec Tues–Thurs and Sun 10–12 and 2–5.30; mid-Dec–early Jan Tues–Sun 10–12.30 and 2–5.30

Périgord claims to have 1001 châteaux; of that number, the most splendid is the Renaissance **Château de Puyguilhem**, northeast of Brântome near Villars. Built in 1524 by the first president of the *Parlement* of Bordeaux, Mondot de la Marthonie, it has a roof-line forest of richly carved dormers and chimneys that is as impressive when viewed from within – it looks like the hull of a ship. Saved from total collapse in the 1930s, Puyguilhem has been refurnished with period pieces and Renaissance tapestries; the jewel is the chimney, beautifully sculpted with the *Labours of Hercules*.

Grotte de Villars
t 05 53 54 82 36; open July and Aug daily 10–7; April–June and Sept daily 10–11.30 and 2–6.30; Oct daily 2–6; adm

From Villars, the D82 continues 3km to the **Grotte de Villars**, the largest underground network in the Périgord, with 13km explored to date. Unlike most caves in the Dordogne, this combines natural art – brilliant white translucent stalactites and draperies – with prehistoric drawings in magnesium oxide, dating way back to the Aurignacian period (30,000 BC). The authenticity of the blue outline of a galloping horse and 'sorcerer' was confirmed by the dense layer of concretions formed over the pictures.

Two kilometres away from Villars, out in a meadow, stand the impressive ruins of the chapterhouse and cloister with the curiously asymmetrical arches of the **Abbaye de Boschaud** (1154–9), one of four Cistercian foundations in Périgord.

Bourdeilles

Château de Bourdeilles
t 05 53 03 42 96; open July and Aug Wed–Mon 10–7; rest of year Wed–Mon 10–12.30 and 1.30–6

From Brantôme, take the lovely D78 and D106/E2 7km southwest along the Dronne to reach Bourdeilles, seat of the oldest of Périgord's four baronies – so old that the first barons lived back in fairytale times, when they slew griffins and transported themselves to Jerusalem and back by means of an ointment extracted from a dragon's ear. Their **château**, guarding the frontier between English Guyenne and France, stands in a commanding position over the river, next to a medieval bridge and quaint boat-shaped watermill. In 1259, St Louis ceded Bourdeilles to the English. However, not all members of the baronial family agreed to the switch in allegiance, and they built the magnificent octagonal keep 34m high; nevertheless, this failed to keep the English out. In 1376 Du Guesclin took the castle back for France. Brantôme was born here, in 1540, and the adjacent Renaissance château was built by his wealthy and widowed sister-in-law, Jacquette de Montbron. Jacquette had invited Catherine de' Medici to visit, and the old medieval keep simply wouldn't do, nor would she trust an architect; she designed the château herself.

The tour includes both the keep with its four vaulted levels and 2.7m-thick walls, and views from the top that make the long slog up worthwhile, as well as the refined château, richly furnished with 16th- and 17th-century furniture from Spain and Burgundy (donated by the collectors who oversaw the château's restoration in 1962). Jacquette worked especially hard on her sumptuous Salon Doré, its ceiling beautifully painted by Ambroise Le Noble, a member of the Mannerist Fontainebleau school. But when Catherine de' Medici and her Flying Squadron (*see* p.180) swooped through Périgord, she snubbed Bourdeilles, and the furious Jacquette abandoned the building. Among the furnishings and paintings, note the 16th-century German *Dormition of the Virgin*, and the Burgundian tomb of Jean de Chabannes, the gilt Spanish bed of Emperor Charles V and a tapestry showing his archrival, François Ier, with his falconers.

Market Days in Brantôme

Friday; also farmers' market **Tuesday** July and August, and truffle market Friday Dec–Feb.

Activities in and around Brantôme

Ask at the tourist office about local walks, mountainbike hire, pleasure trips on the river, and canoe trips down the Dronne. Or hire canoes or kayaks at Allô Canoë, Boulevard Coligny (**t** 05 53 06 31 85) or Brantôme Canoë (**t** 05 53 05 77 24).

You can also fly about town on a piloted **ultralight** (**t** 06 15 15 42 38).

Where to Stay and Eat

Brantôme > *Abbey,* **t** *05 53 05 80 52, www.ville-brantome.fr; closed Tues exc July and Aug*

Moulin de l'Abbaye >

Brantôme ✉ 24310

****Moulin de l'Abbaye, 1 Route de Bourdeilles, **t** 05 53 05 80 22, *www.moulinabbaye.com* (€€€€€–€€€€). A dreamy, romantic, ivy-covered hotel just outside the centre on the Dronne, spread among several buildings – a converted watermill, a carpenter's house and an old curate's residence – and set in a delightful garden. The restaurant (€€€) serves exquisite dishes based on local ingredients, including luscious dessert soufflés. *Closed Nov–late April.*

***Domaine de la Roseraie, Les Courrières, on Angoulême road, **t** 05 53 05 84 74, *www.domaine-la-roseraie.com* (€€€€). A Relais du Silence hotel out of the centre, in a rose garden, with 10 well-equipped rooms, a pool, tennis and riding nearby, and a restaurant (€€€€–€€€). *Closed Nov–April.*

***Hôtel Chabrol, 57 Rue Gambetta, **t** 05 53 05 70 15 (€€–€). A handsome old white building on the Dronne, with an excellent, elegant restaurant (€€€€–€€) serving generous portions of favourites such as *millefeuille* of veal kidney with duck liver and truffles, plus wonderful hot desserts. *Closed mid-Nov–mid-Dec, Jan and Feb; and Sun and Mon eves Oct–June.*

Périgord Vert, 6 Avenue de Thiviers, **t 05 53 05 70 58, *http://pros.orange.fr/hostellerie-perigord-vert* (€€–€).

A stylish, reliable, ivy-swathed Logis de France hotel with a restaurant (€€). *Closed mid-Dec–mid-Jan; restaurant lunch Mon–Fri.*

Chez Mérillou, Rue André Maurois, **t** 05 53 05 74 04 (€). A pleasant, good-value B&B.

Au Fil de l'Eau, 21 Quai Bertin, **t** 05 53 05 73 65 (€€). A restaurant owned by the Moulin de l'Abbaye (*see* opposite), beside the Dronne with an outside eating area. *Closed Oct–April.*

Resto-Grill, 40 Rue Gambetta, **t** 05 53 05 86 25 (€€). Quite simple meals served in a pleasant, intimate atmosphere a stroll away from the tourist hub, with a shaded terrace. *Closed lunch exc July and Aug.*

Le Vieux Four, 7 Rue Pierre de Mareuil, **t** 05 53 05 74 16 (€€–€). A troglodytic restaurant in a prehistoric cave, serving some of the best pizzas in Périgord. *Closed Mon Oct–June.*

Champagnac-de-Belair ✉ 24530

********Moulin du Roc**, **t** 05 53 02 86 00, *www.moulinduroc.com* (€€€€–€€€). Big, beautiful rooms in a charming old mill on the Dronne northeast of Brantôme, with a pool and tennis courts. The restaurant (€€€€–€€€) does wonders with traditional Périgourdin recipes. *Closed Tues mid-Oct–early Mar; restaurant Tues and Wed (exc Wed eve mid-May–mid-Oct).*

Bourdeilles ✉ 24310

*****Château de la Côte**, Biras, southeast of Bourdeilles on D106, **t** 05 53 03 70 11, *www.chateaudelacote.com* (€€). A 15th-century château in an immense park, with 16 beautiful rooms, a restaurant (€€€€–€€€), a helipad, a pool and table tennis. Golf, riding and canoeing are available nearby. *Closed mid-Nov–mid-Mar; restaurant lunch.*

Northeast Périgord

Green and peaceful and full of happy cows, this corner of Green Périgord manages to stay aloof from most of the tourist madness; in winter the roads are often deserted.

Up the Côle, to St-Jean-de-Côle and Thiviers

To the east of Brantôme the D78 follows the little river Côle; one of the first villages you'll pass, **La Chapelle-Faucher**, sleeps peacefully on its hill with the ruins of its château, burned a century ago, and its church with a pretty portal, all belying the horrible event of 1569, when the Protestant Amiral de Coligny massacred 300 Catholics – an act avenged three years later by Catherine de' Medici, who made sure he was a target of the St Bartholomew's Day massacre in Paris.

Northeast, **St-Jean-de-Côle** is as pretty a village as you could ask for, gathered on the banks of the Côle (spanned here by a Gothic humpback bridge), each house crowned by a steep tile roof. It was a busy place in the Middle Ages; the Templars were here, and in the 12th century the inhabitants built themselves a domed church. No one knows how the secrets of dome building were passed on, but in St-Jean they bungled it so often that they settled in the end for a less precarious wooden roof. The belltower has some delightful

Getting around Northeast Périgord

There are no trains servicing the area, but **buses** link Excideuil and Périgueux; contact CFTA, **t** 05 55 17 91 19, *www.cftaco.fr*.

carvings, especially one of God modelling Adam out of clay. St-Jean's handsome 15th–17th-century Château de la Marthonie was remodelled by the same Marthonie responsible for Puyguilhem.

More excellent Romanesque awaits 7km east in the 12th-century church of **Thiviers**. Built over Merovingian foundations, it boasts a Renaissance porch and capitals sculpted with stone monsters, Samson killing a lion, and Jesus giving St Peter the keys to the kingdom; among the statues there's an unusual *Angel and Vagabond*. Thiviers pays tribute to the goose that lays its golden egg, or rather contributes its gorged liver, at the **Musée du Foie Gras, Maison de l'Oie et du Canard**. There is also a display of ceramics at the *mairie* (**t** *05 53 62 28 00*). Opposite the Maison de la Presse is a plaque commemorating Jean-Paul Sartre, who spent his miserable early childhood and summer holidays in a house here with a grandfather who for 40 years refused to speak to his wife because she had no dowry – probably the inspiration for Sartre's famous remark that 'Hell is other people.' If Sartre hated Thiviers (he wasn't very kind about it in *Les Mots*), Thiviers returned the favour, and the plaque was only put up after a bitter fight between the *mairie* and the association Les Amis de Sartre.

Musée du Foie Gras, Maison de l'Oie et du Canard
t *05 53 55 12 50; open Mon–Sat 10–12 and 2–6, with possible variations; adm*

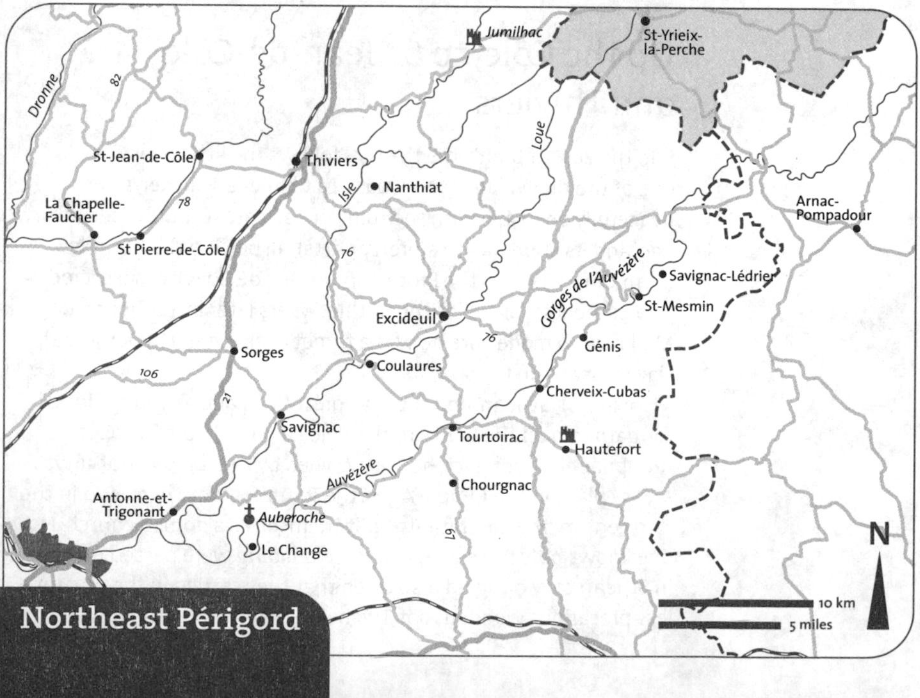

Northeast Périgord

Around Thiviers: Jumilhac-le-Grand

Château de Jumilhac
t 05 53 52 55 43; open Sun 2–5; guided tours June–Sept daily 10–7; mid-Mar–May Sat, Sun and public hols 2–6.30

North and east of Thiviers, the ferny forested frontier of the Limousin is the least populated area in Périgord. Here, like Sleeping Beauty's forgotten castle, at the top of a boulevard, stands the **Château de Jumilhac**. Antoine Chapelle, the brain behind it, was a master of forges who made such fine cannons for Henri IV that the king knighted him and gave him a former Templar stronghold. Chapelle converted it into a fantasia of towers, turrets and chimneys coiffed with blue-slate pepperpots ('the most romantic roofs in France', according to Gustave Doré, who borrowed them for some of his fairytale engravings) topped with an equally fantastic array of forged-iron decorations. Right angles are rare inside as well as out. The Chambre de la Fileuse, built into the thickness of the wall, has naïve murals imitating tapestries, painted for the lady whose portrait is over the door and who had nothing to do but spin when her jealous husband confined her here. The fairytale of Rumpelstiltskin comes to mind. Indeed, there is a **Galerie de l'Or**, a museum of gold at the tourist office, including pieces in their raw state discovered in the Gallo-Roman mines at nearby Fouilloux.

To the south of Jumilhac and the east of Thiviers, there's some fine countryside along the upper reaches of the river Isle, especially around the D67. **Nanthiat** has a château with a pair of pepperpots of its own, and a handsome Romanesque church, with a rare altar cross in front.

Down the Isle and Auvézère

After Jumilhac the river Isle loops down to pick up the waters of the Auvézère just before Périgueux. In the 1500s this little mesopotamia was full of iron forges, one of which remains in the wooded gorges of the Auvézère. This is the country of the battling troubadour Bertran de Born, and of fungi that are worth their weight in gold: truffles.

Excideuil and Around

The busiest market town in the region, Excideuil once belonged to the *vicomtes* of Limoges, who built its vertiginous fortress on a *butte* of Jurassic limestone – a redoubt that three times repelled Richard the Lionheart. Its former **priory church** has a Flamboyant portal and 17th-century retable and overlooks Place Bugeaud, named for a local aristocrat who conquered Algeria in the 1840s, and gave the town a fountain. A *Circuit Découverte* has information plaques on buildings of historical interest.

Excideuil is on the river Loue, which flows into the Isle at **Coulaures**, a pretty village with a double-breasted Romanesque church containing a 14th-century fresco. The best scenery around, however, is along the Auvézère, beginning at **Cherveix-Cubas**, a village with a ***Lanterne des Morts*** in its cemetery – a slender version of the mysterious towers in Atur and Sarlat (*see* p.160). From here you can drive, ride or trek along the delicious Gorges de l'Auvézère. Highlights along the way include **Génis**, a village of schist houses, the belvedere at the **Moulin du Pervendoux**, and at **St-Mesmin** the 15-minute walk to the laughing falls of the Auvézère. You can also follow an interpretative trail around the old riverside forge at **Savignac-Lédrier**. This evocative site dates back to the 15th century, although the remains are mostly early 19th century; the forge was in use until 1975.

Papeterie de Vaux
t *05 53 62 50 06; open Easter–Oct Tues–Sat 10–12 and 2–5.30, Sun 2–6*

Maison de la Pomme d'Or
4 Place Thomas Bugeaud, ***t*** *05 53 62 17 82; open July and Aug daily 10–12.30 and 2–6.30; rest of year Mon–Fri 2–5*

Just north of here, at Payzac, the **Papeterie de Vaux** beside the Belles Dames stream is an old paper factory where you can learn about production. At Lanouaille, you can learn everything there is to know about apples at the **Maison de la Pomme d'Or**.

The Château de Hautefort

Château de Hautefort
t *05 53 50 51 23; open June–Sept daily 9.30–7; Oct daily 2–6; Mar and Nov Sat, Sun and public hols 2–6; April and May daily 10–12.30 and 2–6.30; adm*

South of Cherveix-Cubas, the high-domed towers of one of Périgord's most famous citadels, the Château de Hautefort, dominate much of the Auvézère valley. In the 12th century a fortress on this spot belonged to the troubadour Bertran de Born (*see* pp.33–35). In 1640 it was rebuilt by a famous miser, Jacques-François de Hautefort. According to the gossip of the day, Jacques-François was the model for Harpagon in Molière's *L'Avare* (though Molière lowered his miser to bourgeois status); when the miser fell ill his doctor prescribed English pills, which brought about his death – they cost so much that Jacques-François couldn't bear to swallow them. His sister, Marie, was the most beautiful woman of her day, and was nicknamed *Aurore* by the French court. Even rarer than her great beauty was her evenhandedness – Marie was both the lover of the melancholic Louis XIII and the best friend of the wife he abhorred, Anne of Austria. Marie's devotion to the queen made her the enemy of Cardinal Richelieu, who went to the extreme of presenting a rival for the king's affections, a young man named Cinq-Mars; when that ploy only resulted in the king having two loves instead of one, Richelieu threatened to leave the king's service himself if Louis didn't dump Marie. She was only reinstated in court after Louis's death in 1643.

In 1836, novelist Eugène Le Roy was born here into a family of château labourers – a background that inspired his most famous work, *Jacquou le Croquant* (1899), describing the abject poverty in which Périgord's peasants lived so that the Hauteforts of the world could afford such dishy spreads (a *croquant* is a local word for a 17th-century peasant rebel; the name invokes a crunching or gnashing of angry teeth). There's a museum dedicated to his life in Montignac (*see* p.118). In 1929, the castle passed to the Baron and

Baronne de Bastard, who undertook the complete restoration of Hautefort and its gardens. After the baron died, his wife continued alone, finally finishing it in 1968. In the autumn of that same year Hautefort went up in a blaze that could be seen across half of Périgord. But after the shock of losing 39 years of work in one night, the Baronne de Bastard amazed everyone by starting all over again. Now completed, the château is one of the most inspiring in Périgord open to the public, and you can visit the panoramic terraces and immaculate French gardens.

Musée de la Médecine
***t** 05 53 50 40 27; open daily June–Sept 10–7; Easter–May and Oct Mon–Fri 10–12 and 2–6; adm*

The Hospice of Hautefort is a Greek cross with a dome echoing those topping the towers. Founded by the parsimonious Jacques-François on his English pill-less deathbed in 1680, the hospital took in 11 old men, 11 boys and 11 young women and was known as the hospital of 33 years, recalling the age of Christ when he died. It now houses a **Musée de la Médecine**. Ask at the tourist office (*see* p.92) about **guided tours** of Hautefort's medieval streets.

Tourtoirac

Tourtoirac chapterhouse
open July and Aug daily 10.30–12.30 and 3–6; other times by appointment through mairie, ***t** 05 53 51 12 17*

Musée des Rois d'Araucanie
***t** 05 53 51 12 76; open Wed–Mon 10.30–12 and 2.30–5.30*

On the Auvézère to the west of Hautefort lies **Tourtoirac**, which boasts a damaged 11th-century Benedictine abbey behind a lofty *clocher-mur*; the dome of the church has survived, along with some delightful carvings on the capitals of the ruined **chapterhouse**. In the village, a plaque on a small shop notes that His Majesty Aurélie-Antoine Ier, King of Araucania and Patagonia, died here on 17 September 1878. In the cemetery, his tomb is marked with a stele and crown, which were copied by the stonecutter from the king of hearts on a playing card. Aurélie so wanted the French to establish a protectorate in southern Chile that he went off to do it himself. The Chileans thought that he was mad, but he never gave up his claim. He left no direct heir, but the faithful have never failed to produce successors to the throne. The **Musée des Rois d'Araucanie** south of Tourtoirac in **Chourgnac d'Ans** contains books and other information on the king and his claim; the curator speaks English.

Down the Auvézère in **Auberoche**, a Romanesque chapel with a ruined roof and rain-scoured frescoes is all that is left of a once-mighty fortress that saw the very first battle of the Hundred Years' War. In the summer of 1345, the Earl of Derby installed a garrison here to keep an eye on Périgueux. The Count of Périgord, Roger Bernard, besieged it, and when the beset English tried to send an SOS message to Derby, Roger Bernard jeeringly catapulted the message, with the live messenger tied to it, back into the fortress. Nevertheless, Derby somehow got word and (according to Froissart) surprised the count's 10,000 men while they dined, capturing 2,000, including Roger Bernard himself. There isn't much left to see in Auberoche, but don't miss the charming watermill downstream at **Le Change**.

Sorges, Périgord's Truffle Capital

Musée de la Truffe
t 05 53 05 90 11; open summer daily 9.30–12.30 and 2.30–6.30; winter (exc 2wks in Jan) Tues–Sun 10–12 and 2–5; adm

North of Auberoche and the river Isle, **Sorges** is the central market for the truffle trade and home of a **Musée de la Truffe**, with a 3km truffle path and all you've ever wanted to know about that black diamond stud in your foie gras. According to the French, in AD 300 the afflicted St Anthony was clawing the ground in distress when the angels rewarded him with the first truffles. St Anthony is the patron saint of animals, and in art is usually depicted with a pig: for centuries these were used to root for the delicacy. Nowadays their very uncontrolled pigginess has led many truffle-hunters to prefer keen-nosed hounds whose mothers' teats were rubbed with truffle juice so they would associate the scent with their first love. Other hunters rely on savvy, keeping a lookout for fine soil looking as if it had been scorched, in the vicinity of a specially diseased truffle oak, with 'hélomysa' flies circling above. Sorges and the Causses de Thiviers are one of the richest sources of the tasty fungus; in the old days there were so many that the favourite way of eating them was to put them under the ashes in the fire and then wolf them down whole. Outside truffle season, you can buy them in little jars.

Château des Bories
t 05 53 06 00 01; open July–Sept Mon–Sat 3–6; adm

Sorges also has a domed Romanesque church and a 13th-century castle, though you may find the 15th-century **Château des Bories** more rewarding. The last castle on the Isle before Périgueux, it's the archetype of Périgourdin châteaux, with symmetrical round towers, a Gothic kitchen, a huge chimney and a monumental staircase.

ⓘ Thiviers >
Place Foch, t 05 53 55 12 50, www.thiviers.fr

ⓘ Hautefort >
Place de l'Eglise, t 05 53 50 40 27, www.ot-hautefort.com

ⓘ Excideuil >>
1 Place du Château, t 05 53 62 95 56, www.excideuil.fr

ⓘ St-Jean-de-Côle >
Rue du Château, t 05 53 62 14 15, www.ville-saint-jean-de-cole.fr

Market Days in Northeast Périgord

Thiviers: Saturday, and small farmers' market Tuesday.

Jumilhac Le Grand: second and fourth Wednesday of month, and Sunday morning July and August.

St-Jean-de-Côle: Sunday

Excideuil: Thursday; also medieval market weekend closest to 14 July, and Thursday duck and truffle market Nov–Mar.

Hautefort: Wednesday, and first Monday of month.

Sorges: Sunday in summer; plus truffle market in January.

Where to Stay and Eat in Northeast Périgord

St-Jean-de-Côle ✉ 24800

Doumarias, west on D78 towards St-Pierre-de-Côle, **t** 05 53 62 34 37 (€€). A serene *chambres d'hôte* in a huge, well-furnished 16th-century house. There is a quiet courtyard, and evening meals by reservation (Mon, Wed and Fri). *Closed end Sept–Mar.*

St-Jean, t 05 53 52 23 20 (€). The only hotel in the centre, simple but sweet, with a restaurant (€€€–€). *Closed Tues eve, and Sun and Wed out of season.*

Auberge du Coq Rouge, main square, **t** 05 53 62 32 71 (€€). A popular. old-fashioned place for sumptuous Périgourdin cuisine at reasonable prices. Booking is advised. *Closed Tues July and Aug, Mon–Wed out of season.*

Excideuil ✉ 24160

****Hostellerie du Fin Chapon**, 3 Place du Château, **t** 05 53 62 42 38 (€). Eleven comfortable old-fashioned rooms and well-prepared food (€€). *Closed Mon and Jan.*

Cherveix-Cubas ✉ 24390

****Le Favard**, 4km from Hautefort, **t** 05 53 50 41 05, *www.hotelfavard.com* (€).

A pleasant hotel in the village centre, set around a circular pool, with a popular adjoining restaurant (*t 05 53 51 35 69*; €€–€) serving delicious *tourain* (bread and garlic soup), truffled foie gras pâté, country ham, duck *confit*, cheese and homemade dessert. *Closed mid-Nov–mid-Dec and mid-Feb–mid-Mar; restaurant Mon, Thurs eve and 2wks Oct or Nov.*

ⓘ Sorges >
t 05 53 46 71 43

★ Auberge de la Truffe >

Sorges ✉ 24420

******Auberge de la Truffe**, N21, **t** 05 53 05 02 05, *www.auberge-de-la-truffe.com* (€€–€). An excellent, long-established place with a pool, solarium and billiards room. Rooms overlook the garden. The restaurant (€€€€–€€) specializes in truffles, as well as rather less pricey delights, and cookery courses are sometimes organized in autumn. There's an annex, **Hôtel de la Mairie**, **t** 05 53 06 82 00, on Place de la Mairie. *Restaurant closed Sun eve, and Mon and Tues lunch Nov–Mar.*

Antonne-et-Trigonant ✉ 24420

*****Hostellerie de l'Ecluse**, Route de Limoges, **t** 05 53 06 00 04, *www.ecluse-perigord.com* (€€). Attractive rooms beside the Isle, most with a balcony, and a fine restaurant (€€€–€€). *Closed 2wks in Jan.*

*****Hostellerie La Charmille**, **t** 05 53 06 00 45, *www.lacharmille.fr* (€). A large house offering 13 comfy rooms with satellite TV. There's a good restaurant (€€€–€€) serving southwest favourites and more besides. *Closed 2wks in Jan; restaurant Wed lunch.*

Le Change ✉ 24640

*****Château du Roc-Chautru**, **t** 05 53 06 17 31, *www.chateau-roc-chautru.fr* (€€€€–€€€). A 19th-century château on the Auvézère with 10 luxurious rooms. There's table tennis, billiards, bikes for loan and a bar, and you can get evening meals (€), taken around a communal table. *Closed Dec–Feb.*

Périgueux

Set in a privileged, fertile valley on the river Isle, the capital of the Dordogne *département* is a cheery city of 35,000 people producing and marketing truffles, foie gras and fat strawberries, and printing all the postage stamps in France. The old streets around its famous five-domed cathedral have been intelligently restored to give the city a lively and lovely heart; another plus are two excellent museums with exceptional prehistoric and Gallo-Roman displays.

History

The first inhabitants of Périgueux, the Petrocorii Gauls, built their *oppidum* on the heights of the left bank of the Isle, by the sacred spring Vesunna. After Caesar defeated their ally Vercingetorix, they settled down to enjoy the *pax romana* and build a brand new town known as Vesunna (or Vésone in French) on the fertile plains of the Isle's right bank. It was the perfect place for a market town. By the 3rd century, Vesunna had 20,000 Gallo-Roman citizens, famed for their iron-working skills.

Vesunna was still in its first bloom when the barbarian Alemanni crushed it under their heels in 275. Raped and pillaged into a state of shock, Vesunna destroyed its own temples and basilicas for the stone to build a wall, contracting itself into the space of a tiny village. As the years (and more barbarians) passed by, this bristling remnant of Vesunna even lost its proud name: it became known as

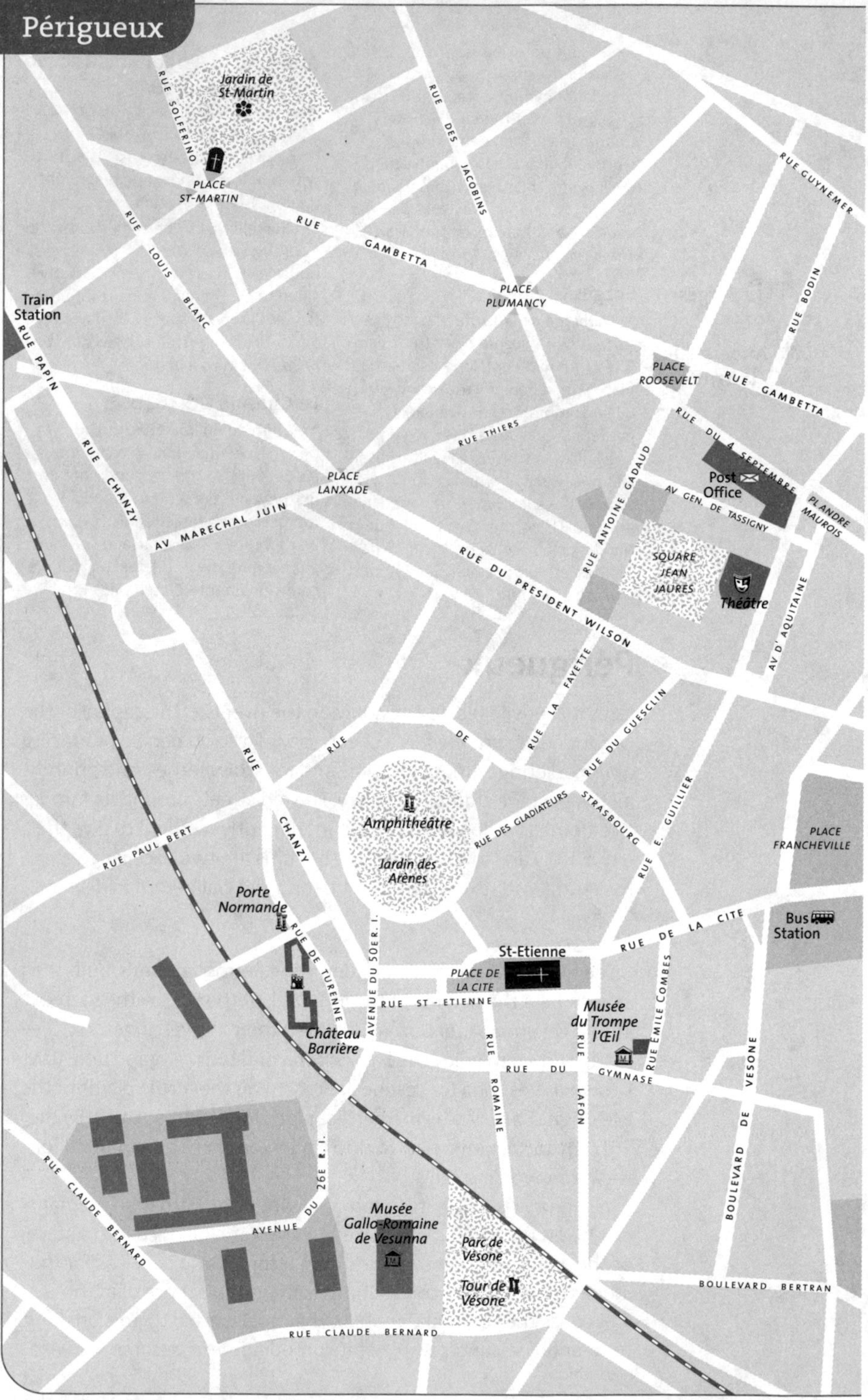
Jardin de St-Martin
RUE SOLFERINO
PLACE ST-MARTIN
RUE DES JACOBINS
RUE GUYNEMER
RUE LOUIS BLANC
RUE GAMBETTA
PLACE PLUMANCY
RUE BODIN
Train Station
RUE PAPIN
PLACE ROOSEVELT
RUE GAMBETTA
RUE CHANZY
RUE THIERS
RUE DU 4 SEPTEMBRE
PLACE LANXADE
Post Office
AV GEN. DE TASSIGNY
PL ANDRE MAUROIS
AV MARECHAL JUIN
RUE ANTOINE GADAUD
SQUARE JEAN JAURES
Théâtre
RUE DU PRESIDENT WILSON
AV D' AQUITAINE
RUE LA FAYETTE
RUE DE
RUE DU GUESCLIN
STRASBOURG
RUE CHANZY
Amphithéâtre
Jardin des Arènes
RUE DES GLADIATEURS
RUE E. GUILLIER
PLACE FRANCHEVILLE
RUE PAUL BERT
Porte Normande
RUE DE TURENNE
AVENUE DU 50E R. I.
St-Etienne
RUE DE LA CITE
Bus Station
PLACE DE LA CITE
RUE ST-ETIENNE
Musée du Trompe l'Œil
RUE EMILE COMBES
Château Barrière
RUE ROMAINE
RUE LAFON
RUE DU GYMNASE
BOULEVARD DE VESONE
RUE CLAUDE BERNARD
AVENUE DU 26E R. I.
Musée Gallo-Romaine de Vesunna
Parc de Vésone
Tour de Vésone
BOULEVARD BERTRAN
RUE CLAUDE BERNARD

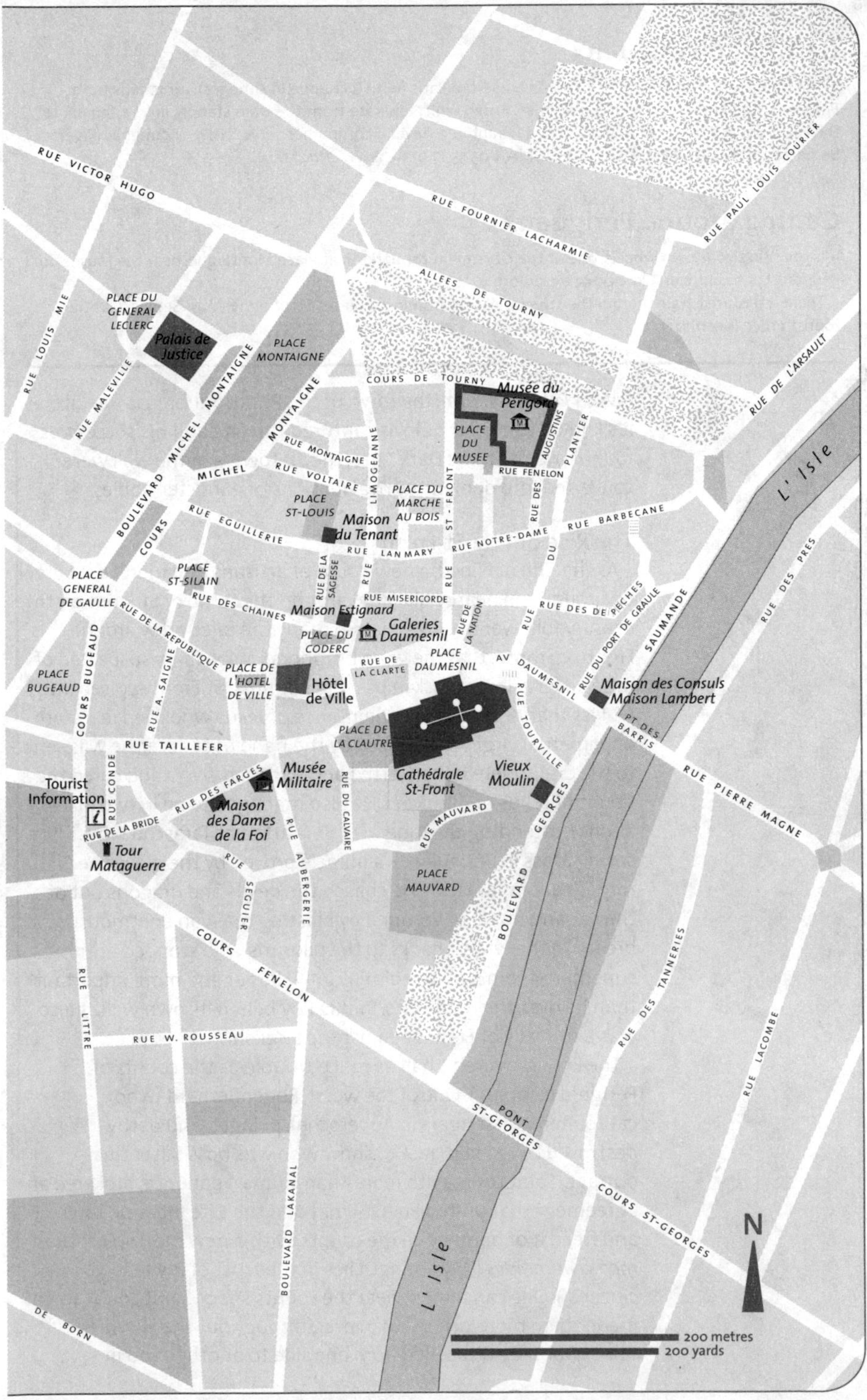
RUE VICTOR HUGO
RUE FOURNIER LACHARMIE
RUE PAUL LOUIS COURIER
ALLEES DE TOURNY
RUE LOUIS MIE
PLACE DU GENERAL LECLERC
Palais de Justice
PLACE MONTAIGNE
RUE MALEVILLE
BOULEVARD MICHEL MONTAIGNE
COURS MICHEL MONTAIGNE
COURS DE TOURNY
Musée du Périgord
PLACE DU MUSEE
RUE DE L'ARSAULT
L' Isle
RUE MONTAIGNE
RUE VOLTAIRE
LIMOGEANNE
RUE ST - FRONT
AUGUSTINS
RUE FENELON
RUE DES PLANTIER
PLACE ST-LOUIS
PLACE DU MARCHE AU BOIS
Maison du Tenant
RUE EGUILLERIE
RUE LANMARY
RUE NOTRE-DAME
RUE BARBECANE
RUE DU
RUE DE LA SAGESSE
PLACE ST-SILAIN
PLACE GENERAL DE GAULLE
RUE DES CHAINES
RUE MISERICORDE
RUE DES DE PECHES
RUE DE LA NATION
Maison Estignard
Galeries Daumesnil
PLACE DU CODERC
RUE DE LA REPUBLIQUE
RUE DU PORT DE GRAULE
SAUMANDE
RUE DES PRES
PLACE BUGEAUD
COURS BUGEAUD
RUE A. SAIGNE
PLACE DE L'HOTEL DE VILLE
Hôtel de Ville
RUE DE LA CLARTE
PLACE DAUMESNIL
AV DAUMESNIL
Maison des Consuls
Maison Lambert
PT DES BARRIS
PLACE DE LA CLAUTRE
RUE TOURVILLE
RUE TAILLEFER
RUE CONDE
Tourist Information
RUE DES FARGES
Musée Militaire
Cathédrale St-Front
Vieux Moulin
RUE PIERRE MAGNE
Maison des Dames de la Foi
RUE DE LA BRIDE
Tour Mataguerre
RUE DU CALVAIRE
RUE AUBERGERIE
RUE MAUVARD
PLACE MAUVARD
BOULEVARD GEORGES
RUE SEGUIER
COURS FENELON
RUE LITTRE
RUE W. ROUSSEAU
RUE DES TANNERIES
RUE LACOMBE
PONT ST-GEORGES
COURS ST-GEORGES
BOULEVARD LAKANAL
N
DE BORN
200 metres
200 yards

Getting to Périgueux

The **train** station, in Rue Denis Papin, is 4hrs from Paris (with a change in Limoges), 1hr 15mins from Bordeaux, and 3hrs from Agen or Toulouse. **Buses**, which operate from the train station, link Périgueux to the Paris–Bordeaux TGV in Angoulême, via Brantôme. Several companies serve Sarlat, Montignac, Ribérac, Bergerac and Brantôme; the biggest is CFTA, **t** 05 55 17 91 19, *www.cftaco.fr*.

Getting around Périgueux

If you bring your own wheels, one of the city's main **car parks** is at Place Montaigne, near the Musée du Périgord. For a **taxi**, call Allô, **t** 05 53 09 09 09.

There is a **tourist train** around the streets, leaving from near Cours Montaigne, May–Sept; ask at the tourist office (*see* p.103).

Civitas Petrocoriorum, the town of the Petrocorii, or just the Cité, as it's known to this day. Clovis captured the Cité and his successors fought over it; in the Dark Ages, the 24 towers of the wall were converted into donjons by rival factions of gangster-nobles.

The Rise of Puy-St-Front

As the Cité declined, a new *bourg* of artisans and merchants grew up around the nearby hill (*puy*) around the tomb of St Front, a 4th-century follower of St Martial. So many tall tales grew around this Front, or Fronto, that the good burghers can be fairly suspected of false advertising to suck in passing pilgrims: St Front evolved into no less than a personal acquaintance of Jesus who lived in a state of perpetual virginity. Baptized by the hand of St Peter, he was sent to the Cité, where he converted and baptized 7,000 and cured the Count Aurélius of his ulcers. He also managed to be in two places at once, attending the funeral of St Martha at Tarascon whilst saying Mass in Périgueux – a miracle proved by the gloves he forgot back in Tarascon. He chased the devils and dragons out of the pagan temple of Vesunna by blasting open an enormous breach in the walls. Thanks to the pilgrims who stopped at this superhero's tomb, bourgeois Puy grew larger and more important than its rival, the noble Cité. In 1182 Puy began its own wall. It also was a firm ally of France against the English.

The English weren't half as much trouble as the counts of Périgord (*see* p.117). One of the worst, Roger Bernard (who catapulted messengers in Auberoche), pillaged and partly destroyed Puy in 1246 just to show who was boss. After this outrage, Saint Louis, with more-than-human patience, brokered an agreement that united Puy-St-Front and the Cité into one town and freed it of homage to the counts, with a new motto: *Fortitudo mea civium fides* ('My strength lies in the trust of my fellow citizens'). One can almost hear the counts sneer. Saint Louis' accord made them more 'ornery' than ever; throughout the Hundred Years' War they weaselled from one side to another, and in 1357, while the French were distracted by the capture of John the Good, Count Archambault V and his brother, Cardinal Hélie de Talleyrand pounced and grabbed Périgueux with English aid. Although Du Guesclin chased the English out in 1369, Count Archambault managed to stay put by promising loyalty to the crown of France; instead, he took money from England to stir up as much trouble as possible until the exasperated French came back to give him the boot once and for all. His castle in the Cité was demolished, his goods confiscated and given to the canons of St-Front.

Périgord's Bastion of Catholicism

In the 15th century the battered survivors slowly rebuilt, putting the city back on its feet just in time for more trouble in the Wars of Religion. Périgueux was as firmly Catholic as Bergerac was Protestant, but the Huguenots were quicker off the mark: in 1575 they killed the Bishop of Périgueux, then, disguising themselves as peasants, entered and captured the city. They held it for six years, wrecking churches and melting down their bells for cannons. Salt was rubbed into Périgueux's wounds when the Treaty of Beaulieu (1576) made the city a safe haven for Protestants; so miserable were the Catholic majority that the triumphal arch they erected for Henri, King of Navarre, read: '*Urbis Deforme Cadaver*'. In pity the Sénéchal André de Bourdeilles offered to buy the town back for the Catholics; failing that, he captured Périgueux in 1581 by using the same peasant-disguise ruse as the Huguenots.

More Trouble

Since the time of St Louis, Périgueux burghers had maintained their privileges. They were exempt from royal taxes and military service; they had their own constitution and elected officials, and to the king owed only 'homage and fidelity'. In 1635, when Louis XIII imposed a tavern tax, there was a riot. The mayor bolted, the tax clerk was murdered and tossed down a well; the *Croquants* took to the forests and fought the king's men until 1641. Louis XIV cast a cold eye on these goings-on, and by the end of his reign he had rubbed out all traces of Périgueux's privileges and independence.

In 1790, when the Revolution divided France into *départements*, the worthies of the Dordogne could not choose a capital: as Périgueux, Bergerac and Sarlat all had valid claims, it was decided that the status would be shared on an alternating basis. Périgueux drew the longest straw and got to be capital first, and inertia has done the rest to make sure it never went anywhere else. As a kind of footnote to its beleaguered past, Périgueux gave birth in 1846 to Léon Bloy, France's most curmudgeonly Catholic philosopher and author, who celebrated the sinking of the *Titanic* with a huge party in Montmartre 'because it drowned so many Protestants'.

The Cité

Musée Gallo-Romaine de Vesunna
t 05 53 53 00 92; open July and Aug daily 10–7; early April–June and Sept–early Nov Tues–Sun 10–12.30 and 2–6; early Nov–early Jan and Feb–early April Tues–Sun 10–12.30 and 2–5.30; adm

In 2003 Périgueux's oldest bits became the stars of its newest and brightest attraction, the **Musée Gallo-Romaine de Vesunna** in the Cité's Parc de Vésone. Designed by Aquitaine native Jean Nouvel, France's leading contemporary architect, it has delicate, almost immaterial glass walls that hang from a parasol roof, which protects the impressive remains of a 1st-century AD *domus* – a fancy patrician villa with paintings, mosaics and heated baths, which you inspect up close from two wooden walkways. The numerous finds excavated over the years are displayed on two balconies, divided into two themes: the City and Public Life, and the House and Private Life.

The museum is next to the 20m **Tour de Vésone**, once the central *cella* of a circular 1st-century AD Gallo-Roman temple. Its great cylinder was originally faced with marble and its walls still bear the breach made by St Front's legendary exorcism, though some say the opening was made intentionally to admit the rays of the rising sun.

St-Etienne-de-la-Cité

From the Tour de Vésone take Rue Romaine up to the centre of the Cité, where **St-Etienne**, Périgueux's oldest church, was founded on the site of a Temple of Mars by St Front. In the 12th century it was rebuilt in a style that became the prototype of the Périgourdin domed Romanesque church, with wide Byzantine cupolas not only over the crossing but cupping the length of the nave. Originally St-Etienne had four of these, culminating in a grand carved portal under a huge belltower porch; the Huguenots unkindly, and none too neatly, tore off the front half. In 1669 the mutilated structure was no longer deemed worthy to be a cathedral and the status was transferred to St-Front.

The two surviving bays are not only an important lesson in the origins of Périgourdin Romanesque but are steeped in a shadowy medieval solemnity so lacking in St-Front. The first dome, from the early 1100s, is solid and primitive, lit only by tiny windows; the second, from around 1160, is elongated, lighter and supported by twinned columns. The interior has a fine if incongruous 17th-century wooden retable and a 12th-century Easter calendar; the arch from the tomb of Bishop Jean d'Asside (d. 1169) frames the Romanesque baptismal font. Nearby, the **Musée du Trompe-l'Œil** has displays on the tricks artists play with our perception, and runs workshops (see the website) on how they're done.

Musée du Trompe-l'Œil
5 Rue Emile Combes, t 05 53 09 84 40, www.museedutrompeloeil.com; open April–Sept Tues–Sat 10.30–12.30 and 2.30–6.30, Sun and public hols 3–6; Oct–Mar Tues–Sat 2–5.30

Rue St-Etienne leads from the church to the **Château Barrière**, a *maison forte*, or strong house, built on the walls of the Cité for a loyal retainer of the counts. Next to the château you can see a rare 13th-century Romanesque house; across the street from it, the

Gallo-Roman **Porte Normande** is a sole survivor of the wall that was thrown together by the citizens of Vesunna after the invasion of the Alemanni; originally it stood about 10.5m high, a jigsaw of columns and temple fragments. The nearby **amphitheatre**, where up to 30,000 spectators cheered gladiators to death, is now practically toothless – as the base for the castle of the bloody-minded counts of Périgord, it had been enthusiastically razed in 1391. Only a few stones and an entrance have survived, now enclosing a pretty garden and a playground.

Puy-St-Front

On the far side of Place Francheville, which once served as the no-man's land between Périgueux's two rival towns, lies the compact and beautifully restored quarter of Puy-St-Front. The tourist office's medieval-Renaissance tour will get you inside some of the courtyards, and into the last remnant of Puy's walls, the **Tour Mataguerre** in Place Francheville. Decorated with fleurs-de-lys, it was repaired in 1477 with the forced labour of men inflicted with the scourge of 15th-century Périgueux – leprosy.

Running just to the left of the Tour Mataguerre, Rue de la Bride/Rue des Farges ('forges') was the main road linking the Cité and Puy-St-Front. Some of Périgueux's oldest houses are situated here – most notably, at No.4, the 12th-century **Maison des Dames de la Foi**, which was built by the Templars, inhabited by Du Guesclin, and occupied by nuns in the late 1600s. At the top of the street you'll find the **Musée Militaire du Périgord**, with items on the French military, including some rare mementos of the colonial wars in this century, as well as memorabilia related to General Daumesnil (*see* below).

Musée Militaire du Périgord
t 05 53 53 47 36; open April–Oct Mon–Sat 10–12 and 2–6; Jan–Mar Wed and Sat 2–6; adm

From here, turn right in Rue Taillefer for **Place de la Claustre**, under the looming belltower of St-Front. This square, site of the Wednesday and Saturday market, was for centuries a graveyard and the theatre for executions; the last walk a condemned criminal would make in this world was up narrow Rue du Calvaire.

The Peg-legged General

Périgueux's feistiest hero fought with Napoleon in Egypt, lost a leg at Wagram near Vienna and was given what seemed to be the equivalent of a desk job as commander of the Château of Vincennes in Paris. When the Allies took Paris in 1814, they demanded that Daumesnil surrender Vincennes. 'Tell the Austrians to give back my leg or else come in and get the other one,' he replied. They didn't, and Vincennes remained the only part of France never to surrender to the Allies. After Waterloo, Daumesnil was besieged again, and again he held out, refusing to give over the fort to anyone but a Frenchman. Finally the new king, Louis XVIII, came in person to accept the keys.

During the Revolution of 1830, Daumesnil was still on the job. The hated ministers of Charles X were imprisoned at Vincennes, and when a mob came to lynch them, the old general kept them out too, saying that he'd ignite the powder room if they tried to storm the place. In Cours Michel Montaigne, there's a statue of him pointing with pride at his peg leg.

The Cathedral of St-Front

Cathédrale St-Front
open daily 9–12 and 2.30–6.30

This is the fourth church built here, on the summit of the *puy* over the Isle. A 6th-century chapel holding the relics of St Front was replaced in 1074 with a much larger church, to draw in pilgrims on the way to Compostela. In 1120, when this new church burned down, it was decided to build one even larger and more extraordinary. Greek architects, it seems, were hired, and they designed a Greek cross plan under five domes. Their model was Agii Apostoli in Constantinople (now gone) – the same design used for St Mark's in Venice. By the 19th century this marvel was a rickety disaster waiting to happen. After the Huguenots had damaged it in 1575 and destroyed the tomb of St Front, a streak of thoughtless restorations exacerbated the typical problems of old age, leaving its domes covered with a sloppy hotchpotch of stones and tiles. The famous medieval re-creator Viollet-le-Duc wanted to have a crack at it but his rival Paul Abadie was given the nod in 1852. Abadie loved Romanesque churches so much that he devoured them whole; he demolished much of St-Front and spent the next 50 years rebuilding it. The result is breathtaking from a distance, especially at night when the cathedral is illuminated and reflected in the waters of the Isle. Close up, it is much harder to overlook its newness, the nakedness, the too precise and orderly cut of the stone. Nor was Abadie above adding improvements to the original, especially the pinnacles on the domes; he liked these so well that he stuck their clones on the bulbous domes of his most famous creation, the Sacré-Cœur in Paris.

From Place de la Clautre you can see what survives from the church of 1074: the austere façade fitted with the odd Roman fragment, lateral walls that now form an open courtyard, the bottom two-thirds of the 56m belltower, two *confessions* (tomb-shrines of saintly confessors) – one under the belltower and the other under the west dome – and the haunting little **cloister** with the original Romanesque pine-cone crown of the belltower as a centrepiece. Inside Abadie's church, the most lingering impression is one of vastness (no wonder – it's one and a half times as long as a football pitch). In its minimal decoration it looks more like a mosque. Abadie designed the 'Byzantine' chandeliers, which originally hung in Notre-Dame, for the pompous wedding of Napoleon III; for a few cents you can shed light on the enormous 17th-century walnut retable made for a demolished Jesuit chapel.

Medieval Streets around St-Front

The north door of the cathedral opens on to **Place Daumesnil**, the centre of a fascinating web of 15th- and 16th-century pedestrian lanes. The pale stone of their urbane houses was mostly quarried from ancient Vesunna, and residents often leave their gates open to let passers-by admire their beautifully curved inner stairs. Steep, stepped streets descend to the river. Houses in **Rue du Plantier** have terraced gardens (see if you can find the carving of Adam and Eve on one of the stairs), while medieval **Rue du Port-de-Graule** is lined with tiny boutiques. Down on the quay, in a cluster of 15th–16th-century houses stands the **Maison Lambert** with its Renaissance gallery and the **Maison des Consuls** with Flamboyant dormers. The **Vieux Moulin**, perched on a river wall, is a relic of the grain monopoly once held by the canons of St-Front.

Back up in Place Daumesnil, enter the picturesque **Galeries Daumesnil** by way of Rue de la Clarté: these are a set of old courtyards opened up to the public, and named after Pierre Daumesnil, born at 7 Rue de la Clarté in 1776.

Rue Limogeanne and Around

From the Galeries Daumesnil, continue along pedestrian Rue Limogeanne, Périgueux's busiest shopping street since the Middle Ages. Most of the houses here date from the 16th century. No.5, the **Maison Estignard**, is especially lovely with its dormers, mullioned windows and carvings; in the courtyard of No.3, note the bas-relief of a salamander, the emblem of François Ier. **Rue de la Sagesse**, parallel to Rue Limogeanne, boasts other fine Renaissance houses; No.1, Maison Lajoubertie, has one of Périgueux's most beautiful staircases, carved with the goddess of Love laying aside her weapons. Rue de la Sagesse gives into handsome **Place St-Louis**, created by demolishing a block of slums. It has a fountain decorated with a dumpling lady, who probably overindulged in the offerings of the *marché au gras* (fattened geese, ducks, foie gras and truffles) held in this square (*see* p.103). The **Maison du Tenant** or **du Pâtissier** (1518), on the corner of Rue Eguillerie, has a sculpted porch and an inscription warning that anyone who speaks badly behind people's backs is not welcome inside, for 'The greatest glory is to displease the wicked.'

Musée du Périgord

Musée du Périgord
22 Cours de Tourny, ***t*** *05 53 06 40 70; open April–Sept Mon and Wed–Fri 10.30–5.30, Sat and Sun 1–6; Oct–Dec Mon and Wed–Fri 10–5, Sat and Sun 1–5; adm*

Just to the north, the Musée du Périgord is a cut above the average, with something for every taste. The ethnographic collection in the first rooms, devoted to Stone Age cultures from around the world (New Caledonia, the Cook Islands, Papua New Guinea and Africa), forms a comparative introduction to the extensive prehistoric section upstairs. The prizes here are three extremely rare complete skeletons: the oldest ever found, the Neanderthal *homme de Régourdou* (70,000 BC), ritually buried with the bears near Lascaux (see p.119); *homme de Combe-Capelle* (20,000 BC), found near Sergeac; and Upper Palaeolithic *homme de Chancelade*, a mere whippersnapper at only 15,000 years of age.

The collection of tools features the very first cut stones found in the Dordogne, dating back a cool million years, and Upper Palaeolithic carvings and engravings on bone and stone, among them the strange, disembodied *Parade of Bison* from Chancelade and a disc carved with does from Laugerie-Basse. In another room are some weapons that laid Vesunna low: a bronze Alemanni sword, and Visigothic and Frankish blades.

Downstairs, stuffed weasels, snakeskins, an Egyptian mummy named Antinoë and a selection of Coptic fabrics are followed by the Gallo-Roman rooms, with finds (jewellery, domestic items and mosaics) found in the Dordogne in general, while items excavated at the original Petrocorii *oppidum* and ancient Vesunna have been moved to the new Musée Gallo-Romaine de Vesunna (*see* p.98). The cloister is lined with some intriguing if poorly labelled stone fragments from Neolithic to medieval times: a 6th-century Visigothic sarcophagus, a lacy fragment of a Carolingian chancel, and strange faces and slatternly mermaids that adorned St-Front.

The Beaux-Arts section begins with ceramics and enamels from Limoges, followed by three rooms of paintings, including the *Diptyque de Rabastens* (1286), a rare work painted on leather from the school of Toulouse; a 16th-century Flemish *Excision de la pierre de folie*, a famous Hieronymus Bosch subject, although here we see doctors simply removing the 'madness stone' from a patient's brain; a fine *Portrait of Fénelon* by Bailleul; a Canaletto; two 19th-century paintings by Paul Guigou; and works by Périgourdins, including sculptures by Jane Poupelet, a student of Rodin.

Around Périgueux

Six kilometres west of Périgueux, **Chancelade** is an enchanting spot with a natural spring and an 11th-century **Augustinian abbey**, sadly no longer open to the public. In 1370 the English gave the monks the bum's rush and converted the abbey into a stronghold that only fell when the great Bertrand du Guesclin personally led the attack, storming up the ladder and splitting open the head of the English captain. You can still see the scars of the battle on the Romanesque Chapelle St-Jean. The main church, with its arcaded, three-tiered belltower, was restored in the 1600s, although 13th-century frescoes of Catholicism's two tallest saints, Christopher and Thomas à Becket, have survived the outrages of time and wars.

In the 12th century, monks from Chancelade founded the **Prieuré de Merlande**, in a forest clearing 6km north, off the D2. One of the original two domes was smashed by the English; the rest was fortified in the 16th century and wrecked again in the Revolution. Somehow the capitals on the blind arcading of the choir have survived, with interwoven designs of animals and monsters.

South of Périgueux (7km on the D2), **Atur** has a Romanesque church and a 12th-century *Lanterne des Morts* (*see* Sarlat, p.160); 21km south on the D8, **Vergt** stands as a rare monument to the seldom-seen constructive side of the counts of Périgord, in this case Archambault III, who founded this pleasant *bastide* in 1285.

ⓘ **Perigueux >** *Rond-Point de la Tour Mataguerre, 26 Place Francheville,* **t** *05 53 53 10 63, www.ville-perigueux.fr; open Mon–Sat 9–7, plus Sun 10–6 in July and Aug*

Tourist Information in Périgueux

Ask at the **tourist office** about guided tours of the historic centre (Mon–Sat), local *son-et-lumière* shows and summer festivals, and foie gras farms you can visit.

For what's on at the **theatre**, call **t** 05 53 53 18 71. The local music venue is Le Réservoir, **t** 05 53 06 12 73.

Market Days in Périgueux

General market: Wednesday and Saturday, Place du Coderc, Place de la Clautre and Place de l'Hôtel de Ville.

Farmers' market: daily 8–1, Place du Coderc.

Clothes and fabric market: Wednesday 8–5, Esplanade du Théâtre.

Marché au gras: Wednesday and Saturday morning, Place St Louis (mid-Nov–end Mar).

Where to Stay and Eat in and around Périgueux

Périgueux ✉ 24000

Hotels here are geared more to foie gras salesmen than ordinary visitors, but there are several fine options (and restaurants) a short drive away – *see* Antonne and Le Change, p.93.

*****Bristol**, 37–39 Rue Antoine Gadaud, **t** 05 53 08 75 90, *www.bristolfrance.com* (€€). A modern hotel near Place Roosevelt, with quite spacious and pleasant rooms and parking.

****Hôtel de l'Univers**, 18 Cours Montaigne, **t** 05 53 53 34 79 (€). An option near the museum, with dining (€€) under an arbour in summer. *Closed Thurs and Fri lunch and Sun eve.*

Le Rocher de l'Arsault, 15 Rue de l'Arsault, **t** 05 53 53 54 06 (€€€€–€€). A Louis XIII dining room northeast of the centre, serving tasty foie gras *tatin* and other regional delicacies. *Closed July.*

Hercule Poireau, 2 Rue de la Nation, **t** 05 53 08 90 76 (€€€–€€). A vaulted Renaissance cellar north of the cathedral, serving *Rossini de canard* (duck topped with sautéed foie gras) and other treats at reasonable prices. *Closed Sat and Sun.*

Aux Berges de l'Isle, 2 Rue Pierre Magne, **t** 05 53 09 51 50 (€€€–€). Traditional dishes such as cassoulet and luscious desserts served on a terrace overlooking the river and St-Front. Booking is recommended. *Closed Sun eve, Mon and Sat lunch.*

Chancelade ✉ 24650

******Château des Reynats**, **t** 05 53 03 53 59, *www.chateau-hotel-perigord.com* (€€€€€–€€€). A turreted 19th-century château with attractive rooms, plus a modern annexe (€€) in its park. It's close to an 18-hole golf course and has a pretty little park with pool and tennis courts. The restaurant (€€€€–€€) serves exquisite regional cuisine with an imaginative slant. *Restaurant closed Sat lunch, Sun eve and Mon.*

****Etang des Reynats**, **t** 05 53 54 79 58, *http://etangdesreynats.free.fr* (€). An option by the lake 3km from the centre, near the golf course, with a pool, pleasant rooms (the most expensive have views of the water and terraces) and a restaurant (€€–€). *Closed Sun eve, and Sat and Mon lunch out of season.*

****Le Pont de la Beauronne**, 4 Route de Ribérac, **t** 05 53 08 42 91 (€). A friendly hotel near the golf course, with a restaurant (€€€–€). *Closed mid-Sept–mid-Oct plus 2wks in Feb; restaurant Sun eve and Mon lunch.*

Razac-sur-l'Isle ✉ 24430

*****Château de Lalinde**, **t** 05 53 54 52 30 (€€–€). An imposing château with a pool. The menu (€€€–€€) has local specialities and veggie options. *Closed Nov–Feb; restaurant lunch Mon–Sat.*

West of Périgueux

The name Dronne may evoke nothing as much as a queen bee's studmuffin, but this is one of the most charmingly bucolic rivers in France. Between the Dronne and the Isle can be found the gentle rolling hills of the Double forest, crisscrossed by streams that feed moody marshes, created by medieval monks to farm fish for Lent.

Down the Dronne

Musée du Costume et de son Artisanat
t 05 53 90 10 40 or t 05 53 90 82 27; open May–Sept Tues–Sun 2.30–6; adm

Tocane-St-Apre, where the D710 running from Périgueux meets the Dronne, is a handsome agricultural village with a good dolmen, the **Pierre-Levée**, the **Musée du Costume et de son Artisanat au XIXe Siècle** illustrating 19th-century dress, and **Gallo-Roman excavations** that suggest folks have long forded the river here. You should, too, following signs for **Montagrier** – the rewards are superb panoramas into the Dronne valley and a 12th-century domed church, Ste-Madeleine, with a three-lobed apse and carved

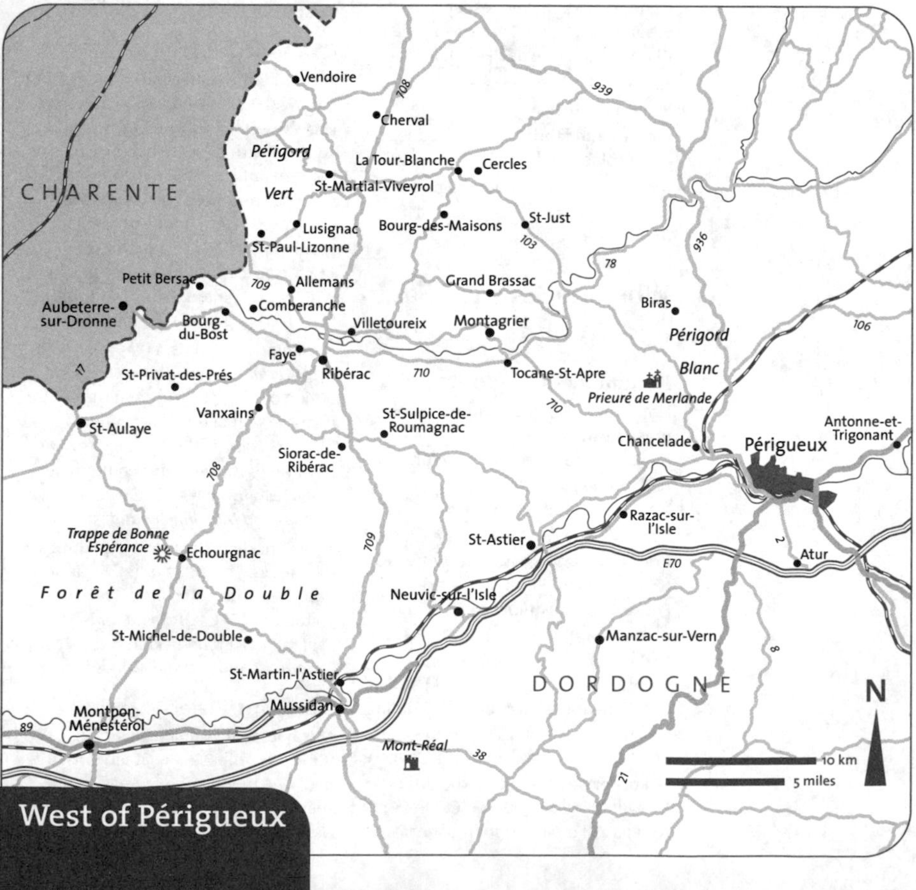

Getting around West of Périgueux

A CFTA **bus** links Ribérac and Périgueux via Tocane-St-Apre at least three times a day, **t** 05 55 17 81 19, *www.cftaco.fr*. For a **taxi**, call **t** 05 53 90 04 99.

---

capitals; here, on the feast day of the doctor-saints Côme and Damien, children with hernias used to gather for a miraculous cure. The Moulin du Pont, an old flour-mill beside the river, has been transformed into the **Maison de la Dronne**, containing the local tourist office and permanent displays on the river and types of mills. Staff here organize boat trips for up to six people.

Maison de la Dronne
t 05 53 90 01 33; open June–Sept daily 10–12 and 2–7

From here you have a choice of roads up to **Grand Brassac**, with an even more extraordinary 12th-century **church**, its north portal decorated with two versions of the same enthronement scene, one made to fit the door, and the other, from a larger door, stuck on top of it, while inside three domes hover on pendentives.

Eglise de Grand Bassac
usually open 9–7, or ask Mme Lacour opposite for key

St-Just, north of Grand Brassac on the D103, has another surprise: silkworms, which you can sometimes visit at the 15th- and 17th-century **Magnanerie de Goumandie**. As you return to the Dronne and head west for Ribérac, keep an eye peeled for the *cluzeaux* (dwellings cut into the limestone in the Middle Ages).

Magnanerie de Goumandie
t 05 53 90 73 60; call for hrs

Ribérac

One of the biggest towns in the area, with nearly 5,000 souls, Ribérac is a quiet and demure place that jumps on Friday, its market day. Its restored domed Romanesque Collegiate church, **Notre-Dame**, which has a handsome apse and bizarre façade, looks more like a school gymnasium than a church; it's used as a concert hall and for exhibitions. Another church up by the river, 12th-century **St-Pierre de Faye**, has a pretty tympanum.

Eglise Notre-Dame
open mid-June–mid-Sept daily 2–7; ask at tourist office (see p.111) for informative church plan

Nothing remains of the castle where the quixotic troubadour Arnaut Daniel (active 1180–1210) was born. Dante met his shade in Purgatory, where Arnaut speaks the only line in Provençal in the *Divine Comedy* (though this was the language that Dante considered using for his great poem before opting for Italian). Arnaut Daniel's verse is so complex that it is well-nigh impossible to translate without losing its charm, but he is credited with the most famous lines ever written by a troubadour:

Ieu sui Arnautz q'amas l'aura,
E chatz la lebre ab lo bou
E nadi contra suberna

(*I am Arnaut, who gathers the wind*
and hunts the hare with the ox
and swims against the incoming tide)

You can hire **canoes** and other boats at Ribérac's camping ground on Route d'Angoulême (***t*** *05 53 90 54 42*).

Around Ribérac

The corner of Périgord to the north of the Dronne practically bubbles with multi-domed Romanesque churches. The signed circuit begins at **Allemans** (up the D709), passes another church at **St-Paul-Lizonne**, then heads to medieval **Lusignac**, which is a delightful film set of a village. Here the fortified church may be domeless, but inside it resembles the Mother of God's attic – it's filled with clutter, discontinued models of saints, vases of dusty artificial flowers and holy pictures that look as if they were clipped from magazines. The next stop, **St-Martial-Viveyrol**, has remnants of frescoes, while **Cherval** to the northeast boasts St-Martin, the most beautiful of them all, with a cluster of five domes – as many as St-Front itself.

Musée de la Ferblanterie/ Musée des Records
t 05 53 91 09 44; open mid-June–Aug daily 3–6; rest of year by appointment

Jardins de Limodore
t 05 53 90 86 83; open April–June Wed and Sat 2–6; adm

Maison des Tourbières
t 05 53 90 79 56; open May–Sept 10–7; Feb–April, Oct and Nov by appointment; adm

La Tour-Blanche derives its name from the ruined *Turris Alba*, which was built in the 10th century over a Gaulish fort. Henri IV lodged here for several weeks, although now he'd be more comfortable in the handsome 1617 Manoir de Roumailhac in the centre. The 'White Tower' also has a little museum devoted to what the French call 'white iron' or tin, the **Musée de la Ferblanterie**, and, on the same site, a museum about rocks and minerals, and the **Musée des Records**, with remarkable, record-breaking objects that are displayed in the Festival des Records every two years in August. The ancient priory of St-Cybard at nearby **Cercles** has excellent Romanesque carved capitals; also in this village is a garden of orchids, the **Jardins de Limodore**, where you can discover 47 species of this beautiful flower.

Bourg-des-Maisons has another good domed Romanesque church; **Vendoire** further to the northwest has yet another, dating from the 17th century, with a façade decorated with columns in the style of the nearby Charente. You can drive up to see the ruins of the 13th-century church of **St-Jean de Grésignac**, and learn all about peat at the **Maison des Tourbières**, which has a nature trail and boat rides.

West to Aubeterre-sur-Dronne and its Eglise Monolithique

Musée Gallo-Romain
t 05 53 90 27 02; open July and Aug daily 2.30–6; adm

To the west of Ribérac and north of the river, you can get a bird's-eye view of the area from the top of **Puy de Beaumont**, located up a little road off the D709, before Allemans. The little bridge at Comberanche will take you back over the Dronne to **Bourg-du-Bost**, which has another Romanesque church; from here you can continue to **Petit-Bersac**, where archaeologists have uncovered a Gallo-Roman settlement and collected the finds in the small **Musée Gallo-Romain**.

Another little road leads due south of Petit-Bersac to **St-Privat-des-Prés**, where there's a venerable Romanesque church wearing a porch and belt of nine blind arches across the façade. St-Privat's **Musée de l'Outil et de la Vie au Village** is chock-full of tools and curiosities recreating a 19th-century village street, as well as a collection of châteaux and cathedrals, all shrunk to one-hundredth their normal size.

Musée de l'Outil et de la Vie au Village
t *05 53 91 22 87; open July and Aug Tues–Sun 3–6 (if closed, ask at* mairie*); adm*

To see the real attraction in this neck of the woods, however, you have to venture 2km into the Charente, to **Aubeterre-sur-Dronne**, 'Dawnland on the Dronne'. A hilltown of ivory stone, rising up at the end of a corridor of 150-year-old unpruned plane trees, Aubeterre has more history and mystery than it has room for. Much of it is concentrated in a church cut into a limestone cliff, known as the **Eglise Monolithique**. First excavations in the cliff began on a small scale in the 5th century, when the rare total-immersion baptismal font was cut into the floor. This early cave church soon became a favourite place for the trump of doom; behind the font a Merovingian necropolis is jammed with 100 corpse hollows chiselled in the stone, with their little round heads all pointing towards Jerusalem.

④ Aubeterre-sur-Dronne

Eglise Monolithique
t *05 45 98 65 06; open daily 9.30–12 and 2–6; adm*

In the 11th century, Benedictines founded a monastery in front of the cave (completely destroyed by the Protestants in the Wars of Religion), and at some point they acquired an important holy relic of an unknown kind, which they housed in a magnificent stone reliquary built in the form of the hexagonal tomb of Joseph of Arimathea in Jerusalem. To set it off better (no one really knows why), they enlarged the holy precinct of the cave, quarrying deep into rock like rabid termites to create a veritable hall of the mountain king – If St-Emilion's rock-cut church (*see* p.196) is the largest in Europe, Aubeterre's is the tallest in the world, rising 20m from the ground and supported by two blackened columns as thick as sequoias. A stairway cut in the rock leads to the upper galleries, with windows peering down into the shadowy depths; a further stair continued up through the rock to the castle overlooking Aubeterre, enabling its *seigneur* to attend services without having to rub elbows with his subjects.

Outside the door are more tombs, these belonging to medieval monks who chose to face the mysterious reliquary instead of Jerusalem; just under the church floor the rock is pitted like a Swiss cheese with their graves. But an even stranger holy place lies below these, discovered by accident in the 1960s when a truck passing down the street made the pavement cave in. The driver found himself in an ancient *mithraeum* – a subterranean chamber lined with benches on either side, where adherents of Mithras (the favourite god of the Roman legions) would be baptized in the hot blood of a bull sacrificed on ground level; you can see where the gore would have flowed into the chamber through the outlets on either side into the square basin. Mithraism, with its monotheistic tendencies, gave Christianity a run for its money in the early centuries AD, which may explain why the entrance to this temple was so well hidden and why the Christians went to such trouble to create an awe-inspiring alternative above. The new paving in the square was paid for by the late French president François Mitterrand, who spent much of his childhood at his grandparents' farm in Aubeterre.

The Eglise Monolithique was an important stop for pilgrims en route to Compostela – a path that was rife with diversions from dogma, just as the pilgrimage itself was a search for something beyond the daily fare at church. The pilgrims had another important stop in Aubeterre, just up the hill: the 11th-century **St-Jacques**. Although the Protestants smashed it up when they demolished the Eglise Monolithique's monastery, they mercifully spared the magnificent three-arched Romano-Hispano-Moorish façade, partly sunken below the level of the modern pavement and fronting a rebuilt church. Bolted on to the upper left of the façade are the black fragments of an equestrian statue, which is believed to have been either Charlemagne or Santiago (St James in his Spanish role as a Moor-slaying crusader), or perhaps even Trajan or some other Roman emperor whom the Christians found lying around and converted.

The façade itself is very Roman in its arches and registers, while the decoration – its lavishly patterned arches, orientalized reliefs and the foiled arch in the centre – are strongly reminiscent of the work of *mudéjar* craftsmen from Spain in the throes of the *Reconquista*. Although the right arch has been eroded by the weather, the central and especially the left arch are richly decorated with abstract patterns and six panels of the zodiac – although, unlike in most zodiacs, each of the scenes features a fellow sitting in a chair by a cooking fire. The monsters on the capitals are a treat: winking cats with two bodies, biting birds and quadrupeds with silly bearded heads (with extra pairs of heads like grinning balloons strapped to their backs). On the far left side of the left arch, note the centaur with a bow, and on the right a horse with an arrow piercing its neck. Inside is the only other bit the Catholics managed to salvage from Huguenot fury: an 11th-century statue of the Virgin holding Jesus in her right arm instead of the usual left – a deviation believed to be mystically significant, although nobody knows exactly how.

Aubeterre also has some museums open in summer, including a doll museum, a museum of butterflies and African art, and a reconstruction of a late-19th/early-20th-century classroom in the old school; the tourist office (***t*** *05 45 98 57 18*) has information.

Some of the prettiest Dronne valley scenery is to be found in these parts: along the D17 between Aubeterre and **St-Aulaye**, a delightful village at the edge of the Double forest, for instance. It is home to a rare 11th-century bridge, a Renaissance château, and a Romanesque church with a handsome white façade, its three arches supported by fine sculpted capitals. While you're in the village, you may want to pay a visit to the **Musée du Cognac et du Pineau du Vin** and learn all about the Charente's famous brandy. Next door to it, the **Ecomusée de la Forêt** contains displays on the forest, its ecosystem and so on.

Musée du Cognac et du Pineau du Vin/Ecomusée de la Forêt
t 05 53 90 81 33; open July and Aug Tues–Sun 3–5; rest of year Sat 3–5; adm

The Forêt de la Double

The emerald forest of La Double, covering some 125,000 acres from the Dronne to the Isle, was long a no-man's-land – a marshy woodland of sand and clay, interspersed with lakes. The trees were all cut down in the 17th and 18th centuries – by barrel-makers, charcoal-burners, glass-blowers and tile-bakers – leaving an impoverished, malarial swamp inhabited by outcasts, memorably evoked in Eugène Le Roy's novel, *L'Ennemi de la Mort*. Napoleon III initiated a scheme to re-colonize the forest, draining swamps and replanting the old forest with pines. The population took a brief upturn, but these days it's as empty as ever – a lonesome, poetic place of old farms and nearly abandoned villages, of quiet paths through the trees.

Vanxains, on the D708 between St-Aulaye and Ribérac, is a nearly deserted village that was once the seat of the Vicomte de la Double. It has an elegant, domed Romanesque church with fine carved capitals, and a Neolithic line of menhirs at **Sauteranne** that's impossible to find unless you get someone to direct you. In 1747 Vanxains was the birthplace of Suzette Labrouse, 'the Prophetess of the Revolution', who as a child so wanted to see God that she kept a jar of spiders handy, ready to swallow in order to kill herself. Then came the day that God told her to go forth, bring down the greats of the world and remedy the ills of the church. She made her way to Paris, where her naïvety was the butt of many jokes; a satirical comedy called her the 'truffled turkey, the patriotic gift of Périgord to the National Assembly'. She met Marat, Dr Guillotin, Desmoulins and, most disastrously, Robespierre, who persuaded her to go to Rome to tell the Pope to give up his temporal power. The Pope disagreed and locked her up in Castel Sant'Angelo the minute she crossed the border. A few years later the French army in Rome liberated her; she returned to Paris and died in 1821, leaving behind a stash of small bottles filled with mysterious liquids, which to the disappointment of alchemists were never analyzed.

East along the D43, **Siorac-de-Ribérac** has yet another domed fortified Romanesque church, while the church of St-Sulpice-de-Roumagnac 3km further boasts a beautiful 17th-century wooden retable. The D43 continues east towards St-Astier on the Isle, with grand views most of the way. Alternatively, some of the marshes south of Siorac are actually little lakes built by monks in the Middle Ages, some of which you can swim in; the largest is the **Grand Etang de la Jemaye** (with lifeguards mid-June–mid-Sept).

Abbaye Notre-Dame de Bonne-Espérance
t 05 53 80 82 50; open Tues–Sat 10–12 and 2.30–5.30, Sun 12–12.30, 2.30–4.45 and 5.45–6.30

Near Echourgnac, in the very centre of La Double, the monks at the **Abbaye Notre-Dame de Bonne-Espérance** arrived in 1868, and were one of the first positive things to happen to the local economy. Now replaced by nuns, they are locally famous for their cheeses, especially La Trappe, which you can purchase at the convent along with other goodies.

Ferme du Parcot
t 05 53 81 99 28; open July and Aug Tues–Sun 2.30–5.30; May, June and Sept Sun 2.30–5.30; adm

Just east of **Echourgnac**, one of the last examples of traditional rural architecture in the region, the **Ferme du Parcot** is open for tours and also doubles as a Double information centre. **St-Michel-de-Double**, further south, has other fine examples of 17th-century rural architecture in its Hameau des Héritiers and the Maisons de Gamanson, close to the Isle.

The Lower Isle Valley

St-Astier lime quarries
open July and Aug Wed 9.30; book with tourist office (t 05 53 54 13 85) at least 1 day ahead

Past Périgueux, the Isle loses much of its charm; the busy N89 that skirts the south bank of the river between Périgueux and Libourne/Bordeaux is not going to win any beauty contests either. If you want to stop, there's **St-Astier**, 15km from Périgueux, named after the 7th-century hermitage of St Asterius. Part of this, it is believed, is conserved in the crypt of the massive 11th-century church. You can tour St-Astier's subterranean **lime quarries**.

Château Mellet
t 05 53 80 86 65; open April–Oct daily 10–12 and 1.30–6.30; guided tours by advance booking; adm

Musée des Arts et Traditions Populaires
t 05 53 81 23 55; open June–mid-Sept daily 10–12 and 2–6; April, May, Oct and Nov Sat, Sun and public hols 2–6

Downriver, at **Neuvic-sur-l'Isle**, are the castle and botanical gardens of **Château Mellet**. **Mussidan**, which is one of the larger villages on the Isle, has twice been singled out for disaster. During the Wars of Religion, all the Protestants in the vicinity took refuge there and fought bravely against the Catholics. They surrendered when their lives were guaranteed, but the Catholics were only joking; many Protestants were hanged, and Mussidan was razed. Henri IV, in honour of the town's sufferings, had it rebuilt. In 1944 the Resistance was very active in the forests that surround Mussidan, and the Maquis were in town on 11 June 1944 when an armoured German train pulled up at the station with a machine gun, and a battle began. In reprisals, 52 people were rounded up and executed; the town was pillaged and was on the point of being razed again when the Gestapo chief – unlike the Catholics – decided Mussidan had suffered enough. Mussidan is the site of the **Musée des Arts et Traditions Populaires**, with the usual collection of tools and furniture and traditional rooms, and a tractor dating from 1920, constructed from parts that were salvaged from a First World War tank.

Château de Mont-Réal
t 05 53 81 11 03; open July–mid-Sept daily 10–12 and 2.30–6.30

Parc de Cervidés du Raymondeau
t 05 53 82 23 76; open for visits mid-June–Aug Tues, Thurs, Sat, Sun and public hols 5pm

Moulin du Duellas
t 05 53 82 39 54; call for hrs

Just north of Mussidan, the 12th-century church at **St-Martin-l'Astier** has a very unusual octagonal choir. The partly medieval, partly 16th-century **Château de Mont-Réal**, 7km to the east of Mussidan just off the D38, belonged to Claude de Pontbriand, who accompanied Cartier to Canada and named the new French town on the St Lawrence after his home in Périgord – or so goes one possible explanation for Montreal's name.

West along the N89 is **St-Martial-d'Artenset** and its **deer farm**. There is also the **Moulin du Duellas** beside the Isle, an old flour and electricity mill hosting art exhibitions. Its staff also organize boat trips, on Sunday afternoon in May, June and September (booking required) and three times an afternoon in July and August.

Montpon-Ménestérol, famous for its organs (musical, that is), is also the site of one of several hatcheries that are busily breeding sturgeons, principally for caviar and commercial uses.

Market Days West of Périgueux

Tocane-St-Apre: Monday (includes walnut market October and November).

Ribérac: Friday (includes walnut market in October and sometimes November, and a *marché au gras*, Nov–Mar); farmers' market Tuesday May–Sept; night markets in July and August (ask at tourist office); antiques fair third Saturday in August.

La Tour-Blanche: Wednesday.

Where to Stay and Eat West of Périgueux

ⓘ Ribérac ›
*Place Charles de Gaulle, **t** 05 53 90 03 10, www.riberac.fr*

Ribérac ✉ 24600

****Hôtel de France**, 3 Rue Marc Dufraisse, **t** 05 53 90 00 61, *www.hoteldefranceriberac.com* (€). A family-run hotel in a 16th-century posthouse – the best and biggest option in town. You can dine in the old-fashioned dining room or out in the garden courtyard (€€) – there are vegetarian and even vegan menus, plus a good choice of fish and duck dishes. *Closed Mon and Tues lunch, plus Sat lunch out of season.*

Le Chevillard, 2km from centre at Gaynet, on Bordeaux road, **t** 05 53 91 20 88 (€€€–€€). An old farm with a large garden and abundant good food at kind prices. *Closed Mon and Tues exc July and Aug.*

La Bergerie, 4km north of Ribérac on D708, **t** 05 53 90 26 97 (€€). A restaurant out among the cornfields in an old *bergerie* with a pretty patio. Call ahead to check it's open.

St Martial-Viveyrol ✉ 24320

*****Hostellerie Les Aiguillons**, **t** 06 85 18 30 62 (€€€–€€). Pretty, spacious rooms in a calm location with a welcoming garden and a swimming pool. The restaurant offers imaginative regional fare such as panfried foie gras with gingerbread and onion jam, and there's a good fish selection. *Closed mid-Oct–Mar.*

Manzac-sur-Vern ✉ 24110

Château de Monciaux, Bourrou, 2km from town, **t** 05 53 80 75 48, *www.chateau-de-monciaux.com* (€€). *Chambres d'hôte* in an elegant Dordogne château built in the 18th and 19th century and set in a lovely park with tennis courts and a pool. It's packed with period furniture, and the lovely bedrooms have pleasant views and modern bathrooms. Three gîtes are available too. With prior booking you can enjoy evening meals (€€€) based on local produce.

****Le Lion d'Or, t** 05 53 54 28 09 (€). A hotel with bay windows overlooking its garden and a restaurant (€€€–€) serving sturgeon, civets and other treats. *Closed Mon, Sun eve Sept–June, Feb and 2wks in Nov.*

Mussidan ✉ 24400

Le Chaufourg, in nearby Sourzac, **t** 05 53 81 01 56, *www.lechaufourg.com* (€€€€€–€€€€). An enchanting 17th-century family residence with eight rooms, a billiards table and a piano, in lush leafy gardens with a heated pool and fishing. The excellent restaurant (€€€€–€€€), open to residents only (advance booking required Dec–Mar), often serves sturgeon from Montpon. *Closed mid-Nov–Mar exc prebooked groups.*

****Hôtel du Midi**, 9 Rue Villechanoux, **t** 05 53 81 01 77 (€). A very decent budget option near the station, with a pool but no restaurant.

Montpon-Ménestérol ✉ 24700

Auberge de l'Eclade, 2km north of town on D730, **t** 05 53 80 28 64 (€€€–€). An old barn with a pretty terrace, offering the likes of foie gras served three ways at some of the most reasonable prices in Périgord. *Closed Tues eve and Wed, plus Mon eve Sept–June.*

ⓘ Mussidan >
Pl de la République,
***t** 05 53 81 73 87*

ⓘ Montpon-Ménestérol >>
Place Clemenceau,
***t** 05 53 82 23 77, www.tourisme-montpon.com*

The Dordogne: the Vézère Valley

Some 400,000 years ago, when Lower Palaeolithic pioneers first settled on the fair banks of the Vézère, it was more than gorgeous scenery that attracted them – the Vézère's bulging cliffs were pocked with caves and shelters, there was fresh water, river pebbles and flint for manufacturing tools, and, most importantly, thundering herds of bison and reindeer that funnelled down the valley before the glaciers of the last ice age. Over the millennia, the hunters turned to art, and they left an extraordinary record of their passing in the valley's most secret caves, a wealth of finds that led UNESCO to place the valley on its famous list of world heritage sites.

08

Don't miss

1. Perfect reproductions of prehistoric art
   Lascaux II p.118
2. A Magdalenian-era masterpiece
   Grotte de Font-de-Gaume p.127
3. A 'crystal cathedral'
   Gouffre de Proumeyssac p.130
4. A hundred mammoths
   Rouffignac p.122
5. Bloody history
   Château de l'Herm p.123

See map overleaf

The Vézère Valley

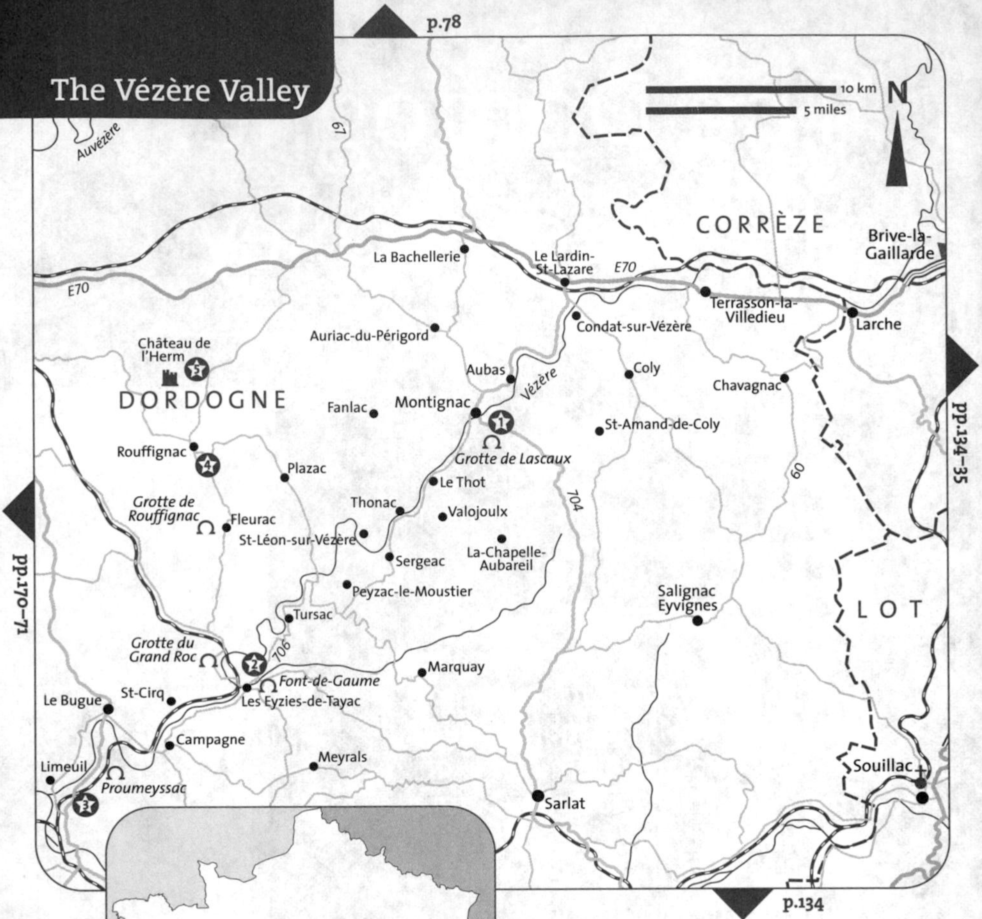

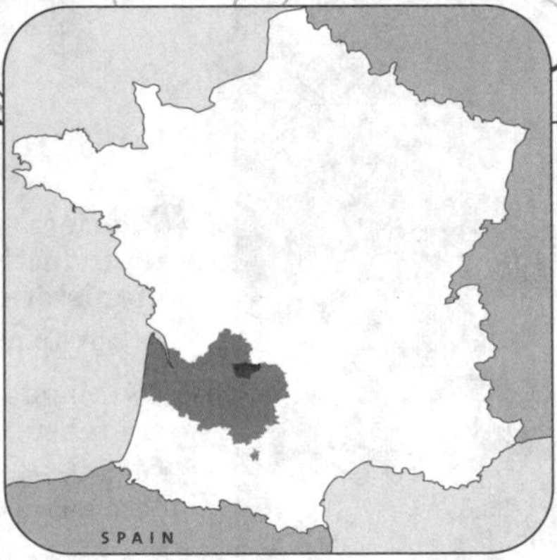

Don't miss

1. **Lascaux II p.118**
2. **Grotte de Font-de-Gaume p.127**
3. **Gouffre de Proumeyssac p.130**
4. **Rouffignac p.122**
5. **Château de l'Herm p.123**

When the earth heated up and big game animals retreated northwards, they took the artistic inspiration with them, leaving the hunters the slow, Mesolithic drudgery of inventing agriculture. The Vézère valley yielded the first hint of its prehistoric past in 1862, when a deposit of carved flints and bones was uncovered at a place called La Madeleine. The finds suggested for the first time that mammoths and humanity coexisted at one period, which has since known as the Magdalenian (c. 15,000–10,000 BC). This discovery set off a quest for signs of 'antediluvian man', leading to a torrent of accidental and organized discoveries. One of the most important occurred in 1888, during excavations for a rail line between Périgueux and Agen, when workers at a hamlet called Cro-Magnon, near Les Eyzies, discovered five Magdalenian-era skeletons, among them a woman, a foetus and a man more than 6ft tall, with a long nose, high forehead and big brain cavity – a race from then on known as *Homo sapiens sapiens*, or Cro-Magnons.

Seven years later the first Magdalenian paintings in France were discovered at Les Eyzies' Grotte de la Mouthe. In 1908, in the caves of Le Moustier, the finding of some 70,000-year-old, Neanderthal-like bones of Cro-Magnon's Middle Palaeolithic predecessors and their effects made Mousterian synonymous with Middle Palaeolithic culture (c. 80,000– 40,000 BC). All this remained the fare of scholarly journals until the accidental discovery of Lascaux in 1940 electrified the imagination of the entire world.

To date, some 200 Palaeolithic caves, shelters and deposits have been discovered along the Vézère. The sacredness of the place has drawn holy men from the other side of the world – near Le Moustier you'll find one of Europe's most important Tibetan monasteries. But the Vézère also attracts thousands of more worldly visitors every year, their fiscal wellbeing threatened by a score of recent roadside attractions. Even worse, the *département* has spent millions of euros to increase tourist access to the riverbanks – a project that local property owners translated into bonanza profits for firewood, in a chainsaw massacre of the lovely old groves that gave the river its special charm.

The Northern Vézère

Most people never make it this far north, and if they do, the Vézère is too busy with roads and train tracks. If you're driving, follow for preference the D60 and D63 between Larche and Terrasson, passing by way of **Chavagnac**, a little village with a Romanesque church guarded by a mighty watchtower.

Terrasson-la-Villedieu

The Vézère spills down the *causse* of Corrèze towards **Terrasson**, a striking medieval truffle and walnut town spanned by the Pont Vieux, a 12th-century bridge some 100m long. Terrasson is built around an abbey founded in the 6th century by a certain St Sour, who according to the story let his two pet doves decide the exact spot. They flew around and around, and when they finally landed, the cry went up: '*Terra sunt!*' ('They've landed!'); hence, supposedly, Terrasson. **St Sour's church**, last repaired in 1889, has, in spite of its name, some sweet 16th-century stained glass; the church of Villedieu has a Carolingian bell. Climb to the top of the old town

Getting around the Northern Vézère

Public transport is pretty thin on the ground in the Vézère valley, though on the Brive–Périgueux line there are **train** stations at Terrasson and Condat-Le Lardin.

There are **bus** connections to Montignac from Périgueux and from Brive (if you change). These are operated by CFTA, **t** 05 55 17 91 19, and run at least twice a day Mon–Fri.

Jardins de l'Imaginaire
t 05 53 50 86 82; open July and Aug daily 9.50–11.50 and 12.50–6.10; April and Oct daily 9.50–11.20 and 1.50–5.20; May, June and Sept daily 9.50–11.50 and 1.50–5.20; adm

Musée du Chocolat
t 05 53 51 57 36; open Tues–Fri 10–12 and 2–6 and Sat 2–6, plus Mon in Aug

for the view, and come on Thursday for the lively market. The **Jardins de l'Imaginaire** condense defining elements of gardens through the centuries and across cultures into a six-acre site, with an abundance of roses, mirrors and synchronized fountains to be found among the trees. There is also a **chocolate museum**.

Terrasson to Montignac

Downriver, **Le Lardin-St-Lazare** offers the 15th-century Château de Peyraux and a 7km detour west to **La Bachellerie**, which derives its name, like the English 'bachelor', from *bas-chevalier* – the lowest, youngest order of knights. It is the address of the singular neoclassical Château de Rastignac (1811–17), built not for Balzac's immortal social climber but for the Marquis Chapt de Rastignac by Périgourdin architect Mathurin Blanchard. Blanchard studied Victor Louis's works in Bordeaux but no one knows much else about him, especially how he came up with what looks like the prototype for the rear façade of the White House in Washington. Apparently the resemblance is only a coincidence, but it was enough to infuriate the retreating Nazis in 1944, who got symbolic revenge on Roosevelt by burning the original: what you see today is a careful restoration. It's not open to the public.

Château de Sauvebœuf
t 05 53 51 89 46; open mid-June–mid-Sept daily 10–12 and 2–6; adm

Condat-sur-Vézère, a paper-making town, was formerly run as a hospital inn for medieval pilgrims by the Knights Hospitallers. At **Aubas**, the Vézère flows past the classic, severe 17th-century **Château de Sauvebœuf**, which was built after the 15th-century original was flattened on the orders of Richelieu, to punish the owner for killing a man in a duel. The king's mistress, Marie de Hautefort, was so upset over this scarring of her native Périgord that she had it rebuilt. Her two monumental fountains of 1610 have gone elsewhere – one to New York, another to Clairac (*see* p.359). The village **church** has some fine works, from its 11th-century carved capitals to a pair of 16th-century retables, one in painted wood and the other in stone fragments.

Just before Montignac, the D67 makes a detour 5km north to Auriac-du-Périgord, with its 14th–16th-century **Château de la Faye** built around a medieval keep. The château's chapel of St Rémy was famous throughout Périgord; nicknamed St Remèdi, the saint was so reputed for his healing juju that all the features of his statue were rubbed off by ill people vigorously rubbing the afflicted parts of their bodies against him.

Montignac

Montignac, once a busy river port, now sits on the right bank of the Vézère, its wooden balconies reflected peacefully across the waters. Although feared for its ferocious counts in the Middle Ages, it rocketed to sweeter fame in 1940, when a pit used as the occasional dead donkey dump was found to house the nonpareil masterpiece of prehistoric cave painting. As extraordinary a sight in its own way is the mutant orange-coloured housing estate blighting the hills to the south of town.

Château de Montignac and the Counts of Périgord

Montignac had its share of glory and defeats between 15,000 BC and the discovery of Lascaux, most of it centred in the ruined Château de Montignac at the top of Rue de Juillet. Now only vertiginous terraces, vaulted casements and a single square tower out of a dozen that originally punctuated its thick walls remain of what was once the most important military castle in the region.

From the 11th to the 14th century, Montignac was the key to Périgord Noir and the chief citadel of the fierce bad counts of Périgord. Their name Taillefer (later Talleyrand) came from an ancestor who made a big impression by slicing a Viking in two with one swipe of his sword. They were unique among the vassals of the kings of France in having absolutely no redeeming virtues; even the hawkish troubadour Bertran de Born stood in awe of them and wrote that one count, Hélie V, was such a cuss that he slept standing up. Hélie was succeeded by his brother Roger Bernard, an ex-priest who thought that the best way to govern Périgord was to crush its inhabitants, to 'destroy and pull out their vines' and 'fill their churches with soldiers and pillagers'. Yet the king supported Bernard, appreciating him for his skill at stomping on lesser barons – to the king's mind the fewer nobles the better, especially in this den of cut-throats.

But Bernard's even nastier son, Archambault V, changed sides and swore allegiance to England, and took advantage of a truce to surround Périgord with castles. He captured Domme by surprise, burned the church with all the people inside, then hunted down all the women who escaped, forcing them to cut off their dresses at the waist, for easier raping. Archambault attacked even the monasteries and royal officers, declaring himself the absolute sovereign of Périgord, and to show that he meant business he destroyed half of Périgueux. The good folk of Périgord begged Charles VI for relief and in 1394 the king sent down an army to punish Archambault, destroying his fortresses and besieging Montignac for a month. Archambault sued for a truce and offered to pay a huge fine; but as soon as the royal army turned its back, Archambault tortured and hanged the king's commander.

Archambault died before the king could punish him again, leaving an heir, Archambault VI, who proved to be even worse, terrorizing Périgord with murder and mayhem, laughing at royal orders to behave. He didn't laugh so hard in 1397, when once again Montignac was besieged by 1000 men, and Archambault was forced to surrender. The king gave Montignac to his brother, Louis d'Orléans (who had to sell it for ransom money when he was captured at Agincourt), while Archambault hightailed it to London, where he connived and made everyone around him miserable until his death in 1430. By the 18th century, Talleyrand blood had cooled enough to produce a diplomat, the famous sallow-faced Charles (1754–1838), who quit Napoleon's foreign ministry in protest against his wars, and then after Waterloo successfully negotiated to keep France's old borders.

Musée Eugène Le Roy
open April–Sept daily 10–12 and 2–6

The town was the last home of Eugène Le Roy, who worked as Montignac's tax collector before he hit the big time with his novel *Jacquou Le Croquant* (*see* p.90). There's a **museum** dedicated to his life next to the tourist office. Nearby, the 18th-century house with columns is by Nicolas Ledoux, the architect of the famous Paris tollhouses. In medieval Rue de la Pégerie is a house Henri IV gave to his mistress, Gabrielle d'Estrées.

Lascaux I and II

Lascaux I and II
*t 05 53 51 95 03, www.culture.fr/culture/arcnat/lascaux/en; **open** July and Aug Tues–Sun 9–7; Sept–Dec and Feb–June Tues–Sun 9–6; closed Jan; between Easter and Nov **tickets** stamped with a time can usually only be bought at a booth by Montignac tourist office; otherwise, you get them at the site; **guided tours** 40mins, ask for details of tours in English; tickets available for **joint adm** to Centre d'Art Préhistorique du Thot (see p.121); bring a sweater*

One morning in September 1940, two local lads and two young refugees from Paris set off up the hill above Montignac with lanterns, determined to descend into an old dump to find a legendary secret treasure their elders believed was nothing more than an old folk tale. With difficulty they enlarged the overgrown opening and fumbled their way down into a treasure beyond anyone's dreams, one that had been virtually vacuum-sealed when the original entrance was blocked by an ancient landslide.

Within a week the world's authority on Palaeolithic painting, the 73-year-old Abbé Breuil, had made his way to Montignac and was ravished by what he called the 'Sistine Chapel of Prehistoric Art'. He made Lascaux's young discoverers responsible for guarding the cave – which they did vigilantly, with shotguns. But by the early 1960s it was clear the Lascaux's worst enemy wasn't something to shoot at but the 'white disease' caused by carbonic acid from the breath of a million visitors; within 15 years of its discovery, the masterpiece that had endured for millennia was fading under a film of white calcite deposits. On 20 April 1963 Lascaux was closed forever to the public; although the deterioration has completely stopped, admission is limited to five prehistorians twice a week.

Disappointment at the cave's closure was so universal that the Dordogne *département* financed the 15-year-long construction of **Lascaux II** 200m below the original. This incredibly painstaking reproduction of the two most beautiful chambers, the Hall of the Bulls and the long narrow Diverticule Axiale (which comprise 90 per cent of the paintings found in the original cave) was painted by Monique Peytral with the same colours and techniques used 17,000 years ago. Far better than any photograph, Lascaux II reproduces the exuberant life, movement and clever use of natural protuberances, faults and shadows of the original, although it hardly explains how an artist limited to a lamp of animal fat and juniper twigs could get the proportions of a 5m bull so perfectly. For Cro-Magnon artists not only drew with the unerring line of a Matisse but mastered techniques forgotten until recently – note the three-quarter, twisted turn in the animals' heads, the Impressionistic use of perspective in the legs of running horses. Scattered among the animals is a vocabulary of mysterious unexplainable symbols reminiscent of a Joan Miró. And what of the Dr Seuss-ish beast dubbed the 'unicorn', the only known 'imaginary' creature discovered in prehistoric art? Was the painting done for a single religious rite and sealed off, never to be revisited? No signs of habitation were discovered here, and the original entrance to Lascaux I has never been found.

Humble awe is a common response to this magical place, or even a sneaking suspicion that LSD guru Terence McKenna might be right (as he claims in his book *Food of the Gods*) that Upper Palaeolithic culture was built around magic psilocybin mushrooms, which afforded a healthy psychedelic experience that lost with the climatic changes at the end of the last ice age. Whatever the truth, more than 300,000 visitors a year get a glimpse into the world of their Magdalenian ancestors.

Gisement du Regourdou
t 05 53 51 81 23; open daily July–Aug 10–7; rest of year 11–6; adm

Nearly 1km north of Lascaux, the privately owned **Gisement du Regourdou** has yet to be thoroughly explored. The Cro-Magnon painters of Lascaux ground their red ochres and magnesium oxides here, but the real fascination of Regourdou is its evidence of a Neanderthal bear cult, predating Lascaux by 60,000 years (*see* pp.36–38). In a collapsed cave, 20 bear tombs were discovered: after being ritually cut up, the bear's bones were placed around its skull, sprinkled with red ochre dust and covered with a slab. Around the tombs fossilized bones of smaller animals were found – presumably funerary gifts to the bear. Fossilized bear turds were found as well. Nearly 2m from the bear sepulchre, the skeleton of a Neanderthal man was found; the flint tools found here and elsewhere suggest he was left-handed. Five bears are living on the site.

Around Montignac

Six kilometres southeast of Montignac, by the D704, stands one of the Dordogne's dreamiest châteaux, the golden limestone *lauze*-topped Château de la Grande Filolie (14th–15th century)

– so perfect that, as Périgord novelist Marc Blancpain put it, 'one could believe it grew here, as mushrooms grow in the humid sweetness of an autumn night'. Unfortunately it can't be visited.

Eglise Monastique de St-Amand-de-Coly
t 05 53 51 04 56; open July and Aug daily 10.30–12.30 and 3.30–7; Sept daily 3–6.30; adm

Just as visually striking, the fortified **church of St-Amand-de-Coly** 6km east of Montignac on the D704 has a massive *clocher-mur* pierced by a shallow arch and topped with a superb roof of *lauzes*, looming like a skyscraper over its narrow valley and hamlet. Built after 1124 as an Augustinian monastery, it lost its cloister and abbey in the Hundred Years' War, but it was fortified so well after that calamity that the Huguenots who took shelter here in 1575 withstood six days of close cannon fire. Defensive traces remain inside as well: just under the roof you can see the path from which the monks and villagers could fire down on their besiegers. It is stirring, wholesome Romanesque, unusually built on a slope (the walls of the nave converge slightly, to create a curious perspective). The dome hovers 20m over the nave: stand under it and sing, and like all true Romanesque churches it rings like a bell. Concerts are often held here; contact the tourist office.

ⓘ **Montignac >>**
Place Bertran de Born, t 05 53 51 82 60, www.bienvenue-montignac.com

★ **Relais du Soleil d'Or >>**

ⓘ **Terrasson-la-Villedieu >**
Espace Jean Rouby, t 05 53 50 37 56, www.ot-terrasson.com

Market Days in the Northern Vézère

Terrasson-la-Villedieu: Thursday.
Montignac: Wednesday and Saturday.
St-Amand-de-Coly: Farmers' market Tuesday evening July and August.

Actitivies in the Northern Vézère

Canoes can be hired at several places, including Canoes APA (**t** 05 53 50 67 71) at St Léon-sur-Vézère and Kanoak (**t** 06 75 48 60 47) at Montignac.

Where to Stay and Eat

Terrasson-la-Villedieu ✉ 24120

*****Hostellerie L'Imaginaire**, Place du Foirail, **t** 05 53 51 37 27, *www.l-imaginaire.com* (€€€). A 17th-century building near the Jardins, with refined rooms and a Michelin-starred restaurant serving inventive meals. *Closed several wks in Mar and Nov.*

Les Saveurs de Jardin, at entrance of Jardins de l'Imaginaire, **t** 05 53 50 30 91 (€€–€). Snacks on a terrace, plus local dishes flavoured with various flowers. *Closed Nov–Mar and Mon, plus Tues exc July and Aug.*

Condat-sur-Vézère ✉ 24570

*****Château de la Fleunie**, **t** 05 53 51 32 74, *www.lafleunie.com* (€€€–€€). A 12th–15th-century château in a park, with tennis courts, a pool, a sauna, stables and gourmet meals (€€€). Half board is obligatory in July and August. *Closed mid-Nov–mid-Feb; restaurant Sun eve and Mon mid-Feb–early April, plus Sat Oct–mid-Nov.*

Montignac ✉ 24290

******Château de Puy Robert**, 2km from Lascaux on D65, **t** 05 53 51 92 13, *www.puyrobert.com* (€€€€€–€€€). A lovely château-hotel in the process of being sold at the time of writing; see the website for the latest information.

*****Relais du Soleil d'Or**, 16 Rue du Quatre-Septembre, **t** 05 53 51 80 22, *www.le-soleil-dor.com* (€€€€–€€). A venerable old inn surrounded by a shady park (itself a historic monument), with plenty to pass the time, including a heated pool, and tennis and canoeing nearby. The restaurant (€€€–€€) serves traditional southwest cuisine with a light modern touch, and there's a cheaper bistro. *Closed Feb; restaurant Sun eve and Mon lunch Nov–Mar.*

*****La Roseraie**, Place d'Armes, **t** 05 53 50 53 92, *www.laroseraie-hotel.com*

(€€€€–€€). A charming large 19th-century house where you can forget about the world, with attractive gardens with a pool, and a good restaurant (€€€–€€). *Closed Nov–Mar.*

****Le Lascaux**, 109 Av Jean Jaurès, **t** 05 53 51 82 81, *www.hotel-le-lascaux.fr* (€€–€). Pleasant, simple Logis de France hotel with decent restaurant (€€). *Closed mid-Dec–mid-Jan, Sun eve, and Wed and Sat lunch Oct–April.*

La Grotte, 63 Rue du Quatre-Septembre, **t** 05 53 51 80 48, *hoteldelagrotte@wanadoo.fr* (€). Basic rooms, a riverside terrace, canoeing, and a playground. The restaurant (€€€–€) serves lots of asparagus in season.

Le Moulin de Bleufond, on D65, **t** 05 53 51 83 95, *www.bleufond.com* (€). The campsite nearest Montignac, with tent pitches and mobile homes, pools and a sauna. *Closed mid-Oct–Mar.*

La Chapelle-Aubareil ✉ 24290

****La Table du Terroir**, 7km south of Montignac, **t** 05 53 50 72 14, *www.tableduterroir.com* (€). A handsome farm-hotel-restaurant with panoramic views from its park and hilltop pool, mini-golf and good local food (€€€–€). It's somewhat off the beaten track but signposted. *Closed Dec–Feb.*

St-Amand-de-Coly ✉ 24290

La Gardette, **t** 05 53 51 68 50, *http://hotelgardette.free.fr* (€). A good-value, family-run hotel offering nine quiet rooms and simple meals (€€). *Closed Nov–Mar.*

Coly ✉ 24120

*****Manoir de Hautegente**, about 3km north of Coly on D62, **t** 05 53 51 68 03, *www.manoir-hautegente.com* (€€€€–€€). A quite magnificent, ivy-covered 18th-century manor with 15 elegant, antique-furnished rooms, an idyllic garden crossed by a clear, ambling trout stream, and swimming in a heated pool. Half-board is mandatory in season, but that's no hardship – the Perigordian cuisine (€€€) is excellent. The restaurant is open to non-guests by reservation only. *Open Nov–early April.*

ⓘ St-Amand-de-Coly >>
t 05 53 51 04 56, www.saint-amand-de-coly.org

★ Manoir de Hautegente >>

Downriver from Montignac to Les Eyzies

Centre d'Art Préhistorique du Thot
t 05 53 50 70 44; open July and Aug Tues–Sun 9–7; Sept–Dec and Feb–June Tues–Sun 9–6

The ticket to Lascaux II includes entry to the **Centre d'Art Préhistorique du Thot**, well signposted along the D706. Displays inside reveal the daily lives of the Lascaux artists, and there are audiovisuals on Palaeolithic art and on the meticulous creation of Lascaux II, as well as a replica of the tiny chamber at the back of Lascaux, showing a stick man in a bird mask, dropping what looks like a bird decoy as a wounded bison charges and gores him. Another chamber at the back of Lascaux was painted with felines; as a rule, the artists didn't shy away from depicting dangerous animals but hid them, either at the back or amidst other drawings (see the bear in the Chamber of the Bulls).

Outside are living examples of the subjects of Lascaux – the deer and bulls, and animals that found a last refuge in Poland: European bison and Przewalski's horses, and oxen representing the wild aurochs that died out in Poland in the 1660s. Even the extinct woolly rhinos and mammoth are animated to wiggle and roar. You can have a go at cave painting yourself on a replica wall, using, as far as possible, materials available to the Magdalenians.

Château de Losse
t 05 53 50 80 08; open mid-April–May and Sept daily 11–6; June–Aug daily 10–7, but times subject to frequent change so call ahead; adm

Further south on the D706, a signposted lane leads you to the riverside **Château de Losse**, associated with the Ophelia of Périgord, the fair Hélène of Château de Sauvebœuf, who drowned on her wedding day rather than marry the horrid old *seigneur* of Losse. In 1576, the medieval castle with its moat was converted into an elegant Renaissance palace by Jean II de Losse, governor of Guyenne under Henri IV; it has now been completely furnished with tapestries, porcelains and other 16th- and 17th-century pieces. There are also gardens and a picnic area.

Thonac, the nearest village, is dominated by a huge belltower, but the main attraction is a leaning tower 2km away on the Plazac road, the Tour de Vermondie. The story goes that a girl was imprisoned here to keep her away from her lover. When he came and sang at its foot, the tower was so moved that it bent over to allow the two to kiss. There are lovely views from here, and towards **Plazac** –a pretty little place in its valley, with a 14th-century church and episcopal palace. If you're in need of relaxation, stop off at **La Fleur de Vie**, a hammam, Jacuzzi and tearoom with separate men's and women's days.

La Fleur de Vie
t 05 53 51 98 72; call for hrs

Due north of Thonac, the village of **Fanlac** is so perfectly intact it was chosen as the location for the French TV film based on *Jacquou le Croquant*. There's a bridge at Thonac crossing the Vézère to Baleinie; upriver from here are some of the most striking dry-stone *cabanes* in the *département*, believed to date from the 13th century.

Rouffignac, Mammoths and the Château de l'Herm

While you're travelling in this corner of the Dordogne, you may notice that village after village has been twinned with one in Germany. In the case of Rouffignac this marks a special act of forgiveness – in 1944, in reprisal for local Resistance activity, the retreating Nazis burned the village to the ground. Only the church of St-Germain remained, or at least most of it – the Romanesque apse is rebuilt, but under the belltower an admirable Renaissance doorway of 1530 survives, its lintel carved with mermaids. If it's open, don't miss the Flamboyant Gothic interior, with elaborate vaulting and twisted columns.

Rouffignac has even greater claims to fame. Five kilometres south, off the D32, is the **Grotte de Rouffignac**, 'the Cave of a Hundred Mammoths'. First off, this is the cave to visit if you have trouble walking: a little electric train waits to trundle you 4km down into the bowels of the earth as the guide illuminates the vivid etchings, drawings of mammoths and woolly rhinos, and niches in the clay floor formed by generations of hibernating bears, restlessly spinning. The ceiling of the innermost chamber is an excellent pastiche of horses, mammoths, bison and an ibex.

★4 Grotte de Rouffignac
t 05 53 05 41 71; open mid-Mar–June, Sept and Oct daily 10–11.30 and 2–5; July and Aug daily 9–11.30 and 2–6; adm

Rouffignac is a good example of the way people sometimes only see what they expect to see. Unlike many caves, its entrance has always been open, and for centuries locals would come down and take scary walks or even Sunday afternoon promenades, leaving their names and dates behind on the walls and ceilings. Only in 1956 did someone notice that the graffiti covered vigorous prehistoric masterpieces. When their authenticity was questioned, a description of them dated 1575 was produced; interestingly, even back then the author sensed that Rouffignac was a sacred place but somehow mistook the drawings for erotic 'Love's larcenies' of our 'idolatrous forefathers'.

Château de l'Herm
t 05 53 05 46 61; 45min tours of interior April–early Nov daily 10–7 but call ahead; rest of year by appt; adm

Other signs from Rouffignac lead you 6km to the northwest, to the sinister **Château de l'Herm**, its savage, ruined towers looming over the trees – a remnant of the Fôret de Barade, which was once Périgord's darkest wood. Few castles in France are so bloodstained: legend tells of the 13th-century Baron de l'Herm, the builder of the two heavy round towers, whose daughter Jeanne fell in love with a page. By a freak accident, the young man accidentally cut Jeanne's hand off when they first embraced; a wax one was made in its place, and in remorse the young husband swore to obey his bride blindly whenever she raised it. Unfortunately he became a violent drunkard. One day he came home to find Jeanne listening to a troubadour – in a jealous rage he would have slain the singer, but Jeanne raised her wax hand, and the troubadour made good his escape, only to hear Jeanne's screams as her husband cut the rest of her to bits.

Windows and openings were cut into the round feudal towers when a third tower was added by l'Herm's later owner, an ambassador of François Ier named Jean III de Calvimont. Calvimont had spent long periods in Italy, and graced his residence with a Flamboyant Gothic portal guarded by men-at-arms, a superb stone spiral staircase and carved fireplaces, now surreally suspended over the floorless void. Calvimont died a mysterious violent death and left l'Herm to his five-year-old daughter, Marguerite. His widow immediately married a neighbour, Foucauld d'Aubusson, and married the child Marguerite to his diabolical son, François, to make sure the property stayed in the family. But François was already in love with Marie de Hautefort (aunt of the mistress of Louis XIII), and as Marguerite grew older and François's debts grew larger, he had her strangled, beginning a new 80-year-long streak of murders at and around l'Herm involving the Calvimonts, d'Aubussons and anyone remotely connected with them. By 1652, when all the claimants had self-destructed, the château was put up for auction; not surprisingly, no one wanted the cursed place. It was eventually converted into a farm and abandoned in 1862.

Palaeolithic Agglomerations along the Vézère

Back along the Vézère, **St-Léon-sur-Vézère**, now a charming, sleepy backwater off the D706, was once a stopping point for pilgrims to Compostela: its handsome, forthright Romanesque church, built on a Gallo-Roman wall, overlooks the willows weeping into the river and a pedestrian bridge. Inside, only some battered frescoes and reliefs have survived of the decoration. The village cemetery has a pint-sized version of Sarlat's *Lanterne des Morts* and some extremely rare *enfeux* – wall niche tombs dating from the 1200s.

Parc de Loisirs Préhistorique Le Conquil
t 05 53 51 29 03; open April–June daily 10–6; July and Aug daily 10–7; Sept, Oct and Nov daily 2–5; adm

Above St-Léon, you can tour the various cave and cliff dwellings (and a dovecote) at **Le Conquil**, which some believe were used and fortified from prehistoric times until the Middle Ages. There is also a **dinosaur park** with lifesize models, some of which make a noise; it also houses a little museum with some prehistoric finds and a very popular adventure trail through the treetops, for children and fit adults.

St-Léon's bridge leads in a kilometre to the hamlet of **Sergeac** (by car, cross the Vézère further up or downstream), with a pretty Romanesque church of its own and a beautifully sculpted 15th-century roadside 'Hosanna' cross at the entrance to the village. In prehistoric times, the Sergeac area was the most densely populated outside Les Eyzies, with nine known shelters inhabited from 35,000 to 10,000 BC; by coincidence (or not), this favoured spot is exactly on the 45th parallel, halfway between the North Pole and the Equator. Several shelters are open to the public just southwest of Sergeac at the **Site de Castel-Merle** on the D65. In one were found Magdalenian-era sculptures, and blocks of stone carved with mysterious symbols dated 32,000 BC that may have been part of a portable sanctuary.

Site de Castel-Merle
t 05 53 50 79 70; open April–Sept daily 2–6; adm

The D66 continues south to **Peyzac-le-Moustier**, another hoary site in the annals of prehistory. Excavations begun in 1908 in the **Abri du Moustier** have produced such a wealth of material that the last half of the Middle Palaeolithic era is known as the Mousterian culture (roughly 100,000–35,000 BC).

Abri du Moustier
open by reservation with Font-de-Gaume *(see p.127)*

The bridge from Le Moustier crosses to the curved prow of the **Roque St-Christophe**, a sheer cliff more than 0.8km long, sliced into five shelves, one of which is the largest natural terrace in Europe. It's a fascinating place to explore. Inhabited from Mousterian times, then fortified in the 900s against the Vikings sailing up the Vézère, Roque St-Christophe was later a Protestant stronghold until the 16th century, when it was destroyed by the troops of Henri III. At its peak more than 1,000 people lived under the rock tiers, with their own church, cemetery and little river port; the winches they used to bring goods up have been reconstructed.

Roque St-Christophe
t 05 53 50 70 45; open April, June and Sept daily 10–6.30; July and Aug daily 10–8; early Nov–Jan daily 2–5; Feb, Mar and Oct–early Nov daily 10–6, adm

If, after all this, you still can't imagine daily life as it was at the dawn of time, pay a visit to Tursac's **Préhistoparc** with its life-size outdoor dioramas featuring hunters killing mammoths, woolly rhinoceri and bears. You can also have a stab at various activities, such as cave painting.

Préhistoparc
t 05 53 50 73 19; open July and Aug daily 9.30–7.30; mid-Feb–June and Sept–early Nov daily 10–6; adm

Maison Forte de Reignac
t 05 53 50 69 54; open May, June and Sept daily 10–7; July and Aug daily 10–8; Mar, April and Oct–mid-Nov daily 10–6; adm

Tursac is also home to the recently opened **Maison Forte de Reignac**, a fortress-like manor that was built beneath and into the rock, and is the only residence of its kind in France to have survived intact. Set in a naturally defensive position, it also has such features as loopholes and bartizans. Inside you can see a number of furnished rooms (including a dining room, a kitchen, some bedrooms, a chapel and a prison), underground vaults and a display of prehistoric finds made here.

La Madeleine
t 05 53 46 36 88; open July and Aug daily 9.30–7; rest of year daily 10–6

Downriver, over the Lespinasse bridge from Tursac, excavations at **La Madeleine** have produced approximately 600 pieces of *art immobilier*, giving the name Magdalenian to the greatest age of Palaeolithic art. Although the finds are now in Les Eyzies' museum, the path from the parking lot leads to the ruins of a **troglodyte village** similar to the Roque St-Christophe – a 10th-century fort carved into the living rock, a 15th-century chapel, and, on the promontory, a ruined château.

Where to Stay and Eat Downriver from Montignac to Les Eyzies

Valojoulx ✉ 24290

La Licorne, t 05 53 50 77 77, *www.licorne-lascaux.com* (€€). Five peaceful *chambres d'hôte* accommodating 2–4 people, on a tranquil, honey-coloured square. Meals are available for guests. *Closed Nov–Mar.*

St-Léon-sur-Vézère ✉ 24290

Auberge du Pont, town centre, **t** 05 53 50 73 07 (€€€–€€). A 19th-century inn that has retained its *lauze* roof, serving a variety of Provençal and Périgord dishes, including a number of vegetarian options. *Closed Tues eve and Wed exc July and Aug.*

Sergeac ✉ 24290

Auberge de Castel-Merle, t 05 53 50 70 08 (€). A pretty hotel by the museum, with five rooms and a terrace overlooking the Vézère where you can feast on well-prepared Périgord specialities (€€). *Closed mid-Oct–Mar; restaurant lunch Mon–Sat.*

Auberge du Peyrol, near Castel-Merle, **t** 05 53 50 72 91 (€€€–€). A restaurant serving lush dishes such as foie gras in Monbazillac and grilled duck *magret* in garlic and parsley sauce, which you can enjoy as you take in the lovely picture-window views of the similarly lush Vézère landscape. There's a vegetarian option available at lunchtime. *Closed Mon out of season, and Dec and Feb.*

Rouffignac ✉ 24580

Château de Fleurac, Fleurac, just southwest of Rouffignac, **t** 05 53 05 95 01, *www.fleurac.com* (€€€€€–€€). A 19th-century château with 15 comfortable rooms and suites and a couple of luxury self-catering apartments, all of them with period furnishings. There are also a swimming pool and tennis courts on site. The property is non-smoking throughout. *Closed Oct–May.*

Thonac ✉ 24290

Archambeau, Place de l'Eglise, **t** 05 53 05 29 83, *www.hotel-restau-archambeau.com* (€€–€). A hotel offering pleasant, calm rooms and a restaurant with a shaded terrace where you can enjoy largely southwest dishes featuring lots of duck, *cèpes* and truffles, plus a wide choice of fish dishes. There's a swimming pool where you can cool off in the warmer months.

Les Eyzies-de-Tayac, the 'World Capital of Prehistory'

The Vézère and Beune rivers meet at Les Eyzies, where the first known bones of *Homo sapiens sapiens* were discovered just above the train station at a place called Cro-Magnon. As the valley's chief crossroads, with an important prehistoric museum and sites in every direction, Les Eyzies gets swamped with summer visitors, all watched over by a lumpish creature representing Cro-Magnon man, sculpted in 1930 by Paul Dardé and a grave insult to the painters of Lascaux.

Musée National de Préhistoire

Musée National de Préhistoire
t 05 53 06 45 45, www.musee-prehistoire-eyzies.fr; open July and Aug daily 9.30–6.30; Sept–June Wed–Sun 9.30–12.30 and 2–5.30; adm

Tucked under the overhanging cliffs that dominate Les Eyzies, and sharing the terrace with the hapless caveman statue, the 16th-century castle belonging to the barons of Beynac was slowly being cannibalized for its stone when it found a new role in 1918 as a museum. Now located in a modern building at the foot of the château, it's the perfect prehistory apéritif, especially if you're not entirely familiar with the subject; tables and charts help put the mind-boggling millennia into perspective.

If, technologically, humankind got off to a slow, painstaking start (see the flint blades), the opposite is true in art: some rooms form a kind of Louvre of prehistory, with the largest collection anywhere of Palaeolithic reliefs and sculpture in stone, bone and ivory. These come in five chief styles. In the Primitive (35,000–25,000 BC) figures are very rare, stiff and roughly shaped; in the Archaic (25,000–15,000 BC) animals were drawn in rigid profile on walls (the Abri Pataud Venus, the animal from Abri Cellier) and the first sculptures in three dimensions were made. The final three styles belong to the Magdalenian era (*c.* 15,000–10,000 BC): the Preclassical, marking the beginnings of the great period of cave paintings; the Classical, marked by a scrupulous attention to proportions, movement and detail, which gradually reveals a decline of spontaneity until reaching the Final period at the end of the Upper Palaeolithic. There are bas-reliefs of shapely Magdalenian women, mammoths butting heads etched on a staff, the famous *Bison licking its Flank* from La Madeleine and the *Aurochs du Fourneau-du-Diable*; there are rough carved vulvas and delicate ornate phalluses that make you wonder which sex carved which. There is also a collection of casts of *art mobilier* found for the most part along the Vézère in the 19th century, including a case of those first subjects of prehistoric sculptors, the lozenge 'Venuses' – buxom, balloon-bottomed beauties common from the Urals to the Pyrenees. And there are casts of Neanderthal and Cro-Magnon skulls, animal bones, and several sepulchres: the remains

Getting to and around Les Eyzies

Les Eyzies station has regular **trains** linking the town to Sarlat, Périgueux and Agen.

Parking in the town in season is notoriously frustrating; excursion buses fill the streets like whales in a goldfish pond. For a **taxi**, call **t** 05 53 06 93 06.

Abri Pataud
t 05 53 06 92 46; open early April–early June Sat–Thurs 10–12.30 and 2–6; early June–early Sept daily 10–7; early Sept–early Nov Sat–Thurs 10–12.30 and 2–5; early Nov–mid-Dec Sat–Thurs 10–12 and 2–5.30; mid-Dec–early Jan Sat–Thurs 10–12.30 and 2–5.30; early Feb–early April Mon–Thurs 10–12.30 and 2–5; adm

Jardins de la Licorne
t 05 53 06 15 29; call for times

of bodies covered with ochre and rare seashells. Note especially the Magdalenian **tomb** from St-Germain-la-Rivière in the Gironde, where a young woman was laid out in a foetal position under what looks like a dolmen, surrounded with funerary gifts: shells, tools, ornaments and animal bones.

The Rest of Town

Under a rocky overhang in the centre of Les Ezyies is the equally remarkable **Abri Pataud**, where Upper Palaeolithic hunters lived on 40 separate occasions over a span of nearly 20,000 years. A museum in the nearby shelter contains the finds, including one of the oldest known bas-reliefs, an ibex dated 18,000 BC. *Homo sapiens sapiens* was discovered near the station; here too is the 13th-century **St Martin-de-Tayac**, an imposing fortified church with antique columns on the porch.

Two kilometres outside town, in the direction of Périgueux, are some medieval-style gardens, the **Jardins de la Licorne**.

Font-de-Gaume

Font-de-Gaume
t 05 53 06 86 00, www.leseyzies.com/grottes-ornees; reservations essential; open for guided tours mid-Sept–mid-May Sun–Fri exc public hols 9.30–12.30 and 2–5.30; mid-May–mid-Sept 9.30–5.30 Sun–Fri exc public hols; adm

Although the Grotte de la Mouthe (where the first cave paintings in France were discovered just south of Les Eyzies) has been closed since 1981, 200 visitors a day are allowed into the Grotte de Font-de-Gaume, a 10-minute walk east along the D47. This has nothing less than the finest polychrome prehistoric paintings open to the general public in France, although as in Rouffignac the cave was visited centuries before the paintings were 'discovered' in 1901.

A path from the ticket booth/shop leads up to the entrance; inside, beyond a narrow passage called 'the Rubicon', the walls are adorned with beautiful paintings and engravings in remarkable flowing lines dating from *c.* 12,000 BC, created with the same drawing and colour-blowing techniques used at Lascaux, and similarly using natural relief to lend volume to the drawing. Although calcite build-ups and graffiti over the years have damaged some of the paintings, others look as if they were made yesterday: magnificent friezes of red and black bison on a light background, reindeer, horses with legs and heads partially formed by natural features in the cave walls. The guide adjusts the lighting to bring out the extraordinary fullness and depth of the art – it's almost impossible to believe that anyone could make such perfect lines and shading on an irregular stone surface with only a dim smoking lamp of mammoth fat to guide their hand. The partially painted, partially engraved black stag and kneeling red doe, unique in the canon of Upper Palaeolithic art, only become visible after the guide carefully traces out the lines with a light. The stag is leaning over delicately to lick the doe's brow – an image of tenderness as sublime as it is startling, and one that questions a lot of commonly held assumptions about life 14,000 years ago. Font-de-Gaume is the rendezvous for visiting Laugerie Haute; *see* p.129.

East of Les Eyzies, along the Beune Valley

Grotte des Combarelles
t 05 53 06 86 00; open for 40min guided tours mid-Sept–mid-May Sun–Fri exc public hols 9.30–12.30 and 2–5.30; mid-May–mid-Sept Sun–Fri exc hols 9.30–5.30; adm (buy tickets at Font-de-Gaume)

Grotte de Bernifal
t 05 53 29 66 39; open June daily 10–5; July and Aug daily 10–6; rest of year by appt; adm

Roc de Cazelle
t 05 53 59 46 09; open May, June and Nov daily 10–7; July and Aug daily 10–8; Mar, April and Oct daily 10–6; Sept and Dec–Feb daily 11–5

Abri du Cap Blanc
t 05 53 06 86 00; by reservation at Font-de-Gaume, see p.127; adm

Château de Commarque
t 05 53 59 00 25; open April daily 10–6; May, June and Sept daily 10–7; July and Aug daily 10–8

A kilometre up the D47, the **Grotte des Combarelles** was discovered in the same year as Font-de-Gaume. Approximately 800 different engravings dated 12,000–10,000 BC have been distinguished in the cave's last section, including 140 horses and 48 rare human representations – hands, masks, women and a seated person. Many are incomplete, most are superimposed in wild abandon, and others only appear when lit from various angles. Most beautiful of all is the reindeer leaning forward to drink from a black cavity suggesting water.

A year later and 3km down the road, 100 paintings and engravings were found in the **Grotte de Bernifal** , near the left bank of the Petite Beune, in Meyrals. The dominant animal is the mammoth, stylistically similar to the ones in Rouffignac (c. 12,000 BC), in the company of many 'tectiform' (roof-shaped) symbols. But the star of the show is a rare, engraved ancestor of the ass. At the **Roc de Cazelle**, kids can learn how to sharpen flint, cavepaint and carry out other prehistoric skills. There is now also a display of lifesize mammoths, and here are re-creations of daily prehistoric life in the caves and tunnels.

More prehistory waits around **Marquay**: the **Abri du Cap Blanc** has a remarkable, vigorous frieze of nearly life-size horses in high relief, following the natural contours of the limestone cliff; the shelter also yielded a Cro-Magnon tomb and tools from the end of the Magdalenian age. Just beyond rise the majestic, romantic ruins of the 12th–13th-century **Château de Commarque**, a castle betrayed and ruined by the English in the Hundred Years' War; the elegant keep was added in the 16th century. On the cliff opposite, the much-restored 14th-century Château de Laussel sits over the Gisement de Laussel (100,000–17,000 BC), which produced the famous relief of the *Vénus de Laussel*, holding her bison horn (now in Bordeaux, but there's a cast in the museum in Les Eyzies).

North of Les Eyzies

Along the opposite bank of the Vézère from Les Eyzies, the D47 is chock-a-block with the works of nature and humankind. A number of shelters are scattered in the pretty Parc Gorge d'Enfer (*closed to visitors*), but you can see the famous **Abri des Poissons** by special appointment with the reservation service at Font-de-Gaume (*see* p.127). This has a rare relief of a fish – a salmon nearly a metre long. It is nearly detached from the ceiling; an enterprising German had sold it secretly to a museum in Berlin but the French found out just in time and classified the site, preserving the fish *in situ*.

Grotte du Grand Roc
t 05 53 06 92 70; open July and Aug daily 9.30–7; Feb–Nov and Christmas hols daily 10–6; adm

Gisement de Laugerie Basse
same hrs as Grand Roc; combined adm possible

Gisement Laugerie Haute
open by arrangement with Font-de-Gaume (see *p.127*)

Further along the D47 is a fairy work by Mother Nature, the stalactite **Grotte du Grand Roc**, halfway up a cliff. This cave is known for its extremely rare triangular formations; others resemble coral, some thumb their nose at the law of gravity. Nearby, you can also tour the **Gisement de Laugerie Basse**, one of the first shelters excavated, in 1863, and a rich source of *art immobilier*. The adjacent Abri de Marseille was occupied continuously from the Magdalenian to the Gallo-Roman periods.

Further up the D47, at the **Gisement Laugerie Haute**, 42 levels of human habitation have been excavated over the last 130 years, at the bottom of the cliff. When the massive top terrace of the cliff collapsed c. 14,000 BC, it had already been home to people for 11 millennia. There are a number of Solutrean (20,000 BC) engravings as well as a sort of carved gutter, an early attempt to solve a problem that would ever after plague humanity – leaking roofs.

ⓘ Les Eyzies-de-Tayac >
t 05 53 06 97 05, www.leseyzies.com; open June and Sept Mon–Sat 9–7, Sun 2–5; July and Aug Mon–Sat 9–7, Sun 10–12 and 2–6; Oct–Mar Mon–Sat 9–12 and 2–6; April and May Mon–Sat 9–12 and 2–6, Sun 10–12 and 2–5

★ Hôtel du Centenaire >

Tourist Information in Les Eyzies-de-Tayac

The opening hours and booking requirements of the sites here are prone to change, so check the latest details with the **tourist office**. Staff there can also provide information on canoe and kayak hire, horse-riding and trails, and the small tourist train, the Cromignon (Easter–Sept). One place for canoe hire is Canoës Vallée Vézère, t 05 53 05 10 11.

Market Days in Les Eyzies-de-Tayac

Monday April–Oct, plus night markets in July and August.

Where to Stay and Eat in Les Eyzies-de-Tayac

Les Eyzies-de-Tayac ✉ 24620

***Hôtel du Centenaire, Rocher Penne, **t** 05 53 06 68 68, *www.hotelducentenaire.fr* (€€€€–€€€). A member of the plush Relais et Châteaux group, in the centre yet far from the summer brouhaha. Along with extremely pleasant rooms and several apartments, it offers an outdoor heated pool, a sauna and a gym. What really draws the crowds, however, is the rather formal dining room (€€€), with some of the most exquisite meals and one of the best wine cellars in the region. You can also buy gift sets of local delicacies. *Restaurant closed Mon, Tues, Wed and Fri lunch and Nov–Mar.*

*****Les Glycines**, by river, **t** 05 53 06 97 07, *www.les-glycines-dordogne.com* (€€€–€€). Pretty rooms in a garden setting, with a pool. The restaurant (€€€€–€€€), which has its own kitchen garden, serves fine regional lamb and beef dishes and other Périgourdin faves. *Closed eves Nov–Mar.*

*****Hostellerie Cro-Magnon**, 54 Avenue de la Préhistoire, **t** 05 53 06 97 06, *www.hostellerie-cro-magnon.com* (€€€–€€). A comfortable hotel with 15 rooms with satellite TV and minibars, a pool and a restaurant with a terrace.

*****Hôtel des Roches**, on road to Sarlat, **t** 05 53 06 96 59, *www.roches-les-eyzies.com* (€€). Comfortable rooms in a tempting position at the foot of the cliffs, with a large lawn and a pool but no restaurant. *Closed Nov–mid-April.*

****Hostellerie du Passeur**, Place de la Mairie, **t** 05 53 06 97 13, *www.hostellerie-du-passeur.com* (€€). A big house by the river, with comfy rooms and a welcoming dining room (€€€–€€) offering southwest dishes such as foie gras three ways, with outside dining in summer. *Closed Nov–Mar; restaurant Tues and Sat lunch exc July and Aug.*

****Hôtel de France et Auberge du Musée**, 4 Rue Moulin, **t** 05 53 06 97 23, *www.hoteldefrance-perigord.com* (€€). Another central choice, with a shady terrace, a pool by the riverbank, and a restaurant. *Closed Nov–Easter.*

****Moulin de la Beune**, **t** 05 53 06 94 33, *www.moulindelabeune.com* (€). A former mill converted into a friendly hotel, with a fine restaurant (€€€–€€) serving local recipes with innovative twists. *Close Nov–Mar; restaurant also Tues, Wed and Sat lunch.*

Les Falaises, 35 Av de la Préhistoire, **t** 05 53 06 97 35 (€). A good budget choice, with parking and a little garden. Be sure to book a few days ahead from October to April.

La Rivière, **t** 05 53 06 97 14, *www.leseyzies.com/la-riviere-hotel* (€). Six tidy rooms and a large pool. *Closed Nov–Mar; restaurant Wed and Sat lunch.*

Outside Les Eyzies

*****Hôtel de la Ferme Lamy**, Meyrals, **t** 05 53 29 62 46, *www.ferme-lamy.com* (€€€€–€€€). Pretty rooms full of character, with bare beams, plus a garden and a vast pool.

Ferme-Auberge de la Rhonie, Boyer, Meyrals, **t** 05 53 29 29 07, *www.coustaty.com* (€). A pleasant family house on a goose farm, with eight comfy bedrooms (some quite small). Farm products are available, and Madame's cooking is based on all things 'goosy'. Half board is good value, or there's a gîte. *Closed Sun.*

Marquay ✉ 24620

****Les Bories**, **t** 05 53 29 67 02 (€€–€). A large country house with a pool and restaurant (€€€–€€). *Closed Nov–Mar.*

****Hôtel La Condamine**, **t** 05 53 29 64 08 (€). A rural Logis de France hotel – unpretentious, calm and comfortable, with a pool and restaurant (€€). *Closed early Nov–Easter; restaurant lunch.*

To Le Bugue-sur-Vézère

There are even more caves south of Les Eyzies, around Le Bugue, a major crossroads of the Dordogne with a few attractions of its own.

Caves, Bears and Fish

Grotte de Bara-Bahau
t 05 53 07 44 58; open July and Aug daily 9.30–7; Sept–Dec daily 10–12 and 2–5; Feb–June daily 10–12 and 2–5.30; adm

Gouffre de Proumeyssac
t 05 53 07 27 47; open May and June daily 9.30–6.30; July and Aug daily 9–7; Mar, April, Sept and Oct daily 9.30–12 and 2–5.30; Feb, Nov and Dec daily 2–5; wheelchair access; adm

From Les Eyzies, the D706 follows the Vézère down to the village and Romanesque church of **Campagne**, and the 15th-century Château de Campagne, given a William Morris neogothic facelift in the 19th century. There's been no tinkering, however, with the magnificent trees in its park and its forest stair, the Chemin des Dames. Sadly, the château is private and inaccessible to the public.

The Vézère flows broadly past **Le Bugue**, a market town full of attractions, including a pair of caves. The prehistoric **Grotte de Bara-Bahau**, 2km northwest, belonged to the bears before graffiti artists moved in 35,000 years ago. Its walls, 'as soft as white cheese' as one prehistorian put it, are covered with rustic flint-blade carvings from the Aurignacian culture; among them are animals (including a rare silhouette of a bear), hand or claw marks, and other mysterious signs. The second cave is a chasm 3km south on the D31E, the **Gouffre de Proumeyssac**. For centuries protected by

Getting to and around Le Bugue-sur-Vézère

Le Bugue, the 'Crossroads of Périgord', has a **train** station (**t** 05 53 06 97 22) on the same line as Les Eyzies (*see* p.127) and lots of traffic jams. For **taxis** round the clock, call **t** 05 53 07 22 97.

Aquarium du Périgord Noir
t 05 53 07 10 74; open June daily 10–7; July and Aug daily 9–7; April, May and Sept daily 10–6; adm

Jardins d'Arborie
t 05 53 08 42 74; open mid-June–mid-Sept daily 9.45–7; Easter–mid-June and mid-Sept–frosty weather daily 10–12 and 2.30–6

Musée de Paléontologie
t 05 53 08 28 10; open Mar–June daily 2–6, July and Aug daily 10–1 and 3–7

Terre des Oiseaux
t 05 53 07 12 81; call for times

demonic legends, Proumeyssac was only explored in 1907; its nickname, the 'Crystal Cathedral', comes from its extraordinary domed chamber of yellow and white stalactites and draperies. You can go down in a sort of small, suspended cage. There are also information panels on the site describing the geological evolutionary eras and the formation of the cave.

Although freshwater fish lack the glamour of their salty kin, Le Bugue's **Aquarium du Périgord Noir** brings out the charms of pike, sturgeon, eels and turtles in imaginative indoor and outdoor settings; in one hall the fish swim right over your head. A section of exotic fish add a splash of colour. You can can also feed the fish. The **Jardins d'Arborie** display trees and bushes from around the world: bonsai, cacti and giant vegetables. There is also a **Musée de Paléontologie et Maison de la Vie Sauvage**, which concerns itself mainly with birds, and the **Terre des Oiseaux** on the way out to Bordeaux if you prefer your birds exotic and living.

Market Days in Le Bugue-sur-Vézère

Le Bugue has general markets every **Tuesday** and **Saturday**.

Activities in Le Bugue-sur-Vézère

Hire canoes at **Canoës Courrèges**, Route du Buisson, **t** 05 53 07 27 44.

Where to Stay and Eat in and around Le Bugue-sur-Vézère

Campagne ✉ 24260

****Le Château, t** 05 53 07 23 50 (€). Twelve tranquil rooms furnished with antiques, plus a good restaurant (€€€–€€): try the escalope of foie gras with a crumble of dried fruits. *Closed mid-Oct–Easter.*

Le Bugue ✉ 24260

*****Domaine de La Barde**, Route de Périgueux, **t** 05 53 07 16 54, *www.domainedelabarde.com* (€€€€–€€€). The fanciest rooms in the area, a pretty garden with a swimming pool, a sauna and tennis and table tennis facilities, and a restaurant (€€€). *Closed Jan–mid-Mar.*

Manoir de la Brunie, Le Coux et Bigaroque, 7km south of Le Bugue, **t** 05 53 31 95 62, *www.manoirdelabrunie.com* (€€€). A lovely big manor house in its own park, affording panoramic views over the valley. The five comfortable rooms have a subtle mix of rustic and modern décor. Dinner (€€) is available by advance booking.

*****Royal Vézère**, Place de l'Hôtel de Ville, **t** 05 53 07 20 01 (€€€–€). A large Best Western hotel beside the river, with an excellent restaurant, **Les Trois As** (€€€–€€) with a wonderful river terrace, plus a pool on the roof. *Closed mid-Nov–early April.*

****Le Cygne**, Le Cingle, **t** 05 53 07 17 77, *www.lecygne-perigord.com* (€). A Logis hotel in a busy spot but not too noisy at night; has a shaded garden. The very good, popular restaurant (€€) serves regional favourites. *Restaurant closed Fri noon, Sun eve and Mon exc July and Aug.*

****Paris**, 14 Rue de Paris, **t** 05 53 07 28 16 (€). Simple rooms in the centre, with a bar serving snacks.

ⓘ Le Bugue >
Pl de l'Hôtel-de-Ville, t 05 53 07 20 48, www.perigord.com/bugue

Village du Bourant
t 05 53 08 41 99; open May–Sept daily 10–7; mid-Feb–April and Oct–mid-Nov daily 10–5; guided tours in English July and Aug 1pm; adm

Sangliers et Cerfs de Mortemart
t 05 53 03 21 30; open June–mid-Sept daily 10–7, plus Wed in school hols; guided tours 3pm

Musée Napoléon
t 05 53 03 24 03; open July and Aug daily 10.30–12.30 and 2.30–6.30; June and first half Sept daily 3–6; by reservation rest of year (for four or more)

Just beyond the Terre des Oiseaux, the **Village du Bourant** makes a game attempt to recreate Périgord of a century ago with craft demonstrations such as walnut-oil pressing and the carving of *sabots* (wooden clogs) – you can understand how one of these tossed into a machine could mother a new word, 'sabotage'. There are fairground rides in summer. You can also visit the wild boars and stags at the **Sangliers et Cerfs de Mortemart**.

To the north of Le Bugue, off the D710, is the **Napoleon museum** at Cendrieux, with more than 500 objects that belonged to France's famous emperor and his family. The museum is today run by one of his descendants.

From Le Bugue the D31E follows the Vézère to its confluence with the Dordogne at Limeuil (*see* p.180); becoming the D51, the road crosses the Dordogne for Le Buisson, from where the D25 goes to Cadouin (*see* p.176).

Down the Dordogne I

The 'Dore water' ('Dore d'eau') begins with a waterfall in the Auvergne, but by the time it makes its first appearance in Quercy, its regal character has been formed. From here on it meanders dreamily to the ocean in a series of elegant hairpins, or cingles. At Bergerac, it becomes a wine river, creating the perfect conditions for the likes of Monbazillac and St-Emilion. To defend such a prize, enough castles were built along its banks to make it the Loire valley of the Middle Ages. It's also one of the finest rivers in France for swimming, kayaking and canoeing: statisticians have rated it the republic's cleanest river.

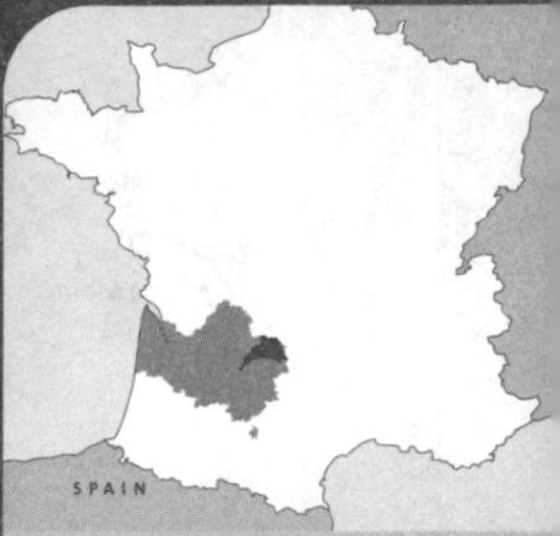

09

Don't miss

1. Golden Renaissance curlicues
   Sarlat p.159
2. A town stood on its side
   Rocamadour p.143
3. Riding a gondola into the Earth's bowels
   Gouffre de Padirac p.141
4. Seven towers
   Martel p.151
5. Romanesque charms
   Souillac p.154

See map overleaf

Down the Dordogne I

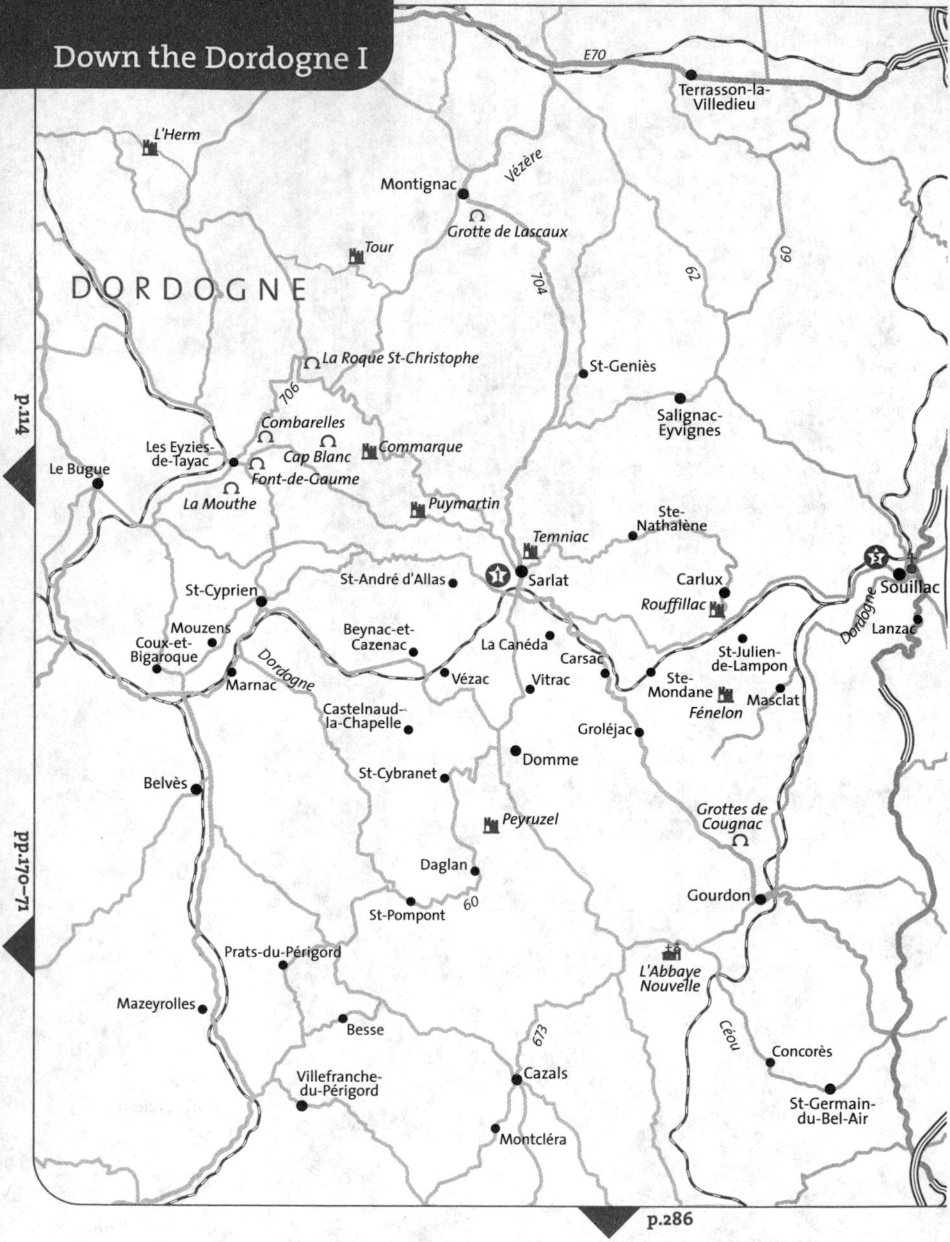

p.114

pp.170–71

p.286

Don't miss

1. Sarlat **p.159**
2. Rocamadour **p.143**
3. Gouffre de Padirac **p.141**
4. Martel **p.151**
5. Souillac **p.154**

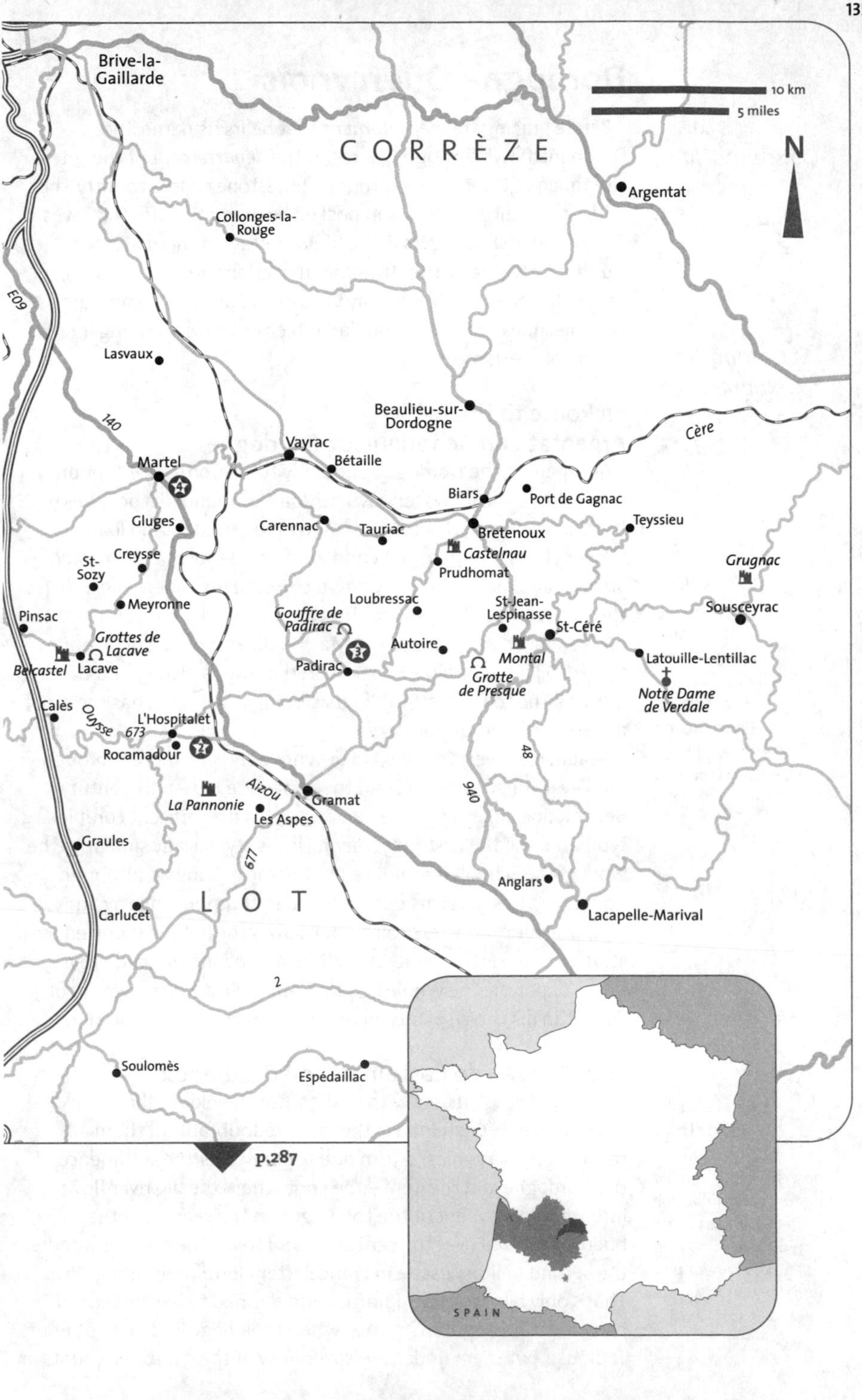
Brive-la-Gaillarde
10 km
5 miles
N
CORRÈZE
Argentat
Collonges-la-Rouge
E09
Lasvaux
140
Beaulieu-sur-Dordogne
Cère
Vayrac
Martel
Bétaille
4
Biars
Port de Gagnac
Gluges
Carennac
Tauriac
Bretenoux
Teyssieu
Castelnau
Creysse
St-Sozy
Prudhomat
Grugnac
Meyronne
Loubressac
St-Jean-Lespinasse
Sousceyrac
Pinsac
Gouffre de Padirac
St-Céré
Grottes de Lacave
Autoire
3
Montal
Latouille-Lentillac
Belcastel
Lacave
Padirac
Grotte de Presque
Notre Dame de Verdale
Calès
Ouysse
673
L'Hospitalet
Rocamadour
2
48
Aizou
Gramat
La Pannonie
940
Les Aspes
Graules
677
Anglars
LOT
Carlucet
Lacapelle-Marival
2
Soulomès
Espédaillac
SPAIN

p.287

Dordogne Quercynois

...Laisse,
laisse-moi faire,
et un jour,
ma Dordogne
Si je devine bien,
on te connaîtra
mieux
Et Garonne et le
Rhône, et ces
autres grands
dieux
En auront
quelque envie
et possible
vergogne
La Boétie,
born in Sarlat

Before gracing the *département* that bears its name, the Dordogne flows through Quercy, or the *département* of the Lot. Like much of Quercy, this is rugged limestone causse country, shot with green velvet valleys and pocked by dramatic cliffs and caves. One of the first such pits is the biggest maw of them all, the Gouffre de Padirac; other five-star attractions are Rocamadour, which draws in nearly as many visitors as Euro-Disney, and the Romanesque carvings in Souillac, which outclass anything in snooty old Périgord.

En Route to the Lot: Argentat and Beaulieu-sur-Dordogne

Maison du Patrimoine
t 05 55 28 10 91; open June–Sept daily 10–12 and 3–6

At **Argentat**, the Dordogne suddenly turns from a swift mountain river into a civilized waterway. The Romans founded a port town here, and for centuries the boatmen of Argentat would load timber, cheese, leather, pelts and wine on to their flat-bottomed *gabares* and make their way down to Bordeaux, where the *gabares* themselves would be sold for firewood. The old quay at Argentat has several on display, and the **Maison du Patrimoine** on Avenue Gilbert Dillange has information on the town's history and the *gabares*. The town itself, under its sloping *lauze* roofs, has the air of a merry, prosperous pensioner.

Beaulieu, a lovely town 25km downriver, is even more thoroughly medieval, constructed around the showcase 12th–13th-century Benedictine abbey church St-Pierre, with a magnificent complex tympanum of the *Last Judgement*. This is stylistically similar to the work of the School of Toulouse in Moissac or Soulliac, although here Christ has his arms outstretched in triumph while a carnival of apocalyptic monsters roll below across the lintel, supported by a strange figure Freda White described as 'flowing upward like a flame of prayer'. The whole inspired Abbot Suger, the inventor of Gothic, in his choice of a tympanum for Paris's St-Denis in 1140.

The Château de Castelnau and Bretenoux

Château de Castelnau
t 05 65 10 98 00; open for 30min guided tours May and June daily 9.30–12.30 and 2–6.30; July and Aug daily 9.30–7; Sept and April daily 10–12.30 and 2–5.30; Oct–Mar Wed–Mon 10–12.30 and 2–5.30

The Dordogne bristles with castles, but the oldest, the burnished red **Château de Castelnau** is the most redoubtable of them all, rising high on a conical, 230m outcropping over the confluence of the Dordogne and the Cère – the spot where the big river flows into the *département* of the Lot. Begun in the year 1000, the building evolved over the centuries, and today the castle is rated the second military castle in France after Pierrefonds in the Oise. That's only fair, for its disdainful lords claimed to be 'the second barons of Christendom'. In 1184, when their liege lord. the Count of Toulouse. put them under the suzerainty of the nearby viscounts of

Getting to and around Bretenoux and Environs

The main SNCF **train** line between Paris and Toulouse (via Limoges) stops at Brive-la-Gaillarde, where you get off to transfer to Bretenoux on the Brive–Aurillac line.

Buses link St-Céré with Bretenoux, and with Lacapelle-Marival and Figeac in Quercy (*see* p.293 and p.297). For times, call Car Delbos, **t** 05 65 38 25 04.

For a **taxi** in Bretenoux, call **t** 05 65 10 90 90. You can hire **bikes** and mountain bikes in Bretenoux at Cycles Peugeot, Avenue de la Libération, **t** 05 65 38 41 56; in St-Céré at 45 Rue Faidherbe, **t** 05 65 38 03 23. In July and August you can also hire a **canoe** in Bretenoux, **t** 06 15 84 02 20, *www.knoe.fr*.

Turenne, they were so insulted that only after the King of France intervened did they agree to pay the most begrudging tribute to Turenne: one egg, ceremoniously transported by a yoke of four oxen. In 1851 much of the château was damaged by arson, but Jean Mouliéret, tenor at the Opéra Comique, came to the rescue, rebuilding and sumptuously refurnishing one wing; his *objets d'art* and collection of triptyches remain. Inside you can see the Grande Salle, where the Etats du Quercy met, fragments of 11th-century sculpture, the chapel, vaulted cellars and the deep, long-forgotten *oubliettes*, where seven skeletons were discovered.

Clustered at the foot of the stone behemoth, the hamlet of **Prudhomat-Castelnau** is worth a stop for its 15th-century Collégiale, with Renaissance windows and sculptures. The main urban venture of the lords of Castelnau, however, was the *bastide* of Bretenoux founded on the left bank of the Cère in 1277. Now making some claim as 'Jam Capital of Europe' thanks to its two large jam companies, it retains its typical grid plan, as well as some medieval arcades and houses in Place des Consuls, the old market square. It also has one of the most pleasant swimming holes on the Dordogne, on the Ile de la Bournatelle. Ask at the tourist office (*see* p.140) about a night tour you can make by car to see the best bits of local villages illuminated.

St-Céré and St-Laurent-les-Tours

From Bretenoux it's 9km south on the D940 to **St-Céré**, a charming town set romantically on the banks of the Bave, or 'babbler', which tumbles down the *causse* to join the Dordogne. St-Céré reached its peak in the 15th century and has never had any

Vin des Côteaux de Glanes

Just east of Bretenoux, Glanes is the epicentre of one of France's least-known *vins de pays*. Grown on the slopes of the mountains of Auvergne, a combination of 45% Gamay-Beaujolais, 45% Merlot, and 10% Ségalin, Côteaux de Glanes was first mentioned in 840 and began to make a comeback in a serious way in 1966. In 1976, the growers formed a cooperative, now called the **Vignerons du Haut-Quercy, t** 05 65 39 73 42; to maintain quality, production is limited to 30 hectares.

Côteaux de Glanes, red or rosé, can be drunk after the first year, when it has a cherry fragrance; after three to five years it grows spicy, with grace notes of cinnamon and cloves. You can take in most of the wine-growing area, and a good bit of first-rate scenery as well, in a circular tour, continuing east of Glanes to Teyssieu, then continuing down to St-Céré on the little D40.

Jean Lurçat and the Renaissance of French Tapestry

After extensive travels in Spain, North Africa and the Middle East, painter Jean Lurçat (1892–1966) spent four decades covering canvases with his memories of the colourful designs of the indigenous peoples he had met, marked by a streak of fantasy and an interest in natural forms. In 1939 he was appointed head designer of the Aubusson tapestry factory – a task that marked a turning point both in his career and in the history of French tapestry. For by the 20th century, the proud art of Aubusson, the Gobelins and Beauvais had hit rockbottom, reduced to endlessly reproducing cartoons from the age of the big Louis, themselves servile imitations of paintings. Lurçat's great contribution was to return the art of tapestry to the weavers, creating cartoons that respected the medium and its techniques, combining abstract forms with a return to medieval stylization (see his famous *Apocalypse* of 1948 in Assy, Haute-Savoie). His main leitmotif at this time, a colourful cockerel or *Coq Arlequin*, was a symbol to restore Gallic pluck after the war.

compelling reason to change anything since. Before it found its destiny as a small art colony, tourist base for the upper Dordogne and centre of a renowned Festival of Voice in the summer, the visitors to St-Céré were pilgrims, come to visit the relics in the church of Ste-Spérie. Spérie, the daughter of the lord of St-Laurent-les-Tours, refused to marry a noble pagan and literally lost her head over him. She picked up her detached noggin and, a tidy soul, gave it a last wash before expiring (794). The exact spot of her martyrdom is marked with a black grid in front of the altar steps, and her bones lie in the Carolingian crypt, along with a curious Celtic altar, but it's only open on 12 October for her feast day. The rest of the church had to be rebuilt after the Wars of Religion, but there's an interesting *Nativity* in one of the right-hand chapels.

Place du Mercadial, St-Céré's beautiful main market square, is surrounded by half-timbered buildings; the stone benches on the Rue Pasteur corner were for centuries used by fishermen to display their catch. Other medieval-Renaissance houses are everywhere, especially along Rue du Mazel, Rue d'Ollier, Rue St-Cyr, Impasse Lagarouste and Quai des Récollets. On the latter, look out for the 18th-century Chapelle des Récollets, decorated with a charmingly painted casement ceiling.

Galerie d'Art Le Casino
t 05 65 38 19 60; open daily 8.30–12 and 2.30–8.30 exc Tues out of season

Atelier Musée Jean Lurçat
t 05 65 38 28 21; open part of April and mid-July–Sept daily 9.30–12 and 2.30–6.30; adm

The first artist to establish himself in the area was Jean Lurçat (*see* above), whose works are on permanent display in St-Céré's **Galerie d'Art Le Casino** and up at the craggy medieval towers of St-Laurent-les-Tours. These were purchased in 1945 by Lurçat, who had fallen in love with the area while fighting with the Maquis; they now form the **Atelier Musée Jean Lurçat**.

West of St-Céré: Château de Montal to Autoire

Château de Montal
t 05 65 38 13 72; open April–Oct Sun–Fri 9.30–12 and 2.30–6; adm

Only 2km from St-Céré, the golden **Château de Montal** was the special project of Jeanne de Balzac, daughter of Robert de Balzac, who had served as governor of Pisa during the wars of Italy. Jeanne, who had accompanied him, was enraptured by the Italian Renaissance, and decided to replant some of it in this corner of *la France profonde* as a surprise gift for her own son, Robert, while he was fighting in Italy; much to Jeanne's despair, he was killed before ever setting eyes on it. After surviving all subsequent wars and the Revolution, the château fell at the end of the 19th century into the hands of a greedy speculator who spent 22 years stripping it of every decoration. In 1908, when only the frame of the staircase remained, an oil tycoon named Maurice Fénaille stepped in, bought Jeanne's château, repurchased as many of its original works as he could, and had copies made of the bits the Americans wouldn't sell back. The sculptures that had been purchased by the Louvre were returned when Fénaille donated the château and all its fittings to the state in 1913.

From outside, Montal looks like a typical medieval castle, but inside the rough walls a magical courtyard opens up, decorated with lovely façades, ornate dormers and an imaginative frieze more than 30m long, attributed to the same sculptors who worked in Biron (*see* p.350); note the intertwined initials of Jeanne and her sons Robert and Dordé. Seven of the finest Renaissance portrait busts in France occupy the niches between the windows and are said to depict accurately the features of Jeanne and her family. The decoration around one of the windows, where legend has it Jeanne often sat, watching for Robert's return, sums up her sorrow – a knight holds a scroll reading *Plus d'espoir* ('no more hope'). Death accompanies a decapitated youth gripping his skull.

The interior is just as beautiful: the meticulous grand stair in the Italian style, in golden cream stone, the grand chimney supporting a heraldic stag with golden antlers, the guard room vaulted with 'basket handle' arches, the walnut table carved from one tree, the rooms full of Renaissance furniture, ceramics, paintings, tapestries and 17th-century German stained glass. Even the graffiti on the walls is quality – left by Léon Gambetta of Cahors, the hero of 1870. After the château you can play the pretty nine-hole **Golf de Montal**, with three practice holes, and pitching and putting greens.

Golf de Montal
t 05 65 10 83 09; open daily, call for times

From here the D673 ascends past **St-Jean-Lespinasse**, with some Romanesque carvings in its fort-like church, to St-Médard-de-Presque and the **Grotte de Presque**, with chambers full of draperies, stone waterfalls and other geological wonders, most strikingly the 'candles' in the 'Hall of Wonders', brilliant white and 8.5m tall.

Grotte de Presque
t 05 65 38 07 44; open for 40min visits July and Aug daily 9.30–6.30; mid-Feb–June and Sept daily 9.30–12 and 2–6; Oct–early Nov daily 10–12 and 2–5; adm

Another 4km down the D673, turn right for the **Cirque d'Autoire**, where a belvedere overlooks the real, 30m falls of the Autoire; cross the bridge and follow the path for a bird's-eye view from the *cirque* (natural amphitheatre) to little **Autoire** and the Dordogne valley. Often picked out as an example of a true Quercynois village, Autoire has steep brown-tiled roofs forming an exquisite ensemble around its Romanesque/Renaissance church; even in the 1700s various nobles and bourgeois of Paris chose it for holiday homes.

Ferme de Siran
t 05 65 38 74 40; call for times

From here the D135 leads to another exceptionally lovely village, **Loubressac**, a 15th-century eagle's nest with sloping brown-tiled roofs and 'one of the finest views in the realm' according to 17th-century writer Savinien d'Alquié, overlooking the confluence of the Bave, the Cère and the Dordogne. It's home to the **Ferme de Siran**, where you can stock up on luxury woollies made from the angora provided by its goats.

East of St-Céré: the Ségala

The region to the east of St-Céré is called the Ségala, the 'rye land' (*seigle*), where wheat refuses to grow. Limestone gives way to grey granite here on the frontier of the Cantal – the cold spot of France. There are a few things to see in this far corner of Quercy, although the deep chestnut forests, heather and pure air have something to be said for them. One place to aim for is the striking 15th-century pilgrimage church of **Notre-Dame de Verdale**, near Latouille-Lentillac, clinging precariously to the rock face high over the Tolerme gorge – take the narrow road off the D30 to the top and walk down. At Latouille-Lentillac is a nature walk, *Sentier Art Nature*, bordered by 20 various sculptures by local artists.

Plan d'Eau de Tolerme
open July and Aug daily 9.30–6.30

Further east, old grey **Sousceyrac** is the largest town in the region, once fortified (see the Porte Notre-Dame, topped by a chapel) and ruled by the viscounts of Turenne. They are responsible for the 15th-century **Château de Grugnac**, 1km north, still bearing its charming *lauze* roof; more recent bosses have recently endowed Sousceyrac with the **Plan d'Eau de Tolerme** (8km south), the largest body of water in the whole *département*, with windsurfing, rowing and other activities for a pleasant day by or on the lake. You can also stroll through the **forest of Luzette**, following a path lined by more than 70 species of trees and bushes, with information panels. The tourist office (*see* opposite) will tell you about many other walks and sporting actitivies in the area.

ⓘ Argentat >
Place de Maïa, t 05 55 28 16 05, www.argentat.fr

ⓘ Bretenoux >
Avenue de la Libération, t 05 65 38 59 53, www.ot-bretenoux.com

Market Days in Bretenoux and Environs

Argentat: Thursday mid-June–mid-Sept.
Bretenoux: Thursday and Saturday.
St-Céré: Saturday, plus fairs first and third Wednesday of month.

Where to Stay and Eat in Bretenoux and Environs

Bretenoux ✉ 46130

****Domaine de Granval**, St-Michel Loubéjou, halfway to St-Céré, **t** 05 65 38 63 99, *www.domainedegranval.com* (€€). Seven well-furnished rooms in a nicely restored farmhouse, plus a pool, playground and restaurant. *Closed several wks in winter (call for details); restaurant lunch Mon, Sat and Sun, and Sun eve in winter.*

Ferme de Borie, t 05 65 38 41 74 (€). A *chambres d'hôte* on a 14th-century farmhouse, with a panoramic terrace.

Port de Gagnac ✉ 46130

****Le Vieux Port, t** 05 65 38 50 05 (€€–€). A modest option east of Bretenoux, in a calm location by the river, with its own restaurant (€€€–€€). *Closed mid-Dec–early Jan; restaurant Sun eve and Mon lunch.*

St-Céré >
Place de la République, t 05 65 38 11 85, www.quercy-tourisme.com/saint-cere

Sousceyrac >>
Place de l'Eglise, t 05 65 33 02 20, www.sousceyrac-ot.net

St-Céré ✉ 46400

***Ric**, 2km south of town towards Leyme, **t** 05 65 38 04 08, *www.jpric.com* (€€€–€€). Five rooms with great views over St-Céré, a lovely pool, and a pretty restaurant (€€€) serving southwest classics with a creative touch. It's half board only in season. *Closed early Nov–Easter; restaurant lunch.*

***Trois Soleils de Montal**, St-Jean Lespinasse, **t** 05 65 10 16 16, *www.lestroissoleils.fr.st* (€€€–€€). A large villa with spacious rooms with balconies, a pool, tennis and mini-golf (and real golf up the road), and a restaurant (€€€€–€€). *Closed Jan–mid-Feb; restaurant Mon lunch, plus Sun and Mon eve and Tues lunch out of season.*

Le France, 181 Avenue F. de Maynard, **t** 05 65 38 02 16, *www.lefrance-hotel.com* (€€–€). Cosy modern rooms, a flowery garden and a pool, and an elegant restaurant (€€€–€€). *Closed mid-Dec–Jan and Fri out of season; restaurant lunch Mon–Sat.*

Hôtel Le Touring, Place de la République, **t** 05 65 38 30 08, *www.hoteldutouring.com* (€). A central hotel with serviceable rooms with TVs and telephones. *Closed Jan and Feb.*

Victor Hugo, 7 Avenue Victor Hugo, **t** 05 65 38 16 15, *www.hotel-victor-hugo.fr* (€). A 16th-century inn in the centre, with 16 pretty rooms and excellent food (€€€–€€). *Restaurant closed Mon, Sun eve in summer, and a couple of wks in Mar and Oct.*

Hôtel-Restaurant Lescure, on road to St-Céré, Leyme, **t** 05 65 38 90 07 (€). A well-positioned, pleasant hotel with a pool, run by the same family for more than 50 years. The *patron* is an avid art collector. The restaurant (€€–€) offers solid regional cuisine. *Closed Christmas hols; restaurant Sat and Sun eves out of season.*

Loubressac ✉ 46130

***Relais de Castelnau**, **t** 05 65 10 80 90, *www.relaisdecastelnau.com* (€€€–€€) Well-equipped rooms, a pool and a tennis court. The restaurant serves local specialities. *Closed Sun and Mon.*

Lou Cantou, **t** 05 65 38 20 58 (€€–€). An old stone building with fine views and a restaurant (€€€–€). *Closed 2wks Feb and mid-Oct–mid-Nov; restaurant Sun eve and Mon Nov–Mar.*

Sousceyrac ✉ 46190

Au Déjeuner de Sousceyrac, **t** 05 65 33 00 56. Eight pleasant rooms (€€) and a restaurant (€€€–€€) serving appetizing dishes featuring local ingredients. Booking is advised. *Closed 2wks in Feb; restaurant Mon and Sun eve out of season.*

Latouille-Lentillac ✉ 46400

Chez Gaillard, **t** 05 65 38 10 25, *www.hotel-gaillard.fr* (€). Comfortable rooms near the river and a restaurant (€€) serving the usual southwest offerings. *Closed 1wk in early summer, Nov and Sun out of season.*

Padirac and Rocamadour

A *gouffre* is an immense hole – easy to remember once you know that French trappers named the burrowing critters they found in America *gaufres*, or gophers. Of the *gouffres* dotting the area southwest of Bretenoux, the most awesome is the Gouffre de Padirac, near the vertical cliff-dwellers' town of Rocamadour.

Gouffre de Padirac

Gouffre de Padirac
t 05 65 33 64 56, www.gouffre-de-padirac.com; open April–early July and Sept daily 9–12 and 2–6; rest of

Had a gopher dug the pit in Padirac, it would have to have been the size of the *Titanic* – this chasm plunges down 90m through the limestone of the Causse de Gramat before forming 21km of galleries – at least, that's the length that's been explored so far. But not only is the Gouffre de Padirac spectacularly huge, much of it is spectacularly beautiful. For centuries this great opening,

Getting to and around Padirac and Rocamadour

The main SNCF **train** line between Paris and Toulouse (via Limoges) stops at Brive-la-Gaillarde, where you can get off and transfer to Padirac-Rocamadour station on the secondary Brive–Toulouse line. For train times, call the station at nearby Gramat (**t** 05 65 38 71 27). The station is 4km from Rocamadour; for a **taxi** to take you to Rocamadour or to Padirac, call **t** 05 65 50 14 82.

Only visitors booked at Rocamadour hotels are allowed to bring **cars** in. In July and August the nearer car parks outside the town gates fill up fast – park on top at the château or a 0.5km walk away at L'Hospitalet and walk or take the **lifts** (€2 one way; €3 return) to the shrines. The lifts are also handy if you have trouble walking (the steps aren't steep, but there are 223 of them). A second lift goes from the shrines to the castle. A little **train** runs between car parks in the valley and the site 10–7.30 (**t** 05 65 33 67 84; adults €3.50 return); it also does summer tours of Rocamadour by night, when it's lit up.

July daily 9–6; Aug daily 8.30–6.30; Oct–early Nov daily 10–12 and 2–5; long queues, so get here at least 30 mins before opening; adm exp; bring sunhat and sweater; picnic tables, snack bars and restaurants by site

35m in diameter, was regarded as the entrance to hell itself. The story goes that St Martin was riding his mule through Padirac, downcast at his failure to convert any pagans on the *causse*, when the Devil happened by with a squadron of demons, all bearing sackfuls of condemned souls. Satan offered to hand them over to Martin if the saint could get over an obstacle of his creation. Martin agreed, and Old Nick stomped his foot and opened up a great chasm. Martin said a little prayer and spurred on his mule, which leapt across the abyss (you can still see the hoofprints); the furious Satan gave Martin the souls and leapt with his devils into the pit, which took them straight to hell. In 1889, Edouard Martel, one of the founding fathers of speleology, made the first scientific exploration of the *gouffre*; by 1898 it had been opened to the public. Investigations uncovered tools and animal bones from around 50,000 BC 8km from the entrance.

The 90-minute guided tour starts with a long descent by lifts or stairs into the cool depths of the cavity, formed by water dissolving the limestone over millions of years. The chamber was domed until the weight of the roof grew too great and it collapsed; now the floor is covered by a pyramid of rubble. You're left to wander past a spring and down a long underground canyon formed by a river. At the end, there's often another long wait to board the gondolas that row you along the Rivière Plane, the 'smooth river', which flows underground into the Dordogne; in 1996 a diver-speleologist found the exact point of its resurgence, under the Cirque de Montvalent. Along this shadowy River Styx (with a little imagination, some of the gondoliers could pass for Charon), the most extraordinary decoration is the *Grande Pendeloque*, or Great Pendant, an enormous stalactite that almost touches the water.

When you disembark on the far bank, you may have yet another wait for a guide, who will lead you on foot up the narrow *Pas du Crocodile*, past a 40m stalactite pillar into the *Salle des Grands Gours*. A *gour* is a natural limestone dam, and here the *gours* create a fascinating series of basins of clear water, flowing one into the other, with a 6m waterfall and a green lake at the end. Beyond lies another little lake, *Lac Supérieur*, fed only by rainwater penetrating the limestone. None of this prepares you for the climactic *Salle du Grand Dôme* – an uncollapsed *gouffre*, a vaulted space that soars up to 93m and in volume could contain two cathedrals of Notre-Dame; as you climb the steps through this fantastical space, with a grandiose view over the lakes, the only way you can take in the immensity is to note how tiny the people are on the far end.

Rocamadour

Rocamadour

Just southwest of Padirac lies Rocamadour, which proudly bills itself as the 'Second Site in France', after the Mont St-Michel in Normandy. The two share extraordinary, fantastical settings, the very kind of natural sacred, magical places that attract legends like lightning rods. Rocamadour is the medieval French version of a Pueblo village in North America, a vertical cliff-dwellers' town, the beautiful golden stone houses and chapels piled on top of one another over a deep ravine, while far, far below the little Alzou continues its work of aeons, cutting even deeper into the gorge.

There are several approaches: the most dramatic is via **Carlucet**, east of the N20 and south of Rocamadour – a narrow winding road that comes out directly under Rocamadour. Wider roads south of Lacave, east of the N20, go via **Calès**, a picturesque hamlet with a midget château, and, a bit further on where the road crosses the blue-green Ouysse, a 13th-century working mill, the **Moulin de Cougnaguet**, that was built by Cistercian monks and fortified against flour thieves and – by the looks of it – against time as well.

Moulin de Cougnaguet
t 05 65 32 63 09; open for demonstrations April–Sept daily 10–12 and 2–5; 1st half Oct daily 10.30–12 and 2–5; adm

Coming from Lacave, you know you're almost there when the road leads up to **L'Hospitalet**, where everyone stops for the picture-postcard view across to Rocamadour, wedged improbably under its overhanging cliff. It is a view that has been enjoyed especially after 1050, when a hostel-hospital was founded by Hélène de Castelnau for pilgrims en route to Compostela. L'Hospitalet was inhabited as early as the Upper Palaeolithic era; its **Grotte des Merveilles** has, besides stalactites, lakes and other subterranean fancies, mostly fantastical rock formations, and some rather deteriorated artwork (negative hands, animals) that dates back to 20,000 BC. It suggests, if nothing else, that the remarkable site of Rocamadour was a holy place long before any of its stories were written.

Grotte des Merveilles
t 05 65 33 67 92; open April–June and Sept daily 10–12 and 2–6; July and Aug daily 9–7; Oct–mid-Nov daily 10–12 and 2–5, or until 6 in Nov school hols; adm

Legends and History

The late 11th-century origins of Rocamadour's cult of the Black Virgin are murky enough, and coincide neatly with the founding of the hostel at L'Hospitalet and the sudden flood of passing pilgrims. On the other hand, the Benedictines of Tulle, the promoters of Rocamadour, were hardly the only ones to suddenly find miracles and saintly relics – the money-generating roadside attractions of the Middle Ages – along the busy Way to Compostela. The cult's legitimacy was given a big boost in 1166 when a man's body was discovered buried near the altar. Over the centuries, the story evolved that this unknown was none other than St Zaccheus, the publican who climbed the tree to see Jesus. Later, he and his wife, St Veronica (of the holy handkerchief), fled Palestine in an angel-powered boat and lived near Limoges; when Veronica died, Zaccheus came here as a hermit and built the first sanctuaries in the cliff-face. The locals called him 'the lover' or *Amator* for his devotion, hence Roc-Amadour, the rock of the lover or lover of rock. A second attraction was Durandal, the famous sword of Roland; just before he died at Roncesvalles, the hero confided his blade to St Michael, and the Archangel hurled it from the Pyrenees like a javelin straight into Rocamadour's cliff.

Yet always the chief attraction was the blackened, goddess-like statue of the Virgin, whose cult, along with that of chivalry, grew by leaps and bounds at the time of the crusades. Rocamadour's first important patron was Henry II of England, who endowed much of its treasure. His wayward eldest son, the Young King, Henry Court-Mantel – companion of Bertran de Born (*see* pp.33–35) – stole it in 1183 in order to pay his *routiers* in his war against his own father; he even, according to some, replaced the famous Durandal with his own sword. By the time the plunderers reached Martel, the Black Virgin got her revenge, striking young Henry down with a killer fever. Full of remorse, he asked his father's forgiveness, had a halter placed on his neck and laid himself naked in a bed of ashes and died. The Bishop of Limoges refrained from excommunicating the dead man when his grieving father promised to replace Rocamadour's losses.

The story had the same effect as the doings of the royals in today's tabloids, and made Rocamadour more famous than ever. It quickly recovered from pillaging to become one of the busiest pilgrimage shrines in France. Saints Louis, Dominic, Bernard, Anthony of Padua, Engelbert and the blessed Raymond Lull came, as did the kings of France and countless others, especially on the days of pardon and plenary indulgence, when the chronicles say that 30,000 thronged into the village to pick up their Get Out of Purgatory Free card. Others who came were less willing: thousands of criminals, Albigensian heretics and men who broke the Truce of God by fighting during Lent were ordered by ecclesiastical courts to make the pilgrimage to Rocamadour, to climb up the famous steps on their knees, to be bound in chains and led to the Virgin to confess and apologize (*amende honorable*) and be purified by the priest. The priest would then strike off the chains, and present the shriven one with a certificate and a little lead medal with a picture of the Virgin to take back home.

Rocamadour suffered a near-fatal setback during the Wars of Religion, when the Huguenot Captain Bessonies came to lay waste and desecrate the shrine, hacking the relics of St Amadour to bits and leaving only the Virgin and her bell intact. After nearly three centuries of neglect, the bishops of Cahors began to restore – read over-restore –the shrines in the 1850s, giving the buildings a Disneylandish air that only increases in high summer, when Rocamadour is swamped by coach parties, and visitors have to queue just to get into the narrow lanes of the village. Arrive early in the morning to avoid the worst; better still, come in autumn when Rocamadour is at its most magical.

The Village

The holy road from L'Hospitalet enters Rocamadour by way of the 13th-century Porte du Figuier, one of four gates that defended the village's one real road. Once you're in, past the gauntlet of souvenir stands and a waxworks museum, you'll find the lift near the second gate, towered Porte Salmon. Beyond, the 15th-century Palais de la Couronnerie is now the **Hôtel de Ville,** where two tapestries of local flora and fauna by Jean Lurçat are on display. The street continues through another gate into the **Quartier du Coustalou**, the prettiest and least restored part of the village, with jumbly little houses and a fortified mill.

Hôtel de Ville
t 05 65 33 62 59; open May–early June and late Aug–early Sept daily 10–12.30 and 1.30–6.30; July and early Aug daily 10–7.30; early Sept–Oct daily 10–12.30 and 2–5.30; Nov–mid-Mar daily 2–5; mid-Mar–April daily 10–12.30 and 1.30–6; adm; tickets from tourist office in cité

The *Grand Escalier* into the holy city begins back at **Place de la Carretta**. The first 144 steps lead up to Place des Senhals, where merchants sold lead holy medals (*senhals* in Occitan) stamped with a picture of the Virgin. Rocamadour's oldest street, Rue de la Mercerie, extends from here, with the 14th-century Maison de la Pomette at its end. From here, continue up through the gate under the over-restored **Fort**, sometime residence of the bishops of Tulle. Tulle remained in charge of Rocamadour throughout the Middle Ages, despite the attempts by Marcilhac and other abbeys to muscle in on the action.

At the top of the steps the small square, **Parvis de St-Amadour**, is the centre of the holy city, where the pilgrim could visit seven churches – just as in Rome but in a much abbreviated space. These days only **Notre-Dame** and the **Basilique St-Sauveur** are open all year round; for the other chapels of **St-Michel, St-Anne, St-Blaise** and **St-Jean-Baptiste**, and the **Crypt of St-Amadour**, you need to join a guided tour.

Parvis de St-Amadour
Notre-Dame and St-Sauveur open summer daily 8am–9pm; rest of year daily 8.30–6.30
St-Michel, St-Anne, St-Blaise, St-Jean-Baptiste, and Crypt of St-Amadour open for tours by appt with tourist office (see p.147)

The 11th–13th-century Basilique St-Sauveur makes good use of the cliff for one of its walls. It was originally built with two equal naves; another was added to cope with the crowd of pilgrims. Over the altar hangs a painted wooden 16th-century Christ shown crucified on a tree, His right side pierced by the lance instead of the customary left. A Basque-style wooden gallery runs along the side.

Steps lead down into another of the seven churches, the simple 12th-century Crypt St-Amadour, where the body of the mysterious hermit was venerated.

Musée Trésor d'Art Sacré
t 05 65 33 23 23; open July and Aug daily 9–7; rest of year daily 9.30–12 and 2–6; adm

The Parvis also has the **Musée Trésor d'Art Sacré**, with documents and precious works of sacred art – medieval reliquaries from Limoges, stained glass, 17th-century *ex votos* – dedicated to atheist composer Poulenc, who converted to Catholicism and composed his *Litanies à la Vierge Noire de Rocamadour* after a vision here in 1936.

Château de Rocamadour
t 05 65 33 23 23; open April–Oct daily 9–9; Nov–Dec daily 9–6; Jan–Mar daily 9–5; adm

On the other side of St-Sauveur, another 25 steps lead up to the church of Notre-Dame and above it, the holy of holies, the Flamboyant Gothic Chapelle Notre-Dame. This dates only from 1479, after a rock crashed off the cliff through the original sanctuary. Inside, darkened by candle smoke, the miraculous Black Virgin still holds court. Carved from walnut in the 11th century, she sits stiffly on her throne, almost a stick figure; the Christ Child balanced on her knee looks like Pinocchio. But the Black Virgin's primitive appearance only heightens her mystic power.

Rocher des Aigles
t 05 65 33 65 45; open April–June daily 1–5; 1st half July and last wk Aug daily 1–6; rest of July and Aug daily 11–6; Sept Mon–Sat 1–5 and Sun 1–6; Oct and Nov Mon–Sat 2–4, Sun 2–5; hourly flight shows, call for times; adm

The proof is in the pudding, or rather in the *ex votos*. Many are from Breton sailors (including two model boats) saved from shipwreck by the Virgin. Whenever she came through, the miracle would be foretold by the ringing of the 9th-century bell hanging from the roof. Chains from pilgrim petitioners still hang in the back of the chapel. Outside, high in the rock above the door, you can see the supposed Durandal, a rusty sword embedded in the stone, fastened by a chain to keep it from falling on someone's head.

Royaume des Abeilles
t 05 65 33 66 98; open May and June daily 10–12 and 1–6; July and Aug daily 10–6.30; April and 1st half Sept daily 10–12 and 1–5.30; last half Sept Mon–Fri 10–12 and 1–5.30, Sat and Sun 1–5.30; Oct daily 1–5

Sharing this upper square with Notre-Dame is the **Chapelle St-Michel**, with the overhanging cliff for a roof, decorated on the outside with good *modillons* and colourful 12th- or 13th-century frescoes representing the Annunciation and Visitation. The patron of travellers, St Christopher, is painted below; to catch a glimpse of him was good luck, so he was always made extra big. To see the faded fresco of *Christ in Majesty*, inside, you must take the tour.

Forêt des Singes
t 05 65 33 62 72; open May and June daily 10–12 and 1–6; July and Aug daily 9.30–6.30; April and 1–15 Sept daily 10–12 and 1–5.30; 16–30 Sept Mon–Fri 1–5.30, Sat and Sun 10–12 and 1–5.30; 1–5 Oct and weekends in Oct 9–12 and 1–5; early Nov and rest of year Sat, Sun and school and public hols 10–12 and 1–5; adm

Further up, a hairpin walk lined with the Stations of the Cross (or the much easier lift from the Parvis de St-Amadour) takes you up to the ramparts of the **château**, built in the 15th century, offering a vertiginous view high over the *causse*. This eagle's nest is also a true one, thanks to the breeding programme for birds of prey at the **Rocher des Aigles**.

Roadside Attractions

Rocamadour, the original medieval roadside attraction, has spawned its own share of secular distractions over the past quarter century. In L'Hospitalet the **Royaume des Abeilles** has exhibitions and courses on apiculture, while the **Forêt des Singes** allows you to meet, perhaps more intimately than you might wish, the 130 Barbary apes and macaques at liberty there. And there's

Féerie du Rail
t 05 65 33 71 06; performances April–mid-Nov; call ahead for schedules

Rocamadour Aérostat
t 06 79 24 28 21

Ferme de Découverte des Causses du Quercy
t 05 65 38 87 76; open April-Oct daily 10–6.30

the **Féerie du Rail**, an enormous model 1:87 diorama with 60 trains and a giant sound and light show. There are even some roadside geological attractions just to the south of Rocamadour – the **Gouffre de St-Sauveur**, a round, deep, blue-green pit, and the **Gouffre de Cabouy**, the resurgence of an underground river in the canyon of the Ouysse. Or you can float above it all in a *montgolfière* – a hot-air balloon – year-round depending on the weather, from **Rocamadour Aérostat**.

On the road going out to Lacave is the **Ferme de Découverte des Causses du Quercy**, where you can learn how a 19th-century farm worked and about the *causses*. There's a garden, a farmyard full of animals, a walk and demonstrations of goats'-cheese production.

ⓘ L'Hospitalet >
Maison du Tourisme,
t 05 65 33 22 00,
www.rocamadour.com

Tourist Information in and around Rocamadour

As well as the main **tourist office** in L'Hospitalet, there's a smaller branch in the *cité*. Both have information about guided tours and bike hire.

For details of events and visits to do with the **shrines**, contact Pèlerinage de Rocamadour, **t** 05 65 33 23 23, *www.notre-dame-de-rocamadour.com*.

Where to Stay and Eat in and around Padirac and Rocamadour

Padirac ✉ 46500

Montbertrand, 2.5km out of town on St-Céré road, **t** 05 65 33 64 47 (€€). Comfortable rooms, a swimming pool and a restaurant. *Closed Dec–Feb.*

****Auberge de Mathieu**, 300m from Gouffre, **t** 05 65 33 64 68, *www.promenades-gourmandes.com/pinquie.htm* (€). Seven comfortable rooms and a restaurant (€€€–€€) with a terrace. *Closed mid-Nov–mid-Mar.*

****Padirac Hôtel, t** 05 65 33 64 23, *www.padirac-hotel.com* (€). Another budget option near the Gouffre, part of Logis de France, a restaurant (€€€–€) with a shaded terrace. *Closed Dec–Mar.*

Camping Les Chênes, 0.5km from Gouffre, **t** 05 65 33 65 54, *www.campingleschenes.com* (€). A well-sited, shady camping ground, with chalet, bungalow, and mobile home hire, a pool, kayaking and other activities, and a restaurant. *Closed Oct–April.*

Rocamadour ✉ 46500

Rocamadour has a vast range of hotels, packed like sardines and all booked up well ahead in summer. One of the advantages of staying here is seeing the place first thing in the morning, or in the evening after all the coachloads have departed.

Rocamadour is famous throughout the southwest for its creamy, flat cylinders of goat's cheese, so special they've been classified like wine: AOC *cabécou de Rocamadour*. Connoisseurs like them ripe, pungent, and coated with a tawny crust – the perfect accompaniment to a well-aged Cahors, at their best June–Nov. If you and goat's cheese haven't been previously introduced, try a mild fresh white *cabécou* to start with, or have it grilled – heat takes away some of the immediately goaty impact and leaves a warm, soft, distinct taste. It's delicious as a starter with salad.

*****Domaine de la Rhue**, just outside town on N140, **t** 05 65 33 71 50, *www.domainedelarhue.com* (€€€–€€). A tranquil hotel with comfy rooms with stone walls and exposed beams. There's a pool, and the breakfasts are good. *Closed mid-Oct–Mar.*

*****Grand Hôtel Beau Site**, *cité médievale*, **t** 05 65 33 63 08, *www.bw-beausite.com* (€€€–€€). The fanciest place in town, a Best Western in a medieval house, with a pool and restaurant. Some rooms have four-posters. *Closed early Nov–early Feb.*

*****Le Troubadour**, Belveyre, 1km from town, **t** 05 65 33 70 27, *www.hotel-troubadour.com* (€€).

A well-kept little hotel, with a garden, a pool, magnificent views of the *causse* and a restaurant (€€€–€€). *Closed mid-Nov–mid-Feb.*

****Bellevue**, L'Hospitalet, **t** 05 65 33 62 10 (€). Decent rooms, parking and, just up the road, a restaurant (€€€–€€) serving traditional meals. *Closed Nov–Mar; restaurant Fri out of season.*

****Terminus des Pèlerins**, Place de la Carretta, **t** 05 65 33 62 14, *www.terminus-des-pelerins.com* (€€–€). A Logis de France hotel, and the best option in the centre for those on a budget. *Closed Nov–Easter.*

****Lion d'Or**, just beyond Porte du Figuier, **t** 05 65 33 62 04, *www.liondor-rocamadour.com* (€). An option that's as old-fashioned and traditional as it gets, with comfy rooms and solid Périgord cuisine such as tatin of foie gras with walnut sauce and duck with *cèpes* sauce in the restaurant (€€€–€), which looks out over the Alzou gorge. *Closed early Nov–Easter.*

****Panoramic**, L'Hospitalet, **t** 05 65 33 63 06, *www.hotelrocamadour.com* (€). A family-run hotel with a restaurant (€€€–€€), a pool and views on to Rocamadour. *Closed mid-Nov–mid-Feb.*

****Ste-Marie**, Place des Senhals, **t** 05 65 33 63 07, *www.hotel-sainte-marie.fr* (€). A simple family place in the heart of things. Pricier rooms have superb views, and the restaurant (€€) is one of the best in town – leave room for dessert. *Closed early Nov–Easter.*

Jehan de Valon, Grand Hôtel Beau Site (*see* p.147), **t** 05 65 33 63 08 (€€€–€€). A great place to try Rocamadour goats' cheese, in a panoramic dining room. The exquisite food also includes Causses du Quercy farm leg of lamb. *Closed mid-Nov–early Feb.*

Chez Anne-Marie, by Hôtel de Ville, **t** 05 65 33 65 81 (€€€–€). Filling dishes, many with local goats' cheese, and a famous walnut cake. *Closed lunch in winter.*

Around Rocamadour

******Château de Roumégouse**, 6km east at Rignac, **t** 05 65 33 63 81, *www.chateauroumegousse.com* (€€€€€–€€€). A romantic Relais et Châteaux hotel in a pretty park. The well-reputed restaurant (€€€) with its Louis XIII and Louis XV dining rooms offers traditional Quercy foie gras and truffle dishes, and seasonal dishes, beautifully finished with fresh herbs plucked daily from the owner's garden There's a shuttle to and from the station for guests. *Closed late Dec–Mar; restaurant Mon–Thurs lunch, plus Tues out of season.*

****Les Vieilles Tours**, 3km west at Lafage, **t** 05 65 33 68 01, *www.vieillestours-rocamadour.com* (€€€–€€). A sturdy manor house constructed between the 13th and 17th centuries, with two annexes, rooms giving on to the garden, and a swimming pool. The restaurant is one of the best in the area; half board is obligatory July and Aug. *Closed mid-Nov–mid-Mar; restaurant lunch exc Sun and public hols.*

****Le Petit Relais**, Calès, **t** 05 65 37 96 09, *www.le-petit-relais.fr* (€€–€). A pleasant country inn with a good restaurant (€€) offering unusual desserts. *Closed mid-Dec–mid-Jan and Sun out of season.*

Carennac to Lacave

This stretch of the Dordogne hugs islets and high cliffs as it flows past châteaux, a fascinating Romanesque abbey connected with the sweet-tempered archbishop Fénelon, the handsome medieval town of Martel and the splendid stalactite grotto at Lacave.

Prieuré St-Pierre
t 05 65 10 97 01; cloister open July and Aug daily 10–1 and 2–7; rest of year Mon–Sat 10–12.30 and 2–6.30; adm

Carennac

From the river, Carennac presents an enchanting higgledy-piggledy cluster of roofs, walls and turrets round its famous honey-coloured **Prieuré St-Pierre**. Founded in 932 by Frotard, Vicomte de Cahors, the priory was given by the bishop of Cahors to Cluny *c.* 1040. Fortified

Getting to and around Carennac, Lacave and Environs

The main SNCF **train** line between Paris and Toulouse (via Limoges) stops at Brive-la-Gaillarde, where you can transfer to a train heading south to Bétaille (4km from Carennac) or Vayrac on the Brive–Aurillac line. There is a **bus** that calls at Martel on its way between Souillac and Brive; for details, contact Voyages Belmon, **t** 05 65 37 81 15.

The steam **Train Touristique du Haut Quercy** (**t** 05 65 37 35 81) from Martel to St-Denis just east (at 11, 2.30 and 4 Sun and public hols April–Sept; plus Wed 1st half of July and Mon, Tues and Thurs 2nd half July–end of Aug) offers thrilling 1hr rides on the old railway line skirting cliffs over the Dordogne. A diesel train runs more regularly.

You can hire a mountain **bike** or **canoe** from Saga Team in Carennac, **t** 05 65 10 97 39.

in the 16th century, it repulsed Protestant attacks, preserving some of the finest Romanesque art in the area: the beautiful 12th-century tympanum over the porch, sculpted by the school of Toulouse with their favourite scene from the *Apocalypse* (Christ blessing in a mandorla), surrounded by the Evangelists and Apostles, divided into registers (as on Cahors cathedral). The frieze below is decorated with an unusual zigzag pattern of animals; in the shadowy interior, capitals carved with primitive birds, animals and monsters add to its atmosphere of archaic mystery. The interior has, unusually, a narthex made of columns. A painting of the Evangelists survives in one 15th-century chapel.

The **cloister**, which has one Romanesque and three Flamboyant Gothic galleries, was rescued from its fate as a pigsty in 1928. After the Revolution, when most of the carvings were hammered, the villagers sold off the priory's art, except for a piece that they particularly loved, the 15th-century *Mise en Tombeau* (found in the Salle Capitulaire off the cloister) – a poignant composition of eight intricately detailed figures. The Virgin's arms reach out stiffly in grief; Nicodemus and Joseph of Arimathea, who are dressed in Renaissance costumes, hold the shroud, while John, Mary Magdalene and the women in biblical draperies mourn (within the folds you can see the original paint). Here too are some 17th-century bas-reliefs on the life of Christ and a moving pietà carved from Carennac's stone.

At the south end of the cloister, the old kitchen with its monumental fireplace and refectory have been converted into a conference centre for the commune. During the work a 15th-century mural was uncovered, known as the *Dit des Trois Morts et des Trois Vifs* – three skeletons warning three cavaliers to reflect on earthly vanity. Over one of the fireplaces is a portrait of a dean of Carennac, François de Salignac. In the 17th century, the deanery became a personal fief of the influential Salignac de la Mothe-Fénelon family, who owned châteaux on either bank of the Dordogne; in 1674, the post was inherited by this dean's nephew, François de Salignac de la Mothe-Fénelon (1651–1715), who went on to further glory as the Archbishop of Cambrai (*see* p.150).

Fénelon, or the Price of Being a Good Man in Bad Times

If I could come back as anyone, I'd like to be Fénelon's valet.

Voltaire

Known for his gentle eloquence as the 'Swan of Cambrai', young François was bred for the Church from the earliest age and attended the seminary of St-Sulpice in Paris. In 1674, he inherited Carennac from an uncle and was given the task of bringing Protestant women back to the Catholic fold. Well-spoken and very tolerant for his bigoted age, Fénelon was so successful he attracted the attention of the pious Madame de Maintenon, morganatic wife of Louis XIV, herself a convert to Catholicism. In 1689 she had Louis appoint Fénelon tutor of his grandson and heir, the charmless Duke of Burgundy. The task took up so much of Fénelon's time that, in spite of tradition, he hardly had the chance to return to Carennac to compose his celebrated allegory for the duke's instruction, *Télémaque*. Fénelon's book, a lesson in truth, justice and virtue, follows the life of Odysseus' son Telemachus in Salentum, an aristocratic utopia where seven strictly defined classes lived a simple life and dressed according to their station, eliminating one of the banes of his time: luxury born of pride and the need to pay for it by soaking the poor. Tradition has it that Fénelon wrote his romance in Carennac's 'Tour de Télémaque'; Ile Barrade, facing Carennac in the Dordogne, was renamed Ile Calypso after the island in the novel.

It was during this period that the unworldly Fénelon became attracted to the quietist ideals of the mystic Madame Guyon, who preached the possibility of abandoning the soul to God's love without any of the outer disciplines or authority of the Church. In 1695, newly appointed to the princely post of Archbishop of Cambrai, Fénelon undertook to defend her preachings against the doughty Bishop of Meaux, Jacques Bénigne Bossuet, who upheld the authority of the Church. 'It is hard to get a great prelate condemned for trusting overmuch in the love of God,' as Albert Guérard commented, but by 1699 Bossuet had succeeded so completely that Fénelon's work had been condemned by the Pope, and the king dismissed him from his tutorial post (all of Fénelon's work went down the drain anyway, when the duke died three years before his terrible grandfather). Worse, *Télémaque* was published in court without its author's permission, and read by Louis as a satirical comment on his arrogant, bankrupt reign. Fénelon spent the rest of his life an outcast in Cambrai. His beloved Carennac fell into ruin and no longer sent him rents to relieve his poverty. He still asked to be buried there when he died, but this was denied. As a posthumous apology for Fénelon's treatment from Louis XIV, the regent had *Télémaque* printed; in the 18th century it went into more than 180 editions.

Centre d'Interprétation de l'Architecture du Patrimoine
t 05 65 33 81 36; open July–Sept Tues–Sun 10–12 and 2–6; Easter–June and Oct–early Nov Tues–Fri 10–12 and 2–6

Musée des Alambics et Aromathèque
t 05 65 10 91 16; open daily 10–1 and 2–7, with demos from 4.30 mid-June–Nov

Parc Aquatique La Saule
t 05 65 32 55 75; open mid-June–Sept daily (supervised bathing 12–7)

Besides its priory, Carennac, like any town worth its salt on the Dordogne, also has a château, this one dating from the 1500s and now housing the **Centre d'Interprétation de l'Architecture du Patrimoine et du Paysage du Pays de la Vallée de la Dordogne**, with exhibits on the river, from prehistoric times to the present, and covering art, history and the natural environment.

You can also visit the **Musée des Alambics et Aromathèque** to learn about different aromas and distilling lavender, and buy essential oils. And small fry will love a day splashing and sliding around like otters at the **Parc Aquatique La Saule** towards Bétaille.

Around Carennac

Cross the bridge over the Dordogne from Carennac and then make a right turn to reach **Tauriac**; its church houses some well-preserved 15th-century murals of ladies. A left turn at the bridge takes you to **Vayrac**, and the D119, leading up a steep hill to **Puy-d'Issolud**, a broad plateau that archaeological work has confirmed as the probable site of Uxellodunum, where the Gauls made their last stand against Julius Caesar's relentless legions. Ruins on the

Musée Gallo-Romain
t 05 65 32 52 50; open July and Aug Tues–Sun 10–12 and 4–6.30

plateau have been identified as belonging to Celtic fortifications, camps and temples; some finds are on display in a small **Musée Gallo-Romain** near the Syndicat d'Initiative.

Martel

Martel

Proud, staunchly medieval Martel, the 'City of Seven Towers', resolves under the microscope to a rustic village of 1,500 souls. It was severely depopulated during the last century, and many of its empty houses are being restored as summer homes for people from far away. Still, the population isn't nearly big enough for Martel. However small, this is a real city, and, beautiful as it is, it wears a melancholy air with so few around to share its beauty.

Martel means 'hammer', like the three hammers the city wears on its coat of arms, and like the hammer wielded by Charles Martel, scourge of the Muslims; a legend credits the grandfather of Charlemagne with founding the city in the 700s. In 1219, Martel received its charter as a free *commune*, a fief of the viscounts of Turenne; so it remained until 1738, when it was snapped up by the French Crown. In central **Place des Consuls** are the covered market and the huge Palais de la Raymondie, begun by the Turenne viscounts *c.* 1300, now the town hall and **Musée d'Uxellodunum**, with prehistoric and Gallo-Roman finds from Puy-d'Issolud, old maps and pharmacy jars. Its *beffroi* is the first of the 'seven towers'. Another is the belltower of St-Maur, a fortified but exquisite Gothic church built into the walls that retains a 12th-century portal with a relief of Christ Pantocrator in the style of Moissac. Superbly restored, it contains excellent stained glass from 1531 with scenes of the Passion, believed to be the work of students of Arnaut de Moles, the master of Auch cathedral. A few sculptural decorations can be seen in the odd corners; for a puzzle, see if you can find the three sleeping monks – the two angels under blankets don't count.

Musée d'Uxellodunum
t 05 65 37 30 03; closed for restoration at time of writing but normally open July and Aug Mon–Sat (call for times)

For the other five towers, you'll need to tour the rest of Martel. It won't take long: there are scarcely more than a dozen streets. One of the towers is the **Maison Fabri**, behind the market, where Henri Court-Mantel died from a fever shortly after his pillage of Rocamadour. The Tour de Tournamire at the northern gate doubled as a prison. Beyond this girdle of medieval defences, Martel has modern attractions: the piquant pleasures of **Reptiland**, abode of 104 species (250 specimens) of crocs, snakes, spiders and other cold-blooded beasts. Next door are some big greenhouses where 35 types of orchids are cultivated for sale; you can visit them by guided tour in July and August (same hours as Reptiland). But it's walnuts that are the serious business around here: the big fat tasty variety grown in the three surrounding *départements* (Corrèze, Lot and Dordogne) received their gourmet classification as AOC Noix du Périgord in 1999.

Reptiland
t 05 65 37 41 00; open July and Aug daily 10–6; Sept–mid-Dec and early Feb–June Tues–Sun 10–12 and 2–6; adm

North of Martel, at the northernmost tip of Quercy, the Causse de Martel naps under its cover of oak and beech forests. The villages of **Cavagnac** and **Lasvaux** both have simple Romanesque churches.

Gluges and Lacave

The Dordogne is at its scenic best between Martel and Souillac, meandering through dramatic countryside, often hemmed in by steep cliffs. South of Martel, the riverside village of **Gluges** fairly cowers beneath one of these lofty rock walls. There's an unusual church, half cut into the rock; the local baron, Gérard de Mirandol, built it after his return from the Crusades in 1108. A cave, converted to a fortress in the Middle Ages, can be reached from the village by a stairway carved into the cliff. Another cliff across the Dordogne, the **Cirque de Montvalent**, forms a striking natural amphitheatre; the river formed it ages ago before it chose its present course.

From here, the D23 to **Creysse** follows the river – terrifically scenic, if a bit dangerous, it climbs up and down the cliffs on one lane. Exquisite Creysse was built round a Romanesque church.

Grottes de Lacave
t 05 65 37 87 03; open April–June daily 9.30–12 and 2–6; July daily 9.30–12.30 and 1.30–6; most of Aug daily 9.30–6.30; late Aug–Sept daily 9.30–12 and 2–5.30; 2nd half Mar and Oct–early Nov daily 10–12 and 2–5; adm

Further downstream, well-named **Lacave** can show you one of France's subterranean wonders, the **Grottes de Lacave**, open to the public since 1905 – not as famous as Padirac but offering some unique sights. From the entrance, you travel on a miners' train, then in a lift into the caverns – 1.7km of them, including the 'Lac des Mirages', where the reflections of stalactites give the illusion of an underwater city. Some caverns are illuminated by backlights for strange phosphorescent effects. Lacave excels in unusual formations – 'eccentrics' such as the pillar shaped like a *tarasque*, the mythical monster of Tarascon, and the 'column of the spiders' feet'.

Préhistologia – Parc Préhistorique
t 05 65 32 28 28; open April and May Mon–Fri 2–6, Sun and public hols 10–12 and 2–6; June daily 10–12 and 2–6; July–late Aug daily 10–6.30; late Aug–mid-Sept daily 10–12 and 2–5.30; mid-Sept–Oct Sun 2–5; Nov school hols 2–5

Two kilometres from the caves, the **Préhistologia – Parc Préhistorique** tells the history of the world from the Big Bang to Neolithic times with lifesize dinosaur models and a reconstruction of a Neolithic village, in a wooded setting. It's fun for kids.

From Lacave the D43 continues to Souillac, passing the **Château de Belcastel** in a perfect clifftop setting over the river to meet one of the most graceful iron bridges you'll ever see, at **Pinsac**; an anonymous engineer of the Ponts et Chaussées, France's national public works office, designed it in the 1930s.

ⓘ Carennac >>
t 05 65 10 97 01, www.tourisme-carennac.com

Market Days from Carennac to Lacave

Martel: Wednesday and Saturday, including *marché au gras* in December and January, plus fairs on 23rd of each month.

Tauriac: Wednesday eve July and Aug.

Vayrac: Thursday and Saturday.

Where to Stay and Eat from Carennac to Lacave

Carennac ✉ 46110

******Auberge du Vieux Quercy**, **t** 05 65 10 96 59, *www.vieuxquercy.com* (€€€–€€). A former posthouse with a fair-sized pool, a garden and pretty rooms. The restaurant is an idyllic place to linger over duck *confit* with chives and lemon juice. *Closed mid-Nov–Mar; restaurant Wed and Thurs lunch in summer, rest of year Wed lunch and Sun–Thurs eve exc public hols.*

****Hostellerie Fénelon, t** 05 65 10 96 46, *www.hotel.fenelon.com* (€€–€). Authentic provincial rooms at the village entrance, plus a pool and a garden dining room (€€€–€€) offering *feuilleté* of morels and *cèpes* with cream and a truffle *jus*. *Closed Jan–mid-Mar and Fri out of season; restaurant Mon, Fri and Sat lunch out of season.*

****Hôtel des Touristes, t** 05 65 10 94 31, *www.hotel.touristes.com* (€). Nine basic rooms and a restaurant (€€€–€). *Closed Christmas–New Year; restaurant also Sat and Sun lunch in summer and Fri and Sat eve in winter.*

ⓘ Martel >
Place des Consuls,
t 05 65 37 43 44,
www.martel.fr

★ Château de la Treyne >>

Martel ✉ 46600

*****Relais Ste-Anne**, Rue Pourtanel, **t** 05 65 37 40 56, *www.relais-sainte-anne.com* (€€€€–€€). A pretty place set around a garden courtyard, with a pool. *Closed mid-Nov–mid-Mar.*

****Le Turenne**, Avenue Jean Lavayssière, **t** 05 65 37 30 30 (€). Simple rooms and a restaurant (€€€–€). *Closed Dec–Feb.*

La Mère Michèle, Rue de la Remise, **t** 05 65 37 35 66 (€€). Authentic traditional cuisine served by a genial host. *Closed Wed and Sun eve Mar–June, Sept and Oct, plus Nov–Feb.*

Ferme-Auberge Moulin du Lac de Diane, Les Landes, on St-Céré road, **t** 05 65 37 40 69 (€€–€). A 14th-century inn serving huge portions of traditional cuisine, with plenty of walnut sauces. There's also a walnut oil press where the southwest's favourite dressing is made, open for visits (Tues and Thurs afternoon July and Aug, afternoons Dec–Mar if you call first). *Closed Mon.*

Plein Sud, Place des Consuls, **t** 05 65 37 37 77 (€). Reliable, satisfying pizzas and other budget fare. *Closed Mon exc July and Aug, plus Oct–mid-Mar.*

Gluges ✉ 46600

****Hôtel des Falaises, t** 05 65 27 18 44, *www.les-falaises.com* (€). A hotel with a perfect setting under the cliffs, lovely gardens and a restaurant (€€€–€€) open only to guests; try the smoked salmon. *Closed end Nov–end Mar.*

Camping Les Falaises, t 05 65 37 37 78 (€). A lovely river site. *Closed Oct–April.*

Creysse ✉ 46600

****Auberge de l'Isle, t** 05 65 32 22 01 (€€–€). Lovely rooms, attentive service, a pool and a restaurant (€€) with canal views. *Closed Nov–mid-Mar.*

Meyronne ✉ 46200

*****La Terrasse, t** 05 65 32 21 60, *www.hotel-la-terrasse.com* (€€€–€€). The old riverside château of the bishops of Tulle, with beautiful rooms and suites, a pool and a fine restaurant. *Closed early Nov–early Mar; restaurant Tues lunch, plus Tues eve out of season.*

Camping du Port, near Creysse, **t** 05 65 32 27 59, *www.campingduport.com* (€). A lovely riverside site that featured in a French soap opera. *Closed Oct–April.*

Lacave ✉ 46200

******Château de la Treyne**, just west of town on river, **t** 05 65 27 60 60, *www.chateaudelatreyne.com* (€€€€€–€€€€). A Relais et Châteaux 14th-century castle high above the river, with 16 luxurious rooms and six apartments with river views, stately gardens, antiques, tapestries, a pool, magnificent stone terrace and a highly rated restaurant (€€€€–€€€). You can visit the formal gardens and chapel (*June–Sept Tues–Thurs 3–5*) and explore the forest. There's also the restored **Château du Bastit** 2km along a riverside path, with four rooms and an apartment, available nightly or weekly. Guests there can get meals from the château restaurant. *Restaurant closed lunch Tues–Fri, and mid-Nov–Easter exc Xmas and New Year.*

*****Le Pont de l'Ouysse, t** 05 65 37 87 04, *www.lepontdelouysse.fr* (€€€). A magical hotel in the same family for four generations, with a heated pool, a terrace and a wonderful restaurant (€€€€–€€€). *Closed mid-Nov–mid-Mar and Mon out of season; restaurant Mon and Tues lunch.*

Ferme-Auberge et Camping Calvel le Bougayrou, Calvel, on D23 to Meyronne, **t** 05 65 37 87 20. An arcadian farm offering tent pitches and delicious, filling renditions of *ferme-auberge* favourites (€€). Book ahead. *Closed Mon in summer, Mon–Fri rest of year.*

Into the Dordogne

Souillac

Souillac

Eglise Ste-Marie
open mid-June–mid-Dec daily 8.30–7, rest of year daily 8.30–6; ***guided tours*** *(inc town) July and Aug Thurs 5pm*

Souillac doesn't look like much from the dusty stretch of the N20 that passes through it, but its **church of Ste-Marie** makes it a mandatory stop – it's one of the jewels of Romanesque sculpture and architecture in the Midi. Ask at the tourist office (*see* p.156) about guided tours in English of the church and town. Souillac's current slogan, 'Gateway to the South', is based on the tradition that cicadas, the totem insect of the French Midi, only sing south of the 45th parallel; its name, however, actually comes from the Celtic *souilh*, or mudflat, the kind that boars like best – hence the bristling swine on its coat of arms.

The origins of Souillac are fairly typical: a monastery was founded here in the early 900s (reputedly by beloved smithy saint, St Eloi [Eligius], though he died in 660) and reached its glory days in the 12th century, when it founded some 150 priories in Quercy, Périgord and the Limousin, and there was money to lavish on a great church. A village grew up around its walls, and the monastery took some hard knocks in the wars. A fire in the 1570s finished it off, leaving only the massive 16th-century belltower of St-Martin, with some older fragments of its medieval portal, and the church of Ste-Marie. The philistines of Louis XIV's time worked some outrageous butchery on it, covering the stately domes with a fake gable roof, destroying one of France's finest carved portals, and plastering over everything inside, redecorating it in a way they found more tasteful. All that has been cleared and, though it may be hard to imagine Ste-Marie in its original splendour, the essentials remain.

Its denuded state, in fact, might make it easier to appreciate the authority and perfection of the architecture. Ste-Marie is Romanesque at its most Roman, striving above all for monumental presence. This is best seen outside in the majestic apse; one suspects the architect had taken a long look at the palaces and public baths of ancient Rome (some of which were still in good nick in the 1100s). The interior is even better: a single, domed nave, graceful and strong. Of the three domes, the earliest is oddly squared, showing the Islamic origins of the technique; squarish domes like this are rare, though a few turn up in contemporary churches in southern Italy. Sculptural decoration is sparse – some good capitals, including the popular theme of Daniel in the lions' den and a few grimacing faces hidden in unexpected spots.

The surviving fragments of the portal have been reconstructed inside the main door. The wild scene on top, showing a fellow with some serious devil troubles, represents *St Theophilus the Penitent*.

Getting to Souillac

Trains travelling on the main SNCF line between Paris and Toulouse (via Limoges) usually stop at Souillac (call **t** 05 65 32 78 21 to check); in any case, there are frequent trains to the town from Paris, Brive, Cahors and Toulouse, and bus services between Souillac and Sarlat, Martel, Gourdon and Brive (Voyages Belmon, **t** 05 65 37 81 15). If you come by **car**, be aware that Souillac gets a lot of traffic, though less now that the Paris–Toulouse A20 is completed.

Archdeacon of Adana (in Turkey), this Theophilus was wrongly thrown out of his office and in revenge sold his soul to the devil; of course the devil got it in writing. Theophilus later repented so sincerely and thoroughly that the Virgin Mary went down to hell and snatched the paper away from the devil for him. The three vignettes in the crowded relief show the signing of the contract, the devil attempting to carry Theophilus away and, above, the Virgin and an angel pulling him up into heaven. Just why this obscure saint should have such a prominent place on the portal is a good question, but then perhaps he isn't so obscure after all – this story is one of the sources for the legend of Faust. Flanking the relief are the two figures without which no French portal would be complete: St Peter (with the keys) and St Paul (with the book).

Outstanding as these reliefs are, one's eye is inevitably drawn below to the prophet Isaiah. As Freda White rightly noted, 'this statue is alive.' It's commonly called the 'dancing' Isaiah. Poised on one foot, with stone draperies flowing, the composition is unlike anything else produced in the Middle Ages; the carving, in its detail, is a virtuoso display of careful precision. Most striking of all is the extreme stylization: studied and consistent, a vision of form that is the work of a great artist – one of the greatest between the Greeks and Donatello. From this he can perhaps be identified as the same man who did the portal at Moissac, or at least an equally talented member of the School of Toulouse. Besides Isaiah and the ruined statue of the patriarch Joseph, one of the side pillars of the portal was saved, swarming with monsters often (if doubtfully) claimed to represent the seven deadly sins, with biblical scenes such as the sacrifice of Abraham cleverly mixed in.

Musée de l'Automate
t 05 65 37 07 07; open June and Sept daily 10–12 and 3–6; July and Aug daily 10–7; April, May and Oct Tues–Sun 10–12 and 3–6; Nov–Mar Wed–Sun 2.30–5.30; adm

Facing Ste-Marie is the ambitious **Musée de l'Automate**, which is run in collaboration with the robotic experts of the Cité des Sciences de La Villette in Paris. Here, scores of mechanical dolls, some dating from as far back as 1870, haunt the premises – eating, drinking, playing banjos, jumping through hoops and doing every other trick that clockwork and circuitry can accomplish, all to a range of special sound and light effects. They have some modern robots to keep them company, including a hi-tech Robot Zoo, together with exhibits that explain everything you ever wanted to know about the history of automata, and there are some discovery workshops too. The experts who keep the robots in good repair

Musée de la Vieille Prune
t 05 65 32 78 16, open Mon–Fri 8.30–12 and 2–6

Quercyland
t 05 65 37 33 51; open May–Sept daily 11–10; ***canoe trips*** *April–Oct; adm*

also construct some of their own – you can see these in the fascinating on-site gift shop, Clepsydra. On Avenue Jean Jaurès, the **Musée de la Vieille Prune**, run by the Distillerie Louis Roque offers free tastings to visitors.

If you're here with kids, **Quercyland** at Les Ondines near Souillac has giant inflatable castles, waterslides, mini-golf, bike hire and much more. For adults its offers canoe trips down the Dordogne lasting from an hour to several days in length.

Market Days in Souillac

There's a general market on Fridays, by the handsome old *halles* (market halls). In July and August there's also a famous market in front of the tourist office, on Wednesdays at 5pm, and there are clothes and bric-a-brac markets on the first and third Saturday of each month.

Sports and Activities in Souillac

There's a pretty nine-hole **golf** course at Souillac Country Club (**t** 05 65 27 56 00) at Lachapelle-Auzac, while Aquarêve (Rue Moriet, **t** 05 65 32 07 16) is a **water complex** with a heated indoor swimming pool, a gymnasium, a hammam, massage rooms, a sauna and vibrosauna, a solarium and so on. **Horse-riding** can be arranged with the Club Hippique Souillagais, Chemin Corpus Christi, **t** 05 65 32 64 62.

You can also tour the town aboard a little **tourist train** (July and Aug; ask at tourist office).

Where to Stay and Eat in Souillac

ⓘ Souillac >
Boulevard Louis Jean Malvy, ***t*** *05 65 37 81 56, www.tourisme-souillac.com*

★ Le Redouillé >>

Souillac ✉ 46200

There are lots of places to stay here, many of them old two-star inns offering a sincere welcome and attractive rooms.

*****Les Granges Vieilles**, on D703 from Sarlat, **t** 05 65 37 80 92, *www.lesgrangesvieilles.com* (€€). A large country house set in a lovely shaded park. All rooms have park views, and there is a swimming pool, a mini-golf course and a restaurant (€€€–€) with a patio; menus feature mainly regional dishes. *Closed mid-Nov–mid-Mar; restaurant lunch exc Sun and public hols.*

*****La Vieille Auberge**, 1 Rue Récège, **t** 05 65 32 79 43, *www.la-vieille-auberge.com* (€€–€). An inn offering a whiff of Louis XV by the river, with a swimming pool, a sauna, a hammam and a Jacuzzi, rooms with televisions and mini-bars, and a fine restaurant (€€€–€€). *Closed early Nov–mid Dec and Sun and Mon out of season; restaurant lunch Mon and Sat.*

*****Grand Hôtel**, 1 Allée de Verninac, **t** 05 65 32 78 30, *www.grandhotel-souillac.com* (€). A central options with pleasant rooms, some with balconies, and a popular restaurant (€€) where you can enjoy a choice of classic dishes. *Closed mid-Nov–mid-Mar.*

****Les Ambassadeurs**, 12 Avenue du Général de Gaulle, **t** 05 65 32 78 36, *www.ambassadeurs-hotel.com* (€). A hotel offering a number of simple rooms, some of them ensuite, a swimming pool, table tennis and a restaurant (€€€–€) serving a range of good local dishes to appreciative locals. The amenable staff are happy to organize trips for guests.

****Auberge du Puits**, Place du Puits, **t** 05 65 37 80 32, *www.auberge-du-puits.fr* (€). Simple rooms and a restaurant (€€) that offers a wide choice of entrées done the old-fashioned way. *Closed Dec and Jan, and Sun eve and Mon out of season; restaurant Nov–Feb and sometimes at lunch (call to check).*

Le Redouillé, 28 Avenue de Toulouse, **t** 05 65 37 87 25 (€€€–€€). A restaurant with an owner-chef who earned his stripes in the Mediterranean but is now at home with the very different cuisine of the southwest. *Closed Sun eve and Mon.*

Souillac to Sarlat

Carlux and Ste-Mondane

As you leave the *département* of the Lot for that of the Dordogne and, more specifically, the corner that has become known as the Périgord Noir ('black' for either its truffles or deep forests – no one seems to know which), **Carlux** has a pair of romantic châteaux to look at: a 14th-century castle that was left ruined by the English in the Hundred Years' War, and, on a remarkable site in a holly oak forest, the 16th-century Château de Rouffillac. Nearby there is also a beautiful series of gardens, the **Jardins de Cadiot**, comprising more than 2,000 varieties and including a rose garden, wild garden and *jardin anglais*.

Jardins de Cadiot
t 05 53 29 81 05; open May–Sept 10–7

Just across the river at **St-Julien-de-Lampon**, you can visit a Gothic church with 16th-century mural paintings. From St-Julien the D50 continues westwards to **Ste-Mondane**.

Mothers are often saints, but very few are ever canonized, what with the Church's fantasies about virginity. One mother who did make it into heaven's ranks, however, was Mondane, the mum of Sarlat's patron, St Sacerdos; she spent her later years living in a cave within the riverside village that now bears her name. Although the cave is no longer a pilgrimage site, visitors still pour into Ste-Mondane in order to see the majestic **Château de Fénelon**, which is piled on a set of terraces, defended by a triple ring of walls and gate towers, its roofs still covered with their original *lauze* stones. Begun in the 13th century, the château was mostly reconstructed during the 1600s as a lordly residence by one of the oldest and most aristocratic families of the Dordogne – De Salignac de la Mothe-Fénelon. The magnificent cedar of Lebanon that you will see by the gate was planted to celebrate the birth of François, in 1651 – a 13th child but one whose brains soon attracted attention (*see* p.150). Inside, the current owner has refurbished a number of the rooms, using his own collection of arms as decoration. There are a few relics of the great man himself, and, in the bedroom where he first saw the light of day, you can admire a superb 17th-century walnut fireplace.

Château de Fénelon
t 05 53 29 81 45; guided tours daily May, June and Sept Wed–Mon 10–12.30 and 2.30–6; July and Aug daily 10–7; Oct and Mar Wed–Mon 2–7; Nov and Feb Sat and Sun 2–5; April Wed–Mon 10.30–12.30 and 2.30–5; adm

Carsac-Aillac and the Château de Montfort

If you travel downriver on the D50, you will come to **Groléjac**, a place that reserves its best features for those willing to get out of their car and walk up its medieval streets. Amidst them you will discover a secretive little 18th-century château and a Romanesque church. If you like creepie crawlies, **Insectorama** is a must-visit; as well as the real thing, it has displays of related artworks and photographs. Opposite Insectorama there's a lake with a beach.

Insectorama
Route de Nabirat, t 05 53 29 38 37; open July and Aug daily 10–7; April–June, Sept and Oct Sat–Thurs 1.30–6; Mar and early Nov Sat and Sun 1.30–6

Near the junction of the Dordogne and the little Enéa stands **Carsac**, a village of 16th–17th-century *lauze*-roofed houses with a domed Romanesque church, constructed in the 11th century. Damaged by the English, the nave and chapels were rebuilt in the 1500s with ogival vaults and capitals carved with unusual classical scenes, including a baby Hercules strangling the serpents that crept into his cradle. When the church was restored in 1940, some new works were commissioned from Léon Zack: the stained glass and the Stations of the Cross, with texts taken from Paul Claudel's *Le Chemin de la Croix*.

Jardins d'Eau
t 05 53 28 91 96; open May–mid-Oct daily 9–8; adm

A short distance outside Carsac, at St-Rome, there is a garden of water plants, the **Jardins d'Eau**, which is home to 16 different types of lotus. The **Château de Montfort** (which is no longer open to the public), high over its river loop, or *cingle*, is one of the most photographed of all the castles in the Dordogne. It was named after the ruthlessly effective leader of the Albigensian crusade, Simon de Montfort, although typically for him all he did was burn it to the ground when he captured it in 1214. Still, his name stuck to the spot when the château was rebuilt over the centuries, especially after three sieges by the English in the Hundred Years' War. It is best viewed from the road between Carsac and **Vitrac**, the latter village a popular holiday base spread between the crossroads to Sarlat and its medieval core, the old 'Bourg' with a large Romanesque church.

Indian Forest Périgord
t 05 53 31 22 22

On the road back to Souillac, **Indian Forest Périgord** offers adventures and acrobatics among the treetops for children and and fearless adults.

Where to Stay and Eat between Souillac and Sarlat

Carsac ✉ 24200

****Hôtel Le Relais du Touron, t** 05 53 28 16 70, *www.lerelaisdutouron.com* (€€–€). A very pleasant hotel with direct access to its gardens and swimming pool from most of its guestrooms, and a good restaurant (€€€–€€). *Closed mid-Nov–Mar.*

Delpeyrat, t 05 53 28 10 43 (€). A quiet, well-kept option. The food (€€–€) tends towards the basic but comes in hefty portions, and the owners are friendly. *Closed Oct and Nov; restaurant Sat lunch.*

Vitrac ✉ 24200

******Hotel Domaine de Rochebois,** Route du Château de Montfort, **t** 05 53 31 52 52, *www.rochebois.com* (€€€€€–€€€€). A stylish option occupying a 19th-century mansion, complete with a golf course, a swimming pool, a gymnasium, gardens and a gourmet restaurant (€€€). *Closed Nov–late April.*

****Plaisance**, Le Port, **t** 05 53 31 39 39, *www.hotelplaisance.com* (€€–€). A building of golden stone, with a long garden terrace overlooking the river, a swimming pool, tennis and table tennis facilities, a mini-golf course and a restaurant (€€€–€€). *Closed mid-Nov–mid-Feb; restaurant Sat lunch May–Sept and Sun eve and Fri Oct–April.*

****La Treille**, Le Port, **t** 05 53 28 33 19, *www.latreille-perigord.com* (€€–€). A well-priced choice set right next to the river, with a good restaurant (€€€–€€). *Closed Nov–early Mar; restaurant Mon and Tues lunch.*

Sarlat-la-Canéda

Sarlat

'*Mon Dieu*, there's nothing here but foie gras, foie gras, foie gras!' muttered an old farmer, brought to Sarlat for a Sunday afternoon promenade. Of course he's right: nearly every other boutique glitters with stacks of tiny shiny tins. But such rich stuff fits Sarlat perfectly well, for, cocooned inside its clinking ring of 20th-century sprawl, this golden Renaissance town is architecturally the foie gras of southwest France. It has the greatest number of classified monuments per square kilometre than anywhere else in Europe.

History

It was Clovis, they say, who founded the first church at what is now Sarlat, and Charlemagne who stopped here after Roncesvalles to give it a fragment of the True Cross and the relics of St Sacerdos, Bishop of Limoges. In the 8th century, Pépin, Duke of Aquitaine, added an abbey, and Sarlat grew up around it. It was raging with plague when St Bernard made a memorable visit in 1147 and cured several victims with blessed bread. By the next century, the autocratic rule of the abbot over the increasingly mercantile town had become intolerable to the good burghers, and in 1299, after much strife, the *Livre de Paix* was signed, acknowledging the abbot as boss, but giving the town councillors the authority to run the show. As compensation, Pope John XXII made Sarlat a bishopric in 1317, elevating the church to a cathedral.

Founded as an abbey town, Sarlat has no natural defences and was constrained to add some formidable man-made ones during the Hundred Years' War. In return for defending itself so well against the English, the French simply handed Sarlat over to Edward III in 1360 as part of the ransom for Jean II, although 10 years later du Guesclin and the French won it back by arms. As a reward for its loyalty in spite of it all, Charles VII granted Sarlat enough tax concessions in the 1440s to bring about its golden age and a building boom; nearly all of its *hôtels particuliers*, or townhouses, were built between 1450 and 1500 and grace Sarlat with a rare architectural unity.

In 1574, Catholic Sarlat was captured and pillaged by the irrepressible Huguenot Captain Vivans, who made his way in during Carnival by disguising his troops as harlequins. Smarting from the embarrassment more than anything else, Sarlat held tight for three weeks in 1587 when it was besieged by the fanatical Protestant Vicomte de Turenne. When their ramparts were damaged, the *Sarladais* rebuilt them during the night, and when Turenne offered them terms they replied: 'We have a good master and don't want any other.' Turenne went away muttering, ashamed not to have been able by force or ruse 'to take such a town'.

Getting to and around Sarlat-la-Canéda

There are direct **trains** to Bordeaux, Les Eyzies, Bergerac and Souillac from Sarlat's station on Avenue de la Gare. There are **bus** connections between Sarlat and Souillac, Brive (Voyages Belmon, **t** 05 65 37 81 15) and Périgueux (CFTA Périgord, **t** 05 55 17 91 19, *www.cftaco.fr*).

For taxis, call **t** 05 53 31 62 43 or **t** 05 53 59 02 43; for **bike** hire try McMoto, 2 Avenue de Selves, **t** 05 53 59 06 11, Cycles Sarladais, Avenue Aristide de Briand, **t** 05 53 28 51 87, or the train station.

There's a **cycleway** to Carsac along an old railway track.

In July and August there are daily **guided tours** to Bergerac by train, the *Autorail Espérance*, with tastings of local products along the way; for tickets and information, call the station, **t** 05 53 59 00 21.

After the Wars of Religion, Sarlat sank gently into the role of a local market town, off the main routes of communications and history. In 1827, the town fathers, hoping to drum up some new business by uncongesting traffic, carved a long straight slice out of its heart to create Rue de la République, better known as *La Traverse*. Further 'improvements' were prevented after 1963, when Sarlat was chosen as one of the first towns to be restored and protected by the state under the Loi Malraux.

From Place de la Grande Rigaudie to the Cathedral

Parking is the first hurdle confronting any motorist arriving in Sarlat; the largest and most convenient car parks are south of the *Traverse*, in and around vast Place de la Grande Rigaudie. Here, in 1892, Sarlat erected a statue to its famous son, Etienne de la Boétie, though it unfairly makes the young thinker look like a wimp (*see* opposite). On the hill beyond him and the courthouse is the **Jardin Public**, offering a good overview of Sarlat and its steep *lauze* roofs.

The urban scale becomes immediately more intimate and richly detailed when you walk up Rue Tourny, just to the north of Place de la Grande Rigaudie. A lane on the right leads you into the Cour des Fontaines, with its age-old fountain. Clovis founded Sarlat's first church in the second courtyard, a site that is now occupied by the 12th-century Chapelle des Pénitents Bleus (*not open to the public*). You can follow the narrow passage to the Ancien Cimitière, where 12th–15th-century tombstones have been excavated and arranged on terraces.

A stairway from here leads up to Sarlat's great oddity, the **Lanterne des Morts**, a stubby stone rocket that was constructed at the end of the 12th century. Its original use has been forgotten – it may have commemorated the miracle of St Bernard, or have been used as a funerary chapel. Or perhaps a lantern was lit here during wakes and vigils on the ground floor (there's an upper floor, but it's completely, and mysteriously, inaccessible). There may even be a confusion over its original name; sometimes it was described as the *Lanterne des Maures*, referring to its marked resemblance to Turkish *türbes* and other Muslim mausolea that the crusaders must surely have seen.

Below stretch the flying buttresses and bulb-topped steeple (which is known locally as 'the scarecrow') of the **Cathédrale St-Sacerdos**, dedicated to the 6th-century leper-curing Bishop of Limoges. The first church was built at the same time as the Lanterne des Morts and had to be consecrated twice, the second time in 1273, after Sarlat's abbot was shot down while he was saying Mass by a disgruntled monk with a crossbow. This church was demolished (except for its Romanesque *clocher-porche*) by Bishop Armand de Gontaut-Biron in 1504 in order to construct a much grander cathedral. Unfortunately the project took until the dull 17th century to complete and, although the result is roomy enough, it holds nothing as artistic as the Bishop Armand's own effigy tomb in Biron (*see* p.351).

Place du Peyrou and La Boétie

Adjacent to the cathedral in Place du Peyrou is the former bishopric or **Ancien Evêché** (now a theatre), with handsome, mullioned windows and a top-floor gallery in brick that looks as though it escaped from Italy – not surprising, as it was built by a Florentine cousin of Catherine de' Medici, Cardinal Niccolò Gaddi, who added Bishop of Sarlat to his titles in 1533.

Opposite the cathedral you can admire the most lavishly ornate townhouse in Sarlat, the **Hôtel de la Boétie** (1525). The modern entrance is through the wide round arch of a former shop; richly ornamented mullioned windows dominate the upper three floors, squeezed between a vertiginously steep gable. The decoration reaches a curlicue frenzy in the dormer window, in frilly contrast with the sombre *lauzes* of the roof. The *hôtel particulier* was built by the father of the precocious Etienne de la Boétie, who was born here in 1530. A student of the classics, Etienne was aged 18 when he wrote his most original essay, *Discours de la servitude volontaire*, asking why people willingly give up their liberty to support tyrants, when such tyrants could never exist without people willing to give up their freedom, the most precious thing of all. These were radical ideas in the 16th century, and, even when Montaigne published La Boétie's papers after his premature death at the age of 33, he discreetly omitted the *Discours*. It only appeared in 1576 in a collection of 'libellous' Protestant writings, and even then its influence remained dormant until the advent of Rousseau. But most of all, La Boétie is remembered as Montaigne's perfect pal in the latter's beautiful *Essay on Friendship*.

Place de la Liberté and Rue des Consuls

From Place du Peyrou, duck through the medieval alleyway of the Passage Henri-de-Segogne to see another of Sarlat's architectural gems, the **Hôtel de Maleville**. A 16th-century combination of three older houses, with two distinct Renaissance façades – one of them French, one Italian – it belonged to Jean de Vienne, a local boy who owed his rise to national high office to Henri IV (see the portrait medallions of the king and a woman – either Henri's wife Marie de' Medici, or his favourite mistress Gabrielle d'Estrées). It was later owned by the family that produced Jacques de Maleville, one of the prime authors of the Napoleonic *Code Civil*.

The *hôtel particulier*'s French façade overlooks elongated Place de la Liberté, Sarlat's main square and favoured café stop, and address since 1861 of the shop for the **Distillerie du Périgord**, where you can try the original *Pastis Lapouge*, Périgord's own rendition of the famous Marseille apéritif, and a heavenly array of fruit *eaux-de-vie*. The 17th-century Hôtel de Ville is here; next to it, Rue de la Salamandre leads up past some 15th- and 16th-century mansions to the handsome **Présidial** and its garden (visible through the gate). The Présidial was the seat of a royal court set up by Henri II in 1552, in defiance of local wishes, to administer local justice; note the curious little polygonal lantern on the loggia. It's now a good restaurant by the same name (*see* p.164). More delights – gabled houses and carved portals – wait along Rue du Présidial and Rue Fénelon, which brings you back to the northern extension of Place de la Liberté, the Place du Marché.

Here stands the sad carcass of a church with a massive belltower, **Ste-Marie**, begun in 1365 and completed in 1507. After being used to store saltpetre during the Revolution, it was sold for a pittance to a speculator, who lopped off its chancel and converted its chapels into shops; before the First World War it was a post office; now it houses a market. The picturesque **Rampe Magnanat**, ascending to the right, has been used by a score of French film directors for climactic duel scenes before the brooding backdrop of the 16th-century Hôtel de Gisson and its hexagonal tower.

On the other side of the Hôtel de Gisson is the old goose market, Place du Marché aux Oies, and the narrow Rue des Consuls. Among the magnificent *hôtels* here, the **Hôtel Plamon** (Nos.8–10) stands out; it was owned by a prosperous family of drapers, who added a new floor every century or so – early Gothic on the ground floor, Flamboyant Gothic on the first and Renaissance on the second. Opposite is a curious cave-like fountain from the 15th century; the river Cuze passed openly under the Hôtel de Plamon as a pestilent sewer until it was covered over in the 19th century.

Across the *Traverse*

The *Traverse* cuts the wealthy Sarlat of splendid townhouses from the steeper, more popular and piquant neighbourhood to the west, where some alleys are scarcely wide enough to walk arm in arm. In its intimate scale, the Chapelle des Pénitents Blancs in

Rue Jean-Jacques Rousseau seems like a walrus. Rue J.-J. Rousseau continues to the lovely, nearly intact 16th-century **Abbaye Ste-Claire** (*not open to the public*), occupied until the Revolution. Further south are Rue du Siège and a stretch of Sarlat's walls that survived demolition; here too is the **Tour du Bourreau**, the executioner's tower. In Rue Rousset there's a second tower, the 15th-century crenellated **Tour de Guet**. Ask at the tourist office about **guided tours** of the town, sometimes in English.

Two kilometres north of Sarlat, Pépin the Short built the first citadel on the natural belvedere at **Temniac** in the 8th century (access is off the D704, or via a marked walking path beginning off Avenue Brossard). In the 1200s the bishops of Sarlat used the site for a palace; it was rebuilt in the 15th century, and today stands in evocative, romantic ruins. The bishops' tower and the pure Périgourdin Romanesque Chapelle de Notre-Dame, with its pair of domes and vaulted choir, are nearly intact.

Market Days in Sarlat-la-Canéda

There are general markets on **Wednesday** and **Saturday** (all day), plus a *marché au gras* and truffle market on Saturdays Dec–Feb and a covered market in the church of Ste-Marie Easter–early Nov daily 8.30–1, rest of year Tues, Wed and Fri–Sun 9–1.

Where to Stay in and around Sarlat-la-Canéda

ⓘ **Sarlat >**
Rue Tourny,
t *05 53 31 45 45, www.ot-sarlat-perigord.fr*

Sarlat-la-Canéda ✉ 24200

As the capital of Périgord Noir, Sarlat, with its many small hotels, is a convenient base, but book well ahead in summer.

*****Hôtel Le Renoir**, 2 Rue de l'Abbé Surguier, **t** 05 53 59 35 98, *www.hotel-renoir-sarlat.com* (€€€€–€€). A former distillery, now a comfortable Best Western hotel, in a quiet lane in the centre, with a garden and pool. *Closed mid-Nov–mid-Dec.*

*****Hôtel de Selves**, 93 Avenue de Selves, **t** 05 53 31 50 00, *www.selves-sarlat.com* (€€€–€€). A classy modern place with airy rooms, some with a terrace, relaxing gardens, a pool and a sauna. *Closed most of Jan and start of Feb.*

★ **La Madeleine >**

***La Madeleine, 1 Place de la Petite Rigaudie, **t** 05 53 59 10 41, *www.hoteldelamadeleine-sarlat.com* (€€€–€€). A 19th-century townhouse near the medieval centre, with air-conditioned and soundproofed rooms and the benefit of a private garage. Owned by a chef, it has a restaurant (€€€–€€) that serves both regional specialities and lighter, more modern dishes. *Closed Jan and Feb; restaurant mid-Nov–mid-Mar, and Mon and Tues lunch exc July and Aug.*

*****Relais de Moussidière**, **t** 05 53 28 28 74 (€€€–€€). A traditional stone manor on a cliff at the western entrance to Sarlat, with simple modern rooms, an exquisite landscaped park with a pool and lake, and a bar. Nearby you'll find riding stables, a golf course and tennis courts. *Closed Nov–Easter.*

*****Hôtel de Compostelle**, 64–6 Av de Selves, **t** 05 53 59 08 53, *www.hotelcompostelle-sarlat.com* (€€). Recently refurbished modern rooms with private terraces and TVs, near the centre. *Closed mid-Nov–early Feb.*

****Hôtel des Récollets**, 4 Rue J.-J. Rousseau, **t** 05 53 31 36 00, *www.hotel-recollets-sarlat.com* (€€–€). Small rooms set within a 17th-century cloister in a quiet corner to the west of *La Traverse*.

****Hôtel La Madrigal**, 50 Avenue de Selves, **t** 05 53 59 21 98 (€). Pleasant rooms in a stone house on a road that can be a bit noisy. *Closed mid-Nov–Jan.*

****La Couleuvrine**, 1 Place de la Bouquerie, **t** 05 53 59 27 80, *www.la-couleuvrine.com* (€). Unusual antique-furnished rooms in a building that forms part of Sarlat's 14th–18th-century ramparts; the restaurant (€€€–€€) prides itself on its use of market-fresh produce. *Restaurant closed early Jan–early Feb.*

****St Albert**, Place Pasteur, **t** 05 53 31 55 55, *www.sarlathotel.com* (€). Colourful rooms at the south entrance of the old town and a decent restaurant (€€–€). *Closed Sun eve and Mon late Oct–late Mar.*

Chez Pierre Henri Toulemon, 4 Rue Magnanat, **t** 05 53 31 26 60, *www.toulemon.com* (€). An atmospheric, friendly *chambres d'hôte* bang in the middle of the old town, with big oak doors. The building is a historical monument accessed via steps, and the rooms have old furniture.

Just Outside Sarlat-la-Canéda

*****La Hoirie**, Rue Marcel Cerdan, La Giragne, 5mins from Sarlat, **t** 05 53 59 05 62, *www.lahoirie.com* (€€€–€€). A former aristocratic hunting lodge, with 17 comfortable rooms with minibars, and a pool in its park. *Closed early Nov–late Mar.*

*****Hostellerie de Meysset**, Argentouleau, 2km northwest of town on road to Les Eyzies, **t** 05 53 59 08 29 (€€). A hilltop hotel with views over its park and pool and the Sarlat valley, including from the terrace of the restaurant (€€€–€€), where you can enjoy delicious *confits* served with a garlic cream sauce and other treats. *Closed early Nov–Easter.*

****Hostellerie La Verperie**, La Verperie, **t** 05 53 59 00 20, *www.laverperie.com* (€€–€). A peaceful, cosy hotel good for families, set in a small park with a pool and games, with a restaurant (€€). *Closed mid-Nov–mid-Mar.*

****Le Mas de Castel**, Sudalissant, 2.5km from town towards Souillac, **t** 05 53 59 02 59, *www.hotel-lemasdecastel.com* (€€–€). Traditionally styled pastel rooms around a large garden with a pool. *Closed early-Nov–Mar.*

Les Périères, 1km from Sarlat on D47, **t** 05 53 59 05 84, *www.lesperieres.com* (€). The best campsite around, in a lovely shady park with a pool, sauna, Jacuzzi, tennis, playgrounds and more. *Closed mid-Oct–Easter.*

St-Geniès ✉ 24590

Ferme-Auberge des Genestes, 12km north of Sarlat just off D704, **t** 05 53 28 97 71, *http://mazet.roland.free.fr* (€). Nine rooms at good-value half-board rates. The traditional dining room (€€–€), in a renovated barn with stone walls and beams, serves an interesting range of classic southwest farm dishes, such as duck and foie gras, and tempting homemade desserts. Booking is required. *Closed early Nov–Easter.*

Eating Out in Sarlat-la-Canéda

The best dining options in town are in the hotels (*see* above).

Le Présidial, near Place de la Liberté, **t** 05 53 28 92 47 (€€€–€€). An elegant dining room with a large patio on the site of a royal court, offering extravagant regional dishes such as squab with *cèpes* and wines from around France, with an emphasis on local vintages. *Closed mid-Nov–Jan, plus Mon lunch and Sun.*

Les Quatre Saisons, 2 Côte de Toulouse, just off Rue de la République, **t** 05 53 29 48 59 (€€€–€€). A restaurant serving great seasonal dishes (as the name promises), including some seafood and a vegetarian menu, and an outstanding wine list. Book ahead. *Closed Tues and Wed exc July and Aug.*

Rossignol, 15 Rue Fénelon, near *Mairie*, **t** 05 53 31 02 30 (€€€–€€). A pleasant spot for good-value regional cuisine. *Closed Thurs.*

La Rapière, Place de la Cathédrale, **t** 05 53 59 03 13 (€€). A good place for real Périgourdien cooking and fish-based specialities. *Closed Jan and Feb, and Sun out of season.*

Relais de Poste, Impasse de la Vieille Poste, **t** 05 53 59 63 13 (€€). An inn with some good menus, mostly focused on regional dishes, plus a good wine selection and a range of local eaux-de-vie. There's a secluded walled patio filled with plants. *Closed Jan–Easter, and Wed.*

Criquettamu's, 5 Rue des Armes, **t** 05 53 59 48 10 (€€–€). A restaurant serving all kinds of tasty things involving foie gras, duck breast and morel mushrooms, at pleasing prices. *Closed Nov–Feb.*

The Plateau of Périgord Noir

Moulin de la Tour
t 05 53 59 22 08; open April and May Wed and Fri 9–12 and 2–6; June and Sept Wed and Fri 9–12 and 2–6, Sat 2–6; July and Aug Mon, Wed and Fri 9–12 and 2–6; adm

Distillerie la Salamandre
t 05 53 59 10 00; open Mon–Fri 8–12 and 1.30–6.30

Forêt des Ecureuils
t 06 89 30 92 99; call for hrs

Manoir d'Eyrignac
t 05 53 28 99 71; open June–Sept daily 9.30–7; Oct–May daily 10–12.30 and 2–7, with variations for weather; adm

Château de Puymartin
t 05 53 59 29 97; open April–June, late Aug and Sept daily 10–12 and 2–6; July and most of Aug daily 10–6.30; Nov call for times; adm

Cabanes du Breuil
t 06 80 72 38 59; open June–Sept daily 10–7; Mar–May and Oct–mid-Nov daily 10–12 and 2–6; rest of year Sat and Sun 10–12 and 2–5 but call ahead; adm

Sarlat's hinterland is pretty quiet these days, but there are a few things worth seeing. At **Ste-Nathalène**, 8km east, is a 16th-century watermill, the **Moulin de la Tour**, where you can watch walnut, hazelnut and almond oils being made the old-fashioned way, or just look round and buy some produce. Nearby, the **Distillerie la Salamandre** makes fruit-based liqueur, aperitifs, fruits in alcohol and so on. For more messing about in trees, head for the **Forêt des Ecureuils** ('Squirrel Forest') just south at St-Vincent le Paluel.

Roads from Ste-Nathalène run northeast to the 17th-century **Manoir d'Eyrignac**, where the current owner has won prizes for his restoration of the 18th-century French gardens – a perspective of hedges cut into cubes, triangles, circles and spheres. From here continue northeast to the D61 for **Salignac-Eyvignes**, a picture-postcard Périgord town spread below the 12th–17th-century pepperpot towers of the Château de Salignac (which is closed to the public). Built by Archbishop Fénelon's feudal ancestors, the château was hotly disputed in all the region's wars. Terraces now replace the once bristling ramparts; among the highlights inside are two floors of vaulted cellars, the chapel and a Renaissance fireplace.

Eight kilometres northwest of Sarlat, at Marquay, the twin-turreted 15th–16th-century **Château de Puymartin**, in a handsome park off the D47, was Turenne's HQ when the Protestants besieged Sarlat, but for better or worse it's had little to do with history since. Rooms are fitted with 17th-century furnishings, some with Aubusson tapestries – two (without tapestries) take overnight guests.

For something completely different, head for **St-André-d'Allas** (4km west of Sarlat); at the stately Château du Roc take the narrow road up to the right for the **Cabanes du Breuil**, a hamlet of tiny, dry-stone huts with breast-shaped stone roofs – the kind of place Astérix or Obélix would feel perfectly at home. In season there is a video, guided tours and demonstrations of (and tuition in) dry-stone building. Similar *bories*, or *gariottes*, exist in Provence and in Ireland, where they're called *clochans*, but whole villages of them are rare, and these are classified as a historical monument. No one knows who built them, or how long ago; the most likely answer is shepherds, who kept them in good repair over the centuries.

Domme: the 'Acropolis of Périgord'

Lovely, honey-hued Domme is a *bastide* town from the Hundred Years' War, but one whose grid plan was remarkably transplanted on to a bluff-top eyrie over the Dordogne. Philippe III 'the Bold' built it in 1281, and, although he bestowed many favours on it, he had to resort to threats to get local peasants to build and settle his baby – only to pay the workers in black leather coins 'minted', or rather cut out, at the Mint in Place de la Rode, Domme's oldest building.

Despite its lofty site and walls, Domme was captured several times: by the English, the counts of Périgord and, in 1588 during the Wars of Religion, by Henri of Navarre's invincible captain, Geoffroy de Vivans – although only on the fourth try, after he laboriously established a secret ammunition depot in a cave halfway up the precipitous, undefended cliff. One black night, after laying coats on the bare rock to muffle the noise of their approach, his troops sprung with a thunderous roar upon the unsuspecting town.

A Roam through Domme

If you approach Domme from the east by way of the D46E, you'll enter the town walls through the best-preserved of its three gates, the 13th-century Porte des Tours. This narrow gate is framed by two fat guard towers that were constructed under Philip the Fair, converted into prisons in 1307 when the king ordered the arrest of the Knights Templars; some of them lingered here until 1318, engraving crucifixes and other graffiti that you can still see on the wall. Domme's other two gates are equally worth a look: the arched Porte de la Combe to the south and the Porte del Bos, still grooved for its portcullis.

As with any *bastide*, the focal point of Domme is its central market square, here called **Place de la Halle**, although no other *bastide* square is quite like this: the church gives on to the Belvédère de la Barre, with panoramic views from Montfort to Beynac. It's also easy to see why the locals hadn't bothered to defend the bluff, even from Vivans. Vivans took care to destroy the church, which is why the current one offers little interest.

Musée des Arts et Traditions Populaires
t 05 53 31 71 00; open April–June and Sept daily 10.30–12.30 and 2.30–6; July and Aug daily 10.30–7; adm

However, Place de la Halle boasts other fine buildings: the turreted, asymmetrical Governor's House from the 1500s (now the tourist office) and the Maison Garrigou containing the **Musée des Arts et Traditions Populaires**, with a mammoth tooth, prehistoric and historical collections and traditional arts and crafts. In the middle, the charming 17th-century stone and timber market offers

Les Mai

One thing that may or may not be in Domme when you visit is a tall pine pole in Place de la Halle, decorated with hoops and *tricolores* and a sign reading *Honneur à Notre Maire*; if it's gone down in Domme you may well spot similar poles in other villages or towns, or even next to private homes, reading *Honneur au Patron* or *à Notre Elu*, or with the names of a newly married couple, or perhaps even a newborn baby. They are called *les Mai*, or maypoles, and are erected at boozy confabs known as *Plantations de Mai*. Once up, they are meant to rot away rather than ever be taken down. The Périgourdins apparently have been planting their maypoles ever since Gallo-Roman times, when a newly elected official would be honoured with a similar pole crowned with a garland. Since the Liberty Trees put up during the Revolution, they have taken on an added republican virtue.

Grottes de Domme
t 05 53 31 71 00; open July and Aug daily 10–6.30; rest of year by appointment; adm; tickets from tourist office (see p.168)

Le Family Park
t 06 72 41 93 39; call for hrs

more than the usual turnips and carrots – the entrance into Domme's very bowels, through the **Grottes de Domme**. Although the lower part of the cave was used as a refuge for the inhabitants during the Hundred Years' War, the upper part, where fossilized bison and deer bones were found, was discovered only in 1954; beyond is a well-lit stalactite phantasmagoria that ends with a ride in a glass lift up the sheer cliff, depositing you near the Jardin Public, with the option of walking back to the Belvédère along the cliffside walk. At Port de Domme, **Le Family Park** has bouncy castles and trampolines to keep the kids amused.

Just below Domme, there's some exceptionally lively Romanesque sculpture in Cénac's early-12th-century priory of **St-Julien**, on the edge of town; it's usually open in summer. The Huguenots who smashed it fortunately gave up before reaching the apse: the exterior *modillons* depict carvings of a man-eating pig, grimacing faces and other oddities, while the interior capitals are vigorously sculpted with a bestiary, Daniel in the lions' den, Jonah and the whale, a monkey-trainer, a naked woman with a snake, and more.

South of Domme to Besse and Villefranche

Chai de Moncalou
t 05 53 28 14 47; open July and Aug Mon–Fri 9–12 and 2–6.30, Sat, Sun and public hols 2.30–6.30; rest of year Mon–Fri 9–12 and 1.30–5

Musée de la Pierre Sèche
t 05 53 29 88 84; open July–late Aug Mon–Fri 9.30–12.30 and 3–7, Sun 10–1; rest of year Mon, Wed and Fri 2–5, Tues and Thurs 9–12

All is rural tranquillity south of Domme, where 14 producers have been working hard to rejuvenate Vin de Domme; taste the wine and learn about their endeavours at the **chai at Moncalou**. The D60 is fringed by chestnut forests and meadows. The Brigadoon stillness that reigns here (except during the autumn mushroom hunts) makes the few 'sights' somehow more magical for being unexpected. The elongated old village of **Daglan** with – to the north – its curious, fortified, cross-shaped Château de Peyruzel from the 1600s also has a **Musée de la Pierre Sèche**, with dry-stone cabins and walls that testify to its past as a vine-growing area, before phylloxera struck. The museum tells the story of these cabins and their builders. Medieval **St-Pompont** has a pair of châteaux and a mini-maze of medieval houses huddled together beneath the fortified church; and further to the south lies remote **Prats-du-Périgord**, with an even mightier 12th-century church and 16th-century château.

Jardins de l'Albarède
t 05 53 28 38 91; open 1st half June and 2nd half Sept Wed, Sat and Sun 9–12.30; 2nd half June–mid-Sept daily 9–12.30

West of Domme at St-Cybranet are the **Jardins de l'Albarède**, mixing cultivated and wild flowers, sculptured hedges and some old-fashioned vegetables. From Prats (Occitan for 'meadows'), follow the signs for **Besse**, another tiny hamlet with yet another château and an overbearing fortified church, although this one is special – not only has it held on to its *lauze* roof but also retains its vigorous sculpted 11th-century porch, which is a rarity in these

Musée du Châtaignier
t 05 53 29 98 37; open April–June and Sept Sun–Fri 9.30–1 and 2.30–7, Sat 9.30–1; July and Aug Tues–Fri 9.30–1 and 2–7, Sat and Sun 9.30–1.30; Jan–Mar and Oct–Dec Sun–Fri 10–12.30 and 2.30–5.30, Sat 10–12.30; adm

Musée des Traditions Périgourdines
t 05 53 29 91 35; open July and Aug daily 2–5; May and June by appt

parts. French books claim that the figures represent the 'Mystery of Redemption' – there's a Garden of Eden scene, possibly an Annunciation (under the six-winged angel), a midget Crucifixion and seven deadly sins, although the hunter on horseback, St Michael killing the dragon and the waltzing horses seem to belong to another story altogether.

To safeguard Périgord's southernmost marches, Alphonse de Poitiers founded the *bastide* of **Villefranche-du-Périgord** during the 1260s. Although the grid plan and a fountain have survived from Alphonse's day, Villefranche's central square has taken a lot of licks, leaving only one row of arcades facing the stone-pillared *halle*. The church sharing the square is a more maladroit than usual 19th-century rebuilding of the original; adjacent to the tourist office, the **Musée du Châtaignier, Marrons et Champignons** is devoted to mushrooms and chestnuts. There is also a museum on 19th-century life, the **Musée des Traditions Périgourdines et**

ⓘ Domme >
Place de la Halle, t 05 53 31 71 00, www.ot-domme.com; closed Jan

ⓘ Villefranche-du-Périgord >>
Rue Notre Dame, t 05 53 29 98 37, www.tourisme.perigord-fr.com

★ L'Esplanade >

Tourist Information in and around Domme

Cave tickets and combined tickets to all Domme's sights are sold at its **tourist office**; ask here about guided tours too. There is also a **tourist train** (*Easter–early Nov daily 8–8*), and canoe hire from the little port nearby; call **t** 05 53 31 06 45.

Market Days in and around Domme

Domme: Thursday.

Cénac: Tuesday.

Villefranche: Saturday. There's also a mushroom market June–Oct daily from 4pm, in the *halle*.

Where to Stay and Eat in and around Domme

Domme ✉ 24250

***L'Esplanade, by belvedere, **t** 05 53 28 31 41, *www.esplanade-perigord.com* (€€€–€€). Tranquil, cosy rooms, some overlooking the Dordogne far below. Half board is obligatory in season, but the restaurant (€€€€–€€€) is charming. *Restaurant closed early Nov–early Mar, plus Mon lunch and Wed.*

****Le Nouvel Hôtel**, Grande Rue, **t** 05 53 28 36 81, *www.domme-nouvel-hotel.com* (€€–€). Comfortable rooms, many with exposed stone walls and one with a balcony with rooftop views. The airy restaurant (€€) in a former stables serves varied dishes, from *cassoulet* to prawns flambéed in *vieille prune* (*eau-de-vie*). *Closed early Nov–Easter, and Sun eve and Mon out of season.*

****Les Quatre Vents**, on D46 towards Sarlat, **t** 05 53 31 57 57, *www.hotelles4vents.com* (€). A modern hotel in a quiet park, with rooms and flats, two pools and a restaurant (€€).

Villefranche-du-Périgord ✉ 24550

****Petite Auberge**, **t** 05 53 29 91 01 (€). An option on a hill up a quiet country lane, with a pool and delicious food (€€€–€€). *Closed Fri and Sun eves plus Sat lunch out of season.*

La Bastide, south end of town, **t** 05 53 30 22 67 (€). Six basic rooms, plus good steaks, pizzas and other family faves (€€). *Restaurant closed Sun lunch.*

St-Cybranet ✉ 24250

Ferme-Auberge de Montalieu-Haut, **t** 05 53 28 31 74 (€). A traditional farm dining room serving southwest treats such as foie gras *feuilleté* and duckling flambéed with *vieille prune*. Booking is required. Outside are play areas and walking paths, and views of the Céou valley and Domme. There are also rooms and gîtes. *Closed Oct–May, and Mon and Sun lunch July and Aug.*

Down the Dordogne II

West of Domme and Sarlat the Dordogne bends below celebrated belvederes and beauty spots, some elbow to elbow: from the lofty Château of Beynac, you can count six other châteaux rising along the river, among them the menacing hulk of Castelnaud-la-Chapelle and the whimsical Renaissance château that gave a home to Josephine Baker's 'Rainbow Tribe'. The Dordogne dawdles through walnut country before the Vézère kicks in at Limeuil, and the newly swollen river whiplashes two more times before you see the fine, medieval city of Bergerac and the first vineyards, which will keep it company all the way to the Gironde.

10

Don't miss

1. Wine and subterranean mysteries
   St-Emilion **p.193**
2. Unreal prettinesss
   La Roque-Gageac **p.170**
3. Noble rot
   Monbazillac **p.187**
4. Josephine Baker's dream castle and shrine
   Les Milandes **p.173**
5. Phoney baloney relics
   Cadouin **p.176**

See map overleaf

Down the Dordogne II

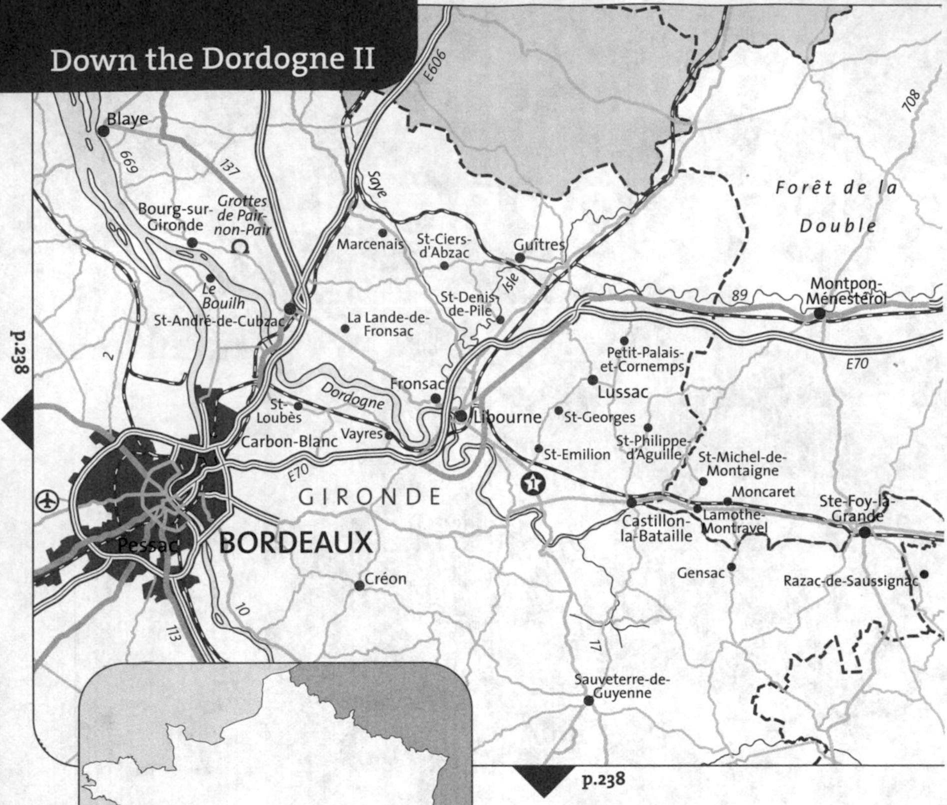

p.238
p.238

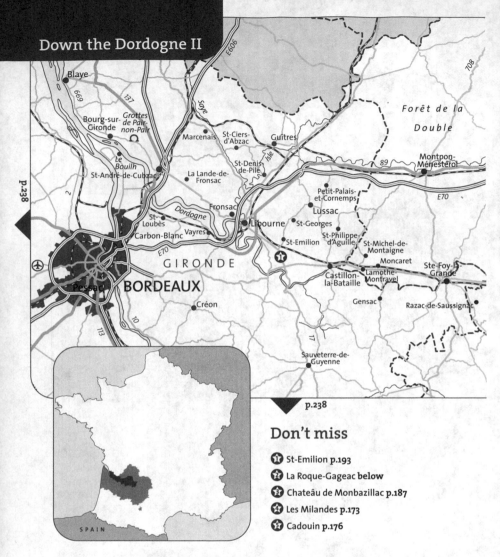

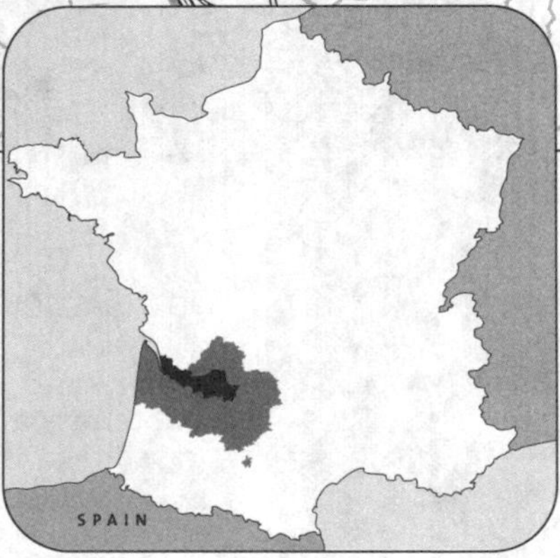

Don't miss

- ❶ St-Emilion **p.193**
- ❷ La Roque-Gageac **below**
- ❸ Chateâu de Monbazillac **p.187**
- ❹ Les Milandes **p.173**
- ❺ Cadouin **p.176**

The Central Dordogne: Beynac to Bergerac

This very pretty region has always been a major crossroads, these days for tourists but in the old days for merchants and armies; few of its imposing castles were built for decoration, but the defensive moats, towers and parapets are offset with fairytale pointed roofs, sprinkled with fleur-de-lys and topped by spindly weathervanes.

La Roque-Gageac and Beynac-et-Cazenac

❷ **La Roque-Gageac**

The car park along the river is five times as large as the entire village of La Roque-Gageac, heightening the sensation that you've

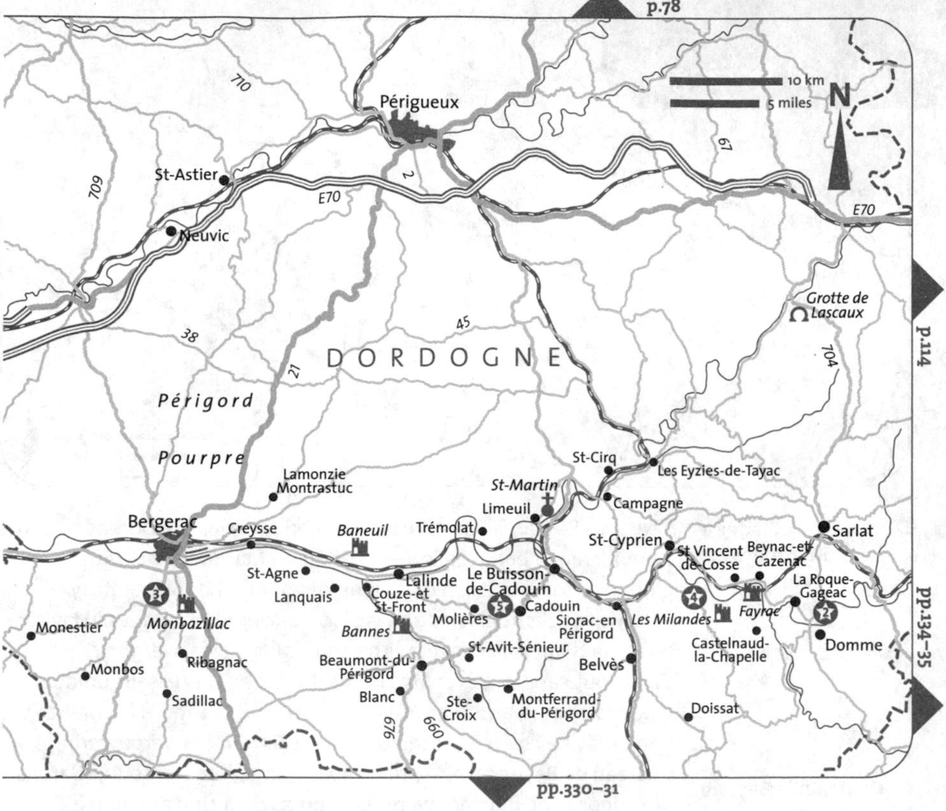

walked onto a 2D stage set. In truth, there isn't room for much depth when you build into the face of an overhanging cliff; the warm stone houses and their brown roofs are piled against it so harmoniously that they hardly seem real. Facing the sunny south (the colours are especially intense at sunset), La Roque-Gageac is sheltered enough that an exotic garden of cacti and palms thrives by the little 16th-century church, set on a throne of rock. Reality does intrude occasionally, when bits from the huge cliff break off and fall like meteors through the roofs.

Fort Troglodytique
t 05 53 31 61 94; open July and Aug daily 10.30–7; April–June and Sept–early Nov Sun–Fri 11–5

Jardin de la Ferme Fleurie
t 05 53 28 33 39; open mid-May–mid-Sept Tues–Sun 10–12 and 4–6

Near the top of town you can visit the **Fort Troglodytique**, once La Roque's main defence. At the eastern end of La Roque stands the manor house belonging to the village's most famous native son, the 16th-century canon Jean Tarde, a humanist scholar and friend of Galileo who left a moving chronicle of the devastation wrought by the Wars of Religion in the area. At the western end, the **Château de la Malartrie** is a convincing reconstruction of the 15th-century original. For garden-lovers there's also the **Jardin de la Ferme Fleurie**, a typical Périgordian farm with a colourful collection of plants, flowers, bushes and vegetables, plus a *chambres d'hôte* (*see* p.174).

Central Dordogne

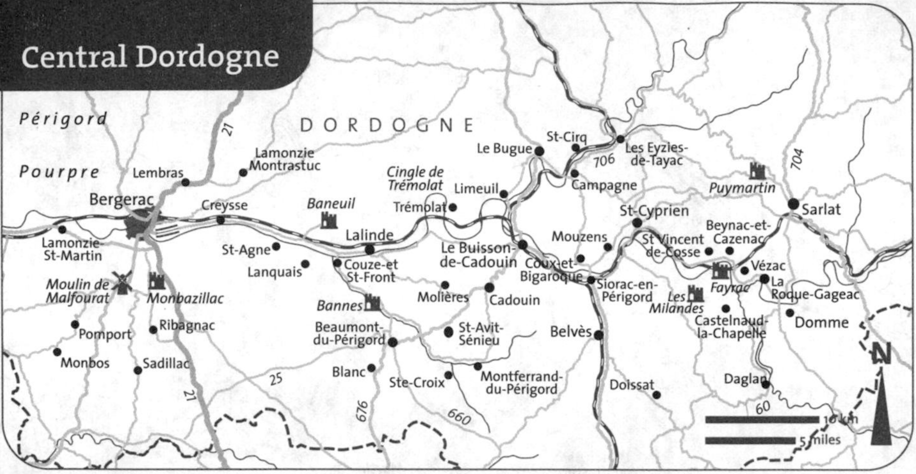

Château Marqueyssac
t 05 53 31 36 36; park open April–June and Sept daily 10–7; July and Aug daily 9–8; Feb, Mar and Oct–early Nov daily 10–6; early Nov–Jan daily 2–5; adm

Château de Beynac
t 05 53 29 50 40; open Mar–May daily 10–6; June–Sept daily 10–6.30; Oct and Nov daily 10–dusk; Dec–Feb daily 11–dusk

Near La Roque-Gageac, **Vézac** has a bridge over the Dordogne and a great French beauty spot – the **Château Marqueyssac**, with gloriously romantic listed gardens laid out in the 16th century, with waterfalls, rockeries and 150,000 ancient box hedges in lavish forms, laid out on terraces with enchanting views over the river. Call about candlelit evenings in summer. A boutique sells unique boxwood items, and there's a restaurant and tea-room (*April–Nov*).

You may have already seen **Beynac-et-Cazenac**'s overpowering **Château de Beynac** from various points along the Dordogne. Barons of Périgord, the Beynacs were every bit as daunting and fierce as their castle appears. When Richard the Lionheart made it known he meant to give it to his devoted Captain Mercadier, the Beynacs joined forces with Fortanier of Gourdon, whose father and brothers had been killed by Richard. In March 1199, when Richard and Mercadier came down with a band of *routiers* to besiege Châlus castle just over the border in the Limousin, Fortanier shot an arrow that caught the king in a gap in his armour. Richard died a few days later, and not long after that the Beynacs liquidated Mercadier.

In 1214 Simon de Montfort attacked Beynac and its lord, nicknamed the '*arca satana*' (Satan's Bow), for being a devoted friend of the Cathar-friendly Count Raymond VI of Toulouse; although he spared Satan's Bow for his loyalty to the King of France, Simon destroyed the château's most imposing towers. The interior has seen numerous transformations: there's a monumental 17th-century stairway, a *Grand Siècle* salon with a sculpted wooden chimney carved with mythologies, a *Sacrifice of Isaac* done with provincial panache, and late 15th-century frescoes in the Oratory of the *Last Supper*, the *Pietà* and the *Man of Sorrows*. In the *Last Supper*, note the rare portrayal of the occasion's *maître d'* – St Martial, the apostle of Limousin and Périgord, and a fitting patron saint for a people in love with food.

Parc Archéologique de Beynac
t 05 53 29 51 28; open July and Aug daily 10–7; adm

Air Parc
t 05 53 29 18 43; open April–June and Sept–early Nov daily 10–6; July and Aug daily 10–8

Behind the castle, the **Parc Archéologique de Beynac** evokes the area's roots from Neolithic to Gaulish times, with reconstructed huts, demonstrations and workshops such as tool-making. At St-Vincent-de-Cosse, the **Air Parc** is another treetop adventure course, on an island in the Dordogne, with features taking you over the water. There's also canoeing, a beach and walking paths on site.

Castelnaud-la-Chapelle and its Three Castles

Musée de la Guerre au Moyen Age
t 05 53 31 30 00; open April, May, June and Sept daily 10–7; July and Aug daily 9–8; Feb, Mar, Oct–early Nov and out-of-season school hols daily 10–6; early Nov–Jan daily 2–5; guided tours in English

④ Les Milandes
t 05 53 59 31 21; open May, June and Sept daily 10–6.30; July and Aug daily 9.30–7.30; April and Oct daily 10–6.15; adm

Opposite Beynac, its eternal nemesis, the **Château de Castelnaud**, hulks arrogantly on the limestone cliffs at the confluence of the Dordogne and Céou. First mentioned in 1214, when its Cathar owner was chased out by Simon de Montfort, Castelnaud was ruled by the Caumonts, who stuck with the English in the Hundred Years' War and built the keep as a base from which to terrorize the surrounds. The Caumonts let the Huguenot Captain Geoffroy de Vivans use Castelnaud for similar exploits, but by then the family had moved out of the stark, dark little rooms of this feudal fort into Les Milandes (*see* below). The castle is now full of catapults and crossbows again, in the **Musée de la Guerre au Moyen Age**, with audiovisuals and summer weaponry demos and swordfights.

A wooded lane follows the river past the private Château de Fayrac, built between the 14th and 17th centuries and romantically restored in the 19th century. Further on, in its own hamlet, is Castelnaud's third château, **Les Milandes**, a Renaissance beauty most famous for its association with Josephine Baker (*see* below).

Josephine Baker, Châtelaine

In the 1930s, while she was on holiday in the Dordogne, Les Milandes cast a spell on Josephine Baker almost as powerful as the spell Josephine had cast over Paris with her joyful, exuberant versions of the Charleston and Black Bottom, performed in a costume made of nothing but bananas. Of all the black Americans who came to France to escape racism at home, Josephine was the most successful, becoming the highest paid performer in Europe – not bad for someone who was born in a cardboard box in St Louis. After earning a medal for her work in the Resistance, she purchased her dream castle and 600 acres to go with it, and, in the late 1940s, after spending millions on the restoration of Les Milandes, she adopted 13 children of every race and creed, her 'Rainbow Tribe', and hosted anti-racism conferences. But her ambitions (which included a 120-acre pleasure garden and amusement park) were unfortunately bigger than her purse, and she and her husband, band leader Jo Bouillon, fell so deeply into debt that Josephine – it broke her heart – had to sell Les Milandes in 1964 and went to live Monaco under the patronage of Princess Grace; she died in Paris during a comeback tour in 1975.

Today Les Milandes is a shrine to her memory: each room has a running commentary in French accompanied by her songs (English translation available): exhibits include her famous skirt of upturned bananas, hundreds of photos, including a series of nude ones (one wonders what Josephine would have thought of that!), posters, forgotten show costumes found in a trunk, and displays on her work in the Resistance and the civil rights movement. A video in French in the snack bar features interviews with her children and locals. Admission includes a charming demonstration of falconry (ring ahead to check hours). If you're very lucky, you'll find the door of the château's lovely Flamboyant Gothic chapel unlocked, where Josephine and Jo were married. Just down the lane from the château, a house has on its corner a statue of the Virgin Mary with children; the Virgin carved with Josephine's features. In 2006 she was also granted her very own statue to celebrate the centenary of her birth.

Terre-Enjeux
t 05 53 29 27 43; open mid-Mar–mid-Nov daily 10–7

Ferme de la Vielcroze
t 05 53 59 69 63; open Easter–early Nov daily 10–7 (pressing demonstrations July and Aug Tues and Thurs)

The castle was built by François de Caumont for his bride, Claude de Cardaillac, and decorated with frescoes and sculptures. François and Claude's grandson, raised as a priest, smashed these lovely, worldly things. He married one of the richest widows of his day, and in 1571 fathered a daughter, Anne, before somebody slipped him a few *amanites mortelles* in his favourite mushroom dish. The king made Anne a marquise, and she became such a marriage prize that she was hauled to the altar three times before her 18th birthday.

The eco-conscious may enjoy **Terre-Enjeux**, which explains, through videos and interactive displays, how hurricanes, droughts and the like occur, and how we can stop them. At the **Ferme de la Vielcroze** you can learn about walnuts and see the oil being made.

Markets in La Roque-Gageac and Beynac

La Roque-Gageac: Friday June–mid-Sept.
Beynac: Monday mid-June–mid-Sept.

Activities in and around La Roque-Gageac and Beynac

You can make **hot-air balloon** trips from La Roque-Gageac (**t** 05 53 28 18 58, *www.perigordballoons.com*), or see the Dordogne from a **light aircraft** from Vézac (**t** 06 89 78 53 07, *www.air-chateaux.com*). There are also 1hr tours of cliffs and châteaux on the Dordogne by flat-bottomed ***gabare*** from La Roque-Gageac (April–Oct daily 10–12.30 and 2–6; **t** 05 53 29 40 44, *www.norbert.fr*) or Beynac (Easter–early Nov 10–6; book out of season, **t** 05 53 28 51 15). The tourist office has details of local **walking paths**.

Where to Stay and Eat in and around La Roque-Gageac and Beynac

ⓘ La Roque-Gageac >
Le Bourg, **t** *05 53 29 17 01, www.cc-perigord-noir.fr*

★ La Plume d'Oie >

ⓘ Beynac >>
Parking de la Balme, **t** *05 53 29 43 08, www.cc-perigord-noir.fr*

La Roque-Gageac ✉ 24250

La Plume d'Oie, t 05 53 29 57 05, *www.guidesdecharme.com* (€€). An attractive modern building with big windows over the Dordogne, pretty rooms and excellent Périgourdin specialities (€€€). Restaurant booking is essential. *Closed early Jan–mid-Feb and early Nov–mid-Dec.*

****La Belle Etoile, t** 05 53 29 51 44 (€€–€). A modest but welcoming family hotel with a terrace and pretty views of the river and village, plus great food (€€). *Closed Nov–Mar.*

****Gardette, t** 05 53 29 51 58 (€). An option that stands out for its lovely garden terrace, good restaurant (€€€–€€) and brasserie and ice-cream parlour. *Closed early Nov–Easter; restaurant Wed.*

****Périgord, t** 05 53 28 36 55, *www.hotel-le-perigord.com* (€). A big house in large, peaceful grounds outside the village, with a pool, tennis court and restaurant (€€€–€€). *Closed Jan and Feb.*

La Ferme Fleurie, t 05 53 28 33 39 (€). A pleasant B&B near the village. *Closed early Nov–Mar.*

Le Près Gaillardou, t 05 53 59 67 89 (€€€–€€). A highly recommended restaurant in a charming stone building. The dishes are Périgordian favourites with a twist; there's a superb five-course menu starting with *amuse-gueules* and a good-value lunchtime bistro menu. *Closed Wed.*

Vézac ✉ 24220

****Relais des Cinq Châteaux, t** 05 53 30 30 72 (€). A modern hotel with a pool, views over the five surrounding châteaux and a good restaurant (€€€–€€). *Closed late Nov–early Dec, and Sun eve and Mon out of season.*

Beynac ✉ 24220

****Bonnet, t** 05 23 29 50 01, *www.hotelbonnet.com* (€€). A traditional hotel between the château and river. The restaurant (€€€–€€) with its riverside terrace is famous for its regional cooking. *Closed Dec–Mar.*

****Hôtel du Château, t** 05 53 29 19 20, *www.hotelduchateau-dordogne.com* (€€). A tranquil hotel on the road up to the castle, with a restaurant making good use of quality ingredients. *Closed mid-Dec–mid-Jan, plus Sun eve and Mon out of season.*

****Hostellerie Maleville-Pontet**, riverbank, **t** 05 53 29 50 06, *www.hostellerie-maleville.com* (€). A pleasant Logis de France established in 1871, with a restaurant (€€) with a terrace right on the beach. *Closed Jan.*

Taverne des Remparts, t 05 53 29 57 76 (€). Rooms with fine views over the castle and ramparts, and tasty Périgord food (€€–€) served on the terrace or near the big fireplace, plus pancakes and ice creams. in the afternoon. *Closed mid-Oct–early Mar.*

Castelnaud-la-Chapelle
✉ 24250

Les Jardins de Josephine Baker, t 05 53 30 42 42, *www.lesjardinsdemilandes.com* (€€). A pleasant *chambres d'hôtes* within the Les Milandes' estate (*see* p.173), and beside the Dordogne, with its own beach, canoes, a pool and a mini-golf course. There's tennis in the park and riding stables nearby. Half board is available; the restaurant offers a range of huge salads in summer. *Closed Oct–April.*

Le Tournepique, on river, **t** 05 53 29 51 07 (€€). A restaurant boasting a flowery terrace, and offering good things featuring duck and walnuts, plus a tapas menu. Note that advance reservations are required for winter evenings. *Closed Mon, Wed and Sat lunch in winter.*

St-Cyprien to Cadouin

The next bridge over the Dordogne is at St-Cyprien, a village overlooking the fertile alluvial plain that has long been the source of its fat, contented air. In the Middle Ages the Romanesque church with its bulky 12th-century belltower had an important relic for pilgrims – the *Sainte-Epine*, or holy thorn, which monks rubbed against the clothes of sick people. You can go truffle hunting here with Edouard Aynaud of **La Truffière** and his dog Titeuf.

La Truffière
t 05 53 29 20 44, http://perso.orange.fr/truffe

At St-Cyprien you can leave the big river for Les Eyzies and the Vézère, or continue down the big river; the south bank is dominated by forests and walnut orchards, and a famous abbey at **Cadouin**.

Belvès and Walnut Country

The bridge from St-Cyprien passes on to the south bank of the Dordogne near **Berbiguières**, a pretty village with a large English population and yet another château; just west, **Siorac-en-Périgord** is a busy market and holiday centre (complete with a nine-hole golf course) that uses its 17th-century château as a *mairie*. There's also a museum on table arts and culinary decoration.

Just 5km south on the D710, the ancient hill town of **Belvès** with its seven bell towers has been inhabited for donkey's years – its name comes from a local Celtic tribe, the Bellovaques. It went from a fortified Roman *castrum* to a walled English town in the Middle Ages; a ring boulevard now replaces the walls. Within the ring, however, the old plan remains intact, as a kind of proto-*bastide*, the straight narrow lanes lined with Gothic and Renaissance buildings.

Getting around from St-Cyprien to Cadouin

Sarlat–Bordeaux **trains** run through the valley 5–6 times a day, stopping at Siorac and Le Buisson-de-Cadouin; Le Buisson is also on the main Périgueux–Agen line.

There's a **bus** from Bergerac to Cadouin (Les Cars Boullet, **t** 05 53 61 00 46).

Musée Organistrum et Vieilles à Roue
t 05 53 29 10 93; open by appointment

Habitations Troglodytiques
t 05 53 29 10 20; open for guided tours, some in English, mid-June–mid-Sept daily 10.30, 11.15, 4, 4.30 and 5.15; Mar–mid-June and mid-Sept–Nov daily 11 and 3.30

In the central Place d'Armes stands a last relic of Belvès's defences, the Tour des Fillols, and a 15th- and 16th-century *halle*, supported by 23 pillars, one bearing the chains from pre-revolutionary days when it doubled as a pillory. The tourist office has a map outlining what's to see, including the **Musée Organistrum et Vieilles à Roue** at 14 Rue J. Manchotte, with medieval musical instruments, old barrel organs and the like. There is also an exhibition of **Habitations Troglodytiques** – underground dwellings occupied from the 13th to the 18th century (entrance near fortified gate). Three kilometres from Belvès is the **Circuit Eco-Archéologique du Camp de César**, a walking trail with information panels on geological and historical sites, including a dolmen; ask at the tourist office for details.

Belvès is known for its nuts; **Doissat**, 7km southeast, off the D54, has the largest walnut plantations in the Dordogne, producing more of them than any other *département*. Doissat's partly collapsed château was the last resting place of the dashing Captain Vivans.

Cadouin

5 Cadouin

In 1115 a holy man, Géraud de Salles, and a group of canons from Périgueux's St-Front founded a monastery at the end of a wooded valley. Four years later they affiliated themselves to the Cistercians and built a vast Romanesque church and cloister in the Norman style; at the end of the 15th century the cloister collapsed and was lavishly rebuilt by masons from Languedoc and the Rouergue. Why

Christ's Turban

The legend goes that in the year 68, during the persecutions in Jerusalem, a converted Jew hid the relic to keep it from coming to harm. After he died his two sons – who hadn't converted to Christianity – inherited it, the younger buying the elder's share, after which he enjoyed a streak of luck while the elder knew nothing but misfortune. The cloth remained in the family as a lucky charm and, when the last member died in 660, Christians and Jews in Jerusalem quarrelled over it and put their case before a Muslim judge. He separated the parties with a bonfire, and threw the cloth in; it proved itself the real McCoy by miraculously not burning, and when it blew over to the Christians' side they got to keep it.

In 1100 Hugues, brother of King Louis the Fat of France, purchased the cloth; when he died he gave it to his confessor. He in turn passed it on to a priest from Périgord, who returned home with it hidden in a vat of Communion wine. He couldn't help blabbing his secret, however, and it wasn't long before the newly arrived monks at Cadouin got it off him – in return for the job of watching over the relic. Pilgrims en route to Compostela poured in, as well as Eleanor of Aquitaine, Richard the Lionheart and St Louis, until the Hundred Years' War, when the monks deposited the holy relic in Toulouse's Eglise du Taur for safekeeping. Toulouse, however, refused to give the cloth back and the Cistercians of Cadouin had to spirit it out of the city by stealth (1456). In 1935, scientific examination of the cloth showed it to be a fine Egyptian weaving from the 11th century. An even greater embarrassment was the discovery that what for centuries had been considered a decorative border was an Arabic inscription in praise of Allah.

such an ambitious enterprise in the middle of nowhere? Because in 1117 the abbey got hold of a precious gift that put it square on the pilgrimage map of France – the *Saint Suaire*, the cloth used to wrap the head of Christ, a lesser Shroud of Turin (*see* opposite).

The Abbey Church and Cloister

Abbaye et Cloître de Cadouin
t 05 53 05 65 65, www.semitour.com; open July and Aug Mon–Fri 10–7, Sat and Sun 10–12.30 and 2–6; rest of year daily 10–12.30 and 2–6

The centre of the village is a sturdy Flamboyant *halle* supported on stone pillars and facing the abbey church, consecrated in 1154. All the austere decoration of the asymmetrical façade is in triplicate: three flat buttresses, three doorways, three windows and nine blind arches, while the interior, with its three naves and domes, has been stripped naked by Cadouin's 19th-century restorers to reveal the vigorous architecture in all its purity. The reliquary holding the *Saint Suaire* originally hung behind the altar in the choir; only the dangling chains remain.

The entrance to the lovely Flamboyant Gothic cloister is just right of the church. It took so long to build that even a remote spot like Cadouin fell under the spell of the Renaissance before its completion; while the first, eastern galleries have pinnacles carved with curly kale leaves and thistles, the west gallery, built in the 1500s, is wholly Renaissance. A handout in English explains the scenes carved on the columns, ceiling pendants and doorways, an altogether hearty mix of sacred and profane – an *Annunciation*, scenes from the Last Judgement, Lazarus and Job keeping company with merchants fighting over a goose, an odd four-eyed, three-headed creature, and an anti-feminist trilogy – Samson and Delilah, a scene from the Lays of Virgil, and a courtesan straddling Aristotle (her name is Phyllis; this is from a medieval legend warning against the vanity of scholars). The debunked *Saint Suaire* is displayed with its copper gilt reliquary in the little museum in the Salle Capitulaire.

Musée du Vélocipède
t 05 53 63 46 60; open daily 10–6; adm

Cadouin also has a **Musée du Vélocipède** with a rare collection of bicycles dating from the early 19th century up to 1947.

Around Cadouin

Les Grottes de Maxange
t 05 53 23 42 80, www.lesgrottesdemaxange.com; open July and Aug daily 9–7; April–June, Sept and Nov–Easter daily 10–12 and 2–6; Oct daily 10–12 and 2–5; adm

Jardins de Planbuisson
t 05 53 22 01 03; open June and Sept daily 2–5.30; July and Aug daily 10–7

If you want to return to the Dordogne, the D25 follows the Compostela pilgrimage route to **Le Buisson-de-Cadouin** with its river-beaches and campsites – the closest point and an important crossroads where you can catch the D710 for Le Bugue and the Vézère valley. Le Buisson also has its own cave: **Les Grottes de Maxange**, which was accidentally discovered in 2000 during quarrying for building stone. It has some utterly unique eccentric calcite formations – little gravity-defying rings and noodles in dazzling crystalline ceiling displays. The only evidence of life were the distinct scratches on the walls left by resident cave bears. The nearby **Jardins de Planbuisson** have 250 types of bamboo, exotic plants and a botanic garden.

Maison de la Noix
t 05 53 57 52 64; open Mon–Fri 10–12.30 and 3–6.30

From Cadouin, consider making a little circuit through the woods to various minor but interesting sights in the area: along the D27 to the tiny, unfinished English *bastide* of **Molières**, boasting a large Gothic church that was built by a Plantagenet architect. Molières, so they say, has a ghost: in the 1360s, Queen Blanca of Castile died here, poisoned by her husband Pedro the Cruel, and she has a habit of wandering the streets. There's a walnut museum, the **Maison de la Noix**, in town.

Eglise de St-Avit-Sénieur
t 05 53 57 52 64; open daily, call for hrs; guided visits July and Aug

Continue south through the valley of the Couze, dotted with prehistoric *abris*, to charming **St-Avit-Sénieur**, a tiny medieval hamlet around an immense **fortified church** from the 11th century, built by Augustinian monks. Despite the terrifying aspect of its towers, the abbey was sacked during Simon de Montfort's crusade; the church's wrecked domes were later replaced with ogival vaulting. Of the abbey, only sections of the cloister, dormitory and *salle capitulaire* survive. In summer you can learn about medieval art, including sculpture and calligraphy, and have a go yourself; see *www.perigord-patrimoine.com* for details.

Just to the west of St-Avit, turn east on the D26, a scenic road passing through the Dordogne's largest wood, the Forêt de la Bessède, to **Montferrand-du-Périgord**, a graceful medieval hilltop village to the southeast, dominated by the ruins of a medieval castle. It has a pretty 16th-century *halle* and a little Romanesque church by the cemetery. Even better is the Romanesque church at **Ste-Croix** (take the D26E), with a stern *clocher-mur* and good carved capitals inside.

Some astute navigation on the wiggly narrow lanes, heading northwest of Ste-Croix, will eventually reward with you with the D660 for **Beaumont-du-Périgord**, a *bastide* that was founded in 1275 by a lieutenant of Edward I, Lucas de Thaney, who honoured Edward's father, Henry III, by laying out Beaumont's wide straight streets in the form of an H. One mighty gate remains of the old ramparts, the Porte de Luzier, as well as the striking 13th-century fortified church, **St-Laurent-et-St-Front**, which could probably lick even St-Avit's church in a pitched battle. Yet for all its military features, an effort was made to embellish the west front, with a carved porch and frieze depicting the four Evangelists, a hunt, a king and a mermaid. You can visit the 15th–16th-century **Château de Bannes**, set high on a crag over the Couze valley, replacing an earlier castle that was destroyed in the Hundred Years' War. Ask at the tourist office (*see* opposite) about night tours of the village in summer and visits to local farms.

One of the southwest's most impressive Neolithic sights, a megalithic gallery known as the **Dolmen du Blanc**, can be seen just over 3km to the south along the D676, on the left side of the road. From Beaumont, the D25 takes you back to Cadouin.

Market Days from St-Cyprien to Cadouin

St-Cyprien: Sunday.

Siorac-en-Périgord: Wednesday.

Belvès: Saturday, and Wednesday-eve farmers' market late June–mid-Sept.

Beaumont-du-Périgord: Saturday and Tuesday.

Le Buisson-de-Cadouin: Friday.

Where to Stay and Eat from St-Cyprien to Cadouin

ⓘ **Belvès >>**
1 Rue de Filhols,
t *05 53 29 10 20, www.perigord.com/belves*

ⓘ **St-Cyprien >**
t *05 53 30 36 09, www.stcyprien-perigord.com*

ⓘ **Le Buisson-de-Cadouin >>**
t *05 53 22 06 09*

★ **Manoir de Bellerive >>**

ⓘ **Beaumont-du-Périgord >>**
Place Centrale,
t *05 53 22 39 12, www.pays-beaumontois.com*

ⓘ **Siorac-en-Périgord >**
t *05 53 31 63 51, www.ville-siorac-en-perigord.fr*

St-Cyprien ✉ 24220

****La Grande Marque**, Marnac, just off road between St-Cyprien and Siorac, **t** 05 53 31 61 63 (€€). A lovely *chambres d'hôte* in its own park, with great views, a pool and a tennis court. When it's not busy, the English owner discusses menus with guests and cooks evening meals (€€€–€€) to order.

****La Terrasse**, Place Jean Ladignac, **t** 05 53 29 21 69, *www.hotel-laterrasse.com* (€). Rooms of differing standards – the best are in the annexe with the small garden at the front – and a rather run-of-the-mill restaurant (€€). *Closed Dec–Feb and Sun eve out of season; restaurant Mon out of season.*

Jardin d'Epicure, just outside town on D703 towards Sarlat, **t** 05 53 30 40 95 (€€€). Superb southwest dishes made with flair in cheerful surroundings. *Closed Wed, Thurs lunch, Sat lunch and 4wks in Nov and Dec.*

Coux-et-Bigaroque ✉ 24220

****Le Petit Chaperon Rouge**, just north of Siorac (head towards village on D703, come off Sarlat road and follow signs), **t** 05 53 29 37 79 (€). Comfy old-fashioned rooms hidden up a drive, and a busy restaurant (€€€–€) with an terrace with fairylights, overlooking the valley. Menus feature southwest favourites with unusual touches. *Closed Nov, Tues, and Wed lunch out of season.*

Siorac-en-Périgord ✉ 24170

****Relais du Périgord Noir**, Place de la Poste, **t** 05 53 31 60 02, *www.relais-perigord-noir.fr* (€€€–€). A handsome stone building with pleasant rooms looking onto a garden and pool, a sauna, billiards and a good restaurant (€€€–€€). *Closed Oct–mid-April.*

****Auberge de la Petite Reine, t** 05 53 31 60 42, *www.petite-reine.com* (€€–€). A club-like hotel with a covered pool and a gym. *Closed mid-Oct–mid-April.*

***Hôtel le Trèfle à Quatre Feuilles, t** 05 53 31 60 26, *www.letrefle4feuilles.com* (€). A simple hotel by the castle, with calm rooms and apartments in a country style. The intimate restaurant (€€€–€€) offers southwest menus and globally inspired dishes, including some vegetarian options. *Closed Wed.*

Belvès ✉ 24170

***Le Home**, Place de la Croix-des-Frères, **t** 05 53 29 01 65, *www.lehomedebelves.fr* (€). A simple option with a restaurant (€€€–€). *Closed mid-Dec–mid-Jan and Sun eve out of season.*

Auberge de Nauze, Sagelat, **t** 05 53 28 44 81 (€€€–€). Excellent fish and meat dishes by the best chef in the area. *Closed Sat lunch, Mon and Tues eve, 2wks in Dec, 1wk in Feb and 1wk in June.*

Le Buisson-de-Cadouin ✉ 24480

*****Manoir de Bellerive**, Route de Siorac, **t** 05 53 22 16 16, *www.bellerivehotel.com* (€€€€€–€€€€). A renovated manor in a large park, with a sauna, tennis court and pool. The superb restaurant (€€€€–€€€) offers a wonderful tournedos of beef Rossini style (on a crouton with truffle and foie gras). *Restaurant closed Jan–mid-Mar and Mon–Wed lunch.*

Cadouin ✉ 24480

*****La Salvetat**, 2.5km east of Cadouin on D54, **t** 05 53 63 42 79, *www.lasalvetat.com* (€€). A well-restored old farmhouse in a pretty garden, with a pool, activities, and great food (€€€–€€). *Closed early Nov–mid-Mar.*

Beaumont-du-Périgord ✉ 24440

Hostellerie de St Front, Rue Romieu, **t** 05 53 22 30 11 (€). Compact rooms, some with balconies, and a restaurant (€€€–€) with good regional food and seafood on occasion. *Closed Sat lunch and Tues.*

Chez Laparre, 4.5km southeast of town at Labouquerie, just off Monpazier road, **t** 05 53 22 40 22 (€). A pleasant farmhouse B&B.

Back along the Dordogne

Before settling down in the western plains around Bergerac, the Dordogne pierces through a last stretch of glorious scenery between Le Buisson-de-Cadouin and Lalinde.

Limeuil and Trémolat

Chapelle St-Martin
open daily 9–6

Parc du Château de Limeuil
open June–Sept Mon–Fri 2.30–6.30; Sat, Sun and public hols 10–12.30 and 2.30–6.30; July and Aug daily 10–7; April, May and Oct Sat–Mon and public hols 10–12.30 and 2.30–6

The lords of lofty **Limeuil**, where the Vézère flows into the Dordogne, defended this important junction with bristling walls, in part intact, along with three mighty gates; the snug village inside, with cobbled streets and stone cottages laced with ivy and roses, is almost too cute to be real (and packed out in July and August). There's a Renaissance statue of the Virgin in the church, and, on the road out to Le Bugue, the domed Romanesque **St-Martin**, jointly financed in 1194 by Richard the Lionheart and Philippe Auguste of France as an expiatory chapel for the murder of Thomas à Becket by Richard's dad (see the Latin inscription over the door, asking for God's mercy). Stroll around **Limeuil castle's park**, dating from the late 19th century, with 60 or so types of tree, an arboretum and, in summer, craft displays, including basketmaking and weaving (see *www.perigord-patrimoine.com* for details). Canoes can be hired from Jean Rivière (*t 05 53 63 38 73*), and the tourist office has details of summer night tours of the village.

Jean Victor Dubois, Emaux d'Art
t 05 53 22 31 21; open Feb–Nov daily 10–7

West of Limeuil the Dordogne's most majestic loop is followed by a scenic corniche road, the *Route du Cingle*. Along the way are a pair of belvederes and charming **Trémolat**, its boundaries exactly matching the outlines of a 6th-century estate owned by the parents of Trémolat's patron, St Cybard. Signs of a Carolingian chapel, built to mark the miracles Cybard performed at home, remain in the nave of the fortified 12th-century church; if things got hot, locals retreated into the mighty belltower keep. Trémolat will be familiar if you've seen Chabrol's *Le Boucher*, filmed here in 1970. The town has a delightful *plan d'eau* for dips. Don't miss the views from the Belvédère de Trémolat, just west, or the **enamel studio and gallery**.

La Douce Limeuil

In the 16th century, Isabelle de Limeuil, daughter of the *seigneur* of Lanquais (*see* below), put the little town's name on the tip of every tongue in Paris. Rhapsodized by Brantôme as 'La Douce Limeuil', she was one of the loveliest of Catherine de' Medici's bevy of ladies-in-waiting, jokingly known as the 'flying squadron'. As queen mother, Catherine employed astrologers and sorcerers to get her way, and, like the wicked witch in *Snow White*, once sent a poisoned apple to an enemy; nor was she above using the virtue of her flying squadron to seduce great Protestant nobles of France, in the hope that a conquest in the bedroom would translate somehow into a conquest for the Faith. Catherine sent the delightful Isabelle to charm one of the most powerful – the Prince de Condé. When a growing waistline betrayed the fact that she'd succeeded only too well, Catherine sent her home in disgrace. After the baby's birth, Catherine had a change of heart, and gave Isabelle in marriage to a social-climbing Italian banker to whom she owed money.

Getting to Trémolat, Lalinde and Environs

Sarlat–Bordeaux **trains** run through this area 5–6 times a day, making stops at Trémolat, Mauzac, Lalinde and Creysse.

Lalinde and Lanquais

The *Route du Cingle* descends through Mauzac to the busy market town of **Lalinde**, a royal English *bastide* founded by Henry III in 1267 and given a 'solemn charter' and tax concessions that set it up from the start. Lalinde has maintained its grid core, *place* and medieval Bergerac Gate; it now extends between the Dordogne and the canal built to avoid the *Saut de la Gratusse*, a dangerous stretch of rapids. Before the canal was built, boatmen from Lalinde made a good living navigating all the flat-bottomed barges on the river through the rapids, helping their business by warning of a great serpent that gobbled up anyone who foundered. A waterside Chapelle de St-Front was built over the worst stretch for heavenly aid, just opposite Lalinde's river terrace. Canoes can be hired from the **Base de Loisirs de la Guillou** (*t* *05 53 61 02 91*). There's also a **private collection of fossils, minerals and stones**.

Exposition Privée de Fossiles, Minéraux et Pierres Taillées
t 05 53 61 23 46; open July and Aug Tues and Fri 10–12 and 3–5; rest of year by appointment

West of Lalinde, cross the Dordogne at **Couze-et-St-Front**, where the river water is so clear that from the 15th to the 19th century the village became the area's chief paper-maker, producing a very high-quality product that was sold throughout Europe. Along the river you can see vestiges of a dozen or so old mills. The **Moulins de Larroque et Pombie** still produce hand-made paper in the traditional way; another, the **Moulin de Couze-La Rouzique**, was restored in 1991 as an *écomusée* of paper, and contains a rare collection of watermarks and paper-making machinery. There are demonstrations of paper-making, too.

Moulins de Larroque et Pombie
t 05 53 61 01 75; call for times

Moulin de Couze-La Rouzique
t 05 53 24 36 16; open April, June and Sept daily 2–6.30; July and Aug daily 10–7 (last entry 1hr before closing); adm

From Couze-et-St-Front, the D37 continues to the delightful **Château de Lanquais**. The stout medieval towers were built in the 15th century, and in the 1570s a Renaissance pavilion, attributed to the builders of the Louvre, was added; the whole is furnished with antiques and fireplaces believed to have been carved by itinerant Italian craftsmen. The 16th-century Grange to the right of the château hosts summer Baroque music concerts. Lanquais is also a great place to go riding, with scenic paths in every direction, and there's a lake, the Etang du Ligal, with bathing beaches.

Château de Lanquais
t 05 53 61 24 24; open May, June and Sept Wed–Mon 10.30–12 and 2.30–6.30; July and Aug daily 10–7; April and Oct Wed–Mon 2.30–6.30; adm

On the other side of the river, between St Capraise and Tuilières, is the ***sentier d'interprétation de Tuilières***, along which you can see a dry dock, a series of locks and other vestiges of the area's fluvial past. There's also a fish lift and eel pass at the hydroelectric works.

To continue west towards Bergerac, you need to recross the Dordogne for the D660, which heads straight and fast across the comparatively dull, flat landscape. In **Creysse**, at Espace Bella-Riva,

Musée Aquarium de la Rivière Dordogne
t 05 53 23 20 45; open Easter–June and Sept–Nov daily 10–12 and 2–6; July–Aug 10–12 and 2–7 daily; adm

the **Musée Aquarium de la Rivière Dordogne** combines a museum with exhibits on flint tools and the Pécharmant area with an aquarium with 33 species of fish from the Dordogne. You can also ride in a *gabare* from April to September (***t** 05 53 23 20 45*) and, on Saturdays in July and August, feast on fish fry-ups on the riverbank, with live music. It's here that you'll see the first of the vineyards the river wears like a green sleeve down to the sea.

ⓘ **Trémolat >>**
t 05 53 22 89 33, www.pays-de-bergerac.com

★ **Le Vieux Logis >>**

ⓘ **Limeuil >**
t 05 53 22 06 09, www.limeuil-perigord.com

ⓘ **Lalinde >>**
t 05 53 61 08 55, www.pays-des-bastides.com

Market Days in Trémolat and Lalinde

Lalinde: Thursday and Saturday, plus fair on second Thursday of month.

Trémolat: Small market on Tuesday.

Where to Stay and Eat in Limeuil, Trémolat, Lalinde and Environs

Limeuil ✉ 24510

****Les Terrasses de Beauregard**, Route de Trémolat, **t** 05 53 63 30 85, *www.terrasses-beauregard.com* (€). A hotel with a swimming pool and splendid panoramic views over the big crook in the Dordogne. Its good restaurant (€€€–€) serves southwest fare. *Closed Nov–Mar.*

Au Bon Accueil, near top of Limeuil, **t** 05 53 63 30 97, *www.au-bon-accueil-limeuil.com* (€). A sweet little hotel with a delightful terrace beneath a pergola, a garden and a good restaurant (€€). *Closed Nov–mid-Mar, and Mon out of season.*

Isabeau de Limeuil, Rue du Port, **t** 05 53 63 39 19 (€). A funny but characterful little hotel on a steep street just up from the riverfront; you have to park down the hill and carry your bags up, but it's not too far. The restaurant (€€–€) serves regional dishes, and the staff are very friendly, though noise from downstairs can carry to the guestrooms. *Closed Oct–April and Wed.*

Le Moulin Neuf Paunat, Ste-Alvère, on D2 northwest of Limeuil, **t** 05 53 63 30 18, *www.the-moulin-neuf.com* (€). An enchanting British-owned B&B in an old mill, with breakfast served under an arbour.

Trémolat ✉ 24510

******Le Vieux Logis**, by church, **t** 05 53 22 80 06, *www.vieux-logis.com* (€€€€€–€€€€). An utterly sybaritic 17th-century manor with a stunning garden and pool. One of our readers said: 'This is the place that everyone should be compelled to go for at least one night and day before they say anything about France.' The restaurant (€€€€–€€€), set in a former tobacco-drying barn with a terrace, serves the best meals for miles around, including heavenly *salade du terroir* (a hearty salad of local produce) and crayfish, and has an excellent wine list.

*****La Métairie**, Millac, west of town, **t** 05 53 22 50 47, *www.la-metairie.com* (€€€). Nine beautifully furnished, tranquil rooms spread out inside a row of traditional Périgourdin houses within a lovely garden, with a pool and prize views over the Dordogne. There are bikes for hire, and a restaurant (€€€–€€) specializing in Périgord treats with a light, modern touch. *Closed Nov–Mar.*

Lalinde ✉ 24150

****Le Périgord**, 1 Place du 14 Juillet, **t** 05 53 61 19 86 (€€–€). A Logis hotel with comfy rooms, some more appealing than others, a restaurant (€€€–€€) and a patio where you can eat simpler, cheaper meals. Most of the paintings on display are the chef's work. *Closed Christmas and New Year, and Sun eve and Mon exc July and Aug.*

Lamonzie Monstatruc ✉ 24520

La Barabie, **t** 05 53 23 22 47, *www.bergerac-tourisme.com* (€). A pleasant *chambres d'hôte* with a two-night minimum stay, with bike loan and dinner with advance reservation from April to October. *Closed Dec–Feb.*

Bergerac

Bergerac, known far and wide as the name of a poetic cavalier with a big nose who never even set foot in the town, is a fine little city where swans swim in the Dordogne and a cluster of half-timbered medieval houses bask by the old river port. It's also been christened the 'Capital of Purple Périgord', rectifying the hitherto unfair colourlessness of this corner, in a *département* elsewhere divided into Green, White and Black. The purple is, of course, for *le vin*: 93 *communes* produce a wide variety of vintages. Perhaps, back in the days when Bogart could seduce Bacall by blowing smoke in her face, it would have been dubbed Nicotine-Brown Périgord: tobacco is still a force to be reckoned with, and the city is not only the home of the national Institut du Tabac but also boasts a unique museum on the much maligned weed, first popularized in France by Catherine de' Medici, who used it to cure her migraines.

History

Medieval *Brageira*, or modern Bergerac, grew up around a feudal castle but really took off as a town in the 12th century with the construction of a bridge – at that time the only one on the river. As a result Bergerac became the chief crossroads on the Dordogne, and the town naturally evolved into a commercial centre and river port. Like most of France's self-reliant mercantile communities, the Bergeracois converted to Protestantism with gusto. During the Wars of Religion it was known as the 'French Geneva' for its ardour.

The strong religious convictions of its merchants spelt the slow death of Bergerac as a prosperous commercial city. First the walls of the city were destroyed by Richelieu in 1620; in 1681 dragoons forced the Calvinists to convert to Catholicism; in 1685 Louis XVI revoked the Edict of Nantes, denying Protestants the right to worship. By the end of the 17th century, an estimated 40,000 inhabitants of Bergerac and its surrounding *pays* had emigrated to England and Holland. The city only revived at the end of the 19th century thanks to tobacco, wine and the national gunpowder works.

Bergerac occupies both banks of the Dordogne, but all the interesting points are in the pedestrian area on the north bank. Here restoration work has uncovered handsome buildings from the 14th–17th centuries, Bergerac's heyday. Some of the finest are in pretty Place du Feu, including the handsome, turreted Maison Peyrarède (1604), now the National Tobacco Museum.

Musée d'Intérêt National du Tabac
t 05 53 63 04 13; open mid-Mar–mid-Nov Tues–Fri 10–12 and 2–6, Sat and Sun 2.30–6.30; rest of year Tues–Fri 10–12 and 2–6, Sat 10–12

The National Tobacco Museum

This museum (non-smoking!) is chock-full of curiosities on the herb, beginning with documents on its role as the sacred medicine of Aztec gods and a binder of peace agreements among North

Bergerac

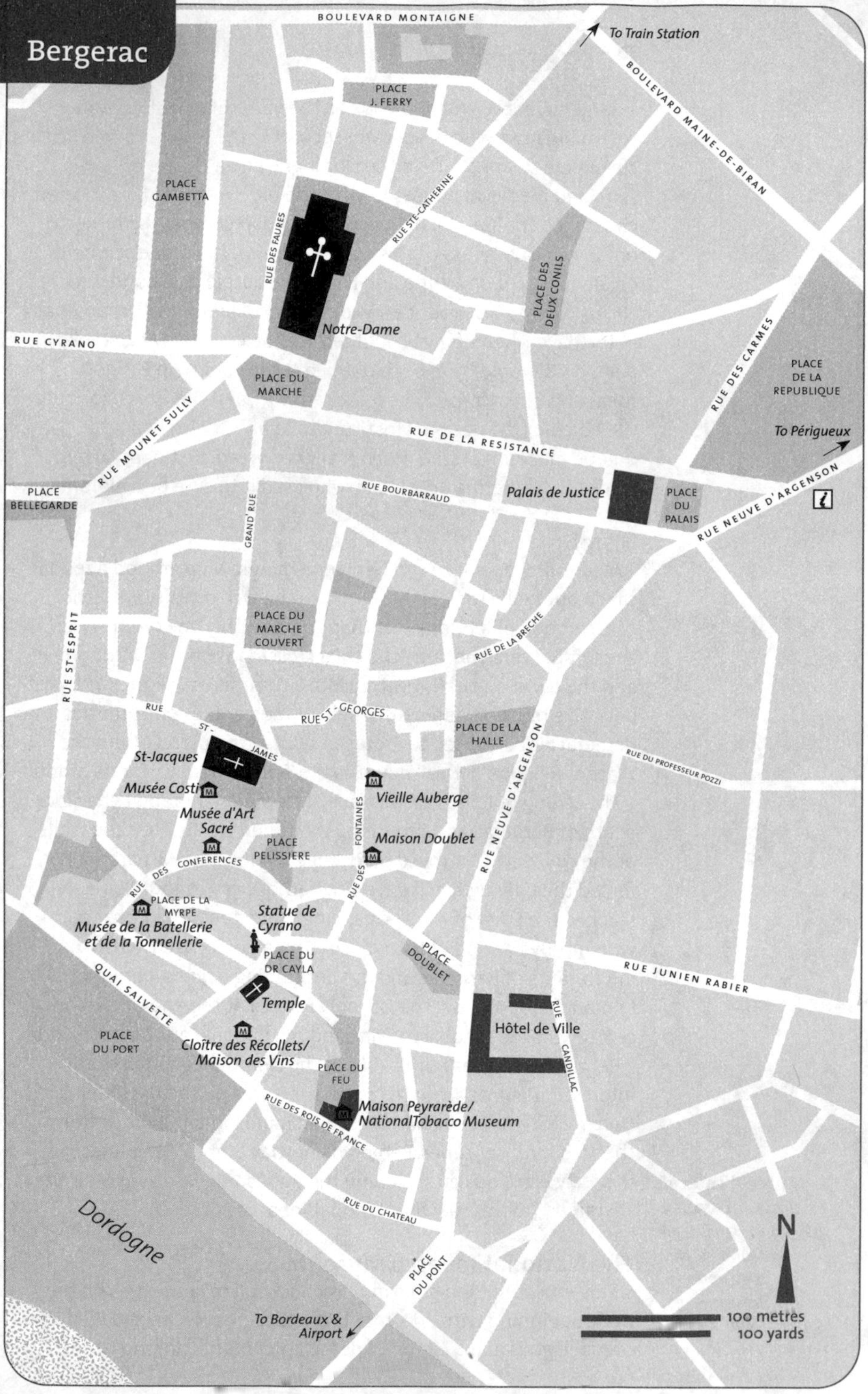

BOULEVARD MONTAIGNE
To Train Station
BOULEVARD MAINE-DE-BIRAN
PLACE J. FERRY
PLACE GAMBETTA
RUE DES FAURES
RUE STE-CATHERINE
PLACE DES DEUX CONILS
Notre-Dame
RUE CYRANO
RUE DES CARMES
PLACE DE LA REPUBLIQUE
PLACE DU MARCHE
RUE MOUNET SULLY
RUE DE LA RESISTANCE
To Périgueux
PLACE BELLEGARDE
RUE BOURBARRAUD
Palais de Justice
PLACE DU PALAIS
RUE NEUVE D'ARGENSON
GRAND' RUE
PLACE DU MARCHE COUVERT
RUE DE LA BRECHE
RUE ST-ESPRIT
RUE ST-GEORGES
RUE ST-JAMES
PLACE DE LA HALLE
St-Jacques
RUE DU PROFESSEUR POZZI
Musée Costi
Vieille Auberge
Musée d'Art Sacré
RUE DES FONTAINES
Maison Doublet
PLACE PELISSIERE
RUE NEUVE D'ARGENSON
RUE DES CONFERENCES
PLACE DE LA MYRPE
Musée de la Batellerie et de la Tonnellerie
Statue de Cyrano
PLACE DU DR CAYLA
PLACE DOUBLET
RUE JUNIEN RABIER
QUAI SALVETTE
Temple
Hôtel de Ville
RUE CANDILLAC
PLACE DU PORT
Cloître des Récollets/ Maison des Vins
PLACE DU FEU
RUE DES ROIS DE FRANCE
Maison Peyrarède/ NationalTobacco Museum
RUE DU CHATEAU
Dordogne
PLACE DU PONT
N
100 metres
100 yards
To Bordeaux & Airport

Getting to and around Bergerac

Bergerac's **airport**, Roumanières, **t** 05 53 22 25 25, *www.bergerac-aeroport.fr*, 10km south of town, is served by Ryanair from London Stansted, Liverpool and East Midlands, and Flybe from Southampton, Bristol, Birmingham and Exeter; *see* p.62 for airline details. The **train** station, north of the centre, is on the Bordeaux–Sarlat line (5/6 trains a day); for the Périgueux–Agen line, you go via Le Buisson-de-Cadouin.

For information about **city buses**, call the *mairie*, **t** 05 53 74 66 40.

There's **car** parking by the river at Place du Port.

American tribes (the Sioux *calumet*, or peace pipe, is one of the prize exhibits). As other items in the first room show, widespread use in Europe came only after the whole west coast of Africa had adopted the vice by the end of the 1500s, thanks to the slave ships that brought it across the Atlantic to trade for their human cargoes. Among the astonishing variety of African pipes displayed is a bowl from the Cameroons that seems to be an intricately carved biography of the smoker.

The upstairs rooms trace the use of tobacco in Europe, beginning with snuff – the most popular way to take tobacco in France from the late 16th century until the Revolution, when clay and porcelain pipes – and later briarwood pipes, with bowls shaped like the heads of famous men – became the rage. There are paintings by Teniers, Meissonnier and others, showing happy snuff-takers and puffers, but it was the 19th-century invention of the cigar (from the Spanish *cigarra* or cicada, for its resemblance to the insect's body) and cigarette that awoke the masses to the delights of smoking. Cigar and cigarette holders were the rage, some reaching rare heights of intricacy, as in the 1850 Viennese meerschaum cigar holder carved with a Sicilian wedding. One of the last exhibits is a curious machine capable of carving a dozen pipe bowls at once.

The rest of the museum covers the history of Bergerac. Not much has survived all the troubles – some 14th-century ceramics, pharmaceutical jars and other titbits.

Cloître des Récollets/Maison des Vins

Cloître des Récollets/ Maison des Vins
t *05 53 63 57 55, www.vins-bergerac.fr; open mid-June–Aug daily 10–7; Feb–mid-June and Sept–Dec Tues–Sat 10.30–12.30 and 2–6*

Behind the tobacco museum, in Place du Dr Cayla, is Bergerac's 19th-century Protestant Temple, where only occasional services are held for the last die-hard Calvinists. Just behind it, on Quai Salvette, the picturesque 16th-century Cloître des Récollets has a wooden gallery and a lone tree. The Récollets were a Franciscan order founded in Spain in the late 1400s, named, according to the *Catholic Dictionary*, 'from the detachment from creatures and a recollection in God which the founders aimed at'. The order was widespread in southwest France, and Louis XIII charged the Récollets with the task of bringing the burghers of Bergerac back to the Catholic fold; after the Revocation of the Edict of Nantes their methods of persuasion included book-burnings.

Today their cloister serves more congenially as the **Maison des Vins**, HQ of the regional wine council. Its Cellier de Récollets offers a wide selection of Bergerac vintages for tasting and other regional products. In summer there are jazz concerts on Wednesdays, other entertainment and exhibitions of painting and sculpture.

Other City Sights

From Place du Dr Cayla it's a few steps up to charming, tree-filled Place de La Myrpe and the town's biggest photo opportunity, its statue of swashbuckling Cyrano de Bergerac. Cyrano owes his appearance here to Edmond Rostand's tremendously successful 1897 play *Cyrano de Bergerac*. Rostand based much of his character on Savinien Cyrano (1619–55), born in Paris of Italian parents. A swashbuckling extrovert and poet (the records say nothing of his olfactory appendage), he was appointed as a musketeer in a company of Gascons; better to fit in with that boastful lot, he added Bergerac to his name. He was a celebrated duellist, and published tragedies, comedies, letters and a humorous essay called 'Le Voyage dans la Lune'. Until the early 20th century, all of the real Cyrano's biographers took the Bergerac in his name as fact; but if he is not literally a native son, he will always be one in a literary sense, and anyway Bergerac is grateful for the free advertising.

Musée de la Batellerie et de la Tonnellerie
t 05 53 57 80 92; open mid-Mar–mid-Nov Tues–Fri 10–12 and 2–5.30, Sat 10–12, Sun 2.30–6.30; rest of year Tues–Fri 10–12 and 2–5.30; adm

At the end of Place de La Myrpe in Rue des Conférences, the **Musée de la Batellerie et de la Tonnellerie** holds an interesting collection of models and tools used by vintners, coopers and boatmen in the days of yore, in a 1700s half-timbered boatmen's tavern.

Rue des Conférences continues to Rue des Fontaines, with two important buildings: **Maison Doublet**, where the future Henri IV and the agents of Henri III negotiated a truce between Protestant and Catholic forces in 1577, and the 14th-century **Vieille Auberge**, at 27 Rue des Fontaines. Rue de St-James leads from here to long Place Pélissière and the **church of St-Jacques**, which began in the 12th century as a pilgrim hostel but was completely rebuilt in the 17th century after the Catholic victory, when the chief Protestant *temple*, a block up on the Grand Rue, was demolished, to be replaced in 1885 with a metal market pavilion.

Musée Costi
t 05 53 58 80 87; open July and Aug daily 2–7; rest of year by appt

By the church, on Place Petite Mission, the presbytery is home to the **Musée Costi**, with statues and busts by Greek artist Costi, a student of Montauban native Bordelle. Costi bequeathed the town his sculpted works before he died in 2004, aged 98.

Further up the Grand Rue stands the lofty neogothic belltower of **Notre-Dame**, a creation of those two 19th-century re-creators of the old, Viollet-le-Duc and Paul Abadie. It boasts two 16th-century Italian paintings, donated from the collections of the Duc d'Orléans: *Adoration of the Magi* by Pordenone and *Adoration of the Shepherds* by Godenzio Ferrari, a pupil of Leonardo da Vinci.

Around Bergerac

Just outside the city, on the D660 towards Lalinde, are the labs and botanical gardens of the **Institut du Tabac** at the Domaine de la Tour. The institute was created in 1927 to improve the product of the region's nearly 300 growers, who have moved from brown tobacco to the lighter, low-tar blond. More than 1,000 varieties of *Nicotiana* (named after 16th-century French diplomat Jean Nicot, who introduced tobacco to France) are grown here, and cigarettes aren't their only use. Ask at the tourist office about occasional exhibitions and visits, or see *www.altadis-bergerac.com*.

Château de Monbazillac
t 05 53 63 65 00; open June–Sept daily 10–7; April daily 10–12 and 2–6; May and Oct daily 10–12.30 and 2–6; Nov, Dec, Feb and Mar Tues–Sun 10–12 and 2–5; adm

Six kilometres south of Bergerac on the D13, high on a ridge, the four-square **Château de Monbazillac** was erected by Charles d'Aydie, Seigneur de Bergerac, in 1550 and – miraculously – remains

Monbazillac, and the Other Wines of Bergerac

Although overshadowed by the elite vineyards of nearby Bordeaux, Bergerac has produced wines since the 12th century and exported them to England since 1250. Although quality controls in the 1300s had already strictly defined the planting area, or *vinata*, and set the date of the harvest, Bordeaux used its position downriver to block Bergerac's vintages and give priority to its own wines until 1511, when the *Parlement* of Guyenne granted Bergerac a charter guaranteeing access to the Atlantic. By that time, however, Bergerac with its Protestant connections had built up an alternative overland trade with Holland and Scandinavia. And in the 18th century, when the Dutch developed a taste for sweet, heavy wines, or *vins liquoreux*, the best vineyards on the chalky clay hills of **Monbazillac** were converted to the production of a strong white dessert wine using mostly Sémillon grapes, with small quantities of Muscadel and Sauvignon. Unusually, the vines are planted on the steep, north-facing slopes to take advantage of a microclimate similar to that of the Sauternes and Barsac areas, where autumnal morning mists help incubate *Botrytis cinerea*, the 'noble rot' that withers the grapes, so concentrating the sugar and thus adding an extra, distinctive sweetness and fragrance that tastes so good when served icy cold with foie gras, melon (with a dash of Angostura bitters) and desserts.

In the 19th century, the reputation of Monbazillac slowly sank, until it became 'the poor man's Sauternes' and then simply cheap plonk. In the 1960s, with the change of fashion to drier wines, Monbazillac's growers uprooted much of the old stock and replanted new vines, especially Sauvignon, to produce dry white wines and drier, lighter *vins liquoreux*. The result is a lovely golden colour that deepens with age, and a scent of wildflowers mellowing into a distinct 'roasted' flavour when aged. Monbazillac averages 13° but goes up to 15° in good years – 1988, 1989 and 1990 were all superb, and may be safely kept, they say, for 30 years. Besides the *pavillon* by the Château, the **Caves de Monbazillac** (**t** 05 53 63 65 00; open June Mon–Sat 9–12.30 and 1.30–7; July and Aug Mon–Sat 9–7 [sometimes Sun in Aug]; Sept–Dec and Mar–May Mon–Sat 10–12.30 and 1.30–7; Jan and Feb Mon–Sat 10–12.30 and 2–6), on the road to Bergerac (D933), has a vast selection.

Some Monbazillac growers also produce a selection of Bergerac's other AOC vintages, in red, rosé or white. The reds are bright and robust when drunk young, while the whites are the perfect summer drink and an accompaniment to seafood or *hors d'œuvre*. Didier Feytout at **Le Bon Dieu**, in St-Antoine-de-Breuilh, **t** 05 53 58 30 83, has produced some of the finest reds in recent years; the Haut-Montravel Moelleux Cuvée Gabriel has a strong, very attractive character. In the tiny AOC region of Saussignac that separates Monbazillac from the vineyards of the Bordelais, **Château Court-les-Muts** in Razac-de-Saussignac, **t** 05 53 27 92 17, produces a singular, exceptional *moelleux* wine, but only in the best years. The estate also bottles a good dry red and elegant white AOC Bergerac. **Château Tour-des-Gendres**, in Ribagnac, **t** 05 53 57 12 43, is another reliable vineyard. Also visit the **Cloître des Récollets** (see pp.185–6) in the middle of Bergerac.

Pécharmant

Making a great comeback after decades of decline, this pocket wine region is on the northeastern outskirts of Bergerac, on a south-facing amphitheatre ('the charming hill') of granite sand and rubble topped with clay. Pécharmant is limited to four *communes*, producing a sumptuous, fragrant, tannin-rich red wine – one of the finest of Bergerac's 12 AOC wines. Made from Cabernet-Sauvignon, Merlot and Cabernet-Franc, with a touch of Malbec for smoothness, it needs at least four years in the cellar.

On the road to Ste-Alvère (known for its truffle market), Colette Bourgès at **Clos Les Côtes** (**t** 05 53 57 59 89), won a gold medal for her Pécharmant in 1992. Prestige, raspberry-scented wines aged in French oak casks are produced at the 17th-century **Château de Tiregand** (**t** 05 53 23 21 08; call in advance) in Creysse. The estate also bottles a fine white AOC Bergerac, and you can tour its beautiful park.

essentially the same as the day it was built, undamaged and unimproved: a fine compromise between the necessities of defence, with its dry moat, machicolations, towers and parapet walk, and beauty, in its array of rooflines covered in flat brown tiles, dormers and mullioned windows, and graceful fleur-de-lys weathervanes that even escaped the Revolution. The owners were Protestants after 1607, made *vicomtes* by Henri IV, and used the castle as a venue for theological discussions and as a refuge for persecuted pastors, until the *vicomtesse* neatly recanted the day she heard of the Revocation of the Edict of Nantes.

The grounds and two lower floors are open to the public, with rooms filled with old Périgourdin cupboards and dressers, antique maps, Flemish tapestries, rare Huguenot books that escaped the book-burnings, prints by engraver Jacques Callot, who presaged Goya's series on the horrors of war, and the flamboyant dining room made for the flamboyant Comédie Française actor Mounet-Sully. Tours end with a free glass of Monbazillac's famous wine; the château is the HQ for the cooperative of one of Bergerac's most famous vintages. The vicinity of the château is planted with vines (in autumn you can examine the famous noble rot firsthand). Other sections are part of a wine study area, with ancient vines that once grew in the Dordogne, and others from around the world that grow on the 45th parallel. You can take a trip in a horsedrawn carriage from the castle to see the vineyards and other sites with the **Ferme Equestre de la Mouthe** .

Ferme Equestre de la Mouthe
t 05 53 46 62 57; open May–Sept by appt

The **Moulin de Malfourat**, just west on the D14E, has a famous bird's-eye view over Bergerac's hills and an orientation table; it's now a good restaurant, the Tour des Vents (*see* opposite). A little west again, at Pomport, the **Château de Sanxet** has, as well as wine, a **car museum** with 23 old models, some rare.

Musée Automobile
t 05 53 58 37 46; open daily 9–7.30

South of Monbazillac, between the N21 and D933, is a beautiful Romanesque church at **Sadillac**, with a dome and excellent animal carvings. There's another, a sturdy, primitive one from the 10th century – one of the oldest in the region – in tiny **Monbos** (west of the D933 just beyond Sigoulès), with a fascinating relief of a hunt.

Market Days in Bergerac

The stalls in the modern covered market are open daily, but **Saturday** mornings and **Wednesdays** are the big shopping days, with stalls outside the market and around Notre-Dame church. There's also an organic market Tuesday mornings in Place Doublet, duck, mushroon and truffle markets in season, and a fleamarket on the first Sunday of each month.

Activities in and around Bergerac

You can take **boat trips** on the river (**t** 05 53 24 58 80) from Quai Salvette, Easter–early Nov, and there's a kids **waterpark** (*www.aquapark-aquitaine.com*) at St-Laurent-des-Vignes.

Ask at the tourist office about **guided tours** of the town.

Where to Stay in and around Bergerac

ⓘ **Bergerac >** *97 Rue Neuve d'Argenson,* **t** *05 53 57 03 11, www.bergerac-tourisme.com; open July and Aug Mon–Sat 9.30–7.30, Sun 10.30–1 and 2.30–7; rest of year Mon–Sat 9.30–1 and 2–7*

Bergerac ✉ 24100

*****Le Bordeaux**, 38 Place Gambetta, **t** 05 53 57 12 83, *www.hotel-bordeaux-bergerac.com* (€€–€). A relaxing modern hotel in the centre, with a garden, pool and restaurant (€€).

*****La Flambée**, 153 Avenue Pasteur, outside centre on Périgueux road, **t** 05 53 57 52 33, *www.laflambee.com* (€€–€). A welcoming family-run hotel and restaurant noted for delicious southwest specialities such as duck *confit* with *pommes sarladaise* (sautée potatoes with truffle), which you can work off in the pool or on the tennis court, or in the panoramic park.

*****Hôtel de France**, 18 Place Gambetta, **t** 05 53 57 11 61, *www.hoteldefrance-bergerac.com* (€€–€). A similar hotel to Le Bordeaux nearby (*see* above), with better sound-proofing and a swimming pool but no restaurant.

*****Hôtel du Commerce**, 36 Place Gambetta, **t** 05 53 27 30 50, *www.hotel-du-commerce24.fr* (€). A Logis de France hotel with comfy, well-equipped rooms; try to get one facing away from the square. The restaurant (€€–€) is unexciting.

Around Bergerac

*****Manoir Le Grand Vignoble**, St-Julien-de-Crempse (✉ 24140), 12.5km north of Bergerac, **t** 05 53 24 23 18, *www.manoirdugrandvignoble.com* (€€€–€€). A 17th-century building amid woods, with a pool, tennis court and restaurant. *Closed early Nov–April.*

****Relais de la Ribeyrie**, Lembras, 5km northeast of Bergerac, **t** 05 53 27 01 92 (€). A traditional hotel in old postal stage, with southwest food (€€–€). *Closed school hols Feb, Oct and Nov, and Sun eve out of season; restaurant also Mon lunch, and Fri eve out of season.*

La Brucelière, Place de la Capelle, Issigeac (✉ 24560), 18km southeast of Bergerac, **t** 05 53 73 89 61, *www.bruceliere.com* (€€–€). An old postal stage with five air-conditioned B&B rooms and an excellent seafood restaurant (€€€). *Closed Wed and Jan.*

Le Mylord, Route de Bordeaux, St-Laurent-des-Vignes, 2km south of Bergerac, **t** 05 53 27 40 10, *www.mylord.com* (€€–€). A pleasant hotel with regional cooking (€€€–€€), plus an Italian eatery serving pizza and the like. *Closed Sun Oct–Mar.*

Eating Out in and around Bergerac

Bergerac ✉ 24100

L'Imparfait, 8 Rue des Fontaines, **t** 05 53 57 47 92 (€€€). Fresh, sunny, simple cuisine, much of it fish-based. Book ahead in winter. *Closed Nov and Dec.*

Le Poivre et Sel, 11 Rue de l'Ancien Port, **t** 05 53 27 02 30 (€€€–€€). Fish, meat and Périgord specialities served on a pretty patio. *Closed Mon.*

Le Sud, 19 Rue de l'Ancien Port, **t** 05 53 27 26 81 (€). Tasty Moroccan tajines and couscous. *Closed Sun exc 1st Sun of month, and Mon.*

Monbazillac ✉ 24240

A La Grappe d'Or, D933, Le Peyrat, **t** 05 53 61 17 58 (€€). Duck dishes galore. *Closed Sun eve and Mon.*

La Tour des Vents, **t** 05 53 58 30 10 (€). Southwest favourites and splendid views. *Closed Sun eve and Mon, plus Tues lunch and Wed eve out of season and 5wks in Jan/Feb.*

West of Bergerac to St-Emilion

From Bergerac, the main and often very busy D936 heads west towards Bordeaux, more or less following the Dordogne. If this is your first trip, leave yourself a good day to dawdle on the way – especially in the haunting medieval lanes of St-Emilion.

Ste-Foy-la-Grande and Castillon-la-Bataille

Maison du Fleuve
t 05 53 61 30 50; open July and Aug Tues–Sun 2–5.30; rest of year ask at tourist office (see p.192); adm

Musée Charles Nardin
t 05 57 46 03 00; open June and Sept Mon–Sat 9.30–12.30 and 2.30–6; July and Aug Mon–Sat 9.30–12.30 and 2.30–6.30, Sun 10–1; Oct–May Mon–Sat 9.30–12.30 and 2.30–5.30

Heading west from Bergerac, take the pretty D4 south from Gardonne towards Duras. Beyond Gardonne, the D936 enters the Gironde at **Ste-Foy-la-Grande**, a market town founded as a *bastide* by Alphonse de Poitiers in 1255. Like Bergerac, it was a Huguenot stronghold, and it retains a big Protestant population. There are some fine half-timbered houses from the 15th–17th centuries, a 13th-century Gothic church, and the arcaded Place Gambetta. In Rue Notre-Dame in the port, the **Maison du Fleuve** has a museum devoted to river traffic and to Ste-Foy's wine, AOC *vin de Montravel*, grown here and in the next town, **Lamothe-Montravel**. You can take a riverboat to the museum from Quai de la Brèche in summer. The **Musée Charles Nardin** at 102 Rue de la République (above the tourist office), is devoted to the area's prehistory up to Gallo-Roman times, with audioguides in English.

Another small AOC wine area encompasses **Castillon-la-Bataille**; just east of the village, along the D936, is a signpost for the **Monument à Talbot**. This marks the spot where the concluding battle of the Hundred Years' War was fought on 17 July 1453. The English commander, John Talbot, Earl of Shrewsbury, was at Mass

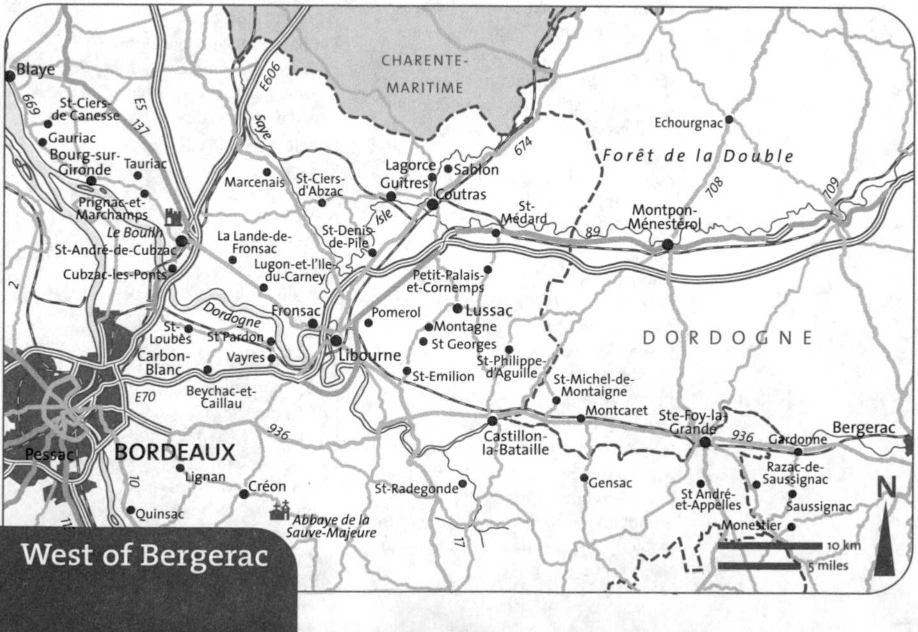

West of Bergerac

Getting to and around Ste-Foy-la-Grande and Castillon-la-Bataille

Sarlat–Bordeaux **trains**, which run through the area 5–6 times a day, stop at Castillon.

Just south of Ste-Foy-la-Grande, at St André-et-Appelles, you can hire **horse-drawn caravans** (**t** 05 57 46 05 45, *www.roulottes-de-campagne.com*).

---

when a spy told him that the French, camped near the Dordogne, were retreating. Talbot hopped on a horse to see, only to learn that, if the French were retreating, it was only to attack – *reculer pour mieux sauter*. As he was so conspicuous in his Sunday finest, Talbot was one of the first of 4,000 to die; the monument in the field marks the spot where he was axed down. The battle is relived with sound and light on weekends from late July to mid-August. In town, the **Maison du Vin** introduces you to the pleasure of *Côtes de Castillon*.

Maison du Vin
6 Allées de la République, **t** *05 57 40 00 88; open Mon–Fri, call for times*

There are fine views from points north of Castillon, especially **St-Philippe-d'Aiguille** and its water tower (*château d'eau*), which has an orientation table. But the main reason to head this way is to continue up to **Petit-Palais-et-Cornemps** to see St-Pierre, its magnificent 13th-century Romanesque church. Though simple in form, it has a façade covered with sculptures of animals and birds. Either side of the main door are figures inspired by antique models, including a relief of a man pulling an arrow or spine from his foot.

Montcaret and St-Michel-de-Montaigne

In 1887, in **Montcaret** just north of the D936, workmen digging the foundations for a bathhouse next to the church struck their shovels on the rock-hard mosaic floors of the luxurious baths of a

Michel de Montaigne

Few men at any time have had the advantage of the wise and gentle upbringing of Michel de Montaigne, the eldest of eight children raised 'without whip or tears' by a Catholic father and Jewish mother. They brought in a tutor to teach him Latin as his first language, and he learned Greek as a child's game. As a young man, he followed the legal and public career destined for him as a court counsellor in Périgueux and Bordeaux; in the latter he met his dear friend La Boétie of Sarlat (*see* p.136 and p.161). He married in 1565, his wife providing him with such a large dowry that in 1572, when he despaired over the hypocrisy of the law and the horror of the St Bartholomew's Day Massacre, he could afford to retreat from the world to his château above the Dordogne. He was 39 at the time, and vowed to spend his life doing nothing at all; instead, he wrote three volumes of *Essays*.

The freest French thinker of the 16th century, Montaigne was also the most sceptical, the product of sober, heartfelt sorrow at the dogmas, cruelty and fanaticism of his day. In his writings he reasoned that if human beliefs throughout history have fluctuated so violently, if one age's reason and common sense would inevitably seem ridiculous to the next, then the only sane response to the world was not to believe in its external things and to accept constant mutability and chaos with a smile. '*Que sais-je?*' ('What do I know?') was his motto, and he had it inscribed over the château door. In such a world one could only be true to oneself and live as tranquilly as possible. 'To live properly is our great and glorious masterpiece,' he wrote. In 1580 he went to Italy, where he learned to his surprise and dismay that he had been elected Mayor of Bordeaux in his absence. He reluctantly returned, and was re-elected for another term – an unusual honour – in recognition of his moderation and justice, and his efforts to bring about a reconciliation between Catholics and Protestants.

Musée des Fouilles Gallo-Romaines
t 05 53 58 50 18; open late May–Sept daily 9.45–12.30 and 2–6.30; rest of year Sun–Fri 10–12.30 and 2–5.30; last adm 1hr before closing; adm

2nd–4th-century AD Gallo-Roman villa. The villa was known to the builders of the church, who incorporated a funerary stele into the apse (along with a primitive Carolingian relief of Adam and Eve) and reused some Roman capitals for its columns; other items (vases, tombs and so on) discovered in the area are now in the **Musée des Fouilles Gallo-Romaines** flanking the excavations. An explanatory sheet gives the fascinating details.

Château de Montaigne
t 05 53 58 63 93; open May, June, Sept and Oct Wed–Sun 10–12 and 2–6.30; July and Aug daily 10–6.30; early Feb–April, Nov and Dec exc Christmas Wed–Sun 10–12 and 2–5.30; guided tours Wed–Sun; adm

To the north of Moncaret, and swathed in vineyards, the hamlet of **St-Michel-de-Montaigne** stands on the outskirts of the **Château de Montaigne**, purchased by the philosopher's great-grandfather, merchant Raymond Eyquem, in 1477. In 1533, it saw the birth of Michel Eyquem de Montaigne, who was baptized in the village church. In 1885, the château went up in flames, but by good fortune the fire spared Montaigne's home within a home – the round tower where he wrote (and rewrote, and rewrote) his famous *Essays*. There's a tiny chapel on the ground floor, its altar painted with a scene of St Michael stabbing the dragon, of which the tolerant Montaigne said: 'I like to light a candle to St Michael, and to his serpent, too.' Stairs wind up to the bedroom on the next floor, equipped with a handy toilet, while upstairs the philosopher installed his famous inner sanctum – a library where he could sit at his desk surrounded by bookshelves and windows, with a stone armchair niche in the wall for quiet readings. The books are all gone now, but the beams still bear the Greek and Latin maxims Montaigne inscribed on them to ponder; you can see a few he scratched out when he tired of them. He died here after a long illness in 1592, and his heart is buried in the village church.

Market Days in and around Castillon-la-Bataille

Ste-Foy-la-Grande: Saturday (one of the loveliest markets in France).

Castillon-la-Bataille: Monday, plus flower market on Sunday.

ⓘ Ste-Foy-la-Grande >
102 Rue de la République, t 05 57 46 03 00, www.paysfoyen.com

Where to Stay and Eat in and around Castillon-la-Bataille

Monestier ✉ 24240

****Château des Vigiers**, 5km south of Saussignac, **t** 05 53 61 50 00, *www.vigiers.com* (€€€€€–€€€€). An enormous 16th-century château that modestly refers to itself as 'Le Petit Versailles', offering bucolic Renaissance splendour amidst a forest with a lake, with a large vineyard, an 18-hole golf course, a swimming pool and a spa. There's delicious, not so old-fashioned food (€€€) in the frescoed dining room, plus a brasserie for less formal eating.

Gensac ✉ 33890

****Les Remparts**, 16 Rue du Château, **t** 05 57 47 43 46, *www.lesremparts.net* (€€). A modest establishment with lovely views across the valley, a sauna, bike hire (and biking holidays) and a very good restaurant: try the veal medallion with thyme cream. *Closed Sun eve, Mon, 2wks Nov.*

Restaurant Le Belvédère, near La Tourbeille on D130, **t** 05 57 47 40 33 (€€€–€€). A place to come for lovely views and good-value regional cooking. *Closed Oct, and Tues eve and Wed out of season.*

ⓘ **Castillon-la-Bataille >**
Place Marcel Paul,
t 05 57 40 27 58

Castillon-la-Bataille ✉ 33350

****La Bonne Auberge**, Rue du 8 Mai 1945, **t** 05 57 40 11 56 (€). Simple rooms with TVs and telephones.

Chez M. et Mme Mintet, Robin, Route de Belvès, **t** 05 57 40 20 55 (€). A B&B among the vines, with a pool.

Ste-Radegonde ✉ 33350

*****Château de Sanse**, **t** 05 57 56 41 10, *www.chateaudesanse.com* (€€€). A restored 18th-century castle with spacious, tasteful bedrooms, most with a terrace or a balcony. It's well-equipped for those with babies, and there's a pool. The restaurant (€€€–€€) uses fresh herbs and veg from the garden, and there's a summer terrace. *Closed Jan and Feb.*

Port-Ste-Foy ✉ 33220

****L'Escapade**, 3km upriver from Ste-Foy-La-Grande, **t** 05 53 24 22 79, *www.escapade-dordogne.com* (€). A 17th-century farm with rustic rooms with exposed stone walls, plus a pool. The restaurant (€€€–€€) serves traditional southwest food, gourmet menus and vegetarian dishes. *Closed mid-Oct–early Feb, and Fri and Sun eves out of season.*

St-Michel-de-Montaigne ✉ 24230

*****Le Jardin d'Eyquem**, **t** 05 53 24 89 59, *www.jardin-eyquem.com* (€€). Five very pleasant self-catering flats in a restored building with a pool, in the middle of a vineyard. Linen is provided.

St-Emilion

St-Emilion

Set in a natural amphitheatre surrounded by its famous vines, St-Emilion is a gem of a town mellowed to the colour of old piano keys, and classed a world heritage site in 1999 – the first vine-growing area to achieve this status. A favourite of medieval popes and English kings, it has been restored to much of its old elegance, but leave your high heels at home: lanes called *tertres*, unevenly paved with granite blocks from Cornwall (the ballast of England's wine ships), are so steep that handrails have been installed down their centres. For all that, the town keeps its greatest secrets underground – not only the ruby nectar in its cellars but Europe's largest subterranean church, where chthonic fertility cults are covered with a thin veneer of medieval Christianity. Come out of season if possible, or at least late in the day to avoid the crowds of day-trippers. Or stay overnight, and see the sights first thing.

History

Known simply as *Ascumbas*, or 'hill', in Gallo-Roman times, the town's destiny was set in motion in the 8th century with the arrival of a Benedictine hermit from Brittany named Emilion. His piety attracted a number of companions, and they enlarged the natural shelters and caves on the site. The largest one was used as a church, slowly excavated until the 11th century to become the Eglise Monolithe. When the founder died, the monastery took his name: *Sent-Melyon* in *langue d'oc*.

As Libourne was not yet founded, the walled town that grew up around the monastery controlled this section of the Dordogne. It received its first charter in 1199 from John Lackland, who also set

Getting to St-Emilion

St-Emilion's **train** station, 2km from town in the countryside, is on the Bordeaux–Bergerac–Sarlat line (5/6 trains a day). Libourne station (*see* p.200), with TGVs from Paris, is only 7km from St-Emilion. For **taxis** from the stations, call **t** 06 09 33 11 58.

There are several Citram **buses** daily between Bordeaux and St-Emilion via Libourne, **t** 05 56 43 68 43.

up a new civil authority of 100 peers from the bourgeoisie known as the *Jurade*. Up until the time of the Revolution, the *Jurade* was responsible for everything from tax-collecting and the local militia to maintaining the quality of the wine – wine that was imported by the *tonne* to the English court, for, unlike Bergerac just upriver, St-Emilion enjoyed the same export privileges as Bordeaux. English interest was so keen that in 1289 Edward I set the limits of the production area – the same limits used to this day.

St-Emilion, On Your Own

Four of the town's principal sights can only be seen on the tourist office's guided tour (*see* p.198), but do take a wander on your own. If you're staying the night, save the tour of the well-preserved town walls for dusk, when the views are at their most romantic.

Entering St-Emilion from the south on the D122, you'll pass a public park built around the **Maison Gaudet**, home of the Girondin deputy Marguerite Elie Gaudet, who managed to flee Robespierre's executions in Paris with seven other Girondins. They hid out for nine months in St-Emilion, in a dark damp tunnel under the garden of Gaudet's sister-in-law, Marie-Thérèse Bouquey. All but one were eventually captured by Robespierre's henchmen and guillotined – ironically, only a few days before 9 Thermidor, when Robespierre himself got the chop. Across the road, rising abruptly out of a vineyard, the **Grandes Murailles**, a single 20m wall with ogival arches, is all that remains of a Dominican monastery built in 1287; as it was outside the town walls, it was destroyed by a marauding French army in 1337.

Just beyond is the main entrance to St-Emilion, the Porte Bourgeoise. Take the first left to see the more substantial remains of the once-sumptuous **Palais Cardinal**, built in 1316 by the Cardinal de Ste-Luce, nephew of Pope Clement V – the same who relocated the papacy to Avignon. Continue up Rue Gaudet, where just beyond Place du Chapitre the Dominicans rebuilt their monastery, the **Couvent des Jacobins**, after a donation in 1378 by the English Lieutenant of Aquitaine, Jean de Neville – a donation that had to be reconfirmed several times in the face of opposition by the *Jurade*, who didn't think St-Emilion *intra muros* had room for any more monks. Nevertheless, until the Revolution, this church held the town's main pilgrimage attraction: a statue of St Valéry, patron of St-Emilion's vintners (now relocated in the *Collégiale*). New

St-Emilion and St-Emilion Grand Cru

A big problem facing the first Roman colonists of Aquitaine was the need to import wine from the Med. Every year, ever hopeful, they tried new varieties of grapes, but none could cope with the climate and soil – until some time around AD 20, when the Biturige druids of Burdigala (Bordeaux) came across vines called *basilica*, with wide-grained wood and fairly loose fruit that the Greeks in Marseille had imported from Epirus (modern Albania). The druids planted them around what is now St-Emilion, where they took so well that the Bituriges, never known for modesty, renamed the vines *biturica*. Just south of St-Emilion's walls at Château Belair, you can see where the vines grew in ancient 'flowerpot' rows gouged into rock; next to Château Belair are the ruins of an imperial Roman villa believed to have belonged to poet and governor Ausonius, whose grandfather and father were said to be druids, and who lent his name to the greatest, most rarefied and smallest St-Emilion estate, Château Ausone.

The reputation of St-Emilion soared in the Middle Ages. The French praised it as the *vin honorifique*, the English as the 'king of wines'. No one can explain why it's so good; the growing area on the north bank of the Dordogne enjoys no special microclimate, and the soil has no prominent characteristic besides its complexity, with clay present in most places – hence the predominant variety (more than 60%) is Merlot, which does well in clay, mixed with Cabernet Franc (or Bouchet, as it's called here) and/or Cabernet Sauvignon. A big factor in the creation of this ruby nectar has been some of the strictest quality control in France. Estates were remarkably small to begin with, compared to others in the Bordelais (St-Emilion's *grands crus* extend only 10–20 hectares), and in 1921 it was decided to limit the growing area to that decreed by Edward I in the 13th century. In 1948 the medieval *Jurade* of St-Emilion was reincarnated, complete with the scarlet caps and robes trimmed in ermine for special occasions; members announce the *Ban des Vendanges*, or beginning of the harvest, with a *fête* the night before and a procession to the top of the Tour du Roi with a blast of trumpets over the countryside. The *jurats* also gather for the crucial *Jugement du vin nouveau* in June, to taste each new wine to see whether or not it merits the proud name St-Emilion. You can make your own mind up the first weekend in May, when 60 or so châteaux open their doors, some for free tastings of the previous year's harvest.

What is especially confusing about St-Emilion is the often changing classifications within the *appellation*. The last revision in 1996 divides the châteaux into *premiers grands crus classés A* (of which there are only two, Ausone and Cheval-Blanc), followed by 11 others distinguished by *classé B*, followed by 55 *grands crus classés*, all of which have to undergo a second tasting two years or so after the harvest to merit their labels. Below these come the St-Emilion, plain and simple (Lussac-Saint-Emilion, Montagne-Saint-Emilion, Puisseguin-Saint-Emilion and Saint-Georges-Saint-Emilion).

Both the **Maison du Vin** (Place Pierre Meyrat, **t** 05 57 55 50 55; *open Mar–Nov daily 9.30–12.30 and 2–6.30, Aug daily 9–7, Dec–Feb daily 10–12 and 2–6*), and the tourist office have booklets containing up-to-date info on *chais* open for visits, languages spoken, and visiting hours – and how much you'll pay for a tasting (the going rate seems to be €2.50 for one *millésime*, but it varies). An alternative is take one of the tourist office's afternoon tours (*May–Sept Mon–Sat*; English translation available).

If you take the road to Pomerol you can ogle two of St-Emilion's greatest vintners, Cheval-Blanc and Figeac, the latter with a handsome 18th-century manor. You can take a quick tour around the vineyards on a tourist train from the Eglise Collégiale (**t** 05 576 31 30 71; *daily Easter–mid-Nov 10.30–12 and 2–6.30*). Vignobles et Châteaux (4 Rue du Clocher, **t** 05 57 24 61 01) and the Maison du Vin offer tasting courses.

brides would gently wipe the statue with their handkerchiefs when wishing to become pregnant; Valéry's exact role in the matter was the cause of many pleasantries.

Continue straight up Rue Gaudet, passing the 14th-century Maison Gothique on the left. The streets fork here: take Rue des Cordeliers for the Commanderie, an old Templar post, and the ruined, partially overgrown Romanesque **Cloître des Cordeliers**, built in 1383 by the Franciscans who had to get a bull from Pope Gregory XI for permission to build in the town walls. In the

Cloître des Cordeliers
open July and Aug daily 10–8; rest of year daily 9–12.30 and 2–6

adjacent chapel, note the carving of two snakes entering a jar, a symbol that goes back to the ancient Greeks. Snakes were commonly used to portray the *daimones*, or genius and identity of a family or tribe; twins were a symbol of fertility; the snake jar may have been like a cornucopia. The Franciscans must have copied it from the Eglise Monolithe, where it appears twice.

Backtrack to Rue Gaudet and Rue de la Cadène, which soon passes under the 16th-century arch of the **La Porte et la Maison de la Cadène**, 'of the chain', by which a street could be quickly closed off in case of emergency. Note the half-timbered house on the left, decorated with a pair of grotesque heads and dolphins. Further up, Rue Gaudet runs into **Place du Marché**, a magnificent urbane stage set built over St-Emilion's first cemetery, its cafés shaded by a Liberty Tree from the Revolution of 1848. Built into the flank of the cliff here is the strange Eglise Monolithe, which is one of the highlights of the guided tour.

The Guided Tour

St-Emilion guided tour
July and Aug daily 10am, from tourist office (see p.198); lasts 45mins

In southwest France the Benedictines were a burrowing order, though the reason they felt compelled to so tediously hollow their churches out of living rock is as obscure as it is remarkable (*see* Aubeterre-sur-Dronne, pp.107–8). They started St-Emilion's **Eglise Monolithe** after Aubeterre, in the 8th century, and when they had attained a cavity measuring 38 x 20m in the 11th century, they gave it up to construct the Collégiale. It is a primitive, sombre and uncanny place, its nave supported by 10 rough, ill-aligned pillars, unfortunately assisted by an equally monumental scaffolding, jarring and brutal, that shows no sign of ever going away. Its colourful 12th-century murals were almost completely obliterated during the Revolution, when it was used as a saltpetre factory; the only decoration that remains are bas-reliefs: four winged angels, signs of the zodiac, and a dedicatory inscription. Bell ropes from the original bell tower hung through the hole in the ceiling.

Next to the Eglise Monolithe is the entrance to the round **Chapelle de la Trinité**, built in the 13th century by Augustinian monks to the memory of St Emilion, and converted into a cooperage during the Revolution. The fascinating wall paintings between the ribs of the apse have been restored. An 8th-century sarcophagus and knight's tomb have been placed here, a preview of the adjacent 8th-century **catacombs**, excavated when the Place du Marché cemetery was filled to overflowing with pious souls who longed to spend eternity near the holy relics of Emilion. Bones were deposited through the funnel-like cupola connecting the catacombs with the cemetery of the canons: around the vault you can make out the engraved figures of three corpses with upraised arms, weird zombies symbolic of the Resurrection.

Lastly, the tour takes in the **Grotte de l'Ermitage**, where the hermit Emilion lived, a cave reshaped over the centuries into a chapel in the form of a Latin cross. The good hermit's one amenity was running water from a natural spring. Worshipped since pagan times, the spring is good for what ails you, especially afflictions of the eye; the story also goes that any young woman who can drop two hairpins into the water in the form of a cross will surely be married within the year. Carved in the stone are St Emilion's 'armchair', where sterile women would sit, praying for offspring, and his bed, which probably originally doubled as his tomb.

The Collégiale

Cloître de la Collégiale
open July and Aug daily 9.30–8; April–mid-June and mid-Sept–Oct daily 9.30–12.30 and 1.45–6.30; 2nd half June and 1st half Sept daily 9.30–7; Nov–Mar daily 9.30–12.30 and 1.45–6; adm

Tour du Roi
closed at time of writing; ask at tourist office (see p.198) for update

Musée Souterrain de la Poterie
t *05 57 24 60 93; open daily 10–7; adm*

From Place du Marché, walk up steep Tertre de la Tente to Rue du Clocher. Left, in Place des Créneaux, St-Emilion's landmark 11th–15th-century belltower rises 53m – the Gironde's second highest after St-Michel of Bordeaux; for a small fee you can climb the 198 steps for a superb view of town. Here, too, is the entrance to the Collégiale, a hotchpotch church begun in 1110 – the period of its west portal, Byzantine cupolas, and frescoes of a devil, St Catherine and the Virgin on the right wall of the nave. The north portal has a tympanum with a *Last Judgement* from 1306, with niches that once held high reliefs of the Apostles; in the choir are 15th-century stalls and the treasury, where the relics of St Emilion are installed.

From the nearby tourist office you can enter the twin-columned Gothic **Cloître de la Collégiale**. Follow Rue des Ecoles to Rue du Couvent and the austere Norman **Tour du Roi**, all that remains of the castle built by Henry III *c.* 1237, with grand views from the top.

Down near Place Bouqueyre, the medieval quarries of La Madeleine in Rue André Louiseau house the **Musée Souterrain de la Poterie**, with an excellent display of pottery and ironware made in southwest France from Gallo-Roman times to the present day.

Pomerol

Tiniest of all the Bordeaux's great red-wine districts, a mere 3 x 4km, Pomerol produces some of the most distinctive wines in France, noted for their power and bouquet. As in adjacent St-Emilion, the soil is very complex, but its cold, even more clayey nature makes for a more intense and tannic wine; the best vintages take many years to come into their own. Merlot is the predominant grape, making up 95% of the most celebrated of all Pomerols, Château Pétrus, considered the best Merlot wine in the world by wine-lovers lucky enough to experience it; the '82 and '83 are said to be among the greatest ever. Unlike St-Emilion and its confusing, constantly changing classifications, Pomerol is simply Pomerol: after legendary Pétrus, the best wines consistently come from La Conseillante, L'Evangile, Trotanoy, Lafleur, Gazin, Le Pin and Vieux-Château Certan. Wines from the gravelly vineyards of nearby Néac and Lalande come under the *appellation AOC Lalande-de-Pomerol*; the best are close to the minor Pomerols and are certainly more reasonably priced as well. Excellent years were 1995 and 2000, and 2004 was good; Château Moulin de Sales, Château La Croix Bellevue, Château Grand Ormeau, Château La Croix des Moines, Château de Viaux and Château Croix Chenevelle won't disappoint.

The Syndicat Viticole (2 Rue du 8 Mai 45, Lalande-de-Pomerol, t 05 57 25 21 60, *www.lalande-pomerol.com; open Mon, Tues, Thurs and Fri 2–5*) has a list of local producers.

Around St-Emilion

Nearly every little village around St-Emilion has a Romanesque church worth a look. One of the best, **St-Martin-de-Mazerat** (1137), is less than 1km west; it has a richly carved south portal but an amputated belltower, chopped off on the order of the *Jurats* to prevent the Huguenots from using it to lob cannonballs on St-Emilion. Due west of St-Emilion, overlooking the Dordogne on the D19, is the largest menhir in the Gironde, the 5m **Pierrefite**. This gets a big summer solstice party – no druids, but old jazz, bonfires, floating candles in the Dordogne, games, food and wine.

Château St-Georges
t 05 57 74 62 11; open Easter–early Nov by appt

Three kilometres north of St-Emilion, the 18th-century **Château St-Georges** is the most beautiful estate in the area, incorporating several towers from the original castle and a magnificent garden stair. In the village of St-Georges, the 11th-century St-Georges-de-Montagne was built on the ruins of a Roman structure and seems too big for its apse; weathered, bizarre heads are carved on the capitals around the door, others decorate the exterior of the apse.

Ecomusée du Vigneron
t 05 57 74 56 89; open April–early Nov daily 10–12.30 and 2–6; adm

Maison du Vin
t 05 57 74 50 35; open daily 9.30–12 and 2–6

Nearby **Montagne** has another handsome Romanesque church, St-Martin, with a lovely dome, and the **Ecomusée du Vigneron**, a better-than-average historical and wine museum with photos, documents, tools and a 2km educational path through a vineyard. **Lussac**, 4km north, produces excellent Lussac-St-Emilion, which you can learn all about in the village's **Maison du Vin**.

ⓘ St-Emilion >
t 05 57 55 28 28, www.saint-emilion-tourisme.com; open July and Aug daily 9.30–8; April–mid-June and mid-Sept–Oct daily 9.30–12.30 and 1.45–6.30; 2nd half June and 1st half Sept daily 9.30–7; Nov–Mar daily 9.30–12.30 and 1.45–6

Tourist Information in St-Emilion

Guided tours of St-Emilion's subterranean monuments (*see* p.196) start at the **tourist office**, which also offers other tours, some in English, and hires out bikes to tour the surrounding country lanes, for €14 a day. The very helpful staff also have information on hot-air balloon trips.

Market Days in and around St-Emilion

St-Emilion: Sunday, Place Bouqueyre.
Lussac: Thursday.
St Georges: Friday night July and Aug.

Where to Stay in and around St-Emilion

★ Hostellerie de Plaisance >

St-Emilion ✉ 33330

****Hostellerie de Plaisance, Place du Clocher, **t** 05 57 55 07 55, *www.hostellerie-plaisance.com* (€€€€€–€€€€). The most luxurious hotel in town, with facilities for the disabled. The elegant gourmet restaurant (€€€€–€€€) serves giant prawns and more. *Closed Jan–mid-Feb*.

Relais du Château Franc Mayne, La Gomerie, **t** 05 57 24 62 61, *www.chateau-francmayne.com* (€€€€). A beautiful 16th-century château offering five luxury bedrooms in the heart of the Bordeaux vineyards; book ahead in winter. Gastronomic meals are available with advance booking, and you can visit the *domaine* and taste some of the produce.

*****Palais Cardinal**, Place du 11 Novembre 1918, **t** 05 57 24 72 39, *www.palais-cardinal.com* (€€€€–€€). A stately classic in the same family since 1876, with a pool and restaurant (€€€–€€). The best rooms overlook the lovely garden terrace. *Closed Dec–Mar*.

*****Logis des Remparts**, 18 Rue Gaudet, **t** 05 57 24 70 43, *www.saint-emilion.org* (€€€–€€). A sweet and pretty option with a little inner courtyard, rooms with baths and televisions, and very hospitable staff. *Closed 2nd half Dec and Jan.*

****Auberge de la Commanderie**, Rue des Cordeliers, **t** 05 57 24 70 19, *www.aubergedelacommanderie.com* (€€). A former Templars' residence in the centre of the old village.

Around St-Emilion

****Château de Roques**, Puisseguin (✉ 33570), 7km northeast of St-Emilion, **t** 05 57 74 55 69, *www.chateau-de-roques.com* (€€–€). A place where you can sleep amid vineyards and enjoy copious country cooking (€€€–€€) and free wine-tastings in the amazing cellars cut in the living rock. *Closed mid-Dec–early Jan (restaurant until Feb).*

La Barbanne, 3km north of St-Emilion on Montagne road, **t** 05 57 24 75 80, *www.camping-saint-emilion.com* (€). An excellent, well-located and well-equipped campsite, with mobile homes for hire, a pool and tennis courts. *Closed mid-Sept–Mar.*

Château Millaud Montlabert, 7km west of St-Emilion on D243 then D245 towards Pomerol, **t** 05 57 24 71 85 (€). An 18th-century house with five rooms among the vines. Guests can use a washing machine and kitchenette.

Eating Out in St-Emilion

St Emilion's wines go especially well with that Bordelaise favourite, **lamprey**. In town you'll see many signs for *macarons de St-Emilion*, a traditional sweet dating back to the town's long-gone Ursuline nuns.

Le Tertre, Tertre de la Tente, **t** 05 57 74 46 33 (€€€€–€€). Excellent cuisine and a good wine list. *Closed mid-Nov–mid-Feb, plus Wed and Thurs in Feb and Mar, and Wed Oct–mid-Nov.*

Les Epicuriens, 27 Rue Gaudet, **t** 05 57 24 70 49 (€€€–€€). Traditional and seasonal cuisine. *Closed Thurs.*

L'Envers du Décor, Rue du Clocher, **t** 05 57 74 48 31 (€€). A great-value wine bar offering 600 wines and a choice of menus. *Closed Christmas–New Year.*

L'Huitrier Pie, 11 Rue Porte Bouqueyre, **t** 05 57 24 69 71 (€€). A brasserie in a 14th-century residence with shaded terraces, serving oyster and duck specialities and brasserie classics amidst painting exhibitions. *Closed Feb, and Wed out of season.*

Logis de la Cadène, 3 Place du Marché au Bois, **t** 05 57 24 71 40 (€). Regional cuisine, including meat grilled over vines, served on a shady terrace. *Closed Jan, and Sun eve and Mon.*

The Libournais

Continuing down the Dordogne, more prestigious vineyards surround the bustling city of Libourne, which may not rate very high as a place to stay in but has a surprising secret: in December it's the address of *Père Noël*. All the letters sent by French kids end up in his special office here, where 60 elves help him sort the post.

Libourne

In 1269, Sir Richard de Leyburn, of Leybourne, Kent, undertook to build the *bastide* port decreed by Edward, son of Henry III and Duke of Aquitaine. Edward wanted to double the export capacities of Bordeaux, and found the perfect site: a languishing hamlet founded by Charlemagne called Fozera, located on the deep tidal waters of the river Isle just before its confluence with the Dordogne. Named Leyburnia after its founder, the name was gradually gallicized to Libourne as the *bastide* grew into a major

Getting to and around the Libournais

Libourne is on the main **train** line from Paris to Bordeaux, with eight TGV stops a day; it also has connections to Périgueux and Thiviers.

Buses for surrounding villages depart from the *gare routière* next to the station, **t** 05 57 51 19 28. Citram Aquitaine (**t** 05 56 43 68 43) runs eight buses a day to Bordeaux in the week; fewer at weekends.

---

port, shipping wine and wood west and seasalt east. After the French sacked Libourne in 1294, the English surrounded the town with high walls and towers; the large cylindrical **Tour Richard**, named after the son of Edward III, still overlooks the Isle at the Grand Port. Here and there are old wine warehouses and merchants' houses, mostly from the 18th century, especially in Rue Victor Hugo and Rue Fonneuve. Both lead into the central square of the *bastide*, **Place Abel Surchamp**, with its arcades, covered market, 16th-century houses and the *Hôtel de Ville*, built in 1429 and restored when the 19th-century infatuation for neogothic was at its peak. Under its pointy clock tower is the entrance to the **Musée des Beaux-Arts** featuring the lively landscape and animal paintings of Libourne native René Princeteau (1844–1914), the first teacher of Toulouse-Lautrec, and a sprinkling of minor works by Le Brun, Bartolomeo Manfredi, Jacopo Bassano, Picabia, Foujita and Dufy. Don't miss the goofy statue on the landing of the monumental stair: *La France* embracing a bust of the worst Bourbon wastrel, Louis XV.

Musée des Beaux-Arts
t 05 57 55 33 44; open Mon–Fri 2–5; guided visits by appt; adm

Libourne's public library or **Médiathèque** is in the 17th-century cloister of the *Récollets* contains a rare survivor: *Le Livre Velu* (the 'hairy book', so-called because of its calf-hide cover), a manuscript of 1476 that transcribes the charters and privileges given to Libourne by the kings of England since its foundation.

Médiathèque
t 05 57 55 30 50; open Tues, Wed, Fri and Sat

North of Libourne: Up the Isle by Barge or Train

From Libourne, the D910 follows the course of the river Isle north to **St-Denis-de-Pile**, a village named after its 12th-century church, with a decorated apse and a painting of *The Visitation* by Le Nain. You can take leisurely barge excursions from Guîtres upstream to **Coutras**, near the confluence of the Isle and Dronne, on the ***Fleur de l'Isle***. At **Guîtres** you can also visit Notre-Dame, a church the size of a cathedral begun by the Benedictines in 1080 and finished in the 15th century. Despite fortifications added during the Wars of Religion, it was damaged on a number of occasions and only restored in 1839. The 13th-century grand portal is especially good.

Fleur de l'Isle
t 05 57 69 11 48; trips July and Aug daily 3pm; mid-April–June and Sept–mid-Oct Sun 3pm; adm

You can hop on another antique form of transport at Guîtres: a **Chemin de Fer** with a narrow-gauge steam engine from 1924 or 1949, with carriages from 1900, which travels to an old watermill,

Chemin de Fer de Guitres
t 05 57 69 11 48; steam train trips May–Oct Sun and public hols 3.30; diesel engine trips May–mid-July, Sept and Oct Wed and Sat, mid-July–Aug Sun (call for times)

Le Moulin de Charlot, now a crêperie, taking 45 minutes and returning after about an hour. In addition there is a 1944 diesel engine with carriages from 1900. Sometimes the trains go on to Mercenais. The old station at Guîtres has a small train museum to get you into the old railroading mood.

Ferme aux Oiseaux
t 05 5 49 13 02; open daily 9–6

Musée du Collectionneur
t 05 57 49 27 80; open July and Aug daily 10.30–7; rest of year Tues–Sun 2–6

In this same area, on the D10 west of Guîtres, **St-Ciers-d'Abzac**'s Romanesque church used to attract pilgrims with weak, stunted children, who came under the protection of St Cyr. Specially venerated here is a massive block of sandstone called La Feyra that once formed part of a Neolithic monument; it is rumoured to turn three times at the ringing of the Angelus.

At Lagorce, near Coutras, is a **bird farm**. At Sablon, in an old mill, the **Musée du Collectionneur** is an interesting array of old cars and toys.

West of Libourne

Maison du Vin
*Place Général de Gaulle, **t** 05 57 74 86 42*

Château de Vayres
t 05 57 84 96 58; visits Easter–June and mid-Sept–Oct Sun and public hols 3, 4 and 5; July–mid-Sept daily 3, 4 and 5; adm

Over on the south bank of the Dordogne, **Vayres** is the centre of its own little AOC wine region, *Graves de Vayres*, which is headquartered at the **Maison du Vin**. It also has a famous castle, the **Château de Vayres**, once owned by Henri IV, built on a partly artifical terrace and endowed with a magnificent monumental stairway sweeping gracefully down to the Dordogne and its riverside park. The buildings, essentially 16th and 17th century, are built around a grand court; the refined, decorative east gallery is attributed to Louis de Foix, architect of the famous lighthouse of Cordouan. The 17th-century French gardens were restored in 1939.

Surfers flock to **St Pardon**, just upstream, to enjoy a natural phenomenon – the *mascaret*, a series of waves created when the river current meets a high tide, reaching up to 1.8m in height and

Fronsac and Canon-Fronsac

Just west of Libourne, along the north bank of the Dordogne and high on a limestone plateau separated by the river Isle from St-Emilion and Pomerol, are the twin appellations of **Fronsac** and **Canon-Fronsac**, producing another venerable wine (Fronsac was one of Charlemagne's favourite thirst-quenchers). In the 18th and early 19th century, these fresh, generous, supple red wines were pricier and had a better reputation than those of St-Emilion. After a century of near-oblivion, they've been making a comeback since the 1980s, thanks to greater care in their elaboration. Merlot again is a dominant grape, with high proportions of Cabernet Sauvignon and Cabernet Franc.

Although the best vintages can be aged for decades, they are also delightfully fruity and ready to drink after four or five years, and go well with chicken dishes. Visitors are welcome at the loveliest estate, the grand 14th-century Château La Rivière with its huge limestone cellars (**t** 05 57 55 56 56; *90min visits June–Aug Mon–Sat 10.30, 2.30 and 6.30; rest of year call for times*; *chambres d'hôtes* also available) and at Château Cassagne Haut-Canon in St-Michel-de-Fronsac on a former hunting estate of Cardinal Richelieu (**t** 05 57 51 63 98; *visits by appointment*), bottlers of a wine called La Truffière, recommended with truffle dishes. The handsome white 18th-century **Château Dalem** at Saillans (**t** 05 57 84 34 18; *visits by appointment*) has led the way in the rebirth of the wine, exporting it to 16 countries. More information on tours can be picked up at the **Maison du Vin** in Fronsac, **t** 05 57 51 80 51.

Association du Mascaret
t 05 57 74 81 04, http://mascaretgironde.free.fr.

attaining a speed of 30km/hr. For times, contact the **Association du Mascaret**. Downriver, the little *bastide* town of **St-Loubès** gave the world one of its first silent film comedians and one of Charlie Chaplin's inspirations, Max Linder (1883–1925), born Gabriel Leuvielle. He shot three of his films in St-Loubès before shooting himself, and is buried in the village cemetery.

Near Fronsac, the church at **La Rivière** houses a tall 14th-century alabaster statue of the Virgin and Child, while **La Lande-de-Fronsac** to the northwest has a minor architectural jewel in the façade of its church of St-Pierre. The tympanum is carved in a rough, oriental style with a scene from the Apocalypse: St John with the Seven Churches and his vision of 'someone resembling the Son of Man', with seven stars in his right hand, with a double-edged sword coming out of his mouth. There is nothing else like it anywhere in France; no one has any idea who sculpted it, or when. And near Cadillac en Fronsadais (near to Lugon) is the **Château Branda**, a castle built during the Hundred Years' War for Edward III, which now offers wine tastings and gardens you can stroll in.

Château Branda
t 05 57 94 09 37; call for times

Market Days in the Libournais

Libourne: Tuesday, Friday and Sunday mornings, Place Abel-Surchamp, and some Wednesday evenings in summer.

Vayres: Sunday.

St-Denis-de-Pile: Thursday afternoon and Sunday morning.

Guîtres: Sunday.

ⓘ Guîtres >
4 Avenue de la Gare, t 05 57 69 11 48

Activities in the Libournais

To float above the vineyards by **hot-air balloon**, contact Agence Lambert Voyages, **t** 05 57 25 98 10. You can hire bikes at **Espace Cycle et Jardin**, 9 Avenue de Verdun, **t** 05 57 51 10 01.

Where to Stay and Eat in the Libournais

ⓘ Libourne >
45 Allées Robert Boulin, t 05 57 51 15 04, www.libourne-tourisme.com

Libourne ✉ 33500

Hôtel de France, 7 Rue Chanzy, **t** 05 57 51 01 66, *www.hoteldefrancelibourne.com* (€€€–€). An 18th-century *relais de poste* in the centre, with comfy rooms and a cosy communal living room.

Hôtel La Tour du Vieux Port, 23 Quai Souchet, **t** 05 57 25 75 56 (€€–€). A modest place with a reasonable restaurant (€€).

****Decazes**, 22 Place Decazes, **t** 05 57 25 19 01 (€). Simple rooms and a brasserie. *Closed 2nd half Aug and Christmas.*

****Hôtel des Ducs de Libourne**, Rue des Treilles, **t** 05 57 74 04 47 (€). An acceptable option with parking.

Chez Servais, 14 Place Decazes, **t** 05 57 51 83 97 (€€€–€€). Fine cuisine, with the emphasis on fish. *Closed Sun eve, Mon, 1wk in May and 2wks in Aug.*

Vayres ✉ 33870

****Le Vatel**, **t** 05 57 74 80 79 (€). A Logis de France with comfy rooms, a pool and a restaurant (€€€–€€). *Closed Sun (and restaurant Sat) mid-Sept–mid-Mar.*

St-Loubès ✉ 33450

****Au Vieux Logis**, 92 Avenue de la République, **t** 05 56 78 92 99, *www.auvieuxlogis.fr.st* (€€). A charming place with an exceptional restaurant (€€€–€€) offering regional dishes and hosting evenings of food from around the world. *Restaurant closed Sun eve in winter and Sun lunch in summer.*

Fronsac ✉ 33126

Le Bord d'Eau, 4 Rue Poinsonnet, **t** 05 57 51 99 91 (€€€–€€). A wonderful spot on the river, with tasty fish and more. *Closed Sun eve, Mon and Wed eve.*

The Haute-Gironde

The Dordogne grows increasingly wide as it reaches its rendezvous with the Gironde, its last stretch lined with limestone cliffs, yet more vineyards, and a charming corniche road; the famous castle of Blaye at the end marks the frontier of Aquitaine.

St-André-de-Cubzac and Around

There are two last towns to visit along the Dordogne before it meets the Garonne. St-André-de-Cubzac, an important crossroads near the Paris–Bordeaux *autoroute*, was the birthplace of the late Jacques Cousteau in 1910; the actual house at 83 Rue Nationale is now a chemist's. Just north of town, wrapped in vineyards, the 16th-century **Château de Bouilh** was partially rebuilt to include a pavilion and hemicycle by Victor Louis in anticipation of a visit by Louis XVI; these were left unfinished when its marquis was guillotined. There's a neo-Greek chapel, 18th-century kitchen and rooms with original panelling. On the edge of St-André, a much smaller spread from the 16th century, the **Château Robillard**, has one of France's oldest plane trees, more than 300 years old.

Château de Bouilh
t 05 57 43 01 45; guided tours mid-July–mid-Aug Thurs, Sat, Sun and hols 2.30–5.30; park open all year; adm

The two iron bridges at **Cubzac-les-Ponts** were designed by Gustav Eiffel in 1882 and 1889 and restored by his engineer grandson. There are also two 18th-century mills, the **Moulins de Montalon**, sitting on the 45th parallel, one with an observatory; ask at St-André-de-Cubzac tourist office (*see* p.206) about visits. The vines you see growing all around here produce white and red Bordeaux and Bordeaux Supérieur, including one label from Marsas (north of St-André) with the funniest name of all: *La Pissotière de l'Impératrice*, the Empress's Chamberpot.

From St-André, the scenic D669/E1 snakes along the limestone corniche that characterizes this last stretch of the Dordogne. For centuries this pale limestone was the most sought-after building stone of Bordeaux, especially the stone from the old quarries at **Marcamps**, which are photogenic enough to be used as a set in Robert Hossein's 1982 film, *Les Misérables*. Other old quarries are now used as mushroom farms. **Tauriac** near Marcamps has a 12th-century church with Merovingian capitals and two carved tympanums, illustrating the Agnus Dei and a knight.

Just north of the D669 in **Prignac-et-Marchamps**, the **Grotte de Pair-non-Pair** was decorated by earlier residents. Discovered in 1881, the cave yielded a rich store of finds from the Mousterian (80,000 BC) to the Périgordien Supérieur (18,000 BC) – tools of flint and bone, and a great pile of animal bones left over from thousands of prehistoric feasts. Unusually for a dwelling area, it was also decorated with etchings as well as extremely rare Aurignacian paintings (25,000 BC), all tragically washed away in 1899 by an

Grotte de Pair-non-Pair
t 05 57 68 33 40; open mid-June–mid-Sept Tues–Sun 9.30–6.30; rest of year Tues–Sun 9.30–12 and 2–5.30; numbers limited per visit so book ahead

Getting to and around the Haute-Gironde

Citram, **t** 05 56 43 68 43, run **buses** from Bordeaux to Blaye, stopping at St-André-de-Cubzac and Bourg. There is also a Prévost SA bus from Libourne to Cubzac via Fronsac, **t** 05 57 94 12 12.

There's a **ferry** from Blaye to Lamarque in Médoc, **t** 05 57 42 04 49.

---

imbecile who wanted to clean them using a hose from a vineyard pump. The etchings, in places scratched one over the other, include mammoths, deer and bison, and most notably a horse in flight, head turned dramatically back towards an unseen pursuer. The cave's funny name, 'Even-Odd', is derived from a village that once stood nearby, lost by its *seigneur* in a game of heads-or-tails.

Medieval **Bourg-sur-Gironde** is a misnomer – it's still on the Dordogne, although just beyond Bourg the river finally contributes its waters to Europe's largest estuary. The white limestone that built Bordeaux was shipped from here. These days, pleasure craft bob in Bourg's port, along with a 19th-century *gabare* that offers weekend excursions in the direction of Blaye and Vayres (schedules vary; call tourist office for details; *see* p.206). You can also learn to jetski (***t** 05 57 68 30 87*), sail and race in a regatta (***t** 06 71 59 80 47*).

Musée Hippomobile
t 05 57 68 23 57; open June–Aug daily 10–1 and 2–7; Mar–May, Sept and Oct Sat and Sun 10–1 and 2–7; Nov–Feb by appointment; adm

There are fine views over the water from the Terrasse du District and the handsome, clifftop **Château de la Citadelle**. Home from home for the archbishops of Bordeaux, this was reconstructed in the 18th century as a folly. In 1944, the retreating Germans torched it out of spite, but it's been beautifully restored, complete with its gardens of magnolias and pistachios. Since 1995, the grounds have hosted the **Musée Hippomobile**, with landaus, omnibuses, phaetons, cabriolets, gigs and coupés, plus retired merry-go-round horses.

Côtes-de-Bourg, Côtes-de-Blaye and Premières Côtes-de-Blaye

The attractive wooded hills around Bourg give way in places to the vineyards of AOC Côtes-de-Bourg. Limestone dominates the soil, and Cabernet Sauvignon and Merlot are the two leading varieties. Like most minor *appellations*, Côtes-de-Bourg wines mature earlier than Bordeaux's *grands crus*, and are often good value: the red 1995s are exceptional, and the 2000s are very good. Among the finest are **Château Mercier** in St-Trojan, **t** 05 57 42 66 99, **Château Gravette Samonac** in Samonac, **t** 05 57 68 21 16, **Château de Barbe** at Villeneuve, **t** 05 57 42 64 00, **Château Mendoce** at Bourg, **t** 05 57 68 34 95 (the 15th-century property of Diego de Mendoza, François I's *maître d'hôtel* and cousin of the Mendoza grandees of Spain), **Château Grand Launay**, **t** 05 57 64 39 03, and **Château de Cambes**, *www.roc-de-cambes.com*. Some of the old subterranean limestone quarries are now used to store the local bubbly, Crémant de Bordeaux white or pink (and an *appellation* since 1990). In the centre of Bourg, the **Maison des Côtes-de-Bourg**, Place de l'Eperon, **t** 05 57 68 22 28, *www.cotes-de-bourg.com*, has a list of producers.

AOC Premières Côtes-de-Blaye is the much larger northern extension of Côtes de Bourg and produces red and a bit of white. There is yet more limestone in the soil here, and wines are fruity with some body yet very drinkable after just three or four years. The **Cave Coopérative des Hauts-de-Gironde** in Marcillac, **t** 05 57 32 48 33, has fine examples, as does **Château Haut-Bertinerie** in Cubnezais, **t** 05 57 68 70 74, for its whites, and **Château Frédignac** in St-Martin-Lacaussade, **t** 05 57 42 24 93, and **Château Loumède** in Blaye, **t** 05 57 42 16 39, for reds. Many also make a Fine Bordeaux, a double-distilled *eau-de-vie*, from Colombard and Ugni Blanc. For a map and details, stop at the **Maison du Vin**, 11 Cours Vauban, Blaye, **t** 05 57 42 91 19. You can also learn tasting (*Mon–Sat 8.30–12.15 and 2–6*), and there's a wine festival in March.

La Corniche de la Gironde: Bourg to Blaye

West of Bourg, the great confluence of the Dordogne and Garonne and estuary islands are watched over by **Pain-de-Sucre**, the local version of Rio's Sugarloaf Mountain. Further up, **Gauriac** has troglodyte houses cut into the limestone, while at **Plassac** you can visit the excavations of three Gallo-Roman villas from the 1st–6th centuries AD and the **Musée Gallo-Romain**. It is interesting to note the development of the Aquitaine style of Roman villas, along with that of their polychrome mosaics; the museum has wall paintings, bronzes, coins, ceramics and other finds. Plassac is also the location of the **Conservatoire Vinicole**, set in a century-old wine cellar and devoted to the history of the wines of Blaye.

Musée Gallo-Romain
t 05 57 42 84 80; open May–Sept daily 9–12 and 2–7; April and Oct Mon–Sat 9–12 and 2–6; Sun 2–6, rest of year by appt on t 05 57 42 07 05

Conservatoire Vinicole
t 05 57 42 16 63; open July–mid-Sept Tues–Sat 2.30–6.30

You can admire the corniche from a *gabare*: contact the tourist office at Bourg (*see* p.206) for information.

Blaye

Occupying a limestone spur overlooking the narrowest, most defensible part of the Gironde estuary, Blaye was inhabited since Neolithic times (5000 BC) but entered history as *Blavia*, a camp of Roman legionnaires, and grew into a town sung by Ausonius. 'The Star and Key of Aquitaine', as its Latin motto proudly proclaims, the town is dominated by a massive citadel built to defend Bordeaux from the English in 1686–89 by Louis XIV's engineer Vauban, along with two less important forts, on the Ile Pâté and at Fort Médoc. As was so often the case, defending the town entailed its partial destruction – 250 houses were razed to make room for the walls. The greatest loss was the Romanesque Basilique de St-Romain,

Jaufre Rudel

Blaye was on love's map even before Marie-Caroline (*see* p.206), thanks to the passion that fired the heart of the handsome troubadour Jaufre (or Geoffroi) Rudel, the Prince of Blaye. Though his triangular castle was engulfed and mostly destroyed by Vauban's citadel, two towers and low walls remain north of the Place d'Armes to give at least some credence to his strange and mystical story.

In 1147 Jaufre heard tell of Melisande, Countess of Tripoli, and, just from the description of her beauty, fell in love with her. He composed many fine songs for her, and begged his liege lord, Count Alphonse Jourdain of Toulouse, to let him accompany him on the next crusade. Seeing how pale he was for love, Alphonse Jourdain reluctantly took him along, but, as they approached the Holy Land, Jaufre became feverishly ill and the Crusaders left him to die alone in a poor fisherman's hut. Suddenly a lovely damsel entered and tenderly took Jaufre's head in her hands, saying, 'You were right to seek me, Jaufre, even if it has cost you your life. I am she whom you have long sought. Rest assured that you will find me as you dreamed.' At that the troubadour smiled and died, and the Countess of Tripoli buried him with the Knights Templars. In grief, she entered a convent and was never seen again.

The story inspired writers from Petrarch to Rostand (*La Princesse lointaine*) and Heine, who has the lovers reunited as tender ghosts in a poem from *Romanzero* (1851):

'Melisande! Was ist Traum?	***('Melisande! What is a dream?***
Was ist Tod? Nur eitel Töne.	***What is death? Just empty sounds.***
In der Liebe nur ist Wahrheit,	***In love alone is truth,***
Und dich lieb ich, ewig Schöne.'	***and I love you, eternal beauty')***

founded in 350, where Roland, lord of Blaye, nephew of Charlemagne and hero of France's greatest medieval epic, the *Chanson de Roland*, was buried in the 8th century after blowing his brains out at Roncesvalles. The foundations of the basilica have been excavated; it was an important pilgrimage site on the road to Compostela.

Cellier des Vignerons
t *05 57 42 36 14; open July and Aug daily 10–12.30 and 3.30–7*

Conservatoire de l'Estuaire
t *05 57 42 80 96; open mid-April–Oct daily 1.30–7*

The 44m walls of the **Citadel** offer great views over the estuary and its defences, especially from the Tour de l'Eguillette; guided tours are run by the tourist office in July and August. The **Cellier des Vignerons** has wine-tasting and exhibitions, the **Conservatoire de l'Estuaire** changing displays on the history of the estuary. There is also an **archaeological exhibition** and a **bread-making museum**, presented around two ovens built by the military in the old prison. Some of the barracks have been taken over by artists. The former commander's quarters, the **Pavillon de la Place**, had an unexpected 'guest' in 1832: Marie-Caroline de Bourbon-Sicile, Duchesse de Berry, arrested in Nantes while trying to overthrow Louis-Philippe in favour of her son, the Duke of Bordeaux, a pretender to the throne. The flamboyant Marie-Caroline was a political hot potato for Louis-Philippe until the next year, when, though a widow for 12 years, she gave birth to a daughter. Once she was neutralized by the scandal, Louis-Philippe packed her off to Palermo.

For **trips round the estuary**, call **t** 06 12 65 32 23; to hire a boat or jetski, call **t** 06 77 42 29 79.

Market Days in the Haute-Gironde

St-André-de-Cubzac: Thurs and Sun.
Bourg: Sunday morning, and 1st and 3rd Tuesday of month.
Blaye: Wednesday and Saturday.

Where to Stay and Eat in the Haute-Gironde

ⓘ St-André-de-Cubzac >
9 Allée du Champ de Foire, **t** *05 57 43 64 80, www.saint-andre-de-cubzac.com*

ⓘ Blaye >>
Allées Marines, **t** *05 57 42 12 09, www.tourisme-blaye.com*

ⓘ Bourg-sur-Gironde >
Hôtel de la Juarde, **t** *05 57 68 31 76, www.mairie-bourg-gironde.fr*

St-André-de-Cubzac ✉ 33240

Au Sarment, 50 Rue Lande, 3km north of town, **t** 05 57 43 44 73 (€€€–€€). Spicy Martinique dishes served in an old schoolhouse. *Closed Mon, Sat lunch, Sun eve.*

Bourg-sur-Gironde ✉ 33710

******Closerie des Vignes***, St-Ciers-de-Canesse, 8km northwest of Bourg, **t** 05 57 64 81 90, *www.la-closerie-des-vignes.com* (€€). A modern house amid peaceful vines, with a park, pool and very good restaurant (€€€–€€). *Closed Nov–Mar; restaurant lunch.*

Château de la Grave, towards Berson from Bourg, then second right, **t** 05 57 68 41 49, *www.chateaudelagrave.com* (€€). A castle amid vineyards. *Closed Feb and 2nd half Aug.*

La Filadière, Gauriac, **t** 05 57 64 94 05 (€€). Local caviar, plus Thai dishes by advance request. *Closed Wed, plus Tues eve mid-Sept–June.*

Le Troque-sel, 1 Place Jeantet, **t** 05 57 68 30 67 (€€–€). Well-prepared fish and meat. *Closed Sun–Tues eves.*

Blaye ✉ 33390

Buy *Praslines de Blaye* (pralines with burnt almonds, invented by a citadel governor's chef in 1649) in bakeries.

****La Citadelle**, **t** 05 57 42 17 10, *www.hotellacitadelle.com* (€€). A Logis de France with a pool and restaurant (€€€–€€). *Restaurant closed Nov–Mar.*

Camping Municipal, **t** 05 57 42 00 20 (€). A small site inside the citadel. *Closed end of Sept–April.*

Le Premayac, 25 Rue Premayac, **t** 05 57 42 19 57 (€€–€). Simple meals, including grilled meats. *Closed Mon.*

Bordeaux

Bordeaux, that warm, magic, generous name on the bottle, can be both terribly grand and terribly monotonous, a hallucinatory city of long flat vistas tinted in a thousand nuances of white, from golden cream to unwashed tennis socks. It offers a neat counterweight to confident, rosy and resolutely southern Toulouse, the other metropolis of southwest France – it's Gothic and 18th-century, splenetic, nostalgic, a stone necropolis that has always looked to the north for tutelage while it made a living from its port.

11

Don't miss

1. **Mysterious and mystic objects**
   Musée d'Aquitaine **p.219**
2. **Superb city views**
   Cathédrale St-André **p.220**
3. **A cache of great artists**
   Musée des Beaux-Arts **p.221**
4. **Good taste and *luxe* shopping**
   Golden Triangle **p.226**
5. **Modern art, architecture, and antiques**
   Les Chartrons **p.230**

See map overleaf

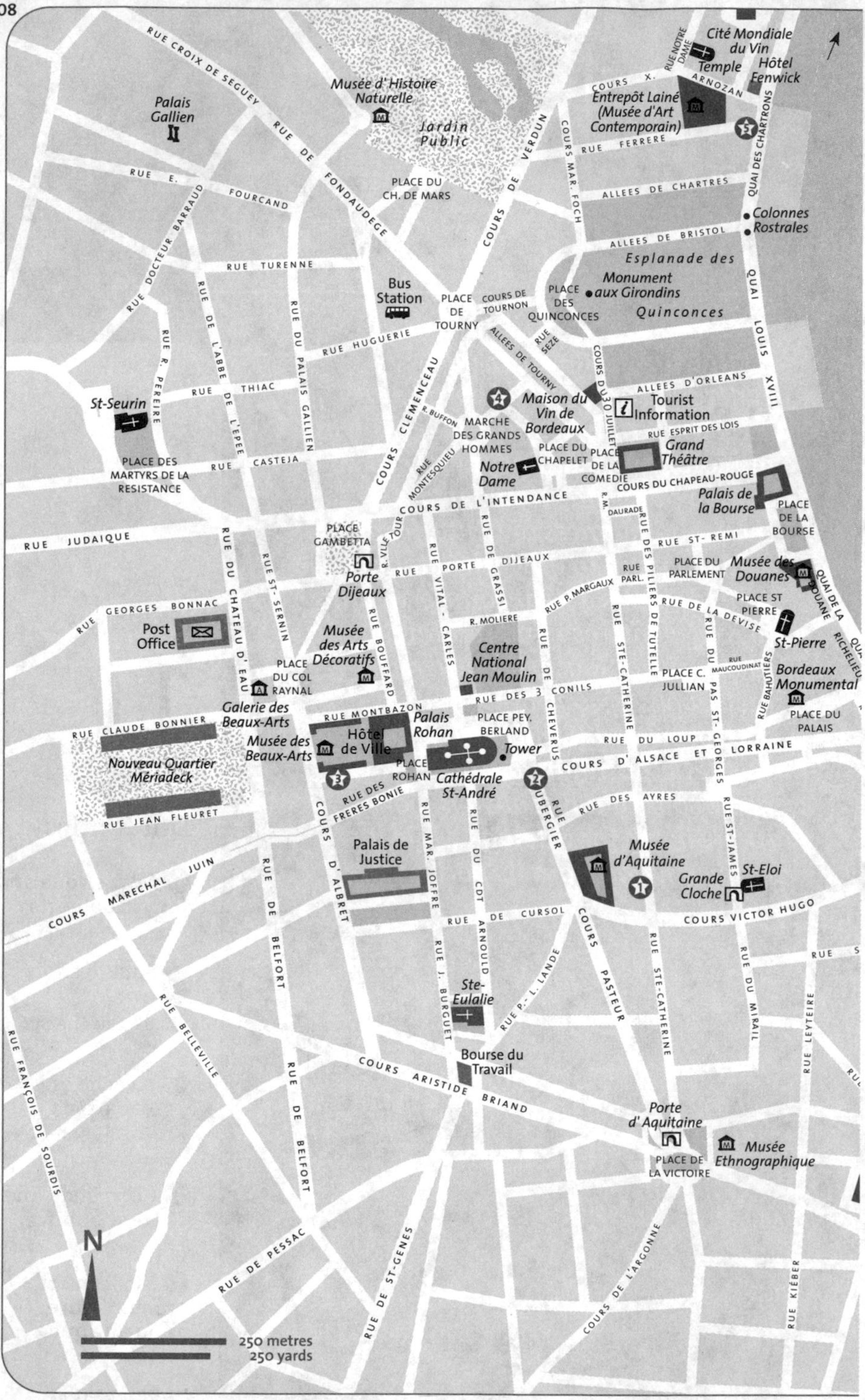
Cité Mondiale du Vin
Temple
Hôtel Fenwick
Palais Gallien
Musée d'Histoire Naturelle
Jardin Public
Entrepôt Lainé (Musée d'Art Contemporain)
Place du Ch. de Mars
Colonnes Rostrales
Esplanade des Quinconces
Monument aux Girondins
Bus Station
Place de Tourny
Place des Quinconces
St-Seurin
Maison du Vin de Bordeaux
Tourist Information
Marche des Grands Hommes
Grand Théâtre
Place du Chapelet
Place de la Comedie
Notre Dame
Place des Martyrs de la Resistance
Palais de la Bourse
Place de la Bourse
Place Gambetta
Porte Dijeaux
Place du Parlement
Musée des Douanes
Place St Pierre
St-Pierre
Post Office
Musée des Arts Décoratifs
Centre National Jean Moulin
Place du Col Raynal
Place C. Jullian
Bordeaux Monumental
Place du Palais
Galerie des Beaux-Arts
Palais Rohan
Place Pey. Berland
Hôtel de Ville
Musée des Beaux-Arts
Tower
Nouveau Quartier Mériadeck
Place Rohan
Cathédrale St-André
Palais de Justice
Musée d'Aquitaine
Grande Cloche
St-Eloi
Ste-Eulalie
Bourse du Travail
Porte d'Aquitaine
Place de la Victoire
Musée Ethnographique
Rue Croix de Seguey
Rue de Fondaudege
Cours de Verdun
Cours X. Arnozan
Rue Notre Dame
Quai des Chartrons
Rue Ferrere
Cours Mar. Foch
Allees de Chartres
Allees de Bristol
Rue E. Fourcand
Rue Docteur Barraud
Rue Turenne
Rue de l'Abbe de l'Epee
Rue du Palais Gallien
Cours de Tournon
Rue Huguerie
Allees de Tourny
Rue Seze
Cours du 30 Juillet
Allees d'Orleans
Quai Louis XVIII
Rue R. Pereire
Rue Thiac
Cours Clemenceau
R. Buffon
Rue Esprit des Lois
Rue Casteja
Rue Montesquieu
Cours du Chapeau-Rouge
Cours de l'Intendance
R. M. Daurade
Rue Judaique
R. Vlle Tour
Rue St-Remi
Rue Porte Dijeaux
Rue du Chateau d'Eau
Rue St-Sernin
Rue Vital-Carles
Rue de Grassi
Rue Parl.
Rue des Piliers de Tutelle
Rue P. Margaux
Rue de la Devise
Quai de la Douane
Quai Richelieu
Rue Georges Bonnac
Rue Bouffard
R. Moliere
Rue de Cheverus
Rue Ste-Catherine
Rue du Pas St-Georges
Rue Maucoudinat
Rue Bahutiers
Rue des 3 Conils
Rue Montbazon
Rue Claude Bonnier
Rue du Loup
Cours d'Alsace et Lorraine
Rue des Freres Bonie
Rue Jean Fleuret
Cours d'Albret
Rue Mar. Joffre
Rue du Cdt Arnould
Rue Duffour Dubergier
Rue des Ayres
Rue St-James
Cours Marechal Juin
Rue de Belfort
Rue de Cursol
Cours Victor Hugo
Cours Pasteur
Rue du Mirail
Rue J. Burguet
Rue P.-L. Lande
Rue Belleville
Rue François de Sourdis
Cours Aristide Briand
Rue Leyteire
Rue de Pessac
Rue de St-Genes
Cours de l'Argonne
Rue Kieber
N
250 metres
250 yards

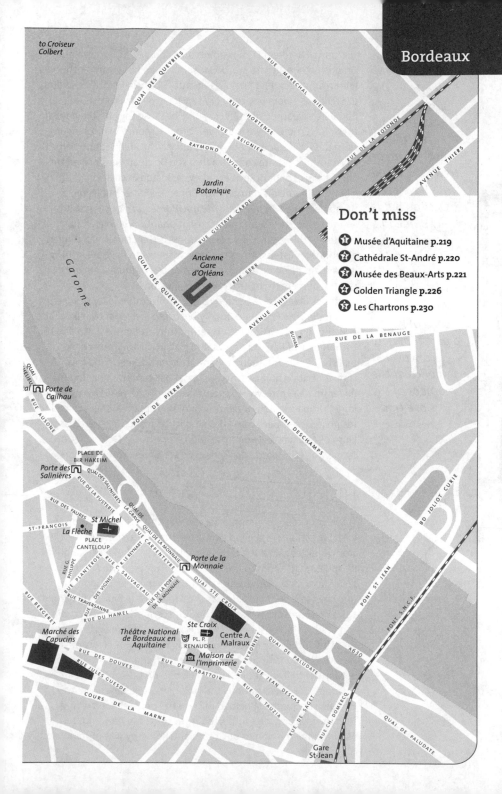

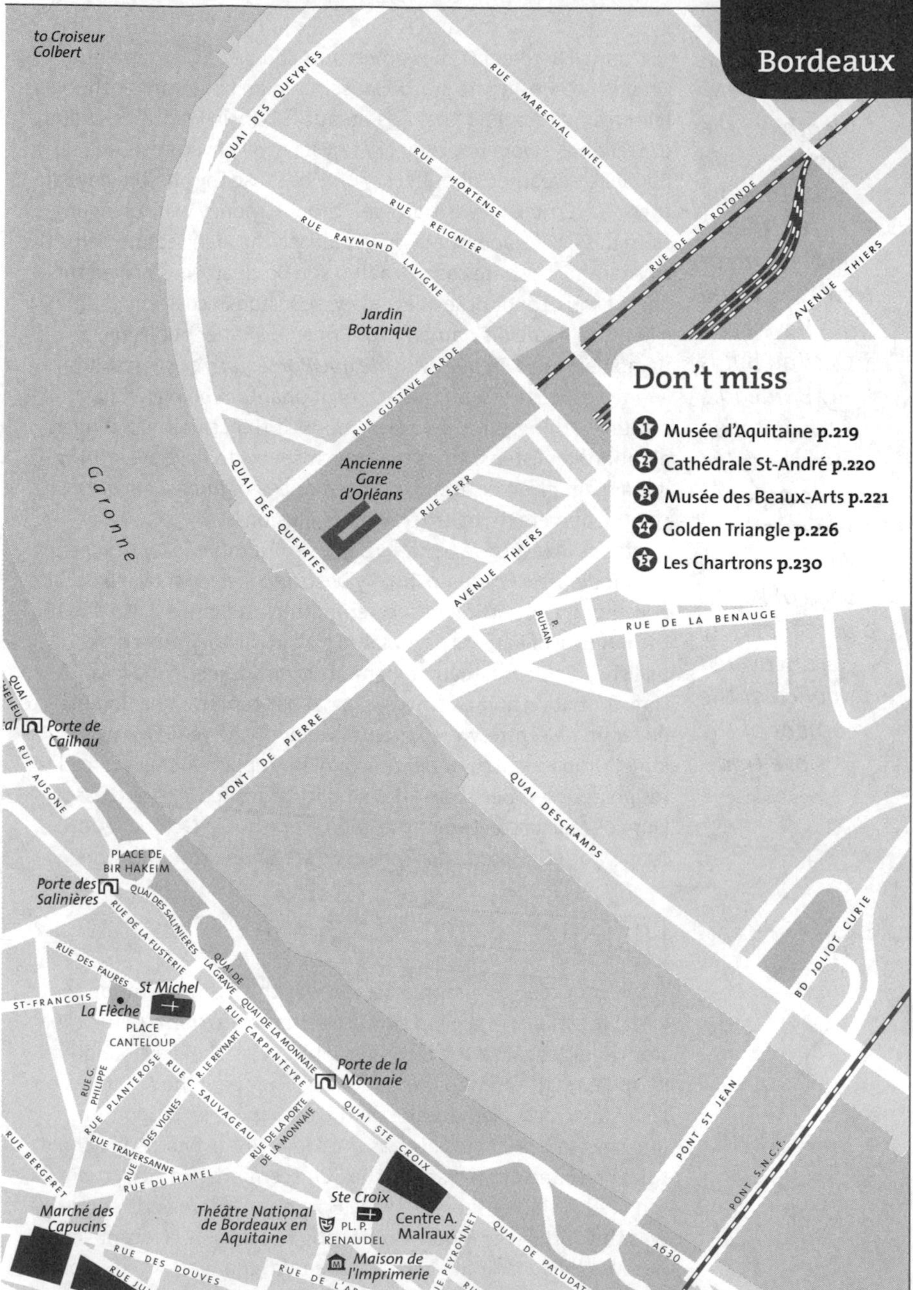

Don't miss

1. Musée d'Aquitaine p.219
2. Cathédrale St-André p.220
3. Musée des Beaux-Arts p.221
4. Golden Triangle p.226
5. Les Chartrons p.230

> *...Bordeaux, squatting in the depths of the Gironde, could be London, Carthage, Rotterdam or New York, could have been Occitan but is only Bordeaux, capital on paper, capital of provincial paper, former satellite of London, and today of Paris... a port that only discovered America at the moment of the slave trade.*
>
> Yves Rouquette, *Occitanie*

Nearly all Bordeaux's monuments, its squares, its uniform quayside Grande Façade and its proto-Haussmannian boulevards – the very features that made it 'the most beautiful city in France' according to Stendhal – were imposed on it by its royal governors. The Bordelais screamed about every one, because they had to pay for them – a terrible imposition even though money was rolling in from the slave trade. These days, at least, the architecture helps the city earn some spare cash as a film set; Bordeaux has played the part of Paris, London, Seville and even Boston in costume dramas.

In 1857 a Bordelais named Paul-Ernest de Ratier published a pamphlet called *Preuve évidente que Bordeaux n'existe pas*. It is a 'whited sepulchre', a phantom city of phantom beings. 'It has created nothing, it receives everything. It thinks nothing, it hears all, but never listens. It has nothing, it seems to have everything. It is a magnificent scaffold of appearances, of *faux-semblants*, of colours, of pretexts, of reflections, of illusions.'

Perhaps in response to Ratier's jibes – but more likely to keep up with Toulouse – Bordeaux finally bestirred itself just over a decade ago, though its portion of the aeronautics industries (also due to the largesse of Paris) is dominated by the military, and cranks out ballistic missiles instead of glamorous Airbus jets. A massive transformation and facelift (*see* p.217) has tempted the Bordelais to linger in the centre, which grows livelier by the year. This was largely implemented under mayor Alain Juppé, who was forced to resign in December 2004 after a political scandal. His successor Hugues Martin continued the good work, but in October 2006 Juppé was re-elected. More changes are undoubtably in store.

History

Ancient Greek geographer Strabo was the first to mention the Gironde estuary: in the 3rd century BC, he wrote that a Celtic tribe from Bourges called the Bituriges Vibisci was 'the only foreign people to settle among the Aquitains'. They paid the Aquitains no tribute and occupied the site on the estuary as an emporium. *Bituriges*, after all, translates as the 'kings of the world', a big bold title for a band of tin-traders; their crescent-shaped city, Burdigala, founded at the confluence of the Garonne, Dévèze and Peugue, was the 'Port of the Moon' – reflecting not only its crescent shape but also the lunar influence over the tidal changes of the Gironde estuary, 'with its river filled with the boiling tide of the ocean', as Ausone, Bordeaux's famous Gallo-Roman poet, described it. Besides tin, Burdigala helped initiate the barley-beer-swilling Gauls into the joys of wine – imported from southern Italy and the Mediterranean colonies of Greece and Rome by way of Toulouse.

Getting to Bordeaux

By air: Bordeaux International **Airport**, **t** 05 56 34 50 50, *www.bordeaux.aeroport.fr*, is 12km west of the centre at Mérignac. At the time of writing, there were flights from Paris and other French cities with Air France, plus flights from the UK and Ireland from London Gatwick (British Airways), London Luton (easyJet), Manchester and Birmingham (BMIbaby), Bristol, Norwich and Southampton (Flybe) and Dublin (Aer Lingus); for airline contact details, *see* p.62. A **shuttle bus**, 'Jet' (**t** 05 56 34 50 71), runs from the the airport to the train station via the tourist office, and to the Barrière Judaïque, from 7.45am Mon–Fri and 8.30am at weekends, every 45mins (from the station they start at 6.45 in the week). A **taxi** (**t** 05 56 97 11 27) to the centre costs €16–30.

By train: Trains arrive at and depart from Bordeaux St-Jean station in Rue Charles Domerq, **t** 05 47 47 10 00. TGVs from Paris-Montparnasse take 3hrs, regular trains from Paris-Austerlitz 4hrs 30mins. Other connections are Périgueux (2hrs); Sarlat (3hrs) via St-Emilion and Bergerac; Tarbes via Orthez, Pau and Lourdes (3hrs; 1hr 50mins by TGV); TGVs or regular trains to Hendaye (2hrs 20mins) via Dax, Bayonne, Biarritz and St-Jean-de-Luz, or to Toulouse (2hrs) by way of Agen and Montauban; other trains make stops in Marmande and Moissac. There are also local lines to Mont-de-Marsan, Pointe-de-Grave and, once an hour, Arcachon.

By bus: The stations for **Citram** buses (**t** 05 56 43 68 43, *www.citram.fr*) serving most towns and villages in the Gironde are at Allée de Munich and Allée d'Orléans. For international buses to London, Portugal, Spain and elsewhere, contact Eurolines, 32 Rue Charles Domercq, **t** 05 56 92 50 42, *www.eurolines.com*.

By road: Bordeaux's great **ring road**, the *rocade*, sucks up all the *autoroutes* and national roads and can make it easier to circumvent the city than penetrate to its centre. There are a number of car parks in the centre, and near the station; *www.bordeaux.fr* has a useful map. The first Sunday of each month (10–7; 10–6 in winter) the centre of Bordeaux (roughly between the Hôtel de Ville and the river) is a car-free zone.

Getting around Bordeaux

The city's frequent, convenient **buses** (**t** 05 57 57 88 88) are backed up by a **tram** system; see *www.infotbc.com* for routes and times for both, or pick up a free bus map at the tourist office or train station. Perhaps the most helpful public transport route is La Navette, an **electric loop bus** that circles through the centre between Place des Quinconces and Place de la Victoire, following a blue line on the pavement (you just flag it down). The same tickets are good for all services; you can buy a *carnet* of 10 at kiosks.

Cabs can't cruise here; there is a 24hr **taxi** rank at the train station, plus daytime ranks in key locations, or call **t** 05 56 51 17 16/**t** 05 56 99 28 41. You can hire **bikes** at Le 63, 63 Cours Alsace Lorraine, **t** 05 56 31 39 41.

You can also see Bordeaux from a **horse-drawn carriage** or 1920s **convertible**: ask at the tourist office (*see* p.233). Or a **tourist train** runs from near the tourist office in July and August. There are several **boat trips** on the river, including *L'Aliénor*, **t** 05 56 51 27 90, and *Ville de Bordeaux*, **t** 05 56 52 88 88; both leave from the Quinconces landing stage, Quai Louis XVIII. There is also a **river bus** between Pont de Pierre and Pont d'Aquitaine, **t** 05 57 57 88 88, or you can hire your own **river taxi** (**t** 06 07 19 75 86, *www.evolutiongaronne.com*). The tourist office has information on these and other ways to cruise the river and estuary.

Burdigala knew on which side its bread was buttered and posed no objection to being captured in 56 BC by Crassus. Quickly Latinized, the Bituriges soon tidied up their trading centre to conform to the basic Roman town grid, with a north–south *cardo* (Rue Ste-Catherine) and east–west *decumanus* (Cours de l'Intendance). To slake the new Gaulish thirst for wine, the traders of Burdigala attempted to grow vines, but it took until AD 20 to discover a grape suited to the humid climate.

Although Vespasian acknowledged Bordeaux's increasing prestige by making it the capital of Aquitaine in place of Saintes (Civitas Santonum), the city had hardly begun to make a name for itself when it was severely mutilated during the barbarian invasion of 276 and retreated into a more defensible *castrum*. Much of the reconstruction was by Christians, devoted to the cult of St Seurin

(Severinus), bishop of Bordeaux (d. 420), whose name is confusingly similar to Toulouse's St Sernin, and whose tomb became the focal point of one of the most desirable burial grounds during the early Middle Ages.

Medieval Bordeaux

In the 7th century the Merovingian king Dagobert made Bordeaux capital of the duchy of Aquitaine. The son of one of his dukes, Huon de Bordeaux, shares a *chanson de geste* with Charlemagne and the 'Elf Oberon'; Huon was followed by a string of 10 Duke Guillaumes (as in Toulouse, there was a wretched lack of originality in given names), who ruled an Aquitaine that stretched from Poitiers to the Pyrenees. The most famous was Guillaume IX (d. 1126), the first known troubadour, and one of the bawdiest, as well as grandfather of the great Eleanor, who ended the streak by being the only child of Guillaume X. Eleanor inherited the duchy and gave Bordeaux first to France when she wed Louis VII (1137), then to Anjou and England when she divorced the pious and dour Louis to marry the far more amusing Henry Plantagenet.

Bordeaux blossomed under the English and grew so much that the walls had to be rebuilt twice; for the Bordelais, English rule meant paying fewer taxes and an eager, guaranteed market for their wine. Their beloved duchess Eleanor granted the wine-growers special privileges, privileges that were confirmed by her son John Lackland in 1206, after Bordeaux was besieged by his brother-in-law, the king of Castille. The siege revealed John's inability to defend the city; to keep it loyal he also granted it considerable municipal power – a mayor and councillors, the *jurats*, and in 1214 he went even further with letters of patent that gave the bourgeoisie of Bordeaux the right to sell their wine and other goods duty-free. Under Henry III, Bordeaux's Château de l'Ombrière became the seat of the Seneschal of Aquitaine. Another plus in Bordeaux's eye was the powerful English fleet, able to protect the city's vital sea trade; among the many things brought back by the English crusaders were the maritime laws of ancient Rhodes, which they re-established in Bordeaux.

Medieval Bordeaux was a tough town that produced some tough *hombres*. One was the archbishop of Bordeaux, Bertrand de Got, who was elected Pope Clement V in 1305 after an 11-month conclave. Clement V stirred the pot like few popes before or since. He earned himself the everlasting hatred of Rome by moving the papacy to Avignon, then colluded with King Philippe IV le Bel to put an end to the powerful and extremely wealthy order of the Knights Templars (Philippe was broke and wanted their possessions, and Clement gave him the moral justification for annihilating the Templars by declaring them heretics). Like any medieval pope, he also diverted as many papal favours as possible to his relatives. He loaded the Curia with 11 Gascon cardinals, who if nothing else kept right on electing popes from southwest France. However, to pay for his extravagances, Clement soaked Bordeaux so badly with tithes and taxes that he had to avoid it when he travelled in Aquitaine.

Philippe IV's grandson, Edward III, opened the Pandora's box that became known as the Hundred Years' War by claiming the French throne. After English victories in Crécy and Calais, Edward III's eldest son, Edward of Woodstock (known as the Black Prince for his fashionable black armour) won the first round of the war at Poitiers (1356), capturing the French King Jean II and his greatest captain, Bertrand du Guesclin, as well as a bouquet of the 'flowers of French chivalry'. In 1360, Jean signed the treaty of Calais, giving Edward III, in exchange for his claims on France, a sure title to the independent duchy of Aquitaine, which then extended from Poitou to the Bigorre. The Black Prince became duke and made Bordeaux his capital, where he minted his own leopard coins. For the French, however, the prince in black armour was definitely the bad guy: not satisfied with the frontiers of Aquitaine, he campaigned to recapture the rest of the 'old duchy of the Plantagenets'. But cash, or rather the lack of it, dealt a deathblow to his ambitions; in spite of his string of victories, the financing he needed to continue his campaigns was withheld by the *jurats* and aristocrats of Aquitaine – especially the Armagnacs and the Albrets who, rather than pay the Black Prince's high taxes, turned to France and Charles V. With their encouragement, King Charles began another round of the Hundred Years' War in 1369; the Black Prince, disillusioned, Ill and exhausted, died in 1376.

The French finally took Bordeaux in June 1451, an event known in the city annals as the *Male Jornade*, the Rotten Day – 10,000 Bordelais were massacred in the marshlands near the present Pont d'Aquitaine before the city's archbishop Pey Berland was able to negotiate an honourable surrender. The final French conquest in 1453 was so unpopular that the Bordelais rebelled off and on until the end of the 17th century, never forgetting the massacre, or their old rights and trading privileges, and their say in the taxes imposed on them. The French monarchy, rather than try to console the Bordelais, built three fortresses to police them: the vast Château Trompette (now Place des Quinconces), the Fort du Hâ and Fort Louis. All have long since vanished. The machinery of French power over Bordeaux included a *parlement* of royal appointees and an *intendant*, or governor, also appointed by the king.

Thanks to its position near the Gironde estuary, Bordeaux controlled the export of wines from the *haut pays* (Bergerac, Cahors, Gaillac and so on), many of which were greatly preferred back in those days when all wines were drunk young. As a sop to

Bordeaux (about the only one, too), a law was passed in Paris in the 16th century to block the sale of wine from the hinterlands – none could be shipped down to the sea until all the wine from Bordeaux was sold. Frustrated English drinkers turned to port and sherry. A happier event was the big welcome that Bordeaux gave in 1540 to the hundreds of Jews chased out of Portugal by the Inquisition; by 1753 Bordeaux had seven synagogues.

Bordeaux Booms Again: the Slave Trade and Urban Renewal

At the start of the 18th century, Bordeaux made a living much as it had since the Middle Ages, exporting its claret to the north and supplying passing ships. After Louis XIV's death, new markets opened up in the New World, especially the Caribbean, and merchants from Britain, Germany, the Netherlands, Portugal and elsewhere were on hand to help the Bordelais make fortunes in the triangular trade: glass, fabrics, weapons and gimcracks were shipped to slave counters in west Africa in exchange for human cargo (one ship, with a nice touch of irony, was named the *Contrat Social*). The slaves were sold in America and the Caribbean for cotton, tobacco, indigo and, most importantly, sugar. Sugar was so fashionable in 18th-century Europe that, imported raw, refined in Bordeaux and re-exported, it brought the city as much money as its wine. The local glass industry took off when it was discovered that wine in bottles survived the journey to America better. By the end of the century, Bordeaux was the first port of France.

To create a city equal to its sweet, intoxicating ambition, Bordeaux's *intendants* started demolishing its poky medieval streets to give the city light and air – in the face of fierce local opposition. Begun by Intendant Boucher, who laid out the Place Royale (now Place de la Bourse), the destruction and re-creation of central Bordeaux was enthusiastically continued under his successor, Louis Urbain Aubert, Marquis de Tourny. 'Bordeaux being one of the cities in the kingdom where one meets the most foreigners, it is fitting to try to give them a favourable opinion of France… I will make you the most beautiful city in the realm, if you will only have confidence in what I shall propose and help me in the execution.' Tourny laid out wide *cours* or *allées* planted with trees linking his new squares and the first public gardens; to adorn them, 5,000 new buildings went up, including the riverfront Grande Façade.

By the beginning of the Revolution, Bordeaux was the third largest city in France, and one of the most cosmopolitan, with a population of more than 100,000. Its close trading contacts with the new United States and the influence of Montesquieu and the *Philosophes* combined to make the local Girondin party a moderate force at the Convention in Paris. They clashed with the

Jacobin fanatics – mainly from the north – who believed in a centralized dictatorship; in 1793, suspected of fomenting a federalist insurrection, 20 Girodin leaders were arrested by Robespierre and died on the guillotine after an all-night fling in the Conciergerie. In Bordeaux the only surviving signs of the Revolution are the quaint, enthusiastic street names engraved into the buildings (Rue de l'Amour de l'Egalité, Rue du Peuple Souverain).

Bordeaux in the 19th and 20th Centuries

During and immediately after the Napoleonic wars, Bordeaux hit one of its lowest ebbs: the continental blockade destroyed the city's commerce, the slave trade was abolished in 1815 and the competition of sugar beets undercut the product from its sugar refineries. Ships from the North and Baltic Seas began to sail across the Atlantic without stopping to be provisioned in Bordeaux. The grand urban plans of the *intendants* ground to a halt. It was only with Louis XVIII (and the demolition of the hated Château Trompette, symbol of Paris' tyranny) that Bordeaux began to get on its feet again and build its first ever bridge over the Garonne (1822). Although it had one of the first railways in France (1841) and modernized its quays, little new industry came its way. Inexorably, port traffic moved to the north.

In spite of an economy just puttering along and the catastrophic phylloxera that wiped out the vines in 1878, Bordeaux began to spread out; these days the 230,000 Bordelais have the dubious honour of taking up more room per capita than other city-dwellers in France, many living in single-storey terraced houses (*échoppes*). With the installation of tramlines in the 1900s, the suburbs (now with a population of 660,000) fanned out, a situation compared by one Bordelais writer to the universe of Pascal, where 'the centre is everywhere and the circumference nowhere'. Even the vineyards that provided Bordeaux's fermented lifeblood for centuries fell victim – today you'll find some of the most august wine châteaux of France totally immersed in sprawl.

Meanwhile the heart of Bordeaux, so proudly and grandly moulded to fit the French idea of a capital, actually served as one three times, all in circumstances France would rather forget: in 1870, 1914 and 1940. Bordeaux remembers 1914 most fondly, when it hosted *le tout Paris* and became one of the chief debarkation points for the American army, while June 1940 leaves the bitter memory of First World War hero Philippe Pétain negotiating the armistice with Hitler, announcing to France over the radio from Bordeaux, '*Je fais don de ma personne à la France*' before moving the government to Vichy, because the Germans wanted the Atlantic coast for themselves. The four years and two months under the Occupation left deep scars that were covered up, in

Bordeaux as elsewhere, in the name of national unity; there were just too many skeletons, especially in the closets of France's governing *classe politique*.

The post-war years were dominated by Jacques Chaban-Delmas, a 31-year-old Resistance general who De Gaulle sent to sort out Bordeaux in 1946. That year he became a deputy, the next year, mayor; from 1969 to 1972 he was Pompidou's PM and played a role in national politics. Pragmatic, dynamic, foxy and a brilliant manipulator of his own image, he was an updated *intendant*, changing the face of Bordeaux with the urban-renewal project of Mériadeck (a flop) and the more successful Quartier du Lac, a congress and leisure complex north of the centre. The best of the old was preserved by the 1966 **Loi Malraux**, which safeguarded 370 acres of 18th-century Bordeaux (especially the Quartier St-Pierre).

Bordeaux found itself in the national news, as official France took its first halting steps to come to terms with its role in the war. The death in 1996 of former President François Mitterrand, whose somewhat shadowy past included service in the Vichy government before he joined the Resistance, has released at least some *mea culpas*, half a century after the fact, notably from President Jacques Chirac. The whole issue – whether or not ever to admit to mistakes – has exacerbated the tension between the democratic right to know what's going on in its elected government ('*la transparence*') and France's deeply ingrained system of elevating its best and brightest to create a *classe politique* that rather smugly knows what's best for the country, even if it occasionally has to resort to the moral low ground to attain its ends. Bordeaux's mayor from 1995 to 2004, former Prime Minister Alain Juppé, is the intelligent, arrogant, classic product of the *classe politique* system; his intense unpopularity on a national level derived not only from the country's record unemployment and economic doldrums but his inability to grasp the concerns of the typical French citizen. He was nevertheless re-elected to Bordeaux's top job in October 2006.

Bordeaux was the scene of the last trial of a man accused of crimes against humanity in the Second World War. One could well imagine that Mitterrand and the whole of the *classe politique* had wished that Maurice Papon would just die and go away ever since his embarrassing past was exposed to the general public in 1983, when two journalists came across his files, but he held on for *14 years* awaiting his day in court (France's second last war criminal, René Bosquet, was mysteriously assassinated just before he was about to go on trial). Papon served as general secretary of the *préfecture* of the Gironde in 1942–4, where the records say he signed for the deportation of 1,500 Jews, in his own words 'only as part of the job'. He wasn't the only one. What is just as dispiriting is Papon's subsequent career as a member of the old boy's club that runs France: in 1945, Paris appointed him *préfet* of the Landes, the *département* just to the south of the Gironde, although at the same time there were enough members of the Resistance in the area to block the appointment. From 1958 to 1967, however, Papon served as police prefect in Paris, and in 1979 he became Minister of the Budget under Giscard d'Estaing. A kind of justice was served in the tribunal in Bordeaux in April 1998, when Papon, aged 87, frail and in ill health, was found guilty, as much as it upset certain members of the *classe politique*, who saw it as a reopening of the wounds best left forgotten. They were reopened again with a fury in summer 2002 when Papon was released from his life sentence in prison 'due to ill health', while his lawyers lodged a fresh appeal. In 2004 he was in trouble again for wearing a Légion d'Honneur medal that had been stripped from him – he was fined €2,500.

For all that, it must be said that Bordeaux has seemed a merrier place over the last decade or so. In 1998, it held its first wine festival ever, **Bordeaux Fête le Vin**, now held every two years in June/July. An energetic committee, Renaissance du Vieux Bordeaux, has rehabilitated the old port buildings and warehouses into a new cultural centre; the lovely pale golden stone of the city's monuments is being liberated from a century of grime, and a project to better integrate the city with its river is well underway. Landscaper Michel Corajoud and his team are knocking down or renovating the old warehouses and other buildings to create a lively waterfront accommodating several means of transport, where Bordeaux's residents can relax, be entertained, and walk in pleasant surroundings. The city's squares and boulevards, and some public buildings and parks, are also getting a facelift.

Perhaps the most striking difference is the tram system – elegant, hi-tech streetcars that have changed the look of the centre. Plans are afoot to extend the lines. The long-neglected industrial right bank is also getting a makeover. Two new districts of homes, office buildings and facilities are being created. The energetic tourist bureau has promotional schemes bringing more visitors every year.

Lamprey (*Lamproie à la bordelaise*)

Bordeaux's setting between land, river and sea has led to the invention of a wide range of specialities, including lamprey, which like shad, the other local favourite, is 'in season' in April and May. This is not a recipe for the squeamish, nor one that would have survived Brigitte Bardot's animal rights squads if the beast in question weren't a remarkably uncuddly, ugly, blood-sucking parasite that missed the evolutionary boat back in the night of time, probably because it doesn't seem to have any eyes.

Nail a live lamprey to the wall and cut it across the tail, carefully catching all the blood that drains out (for thickening the sauce). Cut off the poisonous dorsal cartilage (ingesting some by mistake is said to have killed Henri I) and plunge your lamprey into boiling water to make it easier to remove the skin. Slice the delicate white flesh into rounds and add it to a mixture of leeks, onions, chunks of ham and a bottle of St-Emilion that has been stewing for three days. Poach the lamprey in the wine mixture, and add the blood and a touch of chocolate. It comes in tins if you don't feel like doing it yourself.

Ste-Croix and St-Michel

From the railway station, spare yourself the anomie of the long, straight, endless Cours de la Marne by proceeding up Rue de Tauzia. The first monuments that beckon in this busy medieval but now genteelly dilapidated neighbourhood are in the vicinity of the former monastery **church of Ste-Croix**. Built in the 12th century, this once had a remarkably exuberant Old Curiosity Shop of a façade that was sadly entrusted in 1860 to Paul Abadie (*see* p.84) who, full of the destructive self-confidence of his time, completely dismantled it and put it back together all wrong. The south tower, portal, figures of Avarice and Luxury, and some carved capitals in the transept survived the Abadie touch; the relics in the parish chapel were reputed in the Middle Ages to cure madness. Note the unusual 15th-century crucifix with a 'bald Christ'. An abbey building of 1672 houses the school of fine arts, while the new monster along the Quai Ste-Croix proves Abadie had no patent on dubious taste; this 1980s bunker housing the national conservatory is called the **Centre André Malraux**, a backhanded compliment to the Minister of Culture who passed the national preservation law. In nearby Place Pierre Renaudel, an 18th-century sugar refinery has been turned into the Théâtre du Port de la Lune, now grandly called the **Théâtre National de Bordeaux en Aquitaine** (TNBA).

Crypte de la Flèche St-Michel
open for guided tours June–Sept daily 2–7

Eglise St-Michel
open Thurs and 1st and 3rd Sun of month 2.30–6

Since the time of Charlemagne a church has stood at the site of **St-Michel**, in what is now a lively Portuguese/North African neighbourhood. Its denizens hold a morning fleamarket under the detached hexagonal belltower, the 'arrow' or **Flèche** as the Bordelais call it, built 1472–92 and shooting up 115m, the highest monument in southwest France. It was financed in part by Louis XI, a devotee of the archangel Michael, and over-restored in the 19th century by Abadie. There's a once-celebrated **crypt** beneath the tower, where Victor Hugo and other 19th-century tourists came to gape at the naturally mummified bodies.

Grimy, Flamboyant Gothic **St-Michel** was a product of Bordeaux's medieval prosperity, largely built by the city's guilds. It is missing one of its most remarkable features – the original stained glass, blasted away by Allied bombers in the last war. Inside, the chapels furnished by the guilds contain the best art: the Chapelle Ste-Ursule in the right aisle has a rare 15th-century sculpture of *St Ursula and the 11,000 Virgins* (she also shelters a pope, emperor and several prelates under her cloak); in the left aisle, note the Chapelle de St-Sépulchre with a beautiful *Descent from the Cross* carved in 1492; the Chapelle Notre-Dame has a Flemish painting of the *Annunciation* (1500); and the Chapelle St-Joseph has nine alabaster Renaissance bas-reliefs on the altarpiece. In 1994 these were rather embarrassingly discovered for sale at an auction in

New York; 10 years earlier thieves had made off with them, leaving in their place some run-of-the-mill plaster copies that managed to completely fool everyone.

From behind St-Michel, Rue de la Fusterie (once lined with coopers' shops) leads to the **Porte des Salinières**, the 'salt' gate built in 1755 by Jacques-Ange Gabriel, though money ran out before it could be festooned with statuary. This overlooks the **Pont de Pierre**, the oldest of Bordeaux's three bridges, built in 1842 and lit at night by a necklace of street lamps. From here, turn left up busy Cours Victor-Hugo. The corner at Rue St-James was the road to Compostela, and the gate that defended it is known as the **Grande Cloche**, 'Big Bell'. Built next to and dwarfing the odd little **church of St-Eloi**, this gate was part of the second wall built by the English in the 14th century; it figures on the city's coat of arms. Each year its great bell would ring out at the start of the *vendange*. Across Cours Victor Hugo, the continuation of Rue St-James had, until 1840, a well, home to a serpent so horrifying that a mere glance at it meant certain death. One day a soldier, covering his own face and taking a mirror, went down a rope into the well and made the serpent look at itself. It keeled over, the local water problem was solved and the street had a new name, Mirror Street, or Rue du Mirail.

Musée d'Aquitaine

11 Musée d'Aquitaine
20 Cours Pasteur,
***t** 05 56 01 51 00;*
open Tues–Sun 11–6
exc public hols

This is one of the most compelling and beautifully arranged museums in southwest France. Its subject is the history of Aquitaine, and one of its first works is the unique, utterly mysterious 25,000-year-old bas-relief of the *Venus with a Horn* from Laussel in the Dordogne. The horn she holds curves like the moon, her hair is coiffed in 'corn rows' and her outline, even after all the millennia, still bears traces of red ochre, used in Upper Palaeolithic tombs and sacred sites. She keeps company with two other Venuses from Laussel: one an even fatter, saggy-breasted fertility figure with prominent hands, the other a slender dancing form. Another evocative, if less clearly defined relief has two figures holding hands, one above the other, their arms forming the shape of an egg. Among the Neolithic artefacts is a treasure horde – of flint slices – and burials from the Grotte aux 80 Morts at Coux-et-Bigaroque, with a double-trepanned skull. There are pots, swords and jewels from the Metal Ages, a curious face carved on a wooden post from Larrau in the Pyrénées-Atlantiques, and the golden Celtic treasure of coins and a torque from Tayac.

The excellent Gallo-Roman section has another treasure of coins, 4,000 from the time of Claudius found in the Garonne, as well as mosaics, sculptures and a fascinating set of reliefs from everyday life in ancient Burdigala. Ironically, it's the funerary steles that really bring the dead to life: thin-faced Tatiana gazing at eternity with a wry look and wrinkled brow, and the delightful child Laetus, clutching a kitten the way toddlers do, while a rooster at his feet nips at the kitten's dangling tail.

Further on is a legless but still impressive life-size bronze Hercules, and a room full of finds from a **mithraeum** discovered in 1982 during the construction of a car park in Cours Victor-Hugo. In the 2nd and 3rd century, Mithraism, an all-male, monotheistic religion from the East, posed serious competition to Christianity. A small statue shows the birth of Mithras, rising from earth with the cosmic globe in one hand and a knife to slay bulls in the other; there are statues of Cautes and Cautopatès, his two companions, in Persian costumes, and a rare *Leontocéphale*, a lion-headed man holding keys, his legs entwined with chicken-headed snakes.

Beyond the Early Christian sarcophagi and mosaics are a few strange 11th-century capitals from the Abbaye de La Sauve-Majeure and from La Brède, along with English alabasters, which the Bordelais traded for wine. Montaigne's cenotaph with its Greek inscription stands among the section on French rule. Upstairs are rooms devoted to Aquitaine's last 300 years: its agriculture, industries, port and wine, with the copy of a letter from Thomas Jefferson to the count of Lur-Saluces praising his Sauternes – and a letter from Ronald Reagan to the count's descendant, thanking him for hosting a banquet celebrating the bicentennial of the Battle of Yorktown. There are also ethnographic collections from Africa and Oceania, and temporary exhibitions on world history.

Musée Goupil
t 05 56 01 69 40; open Tues–Fri by appt

One wing of the building is occupied by the **Musée Goupil**, with photos and engravings from the archives of Parisian printer and editor Adolphe Goupil (1827–1920).

South of the Musée d'Aquitaine

Cours Pasteur leads down to Place de la Victoire, where the **Porte d'Aquitaine** (1753), guarded by a pair of sea gods, closes the south end of busy, pedestrian-only **Rue Ste-Catherine**, Bordeaux's main shopping street since Roman times. Fans of Art Deco in its morose, idiosyncratic French version might like to stroll briefly from Place de la Victoire up Cours Aristide Briand to see the **Bourse du Travail** (1934–8), commissioned by Bordeaux's Socialist mayor Marquet and decorated with reliefs on the outside and frescoes inside.

27 Cathédrale St-André
open Mon 2–6, Tues–Fri 7.30–6, Sat 9–7, Sun 9–6; Tour Pey-Berland July and Aug daily 10–6

Cathédrale St-André

Bordeaux's Gothic cathedral is the fourth church erected on this site since the 6th century, and the successor of the church where Eleanor of Aquitaine married Louis VII in 1137. What you see now was built under English rule between the 13th and 15th centuries; in 1440, as the ground was marshy and the architects were reluctant to add more weight to the church, it was given a detached tower, named the **Tour Pey-Berland** after the archbishop who built it. The tower was used as a lead ball factory from 1793 until 1850, when it was repurchased by the archbishop, truncated and crowned with a shiny Notre-Dame-de-l'Aquitaine. Climb it for a superb view, more interesting now an orientation table has been added.

The cathedral is built in the form of a Latin cross and supported by an intricate web of buttresses. A fine 14th-century tympanum crowns the north transept door, carved with the *Last Supper*, *Ascension of Christ* and *Triumph of the Redeemer*. The nearby Porte Royale (used by visiting kings and dignitaries) has another, decorated with a throng of saints and a serene 13th-century *Last Judgement*, in which the lids of the open tombs on the lintel add a nice rhythmic touch. The west front, which originally formed part of the city wall, is strikingly bare. The south portal, dedicated to the Virgin, lost its tympanum to make room for carts when the church was converted into a feed store during the Revolution, but carvings of the Wise and Foolish Virgins, angels and apostles have survived; these doors are usually left wide open, as in the Middle Ages, admitting both worshippers and pedestrians taking a short cut. The single nave is nearly as long and wide as Notre-Dame in Paris, 125 by 44m, and was the only place large enough to hold the tremendous pageant on 6 April 1364 when 1,447 nobles came to pay homage to the Black Prince, 'the most magnificent lord of his time'. The wrought-iron grille in the choir is 18th-century, and there are fine statues in the seven chapels radiating from the ambulatory, especially the 16th-century alabaster *Notre Dame de la Nef*. There are regular organ recitals.

North of the Cathedral

Centre National Jean Moulin
t 05 56 79 66 00; open Tues–Sun 2–6

The **Centre National Jean Moulin** is devoted to the Occupation, Resistance and Deportation, and items on display range from posters (one with a mother telling her daughter 'Hard Times are Over. Papa's Gone to Work in Germany!') to an ingenious folding motorcycle (part of a parachute drop to the Resistance). On the first floor, the office of the Resistance leader Jean Moulin has been reconstructed, containing a collection of his drawings – his cover was running an art gallery in Nice.

Musée des Beaux-Arts
t 05 56 10 20 56; open Wed–Mon 11–6 exc hols; ask about guided tours in English

Musée des Beaux-Arts

There's talk of moving it across the river some day, but for the moment Bordeaux's cache of paintings occupies two wings of the large and luxurious **Palais Rohan** at 20 Cours d'Albret, built in the

1770s by the Prince Archbishop Mériadeck de Rohan to replace an insufficiently princely medieval archbishop's palace. To make space for this ecclesiastical bachelor's pad, Rohan got permission from the king to knock over several acres of medieval Bordeaux, and to finance the building by selling off the archbishopric's properties. He kept a close eye on the construction, ensuring the most fastidious fittings, but before he got a chance to move in he was appointed Archbishop of Cambrai.

Hôtel de Ville
guided tours Wed 2.30; adm

Since 1835, most of the palace has been Bordeaux's **city hall**; the **Musée des Beaux-Arts** occupies the rest of the spread. It has paintings by artists rarely seen in French provincial museums – works by Titian (*Lucretia and Tarquin*); a serene Perugino (*Virgin and Child, with SS. Jerome and Augustine*); a portrait of a senator by Livinia Fontana (1552–1602), a rare female painter from Bologna; a chubby *Magdalen* and equally chubby *Marie dei Medici* by Van Dyck; Rubens' *Martyrdom of St George*; and the jolly *Fête de la Roserie* by Jan Brueghel de Velours. Amid a room of 17th-century, rosy-cheeked portraits and mythologies are a pair of paintings of the cruel world of galley slaves (*Arrivée des galériens dans la prison de Gênes* and *Débarquement des galériens dans le port de Gênes*) by the Genoese Alessandro Magnasco (1667–1749), that singularly uncanny 'painter of phantasmagorias' completely out of synch with his time, both in his choice of subject matter (you wonder who would have commissioned these disturbing scenes) and in his technique of quick, nervous, impromptu brush strokes that lend his works their strange light, and his often tormented figures their peculiar phantom-like unreality.

Later paintings from the 18th century include Reynolds' portrait of Baron Rockeby, Dutch landscapes by Ruysdael and co. (favourites of Bordeaux's *nouveau riche* merchants) and a *Nature Morte* by the inimitable Chardin. The next room has representatives of all the 19th-century grand -isms, from the neoclassical (*L'Embarquement de la Duchesse d'Angoulême* by Gros) and antiquating neoclassical (Guérin's *Hippolytus and Phaedra*, with protagonists with identical features and Phaedra looking as if she's just sucked a lemon) to the highly charged Romanticism of Delacroix (*Grèce sur les ruines de Missolonghi*) and Isabey (*Incendie du Steamer Austria*). There are several glossy nudge-nudge nudes that became popular in the decorously pornographic Second Empire, including Henri Gervex's notorious *Rolla*, inspired by a poem by De Musset and the source of a scandal at the 1878 salon (the fact that the naked girl on the bed was neither a goddess nor an allegory and had left her clothing piled to one side was indecent according to the hypocritical taste of the time). There are paintings by proto-Impressionist Boudin, and Bordeaux native Odilon Redon (1840–1916), the introspective precursor of the Surrealists.

Bordeaux produced two other influential artists, displayed in the last room: Albert Marquet (1875–1947), a fellow student of Matisse and co-founder of Fauvism before becoming a painter of simple landscapes, and André Lhote (1885–1962), represented by his hallmark colourful, geometric compositions on various planes. A lesser-known Bordelais is Impressionist Alfred Smith, whose best works resemble early Monets. Here too is a selection of minor paintings by major 20th-century artists – Matisse, Bonnard, Renoir and Seurat. Temporary exhibitions are held nearby in the **Galerie des Beaux-Arts** in Place du Colonel Raynal.

Around the Musée des Beaux-Arts

Behind the fine arts museum, on one of the *axes* so beloved of French urban planners (in this case, aligned with the Palais de Rohan), is the **Nouveau Quartier Mériadeck**, named after the aforementioned Cardinal de Rohan (who went on to become an enthusiastic patron of Cagliostro, and play a major role as the big dupe in the Diamond Necklace Affair). Mériadeck was a fragrant slum before it was flattened in 1954 by Mayor Chaban-Delmas, clearing 30 hectares to create France's largest single urban renovation scheme . Seven hectares were set aside for greenery and fountains, and the buildings facing this central mall were designed in cruciforms (as in the reflecting-glass *Préfecture*) by J. Willerval, to spare pedestrians the sight of Mériadeck's plain-jane skyscraper. As corporate bosses haven't been beating down the doors for office space here, most of Mériadeck is occupied by government bureaucracies and chain hotels. It did, however, earn an environmental gold star as the first major project in Europe to make large-scale use of geothermal heating (1981).

Musée des Arts Décoratifs
*39 Rue Bouffard, **t** 05 56 10 14 00; open Wed–Sun exc public hols 2–6, or 11–6 during special exhibitions*

Around the corner from the Musée des Beaux-Arts, the excellent **Musée des Arts Décoratifs** has a perfect home in a neoclassical *hôtel particulier* built in 1779 by Bordelais architect Etienne Laclotte; furniture, wallpaper, pharmacy jars and fine ceramics (including some beautiful pieces from Delft), French tin-glazed ware, wrought iron, paintings, gold- and silverwork, glass and jewellery and costumes all evoke the good life in the 18th and 19th centuries. There are fine engravings of Bordeaux, back when its port and quays were bustling; there are also period documents, famous signatures, and more. In the summer you can eat lunch in the elegant courtyard.

Rue Bouffard continues up to **Place Gambetta** (originally Place Dauphine), laid out with uniform façades by Tourny in 1743; its simple gateway, **Porte Dijeaux**, was added shortly after. During the Terror in the autumn of 1793 a guillotine was installed that parted the heads from the rest of 300 Bordelais, including the Girondins who hid out in St-Emilion (*see* p.193); their last words here were muted by the beating drums. The chief of the revolutionaries in Bordeaux was the fiery redhead Tallien, former editor of the *Ami du Citoyen*. Tallien would have given many more Bordelais the chop had it not been for the gentle pleadings of his beloved, soft-hearted Spanish mistress, Teresa Cabarus. When Tallien was recalled to Paris and Teresa was imprisoned by Robespierre, he freed her – by toppling Robespierre himself on the 9th of Thermidor. Legend has it that Tallien's name was among those on a list that an acquaintance accidentally found while rifling through Robespierre's famous sea-green coat, looking for a piece of paper to answer to a bodily need. Tallien and the others on the list joined forces and acted first, so it was Robespierre's head that rolled instead of theirs.

St-Seurin

Northwest of Place Gambetta, **Place des Martyrs-de-la-Résistance** marks the site of a famous Gallo-Roman-Merovingian cemetery. Consecrated, according to legend, by Christ himself in the company of the first saints of Gaul, it was one of several supposed burial places of Roland's paladins, slain in the famous ambush at Roncesvalles. The cemetery is long gone, but **Basilique St-Seurin**, founded by the city's 5th-century bishop Severinus, still stands, although in an often remodelled and expanded state. Its antiquity allowed its medieval canons to concoct pretty stories, including a famous one, that Charlemagne chose it as the shrine for Roland's great horn Oliphant after the hero popped out his brains by blowing it too hard. Although Oliphant has sadly gone missing, there are other things to see at Bordeaux's oldest church: the 14th-century porch with lavish sculptures of the Last Judgement and Resurrection, and, hidden behind the undistinguished main façade of 1828, a second 11th-century porch, holding the tomb of St Severinus, supported by carved capitals depicting the sacrifice of Isaac. Inside, a 7th-century sarcophagus does duty as an altar in the Chapelle St-Etienne, and there are beautiful 15th-century alabaster works: the retable in the Chapelle de Notre-Dame-de-la-Rose and 14 panels in the choir, on the lives of St Severinus and St Martial, the apostle of Gaul. Note, too, the magnificent episcopal throne, curiously made of stone imitating wood, and the sculpted choir stalls: try to find the fat man pushing his stomach in a wheelbarrow, and the man grilling tongues.

Basilique St-Seurin
open Tues–Sat 8.30–11.45 and 2–7.45, Sun 9–12.15 and 6–8.15

The **11th-century crypt** (which you may have to ask the sacristan to open) has a fine collection of 6th- and 7th-century sarcophagi, medieval tiles, Merovingian plaques and the tomb of St Fort, supposedly the first bishop of Bordeaux, way back in the first

Ausonius

Near St-Seurin was the Pagus Novarus, city address of Decimus Magnus Ausonius (*c.* AD 310–94), scion of one of Burdigala's most noble families. After his studies in Toulouse, Ausonius returned to Bordeaux as a professor of rhetoric, with such a reputation that he was appointed tutor of Gratian, son of Emperor Valentinian; Emperor Gratian in turn appointed him prefect of Gaul (377). A familiar of St Ambrose of Milan and Emperor Theodosius, Ausonius managed to live blithely through the golden twilight of the Roman Empire, an empire overextended and attacked from all sides, but cosy enough for a patrician to retire in a choice of villas sprinkled across the Gironde, to hunt, fish, grow grapes for wine and write elaborate, exceedingly bland poetry; he might just have left us something more interesting for the interesting times he lived in. His surviving letters to his Bordelais disciple, the poet-saint Paulinus de Nola, are more illuminating than his verse; the two broke their long friendship towards the end of Ausonius's life, when Paulinus austerely rejected his master's conviction that the new religion could be reconciled with the Olympian muses and the sweet worldly life he loved.

century; the Bordelais would bring their young sons to his tomb and touch their foreheads on the stone to make them strong (*fort*) by mystic osmosis. Excavations under the crypt have revealed the 4th-century **palaeo-Christian crypt**, which goes back to the very origins of Christianity in Bordeaux. Inside you can see sarcophagi, amphorae and frescoes.

Site Paléochrétien
open for guided tours June–Sept daily 2–7

Music-lovers should note that the basilica hosts free organ recitals in July and August, on Thursdays at 6pm.

Quartier St-Pierre

From the 3rd century to the 12th century, St-Pierre was a separate walled quarter outside the city walls, built around the Palais de l'Ombrière, home of the dukes of Aquitaine and kings of England and, later, the *Parlement* of Bordeaux. Although the Palais de l'Ombrière was destroyed in 1800, its triumphal arch-gate, the **Porte de Cailhau**, still overlooks the river with its asymmetrical turrets and tower. One of only two gates spared by Tourny's demolition squads (the *Grande Cloche* is the other), it was begun in 1493 to celebrate the Battle of Fornovo, where Charles VIII and the French fought to a draw against the united Italian republics; the nobility of Guyenne played a prominent role. From here you can see the effect of the 18th-century **Grande Façade** project, conceived by Jacques Gabriel and *intendants* Boucher and Tourny to create a homogenous kilometre of architecture from Cours du Chapeau Rouge to Porte de la Monnaie, a row of pale stone houses, all the same height, with ground-floor arcades, each arch with a *mascaron* at its key, topped by two floors of large windows, and a slate mansard roof with stone dormers.

Porte de Cailhau
guided tours June–Sept daily 2–7; adm

In the Middle Ages, the parish of St-Pierre was inhabited by English merchants and craftsmen remembered only in the street names – Rue Maucoudinat ('badly cooked', the address of the tripe butchers) and Rue des Bahutiers (cabinet-makers). The presence of the *Parlement* of Bordeaux from the 15th century on led to the construction of a number of stately 18th-century *hôtels particuliers*, now restored for the most part by the Association pour la Renaissance du Vieux Bordeaux (12 Rue des Faussets). One of these, in Rue des Argentiers (silversmiths) is now the **Bordeaux Monumental**, which evokes the city's past and its changing faces. You can see the best of the *hôtels* by walking straight through Porte Cailhau to **Rue du Loup** (note especially No.71, and also the 200-year-old wisteria, in the courtyard in the Hôtel des Archives); cross busy Rue Ste-Catherine, and turn right in **Rue de Cheverus** (no.8 is now the offices of *Sud-Ouest*, Bordeaux's paper), and from here turn up **Rue Poquelin-Molière**. In 1656 Molière and his troupe performed at No.9, then a *jeu-de-paume*, a walled court for real tennis, although after a fire in 1728 it was replaced by a handsome *hôtel particulier*. From here find Rue de Grassi and turn right into **Rue de la Porte-Dijeaux/Rue St-Rémi**.

Bordeaux Monumental
28 Rue des Argentiers, t 05 56 48 04 24; open Mon–Sat 9.30–1 and 2–7, Sun 10–1 and 2–6

Rue St-Rémi leads right into the centre of Bordeaux's neoclassical showcase, Jacques Gabriel's **Place de la Bourse**, commissioned in 1735 by Intendant Boucher, who wanted to give the city a touch of Parisian class in spite of itself. Originally called the Place Royale, it had for a centrepiece a bronze equestrian statue of Louis XV that was gleefully pulled down and melted into cannons to fire at other kings in the Revolution; today a fountain of the *Three Graces* (1864) holds pride of place, the Graces in this case representing the Empress Eugénie, the Queen of Spain and Queen Victoria. On one side stands the **Palais de la Bourse**, or stock exchange (now the Chamber of Commerce), enlarged in 1862 and 1925, and repaired after bomb damage in 1940; on the other, the **Hôtel des Douanes**, which must be the most grandiose customs house in the world. Installed in the grand, vaulted clearance halls of the former Fermes du Roy (i.e. the king's tax farms) is a museum devoted to a subject that infuriates people to this day – French customs. The **Musée des Douanes** traces the history of taxes on imports from the days of the ancient Gauls to displays of more recent uniforms, weapons, weights and measures (including a grand 200-year-old scale) of France's *douaniers*, as well as examples of the forgeries and contraband they've nabbed. Among the originals is Monet's *La Cabane des douaniers, effet d'après-midi* (1882).

Musée des Douanes
1 Place de la Bourse, t 05 56 48 82 82; open Tues–Sun 10–6

The Golden Triangle (*Triangle d'Or*)

4 Golden Triangle

Bordeaux's Golden Triangle of good taste and luxury shops is formed by Cours de l'Intendance, Cours Georges-Clemenceau and Allées de Tourny. No.57 Cours de l'Intendance was the last address of Goya, the painter, who in 1824 asked permission of Ferdinand VII to settle in Bordeaux with his former nursemaid and mistress. Then Goya was still the official painter of the Spanish court, but serious illnesses, deafness and political disillusionment had made him ever more reclusive. In his last four years, in the company of his fellow exiles, he turned to a new medium, lithography (*The Bulls of Bordeaux* and *La Laitière*) and evolved a nearly Impressionistic freedom in his handling of paint. He died suddenly in 1828, age 82, while painting a portrait of his friend Molina, and was buried in Bordeaux until 1889, when his remains were transferred to Madrid. Unfortunately you can no longer visit his rooms.

Just off the Cours, in Place du Chapelet, is Bordeaux's chief Baroque church, **Notre-Dame** (1684–1707), directly inspired by the Gesù in Rome. Originally a Dominican chapel, its luxurious altar, organ and paintings show a marked change in the Order's taste since the days of Les Jacobins in Toulouse (*see* pp.435–6). Behind it, in the centre of the Golden Triangle, is the iron and glass shopping mall, the **Marché des Grands-Hommes**, rebuilt in 1991 and soon nicknamed the *bouchon de carafe* ('carafe stopper'). The east end of the Cours de l'Intendance opens into **Place de la Comédie**, a space that once contained 300 houses, a church and a remarkable Gallo-Roman palace, the Piliers de Tutelle – all demolished in the 17th century by order of Louis XIV, who, after the uprising of the Fronde, wanted nothing to stand in the way of his cannons pointed at the city from the Château Trompette (*see* p.229).

In 1773 the Maréchal-Duc de Richelieu, great-nephew of the famous cardinal, governor of Guyenne and a famous libertine who fathered scores of Bordelais (at one of his dinner parties the only guests were the 29 most beautiful society belles of Bordeaux, masked to permit every indiscretion), felt he wasn't being properly entertained in Bordeaux, and rectified the matter by commissioning the **Grand Théâtre** from neoclassical master Victor Louis and making the *jurats* pay for it. If Richelieu rammed the theatre down the city's throat, Bordeaux has since adopted it as its proudest showcase, and in 1992 it underwent a thorough restoration. From the outside it resembles a Greek temple, fronted by a row of mighty Corinthian columns and crowned with statues of goddesses and muses. Louis came up with a number of innovations in its construction, especially the great metal tie-beam ('*clou de M. Louis*') that supports the entablature of the peristyle (shades of Soufflot's Panthéon in Paris; France's technically incompetent 18th-century architects had a hard time making their neoclassical stone confections stand up, and by necessity became leading innovators in the use of iron – a habit that culminated in the Eiffel Tower). If it looks fairly restrained from the outside, all sumptuous hell breaks loose within. Louis's vestibule has more columns, Doric this time, supporting a magnificent coffered ceiling, lit by a 19m cupola; his bold grand stair was copied by Garnier for the Paris Opéra; the auditorium has golden columns and a domed ceiling (repainted in 1919) hung with a massive crystal chandelier weighing 1.3 tonnes. From the day it opened, this high temple of illusion answered a deep-felt need in business-oriented Bordeaux; every single night it was thronged with merchants who paid a king's ransom to bring down the best players and dancers from Paris.

The Grand Théâtre witnessed a curious ceremony in 1965. A literary feather in Bordeaux's cap, although often begrudged by the feather himself, was novelist François Mauriac (1885–1970), 1952 winner of the Nobel Prize for Literature. At 22 he fled Bordeaux for Paris, where, at a distance, he could exorcize an unhappy provincial childhood in books such as *Le Nœud de vipères* (*The Nest of Vipers*), which didn't exactly endear him to folks back home. Nevertheless in 1965 there was an official reconciliation of Bordeaux with its native son, in a ceremony in the Grand Théâtre honouring his 80th birthday. But when it was time to give a speech, Mauriac shocked them into silence: 'The honour that you do me at the very evening of my life gives me a great joy, but a grave joy. Dare I say, a sad joy? I love and I hate Bordeaux like myself.'

Maison des Vins de Bordeaux
3 Cours du 30 Juillet, ***t** 05 56 00 22 66; open Mon–Fri 9–5.30*

You can learn and taste the wide variety of Bordeaux *appellations* on the corner of Place de la Comédie at the **Maison des Vins de Bordeaux**. The labels (Graves, Côte du Blaye, and so on) are generic, but it's a good place to discover some of the nuances between the *appellations*. They run a two-hour wine-tasting course if you want to learn more (*see* p.233).

Esplanade des Quinconces and Around

Just down the Cours du 30 Juillet rises the irresistibly overblown 19th-century **Monument aux Girondins**, a lofty column crowned by Liberty over a fountain mobbed by Happiness, Eloquence, Security, a crowing cockerel and other attractive allegories. Statues of the Girondins themselves were planned, but lack of funds kept them from even coming to their own party. In the fountain basin, two remarkable quadrigas of bronze horses violently rear their sea-monster paws to the sky while expressive figures of Falsehood (holding a mask), Vice (with pig ears) and shameful Ignorance cower under the utterly vacuous gaze of the Republic. The Nazis stripped the fountain of its bronzes in 1943; to everyone's surprise they weren't melted down but were found squirrelled away in Angoulême, although they had to wait in storage until the hotly contested mayoral election of 1983, when Chaban suddenly pulled the money out of a hat to restore the fountain.

Stretching out endlessly from here to the river is Europe's largest, and one of its least interesting, squares, the **Place des Quinconces**. When speculators purchased the hated royal Château Trompette and began dismantling it just before the Revolution, their intention was to lay out new streets and build 1,800 new houses. You're hard put to it to find any quincunxes at all. (What's a quincunx, you ask? A pattern like the five on a dice; all French farmers plant their trees in rows like this. Supposedly the fashion was started by the granddad of all gardeners, King Cyrus of Persia.) At the river end, the *place* is closed by two columns, the **Colonnes Rostrales**, erected in 1829, decorated with the prows of ships and topped by allegories of Commerce and Navigation.

Jardin Public
t 05 56 10 20 30; open June–Aug daily 7am–9pm; April, May, Sept and Oct daily 7am–8pm; rest of year daily 7am–6pm

In 1745, Tourny laid out a promenade lined with linden trees, now called the Allées de Tourny, to give the Bordelais a place in which to stroll; the houses were designed with uniform façades, but limited to two storeys to allow cannonballs from Château Trompette to fly over them. In 1756, Tourny added the city's first patch of greenery, the **Jardin Public**, which the *intendant* had to promote as something practical to make it palatable to Bordeaux's conservative business class: 'In a commercial city, one must look at such public gardens as very useful, where merchants, often meeting one another there, transact much business. It is like having a second Exchange.' Originally laid out by Jacques-Ange Gabriel in the various perspectives of a *jardin à la française*, it was destroyed by Napoleon's troops. When the garden was finally replanted in 1856, it was designed in the romantic *style anglais* popularized by Napoleon III, who spent his early years in exile in London. It makes for a delightful wander: on sunny Sundays, expect to see half of Bordeaux here. The Cours de Verdun entrance has a bust of François Mauriac by Zadkine.

Musée d'Histoire Naturelle
t 05 56 48 29 86; open Mon and Wed–Fri 11–6, Sat and Sun 2–6; adm (free 1st Sun of month)

At the west end of the garden, a *hôtel particulier* of 1778 has housed, since 1862, the **Musée d'Histoire Naturelle**, containing an important collection of Quaternary fossils, many from the Grotte de Pair-non-Pair near Bourg-sur-Gironde (*see* p.203), as well as a selection of stuffed animals from around the world, and mineralogy and geology sections.

Palais Gallien
guided tours June–Sept daily 2–7

Two streets behind the museum in Rue du Docteur A. Barraud, a monumental entrance and a few arches known as the **Palais Gallien** are all that remain of the 15,000-seat Roman amphitheatre of Burdigala, built in the 3rd century AD. The barbarians, who were not as keen on gladiator sports as the civilized Gallo-Romans, burned it soon after construction. Its name comes from a tangled tale that Charlemagne built it as a palace for his wife Galliene; old engravings show that the arena remained fairly intact until the 18th century, when its walls were incorporated into surrounding buildings; today you can only trace its oval shape from a plane.

Les Chartrons

Les Chartrons

In the 14th century, Carthusians chased out of Périgord found refuge in the swamp north of Bordeaux's walls and drained the land. For centuries, the massive Château Trompette in the Place des Quinconces kept the Chartrons apart from the rest of Bordeaux, and in the 17th century Flemish wine merchants ('*courtiers*'), feeling discriminated against by the pro-English *jurats*, set up their own business and quay here. They were soon followed by German, Dutch and Irish traders affiliated with the Hansa of Bruges, then by the English. The most successful merchants, brokers and shippers bought vineyards, founding fabulously wealthy wine dynasties, the *aristocratie de bouchon*. Their smug social circle – the source of Anglophile Bordeaux's reputation for snobbery, clubbiness and mannerisms (as in replacing many French words with English) – first suffered with the Revocation of the Edict of Nantes. This sent the Protestants among them to seek refuge abroad, although many of them kept up their commercial ties with Bordeaux and helped enlarge the market for its wine across Europe.

The decline of the Chartrons began with the Revolution, when many Chartrons merchants were guillotined and others moved abroad. Under Napoleon, commerce came to a standstill – for 30 years the Chartrons lived by fitting out corsairs. Though commerce revived, it was never the same; if in the 1950s the brokers still had their offices in prestigious but shabby waterfront buildings, by the 1960s the relocation of port activities north, to Bassens and Ambès, and the switch to land transport of wine made even this vestige of the past irrelevant. Ever since, Bordeaux has sought a new role for the quarter while maintaining as much of its wine business as possible, first by constructing the shiny new (and sterile) **Cité Mondiale du Vin** on Quai des Chartrons, concentrating on hotels and an ultra-modern conference centre, with exhibitions and shops open to the public. The snobbiest of the Chartrons nobility lived on the Pavé des Chartrons (now Cours Xavier Arnozan), paved by Tourny and planted with trees at the same time as he laid out the nearby Jardin Public. Where it meets the quay stands the **Hôtel Fenwick**, built in 1790 for Joseph Fenwick, who combined his duties as the first American consul in Bordeaux with his mercantile activities – represented in the ship's-prow decoration.

Musée d'Art Contemporain
t 05 56 00 81 50; open Tues and Thurs–Sun 11–6, Wed 11–8, exc public hols

Arc en Rêve Centre d'Architecture
t 05 56 52 78 36; same hrs

One of the success stories of the Chartrons is the restoration of the austere neoclassical **Entrepôt Lainé**, at 7 Rue Ferrère, built in the 1820s; it's where spices and other goods imported from France's colonies were unloaded, exempt from duty. Its vast spaces are used for the giant-scale exhibitions and installations of the **Musée d'Art Contemporain**, with a charming café. The same building contains the **Arc en Rêve Centre d'Architecture**, with architectural exhibits, often on Bordeaux itself. Not far from these is the **Village des Antiquaires**: antiques dealers line Rue Notre-Dame on all sides of the austere Protestant temple, its only ornament the relief of a Bible exploding out of the clouds.

Musée des Chartrons
t 05 57 87 50 60; open Mon–Fri 2–6

The old wine trade is remembered in the *hôtel particulier* of Irish broker Francis Burke (1720), now the **Musée des Chartrons** at 41 Rue Borie; this has a collection of lithographed wine labels and bottles going back to the 1600s. You also learn about the long-lost wine of the islands – in the old days brokers loaded Caribbean-bound ships with 900-litre casks of the finest Bordeaux *crus*, accompanied by a vintner to keep an eye on evaporation and top up casks when necessary. This precious cargo was not for the colonies, however; when the ship arrived in the Antilles, wine and vintner stayed on board and sailed straight back to Bordeaux. The journey improved the wine so much that, as *Bordeaux retour des îles*, it commanded a premium price in Paris restaurants. When steamers took over the route, the wine didn't improve; the secret had been the gentle rolling motion of a sailing ship, and *retour* went the way of the dodo.

***Croiseur* Colbert**
t 05 56 44 96 11; open July and Aug daily 10–7; April, May and Sept Mon–Fri 10–6, Sat, Sun and public hols 10–7; Oct–Mar Wed, Sat, Sun and hols 10–6

Cap Sciences
t 05 56 01 07 07; open Tues–Fri 2–6, Sat and Sun 2–7

Vinorama
12 Cours du Médoc, t 05 56 39 39 20; open July and Aug Mon–Sat 10.30–12.30 and 2.30–6.30, Sun 2–6.30; rest of year Tues–Fri 2–6.30, Sat 10.30–12.30 and 2.30–6.30

Further north, visitors are welcome aboard the retired battleship the ***Croiseur* Colbert**, used by the French navy between 1960 and 1990, opposite 60 Quai des Chartrons near Cours de la Martinique. At Hangar 20, Quai Bacalan, nearly opposite Rue Lucien Faure, **Cap Sciences** aims to introduce scientific subjects, innovations and techniques to the public through a changing exhibitions and themes. **Vinorama** is a corny, talking waxworks museum that explains the history of Bordeaux's wine from Gallo-Roman times to the present, complete with an 'historic wine tasting' of wine made in the Roman style, in the 19th-century style, and so on.

Base Sous-Marine
t 05 56 11 11 50; open Tues–Sun 2–7 but call ahead

For 50 years, Bordeaux's old docks along Boulevard Alfred Daney (bus 9 from the station or boulevards) have been disfigured by the Germans' submarine base: a vast indestructible concrete bunker with walls more than 4.5m thick, the whole in volume equal to St Peter's, with 11 huge entrances to U-boat pens, each 90m long, dug by Spanish, French, Russian and Vietnamese prisoners of war. Since it would take forever to remove it, the Bordelais converted it in 1993 into a centre for exhibitions and performances, the **Base Sous-Marine**. To the west the last swamps of the Chartrons were concentrated in 1960 into an artificial lake, the centre of the **Quartier du Lac**, with Bordeaux's trade-fair buildings, congress centre, golf courses, an arboretum and recreational facilities.

Jardin Botanique
t 05 56 52 18 77; open summer daily 8–8, winter daily 8–6

Last and least, Bordeaux has a **Right Bank**, where the recent development continues. In addition to the new neighbourhoods (*see* p.217), the **Jardin Botanique** has relocated to Quai de Queyries. The views it affords back across the river are impressive enough, but it also has 11 growing environments reflecting Aquitaine's, a climbing plant walk, a water garden and more.

Pessac-Léognan

Since 1987 the northern third of the traditional Graves growing area has had its own *appellation*, Pessac-Léognan. Its worst enemy is urban sprawl – at the start of the 20th century, the four closest *communes* to Bordeaux (Pessac, Gradignan, Mérignac and Talence) had 119 vineyards; today there are nine. Yet these, especially in Pessac, only 6km southwest of central Bordeaux, produce some of the greatest wines in the *département*, beginning with the prestigious **Château Haut-Brion** (bus route 45, on Avenue Jean Jaurès, **t** 05 56 00 29 30, *www.haut-brion.com*) founded in 1550. The elegant finesse of its reds (50% Cabernet Sauvignon, 35% Merlot, 15% Cabernet Franc) were rewarded in 1885, when the property became the only non-Médoc wine granted *premier grand cru* status. But Haut-Brion was famous before then, especially in London. As far as anyone knows, this was the first wine sold under the name of the estate that produced it rather than the name of the parish; 17th-century Londoners called it 'Ho-Bryan' and made it such a success that the original owners, the Pontacs, even opened one of London's first luxury restaurants, the 'New Eating House', with a French grocer and wine cellar.

Later owned by Talleyrand, the estate was purchased in 1935 by US banker Clarence Dillon, whose granddaughter, the Duchesse de Mouchy, now runs the company. In 1983 she purchased the equally celebrated **Château La-Mission-Haut-Brion** (**t** 05 56 00 29 30), across the street, which until the Revolution belonged to a mission founded by St Vincent de Paul; it produces a powerful wine equal to the finest from Médoc. Today the two vineyards are green islands in Bordeaux's post-war sprawl, which may be ugly but creates an urban climate that protects the vines from spring frosts and accelerates the harvest – a plus in years of heavy autumn rains.

A third vineyard in Pressac (on Avenue Pasteur) is the one with the longest continuous history of all – it was planted in 1300 by Bordeaux archbishop Bertrand de Got before he became Pope, and is hence known as **Château Pape-Clément** (**t** 05 57 26 38 38, *www.pape-clement.com*). It produces a *cru classé* famous for its intense wines that pack an extraordinarily aromatic tobacco bouquet.

Visits and and tastings are available at all three by appointment.

Pessac

Pessac (bus 45 from the Musée d'Aquitaine) may be one of many victims of Bordeaux's 20th-century transformation into an octopus, but it is also the site of a landmark experiment to provide new housing and create something architecturally new: Le Corbusier's first project, the **Cité Frugès** in Avenue Henri Frugès. The name commemorates the industrialist whose desire to transform a tract of land he owned near the railway line into healthy, airy, affordable housing for 300 families led him to give the young Swiss architect a crack at practising his theories of urban housing for the post-Cubist era. In 1926 Le Corbusier produced 51 houses for Henri Frugès: geometric modules with rough concrete skins, brightly painted, with hanging gardens on terraces. They had comforts the old *échoppes* of Bordeaux lacked (central heating, running water and adequate sewerage) but they drove the Bordelais bananas. Frugès was dismissed as a loony, and, when people reluctantly moved in, they tried to make the modules fit their idea of what a house ought to be. In dismay, Frugès never finished the project, although up in heaven he must be gratified to see that his *cité* is now classed as a historic monument and is slowly being stripped of later additions to restore the architect's original intention.

Tourist Information in Bordeaux

ⓘ Bordeaux >
12 Cours du 30 Juillet, **t** *05 56 00 66 00; Gare St-Jean,* **t** *05 56 91 64 70, www.bordeaux-tourisme.com* and *www.bordeaux.fr*

Staff at the **tourist office** have up-to-the-minute lists of events, visits, hotels and ideas for excursions. Ask about the ***Bordeaux Découverte*** package: one or two nights in a 2–4-star hotel, free public transport, a tour of the city and a vineyard, and free access to the main sights and museums (though public ones are free anyway). You need to book at least 10 days in advance.

Bordeaux was the first French city awarded the Government label **Famille Plus**, for its provision for families. Among the many tourist board initiatives are walking, cycling, rollerblading and bus tours on various themes (some in English). You can also take a tour in a taxi, **t** 06 24 88 22 09.

There is also an introduction to wine-tasting at the **Maison du Vin** (June–Sept; 2hrs; €20, charcuterie and cheese included) and some short English-language courses on wine and wine-tasting at its **École du Vin du CIVB**, **t** 05 56 00 22 66, *http://ecole.vins-bordeaux.fr*. The tourist office also runs regular half-day excursions to some of the most famous vineyards with tastings (it's the only way to get into most of them).

For information on the *département* of the Gironde, call or write to the **Maison de Tourisme de la Gironde**, 21 Cours de l'Intendance, **t** 05 56 52 61 40; for all of Aquitaine, the **Comité Régionale de Tourisme d'Aquitaine**, Cité Mondiale du Vin, 23 Parvis des Chartrons, **t** 05 56 01 70 00.

Post office (main): 52 Rue G. Bonnac.

Money exchange: American Express: 14 Cours de l'Intendance, **t** 05 56 00 63 36 (*Mon–Fri 9–12 and 1–5*).

UK Consulate: 353 Boulevard du Président Wilson, **t** 05 57 22 21 10.

US Consulate: 10 Place de la Bourse, **t** 05 56 48 63 80.

Shopping in Bordeaux

Bordeaux has several covered **markets**: at Victor Hugo, Place de la Ferme de Richemont, Mon–Sat mornings; at Place des Capucins, Tues–Sun mornings, and at Chartrons, Rue Sicard, Tues–Sat mornings. There is an open-air **market** beside the river at Chartrons on Sundays, and a fleamarket at St Michel, Place Meynard and Place Canteloup, Tues–Sun. There are a few other markets around the city; the tourist office can provide details.

A bottle is the obvious souvenir or gift: there are lots of **wine shops** selling vinous paraphernalia. If you want to stock up on **foie gras** and other southwest staples head for **Comtesse du Barry**, 2 Place de Tourny.

Pedestrianized **Rue Ste-Catherine** is a favourite shopping street, especially for clothes. **English books** are available at Bradley's Bookshop, 8 Cours d'Albret, **t** 05 56 52 10 57.

There are two streets devoted to **antiques**: Rue Bouffard around the Musée des Arts Décoratifs, and Rue Notre-Dame in the Chartrons, with two-score shops and galleries. Quartier St-Pierre is another good place to look for old things and curiosities, especially along Rue de la Devise.

Not far from here **Saunion**, at 56 Cours Georges Clemenceau, is an essential stop for **chocolate**-lovers; the speciality is *guinettes*, cherries soaked in alcohol and covered in dark chocolate. You can find famous ***canalé*** cakes, with their gooey centres and crusty outsides, at **Baillardran**, 29 Rue Porte Dijeaux, near Place Gambetta.

One of the last remaining shops of its kind in France, founded in 1814, **Au Sanglier de Russie**, 67 Cours d'Alsace et Lorraine, sells a huge range of **brushes** for any imaginable household or personal use, with extraordinarily exotic animal hairs and woods.

Sports and Activities in and around Bordeaux

Besides the Jardin Public (*see* p.229), Bordeaux has a green lung further west, the newly landscaped **Parc Bordelais** (buses 51, 52, 53, 54 and 55). The Centre Mériadeck has a **bowling alley** and indoor **skating rink** (95 Cours du Maréchal Juin, **t** 05 57 81 43 72).

There are four **golf** courses on the outskirts of town: the 27-hole Golf de Pessac, 5 Rue de la Princesse, **t** 05 57 26 03 33; the less expensive 36-hole

Golf de Bordeaux-Lac, Avenue de Pernon, **t** 05 56 50 92 72; the 27-hole Golf de Bordeaux-Cameyrac, **t** 05 56 72 96 79; and the 18-hole Golf de Teynac, **t** 05 56 72 85 62.

The city's beloved **rugby** team plays in Bègles, in the Stade André Moga, **t** 05 56 85 94 01; the 1st-division Girondins **football** team in the Art Deco Stade Chaban-Delmas, Bd du Maréchal Leclerc, Le Parc Lescure, **t** 08 92 68 34 33.

Where to Stay in and around Bordeaux

Bordeaux ✉ 33000

There are plenty of chain hotels at Bordeaux Lac, off the *rocade* ring road, near the airport, and in the Centre Mériadeck (*see* p.223).

******Burdigala**, 115 Rue Georges Bonnac, **t** 05 56 90 16 16, *www.burdigala.com* (€€€€€–€€€€). Elegant, air-conditioned rooms and suites individually styled in wood, stone and marble, and a plush restaurant (€€€€–€€).

★ La Maison Bord-Eaux >

La Maison Bord'Eaux, 113 Rue du Docteur Albert Barraud, **t** 05 56 44 00 45, *www.lamaisonbord-eaux.com* (€€€€–€€€). A trendy boutique B&B within an 18th-century townhouse with a garden and an excellent wine bar (€€€€–€€€) offering seafood- and cheese-based menus including wine. Private visits to vineyards, reduced green fees at golf clubs, and spa and beauty sessions are available.

****Le Continental**, 10 Rue Montesquieu, **t** 05 56 52 66 00, *www.hotel-le-continental.com* (€€€€–€€). An elegant hotel on a pedestrianized street in the centre, with comfy rooms.

*****Le Bayonne Etche-Ona**, 15 Cours Intendance, **t** 05 56 48 00 88, *www.bordeaux-hotel.com* (€€€). A Best Western in an 18th-century building, with rooms with air-conditioning, TVs, minibars and Wifi Internet access.

*****Ste Catherine**, 27 Rue du Parlement, **t** 05 56 81 95 12, *www.bordeaux-hotelquality.com* (€€€–€€). A handsomely restored 18th-century hôtel near the Grand Théâtre, with great rooms for the price. There's no restaurant but regional specialities can be ordered as room service.

****Le Majestic**, 2 Rue de Condé, **t** 05 56 52 60 44, *www.hotel-majestic.com* (€€€–€€). Comfortable air-conditioned rooms, an inner garden and a garage.

****La Tour Intendance**, 14 Rue Vieille-Tour, **t** 05 56 44 56 56, *www.hotel-tour-intendance.com* (€€€–€€). A simple, sweet hotel in a pedestrianized lane, with parking.

*****Hôtel de la Presse**, 6–8 Rue Porte Dijeaux, **t** 05 56 48 53 88, *www.hoteldelapresse.com* (€€€–€). A central choice with simple but well-equipped rooms.

*****Les Quatre Sœurs**, 6 Cours du 30 Juillet (near Quinconces), **t** 05 57 81 19 20, *http://4soeurs.free.fr* (€€). The place where Richard Wagner slept before he was run out of town for dallying with the wife of a local politician. Rooms are cosy and have minibars.

*****Royal Médoc**, 3 Rue Sèze (just off Place Tourny), **t** 05 56 81 72 42, *http://hotelsezemedoc.free.fr* (€€–€). Very comfortable and up-to-date rooms and a handy garage.

****Acanthe**, 12–14 Rue St-Rémi, **t** 05 56 *81 66 58, www.acanthe-hotel-bordeaux.com* (€€–€). Simply furnished but well-equipped bedrooms, the most stylish of which is the family room. It's not the best choice for those with cars.

****Hôtel du Théâtre**, 10 Rue de la Maison-Daurade, **t** 05 56 79 05 26, *www.hotel-du-theatre.com* (€€–€). Fine rooms on a pedestrianized street, with nearby parking. There's no lift.

****Notre-Dame**, 36 Rue Notre-Dame, **t** 05 56 52 88 24, *www.hotelnotredame.free.fr* (€). A pretty little hotel in the quiet Chartrons quarter.

****Stars**, 34 Rue Tauzia, **t** 05 56 94 59 00, *www.jjhotels.com* (€). The best choice near the station – welcoming, with shipshape decor, TVs and a garage.

Around Bordeaux

Les Sources de Caudalie, Chemin de Smith Haut Lafitte, Martillac (✉ 33650), 30km southeast of Bordeaux, **t** 05 57 83 83 83, *www.sources-caudalie.com* (€€€€€). An old hamlet transformed into a luxury complex, with beautiful rooms around a lake, an elegant restaurant (€€€€) and a simpler bistro (€€€–€€) in an old washhouse. But the real story here is wine – you can even bathe in the stuff, during unique treatments using springwater, vine and grape extracts. There's also a Turkish bath, a beauty parlour, a pool, a gym, tennis courts, bike hire and a helipad. Wine tours, cooking classes and tasting courses are also available.

******Hauterive Saint-James**, 3 Place Camille Hostein, Bouliac (✉ 33270), 4km southeast of Bordeaux, **t** 05 57 97 06 00, *www.saintjames-bouliac.com* (€€€€). A quirky post-modern hotel with a sauna, a pool, great views and a restaurant (€€€€–€€€) with some of the best food in the Gironde. *Restaurant closed Sun, Mon exc mid-June–mid-Aug, 2wks in Jan and 2wks at Easter.*

*****Le Chalet Lyrique**, 169 Cours Général de Gaulle, Gradignan (✉ 33170), 8km southwest, **t** 05 56 89 11 59, *www. chalet-lyrique.fr* (€€€€). A very comfy hotel with a good restaurant (€€€–€€). *Closed Sun and Aug.*

La Réserve >

La Réserve, 74 Avenue de Bourgailh, Pessac (✉ 33600), 6km southwest, **t 05 57 26 58 28, *www.hotel-la-reserve.com* (€€). A hotel in its own park with a lake and swans, plus tennis courts, a pool and a good restaurant (€€€–€€).

Camping Beausoleil, Gradignan (✉ 33170), **t** 05 56 89 17 66. A simple but good campsite.

Eating Out in and around Bordeaux

Bordeaux

To dine as well in Paris or on the Côte d'Azur as in Bordeaux would cost an arm and a leg. The Bordelais tend to choose a vintage then create a menu to enhance it, which – combined with Bordeaux's location between land, river and sea – has resulted in a wide variety of specialities, from *entrecôte à la bordelaise* (*see* p.258) to the more rarefied lamprey (*see* p.217).

On Sunday and in August, most of the city's eateries shut as tight as a clam, except the touristy places on Place du Parlement.

Pavillon des Boulevards, 120 Rue de la Croix-de-Seguey, **t** 05 56 81 51 02 (€€€€–€€€). A tasteful house with a verandah at the northern end of town, with delicate, sophisticated dishes, including *lobster au Sauternes. Closed Mon and Sat lunch, Sun, early Jan and most of Aug.*

Le Chapon Fin, 5 Rue Montesquieu, **t** 05 56 79 10 10 (€€€€–€€). The oldest restaurant in Bordeaux (dating from 1825), and still one of the best. When Bordeaux was capital, it got packed out with *le tout Paris*, and Sarah Bernhardt and Edward VII stopped by when in town. Its sumptuous rockery décor and inner garden are match the lovely regional food. *Closed Sun, Mon and most of Aug.*

L'Alhambra, 111 bis Rue Judaïque, **t** 05 56 96 06 91 (€€€–€€). The likes of delicious beef fillet with creamy mustard sauce, and poached pineapple with kirsch sorbet. *Closed Sat and Mon lunch, Sun and 4wks in July/Aug.*

Le Café Gourmand, 3 Rue Buffon, **t** 05 56 79 23 85 (€€€–€€). An elegant bistro with a turn-of-the-century feel. Highlights include knuckle of ham caramelized with honey and artichoke with brie. *Closed Sun and Mon lunch.*

Croc-Loup, 35 Rue du Loup, **t** 05 56 44 21 19 (€€€–€€). Imaginative dishes such as ravioli of cuttlefish with coriander. *Closed Sun, Mon and Aug.*

Gravelier, 114 Cours Verdun, **t** 05 56 48 17 15 (€€€–€€). Very tasty southwest cuisine in the Chartrons district, including *tartine* of foie gras with red wine. *Closed Sat, Sun, and Aug.*

Jean Ramet >>

Jean Ramet, 7 Place Jean Jaurès, **t** 05 56 44 12 51 (€€€–€€). One of Bordeaux's classiest restaurants, serving old-fashioned fare and original dishes. *Closed Sun, Mon, 1wk in Jan and 3wks in Aug.*

La Tupina >>

La Tupina, 6 Rue Porte-de-la-Monnaie, **t** 05 56 91 56 37 (€€€–€€). An award-winning place offering southwestern delights such as brochette of duck hearts, with an adjoining shop selling southwest specialities.

Bistrot de la Porte de la Lune, 59 Quai de Paludate, **t** 05 56 49 15 55 (€€). A haven for jazz lovers near the train station, with a simple but tasty menu.

Bistrot du Musée, 37 Place Pey-Berland, **t** 05 56 52 99 69 (€€). Great *millefeuille* of salmon and more. *Closed Sun.*

Bistro du Sommelier, 163 Rue Georges Bonnac, **t** 05 56 96 71 78 (€€). Simple meals that enhance the wide choice of wines. *Closed Sat lunch and Sun.*

Dubern, 42–44 Allées de Tourny, **t** 05 56 79 07 70 (€€). A plush place for seafood specialities. *Closed Sun.*

La Pâte Casset, 12 Rue de Maréchal Joffre, **t** 05 56 44 11 58 (€€). Imaginative food (mostly southwest fare) in a laid-back atmosphere at kind prices. *Closed Sat lunch and Sun.*

Restaurant de Fromages Baud et Millet, 19 Rue Huguerie, **t** 05 56 79 05 77 (€€). More than 950 wines from around the world to go with 200 or so types of cheese, *raclettes* (melted cheese, potatoes, pickled onions and gherkins) and more. *Closed Sun and public hols.*

La Casa Pino, 40 Rue Traversanne, St-Michel, **t** 05 56 92 82 88 (€€–€). The best Portuguese in the city. *Closed Sun.*

Au Bonheur du Palais, 74 Rue Paul-Louis Lande, **t** 05 56 94 38 63 (€). Excellent, very serious Chinese food. *Closed lunch and Sun.*

Malabar, 7 Rue des Ayres, **t** 05 56 52 18 19 (€). One of Bordeaux's better Indian restaurants. *Closed Sun and Aug.*

Around Bordeaux

Le Bistroy, 3 Place Camille Hostein, Bouliac, **t** 05 57 97 06 06 (€€€–€€). A fish restaurant with the same owner as the Hauterive Saint-James (see p.235). He also owns the **Café de l'Espérance** (**t** 05 56 20 52 16) behind the church – a classy café with simple country cooking.

Le Cohé, 8 Avenue Roger Cohé, Pessac, **t** 05 56 45 73 72 (€€€–€€). Good French cuisine with a modern touch. *Closed Sun eve, Mon and Aug.*

Entertainment and Nightlife in Bordeaux

Theatre, Opera and Music

The tourist office has a calendar of concerts, opera and ballet, or see *www.opera-bordeaux.com*. The premier stage for the classics remains Victor Louis' **Grand Théâtre**, Place de la Comédie, **t** 05 56 52 45 19; followed by the **Théâtre Femina**, 8 Rue de Grassi, **t** 05 56 48 26 26. The **Orchestre National Bordeaux Aquitaine** often performs in the Palais des Sports, Place de la Ferme Richemont, **t** 05 56 00 85 95.

The **Espace Culturel du Pin Galant** (**t** 05 56 97 82 82, *www.lepingalant.com*) at Mérignac hosts global opera, jazz, dance, musicals and theatre.

Film

The **Trianon Jean Vigo** (Rue Franklin, **t** 05 56 44 35 17, *www.jeanvigo.com*) shows good films in their original language (*version originale*).

Clubs and Bars

For what's on, get a copy of *Clubs-et-Concerts* (*www.clubsetconcerts.com*). Students hang out in the bars around **Place de la Victoire**, especially on Thursdays, many headed for **Le Lucifer**, 35 Rue de Pessac, **t** 05 56 99 09 02. The St-Pierre neighbourhood is popular with 20–40-somethings, and clubbers head for the Quais Paludate.

Finish up at the **Marché des Capucins** near St-Michel for onion soup with workers unloading produce. Bars here are open 1pm–5am; try **Le P'tit Déj**, 8 Place des Capucins, **t** 05 56 31 28 45.

Le Bœuf sur le Toit, 15 Rue de Candale, **t** 05 56 91 41 14. A good range of beers and other drinks, and occasional free rock concerts, 7pm–2am.

La Calle Ocho, 24 Rue des Piliers de Tutelles, **t** 05 56 48 08 68. Salsa and mambo to Cuban rhythms, Mon–Sat 5pm–2am, and Thursday salsa classes.

Connemara, 18 Cours d'Albret, **t** 05 56 52 82 57. A good Irish bar with music, games and food, open 11.30am–2am.

El Bodegon Rock Café, 14 Place Victoire, **t** 05 56 94 74 02. A busy lunch brasserie and evening music venue, open Mon–Sat 7am–2am, Sun 2pm–2am.

Rockschool Barbey, Cours Barbey, **t** 05 56 33 66 00, *www.rockschool-barbey.com*. A big music complex with workshops, courses and gigs by bands old and new.

Gironde

Bordeaux's département *is chock-full of superlatives. It's the largest in France (17,225 square km), containing 3,500km of rivers and 116km of Atlantic coast, the whole lined with fine silver sand scarcely touched by development. In the Gironde you'll find France's biggest two lakes, Europe's largest estuary, its oldest lighthouse and highest sand dune, and the northern fringes of Les Landes, its largest forest. This is not to mention the biggest and, by most criteria, the best vine region in the whole wide world.*

12

Don't miss

1. **Europe's largest sandpile**
   Dune de Pilat **p.278**
2. **Gothic glories and beefsteaks**
   Bazas **p.257**
3. **Rarefied birdwatching**
   Parc Ornithologique du Teich **p.280**
4. **Wine touring**
   Around Pauillac **p.265**
5. **Landyachting on the 'Silver Coast'**
   Soulac-sur-Mer **p.269**

See map overleaf

Gironde

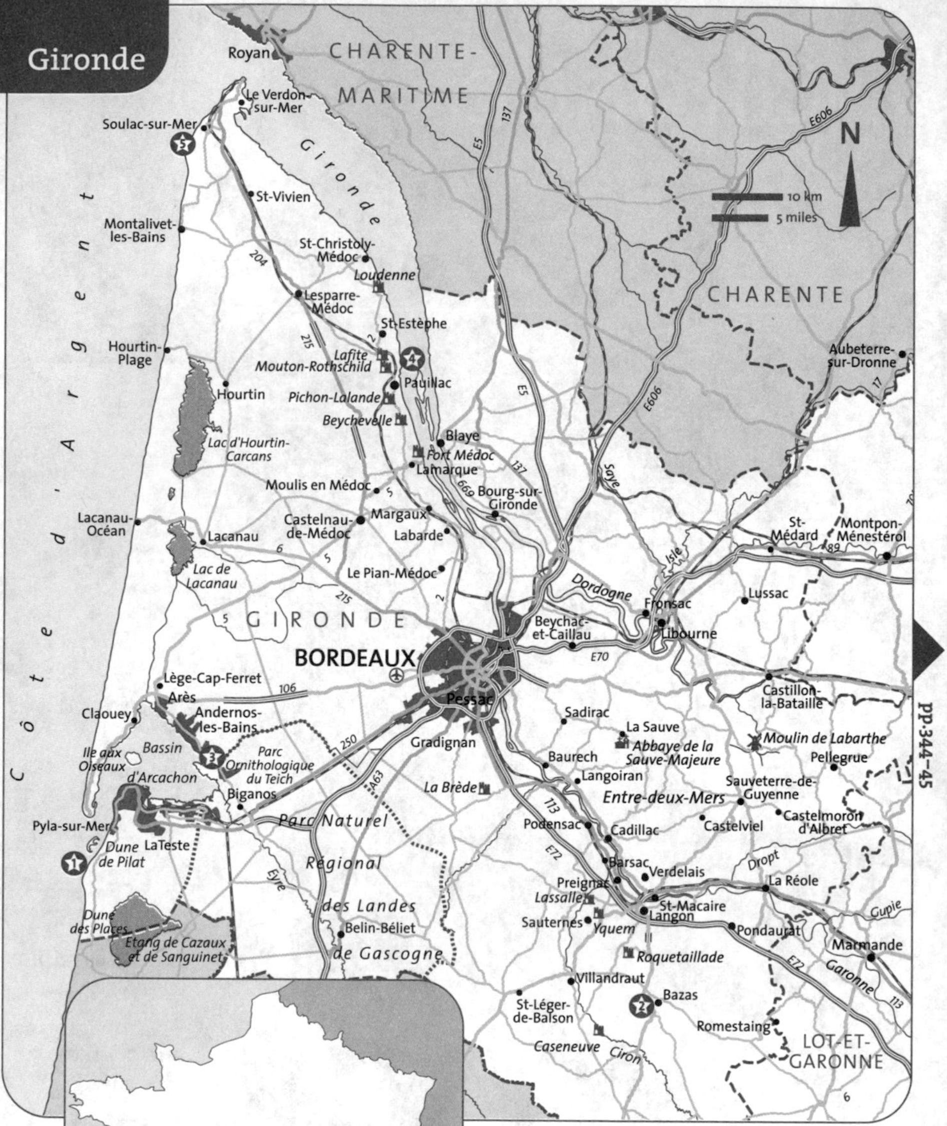
CHARENTE-MARITIME
CHARENTE
GIRONDE
LOT-ET-GARONNE
Côte d'Argent
Gironde
BORDEAUX
Royan
Le Verdon-sur-Mer
Soulac-sur-Mer
St-Vivien
Montalivet-les-Bains
St-Christoly-Médoc
Loudenne
Lesparre-Médoc
St-Estèphe
Hourtin-Plage
Lafite
Mouton-Rothschild
Pauillac
Hourtin
Pichon-Lalande
Beychevelle
Lac d'Hourtin-Carcans
Blaye
Fort Médoc
Lamarque
Moulis en Médoc
Bourg-sur-Gironde
Lacanau-Océan
Castelnau-de-Médoc
Margaux
Labarde
Lacanau
Lac de Lacanau
Le Pian-Médoc
Dordogne
Isle
Saye
Fronsac
Libourne
Lussac
St-Médard
Montpon-Ménestérol
Aubeterre-sur-Dronne
Beychac-et-Caillau
Lège-Cap-Ferret
Arès
Claouey
Andernos-les-Bains
Ile aux Oiseaux
Bassin d'Arcachon
Parc Ornithologique du Teich
Biganos
Pessac
Gradignan
Sadirac
La Sauve
Abbaye de la Sauve-Majeure
Castillon-la-Bataille
Moulin de Labarthe
Pellegrue
Baurech
Langoiran
La Brède
Entre-deux-Mers
Sauveterre-de-Guyenne
Castelviel
Castelmoron d'Albret
Pyla-sur-Mer
Dune de Pilat
LaTeste
Parc Naturel Régional des Landes de Gascogne
Podensac
Cadillac
Barsac
Verdelais
Preignac
Lassalle
Dropt
La Réole
St-Macaire
Langon
Sauternes
Yquem
Pondaurat
Gupie
Marmande
Garonne
Roquetaillade
Dune des Places
Etang de Cazaux et de Sanguinet
Eyre
Belin-Béliet
Villandraut
St-Léger-de-Balson
Bazas
Romestaing
Caseneuve
Ciron
N
10 km
5 miles
E5
137
E606
204
215
669
5
6
2
106
250
A63
E70
113
E72
89
17
PP 344–45

SPAIN

Don't miss

1. Dune de Pilat p.278
2. Bazas p.257
3. Parc Ornithologique du Teich p.280
4. Pauillac p.265
5. Soulac-sur-Mer p.269

Southeast of Bordeaux

Entre-Deux-Mers

The name comes from *inter duo maria*, 'between two estuaries' (the Dordogne and the Garonne), and by the flat Gironde's standards we're talking highlands – a lovely undulating plateau of soft limestone occasionally reaching more than 98m in altitude, pocked with natural cavities. Its fine, blond stone was quarried to build Bordeaux, leaving tunnels converted to mushroom farms that keep the metropolis in fungi. On the whole, though, Bordeaux regards the Entre-Deux-Mers as its backyard Ruritania, a natural base for microtourism, where any village with more than 2,000 souls seems downright urban; it's one of France's best-kept secrets.

In the Middle Ages, this great wedge of land belonged to the Benedictines, headquartered at the great abbey of La Sauve-Majeure, who sprinkled the countryside with good Romanesque churches. A century or two later, this peaceful region found itself on the front lines in the Hundred Years' War, which caused such devastation that in the 15th century the French kings repopulated it with northerners speaking the *langue d'oïl*, the *gavaches* as the Gascons called them, who settled in tiny hamlets or lone farms that to this day appear regularly couple of kilometres. The less said about the peninsula of Ambès (the northern corner of Entre-Deux-Mers) the better, unless you hanker after grey urban dilation, modern port installations and defunct petrol refineries.

Sadirac and Créon

East from Bordeaux along the D10/D10E, a handful of places discreetly bid a detour. The hamlet of **Lignan** was once owned by the Knights of St John, who left behind a little Romanesque **church** with carved capitals and unusual 11th-century tombs carved out of a single rock. There's also a **Musée Archéologique** with prehistoric pieces, old pottery and tools and suchlike.

Eglise de Lignan
open 2nd Sun of month 2.30–6.30

Musée Archéologique
t 05 56 21 23 53; open by appointment

Further east, **Sadirac**, a pottery-wheeling village since the 14th century, has a pair of Renaissance châteaux and a pair of potters: examine their work at the **Maison de la Poterie**, which also exhibits old pots and runs courses. The owner of Sadirac's **Château de Belloc** came up with the genial idea of planting the vegetable garden with old-fashioned, nearly forgotten vegetables – **Oh! Légumes Oubliés**, which you can not only look at but try. It has also a shop selling the farm's produce, including wild-nettle jelly.

Maison de la Poterie
t 05 56 30 60 03; open Tues–Sat 2-5; adm

Oh! Légumes Oubliés
t 05 56 30 62 00; open mid-April–mid-Oct daily 2–6; adm

Southeast is the Gironde's 'Little Switzerland', a green region sliced by valleys, with **Créon** as a chief town – a *bastide* of 1316 founded by and named after English seneschal Amaury de Craon, who hoped to dilute the power of the Benedictines at nearby

Sauve-Majeure. Créon retains three sides of arcades in its central square and a church rebuilt in the 16th century, as described in the ornate Gothic inscriptions on the wall of its pentagonal apse. Inside, the disproportionate 13th-century statue of the Virgin long stood in the niche of the 17th-century *clocher-mur*. Créon's 12th-century priory is owned by **Mathieu Créations** who make paper by hand, incorporating flowers into the sheets. Créon is also a 'Station Vélo': hire bikes from **Point Relais Vélo** to explore the local cycle paths.

Mathieu Créations
t 05 56 23 25 66; shop open Mon–Fri 9–4; free atelier *tours by appt*

Point Relais Vélo
next to tourist office, *t 05 57 34 30 95*

Just south, **St Genès-de-Lombaud** church is built over a Roman villa, with a Romanesque portal sculpted with animals and odd figures.

Abbaye de la Sauve-Majeure

Abbaye de la Sauve-Majeure
t 05 56 23 01 55; open June–Sept Tues– Sun 10–6; Oct–May Tues–Sun 10.30–1 and 2–5.30, exc some public hols; adm

Continue 3km east of Créon for the remarkable ruins of the Benedictine Abbaye de la Sauve-Majeure (*silva major*, the great forest) founded in 1079 by St Gérard de Corbie, who was granted the power of sanctuary and justice by the troubadour Duke Guilhem IX of Aquitaine. By the 1200s it had chapters as far away as England and Aragon. The great Romanesque church dates from

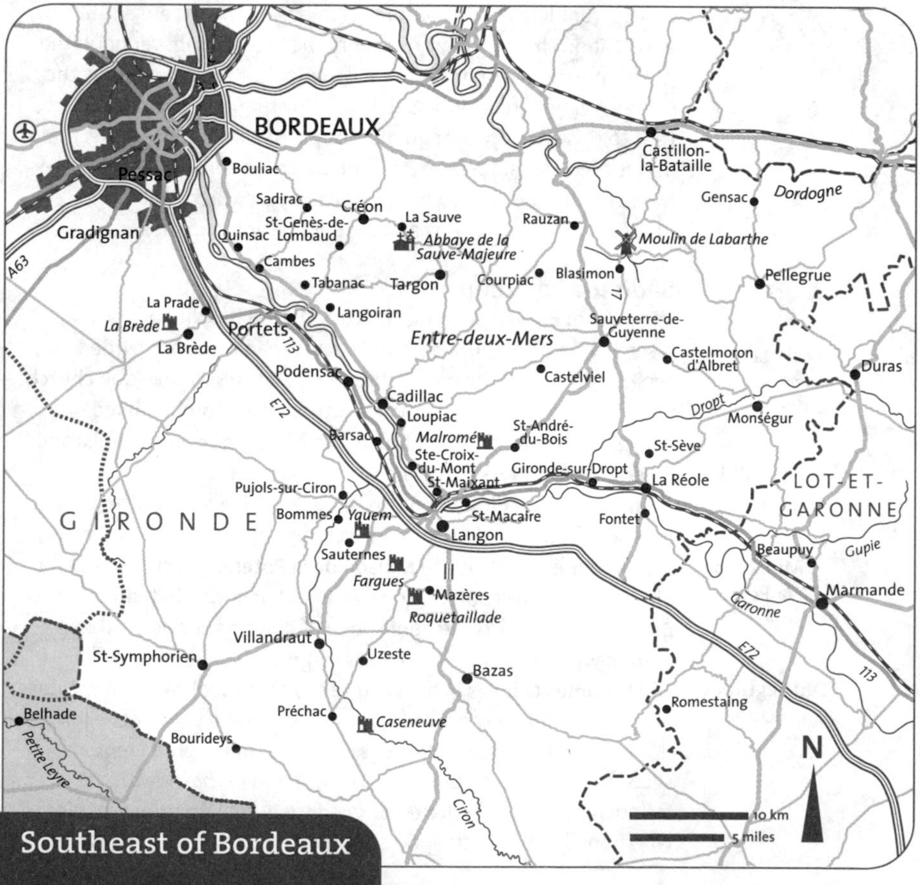

Southeast of Bordeaux

this golden age; it was damaged in the Hundred Years' War and Wars of Religion, and picked apart piece by piece by carrion salvagers from the days of the Revolution until 1882, leaving only the skeleton behind. Few skeletons, however, command such

The Vineyards of the Bordelais

Bordeaux wines come from four principal regions: the **Libournais** along the north of the Dordogne, which encompasses the *appellations* of St-Emilion, Pomerol and Côtes de Blaye and Côtes de Bourg (*see* p.195, p.197 and p.204); the **Entre-Deux-Mers**, between the Dordogne and Garonne (*see* p.243); the **Graves**, south of the Garonne (*see* p.254); and the **Médoc**, along the south bank of the Gironde estuary (*see* p.263). That's the easy bit; the nuances of *terroir* and the names of 10,000 estates, score of *appellations*, growths (*crus*) and other classifications befuddle anyone even before they've careered off on a wine tour.

By the 18th century, much of the best land for growing grapes was consolidated into the hands of Bordeaux's movers and shakers, the *noblesse de robe*, who built splendid manors by their properties. These became the basis for Bordeaux's château system. Many of these estates have been divided and subdivided because of France's strict inheritance laws. Rivalries are fierce, and wine merchants know that any label displaying magic words such Biron and Mouton in its name has an edge over its rivals.

Bordeaux and claret were always popular in Britain (*claret* meant white or rosé, but somehow around 1600 the word got twisted into a name for a light red wine, made of white and red grapes). In 1853, with the construction of the railway to Paris, the market began to expand in France too, especially after the 1855 Paris Exhibition, which saw the famous classifications of Bordeaux wines – without a single one being tasted! – and establishment of stringent rules governing growing and vinification. Bankers (most famously, the Rothschilds) and investors, French and foreign, bought up estates in time for the outbreak of phylloxera in 1878. Vines were quickly replanted, grafted on phylloxera-resistant American roots, and good wine was produced again in quantity by 1893. Even so, bad weather, war, the Great Depression, and more war took their toll, and though some great vintages were produced (such as the legendary 1900), it wasn't for decades that the vineyards of Bordeaux turned a profit again. In the increasingly confident 1960s and 70s, innovations crept into wine-making in spite of the fossilized *règlements* – the use of sprays against rot, mechanical harvesters that can pluck grapes at the moment of perfect ripeness, and adjustments in the temperature of fermentation to an even coolness, especially important for whites.

In the roaring 1980s and 90s, as more people around the world began to drink wine, investors moved in to buy up vineyards, including highfalutin estates such as Château Yquem. William Echikson's recent *Noble Rot: A Bordeaux Wine Revolution*, chronicling the chicanery, feuding and wheeling and dealing, is not exactly popular in many parts of Bordeaux. And many who bought small châteaux are sorry now. Not because their wine was bad (1995–2003 saw a rare consecutive string of superb years, with 2000 considered one of best ever) but because the triumph of world wines has knocked the stuffing out of once-unrivalled Bordeaux. Comeback strategies have included garage wines, and an appeal to younger wine drinkers through the E-Motif range, a good modern tasting wine.

The **Maison des Bordeaux et Bordeaux Supérieur** (**t** 05 57 97 19 24; *open June–Sept Mon–Fri 9.30–5.30, Sat 10–6; Oct–May Mon–Fri 9.30–12 and 2–5.30, Sat 10–6*), in the Entre-Deux-Mers halfway between Bordeaux and Libourne on the N89, is the fief of those wizards of the nose and taste bud who sniff and gargle each estate's wine every year to see whether it merits the proud name of Bordeaux; there's a film, free tastings, commentaries, advice on visiting châteaux, and **Planète Bordeaux**, an introduction to Bordeaux wines using the latest technology. Nearby, the **Musée du Domaine de la Grave** (11 Route de Perriche, Beychac-et-Caillau, **t** 05 56 72 41 28; *open mid-Mar–mid-Oct Mon–Fri 9–7, Sat and Sun 10–1 and 3–6; mid-Jan–mid-Mar and mid-Oct–mid-Dec Sat and Sun by appt*) illustrates wine production from harvesting to tasting, including barrel-making. There's a play area, cart rides and picnics by request.

You can earn more before leaving home at *www.vins-bordeaux.fr* or *www.maisondesbordeaux.com*. If you're really keen, you should book a Dewey Markham tailor-made insider tour of the Bordelais (*www.dmjwineworks.com*).

presence: three of the twelve massive pillars that supported the triple nave still stand, culminating in a row of five 'bread oven' apses, while the lofty hexagonal belltower with ogival windows still rises with panache from the fourth bay, fitted with a viewing platform on top. Two carved Romanesque capitals (the sacrifice of Abraham and beheading of St John the Baptist) are in the second bay, but the most spectacular capitals are in the choir and apses, where the eyes and hair of the figures are lovingly detailed: there are scenes of drinking griffons, fighting centaurs, a battle between an asp and basilisk, and in the apses scenes from Genesis, Daniel in the lions' den and Samson. A pair of others is in the Musée d'Aquitaine in Bordeaux. To see the rest (and the *modillons*, carved by the same hand) you'll have to go the Cloisters Museum in New York. **La Sauve** has an interesting **museum** of its own, in the former monastery, containing a fine statue of St Gérard in a style reminiscent of Chartres, medallions, 13th-century carved keystones, and documents relating to other religious foundations in the Entre-Deux-Mers. The statue of St James on the flat *chevet* of La Sauve's parish church of **St-Pierre** is one of the first known to depict the saint in pilgrim's garb, with cockleshells, staff and broad-brimmed hat; next to him stand Sts Peter and Michael, and the Virgin and Child. Inside, a Roman capital does duty as a font, and there are some simple, softly faded 13th-century frescoes.

Sauveterre-de-Guyenne and Blasimon

Sauveterre-de-Guyenne, another *bastide* founded by the English (in 1283), has kept its arcaded square and its four fortified gates but not much else of interest; from here, however, the D230 heads west to **Castelviel**, where the south portal of the 11th-century **church** is one of the gems of the region, carved with Virtues and Vices, the Labours of the Months and a bevy of other figures; Deadly Sins and saints appear on the capitals. Just a little further down the road, at Gornac, there's a restored windmill transformed into a **museum of wine and rural life**.

Moulin-musée du Haut-Benauge
t 05 56 61 96 15; open mid-June–mid-Sept Sat 3–7 and Sun 4–7; adm

Abbaye St-Nicolas
t 05 56 71 52 12; open Sat and Sun by appt

From Sauveterre it's 7km north on the D17 to **Blasimon**, site of the *castrum* Blavini Mons, which became another *bastide* in 1322, on the orders of Edward II. Outside the centre, the gracefully ruined 12th-century Benedictine **abbey of St-Nicolas** is prettily isolated in the little valley of the Gamage. Part Romanesque, part Gothic, and gracefully ruined, the church itself has somehow managed to survive in good nick, complete with a charming Romanesque façade that takes on a magical golden patina at sunset. The sculptures on the portal (1170) are exceptionally finely chiselled – scenes of Vices and Virtues, animals and scenes from the hunt. In contrast, the interior of the church is simple and pure to the point of austerity; the cloister has a handful of good Romanesque capitals. The tour includes most of the old monastic buildings. Don't miss, just north of the abbey (on the D17), the 14th-century **Moulin de Labarthe**, built by the abbots of Blasimon and one of the most picturesque fortified watermills in southwest France. There's also the **Château Butte de Cazevert**, which organizes walks among the vines (about 2km), followed by wine-tasting.

Château Butte de Cazevert
t 05 57 84 57 03; booking required

To the northwest of Blasimon, **Rauzan** is huddled under the **Château de Duras**, which belonged to England's much-maligned King John before passing to the Duras family. Hotly contested in the various wars, the castle was rebuilt and expanded several times between the 12th and 15th centuries, and has mullioned windows and other details, and a pretty 1200s church. Its impressive 30.5m cylinder of a keep, pierced with narrow slits for archers, offers lovely views over the village and valley.

Château de Duras
t 05 57 84 03 88; open July and Aug Tues–Fri 10–12 and 3–6, by appt rest of year; adm

East of Sauveterre-de-Guyenne to Monségur

Charming medieval **Castelmoron d'Albret**, just to the east of Sauveterre-de-Guyenne, is the smallest *commune* in France (not even 10 acres, with a population of 64), squeezed behind its walls on a promontory overlooking a little valley – a pretty place to stop, even though there's nothing in particular to see. To the east stands the fortified 11th-century Benedictine **abbey of St-Ferme**. The name is a corruption of St Fermin – he of the bull-running in Pamplona. Although the façade has taken a beating, the interior has an excellent, lively set of capitals illustrating the Old and New

Abbaye St-Ferme
t 05 56 61 62 10; open Tues 2–6, Thurs 9–12 and 2–6; adm

Entre-Deux-Mers (*www.vins-entre-deux-mers.com*)

As Bordeaux's largest producer of dry white wines (99 million bottles a year), much of Entre-Deux-Mers is a rolling emerald sea of vineyards. Of its 165,500 acres of vines, most are in the south and along the Garonne valley. The diversity of altitudes, soils and influences from its two great rivers make this mesopotamia a patchwork of microclimates, but for many long years Entre-Deux-Mers was considered second-rate – the *blanc* that became 'plonk' in English. Since the late 1970s pride, perhaps more than anything else, has stirred wine-makers (most of them natives of the area) to improve the quality, bring out the character of the wines, and lift the *appellation* back up to snuff.

As for all white Bordeauxs, Sauvignon is the dominant grape, blended with one or more of Sémillon, Colombard, Ugni Blanc, Merlot Blanc and Muscadelle. Along with white wine, some estates produce reds under the *appellation* Bordeaux or Bordeaux Supérieur. At La Sauve, **Château Turcaud** (**t** 05 56 23 04 41; *visits Sat 8.30–12 and 2–6 by appt*) makes a delightful, floral wine; the cooperative **Les Vignerons de Guyenne** (**t** 05 56 71 55 28; *open Mon–Fri 8–12 and 2–6*) in Blasimon does a fresh, classic pale Entre-Deux-Mers. For a hint of the vast range of this *appellation*, try the elegant cold-fermented wines of the vast 18th-century **Château Bonnet**, north in Grézillac. On the D139 at Rimons, the **Château de l'Aubrade** (**t** 05 56 71 55 10; *visits daily by appt*) has 50 hectares, half white and half red, under five *appellations*; many have won prizes (including the red Château l'Aubrade 2004). Organic Entre-Deux-Mers and Bordeaux *rouge* are produced at the **Château des Seigneurs de Pommiers** (**t** 05 56 71 65 16; *visits by appt*), just southwest of Sauveterre de Guyenne at St-Felix de Foncaude, off the D672; the adjacent 13th-century **Château Pouchaud-Larquey** is one of the finest in the area.

The **Maison de l'Entre-Deux-Mers** (**t** 05 57 34 32 12; *open June–Sept daily 10.30–6, Oct–May Mon–Fri 10.30–12 and 2–5*) is near the abbey of La Sauve-Majeure (*see* p.240); pop in for tastings and to buy.

Testaments, especially a David and Goliath, a Daniel thrown to a pair of snarling lions, along with two giant heads apparently ready to swallow a squatting man; you may have to ask the sacristan to turn on the lights. The *mairie* is in the handsome abbey buildings of 1585, a complex that forms the heart of the peaceful village.

North of St-Ferme is another *bastide*, 13th-century **Pellegrue**, on a rocky spur, with several restored churches and three châteaux on surrounding hills; south of St-Ferme is another, **Monségur**, capital of *La Petite Gavacherie*, where inhabitants, brought from the north in the 15th century to resettle the land, are still called *gavaches* or *gabots*. The word meant uncouth mountainmen, or hillbillies, but these days, realizing that everyone is someone else's hillbilly, this little enclave of northern French descendants living among the twanging Gascons take their nickname in their stride.

A walled *bastide*, Monségur was founded in 1265 by Eléonore de Provence, wife of Henri III (the charter she sent, the *Esclapot*, is preserved in the little museum in the *mairie*); it also has kept its arcaded central *place*, not with the usual medieval *halles* but a 19th-century **covered market** reminiscent of the old Halles in Paris, plus several lanes of half-timbered houses and a simple Gothic church. What it does not have is the famous castle of the Cathars (*that* Monségur is down in the Ariège). Monségur overlooks the river Dropt, and like the *pays de Duras*, just east in Lot-et-Garonne (*see* pp.382–83), busies itself with plums, prunes and prune *eau-de-vie*.

ⓘ **Blasimon >**
14 Place de la République, **t** *05 56 71 89 86*

ⓘ **Sauveterre-de-Guyenne >>**
1 Rue St-Romain, **t** *05 56 71 53 45*, *www.sauveterre-de-guyenne.com*

ⓘ **Créon >**
old station, Bd Victor Hugo, **t** *05 56 23 23 00*, *www.mairie-creon.fr*

Tourist Information in the Entre-Deux–Mers

The **tourist office** for the region is at 4 Rue Issartier, Monségur (**t** 05 56 61 82 73, *www.entredeuxmers.com*).

Market Days in the Entre-Deux–Mers

Créon: Wednesday.

Sauveterre-de-Guyenne: Tuesday.

Blasimon: farmers' market Wednesday eve July–mid-Aug.

Where to Stay and Eat in the Entre-Deux–Mers

Créon ✉ 33670

*****Château Camiac**, 3km northeast of Créon on D121, **t** 05 56 23 20 85, *www.chateau-camiac.fr* (€€€€€–€€). A delightful white-turreted château in its own park, with a pool and tennis court. Meals (€€€) can be served on a magnificent terrace, and vineyard visits arranged. *Closed Nov–April.*

Le Lion d'Or, 2 Place de l'Eglise, Targon, southeast of Créon, **t** 05 56 23 90 23 (€€–€). Good-value southwest dishes. *Closed Sun eve and Mon.*

Lorient-Sadirac ✉ 33670

Camping Bel Air, **t** 05 56 23 01 90, *www.camping-bel-air.com* (€). A year-round site under new (Swiss) ownership since 2006, with a pool and play area, and caravan hire in addition to tent pitches.

Sauveterre-de-Guyenne ✉ 33540

***Hôtel de Guyenne**, **t** 05 56 71 54 92, *www.hoteldeguyenne.com* (€). One of the cheapest hotels in the region, with some ensuite rooms and a restaurant. *Closed Sun; restaurant also Sat.*

Courpiac ✉ 33760

Domaine de Capiet, west of Blasimon. **t** 05 56 23 93 34, *www.domaine-capiet.com* (€). Three rooms in an 18th-century house in the countryside near Laubesc lake, with an attractive shaded terrace. Meals are available.

Rimons ✉ 33580

Le Grand Boucard, just northwest of Monségur, **t** 05 56 71 88 57, *http://grandboucaud.free.fr* (€€). A lovely renovated country house in a calm setting, with a pool and a sweeping garden. Meals (€€€–€€) are offered.

Monségur ✉ 33580

****Grand Hôtel**, overlooking Place Darniche, **t** 05 56 61 60 28 (€). A charming, unpretentious place that belies its name, offering good regional cooking in its restaurant (€€€–€€). *Closed Wed.*

Along the Valley of the Garonne

The most beautiful and dramatic scenery in the Entre-Deux-Mers overlooks the Garonne. Here the vineyards produce AOC Premières Côtes de Bordeaux instead of white wine. The chief towns to aim for are medieval Cadillac, St-Macaire and La Réole, and there is plenty of fine scenery along the way.

Bordeaux to Ste-Croix-du-Mont

From Bordeaux, take the D10 towards **Quinsac**, birthplace of Rosa Bonheur (1822–99), one of France's finest animal painters, an outspoken cigar-chomping, trouser-wearing feminist, and the first woman to be awarded the Grand Cross of the *Légion d'Honneur*. **Cambes**, a small pleasure port to the southeast, has a good Romanesque church with 15th-century English alabasters inside. On the D240 towards Tabanac, you can have a look at the elegant Palladian **Château de Plassan**, generally attributed to Victor Louis and architecturally one of the finest wine châteaux in the Bordelais, the residence and the *chai* (the building where the new wine is stored) built as a harmonious ensemble.

Château de Plassan
t 05 56 67 53 16, www.chateauplassan.fr; visits by appointment

Just after **Langoiran**, the next village upriver, is the half-ruined medieval **Château de Langoiran**, a d'Albret property put to the sack in the Hundred Years' War and again in the Fronde; carved chimneys and some murals survive. The Romanesque **church of St-Pierre-des-Liens** has a beautiful carved 12th-century apse, and the Parc de la Peyruche is pretty. Little **Rions** was peaceful Gallo-Roman *Riuncium* but found itself square on the frontier between the French and English in the Middle Ages, hence the heavy fortifications that have given it the nickname 'the Carcassone of the Gironde' – the ruins of the citadel and a watchtower survive, along with the **Porte du Lhyan** (1304), defended by a 24m tower.

Château de Langoiran
t 05 56 67 12 00; open June–Sept daily 9.30–12.30 and 2–6.30

Cadillac, a riverside *bastide* of 1280, gave its name to America's biggest dream cars but only by an extremely devious route. A local boy named Antoine Laumet from St-Nicolas-de-la-Grave (*see* p.411) went off to seek his fortune in America, where he adopted the grander alias of Lamothe-Cadillac. After a busy career up in the Great Lakes country, where he founded Detroit in 1702, he ended up as governor of the Louisiana territory. In 1902 a Detroit car-maker took the name Cadillac; it was merged with General Motors in the 1920s, and the rest is history. A full-size Caddy would look like Moby Dick in the main square of Cadillac, and trying to squeeze it under the pretty, lantern-topped 18th-century **Porte de l'Horloge**, the main river gate, would be asking for trouble.

Château de Cadillac
t 05 56 62 69 58; open June–Sept daily 10–6; rest of year Tues–Sun 10–12.30 and 2–5.30

But this village does have something even bigger than its eponymous car: the **Château de Cadillac**, built 1598–1620 by Henri III's favourite *mignon* ('cutie-pie', roughly), the fabulously wealthy Nogaret de La Valette, Duc d'Epernon. The story goes that when Henri IV inherited this proud, dangerous and ruthlessly ambitious toyboy from his predecessor, he made him governor of Guyenne and went out of his way to encourage him to spend as much of his time and fortune as possible building himself this palace. The result is architecturally a meld of the styles popular in the time of Henri IV and Louis XIII, but after damage in the Revolution and a century of duty as a women's prison (until 1928) it has lost some of its sparkle. Purchased by the state in 1952, the château has great vaulted guard rooms below and painted ceilings above, tapestries from the 13th and 17th centuries (the latter, showing scenes from the life of Henri III, were made here) and eight monumental chimneypieces, beautifully sculpted in part by Jean Langlois and decorated with rare marbles, cascades of flowers and fruits, cupids and armour. Also displayed are fragments of the grand mausoleum of the ducs d'Epernon, located in a rich marble chapel in the nearby church of St-Blaise until it was bashed in the Revolution. The **Maison du Vin** is in the 18th-century La Closière at 104 Rue Cazaux Cazalet.

Maison du Vin
t 05 57 98 19 20; open Mon–Fri 10–12.30 and 1.30–5

Syndicat Viticole
t 05 56 79 70 53; call for hrs

Villa et Thermes Gallo-Romains
t 05 56 62 93 82; open by appointment

Wine is also the name of the game in **Loupiac**, the next village, where you can visit the **Syndicat Viticole**. It is also the site of the **Villa et Thermes Gallo-Romains**, which may have belonged to Ausonius. Inhabited from the 2nd to 5th centuries AD, the baths and plumbing are fairly well preserved, and the whole is covered with colourful mosaic floors, including one in a pretty heart pattern. The **Lac de Laromet**, 4km from Cadillac, is a stopoff for migrating birds and has a number of walks.

Another vinous vortex, **Ste-Croix-du-Mont**, is perched on an enormous fossilized oyster reef like a great pearl. One of its two châteaux belonged to Pierre de Lancre, a psychotic witch-hunter who terrorized the Basque lands in the 1600s on behalf of the *Parlement de Bordeaux*. The square in front of the reconstructed Romanesque church enjoys a wide-ranging view of the Garonne valley over the Sauternes; in a cave that was excavated in the petrified oysters you can enjoy tastings of Ste-Croix's own golden nectar (***t** 05 56 62 09 02*).

Premières Côtes de Bordeaux (*www.premierescotesdebordeaux.com*)

This area begins in the suburbs of Bordeaux and extends along the hills on the north bank of the Garonne to Langon. Although in the 1970s most of the wine produced here was white, fashions have changed and a very pleasant, fruity red wine made from Cabernet Sauvignon and Merlot is now the main product, while a certain amount of Cabernet Franc is also creeping in. Conditions vary widely, but in general the wines made to the west are lighter, with less capacity for ageing. Some of the best red wines come from the sun-soaked, well-drained vineyards of the 14th-century **Château de Pic** at Le Tourne in Langoiran, **t** 05 56 67 07 51,and **Château Puy-Bardens** in Cambes, **t** 05 56 21 31 14.

Within the area, facing Sauternes-Barsac, are three small communal *appellations*: Superieur AOC Cadillac, Loupiac and Ste-Croix-du-Mont – all sweet, white dessert wines rated just a notch below Sauternes-Barsac, though they tend to be lighter and fruitier. They are grown on pebbly clay soil on steep hillsides, 90m above the Garonne; look for Loupiac's **Château de Ricaud**, producer of a perfumed sweet wine and a dry white (as well as red Premières Côtes) and **Château Loubens** at Ste-Croix.

St-Macaire

Perched on its rock over the Garonne, St-Macaire is one of the Gironde's medieval gems, a busy port called *Ligena* in Roman times. In the Middle Ages it assumed the name of its 4th-century hermit Macaire and got a big boost when the kings of England designated it a coin-minting *ville royale d'Angleterre*. In the 18th century the *Macariens* woke up one morning to find their quays left high and dry when the Garonne slightly altered its course; this took away any economic impulse to modernize its narrow lanes and medieval houses, leaving a village of considerable charm. Another plus is its white wine, AOC Côtes de Bordeaux St-Macaire.

Three fortified gates still defend the town, including the **Porte de l'Horloge**, which is equipped with a watchtower, the town bell and a clock. Best of all is the irresistible, irregular **Place du Mercadiou**, or 'God's marketplace', lined with Gothic arcades and houses in a picturesque variety of styles from the 13th to the 16th centuries. Atop the village ramparts, **St-Sauveur** was part of a 12th-century Benedictine priory, built on the site of St-Macaire's hermitage. The church has an interesting carved portal and tympanum, and a curious interior plan, ending in a choir shaped like a clover leaf. Painted murals from the 1400s, wrecked by over-restorers in the 1850s, decorate the crossing with ghostly memories of their glory: *The Wise and Foolish Virgins*, *St John the Evangelist* and *Christ of the Apocalypse*. St-Sauveur's priory buildings, with their wide views over the countryside, are a favourite setting for summer fêtes.

Around St-Macaire: Mauriac and Toulouse-Lautrec

Centre F. Mauriac
t *05 57 98 17 17, open June–Sept Wed–Mon 10–12.30 and 2–6; Oct–late Dec and Jan–May Wed–Fri 2–5; Sat, Sun and hols 10–12.30 and 2–6*

François Mauriac's beloved summer home **Malagar**, in St-Maixant 3km northwest, belonged to his great-grandfather. Since 1985 it's been in the hands of the the Conseil Régional d'Aquitaine, who have set up a museum, the **Centre François Mauriac**, devoted to the life of the author of *Thérèse Desqueyroux*, and who allow visitors to ramble in its lovely park.

Château de Malromé
t 05 56 76 44 92; visits by appointment; adm

The 14th-century **Château de Malromé**, 6km northeast of St-Macaire in St-André-du-Bois, was completed in the 18th and 19th centuries by the counts of Toulouse-Lautrec. The scion of the family who became a famous artist often spent his summers with his mother, and died here in 1901 aged 37, burned out from alcoholism and syphilis. The château, the seat of a foundation in his name, displays reproductions of his works in a plush Second Empire setting, and has vineyards. 'I'll drink milk when the cows start eating grapes,' Toulouse-Lautrec would thunder at his doctors, and the château's red Bordeaux Supérieur made of 70% Merlot was one of his favourites; now his posters adorn its labels.

Toulouse-Lautrec is buried – rather uncomfortably for such a hard-living, keen-eyed observer of Parisian lowlife, one imagines – in the prim and proper **Basilique Notre-Dame** at **Verdelais**, just southwest. This is Gironde's most famous pilgrimage church, with its miracle-working statue of the Virgin (from the 12th or 14th century), there's an interesting collection of *ex votos* from sailors and landlubbers, testifying to her powers of intervention, in the **Musée d'Art Religieux**, plus temporary art exhibitions.

Musée d'Art Religieux
t 05 56 62 02 04; open Easter–early Nov Wed–Sun 3–7; adm

Further up the Garonne, **St-Pierre-d'Aurillac** has a pleasant river beach and a Merovingian sarcophagus in front of its church. But the most tempting stop between St-Macaire and La Réole is **St-Martin-de-Sescas**, to see the magnificent portal of its 12th-century **church**, with lively carvings of birds, rabbits, trees, leaves and people.

La Réole

In 977,the Benedictines received a charter from the Duke of Gascony to refound a Carolingian-era priory at Squirs on the Garonne, in ruins since the Normans hooliganned their way through in 848. The Benedictines renamed the priory after their Rule (*Regulam* in Latin); this was corrupted to La Réole. Richard the Lionheart gave the priory a set of walls to match its strategic position over the river and defend its river trade, especially in wine from the *haut pays*. Pilgrims from the Limousin brought additional wealth, and until the English created a rival port, Libourne on the Dordogne, La Réole was the second town in Guyenne after Bordeaux. Today it presents a stately river façade, especially with the 18th-century **Prieuré des Bénédictins** on its terrace. You can easily wander about the old priory, used for various municipal services – the panelled and stuccoed Louis XV *salle d'honneur* is the mayor's office, and the impressive vaulted cellars house the library. In nearby Place Rigoulet, the old Benedictine priory **church of St-Pierre** was rebuilt in 1230; it has a pair of pretty Gothic chapels and a *Marriage of the Virgin* (1666) by Valdés Leal of Seville, better known for his delight in morbid religious gore and corpses. Look for the mermaids on the capitals in the nave.

Among the old boutiques and houses in medieval La Réole is the oldest **Hôtel de Ville** in France, built in the early 1200s by order of Richard the Lionheart, with irregularly placed mullioned windows, and, below, a *halle* on Romanesque columns with capitals naïvely imitating antique models. Charming Rue Peysseguin has La Réole's synagogue and medieval houses; Bordeaux's *parlement* met between 1653 and 1678 in a handsome 15th-century *hôtel* on Côte St-Michel. In 1230, an English architect under Henry III Plantagenet designed La Réole's **Château des Quat'Sos** ('of the four sisters'), its name referring to the massive round towers at each angle, of which only one is still intact; this castle suffered 12 different sieges, the last in 1629. It remained the personal property of the kings of England until the end of the Hundred Years' War and was always heavily garrisoned; the Black Prince spent a good deal of time here.

Musées de La Réole
t *05 56 61 29 25; open May, June and mid-Aug–Sept Wed, Thurs and Sat 2–6, Sun and hols 2–6.30; July–mid-Aug daily 10–6; Feb–April, Oct and Nov Wed and Sat 2–6, Sun and hols 2–6.30; Dec school hols Mon–Thurs 2–6; adm*

The former tobacco factory on the N113 hosts the **Musées de La Réole**, one featuring 100 old cars, another on the battles of the Second World War, a third displaying antique tractors, harvesters and combines, and the last devoted to toy trains.

Musée d'Artisanat et Monuments d'Allumettes
t *05 56 71 21 17; open Mar–Sep daily 2–6, Oct–Feb Sun and public hols 2–6; adm*

Nearby **Fontet** has a four-star attraction as well: the **Musée d'Artisanat et Monuments d'Allumettes**, including 'the Largest Matchstick Model in the World' (of Rheims cathedral), 5m long and 1.8m high, made with 350,000 matchsticks and proudly displaying its certificate from *The Guinness Book of Records*.

Just north, on the Dropt, are a pair of attractive watermills: the fortified, 14th-century **Moulin de Bagas**, built by the Benedictines of La Réole, and, 2.5km further up, the Romanesque **Moulin de Loubens**. They may be open once or twice a year; ask at the tourist office (*see* p.250). The Romans liked the area too: the ruins of Gallo-Roman villas have been found about every 2km along the valley.

L'Oseraie de L'Ile
t *05 56 61 21 50; open Thurs–Sat 10–12 and 3–6; call about tours*

West of La Réole, just off the N113 at Barie, **L'Oseraie de L'Ile** demonstrates how osier is cultivated and worked into baskets.

Market Days in the Garonne Valley

Cadillac: Saturday.
St-Macaire: Thursday.
La Réole: Saturday, plus farmers' market Wednesday.
Langoiran: Thursday.

Where to Stay and Eat in the Garonne Valley

ⓘ Langoiran >
4 Place du Dr Abaut, **t** *05 56 67 56 18*

Langoiran ✉ 33550

*__Le St-Martin__, by port, **t** 05 56 67 02 67 (€). A luminous hotel-restaurant looking as if it escaped from New Orleans, with huge windows over the Garonne. Eels, shad and lamprey hold pride of place in the dining room (€€€–€€) in spring, duck breast, confits and foie gras the rest of the year. *Closed Sun eve.*

ⓘ Cadillac >>
8 Place de la Libération, **t** *05 56 62 12 92*

Cadillac ✉ 33410

***__Château de la Tour__, D10, **t** 05 56 76 92 00, *www.chathotel-delatour.fr* (€€€–€€). A plush place overlooking the Château de Cadillac, with a swimming pool and tennis courts in the grounds, and a good restaurant serving the likes of lobster ravioli, plus elegant desserts. *Restaurant closed Christmas.*

La Réole >>
18 Rue Peysseguin,
t 05 56 61 13 55

St-Macaire >
Hôtel de Ville,
t 05 56 63 32 14

L'Entrée Jardin, 27 Rue Pont, **t** 05 56 76 96 96 (€€€–€). Mainly refined local cuisine, including half-cooked foie gras with apple, served beside the river, in a restaurant with a terrace and its own small park. *Closed Sun eve, Mon eve and 1wk Aug.*

Au Fin Gourmet, 6 Place de la République, **t** 05 56 62 90 80 (€€–€). Workaday regional fare popular with locals. *Closed Mon and lunch.*

St-Macaire ✉ 33490

Les Feuilles d'Acanthe, 5 Rue de l'Eglise, **t** 05 56 62 33 75, *www.feuilles-dacanthe.com* (€€). A rustic-style B&B in a 16th-century merchant's house, with stone walls and Gironde tiles. Rooms are attractive and comfy, and there's a garage. Meals are available. *Closed late Dec and most of Jan.*

Apparthôtel Les Tilleuls, 15 Allée des Tilleuls, **t** 05 56 62 28 38, *www.tilleul-medieval.com* (€). Eleven studios with kitchenettes on the edge of the medieval centre of St-Macaire, sleeping 2–6, available by the night, weekend, week or month. There's an adjoining restaurant (€€€–€€).

Camping des Remparts, **t** 05 56 62 23 42 (€€€). A good riverside site.

L'Abricotier, just off N113 east of St-Macaire, **t** 05 56 76 83 63 (€€€–€€). A charming place with innovative menus featuring regional specialities from shad and lamprey to lamb, according to season. Two guestrooms are available. *Closed Mon, and Tues eve.*

La Réole ✉ 33190

Domaine de la Charmaie, north of La Réole outside St-Sève, **t** 05 56 61 10 72 (€€). A charming B&B in a traditional house, with a pool, playground and park. Dinner is available on request.

****Les Trois Cèdres**, N113, Gironde-sur-Dropt, 4km west of La Réole, **t** 05 56 71 10 70 (€). An old-fashioned hotel with 14 rooms. Its restaurant (€€€–€€) serves grilled bass with superb fresh pasta and other delicacies, in the shade of three cedars on the terrace. *Closed Oct; restaurant also Sat lunch, Sun and Mon eve.*

Auberge Réolaise, 7 Rue G. Chaigne (N113), **t** 05 56 61 01 33 (€). A typical French provincial hotel with simple rooms, a bar and a restaurant (€€–€).

Le Martouret, 66 Rue du Martouret, **t** 05 56 61 04 81 (€). Simple rooms, plus a gîte for four people.

Les Fontaines, 8 Rue Verdun, **t** 05 56 61 15 25 (€€€–€€). Garden-fresh cuisine in a dining room with a fountain in the middle; try *pot-au-feu* with foie gras, and leave room for one of the scrumptious desserts. *Closed Sun eve, Mon and Wed out of season.*

Le Régula, 31 Rue André Bénac, **t** 05 56 61 13 52 (€€€–€). A restaurant with a pretty pink terrace looking out over the street, serving global dishes featuring lots of spices but based on local produce. Some wines are from the vineyard at Château Le Luc-Régula up the road. *Closed Sun eve and Wed.*

South of the Garonne: the Graves and the Bazadais

Graves is not exactly the name that a public-relations firm would choose to sell a region, but it isn't so sombre when you remember that here it has more to do with gravel ('*les Grabas de Burdeus*' originally) than with old boneyards; the greatest vineyards in the *appellation* look as if they're growing out of gravel pits, and in some areas there is a deep rivalry between gravel merchants and vineyard owners, each waiting for their chance to pounce whenever any land comes up for sale. The gravel forms a wedge between the river and the deep ferny Landes forest and is endowed with several special microclimates that make it perfect for wine – most famously Sauternes.

Château de La Brède

Château de La Brède
t 05 56 20 20 49; open mid-April–late June Sat, Sun and hols 2–6; rest of June–Sept Wed–Mon 2–6; Oct and early Nov Sat, Sun and hols 2–5.30; no children under 7

One Graves estate has been producing good wine since the days of its most celebrated owner, Charles-Louis Secondat, baron of Montesquieu; from Bordeaux, take the N113 and turn off at La Prade for his ivory tower, the Château de La Brède. Montesquieu described it as 'one of the most pleasant places in France, where Nature puts on her dressing gown as she rises from bed'. Montesquieu wore a number of hats in his life, not only as a successful wine grower who sold his Vin de Graves in England but also as a magistrate in the *Parlement* of Guyenne and, most memorably of all, as a clear-thinking philosopher of the Enlightenment and the author of the best-selling *Lettres persanes*, a satire of French society, and the *De l'esprit des lois* (1748), a work proposing the separation of power into legislative, executive and judiciary branches that became the basis for the Constitution of the United States. His descendants still own the stern Gothic castle he was born in, defended by wide, watery moats and preserving Montesquieu's magnificent vaulted library with more than 7,000 of his books. His bedroom, left as it was when he died, also doubled as his study; Montesquieu sat writing by the fireplace for so long that one of the firedogs is worn down from his foot resting against it. He created the château's park, its pride and glory, shaded by cedars planted at the time of the American Revolution.

Jardin Fruitier de La Brède
t 05 56 20 22 29; open Mon–Sat, call ahead

Top off a visit to the château at the **Jardin Fruitier de La Brède**, Chemin de Mons at Feyteau, and watch how they produce jams from unusual ingredients – shallots, onions and Sauternes wine.

Portets to Barsac

Château de Mongenan
t 05 56 67 18 11; open Easter–Sept 2–6 daily; rest of year Sat, Sun and public hols 2–6; adm

After La Brède the N113 passes through or near various villages synonymous with wine, beginning with **Portets**, on the Garonne, home to the charming Louis XV **Château de Mongenan**, which, besides bottling a fine Graves, has a Masonic temple and lovely botanical garden, planted after the owner read his Rousseau, with 1,000-plus kinds of roses, herbs and medicinal plants. Inside is a museum of 18th-century life, with porcelain, textiles, costumes, dolls and so on. There are temporary exhibitions and concerts in summer.

Maison Lillet
t 05 56 27 41 41; open mid-June–mid-Sept daily 9–5; rest of year Mon–Fri 9–5

Next is **Podensac**, home of the famous Bordeaux apéritif Lillet; at the distillery, **Maison Lillet** on the N113, you can see displays of their famous posters and labels from 1900 to 1930, and taste Lillet Blanc or Rouge. Also at Podensac is the Maison des Vins de Graves (*see* p.255). At **Barsac**, we pass into the magic kingdom of noble rot.

The Barsac–Sauternes Circuit (*www.barsac.fr*).

This is a pretty tour of immaculately kept vineyards and castles from every period; on a fine day, consider hiring a bike at Langon's tourist office and doing the trip in reverse. Beginning in **Barsac**, you

Sauternes-Barsac

Celebrated, simply, as the world's finest dessert wine, or by southwestern autochthones as the only proper drink to wash down a foie gras, Sauternes and its twin *appellation* Barsac are golden in tone but bring out the purple prose latent in many a French pen; give them a glass of Château d'Yquem, the closest thing on earth to the nectar of the gods, and you get:

> *Yquem pushes our sense of taste to the limits of the inexpressible... To taste the apotheosis of taste! The lips make their acquaintance (never a rediscovery, but an endless procession of rebeginnings) with that bewitching freshness. And then, words fail. There doesn't exist, in any language, a way to express the infinite pleasure it consents to offer. Your palate ['palais' in French] suddenly merits its name. It welcomes the sovereign of beverages. The supreme offering of nature dazzles your mouth. You look across at your friend experiencing the same sensations. The force of communion binds you. A kind of complicity is at work. You read your own expressions on his face. He has become the mirror that reflects your ecstasy.*
>
> *The nectar descends on you.*
> *Close your eyes for an instant*
> *And there you are on the other side of life.*
>
> Frédéric Dard

Sauternes and Barsac owe this inimitable quality to the excellence of their *pourriture noble*, or noble rot (*Botrytis cinerea*), nurtured by the autumnal morning mists formed when the waters of the icy little stream Ciron meet the warmer Garonne. Botrytis is a fungus that feeds on overripe grapes, dehydrates them, enhances their sugar content, and puffs them up until they look like turds. Unfortunately for growers of Sauternes-Barsac, this doesn't happen uniformly. The most traditional châteaux (such as Yquem) harvest the berries one by one, selecting each by its degree of noble rot; some years the pickers will go around the vineyard as many as 10 or 11 times. Add to the cost of labour the risk: as the grapes are picked late in the year, a good rainstorm could make the overripe grapes pop and replace all the carefully cultivated noble rot with grey rot. Another factor is the low density of growth: a good Médoc yields 40 hectolitres per hectare; a Sauternes is allowed 25 maximum. Château d'Yquem averages seven and should be aged at least 10 years before drinking. Because of the noble rot, the vinification requires three grape pressings; during fermentation, the wine needs special attention to maintain a balance between sugar and alcohol, which must be a minumum 12.5% – many are over 14. Hence the incredible prices for the finest Sauternes and Barsacs. Conditions in 1989 and 1990 were so superb that in the 20th century you have to go back to the legendary Sauternes of 1928 and 1929 to find their match; 1983,1986, 1988 and 2001 were classic years as well.

The *communes* of the Sauternes *appellation* – Bommes, Fargues, Preignac and Sauternes – lie on the left bank of the Ciron; Barsac is by itself on the right bank, where the soil has more limestone and clay, enough to create a subtle difference noticeable to the few who can afford to drink these classiest of dessert wines more than just on special occasions. Like Médoc, Sauternes-Barsacs were classified in the Paris Exhibition of 1855, and have kept their *cru* classifications, though in many cases quality has gone up or down. Some châteaux welcome visitors, but prices are too high for casual tastings; persistence, however, may be rewarded with a fine Sauternes in the €15 region to put aside for your daughter's or granddaughter's wedding. A good place to start is Barsac, at the **Maison du Vin de Barsac** (*see* opposite), with comparative tastings of Barsac and Sauternes *grands crus*, and sales at château prices.

can pay your respects to St Vincent, patron saint of wine growers, whose church dates from the 16th to the 18th centuries, its Baroque interior a sumptuous feast of woodwork, stuccoes and wrought iron culminating in a wowser of a high altar, carved in 1742. The story goes that up in heaven St Vincent became terribly thirsty for the good French wine he loved, and looked so woe-begone that the Boss gave him permission to return to earth for one last wine tour if he agreed to come back to paradise at a certain time. After drinking himself across the country, Vincent's time ran out, but there was no sign of him. The angels found him in the cellars of La-Mission-Haut-Brion (*see* p.232 and p.254) drinking everything in sight, and so drunk that he was in no state to go anywhere at all, much less to heaven, so they turned him into stone on the spot. And they say he's still there, mitre awry and grapes in hand. The **Maison du Vin** is at Place de l'Eglise.

Maison du Vin
t *05 56 27 15 44; open daily 10–12.30 and 2–6.30*

From Barsac, head south to the handsome neoclassical **Château Nairac** (*deuxième cru classé*), built in 1776 by a Huguenot wine merchant, who added the lovely gardens to show off the façade. Over the railway line stands the fortified 17th-century **Château Menota**; next is an 18th-century *gentilhommière* (country seat), **Myrat**, whose owner in 1975 could no longer afford to make wine and pulled out all the vines, though the latest owner has since replanted them. Beyond is **Château Coutet**, a *gentilhommière* built around a medieval tower in the 17th–19th centuries; and a former charterhouse, the **Château Climens**. The last two are Barsac's two *premiers grands crus classés*, and many œnophiles rate Climens as second after Yquem, though they have very different personalities – Climens is fresh and elegant whereas Yquem is above all luscious. Beyond is **Château Doisy**, now divided into three estates, all of which produce fine *deuxièmes crus classés*, especially Doisy-Daëne.

Château Nairac
t *05 56 27 16 16; visits by appointment*

Château Menota
t *05 56 27 15 06; visits by appointment*

Château Climens
t *05 56 27 15 33; visits by appointment*

Château Doisy
t *05 56 27 15 84; visits by appointment*

Follow the D114 along the Ciron and under the A62 towards Pujols-sur-Ciron. Before crossing the Ciron into the Sauternes, peek at two non-wine châteaux, the handsome 16th-century **Château de Lassalle**, set in a large walled park, and, 4km south, the **Château de Budos**, built in 1308 by a nephew of Pope Clement V in a style similar to Villandraut (*see* p.255), and now a striking white ruin enjoying a lovely view of the Ciron valley.

Cross the Ciron at Pujols. The first Sauternes vineyard belongs to the spectacular 17th-century **Château de Lafaurie-Peyraguey**, set in 13th-century walls. It's a *premier cru classé*, as is the adjacent **Château Rabaud-Promis**, attributed to Victor Louis. Follow the Ciron and D109/E5 up to **Bommes** and the Château de Haut-Bommes, and turn right on the D125E for the hamlet of **Sauternes**, which snoozes away without a care in the world. It has a snooty, disdainful Maison de Vin (*www.maisondusauternes.com*) that you might want to avoid, but a couple of friendly wine shops to sell and tell you about Sauternes. Continue south to the 19th-century Italianate **Château Filhot**, a *premier cru classé*. The stunning park was designed in 1840 and has a *pigeonnier* from the 1600s.

Château Filhot
t *05 56 76 61 09; open Mon–Fri 9–12 and 2–6, Sat and Sun by appt*

North of the village of Sauternes, take the D125 to the D8 and turn right for the hilltop **Château Rieussec** (*www.lafite.com*), a *premier cru* purchased by the Domaines Rothschild, and the **Château de Fargues** (*www.chateau-de-fargues.com*), a *cru* *bourgeois* that has long been as good as a *premier cru*, owned for 500 years by the same Lur-Saluces who founded Yquem, and who sell nearly all of it in the USA. The magnificent **Château d'Yquem** itself is just north of Sauternes on the D125. It's the one château everyone longs to visit, but you are only allowed around the outside (*Mon–Sat*). In the same family for more than four centuries (the Sauvage-Yquems, who in 1785 married the counts of Lur-Saluces), it made headlines when the feuding family sold it for millions to luxury multinational LVMH. The château itself dates from the 15th–17th centuries. The pale gold wines produced on Yquem's 250 acres have been the quintessence of Sauternes since the 18th century – a position confirmed since the 1855 classification that put it in a class all its own. In some years a rich, dry and more affordable white wine is produced too, simply called Y ('*ee-grec*').

From Yquem carry on north, turning right on the D116 then left on the D8E for **Château de Suduiraut** (an excellent *premier cru*), built in the style of Versailles for the president of the Bordeaux court, with a garden by Le Nôtre. From here continue past the 18th-century **Château Bastor-Lamontagne** and turn right for the one Sauternes bailiwick open regularly for visits, the elegant 17th-century **Château de Malle** in **Preignac**. The country house of a Bordelais judge, and later of the Count de Lur-Saluces, Malle with its distinctive breast-shaped towers is one of the few châteaux in France never to have fallen into rack and ruin, and has most of its original furnishings, a pretty set of silhouettes, a fine Italian garden and a nymphaeum with a crazed pebble mosaic depicting figures from the *commedia dell'arte*. Wine-tastings (Malle is a *deuxième cru classé*) are included in the price of admission.

Château de Malle
t 05 56 62 36 86; open April–Oct daily 2–6, mornings by appointment; adm

Vin de Graves: Bordeaux's Rive Gauche (*www.vins-graves.com*)

A 55km gravelly, sandy ribbon between Bordeaux and Langon, 15–20km in width, is the fief of the *appellation* of Graves, a household word in England long before anyone heard of Médoc. As an area it is extremely disparate but is basically known for its soft, full-flavoured wines. The cheap quality and sulphur stink of the whites produced here for many years gave Graves such a mediocre reputation that many buffs learned to dismiss the lot; nor did anyone loudly protest when Bordeaux developers concreted over vineyard after vineyard. Improvements began with the new Graves classification in 1953, when 13 reds were given their credentials as a *cru*, or growth. In 1959 they were joined by eight white Graves.

As these most prestigious *crus* are concentrated in the north near Bordeaux, in Léognan, Pessac and Talence, a vinous civil war of prestige erupted that resulted in 1987 with a secession of the *crus classés* from the common Graves, in an *appellation* of their own, Pessac-Léognan. The *ne plus ultra* here is Haut-Brion, in the middle of Bordeaux's suburbia, along with Mission-Haut-Brion and Pape-Clément (*see* p.232). Other noble names are Haut-Bailly, Chevalier, Carbonnieux, Fieuzal and Olivier. Visits are only possible by elaborate rendezvous; the place to buy them is the **Cave de Léognan** in Léognan, **t** 05 56 64 19 98.

Most of the southern Graves vineyards are in five *communes*: Langon, St-Pierre-de-Mons, Landiras, Illats and Cérons; the last two also produce AOC Cérons – the demi-sweet intermediary between the dry whites and sweet Sauternes that isn't quite as popular as it used to be. In the past 20 years growers here have changed over in a big way to red wines (mostly Cabernet Sauvignon, which has a surprisingly different character here than in the Médoc) with help from Merlot and Cabernet Franc. While the reds of AOC Pessac-Léognan are famous for their nearly infinite capacity for ageing, those in the southern Graves are light and fruity, generally best drunk after 3–4 years. Graves *blancs* (Sémillon and Sauvignon, in various proportions) have benefited greatly from the techniques of cold fermentation *en barrique* and work by the Institut National des Appellations d'Origine, which has researched vine-cloning in Langon: 1995 and 2000 were especially good years for them.

Among Graves to look out for are **Château Rahoul** in Portets (**t** 05 57 97 73 33; *visits by appt exc Aug*), especially their elegant whites; the well-structured reds and aromatic whites of **Château Chantegrive** in Podensac (**t** 05 56 27 17 38, *www.chateaugrive.com*; *open Mon–Sat 9–5*), owned by Henri Lévêque, who bought his first patch of Graves by selling his stamp collection in 1968; **Château Beauregard-Ducasse** in Mazères (**t** 05 56 76 18 97; *visits by appointment*) on the highest part of the Graves, home of a good Sauvignon white and easygoing red; and **Château d'Ardennes** in Illats (**t** 05 56 62 53 66, *www.chateau-ardennes.com*), which uses traditional and novel techniques to produce exceptional, well-priced whites and reds. The **Maison des Vins de Graves**, 61 Cours du Maréchal Foch, Podensac (**t** 05 56 27 09 25; *open Easter–early Nov Mon–Fri 9.30–6.30, Sat, Sun and hols 10.30–6.30, Nov–Easter Mon–Fri 9–6*) has tastings, sales and reams of advice; in general the white Graves are an excellent buy.

The port at **Langon**, the largest town and capital of the southern Graves, is the highest on the Garonne to feel the tide; note the flood markers posted on the corner of Rue Laffargue. For centuries, until the advent of rail, it was important in shipping wine and other products from the hinterland. Trains between Agen and Bordeaux still stop here, and it even boasts an 18-hole golf course at St-Pardon de Conques (***t** 05 56 62 25 43*). Langon is now the incoming port for the components of the giant A380 Airbus being assembled in Toulouse; the tourist office (*see* p.259) runs a minibus along the transit route to the assembly site. Langon's Gothic **church of St-Gervais** contains a surprise: a somewhat atypical Zurbarán (the *Immaculate Conception*, showing the Virgin floating in russet clouds on the heads of two cherubs, her dark mantle flowing all around her like a storm cloud); the local *curé* found it by accident in 1966. All the beautiful capitals were sold off in 1926 and are now in the Cloisters Museum in New York. You can take a little cruise up the Canal des Deux-Mers with **L'Escapade**.

L'Escapade
23 bis Rue des Salières,
***t** 05 56 63 06 30*

South of Sauternes: a Detour into the Landes

Landes in French means moors, sand and maritime pines, and once they begin south of the Garonne they don't stop until the foothills of the Pyrenees, constituting the largest single forest in Europe. South of Sauternes or Langon you can dip into the pines; for more, head up the river Eyre from the Bassin d'Arcachon to Belin-Béliet (*see* p.280).

There is already a definite Landais air about **Villandraut**, the birthplace of Bertrand de Got, who went on to become Pope Clement V in 1305. The papacy then wasn't quite the plummy job that it is now – in 1305 Rome was in the throes of all-out gang warfare and not a very safe place even for the boss of the syndicate; Clement V's predecessor, Boniface VIII, usually avoided the city, but a rival faction eventually caught up with him and delivered the famous 'Slap of Anagni' across the pope's mug that symbolically put an end to the power of the medieval papacy. The slapper, Sciarra Colonna, was acting for Philippe IV of France, and, when this same wily king invited Clement to move to France in 1308, he jumped at the chance. Before moving the papal court to Avignon and the Comtat Venaissin (a piece of French territory that was the papal spoils of the Albigensian crusade), Clement spent a year here in his strong, moat-belted **Château de Villandraut**, on a plain instead of on a hill and without a castle keep, a style made popular in Wales under Edward I; it became a model for several other 'clementine' castles in the area. The other thing to do in Villandraut is hire a canoe or kayak for a leisurely paddle under the big leafy trees that line the river Ciron: contact the **Base Nautique Canoë de Villandraut**. They also have mountainbikes for hire.

Château de Villandraut
t *05 56 25 87 57; open May and June daily 2–6; July–Sept daily 10–7; Oct, Nov and Feb–April Sat and Sun 2–6; adm*

Base Nautique Canoë de Villandraut
2 Marot, ***t*** *05 56 25 86 13; open mid-Jan–mid-Dec, call for times*

Just west of Villandraut on the D3, the **church at St-Léger de Balson** has some unusual medieval frescoes of labourers, with comic-strip-like captions over their heads; further south **Bourideys** awaits as a perfect and utterly tranquil example of a Landes village. **Préchac**, to the northeast, has a late Romanesque church; 4km east, overlooking the gorge of the river Ciron, the irregular polygonal **Château de Cazeneuve** was built in the 11th century by the D'Albrets, then owned by the kings of England, then later by the D'Albrets again; they became kings of Navarre and produced Henri IV, who brought his Queen Margot here for a holiday. The family made the old castle into a pleasure palace in the 17th century, and their descendant, the Duke of Sabran-Pontevès, owns it to this day. It has kept a number of interesting features – the *salles troglodytes* cut into the central court, a Greek nymphaeum (the *Grotte de la Reine*), furnished royal apartments and sculpted chimneypieces, as well as a mill, lake and lovely park along the river.

Château de Cazeneuve
t *05 56 25 48 16; open June–Sept daily 2–6; Easter–May and Oct–early-Nov Sat and Sun 2–6; park opens 11am; adm*

The Pope Clement V tour continues, however, east of Villandraut in the little town of **Uzeste**, founded by Clement's Got (or Goth) ancestors in the 13th century. In 1312 Clement began to pour money into Uzeste for the construction of a small but dignified **collegiate church**, and the next year declared his intention of being buried there, although this wish was granted a lot sooner than he might have hoped. Being in Avignon obliged Clement to go along with Philippe IV's 1312 scheme of abolishing the Templars and confiscating their enormous wealth to fill the king of France's empty treasury. The demise of the Templars culminated in 1314, when their Grand Master, Jacques de Molay, was burned alive at the stake in Paris, but not before he cried-out that both king and pope would follow him to the grave that same year, as indeed they did – the pope from indigestion after eating a plate of ground emeralds, prescribed by his doctor. Clement's monument to himself here in Uzeste suffered when the Protestants took some

Eglise Collégiale
t *05 56 25 87 48; open daily 10–5; ask about guided tours in English*

really good whacks at his church and **tomb** (1315–59): the white marble effigy atop the black slab no longer has a face, although the embroidery of the vestments and anatomy of the dragon at his feet show a great attention to detail. Until the Protestants came, the tomb also sported a black marble baldachin, decorated with alabasters, precious stones and all the sumptuous pomp required by a dead medieval pope. The church's 14th-century *Virgin and Child* was once the object of a local pilgrimage. These days Uzeste is especially zesty in August and September, when a five-day festival of all kinds of music fills its streets.

Bazas and its Cathedral

2 **Bazas**

For the past 2,500 years, **Bazas** (Gallo-Roman *Cossio*) has been the natural capital of a little region of fertile hills south of the Garonne, once the stomping ground of the Vassates Celts. From the 5th century until the Revolution, Bazas even had its own bishop, thanks in part to a unique relic – the blood spilled at the beheading of St John the Baptist, supposedly wiped up with a cloth by a pious woman of Bazas, who just happened to be on the scene and brought the cloth and the new religion back home with her. To shelter the precious relic, a triple church was built on the town's most prominent site, dedicated to Saints John the Baptist, Peter and Stephen. When this threatened to fall over, the present **cathedral** was begun in 1233 by the seneschal of the King of England. Completely contrary to usual practice, the building began with the triple portal (echoing the original triple church) and ended with the choir, and this last bit was only completed thanks to subsidies sent over from Avignon by Clement V. When the rampaging Huguenots turned up to wreck Bazas's pride and joy in 1578, the bishop, Arnaud de Pontac, saved the façade by buying it from the Huguenots for 10,000 *écus*.

It was worth it: you certainly don't get such jammy pieces of theatre in many other places in the Gironde. Around the year 1500, a Flamboyant rose window (the petals of which contain the 64 names of the bishops of Bazas), pinnacles, buttresses and a gallery were added to set off the three great 13th-century Gothic doorways. The **central portal** is devoted to the *Last Judgement*, showing the dead climbing out of their tombs, the good souls blithely heading off to the New Jerusalem as some nasty-looking devils corral the wicked into the maw of hell, while stacks of virtues, prophets, angels, martyrs and confessors rocket vertiginously up the five archings. Along the lintel are scenes from the life of Bazas's patron saint, John the Baptist. The **north portal** is dedicated to the *Mission of the Apostles*, especially that of St Peter; here too are *Adam and Eve*, *Cain and Abel* and *The Wise and Foolish Virgins*. The **south portal** belongs to the Virgin, showing her *Coronation*, *Dormition*

Entrecôte à la bordelaise

Although nowadays a juicy thick rib steak from Bazas is practically synonymous with this dish, until the end of the 18th century this method of cooking was reserved for another kind of meat: rats, specifically the big fat ones caught prowling the vineyards, bellies gorged with grapes. This is obviously just what you'd expect of a people who lust after lamprey (*see* p.217) in blood-thickened sauce, but bear in mind the Belgian restaurant that has thrived serving rat fricassee for a century – it may taste better than it sounds. An added delight in rat Bordelaise was surely the peculiar pleasure derived from eating one's enemy, in the same way French gardeners eagerly tuck into *escargots*.

In most restaurants, what passes for an *entrecôte à la bordelaise* – a slice of beef with a shallot and wine sauce – was invented by Parisian chefs in the 19th century (before or after the 1870 siege of Paris, when rat – and cat – were great delicacies). To make the real McCoy, grill *bœuf de Bazas* over vine cuttings (*sarments*): Cabernet Sauvignon for the heat, and, at the last moment, Merlot, which spreads out the smoke. Top it with finely chopped shallots and serve with *cèpes* cooked with garlic and parsley.

and *Assumption*. The finely detailed archings here are sculpted with signs of the zodiac, scenes of the Virgin's life and the tree of Jesse. The interior, completely destroyed by the Huguenots in 1578, was carefully repaired by Bishop Pontac, his nephew and great-nephew, only to be devasted again in the Revolution. To fill the space, furnishings, paintings and an 18th-century high altar in coloured marbles were brought in from deconsecrated churches in the area. Beside the cathedral , overlooking the Beuve valley, is a magnificent garden, **Le Jardin du Chapître**.

Part of the cathedral's charm is its magnificent setting, on the vast, gently sloping **Place de la Cathédrale**, bordered by arcades and some fine 16th- and 17th-century houses, most strikingly No.3, the **Maison de l'Astronome** (1530), with ogival arcades and carvings of stars, planets, a blazing comet and a wizard astronomer in a pointy hat. Things get very hot indeed here every 23 June, when strings of bonfires are lit in honour of St John, and the *Bazadais* leap over the flames and take embers home for luck, as everyone in Europe did a few centuries ago. A bull is symbolically offered to the mayor, for Bazas means beef as much as Sauternes means wine; the town is home of its very own race of cattle, the *bazadaise*.

Besides *entrecôtes* (*see* box, above), Bazas offers visitors a **Musée de l'Apothicairerie**, a pharmacy from the time of Louis XV, and a **municipal museum**, with historical, religious and archaeological pieces and artifacts. The tourist office (see opposite) organizes tours. In Allées Clemenceau, pick up the pretty tree-lined **Promenade de la Brèche** along the ramparts, with views over the valley.

The **Lac de La Prade**, just east on the D9, is a favourite nest spot for herons and other waterfowl.

Musée de l'Apothicairerie
*Rue St-Antoine, **t** 05 56 25 25 84; open by appt*

Musée Municipal
*1 Place de la Cathédrale, **t** 05 56 25 25 84; open July and Aug Tues 3–6, Sat 10–12 and 3–6; rest of year by appt*

Château de Roquetaillade
***t** 05 56 76 14 16; open Easter–Oct daily, 2.30–6.30, July and Aug daily 10.30–7, Nov–Easter Sun and hols 2.30–6.30; adm*

Around Bazas

North of Bazas towards Langon, the last of the Graves vineyards are in **Mazères**, where you may visit the remarkable **Château de Roquetaillade**, high on a spur that has had some kind of fort on it since prehistoric times. There are actually two castles, one built in the 12th century and partly ruined, and the other built in the 14th century by a nephew of Pope Clement in the 'clementine' style. In the 19th century the owners hired famous restorer Viollet-le-Duc (responsible for Notre-Dame de Paris and Carcassonne) to give it the full medieval treatment, from the exterior to the furniture, and he seems to have had a grand old time with the project. Not one to let an idea go to waste, he built in the castle keep the grand stairway he had designed in the competition for the Paris Opéra. There is also a **farm museum** on life in rural Bazas in the 19th and 20th centuries. The wine that bears the château's name belongs to another family and has won medals both for its reds – especially the 1983, 1985 and 1986 – and its whites (in 2002 and 2005).

Musée de la Métairie
open July and Aug daily 3–7

Market Days in the Graves and the Bazadais

La Brède: Wednesday.
Langon: Friday and Sunday.
Barsac: Sunday.
Villandraut: Thursday.
St-Symphorien: Wednesday.
Bazas: Saturday.

Activities in the Graves and the Bazadais

Both Langon and Sauterne tourist offices hires out **bikes**, including mountainbikes, mid-May–Sept, and organize **minibus tours** of the vineyards in summer, and outings on horse, bike or foot.

Where to Stay and Eat in the Graves and the Bazadais

Sauternes ✉ 33210

Relais du Château d'Arche, on road to Bommes, **t** 05 56 76 67 67, *www.chateaudarche-sauternes.com* (€€€€–€€€). A refined and elegant 17th-century château offering nine rooms among the vines. There's no restaurant, but you can visit the *caves* and taste the wines.

Le Saprien, centre, **t** 05 56 76 60 87 (€€€–€€). Well-prepared fish and other dishes according to the market, rounded off by Sauternes served by the glass. *Closed Sun eve, Mon, Wed eve and Christmas and Feb school hols.*

Les Vignes, Place de l'Eglise, **t** 05 56 76 60 06 (€€). A charming little country inn serving meats grilled over vines. *Closed Sun eve and Mon.*

Langon ✉ 33210

*****Claude Darroze**, 95 Cours du Général Leclerc, **t** 05 56 63 00 48, *www.darroze.com* (€€€–€€). A formal 18th-century building with beautiful, sumptuous rooms and a famous terrace under the plane trees, where some of the best traditional Girondin dishes (€€€€ –€€€) are served – oysters, foie gras, lamprey *à la bordelaise* and lamb and beef dishes prepared with a light modern touch, accompanied by a perfect wine list. *Closed most of Jan and mid-Oct–early Nov.*

****Horus**, 2 Rue des Bruyères, **t** 05 56 62 36 37 (€€–€). A simple hotel with a simple restaurant (€€€–€€) serving southwest favourites. *Restaurant closed mid-Dec–early Jan.*

Bazas ✉ 33430

*****Domaine de Fompeyre**, Route de Pau, **t** 05 56 25 98 00, *www.domainedefompeyre.abcsalles.com* (€€). A bright, modern hotel in lovely grounds overlooking Bazas, with a tropical garden, swimming pools, a floodlit tennis court, a billiards room, and a lovely restaurant (€€€–€€) serving *côte de bœuf bazardais*, lobster and other wonderful dishes. *Closed Sun eve in Oct–April.*

ⓘ **La Brède >**
3 Av Charles de Gaulle, t 05 56 78 47 72, www.otmontesquieu.com

ⓘ **Langon >>**
Allée Jean Jaurès, t 05 56 63 68 00, www.sauternais-graves-langon.com

★ **Claude Darroze >>**

ⓘ **Sauternes >**
11 Rue Principale, t 05 56 76 69 13, www.sauternes.com

ⓘ **Bazas >>**
1 Place de la Cathédrale, www.ville-bazas.fr

ⓘ **Villandraut >>**
Place du Général de Gaulle, **t** *05 56 25 31 39.*

Château d'Arbieu, just east of Bazas on D655, **t** 05 56 25 11 18, *http://chateau.arbieu.free.fr* (€€). Five very comfortable B&B rooms, plus a pool and billiards table. Guests can get meals (€€€) with advance booking, except Saturday evening May–Sept. *Closed mid-Feb–mid-Mar and late Oct–early Nov.*

Les Remparts, Espace Mauvezin, Place de la Cathédrale, **t** 05 56 25 95 24 (€€€). The most succulent *entrecôtes* in town, plus panoramic views over the Jardin du Sultan. If you aren't a beef fan, there are delicious lamb and fish specialities and good salads. *Closed Mon, plus Sun eve out of season.*

Houn Barrade, Cudos, 4km south of Bazas on D932, **t** 05 56 25 44 55 (€€–€). A *ferme-auberge* offering farm home-cooking. Booking is required. *Closed Mon–Fri exc July and Aug, and lunch exc public hols July–Sept.*

Villandraut ✉ 33730

****Hôtel de Goth**, Place Gambetta, **t** 05 56 25 31 25 (€). A typical provincial hotel with a good restaurant (€€–€).

North of Bordeaux: the Gironde Estuary and Médoc

Great freighters and tankers promenade along Europe's largest estuary, along with dainty fishing boats equipped with wing nets, skimming over the water like giant dragonflies, nabbing lamprey, shad, eels and crayfish. From March to September the prize catch is elvers, or ***pibales***, only two inches long – a delicacy that can command as much as €200 a kilo on the market and traditionally must be eaten with wooden forks. Islets in the estuary come and go with the tide; refineries and port installations come and go with the economy, and even the vineyards of Médoc took some hard knocks in the 1920s and '30s, only to rebound – the first great year was 1945, in time to celebrate the end of the war. Birdwatchers may want to keep an eye out for purple herons: the only known nesting areas of these rare birds in this region are in the marshlands along the Gironde. The storms in December 1999 and some fires in 2002 wreaked considerable damage to the pine forest in parts of this area but, despite the gaps in the trees and sheared branches, it remains basically intact and you can enjoy the delicious shade from the summer furnace.

The best time to visit Médoc is early September, when it lets its hair down for the **Médoc Marathon**, with participants from all over the world donning costumes to run through the world's most prestigious vineyards. Music, food, and the chance to visit rarely accessible châteaux are part of the deal, and the 9,000 places fill up fast. For dates and events, see *www.marathondumedoc.com*.

Haut-Médoc: Macau, Margaux and Moulis-en-Médoc

Haut-Médoc begins just beyond the northern suburbs of Bordeaux; aim for Blanquefort and get on the main *route des châteaux*, the D2, from which the great plantation houses are nearly all easy to spot. These mostly date from the 18th and 19th

Getting to the Gironde Estuary and Médoc

Trains from Bordeaux on the Soulac line stop in many of the Médoc villages, including Pauillac; the area is also served by Citram **buses** from Bordeaux.

If you're driving from the north, there's a **ferry** across the Gironde between Blaye and Lamarque near Fort Médoc, sailing roughly every 90mins in July and Aug, much less often other months (call **t** 05 57 42 04 49 for schedules).

---

centuries and lend Médoc its patina of distinction and big money. Yet resident proprietors are increasingly rare; corporations and foreign consortiums, looking for sound investments, have bought some of the most prestigious Médoc vineyards, although foreign ownership is nothing new here – in the 18th century three of the finest châteaux belonged to Irishmen named Kirwan, Dillon and Lynch (the last was once mayor of Bordeaux). Note that while many châteaux welcome visitors, tastings are rarely part of the tour.

The first village of vinous renown is **Macau**, which also produces AOC artichokes and has a little estuary port, where the Bordelais come at weekends to gobble down *bichettes* (little fresh shrimps). At **Labarde**, the next hamlet north, the **Château Siran** and its ample *chais* contain some of the best *cru bourgeois exceptionnel* – the very best is stocked in a nuclear fallout shelter (head there if the sirens start to wail). Siran's park is famous for its cyclamens that burst into bloom from the end of August to early October; several rooms of the château, once owned by the ancestors of Toulouse-Lautrec, contain works of art – a *Young Bacchus* by Caravaggio and engravings by Velázquez, Rubens and Daumier – as well as some 19th-century furniture and ceramics. Another highly rated vineyard in Labarde, 19th-century neo-Renaissance **Château Giscours**, was rebuilt in honour of Empress Eugénie; It welcomes visitors to its *chais* and pretty wooded park, planted in 1881, where you may take in polo matches in the afternoon at weekends in September. There are also rooms to stay in and a souvenir shop.

Château Siran
t 05 57 88 34 04; guided tours daily 10–6

Château Giscours
t 05 57 97 09 09; open Mon–Sat by appt, plus Sun in summer

In **Arsac**, the next *commune* to the west, the **Château d'Arsac**, 'the blue winery', is architecturally one of the most striking, beautifully landscaped with a lake, and features exhibitions of contemporary art as well as tastings of its excellent Haut-Médoc.

Château d'Arsac
t 05 56 58 83 90; visits by appointment

The wines of Siran and Giscours are in the prestigious communal *appellation* of **Margaux**, which is noted for the magnificent finesse and delicate perfume of its wines. The **Maison du Vin** in Place La Trémoille dispenses information and sells bottles, and, just outside the village, you can visit the cradle of its celebrated *premier grand cru*, **Château Margaux**. Here are some of the oldest and most wizened vines in the Médoc, and one of the most severely neoclassical châteaux, designed in 1802 by a student of Victor Louis, and set in a pretty English garden. Note that there are no tastings or sales here.

Maison du Vin
t 05 57 88 70 82; open May–Aug daily 10–1 and 2–7; April, Sept and Oct Mon–Sat 10–12.30 and 2–6.30; Jan–Mar Tues–Fri 10–12 and 2–6; Nov and Dec Mon–Sat 10–12 and 2–6

Château Margaux
t 05 57 88 83 83; call about 1hr tours of chais exc Aug and during harvest; book 24hrs ahead

Gironde Estuary

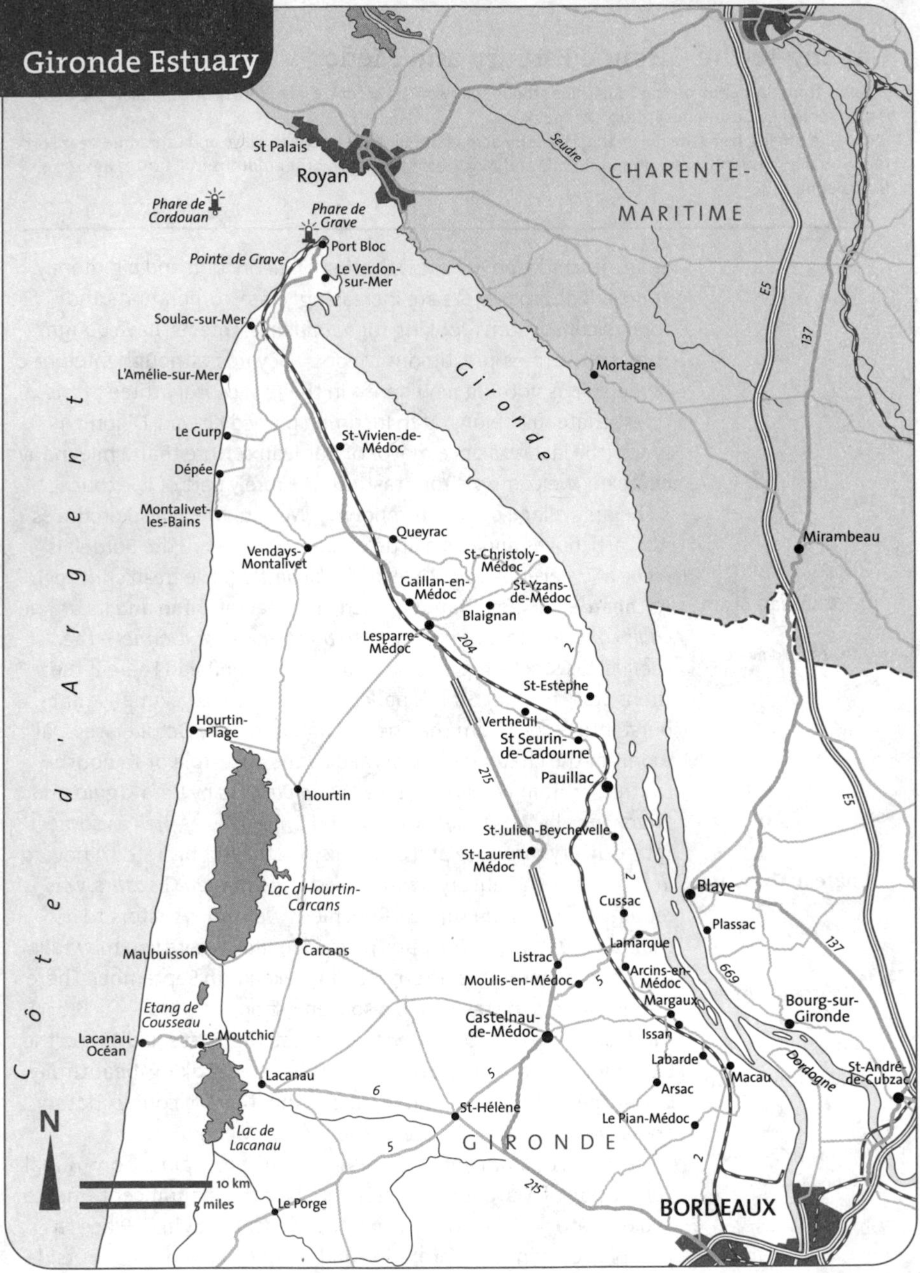

Château d'Issan
t 05 57 88 35 91; open mid-June–mid-Sept Mon–Sat 10–12.30 and 2–6; rest of year by appt

While you're in the area, you should go and have a look at the lovely early-17th-century **Château d'Issan** at Cantenac (*grand cru classé* 1855), a castle that is set amid the moats of its medieval predecessor: 'For the tables of kings and the altars of the gods', reads the inscription on the gate .

Château Palmer
t 05 57 88 72 72; open April–Oct Mon–Fri 10–12.30 and 2–6.30; rest of year Mon–Fri 9–12.30 and 2–5.30; booking required

Château Chasse-Spleen
t 05 56 58 02 37; visits by appointment

Château Poujeaux
t 05 56 58 02 96; tastings Mon–Fri 9–12 and 2–6, plus Sat in summer, but call ahead

Musée des Arts et Métiers de la Vigne et du Vin
t 05 56 58 01 23; open daily 10–12 and 2–6

The adjacent **Château Palmer**, another *grand cru classé* in 1855, was founded by one of Wellington's generals and is still partly British-owned; its wine is often rated just under Château Margaux.

The charming little village of **Moulis-en-Médoc** (inland from Margaux and to the northwest) is the seat of the smallest communal *appellation*, where the top producer has been known as the **Château Chasse-Spleen** ever since Byron commented that a glass of it chases away ill humours. It is closely rivalled by **Château Poujeaux**; both are *cru bourgeois exceptionnel*. Just opposite Moulis station, **Château Maucaillou** (*cru bourgeois supérieur*) is dedicated not only to making wine but to teaching people about it. Its **Musée des Arts et Métiers de la Vigne et du Vin** pulls out all the stops to initiate you into the cult of the 'blood of the vine'; you can take a wine-tasting course here and learn about marrying vintages to food at its *école du vin*. Moulis also has a 12th-century fortified **Romanesque church** with an ornate apse (carved *modillons* outside and capitals inside, one showing Tobias carrying a fish); the holy water stoup built into the façade was set aside for lepers.

Haut-Médoc and Médoc (*www.medoc-wines.com*)

Geographically a continuation of the Graves, Médoc is a 10km-wide ribbon between the Gironde estuary and the sands of the Landes forests, a thick Quaternary terrace of pink and blue gravel and sand. Though its 1961 *grand crus classés* are today the celebrities of Bordeaux wines, protectionists in the Graves prevented anyone from planting vines in this ideal wine region until the late 17th century, when wealthy Englishmen, insisting on better-quality wines and increasingly buying port, Madeira and malmsey instead of claret, became a force in the market that the Bordelais couldn't afford to ignore. The secret behind Médoc's success and consistency is the unusual depth of its poor, gravelly ridges, which forces the vine roots to go deep for water and nourishment; the older the vine (10 years is the minimum age for a Médoc *cru*), the stronger and deeper the roots, and the greater its ability to withstand drought. Equally, in soggy years the perfect drainage of the gravel keeps the roots from getting waterlogged. Because the gravel absorbs heat during the day, damage from spring frosts can be avoided; the vines are pruned quite short as well. Even in the worst years, a *grand cru* usually comes shining through.

Climate, as always, is another important factor. The vast Gironde estuary regulates the temperature, keeping the Médoc from extremes (the great estates all 'see the water'), while the rains and winds off the Atlantic are tempered by the screen of pine forests of the coast. If away from the waterfront, Médoc's great gravel ridges overlook *jalles*, the wide gullies that both drain the Landes and help moderate temperatures. Another factor is the vast size of the estates – enabling the *maîtres des chais* to adjust the blending and proportions of the grape varieties, depending on the vagaries of the weather. Slow-ripening Cabernet Sauvignon is the chief here, accounting for half the vines grown in Médoc, and forming up to 80% of the *grands crus*; Merlot (around 35% of most Médocs) gives the wine strength and suppleness; a dollop of Cabernet Franc adds its characteristic bouquet; and Petit Verdot is also a very important structure grape and perhaps now liked better than Cabernet Franc.

Médocs have been classified and reclassified more than any wines. The Paris Exhibition of 1855 classified 60 vineyards and divided them into five *crus* that, thanks to vested interests, have become fixed in stone; when Mouton-Rothschild moved up into the first-division *premiers crus* in 1973, it was a major event. Though *premiers crus* shatter price barriers, amounts asked for the other growths tend to reflect current quality rather than the 1855 classifications; hence superior fourth growths may cost more than second. In 1920 Médoc estates left out of the Paris rating created a syndicate, the *cru bourgeois*, which, unlike Paris, has undergone adjustments, most recently in 2003. The new classification is based on merit, with three categories: *cru bourgeous exceptionnel*, *cru bourgeois supérieur*, then plain old *cru bourgeois*. A total of 247 châteaux are part of the system; some are unhappy with their grading and have lodged appeals, or have refused to have anything to do with the reclassification, confident they can sell their wine without the new label. And it's true that there are some very good wines in the simple *cru bourgeois* category. The *cru artisan* have also established a classification that became official in 2006.

Besides all these, there are eight *appellations* in Médoc: two ACs (Médoc and Haut-Médoc) and six villages (Saint-Estèphe, Pauillac, Saint-Julien, Margaux, Moulis and Listrac-Médoc). For all the fussiness, there's more than enough to go around: the average production of the whole area is 112 million bottles a year. And studies show that it's good for health – Médoc contains bactericidal ingredients that can knock certain viruses cold; plus it speeds up digestion and has a beneficial effect on arteriosclerosis.

Listrac and St-Julien

Adjacent to Moulis is another tiny communal *appellation*, **Listrac**. Moulis and Listrac are distinguished by their powerful wines, though the fact that they don't 'see the water' prevented them from being classified in 1855; the Rothschild-owned **Château Clarke**, one of the rising stars of Listrac, was re-created from scratch in 1973.

From Listrac, take the D5 down towards the Gironde to see the **Château de Lamarque**, a 12th–14th-century castle that defended the port of Lamarque and Bordeaux from raiders down the estuary until the task was taken over by nearby **Fort Médoc**. Designed by Sébastien de Vauban, Louis XIV's crack fortifications expert, the fort was begun in 1689 and completed only in 1721, owing to the difficulty of building on marshland. Besides the heavily sculpted **Porte Royale**, complete with Louis' sun symbol, you can visit the chapel and a museum dedicated to local customs, and take in the view across the estuary as far as Médoc's sister citadels, at Blaye and the island Fort Pâté.

Fort Médoc
t 05 56 58 91 30; open daily April–June and Oct 10–12 and 1–6.40; July–Sept 9–12.40 and 1–7; Nov 10–12.40 and 1–6; Dec–Mar 10–12.40 and 1–5; adm

To the north of Fort Médoc in **Cussac**, signposted off the D2, the eclectic neo-Tudor-Spanish **Château Lanessan** (1870) is the seat of an estate that has been in the same family since 1790; its *chai* was considered the paragon of modernity during the 19th century, and it produces an excellent Haut-Médoc *cru bourgeois supérieur* that is famous for its long ageing capacity. In the château's stables (which come complete with marble mangers), you can visit the **Musée du Cheval**, where displays include an interesting collection of horse-drawn vehicles from yesteryear, saddles and a variety of other antique horsey gear.

Château Lanessan
t 05 56 58 94 80; open for 1hr guided tours of chais and horse museum daily 9–12 and 2–7, but call ahead; adm

The Duc d'Epernon, who was governor of Guyenne and admiral of France (*see* Château de Cadillac, p.246), inherited by marriage the next estate on the grand Médoc tour, which became known as the **Château de Beychevelle** because every ship that passed in the estuary paid its respects by lowering its sails (*becha vela* in Gascon) before paying the admiral his toll. The current handsome white building that bears the same name started out in life as a charterhouse, and was adapted to its new use in 1757 and decorated with a sculpted pediment.

Château de Beychevelle
t 05 56 73 20 70; visits Mon–Fri, plus Sat in July and Aug; call for times

Château Talbot
t 05 56 73 21 50; open Mon–Thurs 9–11 and 2–4, Fri 9–11 and 2–3

Château Ducru-Beaucaillou
t 05 36 73 16 73; visits Mon–Fri by appt

Château Langoa-Barton
t 05 56 59 06 05; open Mon–Thurs 8.45–11 and 1.30–4, Fri 8.45–11 by appt

Nearby **Château Talbot** is thought to have belonged to John Talbot, Earl of Shrewsbury, loser in the last battle in the Hundred Years' War at Castillon (*see* p.190). Both of these are in the *appellation* of **St-Julien**, wines distinguished for their fruitiness, delicate bouquet and original character; it has the highest density of *crus classés* of any in Médoc, especially the several riverside vineyards of Léoville that once formed the estate of the Marquis de Las Cases, in the 18th century the most famous property in all Médoc. The most distinctive châteaux here are the 19th-century **Château Ducru-Beaucaillou**, home of a *grand cru classé* in 1855, and the similarly classed 18th-century **Château Langoa-Barton**, which unusually for Médoc has its *chais* beneath it.

Pauillac, St-Estèphe and Lesparre-Médoc

(4) wine chateaux around Pauillac

Before settling into the comfortable position of capital of Médoc wines, with more *premiers grands crus classés* than any other *commune* in the Bordelais, the pleasant town of **Pauillac** was an important port, and home to one of the oldest sailing clubs in France. Before the 1930s, when the estuary was dredged, steamers from France's colonies in the Americas, Africa and Asia would call at the **Ile de Patiras**, in the middle of the Gironde, and passengers transferred to and from Bordeaux by smaller craft. Nowadays, instead of exotic steamers there's a marina, and views over the estuary to the looming silhouette of the Braud nuclear plant. But what people come to ponder at Pauillac is another source of power altogether: the most famous **wine châteaux** in France, where the purest gravelly ridges produce more than 7 million bottles a year of the mightiest Médocs of all, full-bodied, presumably non-radioactive wines laced with a distinctive blackcurrant bouquet.

Château Pichon-Longueville
t 05 56 59 19 40; open Mon–Fri 9–11.30 and 2–4 but call ahead

Château Latour
t 05 56 73 19 80, www.chateau-latour.com; visits by appt

Petit Musée d'Automates
3 Rue Aristide Briand, t 05 56 59 02 45; open June–Sept daily 10–12.30 and 2.30–7; rest of year ask at tourist office (see p.267)

Château Mouton-Rothschild
t 05 56 73 21 29; open by appt; adm

Coming from the south, don't miss the **Château Pichon-Longueville**, built in the 19th century by the *grande dame* of Bordeaux wine, the Comtesse Lalande, with a magnificent view over the riverside vineyards and a collection of glasses, china and *objets d'art*.

Further up, the legendary **Château Latour**, a *premier grand cru classé* owned by Allied-Lyons since 1989 (purchase price a record 10,000,000 francs an acre, for 200 acres), has rarely failed to live up to its status or to lead the way in innovation: in the 1960s it revolutionized wine storage in the Bordelais with the introduction of stainless-steel vats. For a break from wine, there's Pauillac's **Petit Musée d'Automates**, full of old-fashioned mechanized figures.

Just north of Pauillac, **Château Mouton-Rothschild** was bought by Baron Nathaniel de Rothschild in 1853. He was devastated when his wine was not selected as a *premier grand cru classé* in 1855 – an omission corrected in 1973, thanks to the enthusiasm of his descendant, Baron Philippe de Rothschild. In the 1920s Baron Philippe took over a property no one else in the family much cared for and made it his life's work until he died in 1988. One of his first moves was to bottle all of his wine at the château, an idea that seemed eccentric at the time. Today it's Baroness Philippine at the helm. The neo-Tudor château, while not terribly interesting in itself, has an exquisite English garden. For oenophiles, the guided tour must be the equivalent of obtaining a private audience with the Pope but is rather easier to arrange. It begins with the perfect *grand chai*, Baron Philippe's 'theatre of wine', its immaculate blond wood barrels lined up with military precision, and the château's collection of wine labels by famous artists (Dalí, Picasso and Warhol) – a tradition begun in 1945. The tour continues to a rich museum of art devoted to wine, **Le Vin dans l'Art** – the oldest pieces are from ancient Mesopotamia – and finishes with a descent into the cellar, the holy of holies, where bottles worth as much as your house and car put together do their silent alchemical work. You can taste the estate's more realistic wines, for a fee.

Château Lafite-Rothschild
t 01 53 89 78 00; visits Nov–July Mon–Fri 2–3.30 by appointment

The big Mouton's eternal rival, the 120-hectare *premier grand cru classé* **Château Lafite-Rothschild**, owned by the Baron's cousins, broods over the Pauillac-Lesparre road from its height – in Gascon *la hite*, hence Lafite. Only a tower survives of the medieval castle, whose lords were in charge of dispensing justice in Pauillac, while the present château dates from the 18th century. In 1868 it was bought by James de Rothschild; his descendants hired the fashionable Catalan Ricardo Bofill to design their extraordinary new round *chais*. Lafite's cellars have bottles going back to 1797.

Château Cos d'Estournel
t 05 56 73 15 50; open Mon–Fri 9–12.30 and 2–5.30 exc Aug and picking season but call ahead; fee for tastings

North lies **St-Estèphe**, the last communal *appellation*, producing vigorous, deeply coloured wines that differ from Pauillac and other Médocs in their need for extra-long periods of bottle-ageing. This is due to their large quantity of Merlot, which can reach as much as 40 per cent of the vintage, as in St-Estèphe's leading producer just north of Lafite along the D2, **Château Cos d'Estournel**, *grand cru classé* in 1855. This is the most striking landmark on the *route des châteaux*, with its *chai* designed in the 19th century as a replica of the palace of the Sultan of Zanzibar. A museum tells the history.

Château Calon-Ségur
t 05 56 59 30 08; tours and tastings by appt

Château La Haye
t 05 56 59 32 18; open for tours and tastings early July–mid-Sept Mon–Fri 10–6, other times by appointment

In this *appellation* you'll also find **Château Calon-Ségur**, another *grand cru classé* dating back to the 12th century and given its heart-shaped device in the 18th century by the Marquis de Ségur because he loved it so much. **Château La Haye**, a *cru bourgeois supérieure*, was built in 1557 and was as a favourite hunting retreat of Henri II and Diane de Poitiers; their initials are engraved in the stones.

Vertheuil, 6km west of St-Estèphe, has an 11th-century abbey **church** with two belltowers and a portal carved with the Elders of the Apocalypse and peasants pruning vines. The interior, if you're lucky enough to catch it open, has three naves and was redesigned in the 15th century with an unusual barrel-vaulted ambulatory, rib-vaulted choir and choirstalls carved with scenes from monastic life.

Château de Loudenne
t 05 56 73 17 80; open Mon–Fri 9.30–12.30 and 2–5.30, advance booking preferred; Sat and Sun by appt

To the north of Loudenne, in **St-Yzans-de-Médoc**, you'll find the riverside **Château de Loudenne**, a handsome 18th-century charterhouse in a stunning setting with English gardens, a little **wine museum** and guided tours and tastings of the estate's white, rosé and red AOC Médoc.

Château Verdus
t 05 56 73 17 31; open Mon–Fri 9–12 and 2.30–7 exc public hols, Sun 2.30–7, but call ahead; adm

Just north of St-Estèphe at **St Seurin-de-Cadourne** is the **Château Verdus**, with an interesting museum on the Médoc from the 15th century to modern times, including marsh-draining in the 17th century, forestation and wine production, told through original documents and artefacts. There is also a dovecote with more than 1,800 nests. Wine tasting is offered at the end of the tour.

Tour de l'Honneur
*t 05 56 41 06 75; open July and Aug Mon–Sat 10–12.15 and 3–6.15; rest of year ask at tourist office (**see p.268**); adm*

The main town in the area is **Lesparre-Médoc**, which until the end of the 14th century was the seat of the *seigneur* of lower Médoc. His castle crumbled away over the course of centuries, leaving behind only an impressive foursquare keep that is known as the **Tour de l'Honneur**, which houses a local-history museum displaying tools and archaeological finds; there are panoramic views from the terrace.

Site Archéologique de Brion
t 05 56 09 02 07; guided visits July and Aug by appt

South again in the hamlet of **Brion** beside **St-Germain d'Esteuil** you can see the site of a 1st-century **Gallo-Roman settlement**, including the remains of a theatre and temple.

Tourist Information around the Gironde Estuary and Médoc

ⓘ Pauillac >
La Verrerie, **t** *05 56 59 03 08, www. pauillac-medoc.com*

Pauillac's **Maison du Tourisme et du Vin du Médoc** offers general tourist information and wine-related services (a video, a guide to châteaux open to visitors, tasting courses, sales of 300-plus wines of all Médoc *appellations*, at château prices), plus bike hire.

Market Days around the Gironde Estuary and Médoc

Pauillac: Saturday.

Lesparre-Médoc: Tuesday, and 1st Friday of month.

Where to Stay and Eat around the Gironde Estuary and Médoc

One of the spin-offs of wine-making in the Médoc was suckling-lamb. All large vineyards had sheep whose task was to graze between the rows and keep weeds down. Lambs, because they bounced around and damaged the vines, were confined to the sheepfold, and fed only their mother's milk until they were slaughtered two months later. Their tender pearly meat was a delicacy that died out when chemical herbicides stole the sheeps' job. Since 1985, however, *agneau de Pauillac*, raised the old way, has made a comeback in local butchers' and on restaurant menus. Another speciality is a refined tripe sausage, *grenier médocain*, rare outside the region.

Le Pian-Médoc ✉ 33290

***Le Pont Bernet**, just north of Bordeaux as you drive onto peninsula, **t** 05 56 70 20 19, *www.pont-bernet.fr* (€€). A rather plush Logis hotel in 15 acres, with a pool and tennis court, set near a golf course. The restaurant (€€€–€€) serves regional dishes. *Restaurant closed Sun eve and Mon.*

Margaux ✉ 33460

****Relais de Margaux**, Chemin de l'Ile Vincent, **t** 05 57 88 38 30, *www. relais-margaux.fr* (€€€€€–€€€€). The place Médoc buyers come to swan around, deducting it all as a business expense. The luxurious hotel is set in an enormous park with lush gardens and a lovely pool. In 2005 a spa was added and in 2006 an 18-hole golf course. A glass gallery links it to the equally beautiful restaurant (€€€€–€€€) offering classic land- and seafood, including roast Limousin beef, accompanied by wines at prices that could melt a credit card. There's also a brasserie (€€€–€€), open daily. *Restaurant closed lunch exc Sun and Sun–Tues eve.*

*****Pavillon de Margaux**, Le Caire, **t** 05 57 88 77 54 (€€€–€€). Fourteen well-equipped rooms in the middle of the vineyards and a restaurant (€€€), making good use of local ingredients such as *grenier médocain* (*see* p.267) in quite elaborate dishes. *Restaurant closed mid-Nov–mid-Mar.*

Auberge Le Savoie, 1 Place Trémoille, **t** 05 57 88 31 76 (€€€–€€). Good seasonal dishes at decent prices, plus a warm welcome. *Closed Sun and Mon eves.*

Arcins-en-Médoc ✉ 33460

Le Lion d'Or, Place de la République, **t** 05 56 58 96 79 (€€–€). Big portions of well-priced, authentic food. *Closed Sun, Mon and July.*

Castelnau-de-Médoc ✉ 33480

Château de Foulon, in woodlands south of Castelnau, **t** 05 56 58 20 18, *www.au-chateau.com* (€€). A 19th-century château with five dreamy, perfectly tranquil rooms and swans fluttering across its lawns.

Listrac ✉ 33480

Château Cap-Léon-Veyrin, in hamlet of Donissan, **t** 05 56 58 07 28 (€). A comfortable little guesthouse in the middle of a vineyard where five generations of the same family have produced an excellent *cru bourgeois*; you can visit their *chais*.

ⓘ **Lesparre-Médoc >>**
Place Dr Lapeyrade, **t** *05 56 41 21 96, www.lesparre-medoc.regioland.com*

★ **Château Layauga >>**

Pauillac ✉ 33250

******Château de Cordeillan-Bages**, Route des Châteaux, **t** 05 56 59 24 24, *www.cordeillanbages.com* (€€€€€–€€€€). A lovely little place in a sea of vineyards, with 29 charming rooms in the Relais et Châteaux tradition and the Médoc's best restaurant (€€€€–€€€), where top-notch local ingredients are enhanced without muss or fuss, by a masterchef who runs cookery courses in conjunction with Le Chapon Fin in Bordeaux (*see* p.235). Even for a restaurant that tends to be patronized by wine merchants and wine-lovers, the cellar is astounding. *Restaurant closed Mon (open to hotel guests in eve), Tues lunch, Sat lunch, and mid-Dec–mid-Feb.*

****Hôtel de France et d'Angleterre**, 3 Quai Albert de Pichon, **t** 05 56 59 01 20 (€€–€). Pleasant riverside rooms in a pretty building with a restaurant (€€€–€€), handy for the stands selling *bichettes* – little shrimps lightly flavoured with aniseed. *Restaurant closed Nov–Feb and Mon.*

Blaignan ✉ 33340

Auberge des Vignobles, west of St-Yzans, **t** 05 56 09 04 81 (€€€–€€). A small stone building in village lost amidst vines, offering simple, good-value meals such as salmon braised with champagne that you can eat among the trees in good weather. *Closed Sun eve and end of Oct.*

St-Christoly-Médoc ✉ 33340

Restaurant La Maison du Douanier, 2 Route de By, on estuary northeast of Blaignan, **t** 05 56 41 35 25, *www.maisondudouanier.com* (€€€–€€). A big house in a quiet village, amidst flowering shrubs. Swifts fly in and out of the eaves as you eat looking out over the riverbank. Highlights include prawn ravioli. There are also rooms (€€€) with river views. *Closed Tues, plus Mon and Wed Oct–Mar.*

St-Julien-Beychevelle ✉ 33250

St-Julien, 11 Rue St-Julien, **t** 05 56 59 63 87 (€€€–€€). Enticing seafood such as lobster salad with garden herbs. *Closed eves Christmas–New Year, and Sun.*

Lesparre-Médoc ✉ 33340

****Château Layauga, 2km from centre, in Gaillan-en-Médoc, **t** 05 56 41 26 83, *www.chateaulayauga.com* (€€€). Seven pretty rooms in a lovely château among vineyards, with a pond, lawns and a restaurant with an emphasis on top southwest ingredients – *cèpes*, truffles, foie gras, duck, lamb and fish – in unusual combinations. The desserts are amazing. *Closed Feb.*

The Côte d'Argent

From Médoc's Pointe de Grave to the Basque lands in the south runs a nearly straight, wide 228km ribbon of silver sand, with the giant rolling waves of the Atlantic on one side and deep green pine forests on the other. Dubbed the Côte d'Argent, the Silver Coast, by a Bordeaux newspaperman in 1905, there is so much sand here that it can be a nuisance (*see* Soulac-sur-Mer, below), but what the rocky French Riviera wouldn't do for a dune or two! Although we only go as far down as the Bassin d'Arcachon, the oldest resort in the northern half of the Côte d'Argent, it's enough to get a taste of the coast, offering broad sweeping vistas of empty space rare in Europe. If that weren't enough, just on the other side of the dunes is a score of lakes and ponds for calmer watersports, which also happen to lie on one of the Continent's major flyways for migratory birds. The whole is France's greatest outdoor playground: the pleasures of surfing, sailing, fishing, birdwatching, delta-planing, land yachting, canoeing, golfing, cycling, building sandcastles on the beach and slurping oysters draw more and more summer visitors every year.

Around Pointe de Grave

From Lesparre to Soulac-sur-Mer

Moulin de Vensac
t *05 56 09 45 00; open June and Sept Sat and Sun 10–12.30 and 2.30–6.30; July and Aug daily 10–12.30 and 2.30–6.30; April, May and Oct Sun 2.30–6.30*

As you continue north of Lesparre, the vineyards begin to give way to coastal plains at **Queyrac**. Just before St-Vivien, you can visit a rare working windmill, the 1858 **Moulin de Vensac**. After a few decades of inactivity, the mill has been on the job again since the 1980s, stone-grinding flour (on sale at the mill). From St-Vivien, the D2 leads to the village's small **oyster ports**. The oyster industry began by accident in 1868 when a captain, bringing oysters from Portugal to Arcachon, was waylaid here during a storm for several days and jettisoned his cargo, believing all the oysters had croaked. Enough of the bivalves survived and proliferated to create a profitable cash crop that employed 700 people before 1970, when the Portuguese oyster parasite struck and the new port at Verdon went into full polluting gear.

Soulac-sur-Mer

Legend has it that **Soulac-sur-Mer** – 'the Pearl of the Côte d'Argent' – is the descendant of *Noviomagus*, the fabled ocean port of the Bituriges, which one cataclysmic day in the 6th century sank into the sea. Recent explorations have proved the legend real, and this comes as no particular surprise to anyone here; the Soulac of today itself replaces an older Soulac that underwent a slower cataclysm, methodically swallowed up by sand in the 18th century. As a result of these roving sand piles, little remains of the medieval

Getting to and around Pointe de Grave

Frequent **trains** in summer and less frequent but regular ones in winter link Bordeaux St-Jean or Bordeaux St-Louis stations to Soulac-sur-Mer, Le Verdon-sur-Mer and Pointe de Grave; there are **bus** links from Lesparre station direct to Vendays-Montalivet. Some trains are replaced by SNCF bus from Pauillac (**t** 05 58 59 00 63).

Ferries (**t** 05 56 73 37 73) from Le Verdon port to Royan (in the Charente-Maritime) run roughly every 2hrs, or every 30–45mins in July and Aug.

In summer, the little PGVS train runs along the shore from Pointe de Grave to Le Verdon and Soulac (*July and Aug daily, April–June and Sept Sat and Sun*; call Soulac tourist office – *see* p.272 – for schedules).

At Soulac you can hire **bikes** (April–Sept) to explore the coastal cycle path, from Cyclo'Star, 9 Rue Fernand-Lafargue, **t** 05 56 09 71 38.

---

port where English pilgrims to Compostela would disembark, except for the **Basilique Notre-Dame de la Fin des Terres**, Our Lady at the End of the Earth, and even this was buried twice by the voracious dunes in the 13th and 18th centuries; in 1859 it was exhumed again, just before the top bit of the tower vanished forever, and it now sits tidily in a sand-lined hollow.

Our Lady at the End of the Earth was founded according to fond legend by St Veronica (*see* Rocamadour, p.143). It became a popular pilgrimage site – Louis XI personally made the journey three times – and it was always the first shrine that English pilgrims visited in France. It has a remarkable apse from the 13th century; inside, the polychrome wooden statue of the Virgin worshipped by the pilgrims is still in place, seated with baby Jesus, holding a lily in one hand and a swollen-sailed ship in the other. The carved capitals show Daniel in the lions' den, St Peter in prison, and the tomb and reliquary of St Veronica, who is said to have been buried here before her body was moved to Bordeaux. Three marble columns from the pre-Romanesque church survive in the apse; the stained glass dates from 1954. It is a classed a World Heritage Site.

Musée d'Art et d'Archéologie
*Avenue El Burgo de Osma, **t** 05 56 09 83 99; open April–June and 1st half Sept Thurs–Tues 3–6; July and Aug daily 3–7*

Soulac also has a **Musée d'Art et d'Archéologie** with interesting prehistoric and Gallo-Roman artefacts and local contemporary art. Ask at the tourist office (*see* p.272) about tours of the old town.

On Boulevard du Front-de-Mer you can see the lighthouse of Cordouan, 8km away, or play the slots at the casino (*closed Feb*). Just south is Soulac's small resort of **L'Amélie-sur-Mer**, named after a ship wrecked here decades ago. The big sand dune here is part of the coastal natural park. Just in from the beaches, dotted here and there along the coast, are crumbling blockhouses and pillboxes from the Germans' Atlantic Wall. Many were originally hidden by the dunes; occasionally you'll find one licked by the tide, covered with barnacles and algae and inhabited by little sea creatures.

Le Verdon and the Phare de Cordouan

From Soulac, the road continues up to the little resort of **Le Verdon-sur-Mer**. Verdon was one of the last places in France held by the Germans in the Second World War; ordered to dig in here, to keep the Gironde and its ports from being used by the Allies, they held out until the April 1945 Battle of La Pointe de Grave. Just before the end they destroyed all Verdon's port installations for ocean liners. In 1967 these were replaced by the rather less glamorous petroleum and container terminals. The tourist office at Soulac (*see* p.272) organizes summer guided visits to the Dune des Graves to look at the animal and plant life.

Further up, at **Port Bloc**, is the ferry terminus for Royan (and for the boat for the Phare de Cordouan). Here, an ancient forest of holm oak survived the war to become a popular picnic spot; a dune divides the ocean from the **Marais du Logit**, a shallow wooded lake, filled with waterfowl during the great migrations. There's a 2km discovery walk through the **Marais du Conseiller** – marshes landscaped by 12th-century Benedictine monks.

Marais du Conseiller
t 05 56 09 65 57

Phare de Cordouan
t 05 56 09 62 93; April–Sept, timetable depends on tide; call for times and bookings in English; tours last 3hrs 30mins; for other sea trips on La Bohème, *see www.littoral33.com/boheme2*

From June to September, *La Bohème II* sails from Le Verdon-sur-Mer to Europe's oldest lighthouse, the **Phare de Cordouan**, sitting on a limestone bump between the Gironde's two main shipping lanes. In the 11th century a tower was built as a first-line defence; and in the 14th the Black Prince made it into a lighthouse, manned by a hermit who fed the fire on the top platform. By 1582 this was falling over, and Louis de Foix, an engineer famous for relocating the mouth of the river Adour, was asked to erect a new lighthouse. When good King Henri IV came to power, De Foix decided to give the lighthouse a second role, as a monument to the glory of the monarchy. The result, on a 7.3m pedestal, was an extraordinary Renaissance confection completed only in 1611 under Henri's son, Louis XIII. Sadly, in 1788 this most froufrou of all lighthouses was truncated to add a 40m no-frills utilitarian white cone. To prevent further depredations, it was designated a historic monument in 1862; in 1981 it became obsolete as a lighthouse and was only just spared demolition. Inside, the first of seven floors houses the king's apartments, and the second a chapel, with a pretty cupola and 17th-century windows and an inscription from an era that was a far cry from our multicultural age: '*Un Dieu, un Roy, une Foy, une Loy.*' From here you can climb up another 250 steps to the lookout and lantern for a bird's-eye view of the estuary.

La Pointe de Grave and Down to Montalivet-les-Bains

At the end of the road and the northernmost tip of the Gironde is La Pointe de Grave (or de Médoc), marked by another lighthouse, the 1852 **Phare de Grave**, which you can climb for the view; one room is dedicated to the history of the Phare de Cordouan, other lighthouses and the Médoc châteaux. Near the lighthouse, a stele commemorating Lafayette's departure for America in 1777 replaces the one destroyed in 1942 by ill-tempered Germans who didn't like people remembering such things.

Phare de Grave
t 05 56 09 61 78; open July–Sept daily 10–12 and 2–6

Most of the Germans who come to the Médoc coast these days couldn't be more harmless; most don't even have any clothes on, leaving them at the gate at one of Europe's largest naturist resorts, the **Centre Hélio-marin** at the modest seaside resort of **Montalivet-les-Bains**. Scandinavians, Belgians, Dutch and increasingly French come to strip down too, usually *en famille*; unlike at posey St-Tropez, the emphasis is good clean naked fun among sand, sea and pines.

There's another naturist centre on the nearby beach of **Dépée**; if you're not ready to let it all hang out, there are non-naturist beaches for *textiles* at Montalivet and to the north at **Le Gurp**.

ⓘ **St-Vivien-de-Médoc >**
Hôtel de Ville,
t 05 56 09 58 50

ⓘ **Vendays-Montalivet >>**
62 Avenue de l'Océan,
t 05 56 09 30 12, www.ot-vendays-montalivet.fr

ⓘ **Soulac-sur-Mer >**
68 Rue de la Plage,
t 05 56 09 86 61,
www.soulac.com

Market Days around Pointe de Grave

St-Vivien-de-Médoc: Wednesday.
Soulac: daily (in evening July and Aug).
Montalivet-les-Bains: daily.

Sports and Activities around Pointe de Grave

Tourist offices at Vendays-Montalivet and Soulac can tell you where to parachute, land-yacht (*char à voile*), surf, kayak-surf, bodyboard, canoe (through the forest from Vensac to St-Vivien), go horseriding on the beach, follow treetop acrobatics circuits, play paintball or tennis, or hire bikes.

At Vendays-Montalivet and Soulac, CAP 33 (**t** 05 56 73 77 28/**t** 05 56 08 82 99) sets up on the seafront in July and August, offering low-cost facilities for nearly every conceivable sport, including some that you may never have even heard of (wave-kayaking, speed-sailing). They also have tuition for children and adults, and beach clubs for kids.

Where to Stay and Eat around Pointe de Grave

Soulac-sur-Mer ✉ 33780

****Hôtel des Pins**, **t** 05 56 73 27 27, *www.hotel-des-pins.com* (€€). A simple Logis de France, with pines and seaviews, 100m from the beach. The restaurant (€€€–€€) is one of the best in the area. *Closed Jan–Mar and Fri out of season; restaurant also Wed lunch and Sat lunch out of season.*

****Michelet**, 1 Rue Bernard Baguenard, **t** 05 56 09 84 18, *www.hotelmichelet33.com* (€€–€). A popular seaside villa with 20 pleasant rooms and a warm welcome. *Closed Nov–Jan.*

****Dame de Cœur**, Place de l'Eglise, **t** 05 56 09 80 80 (€). Pleasant rooms and a tapas bar.

****L'Hacienda**, 4 Avenue Périer de Larsan, **t** 05 56 09 81 34, *www.atlantys-business.com* (€). Another simple Logis de France, centrally located, with a courtyard garden and a restaurant (€€–€).

Camping Palace, Boulevard Marson de Montbrun, **t** 05 56 09 80 22, *www.camping-palace.com* (€). A large three-star campsite with chalets and mobile homes. *Closed mid-Sept–April.*

Camping des Pins, L'Amélie, **t** 05 56 09 82 52, *www.campingdespins.fr* (€). A more rustic site a couple of minutes from the beach. *Closed Oct–Easter.*

Montalivet-les-Bains ✉ 33930

****L'Arberet**, Route de Soulac, Vendays, **t** 05 56 41 71 29, *www.larberet.net* (€€–€). An updated village inn, amidst trees and flowers. The restaurant (€€€–€€) with its pretty terrace serves classics such as snails and *coq au vin*. *Closed Fri and Sun eve out of season.*

****Hôtel de l'Océan**, **t** 05 56 09 30 05, *www.hotellocean.com* (€€–€). A simple oceanfront place.

Euronat, a few km inland at Grayan-et-l'Hôpital, **t** 05 56 09 33 33, *www.euronat.fr*. France's biggest naturist campsite, with thalassotherapy.

Le Soleil d'Or, 100m from beach, **t** 05 56 09 31 37, *www.campinglesoleildor.com* (€). A traditional campsite with mobile-home hire.

Côte d'Argent: the Lakes

More pines, more sand, more water... one of the great selling points of the Côte d'Argent is the proximity of its calm, safe lakes to the Atlantic breakers, which are popular with windsurfers and sailors who don't want to get too wet. Lacanau, the big resort here, is one of the surfing and wave-skiing capitals of Europe.

Lac d'Hourtin-Carcans and Lac de Lacanau

The body of water constituting the Lac d'Hourtin-Carcans stretches 16km from north to south, making it the longest lake in the whole of France. There's no road here, but a cycle track runs between the Atlantic and the lake – it's ideal if you want to seek out your own private stretch of sand between **Hourtin-Plage**, a small family resort in the north, with plenty of activities for kids (*see www.hourtin-medoc.com*), and **Carcans-Maubuisson**, the sports-orientated resort at the southern end of the lake, with a 15km sandy beach (beware – it's as dead as a doornail out of season). Many of the sports activities take place at the **Domaine de Bombannes** 3km from Maubuisson

Domaine de Bombannes
t 05 56 03 95 95

Maison des Arts et Traditions Populaires
t 05 56 03 41 96; open mid-June–mid-Sept Mon–Fri 4–7; adm

Maison du Combattant
t 05 56 03 33 11; open July and Aug Tues and Thurs 3–5.30, Sun 10–12.30 and 3–6

Etang de Cousseau
t 05 56 91 33 95; call about guided visits in summer

One of the curiosities of the lake is an insect-eating plant. the *droséra*; otters, rare in France, are occasionally sighted here. A museum, the **Maison des Arts et Traditions Populaires** evokes life in the Médoc at the beginning of the 20th century, and there is another small museum, the **Maison du Combattant** at Rue des Tilleuls, Carcans, that was put together by World War II veterans.

South of the big lake, dunes and trees encompass the lovely **Etang de Cousseau**, which has 13km of marked paths reserved for cyclists and walkers – it's off-limlts to cars. There's a wide variety of migratory waterfowl here, such as *balbuzards* and water rails, along with some boar, deer, aquatic tortoises, genets, European mink and otters.

Further to the south, the **Lac de Lacanau** has been a favourite weekend escape of the Bordelais since the early 1900s. They built pleasant summer villas at **Lacanau-Océan**, which celebrated its centenary in 2006 – never guessing that the huge rollers that smacked the beach would in the 1960s begin to attract a new breed of tourist, the cream of Europe's surfers. Don't come anywhere near Lacanau-Océan in mid-August without a firm reservation in hand: the place is packed to the gills for Europe's surfing championships. Lacanau town just inland is home to the **Musée Mémoire Canaulaise**, at 77 Avenue de la Libération.

Musée Mémoire Canaulaise
t 05 56 03 53 39; open July and Aug Fri 2.30–5, Sat 10.30–12; rest of year by appt

The area has a numerous cycling paths that were converted from old patrol routes laid out by the Germans, including a 70km trail from Bordeaux (beginning near the Pont d'Aquitaine) to Lacanau; from Lacanau south along the Atlantic to Cap Ferret it's another

Getting to and around the Côte d'Argent's Lakes

In summer there are six Ouest-Aquitaine **buses** (**t** 05 56 70 12 13, *www.groupe-sera.com*) a day from Bordeaux (St-Jean station) to Ste-Hélène, Lacanau, Moutchic and Lacanau-Océan.

The Conseil Général's '**Bus Plage**' (**t** 05 56 52 61 40, *www.cg33.fr*) links many towns with Lacanau and other resorts; fares are very low.

Locacycles
Avenue de l'Europe,
***t** 05 56 26 30 99*

Central Garage
Place de l'Europe,
***t** 05 56 26 99 65.*

40km. You can hire bikes in Lacanau-Océan, at **Locacycles** and **Central Garage**. In July and August there are atmospheric night carriage rides through the pines, tours of early-20th-century residences and boat rides, all organized by the Lacanau tourist board, and a tourist train trundles around Lacanau-Océan both in the day and in the evening, when the casino is open.

ⓘ **Carcans-Maubuisson >**
127 Av de Maubuisson,
***t** 05 56 03 34 94,*
www.carcans-maubuisson.com

Market Days around the Côte d'Argent's Lakes

Lacanau-Océan: Wednesday.
Carcans-Maubuisson: Wednesday in summer.

Sports and Activities around the Côte d'Argent's Lakes

Several places in Lacanau offer **surf-board** hire and tuition, even out of high season: try Lacanau Surf Club, Boulevard de la Plage, **t** 05 56 26 38 84, *www.surflacanau.com*, or Surf Sans Frontières, **t** 05 56 03 27 60, *http://ssf.fr*.

You can hire a horse or pony at Village Cheval, **t** 05 56 03 91 00, *www.jappeloup.com*; play tennis, paddleball or squash at the Pole de l'Ardilouse, **t** 05 56 26 38 06; play golf at the 18-hole Golf de l'Ardilouse, **t** 05 56 03 92 98, *www.golflacanauocean.com*; or sail, windsurf, canoe or kayak at Voile Lacanau Guyenne, **t** 05 56 03 05 11, *http://voilelacanau.free.fr*.

★ **La Vieille Auberge >>**

ⓘ **Lacanau-Océan >**
Place de l'Europe,
***t** 05 56 03 21 01,*
www.lacanau.com

Where to Stay and Eat around the Côte d'Argent's Lakes

Lacanau-Océan ✉ 33680

*****Hôtel du Golf**, **t** 05 56 03 92 92, *www.golf-hotel-lacanau.fr* (€€€). A golf hotel right by the course, with seasonal discounts on green fees.

*****Vitalparc**, Route du Baganais, **t** 05 56 03 91 00, *www.vitalparc.com* (€€€). A hotel, apartments, villas and equestrian centre amid the pines, with a pool, spa and gym. Hotel rooms have balconies, and there's a good restaurant. *Closed mid-Nov–early Feb.*

****L'Oyat**, seafront, Ortal, **t** 05 56 03 11 11, *www.hotel-oyat.com* (€€€). A seaside option with a restaurant serving some of the best food in town, making half-board a tempting prospect. It also has a handy laundrette. *Closed Nov–Mar.*

La Lodgia, Le Drive III, **t** 05 57 70 07 81, *http://lalodgia.free.fr* (€€). Three comfy, colourful rooms with terraces looking onto the garden and their own entrances, opposite the golf course.

Airotel de l'Océan, **t** 05 56 03 24 45, *www.airotel-ocean.com* (€). A campsite in the pinewoods close to the beach, with mobile homes and chalets, and just about every facility you can imagine. Book at least 6 months in advance for August. *Closed end of Sept to early April.*

Les Grands Pins, **t** 05 56 03 20 77, *www.lesgrandspins.com* (€). Another campsite near the beach, with mobile homes, a pool and tennis facilities. Again, book well in advance for August. *Closed mid-Sept–mid-April.*

Le Porge ✉ 33680

La Vieille Auberge, south of Lacanau on way into village on D3, **t** 05 56 26 50 40 (€€). A tasteful, rustic dining room with charming staff, serving traditional meals with Médoc wines. *Closed Mon eve, Tues eve and Wed out of season, and mid-Jan–mid-Feb.*

Arcachon and its Bassin

The straight line of the Côte d'Argent is broken by Gascony's inland sea, the 250-square-kilometre Bassin d'Arcachon. Not only does it sound like something in your bathroom, but like that fixture the actual amount of water in it varies greatly, when the tide sweeps through twice a day – at low tide, large sections turn into sandy mud pies. The Bassin managed to stay out of history most of the time; the Romans and Rabelais wrote admiringly of its oysters, and in the Middle Ages it belonged to the redoubtable Captals de Buch, English allies in the Hundred Years' War. In the 18th century, Louis XVI thought to make the Bassin into a military port and sent down an engineer of the Ponts et Chaussées, Brémontier, to fix the shifting sands. Brémontier built tall palisades 75m in from the high tide, stopping the windborne sand to create barriers: dunes 9–12m high, which he anchored with a long-rooted grass called *oyat*. To stop the dunes from wandering inland, he spread a mix of seeds of

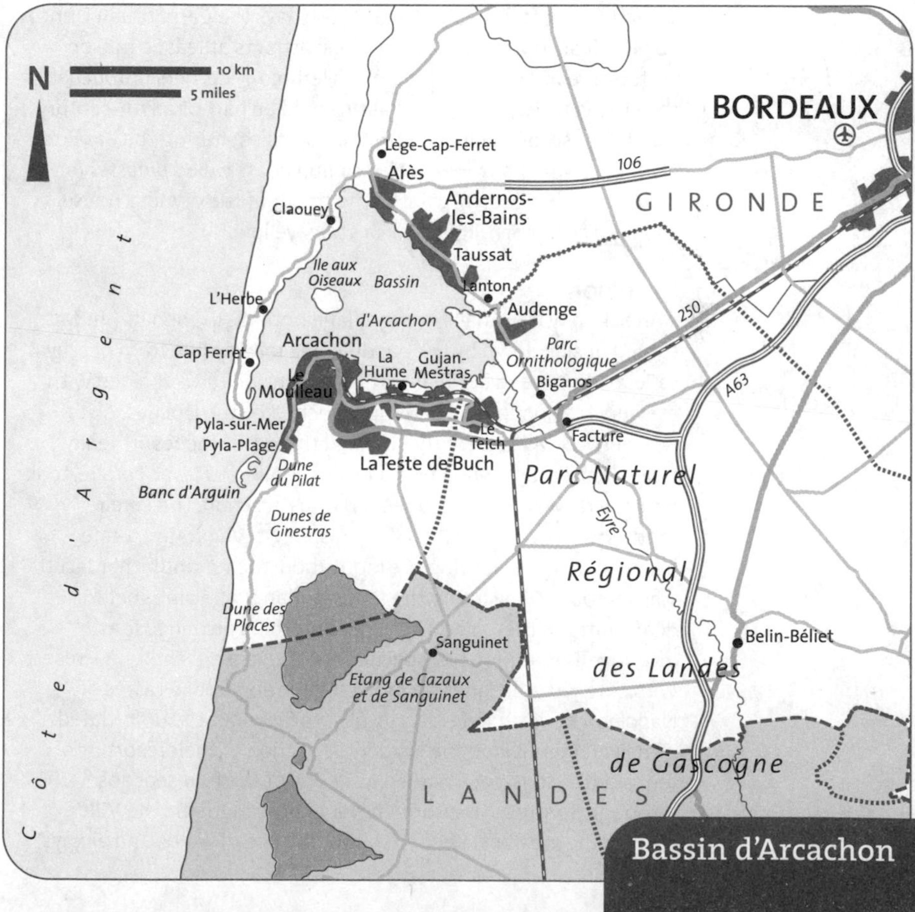

Bassin d'Arcachon

Getting to and around Arcachon and its Bassin

There are **trains** from Bordeaux to Arcachon nearly every hour, and in summer TGVs run directly from Paris-Montparnasse to Arcachon.

Several Citram **buses** a day run from Bordeaux (8 Rue Corneille, **t** 05 56 43 68 43, *www.citram.fr*) and from Arcachon station (coinciding with the TGVs) to Pyla, Andernos, Arès and Cap Ferret. Autobus D'Arcachon (**t** 05 57 72 45 00) runs tourist trips around the area.

For a **taxi** in Arcachon, call **t** 06 08 00 23 24. **Bikes** are a convenient way to get around, and the Bassin has many cycle tracks; you can hire bikes in all the villages. Arcachon Dingo Vélo, Rue Grenier, **t** 05 56 83 44 09, hires out normal bikes plus tandems, quintuplos and an assortment of crazy bikes. Locabeach, 326 Boulevard de la Plage, **t** 05 56 83 39 64, hires out mountainbikes, scooters and motorbikes.

A **tourist train** (**t** 05 57 72 45 00) leaves from in front of Arcachon's tourist office (*see* p.283) in summer.

gorse, broom and maritime pines under a network of branches. The gorse sprouted up quickly, and helped hold down the soil as the slower pines established themselves.

For all that, the Revolution intervened before the military port project ever got under way, leaving the Bassin to daydream to the ebbs and flows of its tides until the mid-19th century, when it discovered its double destiny as a massive nursery for oysters and a summer resort for the Bordelais. These days the gargantuan Dune du Pilat, just south of Arcachon, alone attracts at least a million visitors a year. Yet mass tourism has left many corners untouched: the little villages in the back Bassin could be part of a 17th-century Dutch landscape painting, with their ports sheltering the Bassin's distinctive small, shallow-keeled sailing boats called *pinasses* (or *pinassayres*, in Gascon), painted the colour of the owner's house, usually a cool green, light pink or straw yellow.

Arcachon

Arcachon was a small fishing village until 1841, when its life was turned upside down by the building of a railway line from nearby La Teste de Buch to Bordeaux. This new link neatly coincided with the new fashion for sea-bathing launched by the Duchesse de Berry. Private villas went up here and there, but the resort really took off after 1852, when two brothers, Emile and Isaac Pereire, took over the railway line and extended it to Arcachon. The Pereire brothers were descendants of Spanish Jews who found a safe haven in Bordeaux during the Inquisition; their grandfather Jacob was famous for inventing the first sign-language alphabet for deaf-mutes in the 1700s. The Pereire brothers proved just as inventive, but as property speculators, and laid out their new resort with cute winding lanes according to the anglophile tastes of Napoleon III, designed (successfully) to bewilder the uninitiated.

The Pereires divided the residential section of their resort into four subdivisions, each named after one of the four seasons. Although Spring and Autumn never really caught on, the **Ville d'Hiver**, the area best sheltered from the ocean winds and always

3°C warmer than the rest of Arcachon, attained full fashion status by the 1860s – Gounod, Debussy, Alexandre Dumas, Napoleon III, Marie-Christine of Austria and her future husband Alfonso XII of Spain (who came incognito) were all habitués. Various themed tours are offered by the tourist office, and you can also see it from a tourist train (*see* p.282)

For a centrepiece, the Ville d'Hiver has the **Parc Mauresque**, which was named after its fabulously outlandish pseudo-Moorish casino (1864), inspired by the Alhambra and the Great Mosque of Cordoba – and tragically destroyed by a fire in 1977. Its fantasy in turn inspired the usually staid 19th-century Bordelais who came to build second homes in the Ville d'Hiver – they really let their hair down, indulging in neogothic, Tyrolean, Tudor, pseudo-medieval and other fond fancies; some 200 of these lacy gingerbread villas survive, many now owned by wealthy retirees. Don't miss the fine overall view of the Bassin from the Parc Mauresque gardens, its **Passerelle St-Paul** (over adjacent Allée Pasteur), built by Eiffel in 1862, and the observatory.

A lift up to the Parc Mauresque links the the Ville d'Hiver with the **Ville d'Eté**, facing the Bassin and cooler in summer. This has most of Arcachon's tourist facilities, seaside promenades, sheltered sandy beaches, and the **Musée-Aquarium**, with local sealife, tropical fish, tortoises, seashells and shark skeletons. The Ville d'Eté's most notorious resident was Henri de Toulouse-Lautrec, who had a house by the ocean and liked to swim in the nude, offending the sensibilities of his neighbours. To pacify them, he erected a fence between his house and the beach – then mischievously covered it with obscene drawings. The furious neighbours eventually bought the house and gleefully burned the fence. Their descendants have never really forgiven them. (They should consider the chagrin of the heir of the young man in the Marquesas Islands, charged with tidying up Gauguin's hut after the artist's death. Finding it cluttered with sculptures and paintings, he loaded everything on to his boat and dumped the lot into the Pacific.)

Musée-Aquarium
Rue Professeur Jolyet, ***t*** *05 56 54 89 28; open June–Aug daily 9.45–7; Feb school hols, mid-Mar–May and Sept–early Nov daily 9.45–12.15 and 1.45–6.30; adm*

Since 1950, a new crop of villas has gone up on the oceanfront in **Parc Pereire**, overlooking Arcachon's best beach, **Plage Pereire**. As incredible as it seems, in 1922 someone had the chutzpah to drill for oil right in the middle of the park, but instead of black gold they discovered, at 485m, down a natural spring of mineral water, **Les Abatilles**, now exploited and bottled in the spa. Further south, along Boulevard de la Plage, a **casino** has been installed in the Disneylandish Château Deganne, with a congress centre, the Palatium, to keep it company. The business centre of Arcachon, near its enormous marina, lacks the unique character of the Pereire's residential districts.

The Dune du Pilat

Dune du Pilat

As the afternoon draws to a close in Arcachon, the thing to do is drive or cycle 8km south, through the resorts of **Le Moulleau**, **Pyla-sur-Mer** and **Pyla-Plage**. In the pine trees is a pay car park, and beyond it the extraordinary sight of that Moby Dick of dunes, the **Dune du Pilat**, at 106m the highest pile of sand in Europe, at 2.4km the longest, and at 503m the widest. Excavations in this little chunk of the Sahara have found that Pilat began to form 8,000 years ago with the merging of two huge sets of dunes, and more or less grew to its present dimensions in the 18th century, when a vast sandbank offshore was destroyed and all the sand was blown here. The name first appeared in 1484. Like all dunes, it's in a constant state of flux, and every year it inches a little further inland (at the rate of 5m a year). A useful stair with 190 steps helps you get to the top of the steep behemoth for an unforgettable view – especially at sunset. If you can't resist the urge to roll and slide and scamper down the oceanside slope, be prepared to face the torturous return trip back up the slippery sands.

Often included in the sundown view are schools of bottlenose dolphins and porpoises frolicking just offshore. South of the sand-monster is a beach called **Petit Nice** and beyond that a naturist beach, both with lifeguards and snack bars; further south, the **Plage de la Salie Nord** and **Plage de la Salie Sud** are good for surfing.

Around the Bassin d'Arcachon

Ten *communes*, picturesque little ports with wooden oyster shacks, beaches, a river delta and a bird sanctuary, a trip up the Leyre into the Landes, and a score of rather more commercial amusements await to be savoured around the rim of the Bassin. Try at least once to cross the water the traditional way, in a *pinasse* – trips are offered from the ports of Arcachon, Andernos and Lège-Cap-Ferret.

La Teste de Buch to Le Teich

Zoo de La Teste
Route de Cazaux, **t** *05 56 54 71 44; open April–Sept daily 10–7; Oct–Mar Wed, Sat and Sun 10–7; adm*

Parc Animalier La Coccinelle
t *05 56 66 30 41; open July and Aug daily 10.30–7; rest of year call for times; adm*

Aqualand
t *08 92 68 66 13; open early June–early Sept daily 10–6; adm*

Southeast of Arcachon, pines line the Bassin at La Teste de Buch. Its name recalls the Captals de Buch who lorded it over the Bassin in the Middle Ages, though in those days pine resin rather than oysters was the cash crop. La Teste has handsome houses dating back to the 18th century, and includes in its municipal boundaries not only the Dune du Pilat and a racetrack but also the **Lac de Cazaux**, the second largest in France. There's also a **zoo** with 50 big cats, bears and other animals, plus a farm and activity park.

In the same area, La Hume has sprouted another three roadside attractions designed to keep mum and dad in the poorhouse: a 'zoo' with domestic animals, the **Parc Animalier La Coccinelle**, where children can feed lambs and baby goats, go on rides and play games; **Aqualand**, with rivers, pools with waves and every kind

The Oyster's their World

Oysters from the Bassin were popular among rich Romans of Burdigala, who set up relays to have them brought to their tables in a few hours, and slurped them raw with *garum*, the prized, mysterious fish-gut sauce that culinary archaeologists guess was similar to Vietnamese *nuoc nam*. By the Middle Ages, when the old Roman roads were full of mud and potholes, tastes turned to dried oysters put up in barrels, in sauce or fried. The Bassin's industry remained small and local, however, until 1850, when once again speedy transport – the railway – allowed the tasty bivalves to chug posthaste to Bordeaux, and, from 1857, to Paris – at a time when diners thought nothing of beginning a meal with 10–15 dozen.

Twice, however, Arcachon's bread-and-butter industry was devastated by oyster parasites. The first attack, in 1922, wiped out Arcachon's flat native *gravettes*. These were replaced by *portugaises*, which in turn fell prey to a new parasite in 1970. Since 1972, oysters farmed in the Bassin belong to two species – a new *gravette*, a flat hybrid of Charente and Breton oysters, and a parasite-resistant, elongated Japanese oyster, the *huître creuse*, or *gigas*. However, there are still problems from time to time.

Today the Bassin d'Arcachon is the fourth-largest oyster producer in France, but the first in Europe in 'trapping' microscopic oyster embryos and larvae swishing about the sea in search of a home – they simply can't resist stacks of canal roof tiles, bleached in a mix of lime and sand. After eight months clinging to a tile, the baby oysters are moved into calm nurseries in flat cages; the next year, they are moved once more to oyster parks, in fresh plankton-rich waters, where the oyster farmers defend them the best they can against greedy starfish, crabs and other crustaceans, who will nevertheless devour 15–20% of the crop over the next three years. In the parks, the oysters are constantly turned, to encourage them to develop a good shape and a hard shell (although, increasingly, once they reach a certain size they are raised in the sacks they will eventually be sold in, set on shelves at just the right height (*élevage en surélevé*). When at long last they're ready to go on the market, they are placed for up to four days in special pools that trick them into no longer trusting the tide, so that they remain sealed tight while they are shipped and sold by size, from 6 (the smallest) to 0 (the largest and best).

'Now if you're ready, Oysters dear/We can begin to feed,' as the Walrus said. To prepare the little rascals *à la mode d'Arcachon*, count on a dozen oysters per person (or more if you're really greedy), four or more *crépinettes* (small flat sausages cooked in white wine), plenty of thinly sliced rye bread and butter and lots of dry white Graves, properly chilled at 6–8°C (44°F). Open the oysters and keep them cool, then fry or barbecue the sausages just before serving, and eat – slurp down a cold oyster, take a bite of hot sausage with a bit of buttered bread and wash it down with a swallow of wine.

Kid Parc Ile d'Aventures
t 05 56 66 06 90; open July and Aug daily 10.30–7; rest of year call for times; adm

Jardin Botanique
t 05 56 66 00 71; open early May–June and 1st half Sept daily 2–6; July and Aug daily 10.30–12.30 and 2.30–7

Maison de l'Huître
t 05 56 66 23 71; open daily 10–12.30 and 2.30–6

of waterslide that you can imagine; and **Kid Parc Ile d'Aventures**, an adventure park for younger children. You can also take a stroll around the **Jardin Botanique**.

La Hume is part of the Bassin's oyster capital, **Gujan-Mestras**. Here seven little ports crowded with *oustaous* (oyster huts) provide the perfect backdrop for tasting a plate of oysters, or attending the big oyster fair in early–mid-August (you can eat them in non-R months now); there's even a little **Maison de l'Huître**, at the Port de Larros, where you can learn some of their oyster secrets. The critter on Gujan's coat of arms, however, is the ladybird beetle, the *barbot* in Gascon. The name goes back to the early days of the phylloxera epidemic, when locals noticed that their infected vines swarmed with ladybirds. They accused those helpful insects of spreading the plague, while in fact they were gobbling down the real culprits as fast as they could; the priest at Gujan even held *barbot* exorcisms in the vineyards. When the real, much tinier lice-like pests were discovered, the villagers of Gujan became the butt of jokes from their neighbours, who called them the *barbots*. By the 1920s, Gujan learned to laugh at itself, and adopted the ladybug as its own, even naming its rugby team the Barbots.

Le Teich, the Leyre and a Look into Les Landes

37 Parc Ornithologique du Teich
t 05 56 22 80 93, www.parc-ornithologique-du-teich.com; open July and Aug daily 10–8; rest of year daily daily 10–6; adm; bring binoculars or rent at site

Villetorte Loisirs
30 Rue du Pont Neuf, t 05 56 22 66 80

Parc Naturel Régional des Landes de Gascogne
***Information office**: 33 Route de Bayonne, **t** 05 57 71 99 99, www.parc-landes-de-gascogne.fr; **Centre d'Animation du Graoux**: **t** 05 57 71 99 29*

At Le Teich, the Leyre (or L'Eyre), one of the most important rivers of the Landes, drains into the Bassin d'Arcachon, forming the kind of marshy delta beloved of migratory waterfowl. In 1972, Le Teich's rare environment of saltwater and freshwater *bayous* was set aside as the **Parc Ornithologique du Teich**. The delta is a favourite stop on the great migration route between Africa and Scandinavia, and a nesting ground for several species, especially grey herons, black cormorants, white storks, black and white oystercatchers, egrets, kingfishers, dabbling garganeys and spoon-billed shovelers. Altogether some 280 different species have been sighted. One of the great success stories has been the return of the mute swan, which vanished from France at the time of the Revolution.

The 120-hectare park is divided into four sections: the vast **Parc de Causseyre**, which has several hides and observation posts; the **Parc de la Moulette**, where the geese, swans and ducks are concentrated; the small **Parc des Artigues**, with a collection of ducks from around the world, at liberty, and large aviaries; and the **Parc Claude Quancard**, for wading birds. The latter is inaccessible to the public, although there are two observation posts. There are three paths to walk, covering 2.4km, 3.4km and 6km; the longest one does a circuit through all the zones. There's an information centre in the **Maison de la Nature du Bassin d'Arcachon** at the entrance to the Parc. The Maison also organizes daytrips and evening and weekend visits on various themes and you can hire a canoe for the Eyre or a kayak for the Bassin. There is a fine viewpoint over the delta from the **point d'observation du Delta de l'Eyre**. Also in La Teich, **Villetorte Loisirs** hires out canoes and kayaks to explore L'Eyre from mid-June to mid-Sept.

Le Teich lies in the northern confines of the **Parc Naturel Régional des Landes de Gascogne**, 262,000 hectares (647,000 acres) of forest set aside in 1970. The great pine moors of the Landes may seem monotonous from the car window while you're zooming down the *autoroute* to Spain, but close up they are striking, especially when the heather, gorse or honeysuckle is in bloom and the heady scent of resin fills the air in an aromatherapy overkill. The nearest place to learn about the secrets of the Landes is **Belin-Béliet**, 30km up the Eyre from Le Teich. There's a **park information office**, and canoe, kayak and bicycle hire at the **Centre d'Animation du Graoux**, which also organizes various visits. Belin is a tranquil place, but it can claim a mention in nearly any medieval history book as the birthplace of Eleanor of Aquitaine in 1122, and (some say) of her favourite son, Richard the Lionheart (in a now ruined castle on the outskirts of town, marked by a stele). The **church of St-Pierre-de-Mons**, situated on the outskirts of Belin, was built during Eleanor's reign as a priory on the Compostela road, although its belltower was only fortified a century later, during the Hundred Years' War, that timebomb left by her French and English marriages. Inside are four archaic capitals, carved with scenes of mysterious import; legend has it that St-Pierre's cemetery, like St-Seurin in Bordeaux and the Alyscamps in Arles, has the tombs of Charlemagne's paladins.

The Back Bassin around to Cap Ferret

At **Biganos**, north of the Eyre delta, many of the old picturesque oystermen's *cabanons* have been converted into holiday homes; the oystermen, one presumes, now work in the local papermill. The Roman town of **Boios** is being unearthed nearby: the tourist office (*see* p.283) organises guided visits of historical sites around the area. At nearby Facture is the **Moulin de la Cassadotte**, where trout and sturgeon are raised and caviar produced.

Moulin de la Cassadotte
t 05 56 82 64 42; open mid-July–mid-Aug Wed–Mon, call for times

The next stop, **Audenge**, is a sleepy fishing village where the day's catch is trapped in reservoirs left by the retreating tide – a method of fishing that inspired someone to dig similar tide-fed reservoirs for humans to swim in; if the tide is out you can join the locals in the public seawater pools. There are paths around the wonderful saltwater marshes of **Les Domaines de Certes** and **Graveyron**; ask at the tourist office (***t** 05 56 26 95 97*) about guided visits in summer.

The next town to the north is **Lanton**, which has a long beach and a 12th-century church, the oldest on the Bassin (the *mairie* keeps the key). Family-orientated **Andernos-les-Bains** is a lively summer resort with splendid views across the water, the longest jetty in all of France and the remains of a 4th-century Gallo-Roman villa, finds from which can be seen in the town's **Maison Louis David**, alongside art exhibitions. In late July/early August the town hosts important jazz and oyster festivals; the former has featured the likes of Miles Davis and Lionel Hampton. Like the next village, **Arès**, it has safe beaches for children.

The northwestern curve of the Bassin is sprinkled with little oyster ports/resorts set between the calm waters and the rough Atlantic, all belonging to the *commune* of **Lège-Cap-Ferret**. The prettiest port is **L'Herbe**, an intimate hamlet of wooden houses stringed along tiny lanes, founded in the 17th century. The tourist office at **Claouey/Lège-Cap Ferret** (*see* p.284) organizes guided tours in summer, and has information on a host of watersports, cultural and nature visits and what's going on in general.

The *commune*'s 35km of ocean beaches culminate in the sandy tail of **Cap Ferret**, which has long been doing its damnedest to

Phare du Cap Ferret
open July and Aug daily 10–7.30; April, June and Sept daily 10–12.30 and 2–6; Oct–mid-Nov and mid-Dec–Mar Wed–Sun 2–5

Tramway du Cap Ferret
t 05 56 60 60 20; early April–early Sept daily, call for times

close off the mouth of the Bassin; in the past 200 years the cape has grown 4km and gobbled up several fashionable villas in its wake. A path leads around to the tip of the cape, with splendid views of the Dune du Pilat, most breathlessly from the top of the 258 steps of the **lighthouse**.

Several times a day, the cute little **Tramway du Cap Ferret** covers the several kilometres from the Jetée Bélisaire at the Bassin to the Plage de l'Horizon, one of the ocean beaches, where surfers ride the big rollers expedited by the Bay of Biscay.

ⓘ La Teste de Buch >
Place Jean Hameau, t 05 56 54 63 14, www.latestedebuch.fr

Market Days in Arcachon and around its Bassin

Arcachon: Tuesday–Sunday (plus Monday in high season), covered market, Place de Gracia.

La Teste de Buch: Covered market daily (except Monday in winter), plus daily market near church in July and Aug.

Andernos-les-Bains: Covered market every morning in summer, plus Tuesday, Thursday, Friday and Saturday mornings in winter.

Gujan-Mestras: open-air market Wednesday, Place de la Gare.

Cap Ferret: covered market Wednesday and Saturday, plus Sunday in summer; outdoor market daily mid-June–mid-Sept.

Excursions and Activities in Arcachon and around its Bassin

The tourist office at Arcachon has details all kinds of activities and tours, including the **Oyster and Coastal Heritage Trail**, where you can learn about oyster farming, plus themed **weekend breaks**.

Le Marin Independant Digue Ouest (**t** 06 08 16 32 25, *www.ami-arcachon.com*) and Bateliers Arcachonnais (**t** 05 57 72 28 28, *www.bateliers-arcachon.asso.fr*) make excursions to the **Ile aux Oiseaux**, the Bassin's only island, given over to seabirds, oyster farms and sailing boats, with picturesque *cabanes tchanquées* (huts perched on stilts; in the old days, herdsmen in boats had their horses swim over to the sweet islet pastures). In July and August both also offer days on the shadeless, hot, sandy **Banc d'Arguin**, a wildfowl refuge at the entrance of the Bassin (bring a picnic), and both also offer guided tours of the oyster beds and cruises up the coast.

Bateliers Arcachonnais also make frequent excursions from Arcachon and other ports, up the cool, forested river Eyre, across the Bassin, and out to sea, especially to the Dune du Pilat. They also run painting cruises, but you need to bring your own brushes.

Among the **daredevil sports** practised off the Dune du Pilat are deltaplaning, hang-gliding and *parapente* (paragliding); contact Sand Fly, Camping La Forêt, Pyla, **t** 06 63 21 27 82, *www.sand-fly.com*.

Arcachon owes its passion for **golf** to its sizeable 19th-century British colony. There are two courses in the area; the closest is the beautiful Golf Club d'Arcachon, 35 Boulevard d'Arcachon, La Teste, **t** 05 56 54 44 00.

You can get a bird's-eye view of Arcachon's remarkable setting from a small **plane** with Aéroclub du Bassin d'Arcachon at La Teste, **t** 05 56 54 72 88, *www.acba-fr.com*.

Sailing is popular here, and challenging – there are strong currents, sandbanks, channels and occasional high winds. Each year sees a number of races, including the *18 heures d'Arcachon* in early July. The tourist office has a long list of places to hire your own sailing boat, as well as listings for horse-riding, tennis, diving, water-skiing, fishing, kayaking, cycling and nearly every other sport you can imagine. It also has a list of art galleries, nightclubs, cinemas and events, as well as information on **beach clubs** to entertain the children.

Where to Stay in Arcachon and around its Bassin

ⓘ Arcachon >
*Esplanade Georges Pompidou, **t** 05 57 52 97 97, www.bassin-arcachon.com and www.arcachon.com*

ⓘ Gujan-Mestras >>
*19 Avenue de Lattre de Tassigny, **t** 05 56 66 12 65, www.ville-gujanmestras.com*

ⓘ Biganos >>
*Rue Jean Zay, **t** 05 57 70 67 56*

ⓘ Pyla-sur-Mer >
*2 Avenue Ermitage, **t** 05 56 54 02 22, and at Dune, **t** 05 56 22 12 85, www.pyla-sur-mer.com*

★ Côte Sud >

ⓘ Andernos-les-Bains >>
*Esplanade du Broustic, **t** 05 56 82 02 95*

Arcachon ✉ 33120

Hotels in fashionable Arcachon tend to be more expensive than anywhere else in this book. If you plan to stay a week or more, you'll go less broke in a furnished room, studio or flat – pick up the fat list at the tourist office. Book months ahead for July or August, when it's hard to find anything for less than €50 a night.

********Arc-Hôtel sur Mer**, 89 Boulevard de la Plage, **t** 05 56 83 06 85, *www.arc-hotel-sur-mer.com* (€€€€–€€€). A mid-sized, modern but stylish hotel with rooms with balconies overlooking the water or the garden. A swimming pool, sauna and Jacuzzi are among the amenities.

*****Les Vagues**, 9 Bd de l'Océan, **t** 05 56 83 03 75, *www.hotel-les-vagues.com* (€€€€–€€€). Rooms looking down on the waves, with fresh, light decor, and a restaurant (€€),

*****Le Richelieu**, 185 Bd de la Plage, **t** 05 56 83 16 50, *www.grand-hotel-richelieu.com* (€€€€–€€). An option in the centre, across from the beach. Rooms have TVs and mini-bars. *Closed Nov–mid-Mar.*

****Le Nautic**, 20 Boulevard de la Plage, **t** 05 56 83 01 48 (€€). Some of the best rooms in this category, with a Spanish touch, 1km from the centre of town with a good view of the Bassin.

****Marinette**, 15 Allée José-Maria de Hérédia, **t** 05 56 83 06 67, *www.hotel-marinette.com* (€€–€). A large white house in the Ville d'Hiver, with pleasant, comfortable rooms. You can enjoy breakfast on a flowery terrace. *Closed Nov–mid-Mar.*

****Les Mimosas**, 77 bis Avenue de la République, **t** 05 56 83 45 86 (€€–€). Tidy rooms not far from the sea in the Ville d'Eté, not far from the train station. *Closed Jan and Feb.*

Pyla-sur-Mer ✉ 33115

****Côte Sud**, 4 Avenue du Figuier, **t** 05 56 83 25 00 (€€€). A delightful 1940s villa in the pines, a few metres from the beach, with imaginative rooms and an excellent, intimate restaurant (€€) serving the likes of tuna steak with tomato and cardamon sauce and rice. *Closed Dec and Jan.*

****La Corniche**, 46 Avenue Louis Gaume, **t** 05 56 22 72 11, *http://chez.com/corniche* (€€). A neo-Basque wood and brick hotel built in 1932 at the foot of the mighty Dune, with wide balconies and a stairway to the beach. The restaurant (€€) has good seafood plus southwestern duck dishes. *Closed Wed.*

****La Guitoune**, 95 Bd de l'Océan, **t** 05 56 22 70 10, *www.laguitoune.com* (€€). A favourite weekend retreat among the Bordelais, with comfortable rooms and an excellent seafood restaurant. *Closed early Nov–mid Dec.*

****Ttiki-Etchea**, 2 Place Louis Gaume, **t** 05 56 22 71 15 (€). A Basque-style hotel in a peaceful setting overlooking the beach near the Dune, with a pretty terrace. *Closed mid-Oct–Easter.*

Camping La Dune, **t** 05 56 22 72 17, *www.campingdeladune.fr* (€). An excellent site south of the Dunes, with a pool. *Closed Oct–April.*

Pyla Camping, **t** 05 56 22 74 56, *www.pyla-camping.com* (€). A great site for families, very close to the beach and with plenty to amuse all ages, including a pool. *Closed Oct–Mar.*

Gujan-Mestras ✉ 33470

*****La Guérinière**, 18 Cours de Verdun, on Bordeaux–Arcachon road, **t** 05 56 66 08 78, *www.lagueriniere.com* (€€€). A good option with a pool and an excellent restaurant (€€€€–€€€).

Biganos ✉ 33380

***Hôtel de France**, 99 Avenue de la Libération, **t** 05 56 82 61 08 (€). A refreshingly unpricey choice 15km from the beach. *Closed Sept.*

Taussat ✉ 33148

****Hôtel de la Plage**, 20 Bd de la Plage, **t** 05 56 82 06 06 (€€–€). A Logis de France establishment near the beach, with reasonably priced rooms for these parts and a restaurant (€€). *Closed mid-Nov–Easter.*

Andernos-les-Bains ✉ 33510

****La Belle Vic**, 20 Avenue Thiers, **t** 05 56 82 02 10 (€€). A fairly simple hotel with a restaurant, near the beach.

ⓘ **Lège-Cap Ferret >**
1 Avenue Général de Gaulle, Claouey, **t** *05 56 03 94 49, www.lege-capferret.com*

ⓘ **Arès >>**
Esplanade G. Dartiguelongue, **t** *05 56 60 18 07*

****Hôtel de la Côte d'Argent**, 180 Bd de la République, **t** 05 56 03 98 58 (€€–€). Ten rooms a short walk from the beach. *Closed Sun eve out of season.*

Lège-Cap Ferret ✉ 33970

Cap Ferret is the trendiest spot on the Bassin, but though there are plenty of restaurants, bars and campsites, there are only a handful of hotels.

*****Hôtel des Dunes**, 119 Avenue de Bordeaux, **t** 05 56 60 61 81, *www.hoteldesdunes.com* (€€€€). A recently upgraded dune-side place, with a sauna. *Closed Dec–Mar.*

****La Frégate**, 34 Avenue de l'Océan, **t** 05 56 60 41 62, *www.hotel-la-fregate.net* (€€€–€). Recently renovated rooms and apartments with balconies and shared use of a pool.

Hôtel de la Plage, Port de l'Herbe, **t** 05 56 60 50 15 (€). A simple eight-room wooden hotel by the beach, with a good fish restaurant (€€). *Closed Jan.*

Where to Eat in Arcachon and around its Bassin

Arcachon ✉ 33120

Aux Mille Saveurs, 25 Bd du Général Leclerc, **t** 05 56 83 40 28 (€€€). Popular traditional meals and seafood in a rather downmarket location on a main road opposite the railway tracks. *Closed Sun eve and Mon.*

Chez Yvette, 59 Boulevard du Général Leclerc, **t** 05 56 83 05 11 (€€€). Incredibly fresh, immaculately prepared fish.

Le Patio, 10 Bd de la Plage, **t** 05 56 83 02 72 (€€€). Lobster salad, oysters in flaky pastry and the like served amidst bright clutter and a waterfall. *Closed Tues and several wks in winter.*

Diego Plage, 12 Bd Veyrier-Montagnères, **t** 05 56 83 84 46 (€€). Tasty seafood with a Spanish zing, on the seafront.

Camping Club d'Arcachon, Allée de la Galaxie, Les Abatilles, 1.8km from centre, **t** 05 56 83 24 15 (€). Quick cheap food in a pine grove. *Closed Oct–April.*

Pyla-sur-Mer ✉ 33115

Gérard Tissier, 35 Bd de l'Océan, **t** 05 56 54 07 94 (€€€–€€). A good, quite smart roadside restaurant; traditional dishes plus seafood.

Gujan-Mestras ✉ 33470

L'Escalumade, 8 Rue Pierre Dignac, **t** 05 56 66 02 30 (€€€–€€). A good honest fish restaurant overlooking the oyster farms, also serving a few meat dishes. *Closed Mon eve, plus Sun out of season.*

Les Pavois, Port de Larros, by Musée de l'Huître, **t** 05 56 66 38 71 (€€€–€€). Well-prepared *fruits de mer*, fish and meat on a terrace above the water.

Les Viviers, Port de Larros, **t** 05 56 66 01 04 (€€). Seafood and a few meat dishes, in a light-filled dining room or on a floating terrace. *Closed Tues eve, plus Wed and Thurs eves out of season.*

La Vache sur le Toit, 2 Route des Lacs, **t** 05 57 52 42 51 (€). Solid Belgian food.

Taussat ✉ 33148

L'Esquirey, 9 Av Commandant Allègre, **t** 05 56 82 22 15 (€). Ultra-fresh oysters and super-tasty fish in a real *cabanon*. *Closed mid-Dec–mid-Jan, and Mon.*

Arès ✉ 33740

Le St-Eloi, 11 Boulevard de l'Aérium, **t** 05 56 60 20 46, *www.le-saint-eloi.com* (€€€–€€). An excellent restaurant with shaded patios, offering foie gras, monkfish, scallops and more, plus eight renovated rooms (€€). *Closed Sun eve, Mon and Wed out of season, Mon eve in July and Aug.*

Lège-Cap Ferret ✉ 33970

Chez Hortense, Avenue du Sémaphore, **t** 05 56 60 62 56 (€€€). Something of an institution, serving well-prepared if pricey seafood, and some meat dishes, at the end of the peninsula overlooking the Bassin. *Closed early Sept–Easter.*

Chez Pierrette, 9 Impasse des Sternes, Le Canon, **t** 05 56 60 50 50 (€€€–€€). Dishes based on the market and the day's catch, plus meat specialities, served in a traditional Basque house.

Pinasse Café, 2 bis Avenue de l'Océan, **t** 05 56 03 77 87 (€€€ –€€). A popular lunch spot just above the Bassin.

Pat-à-Chou, Le Grand Piquey, **t** 05 56 60 51 38 (€). The best ice cream on the whole Bassin.

The Lot: Quercy

The Lot is named after a river that twists like a lazy bedspring through its heart, flowing beneath cliffs and through sleepy villages and vineyards. In the spirit of the Slow Food movement, this is the Slow Département; *free of industry (with the exception of foie gras, wine, goat's cheese and lamb), it's one of the least polluted in France, a place of rural idylls, where nothing seems more urgent than deciding what to have for lunch.*

13

Don't miss

1. Winsome spotted horses
Grotte du Pech-Merle p.304

2. Medieval streets and Egyptian surprises
Figeac p.297

3. A devil-built bridge, and black wine
Cahors p.313

4. Relics of a 16th-century braggart
Assier p.294

5. 'An impossible rose in the night'
St-Cirq-Lapopie p.309

See map overleaf

The Lot: Quercy

p.134

p.344–35

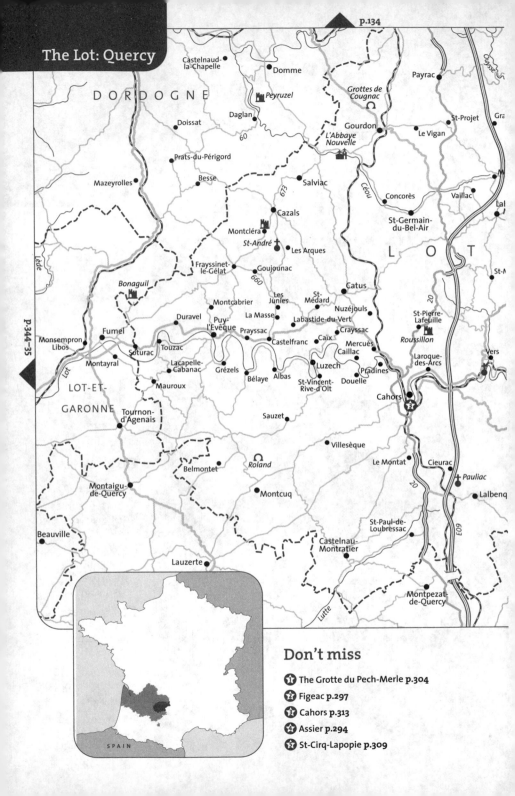

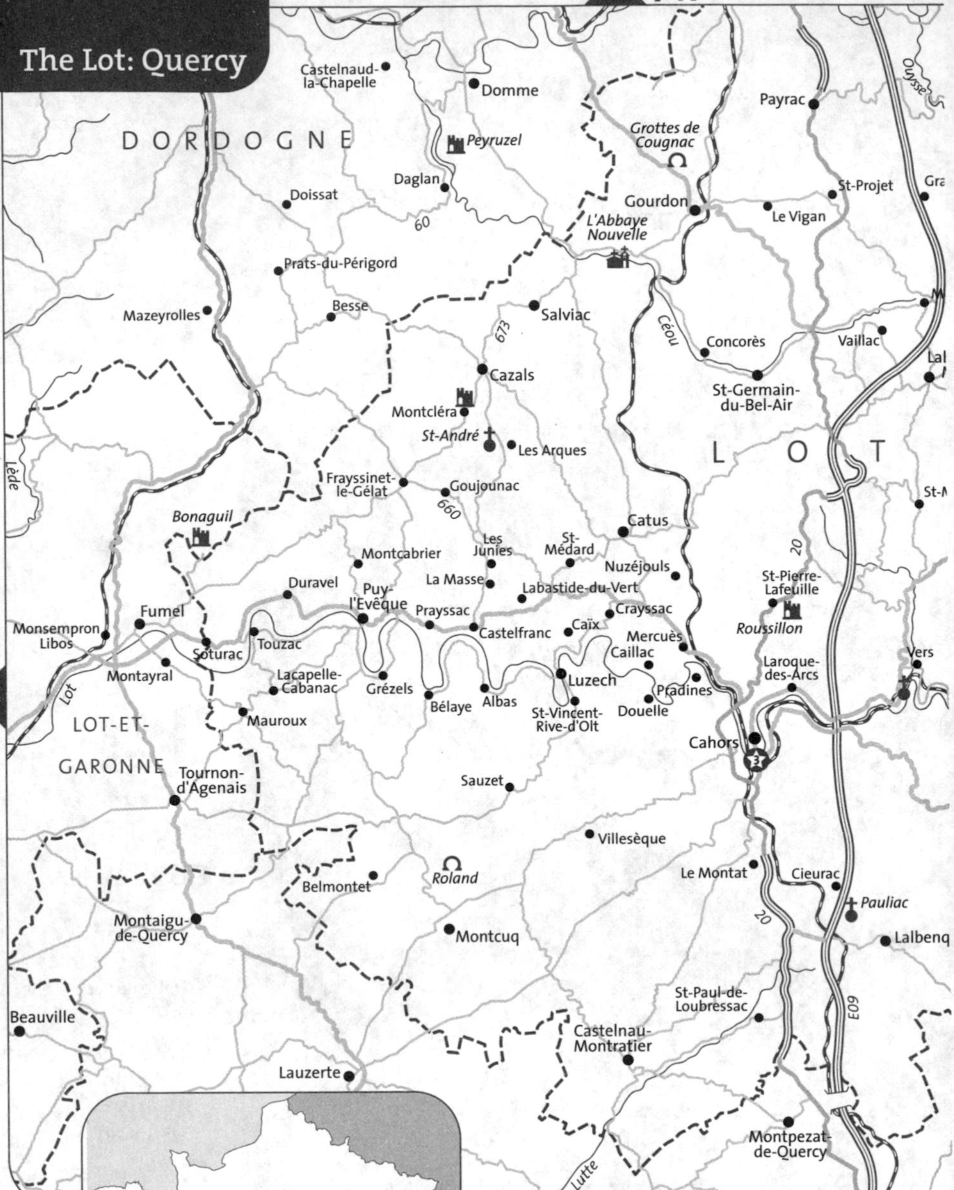

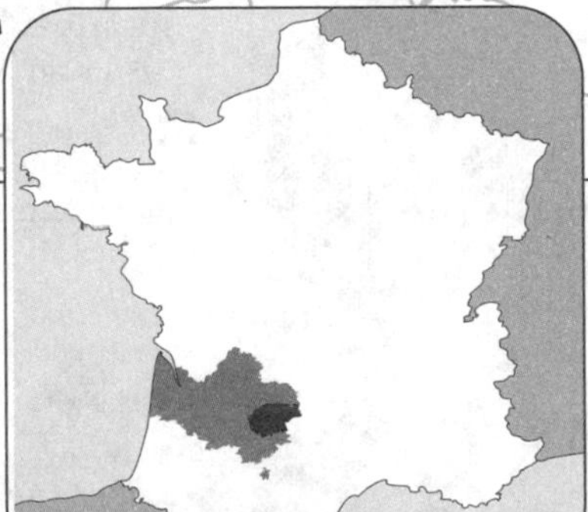

Don't miss

1. The Grotte du Pech-Merle **p.304**
2. Figeac **p.297**
3. Cahors **p.313**
4. Assier **p.294**
5. St-Cirq-Lapopie **p.309**

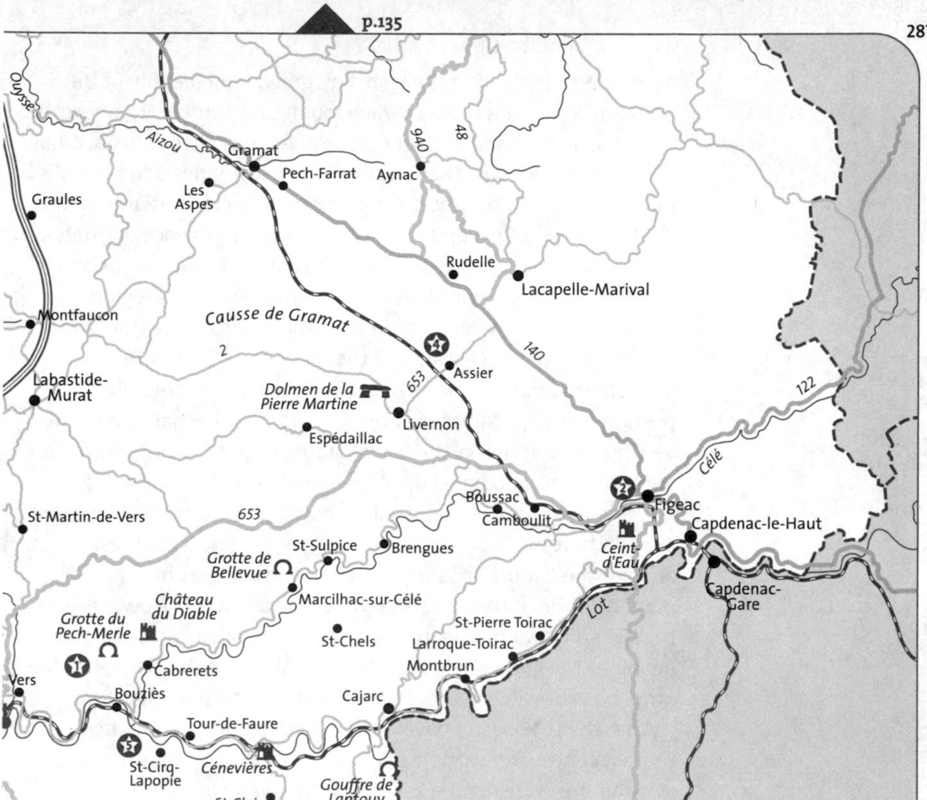

Connoisseurs of tourist slogans will find the 'The Lot: We Are Under a Spell' (*Le Lot: On est sous le charme*) a limp noodle when the *département* is blessed with a name so full of potential. Possibilities race to mind: 'Take the Lot, will you?' – 'We have a Lot to answer for' – 'A Whole Lot to Love' – 'A Lot like Arkansas' – 'What a Lot of ????', or whatever. The truth is, the Lot needs a lick of PR. Outsiders tend to lump it with the neighbouring Dordogne, when the Lot's heartstrings have always pulled it in the other direction –

to the south. Instead of the lush, tidy, green-shire beauty of the Dordogne, the Lot is more cowboy rough-and-tumble, its landscape tossed up in wild and arid limestone plateaux called *causses*. What soil it has is said to be the worst in France (the vines don't mind that at all). The Dordogne belongs to Aquitaine, the Atlantic and Bordeaux; the Lot occupies half of the ancient province of Quercy, the northernmost possessions of the counts of Toulouse, and to this day it belongs to Toulouse and the Midi-Pyrénées region.

'Quercy' may evoke oaks (as in the Latin *quercus*), the tree that covers much of its territory, but the name is derived from its Gaulish residents, the never-say-die Cadurcii, also remembered in the name of their capital, Cahors. In 51 BC, after Caesar's defeat of Vercingetorix at Alésia, the feisty Cadurcii still refused to surrender to the Romans and holed up at an *oppidum* with an ululating nursery rhyme of a name, Uxellodunum. Julius Caesar was niggled enough to come in person to sort out this last pocket of resistance, and got the Cadurcii to surrender by diverting the physical manifestation of their goddess – their water supply. Now it seems that Puy-d'Issolud, in the Lot (*see* p.150) has convinced enough people in the know that it was the last Alamo of the Gauls, but the other possible sites in the *département* hold on to their claims.

What the Lot doesn't have a lot of is people. Many migrated in the last century for work, leaving old stone houses that tumbled into ruins or were restored; in 2006 there were an estimated 18,000 holiday homes – the kiss of death for daily life in smaller hamlets. But the A20 *autoroute* extension to Cahors, linking it to Toulouse, Brive and Paris, has improved access, brought in industry and created more jobs. The Lot has begun taking its vocation for vacations more seriously: you can canoe and rent houseboats on its curling loops; fireworks get better every summer; and there's talk of changing the *département* name to Lot-et-Dordogne to remind visitors it too rules a section of that famous river, from Castelnau to Souillac. Tourist figures for 2005 were up on the previous year.

The *département* tourist office (107 Quai Cavaignac, BP7, Cahors, Cedex 9, **t** 05 65 35 07 09) is one of the best in France, with an excellent website, *www.tourisme-lot.com*. Ask at any tourist office for the great *département*-wide guide, *Le Lot – Guide Pratique*.

Between the Dordogne and Lot Rivers: the Causse de Gramat

The largest and wildest of Quercy's rocky and arid limestone plateaux, the Causse de Gramat is the upper crust of an amazing subterranean world of lakes and rivers, accessible to earth-dwellers through caverns, little canyons and *gouffres*, among them the

Between the Dordogne and Lot Rivers

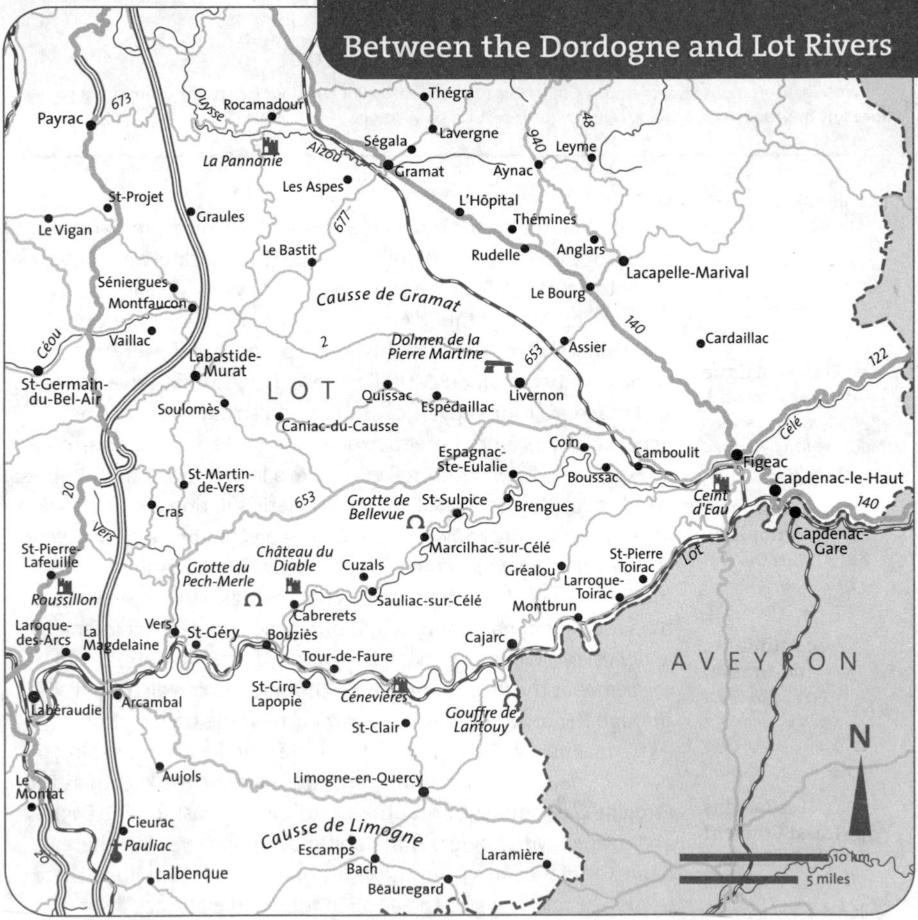

spectacular pit of Padirac (*see* p.141). The *causse* has a peculiar fascination in spring and early summer, when the scrub oak and juniper, wild flowers, eglantine and honeysuckle soften the deserted landscape; the odd-looking flocks – a local breed of sheep called the *caussenarde* whose eyes are protected from the sun by natural black spectacles – forage in the shade, butterflies flutter by and the dark shadows of buzzards and kestrels make slow loops across blue-grey horizons. The limestone soaks in the sun as it soaks in the rain, and the heated scent of juniper in a clearing is like inhaling from a vat of gin. Holiday people fill the houses, and cafés and restaurants are open, which can be a welcome sight after you've travelled for miles without passing any sign of human life.

Come in winter and the *causse* is a study in desolation, the colour drained out of it, the oaks clinging dismally to their brown leaves in the sodden mists. The villages seem sad and empty, or locked up altogether; the buzzards and kestrels are still there, but now they seem sinister as they circle over silent, overcast ridges.

Getting to and around the Causse de Gramat

Brive–Figeac–Toulouse **trains** stop in Gramat as well as nearby Rocamadour (*see* p.142). Gramat is also linked by **bus** to Brive: call SA Cars Quercy-Corrèze, **t** 05 56 38 71 90.

Gramat

Gramat on the river Alzou is the pleasant if not very remarkable capital of the *causse*, with only a 15th-century clocktower and a watchtower that recall the town before the Wars of Religion; Gramat's baron, Gontaut d'Auriolle, was an ally of Henri IV, but, unfortunately for the town's historical preservation, everyone else in the vicinity remained Catholic. These days Gramat serves as Rocamadour's tourist overflow tank, but also as a base for the many potholers who come to explore the pocked *causse* and, more unexpectedly, for pewter-makers – take a look at **Les Etains Maigne** – and police-dog trainers. The Gendarmerie's national kennels are here, now officially known as the **Centre de Cynophilie**, as if it were some kind of New Age cult; you can watch the cops and their best friends do their stuff here . Besides police dogs, you can see more than 1000 European animals and birds (including rare chickens and pigs) in a wooded park on the *causse*, a few kilometres from the centre at the **Parc Animalier de Gramat**. You can also stroll through the convent's splendid **garden**, near the train station.

Les Etains Maigne
1 Rue de Gabaudet, Faubourg St-Pierre, **t** *05 65 10 14 30; open daily, call for times*

Centre de Cynophilie
t *05 65 38 71 59; open mid-June–mid-Sept Thurs 3pm*

Parc Animalier de Gramat
t *05 65 38 81 22; open Easter–Sept daily 9.30–7; Oct–Easter daily 2–6; adm*

Les Jardins du Grand Couvent de Gramat
t *05 65 38 73 29; open May, June, Sept and Oct daily 2–6; July and Aug daily 10–7; adm*

The environs of Gramat are full of little wonders, easily explored by bike. One of the most important tumuli in the Lot, known as the **Etron de Gargantua** ('Gargantua's turd'), is just east (on the D15) and covered with flowers that don't grow anywhere else (the name Gramat comes from the Celtic *grammat*, or tumulus – there used to be one as big as the *etron* in the middle of Place de la République). Other Neolithic sites in the vicinity include good **dolmens** at **Pech-Farrat** (east off the N140), **Ségala** (up the Alzou from Gramat) and **Les Aspes**, to the west on the D39. Les Aspes is also near an impressive *gouffre* at Ligue de Biau (ask about access at Gramat tourist office; *see* p.266). At **La Pannonie**, off the D39, the vast Mansart-roofed **Château de la Pannonie** was begun in the late 1400s as the pleasure dome of a Rocamadour merchant, and has a fine set of windows and dormers.

Château de la Pannonie
t *05 65 33 71 71; open for guided visits 2nd half June Wed–Mon 2–5; July–Sept Wed–Sun 10–5; 1st half Oct by appt*

Northeast of Gramat, **Lavergne** has an impressive *pigeonnier*, unusually built over a gate; the apse of the village's Romanesque church has *modillons* carved with lively human and animal faces. Another 2.5km north, **Thégra** has a harmonious 15th-century château.

South to Labastide-Murat

Further afield (10km south of Gramat on the D677), **Le Bastit**, once an important Templar commandery serving passing pilgrims, has one of the *causse*'s most spectacular *avens* (natural wells), the

The King of Naples

Born in 1767, son of the local innkeeper, young Joachim Murat began his military career by being kicked out of the army for unruly behaviour. The advent of Napoleon gave him a second chance in the wars of Italy and Egypt, where as Bonaparte's *aide-de-camp* he distinguished himself with gut-busting courage and bravado; his subsequent promotion gave substance to Napoleon's saying that each of his soldiers carried a marshal's baton in his knapsack. Murat was the engineer of the great French victory at Marengo, and nudged his destiny along by loyally supporting Napoleon at the *coup d'état* of 18 Brumaire (a gesture rewarded with his marriage to Caroline Bonaparte in 1800); in 1808 he crushed the May insurrection in Madrid with a brutality immortalized in Goya's paintings of the French firing squads. Pleased, Napoleon gave him the throne of Naples, then called on him to lead the cavalry of the Grande Armée into Russia in 1812. After the defeat, Murat tried to talk the allies into letting him keep Naples, and when they refused sailed over to grab it for himself (1815). But Murat had grieviously miscalculated his popularity; when he landed and announced to peasants he met that their king had returned, they tried to kill him; a Bourbon army arrived soon after, arrested and shot him on the spot.

Igue de la Vierge. To the southwest, **Montfaucon** is a charming hilltop *bastide*, erected by Edward II in 1292 on the English frontline as a foil to the new French town of Labastide-Murat; if the **church** is open, pop in to look at the 17th-century altarpieces.

Two kilometres north of Montfaucon, **Séniergues** is a minor gem – a picturesque rural hamlet with a 12th-century Romanesque **church** and splendid views all around; **Vaillac**, 3km south, is the seat of a formidable feudal **castle** and Romanesque **church**, where a medieval relief of the Virgin of Rocamadour was discovered. The fine *causse* country in this area has been sliced by the recent A20 motorway from Brive to Cahors – a project many Lotois vigorously opposed, knowing well that one of the great charms of the area is or, rather, was precisely its lack of motorways.

The agricultural centre of the south *causse* is **Labastide-Murat**, founded in the 13th century by Fortanier, *seigneur* of Gourdon, and named after him until 1852, when the town decided to rename itself in order to honour a hometown boy who spread his name across Europe at the beginning of the 19th century. Yet despite his adventurous career, Murat never forgot the folks back home. He built a château for his brother André – a rare example of the Empire style in this neck of the woods – and sent letters to his mum, which are displayed in the **Musée Murat** in his father's *auberge*; amongst the period furniture and other memorabilia is a giant family tree showing Murat's relationship with most of the crowned heads of Europe .

Musée Murat
t 05 65 21 19 23; open July–Sept Wed–Sun 10–12 and 3–6; adm

Three kilometres southeast, **Soulomès** was one of several Templar *commanderies* or priories in the region; the village's 14th-century Gothic **church** has a Templar baptismal font and unusual frescoes on the *Life of Christ* – scenes of Jesus taking a stroll with Mary Magdelene, Doubting Thomas, and the resurrected Christ with a knight of St John, a member of the Order that inherited most of the Templars' property after their suppression in 1312.

From Labastide-Murat the scenic D32 heads south through the narrow valley of the little Vers river, its clear waters reflecting the deep, steep greenery of its banks. It was favoured by those most picky of water connoisseurs, the Romans; the valley's gem of a village, **St-Martin-de-Vers**, has the beginnings of the ancient aqueduct carved in the rock that once descended to slake the thirst of Cahors – the best parts of it are south, around the village of Vers (*see* p.310), where the little river flows into the Lot.

Closer to St-Martin, to the west, **Cras** lies at the foot of the road up to the haunting, scanty ruins of the **Oppidum de Mursens**, an Uxellodunum candidate.

Into the Heart of the Causse de Gramat

To explore the wildest, most desolate part of the Causse de Gramat, the **Désert de la Braunhie**, head south of Gramat towards Cabrerets, or take the small roads east of Labastide-Murat. On the west edge of La Braunhie, **Caniac-du-Causse** has, under its modern church, a 12th-century **crypt** containing the 11th-century reliquary of St Namphaise, a friend of Charlemagne who fought against the Saracens in Quercy and then returned to live as a hermit, wandering about excavating drinking holes for the flocks of the *causse*, earning himself the sincere devotion of Lotois shepherds. The local answer to fertility drugs is to crawl under his reliquary. There are traces of a Roman road nearby.

Some things do grow in the La Braunhie desert – eglantine, juniper, twisted little oaks, gorse, brambles and other prickly thorny things. East of Caniac, you can visit its most dramatic feature, the **Gouffre de Planegrèze**, a pit descending 270m into one of the *causse*'s innumerable underground rivers. Unlike at Padirac (*see* p.141), you can't descend into the chasm, but explanatory panels tell you what's down there. A path carved out of the stone links the pit to a dolmen nearby, as if it were part of the sacred site.

Other picturesque, sleepy villages to aim for in these lonesome wastelands include **Blars** (south of the D653 to Figeac), with a domed Romanesque church with carved capitals and reliefs, **Quissac** and **Espédaillac**, the former with a *pietà* in its church from the 1600s. Just northwest of **Livernon**, the larger town on the east end of the Causse de Gramat, you can see the biggest dolmen in the entire *département*, the **Pierre Martine** (off the D2; walk through the scrubby trees to the end of the field). Its table stone stretches 2m, but, massive as it is, it would wiggle at the touch of a finger until 1948, when it cracked; now concrete blocks support it. You can scramble over the stone wall nearby to see a second, slightly smaller dolmen in the next field. If you aren't afraid of getting lost, leave the path between the road and the Pierre Martine to see what must have been the quarry of a score of megalithic monuments – the limestone gouged out and scoured bare. Livernon's **church** has a beautiful fortified Romanesque bell tower, and there's a pretty fountain in the centre called the Boudoulou, but there's not much else to stop for; from here the stately D653 leads to Assier (*see* p.294).

Gramat to Figeac: the Limargue

The main N140 between Gramat and Figeac rather neatly separates the *causse* from the Ségala south of St-Céré towards Figeac, running along a broad swathe of land known as the Limargue – a lush micro-region of chestnut forests and meadows of wildflowers. It has some charming villages, and the remains of one of the most blustering castles ever built.

Aynac and Lacapelle-Marival

The N140 traces an important pilgrim route to Rocamadour, remembered in **L'Hôpital** 7km from Gramat, where the Knights of St John ran a hostel, of which a chapel survives. Further southeast, tiny **Thémines** has its fine *halle* with a *lauze* roof, while, yet further along, **Rudelle** is a rather dilapidated 13th-century *bastide*, defended by an astonishing battlemented **church** built by Bertrand de Cardaillac that looks more like an overgrown rook from a chessboard than a house of God.

For a scenic detour, take the D40 north from Thémines up to **Aynac**, once a lead-mining centre, where a **château** was built in the 16th century by the bastard son of the Vicomte de Turenne, its four corner towers crowned with breast-shaped slate-coated cupolas; the delicate bas-relief over the door fits in perfectly, even though it was carved in 1895. Aynac's Romanesque **church** is also worth a look, with its octagonal tower and carved capitals. All in, though, the most extraordinary thing about Aynac is the average height of its inhabitants, who get an entry in the French *Guinness Book of Records* – in the 1980s five out of 710 measured at least 6ft 6in. A skeleton found near the château was just short of 8ft.

For a pretty drive from Aynac, circle around on the D39 to Leyme, then follow the D48 to **Lacapelle-Marival**, an attractive town of sunwarmed limestone and old towers. It grew up around an 11th-century chapel, and after the next century was defended by the Cardaillacs' **Château de Lacapelle-Marival**, one of that powerful family's principal residences, which they built smack in the middle to use its walls as an outer ring of defences; you can stroll along its parapet walk and look at its medieval frescoes. The tiny *halle* on sandstone pillars squeezed into the centre dates from the 1400s.

Château de Lacapelle-Marival
t 05 65 40 80 24; open July and Aug daily 10–12 and 3–7, 1st half Sept daily 3–7; adm

There's another good Romanesque church to be found at **Anglars** (12th-century, with a fortified belltower) and another with interior carvings at **Le Bourg**, down at the N140 crossroads.

Assier and its Cannonballing Egomaniac

Assier

The pleasant, tidy *commune* of **Assier** straddles the dramatic division between the Limargue and the Causse de Gramat. In the 16th century, much of what you see, or at least 2,500 acres of it, belonged to the irrepressible braggart Galiot (Galahad) de Genouillac (1465–1546), François I's Captain General of Artillery, Master of the Horse and Lieutenant General of Guyenne. In 1515 Galiot helped the king beat the redoubtable Swiss pikemen at the Battle of Marignano by blowing them away, on a massive scale, with cannons – the first time anyone ever employed them so in battle. As Galiot bought up the largest property in all Quercy, he made two rich marriages to help finance a building programme that was pharaonic for the Lot in 1526: a Loire Valley-style château in an immense quadrangle, numerous windmills and barns, a vaulted, 55m stable (still standing in the village), a forge, a church, the Rockefeller Center of *pigeonniers*, and a *jeu de paume* for court tennis matches. The pile was inherited by the dukes of Uzès, who cared little for it, and by 1786 it had reached such a state of decay that the owners let builders cannibalize it for a small fee; wherever you see a carved stone incorporated in a local house, you can bet it came from the château. When Prosper Mérimée, inspector of historical monuments, came to Assier in 1841, he was touched by the romantic ruin of Galiot's pride and put it on his register to prevent the rest from going to hell. Only the relatively simple west wing of the quadrangle, the guards' quarters, remains of the once enormous **Château d'Assier**.

Château d'Assier
t 05 65 40 40 99; May, June and early Sept Wed–Mon 10–12.30 and 2–6.45; July and Aug daily 10–12.30 and 2–6.45; rest of Sept Wed–Mon 10–12.30 and 2–5.30, but call first outside high season; adm

The exterior façade of this wing is framed by two of the château's original four towers, one sheathing Galiot's humble medieval birthplace. The ornate dormers have all been stripped off, except for one on the left; the niche over the entrance once held an equestrian statue of Galiot. The interior façade, however, is still a handsome Renaissance work; large stone-framed windows alternate with walls bearing medallions of Roman emperors, while bands of a frieze show swords and cannons relating to Galiot's deeds or those of Hercules, with whom Galiot fancied a resemblance. The interior, described by Brantôme as 'the best furnished in France with its vast piles of silver, tapestries and silks', now contains only one of its score of grand stairways, decorated with a handsome pilaster carved with grotesques, Hercules and the Nemean Lion and Galiot's trophies. A pendant in the vault, showing Hercules wrestling with Ateneus, is inscribed with Galiot's motto: *J'aime fort une* (a play on words, meaning 'I love fortune' or 'I love one very much' – in Galiot's case, read this as Looking Out for Number One). There's an exhibit on Galiot's career, and a hologram of his armour sent by New York's Metropolitan Museum.

The man's overweening self-esteem is most manifest today in the **church** that he built in the middle of Assier between 1540 and 1549, as a shrine to himself and his weaponry. Though Gothic in form, the decoration is Renaissance: the fascinating sculpted frieze that encircles the exterior is devoted to cannons, battles and artillery, with nary a Christian symbol in sight (reminscent of Venice's Santa Maria Zobenigo), although in the tympanum over the door we see the Virgin looking quite pleased to accept Galiot's sword and insignia from an angel, while two other angels unfurl banners reading *Vivit d. Jac. Galeotus!* ('Long live Galiot!'). Inside, under the lovely star vaulting, you can see Galiot's tomb, topped with a statue of you-know-who in his battle gear, leaning nonchalantly against a cannon, with a braggart's epitaph and his *J'aime fort une* motto. The old warrior died peacefully in bed at the age of 81 and, according to the dictates of his will, 500 priests were gathered together from miles around to give him a rousing send-off at his funeral.

On the road to Lacapelle-Marival you can still see Galiot's 11.5m pigeon tenement complete with 2,300 varnished nests, each of them representing an acre of his realm.

Cardaillac

Cradle of one of the oldest and most powerful families of Quercy, the name Cardaillac once made people tremble in their boots, but today it means only a delightful old *village perché* where dogs snooze in the middle of the lane, just 3km off the N140. Only two towers and few walls of its mighty 12th-century citadel have survived the demolition of 1629, ordered by Cardinal Richelieu to punish Cardaillac for being a Protestant safe haven – Jeanne de Cardaillac, mother of Madame de Maintenon and future mother-in-law of Louis XIV, was an important Reformation figure. Another important member of the family was Hugues de Cardaillac, who wrote a code regulating the use of cannons in warfare (1346) – a code that his neighbour Galiot probably broke when he blasted the Swiss at Marignano. The village has marked out a walk through the *quartier du fort*, the site of the old citadel on its rocky spur, still dominated by the Cardaillacs' 21m **Tour de Sagnes** which you can (sometimes) climb for the grand views.

Musée Eclaté
t *05 65 40 10 63; visits 1st half July, part of Aug and Sept Sun–Fri 3pm; 2nd half July and most of Aug Sun–Fri 3 and 4.30*

Cardaillac is also home to the unique **Musée Eclaté**, which contains artefacts related to Cardaillac's history, crafts and traditions, not confined in the walls of a single building but *éclaté* ('burst open') and displayed where they belong, in the old schoolhouse, bakery, farm buildings and so on. The villagers founded the museum and provide an enthusiastic narration – it's one of the most fun and enlightening of Good Old Days museums (if you understand French).

ⓘ Labastide-Murat >> *Grand Rue, t 05 65 21 11 39, www.cc-labastide-murat.fr (summer only)*

ⓘ Gramat > *Place de la République, t 05 65 38 73 60, www.tourisme-gramat.com*

ⓘ Lacapelle-Marival >> *Place de la Halle, t 05 65 40 81 11 (summer only)*

ⓘ Assier >> *Place de l'Eglise, t 05 65 40 50 60, www.tourisme-quercy.com/assier*

Market Days on the Causse de Gramat

Gramat: Tuesday and Friday all year, plus Sunday mornings May–Sept, Place de la Halle; fairs 2nd and 4th Thursday of month.

Labastide-Murat: Sunday 9–12 July and Aug, plus huge fair 2nd and 4th Monday of month.

Lacapelle-Marival: farmers' market Tuesday afternoons and Sunday mornings, including organic produce in July and Aug; fairs 2nd and 4th Monday morning of month.

Where to Stay and Eat on the Causse de Gramat

Gramat ✉ 46500

*****Lion d'Or**, 8 Place de la République, **t** 05 65 38 73 18, *www.liondorhotel.com* (€€). Central, solid and comfortable rooms and one of the Lot's best-known restaurants (€€€€–€€), with a seasonally changing menu and a cellar full of *vin de Cahors*. *Closed several wks in winter.*

****Relais des Gourmands**, 2 Avenue de la Gare, **t** 05 65 38 83 92, *www.relais-des-gourmands.fr* (€€). Cheerful rooms amidst greenery, a pool, a toybox for kids and a restaurant (€€€–€€) popular for its tasty dishes with local ingredients. *Closed Sun eve in winter and several wks in Oct and Feb; restaurant Mon exc July and Aug.*

Domaine du Cloucau, Çavanac, **t** 05 65 33 76 18, *www.domaineducloucau.com* (€€). A charming 18th-century family house with four very pretty and comfortable rooms, a lovely garden and a pool. Meals, available on request, often feature lamb and duck specialities. *Closed Dec and Jan.*

Moulin de Fresquet, in a park less than 1km from centre, **t** 05 65 38 70 60, *www.moulindefresquet.com* (€€–€). Five pleasant B&B rooms in a 17th-century watermill, plus meals (€€) by request. *Closed Nov–Mar.*

****Hôtel de Bordeaux**, 17 Avenue du 11 Novembre, **t** 05 65 38 70 10 (€). A very reasonably priced choice with a restaurant (€€€–€) serving filling southwest dishes. *Closed several wks in Oct and Mar; restaurant Sun in winter.*

****Hôtel du Centre**, Place de la République, **t** 05 65 38 73 37, *www.lecentre.fr* (€). Simple modern rooms and a restaurant (€€).

Thégra ✉ 46500

Giscard, **t** 05 65 38 77 31, *www.hotel-giscard.com* (€). An unflashy choice a world away from the tourists at nearby Padirac, with a pool and a restaurant (€€–€) with good southwest dishes. *Closed Sat out of season.*

Labastide-Murat ✉ 46240

****Hôtel Kyriad**, Place de la Mairie, **t** 05 65 21 18 80 (€€–€). Twenty rooms with air conditioning in a handsome 13th-century château with a restaurant (€€). *Closed mid-Dec–mid-Jan.*

Le Cloître, Montfaucon, **t** 05 65 31 11 80 (€€). Excellent food in a lovely setting. *Closed Mon eve and Sat lunch.*

Lacapelle-Marival ✉ 46120

****La Terrasse**, by château, **t** 05 65 40 80 07 (€). Thirteen rooms in a nondescript building with panoramic views of the castle and a very good restaurant (€€€–€€). *Closed Jan and Feb; restaurant Sun eve, Mon exc July and Aug, and Tues lunch.*

Le Glacier, centre, **t** 05 65 40 82 67 (€). Cheap and basic rooms. *Closed Sat eve, Sun, and Nov–May.*

Lescure, Route de St Céré, north of town, **t** 05 65 38 90 07 (€). A family-run Logis de France hotel in a quiet spot, with a pool and tasty local food (€€–€). *Closed Christmas–New Year, and Sat and Sun eve Oct–Mar.*

Mas de la Feuille, Le Bourg, on N140, **t** 05 65 11 00 17 (€). Three rooms in a restored old farmhouse, plus meals by arrangement (€€). *Closed Nov–Mar.*

Assier ✉ 46320

Chez Noëlle, **t** 05 65 40 56 27 (€). Simple rooms and good, filling food.

Cardaillac ✉ 46100

Chez Marcel, **t** 05 65 40 11 16 (€). A local institution, with five simple rooms and plentiful, well-prepared authentic cuisine (€€–€). *Restaurant closed Mon, and Sun eve in winter.*

Figeac

Figeac

Figeac, metropolis of the Célé valley, has more than one feather in its cap. It gave the world Jean-François Champollion, the linguistic wizard who cracked Egyptian hieroglyphics, and Charles Boyer, the archetypical French lover of the silver screen (and the inspiration for Warner Bros' cartoon skunk Pepe le Pew). Figeac is the second city of the Lot, with all of 11,000 people; it has more obelisks than Paris, and lays fair claim to flexing the *département*'s industrial muscle, thanks to the aeronautics manufacturer Ratier. But for the casual visitor, it's Figeac's medieval heart of golden sandstone that comes as the most charming surprise of all – if none of the individual buildings makes the architectural textbooks, some 700 have been intelligently restored to create a delightful ensemble.

History

The story goes that Pepin the Short was resting on the banks of the Célé in 753 when he saw doves suddenly fly up in the form of a cross. He founded a church on the site (the ancestor of St-Sauveur), which, the legend continues, was consecrated two years later by Pope Stephen II himself. The abbey that grew up around it linked itself with Cluny, and drew in its share of pilgrims en route to Rocamadour or Compostela. As was so often the case during that period, the 11th and 12th centuries saw the hamlet round the abbey expand into a sizable commercial town that chafed at being bossed around by an abbot, and in 1302 Philip the Fair liberated it, replacing monastic rule with that of seven consuls, one for each quarter, with a *Viguier* in charge of administering royal justice in the town. It was the beginning of Figeac's prosperity; apparently, like their brethren in Cahors, they were known for cutting a close deal.

As in many mercantile towns, Protestantism made many converts in Figeac, although the Calvinists only took control in 1568 when their captain bribed the wife of a consul to steal her husband's keys while he slept and toss them over the gate. In 1598 the Edict of Nantes made Figeac a Protestant safe town; Henri IV's brilliant minister, the duke of Sully, took refuge here after the king's assassination. Sully remained Henri IV's right-hand man (and a Protestant) even after the king decided that Paris was worth a Mass; as the powerful superindendent of finances he performed the seemingly impossible task of filling the king's war chest, promoting agriculture and building roads all across France while lowering taxes and balancing the budget. In his retirement he wrote the *Memories of wise and royal economies of the state of Henry the Great*, which subsequent superintendents of finances would have done well to study, rather than abet France's kings down their extravagant road to ruin and revolution.

Getting to and around Figeac

You can **fly** from London Stansted, Paris or Lyon to Rodez, a 45min drive from Figeac; **t** 05 65 76 02 09, *www.rodez.cci.fr*. Figeac's **train** station is on the Brive–Toulouse branch line, with direct services to Gramat, Rocamadour and Capdenac.

The SNCF runs regular **buses** from Figeac to Capdenac, Cajarc, St-Cirq-Lapopie, St-Géry and Cahors; private companies also link Figeac to Toulouse, St-Céré, Cardaillac and Lacapelle-Marival; ask tourist offices for the brochure *Guide Horaire des Transports – Les Bus du Lot*, which contains schedules for all routes.

You can **bikes** or mountainbikes from Base VTT du Pays de Figeac-Carjarc, 2 Avenue du Général de Gaulle, **t** 06 81 15 79 03.

If the Calvinists damaged much of Figeac's ecclesiastical patrimony, the Nazi SS in 1944 cruelly struck at the inhabitants themselves, deporting nearly every able-bodied man who was not employed by Ratier, which at the time made parts for the Luftwaffe. Of the 540 who went, only 395 returned from the labour and concentration camps at the end of the war.

Place Vival and Around

There may be no canals, but there's something vaguely Venetian about Figeac, beginning with its medieval street plan, full of curving lanes and irregular, asymmetrical little squares, offering a wealth of visual surprises for the pedestrian. The stone houses are so tall and densely built that many are topped with covered rooftop terraces that the Venetians call *altane* and the Lotois call *soleihos*, which not only offered city-dwellers a breath of fresh air but came in handy for drying textiles for sale as well as the family's clothes, fruit and other foods. As in Venice as well, the ground floors were given over to stocking merchandise, while the merchants themselves lived upstairs on the *piano nobile*, usually lit with the most elaborate windows of the building. As you stroll through the lanes (an activity that becomes especially evocative in the evening), keep an eye peeled for the myriad sculptural details.

Figeac has no grand central piazza like Venice but a dozen smaller ones that form the focal points of its old neighbourhoods, like Place Vival, site of the elegant 13th-century **Hôtel de la Monnaie**, one of the most beautiful secular buildings of the period in France. Philippe IV granted Figeac the privilege of minting its own coins, a dandy boost to commerce in those days; the ground floor with its pointed arches was used as a bank, while on top is a typical *soleiho*. Sharing the *hôtel* with the tourist office is the little **Musée du Vieux Figeac**, an eclectic collection that includes the beautiful Renaissance door from Sully's mansion, a set of stocks, a carving of a monk playing a drum, and more.

Musée du Vieux Figeac
t 05 65 34 06 25; open July and Aug Mon–Sat 10–7.30; rest of year Mon–Sat 10–12 and 2.30–6; adm

Just west of Place Vival runs **Rue Caviale**, one of Figeac's prettiest streets, where the **Hôtel de Marroncles** at No.30 hosted Louis XI in 1463. Rue Caviale gives into **Place Carnot**, Figeac's ancient market square, since 1988 sadly lacking its 13th-century grain *halle*. Note

Champollion and the Rosetta Stone

Son of Figeac's first bookseller, Jean-François Champollion (1790–1832) astonished his teachers with his precocious aptitude for languages – by age 14 he could rattle away in Latin, Greek, Hebrew and Arabic. He discovered hieroglyphics in his teens; though common opinion held they were mere decorations, Champollion suspected from the start that the 'pictures' were a form of writing and began a serious study of Oriental languages in the hopes of discovering a clue to their meaning.

In 1799 the huge corps of scholars who accompanied Napoleon on his expedition to Egypt began the first systematic study of that country's antiquities (as well as scouting out the possibility of a canal through the Suez and inventing the lead pencil). It's a good thing they were around when French soldiers happened to dig up a fragment of polished black basalt at Rosetta, covered with inscriptions in hieroglyphics, Greek and a cursive demotic script. They saved what became known as the Rosetta Stone and in 1814 it ended up in the British Museum. Attempts by Thomas Young to translate it were frustrated until Champollion got hold of a copy of the text and made the essential discovery in 1822 that the hieroglyphics were not only phonetic ideograms but figurative and symbolic (as described in his *Précis du système hiéroglyphique*, 1824).

Champollion made an expedition of his own to Egypt in 1828 and spent the rest of his abbreviated life as the curator of the Egyptian section in the Louvre, translating texts in Egypt and in Paris, and leaving behind a posthumously published dictionary and grammar of hieroglyphics.

the well-preserved 13th–17th-century **Maison Cisteron** in the corner, with a turret: this was the residence of Pierre de Cisteron, master armourer of Louis XIV and a Huguenot. Just before revoking the Edict of Nantes, Louis sent down a special safeguard for Cisteron, to keep him from the persecutions he had in store for Protestants who weren't so dear to his heart.

To the east Place Carnot flows naturally into handsome **Place Champollion**. For centuries this held Figeac's chestnut market; until the 19th century chestnuts were staple in the local diet and ground into flour for bread. The butchers had their stands under the ogival arches, and the **Templars' commandery** (No.5), on the south side of the square, has little columns on the windows; note, too, the 12th-century **Maison du Griffon** at No.4. In nearby Rue Séguier is the 14th-century house where Champollion (*see* above) was born, now containing the **Musée Champollion**. When this reopens, existing displays on how Champollion cracked hieroglyphics plus some mummies and Egyptian and Coptic art will be joined by an exhibition on the history of writing around the world. Outside the museum in the **Place des Ecritures**, Champollion's bicentenary in 1991 was celebrated with the installation of a giant facsimile of the Rosetta Stone in the pavement and the planting of a papyrus garden, all designed by American artist Joseph Kosuth.

Musée Champollion
closed for renovation at time of writing, due to reopen summer 2007; ask at tourist office (see p.301), for update

Notre-Dame du Puy and St-Sauveur

Figeac's churches haven't withstood the trials of time as well as the mummies or even its secular buildings, but are nevertheless worth a look. From Place Champollion, Rue de Colomb runs past some of Figeac's most aristocratic houses (note especially the fine courtyard off the pedestrian lane, Rue Malleville). You will also find here, in the Hôtel de Ville, the **Espace Patrimoine**, a permanent exhibition of the history and heritage of the town. To the right, other lanes or steps lead up the hill to **Notre-Dame du Puy**. This much-tampered-with 12th-century church replaces an ancient chapel built where the Virgin made a rose bloom on Christmas Day; the church's 14th-century portal retains its carving of animals, and inside there are some carved capitals from the same period. Perhaps best of all are the views over Figeac's medieval roofscape.

The most picturesque descent from Notre-Dame is by way of narrow medieval Rue Delzhens, past the seat of the king's judge, the **Hôtel du Viguier** (1300s, now a superb hotel; *see* opposite), to Rue Roquefort, where at No.12 are the elegant remains of the townhouse built by braggart Galiot de Genouillac (*see* pp.294–95). This street continues to **St-Sauveur**, encased in a forgettable 19th-century façade and belltower crowned with a giant breadbox; only its size and some much-knocked-about bits on the north and south flanks hint that this was Figeac's great, famous medieval church.

The **chapterhouse** (now a chapel off the right aisle) was given its remarkable ogival vaulting in the 15th century; in the 17th century, to cover up some of the damage caused in the Wars of Religion, a local sculptor added the naïve painted reliefs of the Passion: don't miss the *Last Supper*, where the Apostles are served a platter of roast hamster, or the scene of baby Jesus sleeping sweetly on a cross, dreaming of his future torments. In the nave are medieval capitals from the original portal, transformed into holy-water fonts. In the adjacent riverside Place de la Raison stands a small obelisk, a monument to Champollion.

Just before the river, Rue du Balène winds past the **Hôtel du Balène** with its huge ogival door and Flamboyant windows. From here Rue Orthabadial, once the realm of the medieval abbey gardener, returns you to the Hôtel de la Monnaie.

Around Figeac: Obelisks and Capdenac

The classic Figeac excursion is to its mysterious 7.9m obelisk-needles or *Aiguilles*, erected in the 12th century on the summit of two nearby hills – the **Aiguille de Lissac** to the west and the **Aiguille du Pressoir** to the south, on the Colline du Cingle. Their original purpose has long been forgotten, but they may have been set up by the abbey of St-Sauveur, either to lift the spirits of pilgrims approaching over the *causse*, or to set the limits within which fugitives were guaranteed the abbey's asylum.

After the death of Henri IV, Sully divided his time between Figeac and his 14th-century castle 8km south at **Capdenac-le-Haut**, a perched, medieval town fortified with ramparts; this was one of the keys to Quercy, and was constantly besieged over its history. Before the recent finds at Puy-d'Issolud (*see* p.150), Capdenac was a prime Uxellodunum contender, with its Gallo-Roman spring-fountain, claimed to be the very one blocked by Caesar. Excavations at Capdenac-le-Haut have nevertheless revealed artefacts dating back to Neolithic times, most notably the torso of the *Lady of Capdenac*, from *c*. 3000 BC and one of the oldest statues ever found in France. You can see a cast of her as well as Roman coins and other odds and ends in the **local history museum**.

Musée d'Histoire Locale
t 05 65 50 01 45; open July and Aug daily 9.30–12 and 2–6; rest of year Tues–Sun 2–6; guided visits by request

The village itself is a charmer, with a pair of Gothic gates, medieval lanes of sunny limestone houses and a belvedere with a bird's-eye view of the Lot and the village's own ugly stepsister, the industrial railway junction of Capdenac-Gare. East of here the corniche road leaves the Lot to wind into the chestnut forests of the Aveyron.

Tourist Information in Figeac

ⓘ Figeac ›
Hôtel de la Monnaie, Place Vival, **t** *05 65 34 06 25, www.tourisme-figeac.com*

The tourist office runs day and night walking **tours** of the medieval centre (early April–Sept) and themed tours (July and Aug). It's also the place for details of and tickets for the **tourist train** around the old streets.

Market Days in Figeac

There's a market all day Saturday, plus a fair on the second and last Saturday of each month.

Activities in Figeac

To see Figeac and its lovely environs by **air**, call the Aérodome de Figeac-Livernon in Durbans, **t** 05 65 40 57 04.

In July and Aug you can hire a **canoe** or kayak to paddle down the Célé, from Eaux Vives, **t** 05 65 50 05 48.

You can also **horseride** at the Club Figeacois du Cheval et du Poney, Avenue de Nayrac, **t** 05 65 34 70 57, and **swim** in a wave pool at the Domaine du Surgié (**t** 05 65 34 59 00; *open mid-April–June and Sept Sat, Sun and Wed 2–5; July and Aug daily 11–9*), which also has a playground, mini-golf and other kid-pleasers; free minibuses (**t** 05 65 50 05 40) run there from the centre of Figeac.

Where to Stay in Figeac

Figeac ✉ 46100

****Château du Viguier du Roy**, Rue Droite, **t** 05 65 50 05 05, *www.chateau-viguier-figeac.com* (€€€€€–€€€€). The once-ruined lodgings of Philippe le Bel's judge, built in 1302 and added to over the centuries, with a cloister, several 18th-century houses and an enclosed courtyard and terrace with a pool, all impeccably restored. There are 16 rooms, three suites and two apartments, individually furnished with antiques; the 18th-century rooms have gilded overmantels. For **La Dinée du Viguier** restaurant, *see* p.302. *Closed mid-Oct–late April.*

Les Bains, 1 Rue du Griffoul, **t** 05 65 34 10 89, *www.hoteldesbains.fr* (€€–€). Simple rooms directly over the waters of the Célé. *Closed Fri and Sat in winter.*

Hostellerie de l'Europe, 51 Allées Victor Hugo, **t** 05 65 34 10 16, *www.hostelleriedeleurope.com* (€€–€). Thirty pleasant rooms, a garden and a swimming pool. The friendly owners run themed weekends, including local produce tastings.

Hôtel-Bar Le Champollion, 4 Place Champollion, **t** 05 65 34 04 37 (€). A very modern little place with friendly staff and a bright bar full of locals.

Terminus St-Jacques, 27 Av Georges Clemenceau, **t** 05 65 34 00 43, *www.hotel-terminus.fr* (€). The best cheap option, near the station, with a bit of a garden. Its restaurant (€€€–€€) serves tender Quercy lamb. *Restaurant closed Sat lunch and Sun eve.*

Camping les Rives du Célé, Domaine du Surgié (*see* above), 1 km from Figeac, **t** 05 65 34 59 00 (€). Bungalow accommodation and mobile homes, plus a beach on a small artificial lake and a pool. *Closed Nov–Mar.*

Eating Out in Figeac

Figeac ✉ 46100

La Dinée du Viguier, Château du Viguier (*see* p.301), **t** 05 65 50 08 08 (€€€€–€€€). The gourmet shrine of Figeac. *Closed Sat lunch and Mon, plus Sun in winter, 2wks Feb and 1wk Nov.*

La Puce à l'Oreille, 5–7 Rue St-Thomas, **t** 05 65 34 33 08 (€€€–€€). Traditional menus, featuring duck *confits*, and unusual dishes. Book ahead. *Closed Sun eve and Mon exc July and Aug.*

La Table de Marinette, next to Hostellerie de l'Europe (*see* p.301), **t** 05 65 50 06 07 (€€€–€€). Wonderful dishes with mushrooms and other traditional Quercy ingredients – try the foie gras with spices. *Closed Fri, Sat lunch and Sun, plus Jan and Feb.*

La Cuisine du Marché, 15 Rue Clermont, **t** 05 65 50 18 55 (€€€–€). An old wine cellar with a terrace under stone arches, with imaginative fish dishes and other delights such as panfried foie gras. *Closed Sun eve, plus Sun lunch in winter.*

The Célé Valley

The Lot's merriest river, the Célé (from the Latin *celer*, or rapid) is born in the harsh lands of the Cantal, but once past Figeac this clear and shallow stream takes on a softer quality as it splashes through gentle valleys and steep gorges protected by cliff forts, the *châteaux des Anglais* left over from the Hundred Years' War. Off season, the tiny hamlets along the river are almost deserted; come before the first tourist wave of Easter and you may think you've landed in a Quercy Brigadoon. Until the 1700s the valley was famous for its saffron, grown mostly as a dye and marketed by German merchants. There has been a renaissance in saffron growing of late, especially around Cajarc to the south, which helps satisfy the local appetite for paella, introduced by refugees from the Spanish Civil War who settled in southwest France. This is ideal walking country: pick up a copy of the literature describing walks in this area, from the *Promenades et Randonnées* series available at Figeac and other area tourist offices. Ask for the English-language *Walking, Riding and Mountain-Biking in the Lot Département*. The Célé is also an easy and lovely river to float down in a lazy canoe or kayak, and a number of places from Figeac (*see* p.301) on down hire them out to make the descent as far as St-Cirq-Lapopie.

From Figeac to Espagnac-Ste-Eulalie

Six kilometres west of Figeac, leave the D13 for the picturesque riverside D41 near the much-restored, fat-towered 15th–16th-century **Château Ceint d'Eau**. Soon to the right, just beyond a ruined Romanesque chapel, a road leads up to tiny **Camboulit**, a charming medieval hill village as yet not given over to holiday homes. The valley narrows once past Boussac, where overhanging cliffs similar to those along the Vézère in Périgord were used as shelters or fortresses in the Middle Ages. In and around **Corn**, an old farming village, are fortified caves from the Hundred Years' War as well as a pair of 17th-century châteaux on either side of the river.

Espagnac-Ste-Eulalie, another 9km downstream, is the most frequently photographed beauty spot along the Célé – it's a tiny hamlet watched over by a striking *clocher*, a slender tower crowned by an openwork timbered chamber with a bell dating from the 1500s and a pointy octagonal roof, the whole almost too quaint to be real. This belongs to a convent fittingly named **Notre-Dame du Val Paradis**, founded in the 12th century but greatly expanded in the next by its benefactor, Aymeric d'Hébrard of Cajarc, a member of the valley's leading family and bishop of Coimbra in Portugal. The convent, which survived until the Revolution, incorporated all the buildings within the towered gateway, including the pleasant communal gîtes.

The belltower isn't the only quaint thing about the little church of Notre Dame; note how the pentagonal apse rears up abruptly, a full storey higher than the rest of the church. The portal, decorated with carved ivy and fig leaves, leads into an interior half rebuilt after fires in the 15th century, and has ended up unusually short for its height. There are three tombs: those of Aymeric d'Hébrard, the knight Hugues de Cardaillac-Brengues (d. 1342), and his elegant wife, Bernarde de Trian, niece of Pope John XXII. The lofty choir is decorated with the arms of the Cardaillacs and little mitred heads. On the high altar, a gilt wooden retable from the 1700s displays a badly restored copy of an altarpiece by Simon Vouet, showing Louis XIV's mum, Anne of Austria, floating up to heaven in the guise of the Virgin of the Assumption.

The next village, **Brengues**, is an old Cardaillac fief, built on a bluff over the river that conceals a *château des Anglais*. The Hébrards came from the next village, **St-Sulpice**, partially built into and growing out of the curve of its cliff; Its much restored 12th-century château is still in the Hébrard family. In the Middle Ages this was a cradle of bishops, soldiers and diplomats who served in important posts across Europe; the Hébrards owned so much of the Célé valley that it was nicknamed the 'Hébrardie'.

Marcilhac-sur-Célé

Abbaye de Marcilhac-sur-Célé
t *05 65 40 68 44; open July and Aug daily 12–6; Easter–June and Sept–early Nov daily 2–5*

With a population of 240, Marcilhac-sur-Célé is one of the larger villages in the valley. It owes its existence to a powerful **Benedictine abbey** founded by Pepin the Short. By the 12th century this owned more than 100 properties, including Rocamadour (*see* p.143). Its abbots, however, had failed to foresee Rocamadour's potential – unlike the bishops of Tulle, who took it over and transformed it into a prestigious pilgrimage site. When the pilgrims (and profits) starting piling into Rocamadour, Marcilhac wanted it back, leading to an unseemly conflict that saw each side booting out the other's monks. In the end, Marcilhac surrendered its claim in exchange for cash. The abbey was badly pillaged in the Hundred Years' War. The

Hébrards of St-Sulpice took it under their wing in 1451 and rebuilt the damaged bits in the Gothic style; this was destroyed by the Protestants. A few monks stuck it out until the Revolution.

There are more ducks than people here now, but along the Célé they are still defended by the thick medieval buttresses topped with little carved figures mysteriously called 'conspirators' heads'. The path from Place des Platanes leads past the Romanesque chapterhouse, with curious capitals carved with scenes of heaven and hell in two distinct styles. The lofty, grandiose ruins of the bays and narthex of the abbey's Romanesque church form a kind of courtyard around what is now Marcilhac's parish **church**, rebuilt by the Hébrards in the Gothic style to replace the once-vast Romanesque apse and ambulatory. The interior is decorated with Hébrard coats of arms and 15th-century frescoes, 17th-century panelling and a copy of a Van Dyck *Virgin and Child* in the retable. Note the angel's head with a teasing smile, on the pew with the heraldic carvings. The original Romanesque church's south portal has a rare Carolingian tympanum, a triangular composition of bas-reliefs. Christ on top is framed by symbols of the sun and moon, while two angels below grip instruments of the Passion, and at the bottom stand saints Peter and Paul.

Grotte de Bellevue
open July and Aug daily 10–7 (last entry 6.15); adm

Musée en Plein Air du Quercy
t 05 65 31 36 43; open early May–June and Sept Wed–Sun 2–6; July and Aug daily 11–7; adm

Two kilometres northwest of Marcilhac is a steep hairpin road up to the **Grotte de Bellevue**, discovered in 1964, full of curious red and white stalactites and stalagmites. Beyond the old village of **Sauliac-sur-Célé** (with a lovely place for a riverside picnic, overlooking a dilapidated château) is the narrow but well-signposted road up to **Cuzals** and the **Musée en Plein Air du Quercy**, which re-creates two farms with original buildings, one pre-Revolutionary, the other from the 19th century, along with 30 little museums of crafts, agriculture, water and natural sciences; there's a dental surgery from 1900, working craftspeople (especially on Sundays), and more.

Cabrerets and Grotte du Pech-Merle

Musée de l'Insolite
t 05 65 30 21 01; open April–Sept daily 9–1 and 2–8; rest of year call ahead

Grotte du Pech-Merle
t 05 65 31 27 05, www.pechmerle.com; guided tours mid-April–Oct daily 9.30–12 and 1.30–5; book 2 days in ahead July and Aug; get your time-stamped ticket on arrival; adm

Back against the cliffs of the Célé, Cabrerets has a dramatic, cliff-cut *château des Anglais*, begun in 745 by Waiffre, Duke of Aquitaine, though this one is better known as the **Château du Diable** – devils and Englishmen being frequently synonymous in medieval France. Downstream, on a high bluff, is the much restored 14th-century **Château de Cabrerets**, owned until the Revolution by the Gontaut-Birons of Biron (*see* pp.350–51). Outside the centre, the quirky **Musée de l'Insolite**, 'museum of the unusual', has works of art and other things with an unusual/surreal twist. Stop by **La Pescalerie**, an impressive resurgent spring that still powers a mill.

The main reason for visiting, however, is 4km up the road from Cabrerets, the **Grotte du Pech-Merle**, which rivals Font-de-Gaume at Les Eyzies as the finest prehistoric painted cave still open to the

Musée de Préhistoire Amédée-Lemozi
open same hrs as Grotte du Pech-Merle

public since the closing of Lascaux. While waiting for your tour, visit the **Musée de Préhistoire Amédée-Lemozi** by the car park, with a fine collection of tools and art ranging from the Lower Palaeolithic to the Iron Age, plus photos of decorated caves and a film; there's also a snack bar, shady picnic area and a playground.

The original entrance to the cave had been blocked up at the end of the last ice age and was only rediscovered in 1922 by 16-year-old André David, son of the owner of Pech-Merle, and a friend. Inspired by the exploration of caves by Abbé Lemozi, a Cabrerets native, they wormed their way through a narrow 122m passage and found exactly what they dreamed of – a magnificent cave decorated with magnificent Upper Palaeolithic works of art. Some 80 drawings of animals and humans and hundreds of symbols decorate a third of Pech-Merle's 1.6km of passageways, spanning three periods, from the Solutrean to the Magdalenian (20,000–15,000 BC). The tour begins with the **Chapel of the Mammoths**, an arched gallery carved by an underground river with a great spiral frieze of mammoths, horses and bison outlined in black around a horse; one artist took advantage of the bulge in the rock to paint a mammoth in natural relief – a fine example of 'non-polarized' art, void of any north–south or up–down orientation. It's believed to date from the Aurignacian or early Magdalenian age (15,000–14,000 BC), while the traces of red date back from the first cave users. Here too is the **Ceiling of Hieroglyphs**, covered with finger drawings of female and animal figures and mysterious circular signs from all periods.

From here the tour descends to the **Hall of Discs**, named after the rare calcite concentrations in upright concentric circles caused by water dripping through hairline fissures in rock. Yet more stunning are the **footprints** in the upper gallery, left by a woman and her 12-year-old child in the muddy clay of a natural dam at least 12,000 years ago. The next drawing is 'the wounded man' – a long figure hidden along the ceiling, pierced by arrows, with a bull and mysterious red signs, all from the Magdalenian age. Beyond are the famous white or red cave pearls (pisolites), part of the upper **Geological Network**, culminating in the magnificent **Red Hall**, with stalactites and columns formed by dripping limestone and oxides.

The visit re-enters the prehistoric section via the **Bear's Gallery**, with signs of clawmarks and a bear's head carved faintly in the wall. Beyond is Pech-Merle's best-known work, two fat yet graceful **spotted horses** reminiscent of ancient Chinese figures, one with its delicate head drawn on a natural protuberance in the rock. The spots spill out of the outlines while six feminine 'negative hands' (made by blowing paint over hands) seem to yearn to stroke or hold the horses. Lastly, the **Combel Gallery** has the extraordinary root of a living oak through its heart; bears' lairs are hollowed out in the floor and a cache of bear bones was discovered here.

ⓘ **Cabrerets >>**
t 05 65 31 27 12 (summer only)

ⓘ **Marcilhac-sur-Célé >**
Mairie, **t** *05 65 40 68 44, www.quercy.net/quercy/marcilhac (summer only)*

Where to Stay and Eat in the Célé Valley

Boussac ✉ 46100

Domaine des Villedieu, between Figeac and Corn, **t** 05 65 40 06 63, *www.villedieu.com* (€€€–€€). A *ferme-auberge* serving sumptous meals in its apple orchard in fine weather, including garnished duck dishes, cassoulet and *magret Rossini* – duck breast with truffles, foie gras and Madeira sauce. Book in advance. There are also some rooms (€€–€) available on a half-board basis in July and August, plus a pool.

Marcilhac-sur-Célé ✉ 46160

Les Tilleuls, **t** 05 65 40 62 68 (€). A superb B&B in a Quercy house, with a shady lawn and pretty rooms. Book well in advance. *Closed Dec.*

Restaurant des Touristes, Le Bourg, **t** 05 65 40 65 61 (€€). Good family cooking, served by charming staff under a pergola in summer. Book ahead. *Closed Nov–Easter.*

Cabrerets ✉ 46330

****Auberge de la Sagne**, near entrance to Pech-Merle, **t** 05 65 31 26 62, *www.hotel-auberge-cabrerets.com* (€). A charming, tranquil old inn set within lovely gardens, with a good restaurant (€€). *Closed mid-Sept–mid-May; restaurant lunch.*

****Hôtel des Grottes**, **t** 05 65 31 27 02, *www.hoteldesgrottes.com* (€). A pleasant hotel with a pool and restaurant (€€-€). *Restaurant closing days vary, call ahead.*

Chez Bessac, opposite *mairie*, **t** 05 65 31 27 04 (€). A friendly B&B. *Closed Nov– Easter.*

Down the Lot to Cahors

Sometime in the deep dark past, the letters in the Celtic name *Olt* were jiggled to create the Lot, a river with more bends and curls than Goldilocks' ringlets; if you stretched it out from its source in the Lozère to Aiguillon, where it flows into the Garonne, it would measure 471km – compared to 270km as the crow flies. Taking its own sweet way, it wanders through three distinct landscapes. Above Vers it is closed in by blond and ochre limestone cliffs that the feudal lords of Quercy found convenient to carve out as nearly inaccessible *châteaux des Anglais*, or use as bases for their castles.

Beyond Vers the cliffs have been worn into *cévennes*, rounded but arid rocky hills covered with scrub oak where vineyards were planted in the Middle Ages; in the rich alluvial soil of the meanders, tobacco and walnut farms are a big source of income. From Cahors west to Fumel, the typical Lot valley landscape is asymmetrical – *cévennes* on one bank, spacious valley on the other, cut by wayward loops, or *cingles*, similar to those of the Dordogne – much of it covered with oak forests, the rest with vineyards producing *vin de Cahors*. Downriver at Fumel the *cévennes* give way to isolated hills or *pechs*. The river straightens in the wide valleys, and the vines give way to orchards, the source of the renowned prunes of Agen.

Capdenac to St-Cirq-Lapopie

To follow the Lot west of Capdenac, you'll have to cross over the bridge at Capdenac-Gare and take the scenic D86 along the south bank as far as the bridge to **St-Pierre-Toirac**, a pleasant village

Getting around between Montbrun and Cahors

The SNCF runs several **buses** a day between Capdenac (*see* p.300) and Cahors station, stopping at Montbrun, Cajarc, St-Géry and Vers.

In 1990 the Lot was made navigable by **boat** again between St-Cirq-Lapopie and Luzech (to the west of Cahors), thanks to the repair/installation of 14 locks. Safaraid at Bouziès, **t** 05 65 35 98 88, offers excursions (daily April– Oct) as far as St-Cirq, departing from Port de Bouziès. They also hire out boats, canoes and *gabares* for up to 12 people. Nicols Lot Navigations, at Bouziès, **t** 05 65 24 32 20, *www.nicols.com*, hires out **houseboats** by the week, sleeping up to 12 .

---

named after its 12th-century Romanesque church. In the 1300s, this doubled as the base for the town's defensive tower; the walls were thickened, and an upper room was added over the vaults. There are rustic carved capitals inside, and Merovingian sarcophagi outside. There is also a **Musée Rural Quercynois** with figures in traditional garb and various other collections and exhibitions including objects linked to witchcraft.

Musée Rural Quercynois
t 05 65 34 26 07; open July and Aug Sun–Fri 2.30–6.30; adm

Larroque-Toirac is spread under the lofty *donjon* of its singular **château**. Dating from the 12th century, it passed to the Cardaillac family, whose stalwart fidelity to France in the Hundred Years' War invited numerous sieges before the English succeeded in taking the castle in 1372. It burnt down soon afterwards but was rebuilt in the next century and restored in the 1920s. Incredibly, the high, pentagonal donjon, now cut off with a sloping roof, originally stood 30m higher before it was cut down to size in the Revolution; in the manor house, served by a spiral Romanesque stair, are some fine chimneypieces and furnishings.

Château de Larroque-Toirac
t 06 12 37 48 39; guided tours early July–early Sept daily 10–12 and 2–6; adm

Prettily situated **Montbrun**, the next village, has the ruins of another Cardaillac castle, overlooking the grand belvedere on the south bank, known as **Saut de la Mounine** (Monkey's Leap). The cruel lord of Montbrun, furious at his daughter's choice of lovers, had ordered her to be thrown off the cliff; a kindly hermit dressed up a monkey in the girl's clothing and hurled it over in her place. The sight made the lord of Montbrun deplore his cruelty, and when he found out he had been duped he forgave his daughter. What she thought about him isn't recorded.

The next town downriver, spread across a loop of the Lot, is **Cajarc** – a pleasant riverside resort with a beach on its extremely popular *plan d'eau* (artificial lake). One-time French president Georges Pompidou had a holiday home in the village, and he served on the town council when De Gaulle insisted that his ministers hold posts in local government in order to keep in contact with the people. Pompidou's strongest influence on Cajarc was an abiding passion for contemporary art, which is expressed in the changing exhibits displayed the **Maison des Arts Georges Pompidou**. There is also a **railway museum** at the station, with all things pertaining to trains and tracks.

Maison des Arts Georges Pompidou
t 05 65 40 78 19; open Feb–June Tues–Sun 2–6, July–Sept Mon–Sat 1–7 and Sun 2–7

Musée du Rail
t 06 81 74 16 47; open July–Sept daily 3–6

There are many fine medieval houses on the teardrop-shaped *boulevard* (especially the 13th-century Maison de Hébrardie) and, on the edge of town, the ruined 12th-century chapel of an asylum for lepers. Cajarc has now become synonymous with a renewed interest in saffron growing. Less than a kilometre to the north, there's a pretty waterfall, the **Cascade de la Cogne** (it dries up during the summer months).

The area north of Cajarc, between the rivers Célé and Lot, is rich in **dolmens**: there is a pair of good ones to be found along the D82, to the west of Gréalou, and another two on the D17 just north of St-Chels; just to the south of St-Chels, you can enjoy beautiful views over both valleys from Mas-de-Laborie.

Four kilometres south of Cajarc, a path off the D146 towards St-Clair leads to the deep **Gouffre de Lantouy**, with emerald-green water, and, according to the locals, a monster.

Château de Cénevières

Château de Cénevières
t 05 65 31 27 33, www.chateaucenevieres.com; open Easter–Sept Mon–Sat 10–12 and 2–6, Sun 2–6; Oct–early Nov daily 2–5; adm

Perched on a lofty cliff over the river, the Château de Cénevières marks a strategic point that has been fortified since the cows came home. Pepin the Short came here in 763, hunting down Waiffre, the last Merovingian duke of Aquitaine; in the 13th century, the lords of Gourdon constructed the first castle, as a way of spiting the English. In the 1500s its lord was a master of the royal artillery, this one ripely named Flottard de Gourdon, who served François I with his buddy Galiot de Genouillac and married Marguerite de Cardaillac. The château was embellished and enlarged in the Renaissance style; Flottard's son Antoine converted to Protestantism, and in 1580 the future Henri IV stopped here, to plot his attack on Cahors. During the Revolution, local *sans-culottes* arrived ready to burn this symbol of feudalism and tyranny to the ground. The custodian opened the door and invited them in – to the wine cellar, and they were soon drunk as skunks. Afterwards they halfheartedly vandalized a bit here and there and staggered home; Cénevières stands to this day.

Near the entrance to the château you can see the little Protestant temple that was added by Antoine Gourdon. Of the medieval castle only the donjon remains, although it's hardly recognizable behind the ornate dormers and windows that stylistically meld it to the Renaissance sections added by Flottard and son. These are richly appointed with period furnishings and ancient tapestries; there's an ornate chimney, a complex stair, charmingly painted coffered ceilings, a vast kitchen and an unusual *Cabinet d'Alchimie* decorated with 16th-century frescoes; never fully explained, the paintings seem to express some alchemical allegory. In summer, the château hosts exhibitions, concerts and medieval days; see the website for details.

St-Cirq-Lapopie

St-Cirq-Lapopie

Saint-Cirq appeared to me, embraced by Bengal fires – like an impossible rose in the night... I no longer have any desire to be anywhere else
André Breton

If a hard-nosed urban surrealist such as André Breton melts at the sight, you can gather that the prettiest village in Quercy must be quite a looker. The setting is spectacular; St-Cirq (pronounced San-Seer) hovers 100m above the Lot, overlooking the kind of dramatic, sheer cliffs beloved of Romantic poets. Its architecture is pure, harmoniously medieval – and rigorously preserved and protected. In season parking is nearly as difficult as at Rocamadour – there's a car park just west of St-Cirq, next to the belvedere. In summer, get there early to avoid the disgorging coachloads; in winter you may well have it all to yourself.

St-Cirq began as a Gallo-Roman villa called Pompéjac, owned by the 7th-century bishop of Cahors, St Didier. It was the last possession of Waiffre of Aquitaine to be conquered by Pepin, and gave its name to the La Popie family who made it their bailiwick. In the 13th century, its strategic importance was such that the site was shared by the lords of Gourdon, Cardaillac and La Popie (later succeeded by the Hébrards), each of whom had their own castle, linked together at the top of the town. Such rare cooperation failed to keep the English out in the Hundred Years' War: not once but three times in the 14th century they played the same trick on the French barons, scaling the sheer cliff and surprising them. In 1471 Louis XI ordered the contiguous castles to be destroyed in order to punish the Hébrards for throwing in their cap with the English. Enough of the castle, however, remained intact to cause trouble in the Wars of Religion, until the future Henri IV ordered the site razed to keep out the Catholics. This time only a few crumbling but wonderfully panoramic **walls** survived above the church; many of the cut Gothic stones were reused in the houses of St-Cirq. These days many of St-Cirq's residents are artists and craftworkers, following in the footsteps of Man Ray and Foujita, who came to stay with André Breton.

The **church**, which was built by master mason Guillaume Capelle in 1522–40, is now the most prominent building in St-Cirq, its buttressed apse high on the bluff, its turreted watchtower running up the side of the stout belltower. To the left of the portal are two medieval grain measures; inside, the church incorporates a Romanesque chapel, with a carved capital of Judith beheading Holofernes. The font is held up by a Gallo-Roman capital. Near the church you'll find St-Cirq's most medieval and picturesque lane, **Ruelle de la Fourdonne**, and the main street, the Grand-Rue, lined with 15th- and 16th-century houses; along the way keep your eyes peeled for the lampholder with a head carved on it. The Château de la Gardette is home to the **Musée Rignault**, hosting special modern-art exhibitions every summer.

Musée Rignault
t 05 65 31 23 22; open late Mar–June and Sept Wed–Mon 10–12.30 and 2–7; July and Aug Wed–Mon 10–12.30 and 2–6

Musée de la Mémoire du Village
t 05 65 31 21 51; open mid-Mar–early Nov Tues–Sat 2–7, plus Sun in high season; adm

The names of Rue de la Pélissaria and Rue de la Payrolerie recall two formerly important trades in St-Cirq: skin-dressing and copper-cauldron-making. Another was wood-turning: from 1810 until recently the village was famous for the manufacture of boxwood taps for barrels; the **Musée de la Mémoire du Village**, in the Maison de la Fourdonne, has exhibits showing how it was done, as well as old photographs and other items.

St-Cirq-Lapopie to Cahors

Musée Ferroviaire Mémorial Quercy Vapeur
t 05 65 35 46 91; open June and Sept Sun 2.30–6.30; July and Aug daily 2.30–6.30

Stride Studio
t 05 65 31 43 43; open summer daily 10–12 and 4–7; rest of year by appt

One scenic way to continue downriver is to walk the towpath cut in the rock below St-Cirq that runs 5km west to **Bouziès**; it's part of the GR36, marked with red and white signs and decorated with a long relief in the living limestone, carved by sculptor Daniel Monnier. Little Bouziès is the chief pleasure-boat port on the Lot; here in the cliffs is another fortified cave or *château des Anglais*. Don't miss the lovely view from the belvedere on the D40, overlooking the confluence of the Célé and Lot, near a Renaissance château and ochre cliffs. Opposite is the little medieval hamlet of **Bouziès-Bas**, while Pech-Merle is just north (*see* pp.304–5). At St-Géry there's a **railway museum** with mini-train in the grounds.

Vers, situated where the little Vers river ripples down to meet the Lot, has some impressive grooves cut in the rock – they were left by the Roman aqueduct that follows the pretty Vers valley; the church under the cliffs, **Notre-Dame-des-Velles** ('of the sails'), was long a boatman's chapel and has a 12th-century apse decorated with *modillons*. On Place Communal you can visit the **studio of artists Sally and Jeffrey Stride**.

On the south bank, **Arcambal** has a castle, restored in the 19th century; the town marks the eastern limits of the region producing *vin de Cahors* (*see* p.328). The name of **Laroque-des-Arcs** on the north bank recalls the arches of the Roman aqueduct where it crossed the Lot. It had three storeys, like the Pont du Gard, but was demolished in 1370 by the consuls of Cahors to keep the English from seizing it. Nowadays Laroque's chief landmark is its little chapel of St-Roch on a bluff, with the wall of a *château des Anglais* below. Laroque-des-Arc's castle, **Château de Polminhac**, with its great round 13th-century donjon, began as a *borie*, or fortified country farm, built by a branch of the Gourdon family.

Market Days between Montbrun and Cahors

Cajarc: Saturday afternoons, plus fairs on 2nd and 4th Wednesdays of every month.

St-Cirq-Lapopie: Wednesday mornings, June–Sept.

Where to Stay and Eat between Montbrun and Cahors

Montbrun ✉ 46160

La Treille, t 05 65 40 77 20 (€). A pretty spot on the river, with pleasant rooms.

ⓘ **Cajarc >**
La Chapelle, **t** *05 65 40 72 89 (April–Sept)*

ⓘ **St-Cirq-Lapopie >**
Place du Sombral, **t** *05 65 31 29 06, www.saint-cirqlapopie.com*

★ **Claude Marco >>**

Cajarc ✉ 46160

****Ségalière**, 380 Avenue François Mitterrand, **t** 05 65 40 65 35 (€€). A modern hotel named after the fields of rye (*siegle*) that used to cover the area, with well-equipped rooms, some with a terrace. The restaurant (€€€–€€), which opens out on to the swimming pool, serves regional dishes, some featuring locally grown saffron. *Closed Nov–Feb.*

Tour-de-Faure ✉ 46330

****Hôtel Les Gabarres**, just beyond village near bridge over Lot, **t** 05 65 30 24 57 (€). A big, functional modern hotel in a quiet corner, with good views of tree-covered cliffs from some rooms, a swimming pool, equipment for babies, and bikes for hire. *Closed Nov–mid-April.*

St-Cirq-Lapopie ✉ 46330

*****La Pélissaria**, **t** 05 65 31 25 14, *http://perso.orange.fr/hoteldelapelissaria* (€€€–€€). A friendly, intimate place built in the 13th century, with 10 wonderful rooms hanging on the cliff in the lower part of the village, plus a pool. *Closed Nov–late April.*

****Auberge du Sombral**, **t** 05 65 31 26 08 (€€–€). A medieval house in the centre, with eight charming rooms under its steep-pitched roof. *Closed mid-Nov–Mar, plus Wed exc July and Aug.*

Maison de la Fourdonne, centre, **t** 05 65 31 21 51 (€). A hostel in a large Renaissance house that also contains an exhibition about woodwork and the Musée de la Mémoire du Village (*see* opposite). Guests need to bring their own sleeping bags. *Closed mid-Nov–mid-Mar.*

Camping de la Plage, Porte Roque, **t** 05 65 30 29 51, *www.la-plage-camping.com* (€). A riverside site with mobile homes and chalets to let, plus kayak and bike hire. Advance reservations are recommended.

La Truffière, Route de Concots, **t** 05 65 30 20 22, *www.camping-truffiere.com* (€). A campsite on the *causse*, with lots of trees and a pool, and chalets and caravans to let. Book ahead. *Closed mid-Sept–Mar.*

Lou Bolat, on roadside on way up out of village, **t** 05 65 30 29 04 (€€). A pretty café-restaurant-crêperie with a terrace overlooking the village, serving regional dishes such as trout with *vin du Cahors*, a variety of savoury and sweet pancakes and ice-cream desserts. There is also a bustling, shaded terrace bar.

Bouziès ✉ 46330

****Les Falaises**, **t** 05 65 31 26 83, *www.crdi.fr/falaises* (€). A country hotel overlooking the cliffs of the Lot, with a heated swimming pool. Its restaurant (€€) serves good and well-priced Quercy cuisine. *Closed early Nov–early April.*

Vers ✉ 46090

***La Truite Dorée**, **t** 05 65 31 46 13, *www.latruitedoree.fr* (€). Good rooms set within an old stone farmhouse, an amoeba-shaped swimming pool and a restaurant (€€). *Closed early Nov–Mar; restaurant mid-Dec–Feb, plus eves in winter.*

Le Clos des Dryades, on Cahors road, **t** 05 65 31 44 50, *www.closdesdryades.com* (€). Four pleasant *chambres d'hôte* amidst oak trees, with a pool and meals (€€) by request. Two gîtes are also available.

Auberge Rustica, on Figeac road at Cours, **t** 05 65 31 40 96, *www.auberge-rustica.fr* (€€–€). Good-value, traditional southwest dishes, such as duck *confit*, plus four rooms (€) and a bungalow sleeping 4–6 people. *Closed Wed lunch and Nov.*

Lamagdelaine ✉ 46090

Claude Marco, just off roundabout, **t** 05 65 35 30 64, *www.restaurantmarco.com* (€€€€–€€€). The gourmet hotspot on this stretch of the river, located within a 19th-century house. Local ingredients (some of them plucked from the chef's own veg patch out back) are magically transformed into divine dishes such as foie gras *tatin* with a creamed truffle *jus*. The range of excellent-value menus make it an affordable treat. If you fancy staying overnight, there are also four pretty designer guestrooms (€€€–€€), plus an outdoor swimming pool in the garden. *Closed Sun eve and Mon outside high season; restaurant also Tues lunch, plus Mon lunch mid-June–mid-Sept.*

South of the Lot: Truffles and the Causse de Limogne

South of the Lot, the dry, sparsely populated Causse de Limogne, more wooded and less dramatic than the Causse de Gramat, is dotted with dolmens, magnificent *pigeonniers*, abandoned walls and stone huts. Lavender is grown commercially here, and most of the Lot's truffles hide out near the roots of its dwarf oaks. In winter you can watch locals in berets with bulging jacket and trouser pockets (to fool plain-clothes tax inspectors) dickering with owners of the biggest restaurants in Paris at 'the world's biggest truffle market' at **Lalbenque** (*see* p.313). In these hi-tech times, there are fewer truffles every year because no one has the patience to plant the right kind of 'truffle oak' and wait 10–15 years for a possible crop. Lalbenque also has a 15th-century altarpiece in its church and a fine carved 18th-century wayside cross by the fire station.

Château de Cieurac
t 05 65 31 64 28; open June Sat and Sun 2–6.30; July–mid-Sept Tues–Sun 2–6.30, adm

Moulin de Fontvieille
t 05 65 31 52 71; visits by appt

Musée d'Arts et Traditions Populaires
t 05 65 31 48 78; open mid-June–mid-Sept daily 10–12.30 and 3.30–7.30; rest of year by appt

Prieuré de Laramière
t 05 65 31 54 07; open late July–late Aug daily 10.30–12 and 2.30–5.30; late Aug–early Sept daily 2.30–5.30

Escaliers du Temps
t 06 03 93 45 91; open July and Aug daily 11–6; early April–June and Sept–early Nov call for times

Les Sentiers du Quercy
t 05 65 21 01 67; call for hrs

Just northwest are the pretty farms, Cahors vineyards and full-sailed windmill of **Cieurac**, the ruined priory of **Pauliac**, a daughter of the abbey of Marcilhac, and the 15th-century **Château de Cieurac**, with its sculpted portal, carved stair and mullioned windows, beautifully restored after being torched by Germans in the last war. The château usually has an art exhibition, and there are pretty French gardens. The other main 'sight' here is the vast public washhouse (*lavoir*) of **Aujols**. Are the locals laundry-proud, we asked, or do they indulge in too many dandelion (*pissenlits*) salads? 'No, no, that's just the way it is,' little old lady assured us.

Limogne-en-Quercy, capital of the *causse*, has a working windmill at Promilhanes, and a walnut-oil mill, the **Moulin de Fontvieille** at Varaire, operated by donkey power (for information about mills in the area, see *www.moulinsduquercy.com*). There is also a museum of old tools and the like, the **Musee d'Arts et Traditions Populaires**.

The *bastide* **Beauregard** was founded by the abbot of Marcilhac and possesses a 14th-century *halle* with a gorgeous *lauze* roof; you can still see the original grain measures cut into the stone. There are four **dolmens** near Beauregard and more in lavender-scented **Laramière**. Laramière's charming 12th-century **priory** was restored by the Jesuits after damage in the Wars of Religion. There are sculptures from the 1300s in the chapel, a room to put up pilgrims en route to Compostela, and a lovely chapterhouse decorated with geometric designs and effigies of St Louis and his wife, Blanche de Castille. At **Bach**, walk through some late-19th-century phosphate mines, **Les Escaliers du Temps**, open to the air, where unusual fossils and unique vegetation were found. At **Escamps**, **Les Sentiers du Quercy** is a three-hectare park with more 1,000 varieties of iris.

To continue into the Valley of the Bonnette, *see* pp.388–94.

Market Days in Lalbenque and Limogne-en-Quercy

There's a huge **truffle market** in Lalbenque on Tuesdays at 2pm sharp, Dec–Mar (come 30min early to watch the preliminaries). **Limogne** also has a seasonal truffle market, on Fridays.

Where to Stay and Eat in Lalbenque

Lalbenque ✉ 46230

*****L'Aquitaine**, west of town on N20, **t** 05 65 21 00 51, *http://perso.orange.fr/aquitaine.hotel* (€). A white-painted modern hotel with a swimming pool, a tennis court and restaurant (€€). *Closed 1st half of Jan; restaurant Mon and Sun.*

***Le Lion d'Or**, centre, **t** 05 65 31 60 19 (€). Eight simple rooms and a little restaurant (€€€–€€).

Le Café du Monde, old train station, **t** 05 65 24 20 76 (€€). A restaurant famous for miles around, serving a variety of local cuisine and, on Friday and Saturday evenings, dishes from a different 'destination' around the world – perhaps Russia, or China. There are often excellent live music events, too, with the emphasis squarely on blues. *Closed Nov.*

3 Cahors

Cahors

Towards Cahors the country changes, and has something of a savage aspect; yet houses are seen everywhere, and one-third of the area is under vines. That town is bad.

Arthur Young, *Travels in France* (1787–89)

The immediate surroundings of Cahors are some of the most discouraging landscapes in all France. In winter, the barren grey *causse* hills that glower over the town appear desert-like and eerie, and in summer they don't significantly improve. The anomic clutter of the newer parts of town matches them well. But persevere – in the middle is a medieval city of surprising subtlety and character. Its star attraction is the Pont Valentré, which, as any Frenchman will tell you, is the most beautiful bridge on this planet.

History

A man from Cahors is a *Cadurcien*, just to remind us the capital of the Lot *département* began as *Divona Cadurcorum*. Divona was the name of the sacred spring that still flows under the riverside cliffs, or perhaps of the Celtic goddess who presided over it. Cadurcorum refers to the Cadurcii, the fierce local tribe who probably had their capital here before the Romans arrived. Under Roman rule, Divona Cadurcorum was famous for exporting linen; it boasted an aqueduct, well-appointed public baths, and a theatre with room for 1,000. It isn't known whether any of these were still working when the town became embroiled in a civil war among the Franks in the 570s and got thoroughly trashed. Fortunately, not long after, a strong-willed bishop named Desiderius took matters in hand; even more fortunately, this Gallo-Roman gentleman, later to be declared St Didier, was also royal treasurer to King Dagobert, and he found enough loose change to resurrect Cahors at a time when very little was being built anywhere else in Gaul. By the time he died, *c.* 650, Cahors's first cathedral was well underway, and its Roman bridges and aqueduct were restored.

Cahors

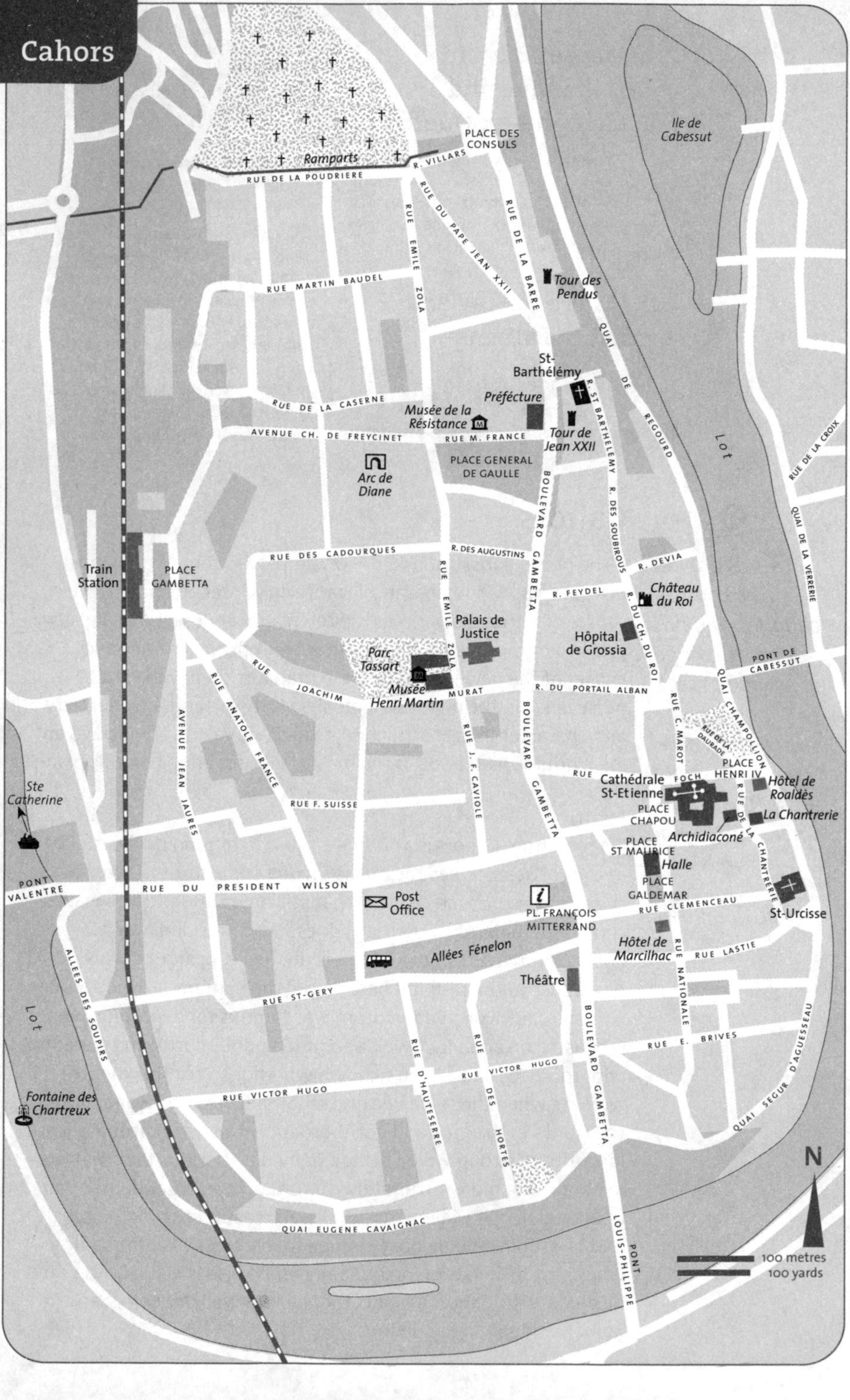
Ramparts
Rue de la Poudriere
R. Villars
Place des Consuls
Rue du Pape Jean XXII
Rue Emile Zola
Rue de la Barre
Ile de Cabessut
Rue Martin Baudel
Tour des Pendus
Quai de Regourd
St-Barthélémy
Préfécture
Rue de la Caserne
Musée de la Résistance
Tour de Jean XXII
Avenue Ch. de Freycinet
Rue M. France
R. St Barthelemy
Place General de Gaulle
Arc de Diane
Boulevard Gambetta
R. des Soubirous
Lot
Rue de la Croix
Quai de la Verrerie
Rue des Cadourques
R. des Augustins
R. Devia
Train Station
Place Gambetta
R. Feydel
Château du Roi
R. du Ch. du Roi
Palais de Justice
Hôpital de Grossia
Parc Tassart
Pont de Cabessut
Rue Joachim Murat
Musée Henri Martin
R. du Portail Alban
Quai Champollion
Avenue Jean Jaures
Rue Anatole France
Rue J. F. Caviole
Rue C. Marot
Rue de la Daurade
Place Henri IV
Rue Foch
Cathédrale St-Etienne
Hôtel de Roaldès
Ste Catherine
Rue F. Suisse
Place Chapou
La Chantrerie
Archidiaconé
Rue de la Chantrerie
Place St Maurice
Halle
Pont Valentre
Rue du President Wilson
Post Office
Place Galdemar
Rue Clemenceau
St-Urcisse
Pl. François Mitterrand
Hôtel de Marcilhac
Rue Nationale
Rue Lastie
Allées Fénelon
Allees des Soupirs
Théâtre
Rue St-Gery
Rue d'Hauteserre
Rue des Hortes
Rue E. Brives
Quai Segur d'Aguesseau
Rue Victor Hugo
Fontaine des Chartreux
N
Quai Eugene Cavaignac
Pont Louis-Philippe
100 metres
100 yards

Getting to and around Cahors

Cahors' **train** station is near the centre, with direct services north to Gourdon, Souillac, Brive, Limoges and Paris, and south to Montauban and Toulouse. The train station is also the base for SNCF **buses** for Fumel and Figeac.

A little **tourist train** can trundle you around old Cahors, from near Pont Valentré, **t** 05 65 30 16 55, Easter–Sept.

Ask at the tourist office (*see* p.321) about ways to explore the Lot from Cahors. They include Safaraid's frequent 90min **riverboat** excursions from Pont Valentré (April–Nov), **t** 05 65 35 98 88. Babou Marine, **t** 05 65 30 08 99, *www.baboulene-jean.fr*, hires out **houseboats** for up to 12 people, and the aerodrome can organize **tourist flights**, **t** 05 65 53 90 58.

Further insults were in store – unwelcome visits by Vikings, Magyars and Arabs – but Cahors survived to find a brilliant and surprising career in the Middle Ages. The bishops still ruled, and did quite well for themselves, gradually gaining control of most of the Lot valley and becoming a factor that even the French and the counts of Toulouse had to take into consideration. Under their stable rule, the town began to learn to make money. The founders of Cahors's great foray into modern capitalism seem to have been Italians, 'Lombard' merchants who fled north to the relative safety of the bishops' domains from the terrors of the Albigensian crusade in the early 1200s; among the old palaces of Cahors you will find family names such as Dominici, Issalda and Grossia.

Throughout the 13th century these families and their native colleagues perfected their merchant finance and moneylending skills. They became familiar figures in all the trade fairs and business centres of Europe, so prominent – and predatory – that *Caorsin* became a common word for a usurer. Dante mentions them in the *Inferno* (Canto XI, 50); he put the Caorsins down with the people of Sodom in the third circle of hell. No doubt they laughed all the way to the bank. The king of France needed them, whenever he was in the mood for a campaign; the noblemen and the Church needed them too, and they got on just fine with the town's bishops. In 1270, the bishop granted the merchants a city charter, establishing rule by elected consuls.

As their wealth piled up, the merchants translated it into impressive palaces. Cahors's golden age, which lasted until the Hundred Years' War, produced not only these but a new set of fortifications, magnificent bridges, a university and the completion of the cathedral. Even more money flowed in after 1316, when a Cahors merchant's son named Jacques Duèze became Pope John XXII. John reigned from Avignon, where he acquired a sinister reputation as an alchemist. One story has him quarrelling with a competitor in sorcery, another bishop of Cahors no less, and eventually having the man burned at the stake for trying to do him in with wax voodoo dolls and potions made of spiders and toads.

Cahors suffered from the Hundred Years' War only indirectly. Its new walls were good enough to keep the English out, but the disruption of trade meant a slow but inexorable strangling of its business affairs. The refined little city carried on, making a modest living off its rents and the wine trade and devoting its energies to higher things. During the Renaissance, Cahors had a reputation as a cultured place, full of academies and libraries; its university lasted until 1751, when the jealous scholars of Toulouse succeeded in having it merged into their own.

During the religious wars, Cahors with its still-influential bishops remained stoutly Catholic. In 1560 there occurred a bloody massacre of Protestants; 20 years later, Henri IV stormed the city, and in retaliation the future king allowed his troops to give the place a thorough sacking.

Not much has happened since then, but there are signs that Cahors, after 600 years of decline and somnolence, is starting to look ahead to a more economically active future, chiefly thanks to to improved communications: the Paris–Toulouse A20 motorway was completed in 2003.

Orientation: Walking Cahors

Cahors's charms are discreet, and most tourists have little time for them. But a bit of knowledge and a careful eye can make this well-preserved and genteel medieval town come alive. First, pay no attention to the broad and leafy Boulevard Gambetta, pretending to be the centre of town. This is merely the course of the city's old walls; everything of interest is squeezed between it and the river. Instead, for a panorama of Cahors's medieval skyline most people never see, start from across the river, over the Pont de Cabessut.

Long and narrow Cahors had a single main thoroughfare (Rue du Château du Roi north of the cathedral, Rue Nationale south of it). Along this are most of the merchants' palaces; to each side, the ranks of tiny alleys crowded with tall houses give an idea of how dense and urban the medieval town must have seemed. Many of these alleys are partially covered; if so they are not called *ruelles* but *botes*, a word meaning 'vaults' that is peculiar to Cahors. The medieval palaces, built in grey stone, are spare and squarish, with big arches facing the street for the business façades and elegant twinned windows on the family quarters upstairs; less imposing buildings were made *en colombage*, in half-timbering, and scores of these survive. In the 1400s, Cahors developed a distinct style of decoration, surrounding doors and windows with carved rosettes and *bâtons écotés* (raised mouldings). Another feature is the *soleiho*, a Venetian-style sun porch on the top storey (as in Figeac); in Renaissance palaces they are often made of brick arches and called *mirandes*.

The Poet of the Nipple

Cahors gave birth to several exceptional, obstinate men, with Pope John XXII and Léon Gambetta (*see* below) at the top of the list. A third was the poet Clément Marot (1495–1544), son of a Cadurcien mother and the Norman poet Jean Marot, *valet de chambre* of François Ier. Sent to Paris aged 11, Marot went into the service of the king's sister, Marguerite d'Angoulême, and soon made his mark at court for his elegant verse, if not for his personal charms; contemporaries described him as looking 'like a skinned rat'. Marguerite was known for protecting Protestants, and Clément Marot was often suspected of being one, especially in 1526 when he was chucked into prison for eating bacon during Lent. His eloquent plea to the king, the *Epître au roi*, got him out of the calaboose overnight, and the next year he succeeded his father as *valet de chambre*.

Although Marot remained faithful to the medieval forms of his father in his ballads and rondels, he was the first French poet to write in sonnets. When he got into trouble again in 1534, and was forced into exile in Italy, he regained favour with the invention of the *blason* (a short poem eulogizing an attribute of a lady) with his *Blason du beau tétin* ('to the beautiful nipple'). It was an immediate success: Clémont, 'the Prince of Poets', was welcomed back to court in 1536. But he was too honest to take much comfort in fashion; bored by the vast number of his imitators that cropped up, he wrote the *Contre-blason du laid tétin* ('anti-blason to the ugly nipple'), setting a new fad for indelicate satires. Then he published *L'Enfer*, inspired by his stay in prison and today considered his greatest work. At the time, however, it caused such an uproar that he was forced to leave France yet again, and for the last time: he died alone in Turin in 1544.

St-Etienne Cathedral and Around

A tour of Cahors should begin in **Place Chapou**, the elongated square in front of the cathedral, filled with vegetable stands on many weekday mornings. Note the bank that has restored an old painted shop sign over its modern façade: *Bazar Genois – Gambetta Jeune et Cie*. This Italian immigrant grocer earned his immortality for being the father of Léon Gambetta, Cahors's great native son. As a lawyer and politician, Gambetta was a strong opponent of the tyranny of Napoleon III. After France's defeat in 1870, he declared the Third Republic in Paris, and then dramatically escaped from the city in a balloon while the Prussians were besieging it. After that, he raised new armies in the south (though the Prussians whipped them too), and eventually became premier; all France mourned in 1882 when he accidentally killed himself while cleaning a gun. The covered market is just down the square.

Cathédrale St-Etienne
open daily roughly 9–7; adm (cloister)

The **cathedral of St-Etienne** provides a sober backdrop. Begun in the 10th century on the site of St Didier's original cathedral, this is the second of the domed churches of Périgord and Quercy, directly inspired by St-Etienne in Périgueux. Not completed until the 1400s, its western and eastern ends were completely rebuilt, resulting in a not unlovely architectural mongrel, a kind of Romanesque-on-Gothic sandwich. The severe façade, the typical broad tower-façade of a Quercy church writ large, was redone in the 14th century, and the original entrance was moved around to the side. The **north portal** is one of the finest in southern France. In the centre, Christ in a mandorla (oval panel) is flanked by angels tumbling down out of the heavens, and scenes of the martyrdom of St Stephen; below are the Virgin Mary and 10 apostles (there wasn't room for 12). Of greater interest are the borders and *modillons*, with a full complement of monsters, scenes of war and violence, and unusual decorative rose motifs that seem to prefigure the trimmings on Cahors's Renaissance palaces.

Once you're inside (through the main portal), turn around to see the finely drawn frescoes (*c.* 1320) high above the west door, a series of scenes from Genesis including the *Creation* and *Adam and Eve*. The other surviving original paintings are in an equally inconvenient spot, under the first of the two domes in the nave. These include figures of eight prophets, and in the centre the '*14 lapidateurs*' with their stones, ready to lapidate poor Stephen and ensure his status as the first Christian martyr. The large organ over the entrance has recently been restored and when in full throttle (the cathedral is a favourite concert hall) swells the domes with its magnificent sound.

In 1330 the original east end was replaced with a Gothic apse, an odd structure constructed on the plan of a pentagon that from the outside looks like a separate building. Inside, it contains some of the best of Cahors's sculptural work in its side chapels, done 1484–91. More of the same can be seen in the **cloister** (1509), which is lavishly spread with flowing Flamboyant decoration. Tragically, Henri IV's lads did a very thorough job of smashing up the capitals in 1580; however, enough remains, or has been restored, to allow you to appreciate one of the finest sculptural ensembles of the southwest. Note in one corner the winsome carved *Vierge des Litanies*. The carvings around the arches in the cloister's grassy centre have an M.C. Escher quality, metamorphosing from a leaf of curly kale into an ocean wave into a dog licking its legs. The **Chapelle St-Gausbert** contains what remains of the cathedral treasure, as well as 15th-century frescoes representing a not very dire *Last Judgement* .

Chapelle St-Gausbert
open June–Sept Mon–Sat 10–12.30 and 3–6 exc public hols

The back door of the cloister leads you to the handsome Renaissance ensemble of the **Archidiaconé**. Through here, in Rue de la Chantrerie, the growers of Cahors wine have beautifully restored the 13th-century **La Chantrerie**, the building containing the cathedral chapter's wine press, and made it into a **wine museum**, with art exhibitions thrown in.

Musée du Vin
t 05 65 23 99 70; open July and Aug Tues–Sat 9.30–1 and 2.30–7

Quartier des Soubirous

To the north of the cathedral extends what was the wealthy merchants' quarter in medieval times; *soubirous* means superior, for the way the area climbs uphill towards the citadel. It has been neglected for centuries, and only recently have the Cadurciens begun to restore some of its old mansions; a few of the old bankers' counting houses now hold swish shops and antique dealers. **Rue du Château-du-Roi**, the spine of the neighbourhood, is an elegant street reminiscent of Siena or Perugia. Its most impressive façade is at No.102, the 13th-century **Hôpital de Grossia**. Take the alley to the right of it, the Bote de Fouilhac, which will bring you to a typically hidden Cahors surprise, a tiny, lovely courtyard decorated with modern murals and a musical fountain that works about half the time. Across from the Hôpital, the **Château du Roi** was one of Cahors' grandest palaces in the 1300s, though it was thoroughly wrecked in the 19th century when the state converted it into a prison and replaced the façade; the tall donjon inside, visible only from the riverfront, is all that survives.

Here the street changes its name to Rue des Soubirous, and continues its way to the northern edge of the city, with the austere **church of St-Barthélémy** and the adjacent **Palais Duèze**. Much degraded by the centuries, this was built by John XXII for his family; he also rebuilt the church, where he had been baptized. The best surviving parts can be seen from Boulevard Gambetta, including the solid and graceful **Tour de Jean XXII**, and, further north, the Barbacane with its massive **Tour des Pendus**, 'Tower of the Hanged Men'. At the top of the boulevard, by the large parking lot of Place Général de Gaulle, the **Musée de la Résistance** has six rooms covering the role of the Resistance in the Lot from the beginning to the end of the war; most of the staff were themselves members.

Musée de la Résistance
t 05 65 22 14 25; open daily 2–6

Opposite the Tour des Pendus you can see the Ile de Cabessut, an island made into a big waterpark, **Archipel**, with a huge pool, whirlpool, children's area, beach and so on.

Archipel
t 05 65 35 31 38; open daily mid-June–mid-Sept 11–8; adm

The Badernes

This was the popular quarter of the city, south of the cathedral, though it too had its share of palaces, mostly along **Rue Nationale**, the southern continuation of Rue du Château-du-Roi. For one example, at the beginning of the street, there is the lovely Baroque carved door at the **Hôtel de Marcilhac** (No.116). The streets to the left off Rue Nationale are worth a digression, with a large number of well-restored half-timbered houses, and a few medieval palaces along Rue Lastié. The neighbourhood's church, **St-Urcisse**, stands at the end of Rue Clemenceau near the river. The 13th-century statue of the Virgin on the façade is one of the oldest sculptural works in Cahors; if the church is open, don't miss the set of carved capitals with fond naïve scenes of Adam and Eve and the life of Christ.

Pont Valentré

If anything is a sign of opulence in a medieval city, it's the bridges. Cahors had three, where one would have sufficed, and the two that have disappeared were almost as good as this one. The city demolished them in 1868 and 1907. Cahors in its decadence cared very little for its ancient monuments; the Roman theatre of *Divona Cadurcorum* survived to the 19th century, when the city fathers had it destroyed to make way for the railway.

The Pont Valentré (at the end of Rue du Président Wilson) survived because it was out of the way and carried little traffic. But it was built well enough for cars to continue to cross over it until 1996, when a new bridge, out of sight down-river, was built to replace it. Now you can happily cross without being squashed like a bug. Begun in 1308, and financed with the help of Pope John, the bridge nevertheless took nearly a century to complete. With the Hundred Years' War in full swing, it isn't surprising that defence became the major consideration. The three towers that look so picturesque are three rings of defences to keep the English out; each had its portcullis, and slits for archers and boiling oil.

Wherever in southern France you find a medieval bridge, you can be sure the Devil had something to do with it. Here, according to legend, this master engineer made a deal for the soul of the Pont Valentré's builder in return for his aid. The builder tricked him by giving him a sieve with which to fetch water, but the Devil got his revenge by coming back each night to steal a cornerstone of the central tower, which had to be replaced every following day. In the 19th century, restorers added the stone with the Devil carved on it to remind us of the tale (on the east side of the tower, near the top).

Nearby, on the riverbank, the medieval **Fontaine des Chartreux** is fed by the underground streams of the *causse*; explorations by archaeological divers, who discovered hundreds of ancient coins in the depths, seem to confirm the popular belief that this was Divona, the spring of ancient times around which Cahors grew up.

There isn't much else to see in the newer quarters of town. In Rue Emile Zola, just north of Rue du Président Wilson, the 17th-century bishop's palace now contains the **Musée Henri Martin**, with a permanent collection of canvases of the Lot by *pointilliste* painter Henri Martin, a native of Toulouse who lived and painted in Labastide-du-Vert, a village west of town; it also holds historical and archaeological collections relating to Cahors and the Quercy, and temporary exhibitions. There's a pretty little park behind it, with a playground and a pair of swans. Nearby, on Boulevard Gambetta you'll find an appropriately Flamboyant monument to Cahors' Republican hero, pointing dramatically, perhaps accusingly, north towards Paris. The only reminder of the Roman town is the '**Arc de Diane**' in a schoolground, visible from Avenue Freycinet; this fragment of stone and brick was a part of the municipal baths.

Musée Henri Martin
t *05 65 20 88 66; open Mon and Wed–Sat 11–6, Sun 2–6; adm*

In recent years Cahors has become very proud of its 250 **gardens**, winning prizes at national and even international level; ask at the tourist office (*see* opposite) about its 'Secret Gardens' tour, which is an alternative way of seeing the sites in the old town.

Castles around Cahors

North of Cahors, visible off the N20 in St-Pierre-Lafeuille, the imposing **Château de Roussillon** is surrounded by a dry moat. It was begun in the 12th century and rebuilt in subsequent centuries as one of the city's chief defences. Cannibalized for its stone in the 19th century, it still makes an impressive sight and has been partly restored by its current owner.

Château de Roussillon
t 05 65 36 87 05; open by appt for minimum of 25

Even more striking is the **Château de Mercuès**, prominent, or rather unavoidable, on its hilltop over the D911 5km northwest of Cahors (note the 'medieval' railway tunnel beneath it). Begun in its present form in the 15th century as a stronghold and pleasure dome of the bishops of Cahors, this castle suffered sackings by the English and the Protestants. In 1563, the latter smoked the bishop out. He was caught climbing out of a window and made to ride backwards on a donkey dressed in mock papal regalia before being rescued; his embarrassment was so acute that he died shortly after. The castle burned in the 17th century; when a plague hit Cahors, the bishop offered hundreds of refugees shelter at Mercuès – in exchange for rebuilding his spread. The bishops gave Mercuès up in 1909, and since then it's settled down to its present career as the poshest hotel in the whole *département* (see p.322). It owes much of its present storybook appearance to 19th-century restorations; any bishop would be proud of the vast wine cellars.

Tourist Information in Cahors

ⓘ **Cahors >**
Place François Mitterrand, **t** 05 65 53 20 65, www. mairie-cahors.fr and www.quercy-tourisme. com/cahors.

Ask at the **tourist office** about guided tours of the town, some at night in summer.

Market Days in Cahors

There's a **general market** on Place de la Cathédrale on Wednesday and Saturday mornings, plus a **covered market** Monday–Saturday. The first and third Saturday of the month sees a big *foire* in Place F. Mitterrand, and on Saturday mornngs the Verrière de la Halle hosts a **fattened duck and goose/truffle market**, Nov–Mar.

Where to Stay in and around Cahors

Cahors ✉ 46000

★★★Le Terminus, 5 Avenue Charles de Freycinet, opposite station, **t** 05 65 53 32 00, www.balandre.com (€€€€–€€).

A hotel that's been in business for at least a century. Charming, resolutely retro and ivy-covered, it has cosy rooms with TVs, disabled access, a garage and Cahors's best restaurant (see p.322). Closed 2nd half Nov.

La Grange de Jaillac, Pelacoy, north of town on N20, **t** 05 65 36 02 36, www.grange-de-jaillac.com (€€). A converted 19th-century barn with exposed stone walls and beams, spacious and calm rooms and a pool. Meals are available by request.

★★★La Chartreuse, Rue St-Georges, **t** 05 65 35 17 37 (€€–€). A similar place to Le Terminus, with better prices, overlooking the Lot by the spring of the same name, not far from the Pont Valentré. Some of the modern rooms are air-conditioned, and there's a pool and a good restaurant (€€€–€€).

★★L'Escargot, 5 Bd Gambetta, **t** 05 65 35 07 66, http://perso.orange.fr/calrou (€). Simple but comfy rooms within the big stone walls of the old Palais Duèze, including two for families. The restaurant serves regional favourites.

****Le Melchior**, Place de la Gare, **t** 05 65 35 03 38, *www.lemelchior.com* (€). A functional hotel with a restaurant (€€–€). *Closed Christmas–New Year and Sun out of season; restaurant Sun lunch.*

Camping Rivière de Cabessut, near Archipel waterpark (*see* p.319), **t** 05 65 30 06 30, *www.cabessut.com* (€). A three-star campsite with mobile homes to let. *Closed Oct–Mar.*

Pradines ✉ 46090

Château de la Roussille, **t** 05 65 21 23 37, *www.chateauroussille.com* (€€). A classy 18th-century château rebuilt in the 1930s, in a large wooded hilltop garden just west of Cahors, with huge rooms with period furnishings and balconies. There's also a pool and a billiards room. Booking is a must out of season. *Closed mid-Nov–mid-Mar.*

****Le Clos Grand**, Labéraudie, **t** 05 65 35 04 39, *www.clos-grand-com* (€). The pick of the two stars – a Logis de France country inn with cosy rooms, a large garden and a pool. The restaurant (€€€–€€) serves hearty meals. *Closed several wks in year (call for details); restaurant Sat lunch.*

Mercuès ✉ 46090

******Château de Mercuès**, **t** 05 65 20 00 01, *www.chateaudemercues.com* (€€€€€–€€€€). A Relais et Châteaux hotel on a spur above the valley. Rooms (two in towers) have marble baths and canopy beds, and there are hanging gardens with a pool and tennis courts. The restaurant (€€€€) is equally classy,; the vast cellars feature owner Georges Vigouroux's celebrated stock of wines, including his prize-winning Château de Mercuès 1990. *Hotel closed Nov–Easter; restaurant also Mon, and lunch exc Sun.*

Le Mas Azemar, Rue du Mas-de-Vinssou, **t** 05 65 30 96 85, *www.masazemar.com* (€€). An 18th-century farmhouse converted into a beautiful B&B, at the foot of the mighty castle. Meals can be booked ahead.

Where to Eat in and around Cahors

Cahors ✉ 46000

Le Balandre, Le Terminus (*see* p.321), **t** 05 65 53 32 00 (€€€€–€€€). An elegant dining room dating from 1910, making a fine setting for a range of delectable Quercy dishes prepared with a twist, including a famous starter of poached eggs with escalope of foie gras and truffle sauce. They're accompanied by bottles from an outstanding wine cellar. *Closed Sun, Mon lunch and public hols in season, Mon eve in winter.*

Auberge du Vieux Cahors, 144 Rue St Urcisse, **t** 05 65 35 06 05 (€€€–€€). Seasonal classics served in a handsome 15th-century house.

La Garenne, St-Henri, 5km north of town on N20, **t** 05 65 35 40 67 (€€€–€€). A 19th-century farm where you can feast on imaginative, well-prepared land and sea dishes such as scallops with truffles and beef Rossini (with foie gras and truffles). *Closed Wed, plus Mon and Tues eves in winter.*

Au Fil des Douceurs, off Quai de la Verrerie, **t** 05 65 22 13 04 (€€€–€). A good place for romantic evenings on the Lot – literally, since this is a floating restaurant across the Pont du Cabessut from the old centre. Try the regional and fish dishes. *Closed Sun (exc lunch in summer) and Mon.*

L'Ô à la Bouche, 134 Rue St Urcisse, **t** 05 65 35 65 69 (€€€–€). A touch of class near the cathedral, with elegant dishes designed, as the name of the restaurant suggests, to make your mouth water. *Closed Sun and Mon.*

Le Marché, 27 Place Jean-Jacques Chapou, **t** 05 65 35 27 27 (€€). A new restaurant situated near the covered market and specializing in dishes featuring market produce.

Le Lamparo, 76 Rue Clemenceau, **t** 05 65 35 25 93 (€). A huge two-level restaurant that looks like a small café from the outside, located opposite the covered market. It's popular at lunchtime, so come early or book ahead. The long menu features generous portions of regional classics and good pasta and pizzas. There are also three beautifully decorated modern B&B suites (€€–€). *Closed Sun.*

Chez Ngo, Place des Consuls, **t** 05 65 22 17 30 (€). The best Vietnamese in town, with alfresco dining in summer. *Closed Mon.*

Crêperie au Cœur du Lot, 71 Rue-du-Château du Roi, **t** 05 65 22 30 67 (€).

A good place for crêpes, omelettes, salads and wonderful ice-cream desserts, popular with families. *Closed Sun and Mon.*

Marie Colline, 173 Rue Clemenceau, **t** 05 65 35 59 96 (€). A rare vegetarian restaurant, offering two *plats du jour* plus a good choice of starters and magnificent desserts. In summer there are tables on the pavement. *Closed eves, Mon and Aug.*

St-Pierre-Lafeuille ✉ 46090

*****La Bergerie**, north of Cahors on N20, **t** 05 65 36 82 82, *www.labergerie-lot.com* (€€€–€€). Delightful modernized versions *of cuisine quercynoise* that attract hungry Cadurciens, together with guestrooms (€€–€) and a swimming pool. *Closed Sun, Mon and Tues eves, early Jan–early Feb, and several wks in Oct.*

South of the River Lot: Quercy Blanc

Quercy shows a markedly different, drier face south of the river, less hilly and forested, with fewer villages and farms. Conspicuous in the open countryside are the slopes where the poor soil has been washed away to expose the pale limestone underneath; this is also used to build the characteristic houses and simple Romanesque chapels, giving 'White Quercy' its name. Beyond the Provence-like sunbaked grandeur of its white hills, its fields of sunflowers and vineyards of Chasselas table grapes, attractions are few; if the sun isn't shining, it can be haunting, impatiently waiting its own Thomas Hardy to do it justice.

Montpezat-de-Quercy

Montpezat-de-Quercy, a half-hour due south of Cahors and west of the N20, may be the most rewarding destination in this area. This thoroughly medieval village retains its gate and arcaded square, as well as plenty of half-timbered houses, many of which are finally getting a long-overdue restoration.

Montpezat grew up in the 10th century. In 1257, its lord Alphonse of Poitiers granted it a charter as a free town, with rights to its own mill, a pigeon-house and an oil press. In the 1300s, the town was home to a dynasty of churchmen named Des Près. Well-connected at the papal court at Avignon, they brought one of the popes' architects home to build the **Collégiale St-Martin** on a shady promenade at the edge of town. It makes a handsome setting for the Des Près Carrara marble tombs and the rich treasure they accumulated, including glittering medieval reliquaries and some lovely carved alabaster plaques from England. The *collégiale*'s real prize, however, is the series of tapestries hung around the apse, perfectly preserved 16th-century Flemish works commissioned by Jean Des Près that tell the *Life of St Martin of Tours* with the colour and vivid directness of a comic strip. Woven to fit the very spot where they are displayed, each of the 16 scenes is accompanied by an Old French quatrain. A few minutes from Montpezat, off the D38 towards Castelnau, the woodland church of **Notre-Dame de Saux**

Getting around the Quercy Blanc

Raynal **buses** (**t** 05 65 23 28 28, *www.raynal-voyages.fr*) from Cahors serve Castelnau-Montratier.

has 14th-century frescoes of the legends of saints George and Catherine, the childhood of Jesus and the Crucifixion (the key is held at Montpezat *mairie*).

Castelnau-Montratier and Montcuq

To the northwest of Montpezat, **Castelnau-Montratier** had the honour of being razed to the ground in 1214 by Simon de Montfort during the Albigensian crusade. Rebuilt soon after as a *bastide*, it has an unusual, triangular arcaded market square and a handful of white stone houses from the 15th century. Castelnau's pride and its symbol, however, are the three venerable stone **windmills** on the hilltop above the village. Two centuries ago, when these were built, almost every village without a dependable river had them. Castelnau's are rare survivals; one, the **Moulin de Boisse**, is a historical monument. They provided a backup for the 13th-century watermill, the **Moulin de Brousse**, which is still in operation with a 3.6m waterfall.

Moulin de Boisse
visits by arrangement with tourist office, *see opposite*

Moulin de Brousse
t 05 65 21 95 81; visits by appt with miller

You can also poke around the **Roman ruins** of a sanctuary or village – no one is quite sure – among the weeds and wildflowers at the **Moulin du Souquet**, or play a round or two of golf at the

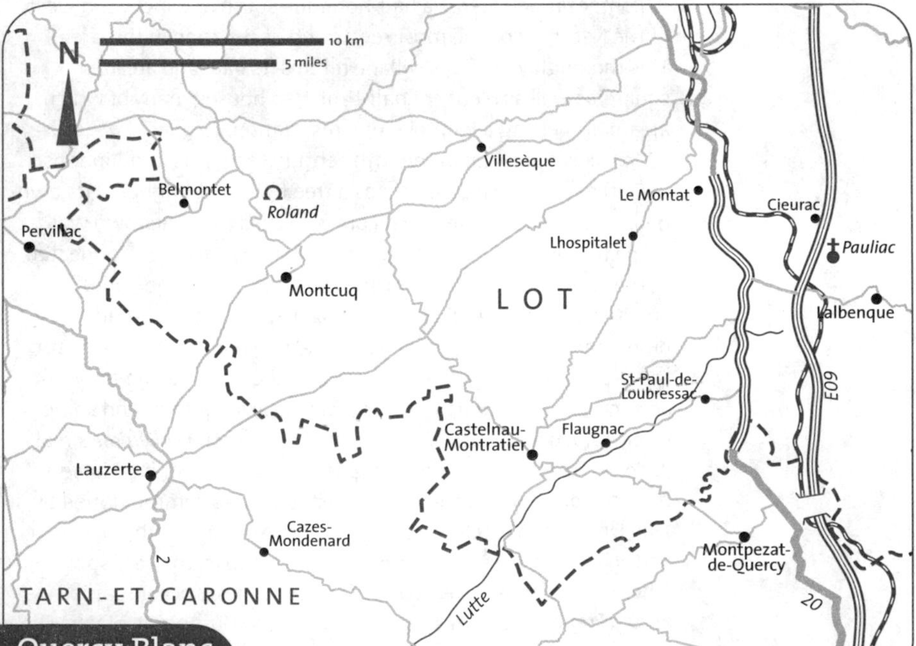

Quercy Blanc

Golf des Roucous
t 05 63 95 83 70, www.golfdesroucous.com

beautiful course in nearby Sauveterre, the nine-hole **Golf des Roucous**; it also has a swimming pool, a tennis court and some bungalows to rent. And don't miss **Flaugnac**, a striking medieval hilltop village just east of Castelnau, or **St-Paul-de-Loubressac**, both perched over the valley of the Lupte.

To the north of Castelnau stretches an open, strangely empty part of Quercy Blanc. It was probably busier in Neolithic times; a number of tumuli can be seen, for instance at **Lhospitalet** and **Villesèque**. The people of the largest village, **Montcuq**, on the D653, claim that their village's name comes from the Latin *Montis Cuci* – Mount Cuckoo. Do pronounce the Q, unless you want to say 'My Arse' and hear the French giggle; a range of silly postcards, most of which are sold outside the village, exploits the joke, although the villagers aren't quite as desperate as the good folk of Condom, just south in the Gers.

Tour Comtale
open late June–early Aug daily 2–6

Montcuq's 26m landmark, visible for miles around, is the 12th-century **Tour Comtale**, all that remains of the castle dismantled in 1229 by Saint Louis. Impressive as it looks, with walls 2m thick, this donjon wasn't strong enough to keep out Simon de Montfort; he called here too, and sacked the village. There are frescoes in Montcuq's 14th–15th-century **church of St-Hilaire**, with its striking octagonal bell tower. In **Rouilhac** just to the south there are remarkable frescoes from the 12th century on the subject of Original Sin; one of the hamlet's main attractions in summer is a clean and pleasant *plan d'eau* with a playground.

Grotte de Roland
t 05 65 22 99 90; 1hr guided visits July and Aug daily 10–12.30 and 2.30–5.30; 2nd half June and 1st half Sept daily 2.30–5.30; May–mid-June and 2nd half Sept Sat and Sun 2.30–5; adm

Distillerie de Lavande de Servat
t 05 65 31 90 17; visits July and Aug Wed 9.30–12 and 2–5; rest of year by appt

Three kilometres to the north on the D28, the pretty stalactite **Grotte de Roland**, complete with an underground lake, was a favourite abode of prehistoric bears and hyenas; it includes a small **museum** on the subject, and the guide makes sure that visitors see every single scratch. The **Servat lavender distillery** in nearby **Belmontet** can be toured.

ⓘ Montcuq >>
La Promenade, t 05 65 22 94 04

ⓘ Castelnau-Montratier >
27 Rue G Clemenceau, t 05 65 21 84 39, www.cc-castelnau-montratier.fr

Market Days in the Quercy Blanc

Castelnau-Montratier: Sunday, plus Wednesday evening in summer.
Montcuq: Sunday, and Thursday in July and Aug, plus fairs on 2nd Wednesday of month.

Where to Stay and Eat in the Quercy Blanc

Castelnau-Montratier ✉ 46170

****Les Trois Moulins**, t 05 65 21 92 95, *www.hotel-restaurant-les-trois-moulins.com* (€). A modern option with the benefit of a swimming pool and its own restaurant (€€–€). *Closed Fri and Sun in winter.*

St-Paul-de-Loubressac ✉ 46170

***La Madeleine**, t 05 65 21 98 08 (€). Simple rooms, a big garden for kids to run around in, and a restaurant (€€–€). *Closed Sat, plus Fri in winter and several wks outside high season; restaurant also Sun eve out of season.*

Montcuq ✉ 46800

****Hôtel du Parc**, Route de Fumel, t 05 65 31 81 82, *www.hotel-restaurant-du-parc.fr* (€€–€). A country inn in a pretty garden, with good food (€€). *Closed mid-Oct–Mar; restaurant lunch.*

Café de France, 5 Place de la République, **t** 05 65 22 90 29. An atmospheric bar and bistro serving food from across the south of France, including Catalan and Basque dishes (€€–€). *Closed Mon eve, and several wks out of season.*

On Dirait le Sud, 6 Allée des Platanes, **t** 05 65 31 47 68 (€). A bar-restaurant run by a Brit chef raised in Catalonia, who changes his menu weekly according to the season, and offers a special €10 menu to passing pilgrims.

Down the Lot: Cahors to Touzac

After Cahors the Lot valley becomes lush and fertile, the heart of the Cahors wine region. Among these landscapes, the river decides it is in no particular hurry to get to the sea, and winds around in big lazy loops. It contains more than its share of modest attractions, as well as plenty of wine châteaux and country inns.

Cahors to Caix

Although the D911 is the obvious route, the scenery is much better near the river, carpeted with vineyards. You have several options, none straightforward, but then again, neither is the river.

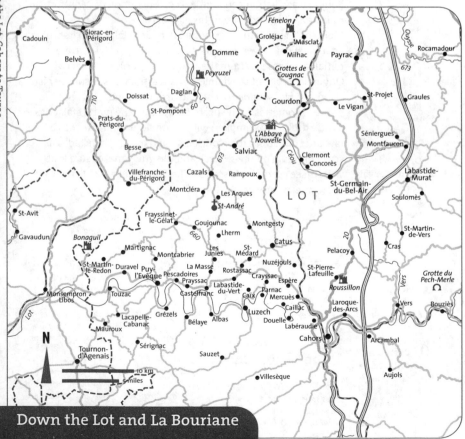

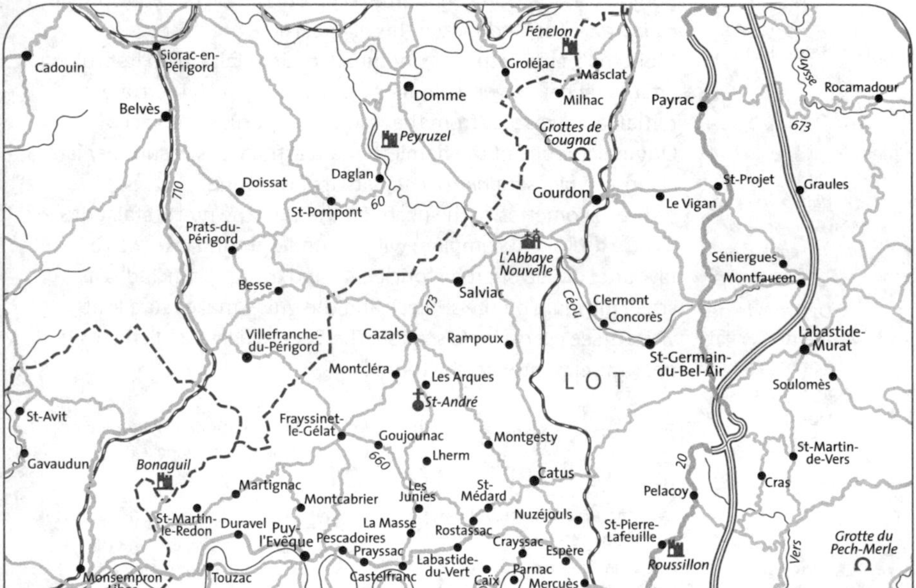

Down the Lot and La Bouriane

Getting around between Cahors and Puy-l'Evêque

There's a regular SNCF **bus** from Cahors train station to Monsempron-Libos west of Puy-l'Evêque, with stops at Luzech and Prayssac. You can hire **bikes** from Mundial Sport in Prayssac, **t** 05 65 30 60 86, June–Aug.

For **boat** hire and excursions, contact Crown Blue Line in Douelle (**t** 05 65 20 08 79), who hire out comfortable houseboats sleeping up to 12. In Caïx, Navilot (**t** 05 65 20 18 19) organizes excursions up the river, with lunch, and hires out *gabares*, canoes, kayaks, pedalos and motorboats by the day or half-day.

If you're in no hurry, leave Cahors via **Pradines**, now a suburb of the town but once a village in its own right, with an 11th–12th-century Romanesque church, **St-Martial**, containing a polychrome statue of the Virgin from the same period. The road then rises and skirts the river and heads west to **Douelle** ('barrel stave'), a favourite river port for barges in the old days, when all the cargo was loaded into enormous barrels. Douelle has seen better days but has been more colourful since Didier Comizo painted the 122m quay wall with a mural on the Creation, wine and humankind. The village has the Lot's **Ecole de Parapente**, if you want to learn to paraglide.

Ecole de Parapente
t 05 65 30 78 20

Cross the narrow suspension bridge in Douelle and then head towards Mercuès via **Caillac**, passing by way of two exceptional wine estates: the handsome Renaissance château, **La Grézette**, overlooking a prestigious vineyard that produces the most expensive *vin de Cahors* of all, the *Pigeonnier*; and a bit further north, the 12th-century **Château Les Bouysses**, donated by its builder, Raymond de Lard, to the Cistercians, who made it a priory (a rather nice one with an orangery) until the Revolution, when the Count of Mosbourg purchased it and made it a wine business, and replaced the chapel with a *chai*. There are art exhibitions in the summer, excellent *vin de Cahors, bien sûr*, and a four-bedroom house to rent (May–Oct). Caillac's Romanesque **church** is also worth a stop for its foursquare belltower and 15th-century porch, with carvings, including Adam and Eve and floral motifs.

Château Les Bouysses
t 05 65 20 08 77; visits by appt

At **Mercuès** (*see* p.321), take the D911 west through **Espère**, 'a town called Hope' here in the Arkansas of France, and a noted speed trap. The D811 rises up the *causse* to Fred Flintstone's job site, the stone quarries of **Crayssac,** with neat piles of stones for sale along the road. A sign on the right, just past the quarries, indicates the **Plage aux Pterosaures**, where in 1995 workers were surprised to find fossils of winged dinosaurs, crocodiles and others going back 140 million years, left *in situ*. A museum is planned.

Plage aux Pterosaures
open July and Aug, call Catus tourist office (t 05 65 20 86 40) for hrs

Turn south here past Crayssac church to the belvedere and narrow corniche road that loops down towards the river to **Caïx**, with a huge panoramic view over the valley. In summer Queen Marguerite of Denmark, who married local boy Henri de Montpezat, stays at the 17th-century family château; surrounding vineyards produce the wine served at the royal table in Copenhagen. Caïx also has an early Romanesque church with good naïve carvings.

The prince consort's father, Comte André de Montpezat, was a rice planter in Vietnam before returning to the Lot to become a founding member of the Côtes d'Olt *vin de Cahors* Cooperative in **Parnac**, the next village west, which still bottles the count's label.

Next along the river, **St-Vincent Rive d'Olt** has a 16th-century church with many original fittings; nearby, **Marcayrac** has a curious tall **menhir** or *pierre levée* in the woods, pierced with natural holes.

Vin de Cahors (*www.vindecahors.com*)

Wine historians rate the deep crimson, full-bodied 'black' wine of Cahors as one of the last 'real' French wines, not drastically changed since the day Julius Caesar sent amphorae back to Rome after his victory over the Gauls at Uxellodunum. It went down so well in Rome that by the next century Italian vintners were whining about the competition, which in those pre-EU days resulted in an order from Emperor Domitian to uproot Cahors's vineyards, in AD 96. The vines were restored in 276 by a prince named Probus; they prospered, and in 1152 they became part of Eleanor of Aquitaine's dowry when she wed Henry Plantagenet. When John XXII of Cahors become pope at Avignon he further boosted the reputation of the wine by declaring it the papal communion wine. François I planted Cahors vines at Fontainebleau, and Peter the Great, finding *vin de Cahors* soothed his ulcer, planted vines in Azerbaijan along the Black Sea, which to this day produces its very own *Caorskoïe Vino*.

Knocked out in the 1870s by a phylloxera epidemic, Cahors wasn't replanted as quickly as other French wines. In 1947 a slow revival began with the founding of the excellent **Côtes d'Olt Cooperative** in Parnac (**t** 05 65 30 71 86; *open Mon–Sat 9–6*), but it wasn't until after the vines froze in 1956 and '57 that wine-growers seriously began to replant the Cahors of yesteryear, at least 70% Cot Noir, or Malbec, mixed with Merlot for bouquet and roundness, and Tannat, the great enhancer of Auxerrois.

Their efforts were rewarded in 1971 with AOC status – partially thanks to the good offices of then president Georges Pompidou, who had a summer residence in Cajarc. The immediate result brought the wine a fleeting popularity, soon tarnished by greed and local feuds that produced many a dire bottle of plonk. In the 1990s, however, the wine enjoyed a great comeback (the 1999–2002 vintages were generally superb, and 2005 shows promise), thanks in part to director general of the Vendôme group (*www.chateau-lagrezette.tm.fr*) and Cahors wine-grower Alain Dominique Perrin (owner of the **Château La Grézette** in Caillac, **t** 05 65 20 07 42), who formed an association of châteaux-vineyards known as Les Seigneurs du Cahors. In order to ensure quality and to promote the wine, Côtes d'Olt are now closely aligned with trader Sud Ouest Millésimes. Also in Caillac, follow the signs to the friendly, family-run, award-winning **Domaine de Chantelle** (**t** 05 65 20 04 66), who produce an excellent *vin traditionnel* that never touches a splinter of oak.

If you want to do some serious wine exploring, pick up the free map to the vineyards and the leaflet *Le Livret du Vin de Cahors*, available at local tourist offices: nearly all (there are some 200 altogether now) welcome visitors who just drop in, but outside of summer it never hurts to ring ahead to make sure someone's running the shop. The less hoity-toity ones sell the most recent *millésimes* by petrol pump (*en vrac*) if you bring your own container; a good way to try over 100 different *crus* is to visit the *Fête du Vin de Cahors*, where the only expense is the special Cahors glass (contact Cahors tourist office for details; *see* p.321). In general, drink young, tannic Cahors with foie gras, duck, goose, meats in sauce, Roquefort cheese and charcuterie; a well-aged Cahors goes well with game dishes, red meats with wild mushrooms, and *cabécou* goat's cheese.

A leading member of Les Seigneurs is the **Château de Haute-Serre**, **t** 05 65 20 80 20, south of Cahors in Cieurac, where Georges Vigouroux has laboriously revived a famous medieval vineyard – planted not in the Lot valley as other post-phylloxera vines but on the traditional limestone *causses*, where the wines take much longer to mature. His gamble paid off: Haute-Serre today is one of the top wines of the *appellation*, and he's even built his own huge shop at the south end of Cahors at Roc de Lagasse, **L'Atrium**, **t** 05 65 20 80 90, as well as adding the Château de Mercuès and its highly rated vineyard to his empire and a couple of other properties (*www.g-vigouroux.fr*).

The oldest of the Cahors dynasties is now headed by the late Jean Jouffreau's daughter at Prayssac's **Clos de Gamot, t** 05 65 22 40 26, first recorded here in 1290 – a history traced in the frescoes in the cellars. The Jouffreaus have in their cellars the oldest known *vin de Cahors*, with bottles from the start of the 20th century; they also conserved Cahors stock predating the phylloxera scourge, which produced the exquisite '92 Vignes Centenaires. Besides the Clos de Gamot, the family also owns the elegant, early-17th-century **Château de Cayrou, t** 05 65 22 40 26, by the river in Puy-l'Evêque, where a botanist planted redwoods and other exotic trees 200 years ago. The wines are organic and, unusually, 100% Auxerrois. Another Cahors thoroughbred, on the plateau south of the river, comes from the immaculately maintained vineyards of the 17th-century **Château de Chambert** at Floressas, **t** 05 65 31 95 75, *www.chateaudechambert.com*; in the same area, **Domaine de Paillas, t** 05 65 36 58 28, also produces highly rated Cahors. Nearby, at Le Boulvé, Brits Mike and Sue Spring can explain how it's done over a tasting of their white, red and rose wine at the **Domaine Le Garinet, t** 05 65 31 96 43.

Every inch of the main road south of Puy-l'Evêque towards Lacapelle-Cabanac is covered with vines: **Clos Triguedina, t** 05 65 21 30 81, is considered by many the very best Cahors, while others favour its rival a bit further up, **Château du Cèdre, t** 05 65 36 53 87. Next to this, the charming Maradenne family's **Château Nozières, t** 05 65 36 52 73, is a local favourite – and they are one of the few in the area who produce loose (*en vrac*) as well as by the bottle. Close by, in Duravel, Stéphane and Véronique Aazemar produce one of the best up-and-coming Cahors, **Clos d'Un Jour, t** 05 65 36 56 01.

Luzech

West of Parnac, **Luzech** enjoys the most striking setting of the river villages, on a narrow isthmus where two loops of the Lot nearly meet – an even more extreme version of Cahors' own setting. Once one of the four baronies of Quercy, captured by Richard the Lionheart in 1188, Luzech began as a Gallo-Roman citadel. Some remains survive on the steep hill above the town at the **Oppidum d'Impernal**, once another Uxelludunum contender.

Musée Municipal Armand-Viré
t 05 65 20 17 27; open Feb–mid-June and mid-Sept–Oct Mon–Sat 10–12.30 and 3–6.30; mid-June–mid-Sept Mon–Sat 10–1 and 3–7; Nov–Jan Mon–Sat 10–12.30 and 3–6; but call ahead

Musée Ichnospace
t 05 65 30 72 32; open July and Aug Mon–Fri 11–1 and 3–7; adm

Below, medieval Luzech was held by its barons with the bishops of Cahors after the latter beat the local Cathars in the Albigensian crusade. Back then Luzech was defended at either end by castles, which successfully repelled every English siege in the Hundred Years' War. The barons' castle is gone, but what remains of medieval Luzech gathers itself under the stout ***donjon épiscopal*** (or *Tour de l'Impernal*), all that survives of the bishops' fortress. In the village centre, the beautiful 13th-century **Maison des Consuls** houses the *syndicat d'initiative* and the small **Musée Municipal Armand-Viré**, with some Gallo-Roman finds from the *oppidum*, including a model of Trajan's column. The **Musée Ichnospace** has dinosaur fossils and footprints.

The wide square that carries the main D8 road through the village was once a canal, cutting off the loop of the river and dividing the village from its *bourg*. For a taste of old France, stop in for a drink at the Café Richard, with its old signs and lace curtains and original bar. From here, you can walk up to the teardrop-shaped hill that forms the river loop. The Flamboyant Gothic church on the top, **Notre-Dame de l'Isle**, was begun in 1505 in the same style as the Cahors cathedral cloister, with a Flamboyant portal; it replaces an older chapel venerated since the 13th century by river boatmen. In the winter much of the local excitement is concentrated to the south, in the tiny village of **Sauzet**, where the basketball team has now joined with that of Cahors.

Albas to Prayssac

Albas, just to the west, occupies an exceptionally picturesque spot on a cliff over the river. The tiny fortified centre includes a church and yet another Cahors episcopal palace, much favoured by the wealthy bishops. In late May the whole village erupts into one of the best wine festivals in all southwest France, drawing people from as far away as Toulouse, with great music spilling out of every vaulted cellar.

Castelfranc, a few kilometres west on the opposite bank, is an austere *bastide* of the 13th century – die-straight streets and a central square with a modern *halle* and a spare, elegant church, typical of medieval Quercy architecture – with its *clocher-mur*, as wide as the church itself, serving as much for defence as for decoration. The village's small but elegant suspension bridge is typical of the structures the Ponts et Chaussées erected all around this area in the early 1900s.

The long ridge to the northwest of Castelfranc was an important Neolithic site. Leaving the village on the D911 west, take the first turn right, which climbs steeply up the hill for a fine view, and then pick up the marked ***circuit des dolmens***. There are only two dolmens on this walk, but in addition you encounter an unusual 'double' *garriote*, a rock-carved niche called 'Caesar's armchair', near an ancient well, and, at the summit of the hill, a circle of three huge menhirs amidst jumbles of rocks known as the Cromlech of Roquebert although everyone calls it 'Chaos'. Call the tourist office at Prayssac (*see* opposite) for information.

Prayssac, like Castelfranc, started out as a *bastide* – only a round one, a mere circle of houses around a marketplace; it has grown greatly since the 19th century, as the biggest producer of the *vin de Cahors* region. Prayssac is worth a mention for its addiction to marble statuary, starting with the quite unforgettable nude **Venus** on Venus Square, the vernal nymph in the lobby of the cinema, and the well-endowed sphinx-like creatures in the fountain by the post office. Also in marble is Jean-Baptiste Bessières, the 'Duke of Istria', across from the *mairie*. One of Napoleon's henchmen, this son of Prayssac oversaw the military occupation of Moscow, and died with a cannonball in his brain at Lützen in 1814.

Just west of Prayssac, **Pescadoires** has a fortified Romanesque church near the river, while **Bélaye** stands perched on the cliffs overlooking the valley. This ancient fortified place was one of the most important towns in the area before the English *routiers* raided it – several times – during the Hundred Years' War. The ruins of its episcopal castle remain, together with a strong-looking fortified church with a retable that was brought back by the souvenir-hunting Maréchal Bessières. Below, on the D45 crossroads to Montcuq, there is an exceptionally pretty little castle, slowly, sadly, simply falling to bits.

ⓘ **Luzech >**
Maison des Consuls,
***t** 05 65 20 17 27,*
www.ville-luzech.fr

ⓘ **Prayssac >>**
*6 Boulevard de la Paix, **t** 05 65 22 40 57*

Market Days between Cahors and Puy-l'Evêque

Luzech: Wednesday, plus fair first Wednesday of month.

Prayssac: Friday, plus Sunday-morning farmers' market in summer, and fair on 16th of each month (except when it falls on a Sunday).

Where to Stay and Eat between Cahors and Puy-l'Evêque

Douelle ✉ 46140

***Auberge du Vieux Douelle, t** 05 65 20 02 03, *www.aubergeduvieuxdouelle.new.fr* (€). Quiet rooms and a good-value restaurant (€€–€). *Restaurant closed Sat lunch out of season.*

La Marine, t 05 65 20 02 06 (€€). One of the best places in the area for seafood, plus a range of regional favourites. *Closed Sun eve and Mon.*

Caillac ✉ 46140

Le Vinois, 10 minutes west of Cahors (accessible by boat), **t** 05 65 30 53 60 (€€€). Local ingredients with a twist – risotto with artichokes and girolle mushrooms, spicy duckling with sweet potato, pork tenderloin with sesame and *citrons confits*, and lovely desserts. Be sure to book.

Nuzéjouls ✉ 46150

L'Oasis, 10km northwest of Cahors on D12, **t** 05 65 30 98 44 (€€). Delicious feasts of couscous or tajines. *Closed Sun eve and Mon.*

Caïx ✉ 46140

La Table de Capitan, t 05 65 20 18 19 (€€€–€€). A place down by the river, by a campsite, where you can hire *gabares*. The fish and regional dishes are accompanied by a good choice of Cahors wine. The cheese course offers *cabécou* goats' cheese just about any way you want. At the time of writing there was live music on Thursdays in July and August, but the place was due to change hands in 2007. *Closed Tues and mid-Sept–April.*

Sauzet ✉ 46140

****Auberge de la Tour**, Route d'Agen, **t** 05 65 36 90 05, *www.aubergedelatour.com* (€). A handsome little hotel in the 13th-century Château de Sauzet, with a restaurant (€€) devoted to Quercy specialities. In summer you can dine on a magnificent wisteria-covered terrace. *Closed Fri eve and Sat in winter, plus 2wks in Nov.*

Albas ✉ 46140

Auberge Imhoptet, 2km east in Rivière Haute, **t** 05 65 30 70 91 (€€€–€€). A little place offering affordable duck feasts and other deftly prepared dishes using ingredients from the farm. The speciality is brochette of curried *magret* with fried potatoes and two types of mushroom, and there's also a fish menu. *Closed Sun.*

Anglars-Juillac ✉ 46140

Hostellerie Clau del Loup, south of river from Prayssac, on main road, **t** 05 65 36 76 20, *www.claudelloup.com* (€€€). Smart rooms in a restored *maison de maître*, attractive grounds and a pool. Fancy seafood dominates the menu, and there are Saturday-night concerts in summer.

Prayssac ✉ 46220

Le Vidal, 3 Rue Garabets, **t** 05 65 30 66 00 (€). A little hotel in the centre, with a popular, friendly bar and restaurant (€€€–€), with tables spilling out into the square. *Hotel closed for few wks in winter; restaurant Nov.*

Ma Chaumière, t 05 65 22 40 52 (€€€–€€). Seafood and regional meat dishes served on a pretty terrace. *Closed Sat lunch, Sun eve and Mon.*

Puy-l'Evêque to Touzac

Puy-l'Evêque and Grézels mark the end of the frontier of the lands owned by the count-bishops of Cahors, but *vin de Cahors* vineyards stretch all the way to the west end of the *département*. In 2007 the new locks should be ready, opening this scenic stretch of the river up to boats.

Puy-l'Evêque and Around

The hills close in on the river again at **Puy-l'Evêque**, giving this village its exceptional riverside setting, best seen from the bridge over the Lot. By now, you should be able to guess to which *évêques* this *puy* (an Occitan word for 'hill' or 'mount') belonged. The Cahors bishops defeated the Cathars to pick up this property in 1227, and soon after built the **donjon**, similar to Luzech's, at the highest point of the town. Not long after, many of the local nobles added their houses in its shadow – none is that impressive individually, but the whole makes a lovely ensemble. In the Revolution, there was a brief movement to change its name to Puy-Libre, but Napoleon changed it back. Though small, Puy-l'Evêque is worth a look around for its quiet medieval streets and the battered Flamboyant Gothic portal of its **church of St-Sauveur** (near the top of the town), said to have been whacked by a hundred Protestant cannonballs in the Wars of Religion; one catapult ball is still embedded in the wall to the right of the door. In early August the whole village becomes the setting for one of the most spectacular fireworks shows in France (contact the tourist office for dates; *see* p.334).

To the north, the **church** of the pretty village of **Martignac** has the remains of some 16th-century frescoes, including large *Allegories of the Seven Deadly Sins* (not well preserved), some Italianate chiaroscuros, and in the apse a strange, looming figure like the king on a playing card that seems to be a pope, or God the Father himself. South of Puy-l'Evêque, is the village of Grézels with its imposing castle. In the 12th century, the bishop of Cahors built the **Château de Grézels** (or de la Coste), to guard that corner of his fief; after keeping the English at bay during the Hundred Years' War and a sacking by the Protestants in 1580, the castle was rebuilt in its current foursquare Renaissance style, squatting high on its hillside like an elegant bunker. Inside is a small **wine museum**.

Château de Grézels
t *05 65 21 34 18; 2hr guided tours in French mid-July–Aug daily 4.30; wine museum open mid-July–Aug daily 3–7; adm*

The next village west is **Duravel**, which is dominated by its massive 11th-century **church** atop a terrace – it's one of the most interesting pieces of Romanesque architecture in Quercy but unfortunately also one of the most restored in the 19th century. You can pick up the key at the tourist office. The outside of its apse is decorated with perforated metopes – openings under the roofline, usually round, alternating with *modillons* or other carvings – a

Getting around Puy-l'Evêque and Environs

The Cahors–Fumel SNCF **bus** serves the river's villages. If speed is no object, Les Roulottes du Quercy in Sérignac (near Mauroux), **t** 05 65 31 96 44, has horse-drawn wooden **caravans** for hire. Or you can hire **canoes** at Camping Le Clos Bouyssac at Mauroux, **t** 05 65 36 52 21.

---

conceit popular in this corner of the Lot. The occasion of this vast building project was the arrival in Duravel of an 11th-century sarcophagus containing 'three holy bodies' brought back from Palestine, by a crusader who perhaps bought them from some sharpsters with less imagination than the ones who peddled Geoffroi de Hardoin the Crown of Thorns. You can see their relics once every five years on the last Sunday in October (next display: 2010); at other times they are stored in the rare Carolingian crypt, with primitive but finely carved capitals, one showing a peacock. Upstairs, the capitals in the nave and chapels (scenes of misers in hell, St Michael pinning down the dragon) are among the very few that still wear their bright paintwork – a bit disconcerting at first, the way the Parthenon would be in all its original Technicolor tones. Also look for a Gallo-Roman relief of – aptly for this wine village – bunches of grapes.

From Duravel you can take the pretty back road by way of quaint **St-Martin-le-Redon** to reach the Château de Bonaguil (*see* p.347). Alternatively, continue along the river until the signs point you back over the bridge to **Touzac**, the site of a lovely deep-blue spring and 12th-century mill, the **Moulin de Leygues**. Just to the west of the bridge you'll find a dirt road that leads to one of the most idyllic locations on the river, with no cars and no buildings – nothing but river and trees.

The road from Touzac continues south up to the villages of Lacapelle-Cabanac and **Mauroux** (pronounce the 'x'). Between the two, to the right of the D5, is the striking Romanesque **church of Cabanac**, with a belltower rebuilt in the 13th century; you can get the key from the nearby Château Latuc vineyard. It stands at the highest point of the lost medieval town of Orgeuil. In the 13th century the knights of **Orgeuil**, sworn enemies of the bishop of Cahors, terrorized the Lot valley, burning, pillaging and raping as far south as Moissac. Although the King of France took Orgeuil into hand by putting it directly under his rule with a charter in 1293, the Hundred Years' War brought new troubles. The lords of Orgeuil sided with the English and gave nearby Puy-l'Evêque to the Duke of Derby. When they were banished, the town became a robbers' den, occupied by English *routiers*. The count of Armagnac came and razed the pit of vipers once and for all in the mid-1300s. It was excavated a few years back (finds are displayed in the Mauroux tourist office; *see* p.334) but the site is now overgrown.

ⓘ **Puy-l'Evêque >**
Place Truffière,
***t** 05 65 21 37 63,*
www.puy-leveque.fr

ⓘ **Mauroux >>**
*Le Bourg, **t** 05 65 30 66 70, www.mauroux.fr*

★ **Maison Rouma >**

ⓘ **Duravel >**
***t** 05 65 24 65 50, www.duravel-tourisme.com*

★ **Domaine de Haut-Baran >**

Market Days in and around Puy-L'Evêque

Puy-L'Evêque: Tuesday and Saturday.

Duravel: Saturday.

Where to Stay and Eat in and around Puy-L'Evêque

Puy-l'Evêque ✉ 46700

*****Bellevue**, Place Truffière (on D911), **t** 05 65 36 06 60 (€€). A stylish hotel-restaurant with bewitching river views from its elegant dining room (€€€€–€€€), plus a cheaper bistro to which locals flock for lunch. *Closed Sun (exc lunch in summer), Mon, last 2wks Nov and mid-Jan–mid-Feb.*

****Henry**, 23 Rue du Dr Rouma, **t** 05 65 21 32 24 (€). Rooms with TVs, a garden and a restaurant (€€€–€). *Closed Mon, Sat lunch and Sun eve out of season.*

****La Truffière**, **t** 05 65 21 34 54 (€). A simple little place with soundproofed rooms, a restaurant (€€–€) and a popular bar with a billiards table and a dartboard. *Closed Sun eve, plus Fri eve out of season.*

Maison Rouma, 2 Rue du Dr Rouma, **t** 05 65 36 59 39, *williamarnett@hotmail.com* (€). Three charming B&B rooms with a pool, smack on the river. Rooms can accommodate up to four.

Grézels ✉ 46700

La Terrasse, centre, **t** 05 65 21 34 03 (€€). A favourite for miles around for its satisfying lunches served under oak beams. There is often no menu; you get what *madame*'s concocted, with as much wine as you can drink. Sunday lunch is an extravaganza. *Closed Mon, plus eves exc July and Aug.*

La Guinguette, right by Lot on edge of village, **t** 05 65 30 86 91 (€€–€). Pizzas and other family fare in a lovely spot, with an adjoining playground and frequent theme nights with music. Call to check it's open out of season.

Duravel ✉ 46700

Domaine de Haut-Baran, signposted off D811 between Duravel and Puy-l'Evêque, **t** 05 65 24 63 24, *www.hautbaran.com* (€€€€–€€€). One of Quercy's most beautiful rural B&Bs, with a pool and Jacuzzi, run on a five-star level by a charming French-American couple. There's a two-night minimum stay, and special rates for bookings of a week or more. Dinner (€€€) is available by prior request, and courses and tours can be organized.

Touzac ✉ 46700

*****La Source Bleue**, **t** 05 65 36 52 01, *www.sourcebleue.com* (€€). A 12th-century mill next to the spring and bamboo forest, once owned by actress Marguerite Moreno, who entertained her friend Colette here. The 12 rooms are charming (try a large one in the mill itself), and there's a sauna, pool, gym and restaurant (€€€–€€). *Closed Thurs lunch, Wed, Sun–Thurs eve out of season exc public hols, and mid-Nov–Easter.*

Le Clos Bouyssac, **t** 05 65 36 52 21 (€). A delightful, shady campsite right on the Lot, with bungalows, chalets and mobile homes. *Closed Oct–April.*

Mauroux ✉ 46700

****Hostellerie Le Vert**, on D5, **t** 05 65 36 51 36, *www.hotellevert.com* (€€€–€€). Seven lovely, utterly tranquil rooms (one with a baby grand piano) in a country manor and outbuildings, plus a pool and a good restaurant (€€€) – try *confit* of roast lamb with spices. *Closed Nov–Mar exc by request; restaurant lunch and Thurs eve.*

Le Mas de Laure, 1km out of village on road to Sérignac and Montcuq, **t** 05 65 30 67 39, *www.masdelaure.com* (€€). A very friendly, popular *chambres d'hôte*. Rooms are fresh and airy, and there's a pool, plus dinner by request. There's also a gîte here. *Closed Jan.*

La Grange, Les Places, just outside Sérignac, **t** 05 65 30 51 10, *www.lesplaces.com* (€). Two B&B rooms on a sheep farm. Meals are available, and there's a riding stable just up the road. *Closed July and Aug..*

Rouge Passion, Place de la Mairie, **t** 05 65 22 97 26 (€€€–€€). A friendly new Belgian-owned bar-restaurant that's brought a breath of fresh air to the village centre, offering satisfying and creative cuisine. Book ahead. *Closed Tues and Sun eve.*

North of the Lot: La Bouriane

Bories in Provence are dry-stone huts, or what the southwest calls *cazelles* or *gariottes*; in this most Périgourdin corner of Quercy *borie* means a farmhouse, especially a fortified medieval country retreat belonging to Cahors' merchant elite; they give this mini-*pays* its name. Scattered farmhouses set amidst lush landscapes of chestnuts, pines and meadows are indeed the order of the day in the Bouriane, but there are some surprises, too: frescoed churches and modern Ukrainian art.

Catus and Les Junies

Catus, the site of another very popular *plan d'eau*, is built around a buttressed priory **church** with a polygonal apse, all that remains of the 10th-century priory; the star attraction is the 12th-century chapterhouse with a dozen magnificent capitals and column bases, carved by the same school as at Moissac. The farms around Catus are especially photogenic, some retaining their *lauze* stone roofs, which are pretty rare in the Lot.

Nearby **St-Médard** is a picture-postcard Quercy village with a famous restaurant (*see* p.340). Legends say that Roland clobbered the Saracens at **Montgesty** to the northwest, in revenge for a town that they had destroyed on the site; all that digging has produced, however, is bits of a Gallo-Roman villa at Mas-de-Rieu.

Sals, a very pretty stone village perched on the hill, is now half taken over by holiday homes; below it on the D911 and the stream, little **Labastide-du-Vert** will look very familiar to anyone who has visited the Henri Martin museum in Cahors (*see* p.320): there is a monument to the Impressionist from Toulouse in the centre of the village, and he is buried in the village cemetery.

Just west of Labastide-du-Vert is the turn-off for **Les Junies**, in the lush valley of the Masse. This has a very picturesque 14th-century **château** in the centre (one of the few you'll see where they hang out their washing out on the line), which was given by the bishop of Cahors as a thank-you-for-stomping-on-the-Cathars present to Bertrand de Jean. The de Jeans built a nuns' priory nearby; the church has lovely 14th-century stained glass showing the founders, along with scenes of Christ and St John. The name de Jean was corrupted to form the village's name, Les Junies.

Downstream, at **La Masse**, is a **church** with the liveliest frescoes of any Bouriane church: a parade of the Seven Deadly Sins, each riding a beast guided by some frisky devils and goaty satyrs. The key is held at the house with white shutters opposite. The spring water flowing into the basin in the centre of La Masse, which is delicious, has never stopped flowing in living memory, even during the worst droughts.

Getting to La Bouriane

Gourdon has a **train** station with connections to Cahors, Souillac and beyond.

Les Arques and Around

From the centre of Les Junies, a narrow road winds its way to the little old village of **Lherm**, a striking ensemble in stone, the site of an ironworks in the Middle Ages that was left so desolated after the passing of English *Grandes Compagnies* in the 15th century that a wolf gave birth outside the church door.

North of Lherm, **Les Arques** is a sleepy village that's always had an artist or two ever since the Cubist sculptor Ossip Zadkine of Smolensk bought a home here in 1934. Some of the works left by his widow to the city of Paris have been transferred here to create the little **Musée Zadkine**. Zadkine is best known for his 1947 *Destroyed City* in Rotterdam, and in peaceful Les Arques his works – several are on display – seem almost too searing and painful. Next to the museum is the superb 11th-century **church of St-Laurent**, which Zadkine loved; he initiated the restoration and contributed three sculptures. Once a priory of Marcilhac, the interior has been stripped down to its mellow ochre stone to reveal its essentials: a single nave ending in three tiny apses, divided by columns with primitive carvings and divided by little Mozarabic horseshoe arches, while below is a tiny, ancient crypt; on one of the exterior portals, note the carved Celtic spiral.

Musée Zadkine
t 05 65 22 83 37; open April–Sept daily 10–1 and 2–7; rest of year daily 2–5; adm

While you are at the museum, you might like to pick up the key for Romanesque **St-André-des-Arques**, 4km on the other side of the D45 (signposted). In 1954 Zadkine discovered its 15th-century frescoes under the plaster in the apse, interesting but sadly damaged by the wet: *Christ in Majesty*, the *Annunciation* and the *Apostles*. St Christopher is painted on one pillar, and baby Jesus, waiting to be carried, on the other.

If your wanderings bring you further north, one of the many pretty routes to follow in the Bouriane is the D12 along the Céou valley, which is dotted with ruined castles at **Clermont**, **Concorès** and **St-Germain-du-Bel-Air**.

Gourdon

Harmoniously piled on a lofty bluff, rose-coloured Gourdon, capital of the Bouriane, is easily spotted from miles around. Easily defended, the site has been inhabited for donkey's years. In 961 Count Raymond I of Toulouse gave the city to the Gourdon family. The clan, and Gourdon itself, were nearly wiped out in 1189 by Richard the Lionheart, who as Duke of Aquitaine often played the baddie – far more like the Sheriff of Nottingham than the good king of the Robin Hood legends. The story goes that the son who survived the massacre of Gourdon got his revenge with his crossbow ten years later at the siege of Châlus, when he shot Richard fatally in the shoulder.

Gourdon in its medieval heyday had four monasteries, although one of its lords, a troubadour named Bertrand I, had a run-in with the Inquisition for protecting the Cathars. In the Wars of Religion the monasteries also made a juicy target for the fierce Protestant captain Duras, who spent a month razing them to the ground and slaughtering their inhabitants. Gourdon's once-mighty castle suffered a similar fate in 1651 when the lord of Gourdon foolishly supported the cause of Marie de' Medici over her son, Louis XIII. In the 18th century the city walls went down to make space for a circular boulevard.

Walking around Gourdon

Start your tour of Gourdon at the top, with the massive **church of St-Pierre**, begun in 1302, its façade flanked by two 30m towers, linked by a gallery over the rose window. The portal has some delicate carving on the capitals; inside, the vast single nave is the most important venue of the town's **summer music festival**. For a view from Gourdon equal to the view of Gourdon from the distance, climb the stairs by the church for the esplanade that once formed the base of the castle: you can see the Dordogne valley, the green Bouriane and just about every roof in town.

Festival de Musique
*Comité d'Animation Culturelle, 8 Boulevard du Docteur Cabanes, **t** 05 65 41 20 06*

Narrow little streets, such as the famous Rue Zigzag leading up to St-Pierre, are lined with well-restored medieval houses. Near the church lies the 13th-century consulate that was converted in the 1700s into the **Hôtel de Ville**, with graceful arcades on the ground floor that shelter the farmers' market. Behind St-Pierre, in Place des Marronniers, note the fine Renaissance portal and carved door of the **Cavaignac house**. The Cavaignacs were nationally prominent in the Revolution and 19th century; the father, Jean-Baptiste, served on the National Convention and ended up as a counsellor of Napoleon. His eldest son, a Republican journalist, created a society that was dedicated to the rights of man, while the younger, who was cast in the same mould as Richard the Lionheart, personally led the massacre of the Parisians in the revolt of 1848. Gourdon's main street, **Rue du Majou**, is lined with relics of the Middle Ages – handsome houses, a fortified gate and chapel, and the town's most interesting shops.

On Gourdon's ring boulevard, the Gothic **church of the Cordeliers** survived Duras' monastic destruction. It's not much from the outside, admittedly, but the honey-hued interior is pure and lovely, and there's a beautiful 14th-century baptismal font carved with the figures of Christ and the 12 apostles. The church is generally only open to the public for festival concerts, however, so you'll have to ask the tourist office (*see* p.341) if you can visit.

There's a third pretty church, **Notre-Dame-des-Neiges**, 1km from the Hostellerie de la Bouriane (*see* p.341). Built near a watermill, the church stands on the site of a miraculous spring; the snow in its name refers to one of the Virgin's 4th-century miracles in Rome, when she caused a summer snowfall on the site of Santa Maria Maggiore. Although only the apse survives from the Romanesque church, the whole is simple and charming and contains an altar by Tournier, although it's always locked tight.

Around Gourdon

Grottes de Cougnac
t 05 65 41 47 54; open Easter–June and Sept 10–11.30 and 2–5; July and Aug Mon–Sat 10–6; Oct Mon–Sat 2–4; adm

North of Gourdon are the two **Grottes de Cougnac**. One cave is full of stalactites and stalagmites, the second, discovered in 1952, is home to the *département*'s second most important collection of prehistoric paintings: black and red outlines of goats, deer, mammoths, symbols and a number of humans, some pierced by lances. The cave walls around them look like trees and mutant cauliflowers. Among them, palaeontological detectives have found fingerprints believed to be 20,000 years old.

From the caves, the D17 continues north to **Milhac**, a delightful medieval village that was the cradle of the lords of Gourdon; another charmer is **Masclat** further north, built around a pretty château and church, only a few kilometres from Lamothe-Fénelon. **Le Vigan**, 6km east of Gourdon, is built around a massive **abbey church** with a giant belfry, founded by the canons of St-Sernin in Toulouse and especially favoured by the popes in Avignon, who gave it the relics of St Gall, uncle of St Gregory of Tours. The English in the Hundred Years' War so thoroughly pillaged the abbey that it never recovered, although stained glass was added to the church in the 15th century. Le Vigan is also the home to the **Musée Henri Giron**, where you can examine the landscapes, still lives and nudes of the inclassable erotic, Modigliani-inspired Giron, a Frenchman who ran a hotel in Brussels in the 1930s and gradually changed career; he still lives in Belgium, but many of his best works are here.

Musée Henri Giron
t 05 65 41 33 78; open June and Sept Wed–Sun 10–12 and 3–6; July and Aug Wed–Sun 10–6; rest of year Sun 10–12 and 3–6 and by appt; adm

East, **St-Projet** has a naïve pilgrims' cross in which the serpent represents evil, the heart triumphant love, the skull and crossbones unredeemed humanity; on the top Christ is crucified. It has an identical twin just to the east near **Graules**; the Graules cross, with its smiling Christ, has preserved its mysterious stone pendants. For a grand bird's-eye view, cross the N20 to Reilhaguet. There's a small **museum of minerals and fossils** at **St Chamarand** to the south.

Musée des Minéraux et Fossiles
t 06 71 10 29 11; open daily July–Sept 10–7

Payrac to the north, a pleasant town sliced in two by the big road, has **Aqua Folies**, with slides, pools and mini-golf, and the **Musée Roger Thières** in the *atelier* of the eponymous artist-blacksmith.

Aqua Folies
open April–Sept daily 11–8; adm

Musée Roger Thières
ask at tourist office, see p.341, for for times

Southwest of Gourdon: More Bouriane, along the D673 to Fumel

Just off the scenic D673, 8km to the west of Gourdon, stand the romantic ruins of the **Abbaye-Nouvelle** at Léobard. A Cistercian abbey (the 'old' one was at St-Martin-le-Désarmat), it was founded in 1242 on a rock overlooking the valley of the Céou on lands donated by Guillaume de Gourdon-Salviac, anxious to get back into good grace with the Inquisition. The Gothic church (1274–87) was damaged in the Hundred Years' War and never properly repaired, and by 1658 the abbey was abandoned. In 1950 it was dynamited by the farmers who owned it; the once-elegant stairs were dismantled for a barn. Now only the lofty, ruined walls of the church stand, originally 27m high – Abbaye-Nouvelle was the only known Cistercian church in France without a transept, and one of the few built with two storeys; the wooden upper floor has long since gone. There is a local organization dedicated to bringing the ruins back to life.

The D673 to **Salviac** has its scenic merits too; Salviac has a Renaissance château, and a Gothic **church** that was built by Jacques Duèze of Cahors, the future John XXII, which has some of its original stained glass. From Salviac a good navigator can get you through the narrow lanes to **Rampoux** to the southeast (it's easier to head south on the D6 from Dégagnac); the reward is a 12th–14th-century Benedictine priory decorated with naïve frescoes from the 15th century and a statue of St Peter from the 1200s.

Cazals

Back on the D673, the most important town in the area is **Cazals**, next to a pretty *plan d'eau*. The town was a *bastide* laid out for the King of England by Guillaume de Toulouse in 1319. Only the main square serves as a reminder of its *bastide* origins, and the church (with some good capitals inside) is said to be built over a Roman temple. Cazals gave the world Hugues Salel (1504–53), one of the poets who drove Clément Marot crazy by imitating his *blasons*, preciously dedicated to pins and the like. See how rural life has changed since 1900 at the **Atelier-Musée des Vieilles Mécaniques**. **Montcléra**, the next village along, has an extremely beguiling fat 15th-century château at its southern end, which is best viewed when you head north up the D673; all it needs is a Rapunzel letting down her long hair.

Atelier-Musée des Vieilles Mécaniques
t 05 65 20 29 68; open mid-June–mid-Sept Tues 3–7, Wed–Sat 9–12 and 3–7, Sun 9–12

Little **Frayssinet-le-Gélat** occupies the crossroads between Gourdon and Fumel, Cahors and Villefranche-du-Périgord. The only thing that's striking about it, aside its attractive medieval church, is the little monument next to it, with the inscription *TO THE MARTYRS OF GERMAN BARBARISM*. This recalls 21 May 1944, when a detachment of soldiers who had been attacked by the Resistance took their revenge, rounding up villagers and shooting them; the old folks in the village still talk about it today. If you follow the D660 east from Frayssinet-le-Gélat, you'll pass through the golden village of **Goujounac**, where the Romanesque **church** has a tympanum on its south side, carved with Christ and the four Evangelists.

The D673 to Fumel follows the valley of the Thèze, passing under **Montcabrier**, a little *bastide* founded in 1297 by and named after Guy de Caprari, the seneschal of Quercy. Its **church of St-Louis** with its arcaded *clocher-mur* was given a pretty Flamboyant portal and rose window in the 14th century; inside its prize is a reliquary of St Louis, one of the few that portray the king with a beard.

The steep heights on the opposite side of the D673 once held the town of **Pestilhac**, Montcabrier's bitter rival; some of its outer fortifications can still be seen from the valley. For three centuries, the two towns fought each other like Kilkenny cats; Pestilhac finally succumbed and disappeared in the 1500s. In its day it must have been one of the most important centres in the region. If you want to see the most evocative ruins in Quercy, climb up and make the acquaintance of the pleasant woman who lives in the smaller of the two houses on the site. The path leads through her back garden, up past a wild, forested jumble of stones that includes parts of the walls and bastions, various buildings and best of all the church of Notre-Dame, still substantially intact, with some lovely carvings and an oak tree growing right through one of its Romanesque windows. From here it's only a few miles to the Château de Bonaguil (*see* p.347).

ⓘ **Catus >**
Maison des Services Publiques, **t** *05 65 20 86 40, www.cccatus.fr*

ⓘ **St-Germain-du-Bel-Air >**
Place Mairie, **t** *05 65 31 09 10*

★ **Le Gindreau >**

Market Days in La Bouriane

Catus: Tuesday; plus fair on last Tuesday of month.

St-Germain-du-Bel-Air: Friday and Sunday mornings July and Aug.

Gourdon: Tuesday and Saturday in front of St-Pierre; farmers' market in Place Noël-Poujade Thursdays in summer; big general fair first and third Tuesday of month.

Where to Stay and Eat in La Bouriane

St-Médard ✉ 46150

Le Gindreau, t 05 65 36 22 27 (€€€€–€€€). The Bouriane's gourmet haven, in the former village school, with a gorgeous terrace overlooking the countryside. The elegant dishes are prepared with authentic ingredients – lamb from the *causse* and the freshest seasonal vegetables. The charming sommelier, a dead ringer for Peter Ustinov, will help you to select the right wine, with Cahors naturally at the top of the list. *Closed half Mar, late Oct–early Nov, and Mon and Tues.*

Les Junies ✉ 46150

Le Château, t 05 65 36 29 98 (€€). A delightful château offering B&B accommodation in two guestrooms. *Closed Oct–June.*

Romulus, just off D660, **t** 05 65 36 74 36 (€€€–€€). An airy Mediterranean restaurant in a beautifully restored mill, without a hint of duck on the menu! *Closed winter.*

Pontcirq ✉ 46150

***Labastide-du-Vert**, Rostassac, between St-Médard and Labastide-du-Vert, **t** 05 65 36 22 85 (€). A comfortable old postal stage with a sunny dining room serving southwest favourites (€€), including Quercy lamb, truffles and *vin de Cahors*. *Closed Jan and Feb, and Sun eve and Mon out of season.*

Les Arques ✉ 46250

La Récréation, **t** 05 65 22 88 08 (€€). A wonderful restaurant that's become even more popular since American author Michael S. Sanders wrote a book, *From Here, You Can't See Paris*, about it. Reserve well in advance in summer. It's set in an old school, and you can dine in the former playground in fine weather. There's something to suit everyone among the delicious and delicate dishes; try *raviolis de homard* – truly scrumptious and excellent value. *Closed Mar, Wed and Thurs April–Sept, Mon–Thurs plus Fri–Sun eve Oct–Feb.*

ⓘ **Cazals >>**
Rue de la République, t 05 65 22 88 88

ⓘ **Gourdon >**
24 Rue du Majou, t 05 65 27 52 50, www.gourdon.fr

ⓘ **Payrac >>**
t 05 65 37 94 27

Gourdon ✉ 46300

*****Bissonnier La Bonne Auberge**, 51 Boulevard des Martyrs, **t** 05 65 41 02 48, *www.hotelbissonnier.com* (€€). A slightly cheaper option than the other three stars, set in the medieval town and run by the same family since the early 18th century, with a restaurant (€€€–€). *Closed Sun eve.*

*****Domaine du Berthiol**, on D704 towards Cahors, **t** 05 65 41 33 33, *www.hotelperigord.com* (€€). A tranquil, large stone Quercy manor house in the woods, with a pool, a tennis court and kids' games. The restaurant (€€€–€€) has a delectable seasonal menu. *Closed Sun eve, Mon and lunch Tues–Sat out of season, and mid-Dec–Mar.*

*****Hostellerie de la Bouriane**, Place du Foirail, **t** 05 65 41 16 37, *www.hotellabouriane.fr* (€€). A large country inn that has long been *the* place to stay in Gourdon, on the edge of town. The rooms are lovely, the food (€€€–€€) – which includes some fish dishes – delicious. *Closed mid-Jan–mid-Mar. Restaurant Mon–Sat lunch, plus Sun and Mon mid-Oct–mid-April.*

Le Paradis, on road to Salviac, **t** 05 65 41 09 73 (€). A popular *chambres d'hôte* in a large house with a big garden with a swimming pool. Evening meals (€€) can be arranged except on Saturdays.

L'Abbaye, on Salviac road next to Abbaye-Nouvelle, **t** 05 65 41 32 70 (€€). A delightful restaurant run by a Dutch couple, drawing in locals with delicious prawns, racks of lamb and fabulous alcoholic sorbets. Booking is essential. *Closed mid-Oct–Feb.*

Le Vigan ✉ 46300

Le Manoir la Barrière, signposted off D1, **t** 05 65 41 40 73 (€€). A rather special *chambres d'hôte*, with huge and beautifully furnished bedrooms, all different; if you fancy sleeping in a four-poster, ask for the Quercy. The 13th-century manor house is in a big garden with tailored lawns and a small pool. *Closed Dec–Feb.*

Cazals ✉ 46250

La Caminade, **t** 05 65 21 66 63, *www.lacaminade.com* (€€). A honey-coloured stone house that began as a priory in the Middle Ages and later housed the imperial *gendarmerie*. It is now a restored family home with four stylish ensuite *chambres d'hôte* with a classy mix of modern and medieval decor. Breakfast is served in one of the gardens and there's a swimming pool. Booking is essential.

Payrac ✉ 46350

****Hostellerie de la Paix**, on N20, **t** 05 65 37 95 15 (€€–€). A pleasant former posthouse with a pool, garden and restaurant (€€). *Closed Jan–mid-Feb.*

Frayssinet-le-Gélat ✉ 46250

La Serpt, signposted from centre, **t** 05 65 36 66 15 (€€). A *ferme-auberge* serving some of the best duck and goose *confits* and *magrets* in the Lot, as well as tempting traditional dishes such as *mique levée* (*see* p.47), and goose cooked in Cahors wine and pastis, smothered in light flaky pastry like a pile of autumn leaves. Booking is required. *Closed Mon.*

Goujounac and Around ✉ 46250

****Hostellerie de Goujounac**, **t** 05 65 36 68 67, *www.hostellerie-de-goujounac.com* (€). A handful of remodelled rooms in the village centre, plus a restaurant (€€€–€) offering reliable, generous menus. *Closed Sun eve and Mon Nov–Jan, Fri eve Feb–early Mar.*

Jeanne Murat, Pomarède, 4km southwest of town, **t** 05 65 36 66 07 (€€–€). Filling dishes containing ingredients from local producers. The place was recently featured, in honour of its centenary, in a book and documentary by Australian media star Mary Moody. Booking is required on Sundays. *Closed Sat.*

La Poule au Pot, **t** 05 65 36 65 48 (€€–€). A *ferme-auberge* full of cycling trophies (the owner's son raced in the Tour de France), serving generous portions of regional favourites. Book ahead, especially on Sundays. *Closed eves in winter.*

Montcabrier ✉ 46700

Chambres d'Hôte Chez les Lemozy, Mérigou, on D68 west of Montcabrier, **t** 05 65 36 53 43 (€). An Arcadian *chambres d'hôte* set on a farm, plus two gîtes that are available in summer only. Foodies and aspiring chefs should enquire about the winter culinary weekends, during which you can learn all about preparing foie gras and *confits*.

Atelier de la Rose, Place du Village, **t** 05 65 23 66 36, *www.french-rose.com* (€). A B&B with an adjoining studio available for artists' and writers' residencies. The owner also runs motorcycle itineraries and walking holidays, and provides her own 'roadbooks' for exploring the area.

Ferme-Auberge Lou Montaïcos, signposted from D673, **t** 05 65 36 55 70 (€€). A friendly hilltop place that raises geese and ducks and serves them cooked in Cahors wine and a dozen other ways, all good. It's open by reservation only.

Lot-et-Garonne

Rolling, rich, fertile, well-rivered département *number 47, the Lot-et-Garonne, is far more agricultural than the plain old Lot to the east: famous across France for its high-class prunes,* pruneaux d'Agen, *it produces masses of other fruit and vegetables as well; when the nightly news shows burly, bereted French farmers with attitudes dumping imported apples and tomatoes in the streets, half the time they are Lot-et-Garonners, a-cussing in their distinctive Gascon twang.*

14

Don't miss

1. The perfect stage-set castle
   Bonaguil p.347
2. Five Goyas and a million prunes
   Agen p.364
3. An august fortified mill
   Barbaste p.373
4. Edward I's *bastide* of 1284
   Monpazier p.350
5. Château architecture and futuristic shows
   Duras p.382

See map overleaf

Lot-et-Garonne

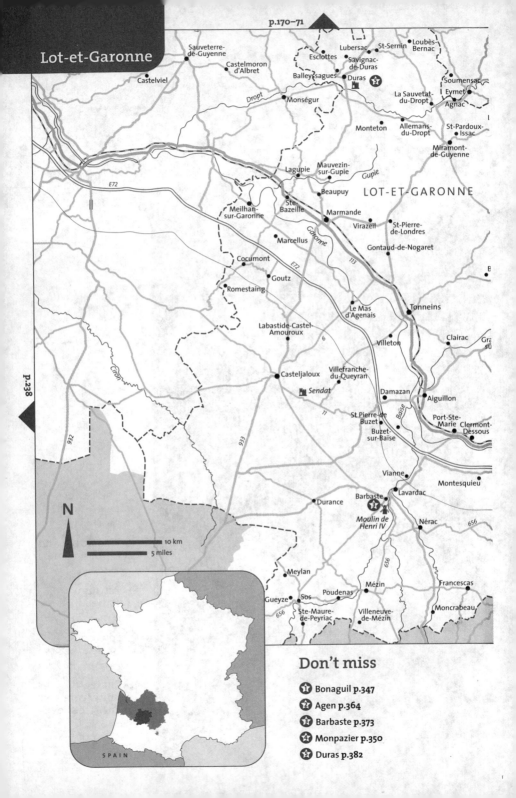

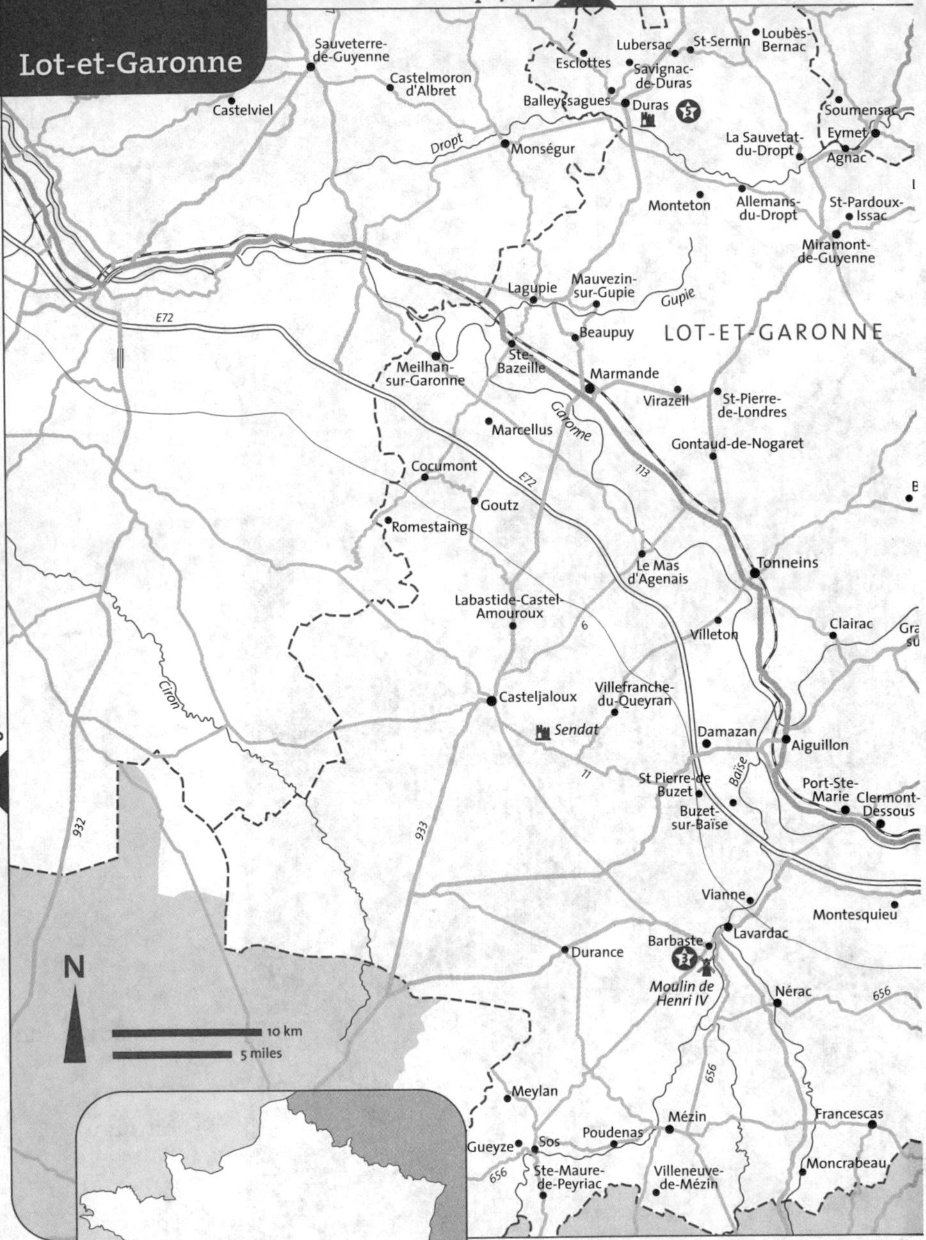

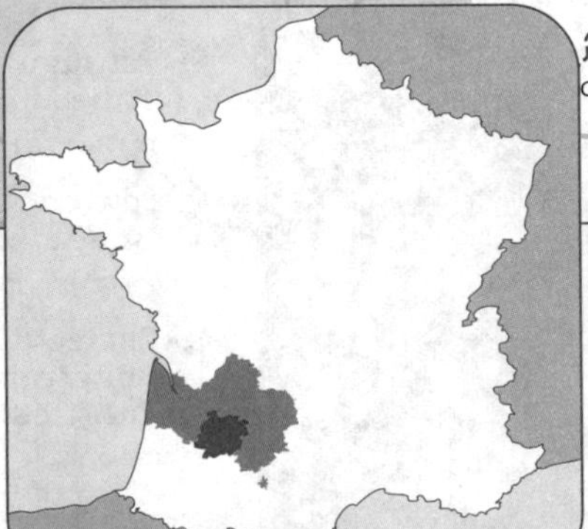

Don't miss

1. Bonaguil p.347
2. Agen p.364
3. Barbaste p.373
4. Monpazier p.350
5. Duras p.382

pp.170–71

pp.286–87

pp.386–87

The Lot-et-Garonne has several personalities. Besides orchards, as Bordeaux's neighbour it has some small but excellent wine regions in the west producing constantly improving but kindly priced bottles. The east is dotted with castles and *bastides* and forests, like the Dordogne and Lot. The southern portion is part of Gascony, stomping ground of King Henri IV. Agen, the capital, has

ⓘ Lot-et-Garonne
271 Rue Péchabout, BP158, 47000 Agen, **t** *05 53 66 14 14, www.lot-et-garonne.fr*

an excellent art museum. All over the *département*, rugby is taken nearly as seriously as prunes, with major clubs in Villeneuve and Agen, and the fine rivers are being reopened to pleasure boats.

The *département*'s **tourist office** produces a constantly improving library of literature, particularly the *Guide des Loisirs*.

Fumel and the Château de Bonaguil

At the eastern end of Lot-et-Garonne, tucked away in some wooded hills, is one of the finest castles in the southwest, the Château de Bonaguil, now property of the *commune* of Fumel, which runs imperceptibly into Monsempron-Libos, the market town for the region.

Fumel and Monsempron-Libos

Just west of the last Cahors vineyards is Fumel, the Lot's rustbelt or, rather, little rust garter. The barons of Fumel, first recorded in the 11th century as protectors of Moissac, were in the Wars of Religion ardent Catholics and buddies of Henri II and Catherine de' Medici; the most famous, François de Fumel, was Captain of the King's Guard and Catherine's ambassador to Constantinople, but he was so unpopular at home that in 1562 his Protestant subjects slaughtered him in his château. Reprisals and mass executions followed, and Fumel only recovered in 1848, when it was chosen to have the first industry on the Lot, a small steel mill making railway bearings and pipes. In the early 1960s it employed 2,700 workers, many from Algeria; today it has been converted to make car parts.

The one sight in town is the **château**. François de Fumel was responsible for converting the medieval donjon into an Italianate villa, and if you walk up the big steps to the library, there's a stucco of François over the door, his nose busted off in Fumel's proto-Revolution. Completed in the 1700s, with immaculately kept garden terraces overlooking the river, the château stayed in the family until 1950, when they sold it to the city to become the *mairie*. You can visit the terrace and gardens. These days Fumel can hold its head a bit higher as the home town of Jean Nouvel, architect of the exquisite Institut du Monde Arabe in Paris.

Past the car parks of **Montayral**, a former Templar fief across the Lot, look for its fortified mill built directly in the river, or its château, a 13th-century residence of the pirate lords of Orgeuil just upriver. **Monsempron-Libos**, on the far side of the steel mill, is spread round a medieval *castrum* on a hill with the exquisite 12th-century church of St-Géraud. The exterior has perforated metopes; the unusual plan inside has innovative vaulting and an entrance under the choir for pilgrims who flocked to see the relics in the crypt. The capitals in the nave are carved with masks and monsters.

Getting to the Fumel Area

The station at Monsempron-Libos has a few **trains** a day to Les Eyzies, Périgueux and Agen. More frequent **buses** run up the Lot valley as far as Cahors.

The Château de Bonaguil and Around

Château de Bonaguil
t 05 53 71 90 33; open June–Aug daily 10–6; April and May daily 10.30–1 and 2.30–5.30; Sept daily 10.30–1 and 2.30–5; Feb, Mar and Oct daily 11–1 and 2.30–5.30; Nov Sun and hols 11–1 and 2.30–5.30; 1st 3wks Dec daily 2.30–5

'It's so perfect that it seems ridiculous to call it a ruin', said Lawrence of Arabia of the great prow-shaped **Château de Bonaguil** in 1908. Of all the castles bristling across France, few are as useless or photogenic as 'the swan song of feudalism', born 200 years behind the times. Begun in the 13th century by a family of knights from Fumel, it passed in the 1460s to hunchback Brengon de Rocquefeuil, who liked to be called 'the noble, magnificent and most powerful lord' of his assorted little possessions. Brengon was a cartoon baddie, a proto-survivalist as nasty and paranoid as he was vain. When Charles VII fined him for brutality to his vassals, he ensconced himself at Bonaguil in a massive donjon reminiscent of the Flatiron Building, filled with years' worth of provisions and weapons, and surrounded it with a moat and surging walls and towers, designed to deflect cannon fire from all sides.

'I will raise such a castle that my villainous subjects will never take it, nor the English, nor even the most powerful soldiers of the King of France,' Brengon boasted. Never mind that none of them ever showed the least interest in Bonaguil. By the 18th century Brengon's lair was such a white elephant that it changed hands for 100 francs and a bag of walnuts. Partially demolished in the Revolution, it was purchased by the town of Fumel in 1860.

Whether you approach Bonaguil from Fumel or from above, via St-Martin-le-Redon (*see* p.333), it is as stunning as a Hollywood set; in summer it's illuminated until midnight. The interior can't match the exterior: there are fireplaces suspended in the void, objects found in the midden, old graffiti and views from the walls. The adjacent castle chapel, St-Michel, has an unusual cinquefoil window. There is a festival of theatre in the summer.

From Bonaguil, little winding roads bring you to **Sauveterre-la-Lémance**, with a large, less glamorous but actually used castle built by Edward I in the 13th century to defend the frontiers of Guyenne. Sauveterre was another popular prehistoric residence and gave its name to the early Mesolithic period, the *Sauveterrien*; you can visit the excavations at Roc-Allan in summer and have a look at the finds at the **Musée Préhistorique** in the *mairie*.

Musée Préhistorique
t 05 53 40 73 03; open June–Sept Tues–Fri 10–12.30 and 2.30–6.30; April, May and Oct Tues–Fri 2.30–6.30; adm (joint tickets available with Bonaguil)

The serene little valley of the Lémance is a pretty place to explore, with more reminders of the armies in the Hundred Years' War that raged up and down its length at **Cuzorn**, just south; here too are relics of the Lémance's old economic mainstays, forges and paper mills; **Montcabrier** (*see* p.340) is nearby.

Tourist Information in Fumel

Fumel >
Place Georges Escandes (near mairie*),*
t *05 53 71 13 70, www.fumel-fr.com and www.cc-dufumelois.com*

The tourist office at **Fumel** has details of *gabare* trips on the Lot, twice-daily in June and Sept, four times daily in July and Aug (note that the ticket gives you access to the Château de Bonaguil; *see* p.347)

Market Days in and around Fumel

Fumel: Sunday, plus several night markets in summer.

Monsempron-Libos: Thursday food and clothes market.

Where to Stay and Eat in and around Fumel

Fumel and Monsempron-Libos ✉ 47500

La Fontaine des Oiseaux, St Vite (just south of Monsempron), **t 05 53 71 26 57, *http://perso.orange.fr/lafontainedesoiseaux* (€). A traditional stone farmhouse with three *chambres d'hôte*, a two-bedroom gîte and a pool within 12 acres full of horses, dogs, birds, ducks and chickens. The British owner offers regional, British, Indonesian and Indian cuisine, and the breakfasts are accompanied by homemade preserves and organic fruits grown on the property.

Le Relais de la Poste, Monsempron-Libos station, **t** 05 53 71 15 44 (€). Simple rooms and reliably good French food.

Auberge Les Bons Enfants, opposite Château de Bonaguil, **t** 05 53 71 23 52 (€€–€). Pizzas, pancakes, ice cream and other family fare, served by the British owner. *Closed Dec and Jan.*

Sauveterre-la-Lémance ✉ 47500

*Le Centre, upper part of village, **t** 05 53 40 65 45 (€). An old country inn with pleasant rooms and a good restaurant (€€€–€€). *Closed mid-Dec–Feb and Sat lunch Oct–Mar.*

Bastide Country

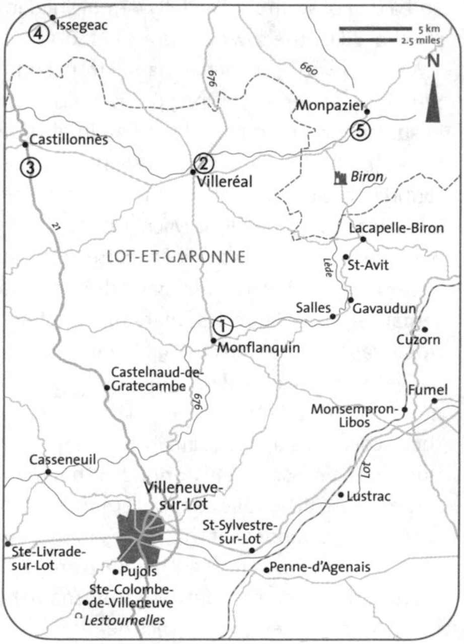

To the west of the Bouriane a similar landscape of rolling hills, woodlands and meadows carries on into the *département* of Lot-et-Garonne and the southern portion of the Dordogne. The writer Stendhal once described this landscape as the 'Tuscany of France', and it's sprinkled with a truly superb array of *bastides* and castles.

Monflanquin, Villeréal and Around

Musée des Bastides
t 05 53 36 40 19; open May, June and Sept Mon–Sat 10–12 and 2–6, Sun 3–6; July and Aug daily 10–7; Oct–April Mon–Sat 10–12 and 2–5, Sun 3–5; adm

Pollen
open Mon–Fri 9–12 and 2–5

Cave des 7 Monts
t 05 53 36 33 40; open Mon 3–6.30, Tues–Sat 9–12.30 and 3–6.30

Espace Forme
t 05 53 49 85 85; some facilities open daily, call for info

Maison de Campagne
t 05 53 36 65 14; call for times

Monflanquin ① is a convenient starting point for exploring the *bastide* country, whether you approach from Fumel to the east or from Villeneuve-sur-Lot to the south. Strategically planted at the top of a 181m hill with views for miles around, the *bastide* of Monflanquin, 'one of the most beautiful villages in France', was founded in 1256 by St Louis' brother Alphonse de Poitiers. Alphonse's interest in these marches had much to do with his marriage to Jeanne, the only child of Raymond VII of Toulouse, which was part of his brother's strategy to Frenchify the lands recently devastated by the Albigensian crusade. Alphonse and Jeanne further obliged by dying childless and leaving Toulouse to the Crown of France. Monflanquin has preserved most of its original *bastide* elements: the central square bordered with wide arcades, or *cornières*, a fortified church still bristling behind its original façade, its grid street plan and blocks of medieval houses; the exhibitions in the **Musée des Bastides** (in the Maison du Tourisme) will tell you all about them.

Monflanquin's most recent vocation is art, and it fills the summer months with events, exhibitions and festivals; you can also visit the artists' commune **Pollen** at 25 Rue Ste-Marie year round. The town also produces a drinkable *vin de pays de l'Agenais*, sold at the cooperative **Cave des 7 Monts**. Additionally, it has a rarity in this neck of the woods: a gym, heated pool and sauna at **Espace Forme**. The late, not so great Robert Maxwell used to have a château on the outskirts of Monflanquin.

It's a 13km beeline north up the D676 to another foundation of Alphonse de Poitiers, the 1269 *bastide* of **Villeréal** ② alongside the river Dropt (or Drot). Villeréal, with its agriculture (mostly orchards and tobacco) and commerce has a more solid air to it than artsy Monflanquin. The shop-filled arcades of the main square overlook the 14th-century *halle*, which had an upper storey added in the 16th century. The façade of the church is framed by two towers and retains the loopholes in the apse, from where the citizens shot at the rampaging English. The **Maison de Campagne** has displays, some of them interactive, on the countryside, animals, flowers and so on, and a nature trail around Brayssou lake.

A decade before Villeréal, Alphonse founded the handsome *bastide* of **Castillonnès** ③ 13km west, down the Dropt midway between Villeneuve and Bergerac, on the N21. Castillonnès has conserved its *cornières* and narrow medieval lanes, and, on Rue du Petit Paris, a fine 17th-century house. The church has a gilded retable also from the 17th century. Ask at the tourist office (*see* p.352) about guided tours in summer. Tiny **Douzains**, just southwest, is famous for its enormous oak tree that figures in several local legends.

Picture-postcard **Issigeac** ④, north of Castillonnès and Villeréal, has changed so little over the centuries that it's a popular film location; it also manages to be less austere than the other *bastides*. Among its charms are a late-Gothic **church** with a good porch, a massive **bishop's palace**, and the half-timbered **Maison de Têtes**, with leering faces. The tourist office (*see* p353) runs tours.

Monpazier

④ Monpazier

Monflanquin, Villeréal and Castillonnès held the frontlines against the English foundations at Beaumont and **Monpazier** ⑤, 'the most perfect *bastide*', 15km up from Villeréal on the Dropt. Founded by Edward I in 1284, the town had a perfectly rotten 14th century as a football kicked from side to side in the Hundred Years' War – even the Baron of Biron got into the act and put it to the sack, *routiers* pillaged it, and a streak of bad harvests was followed by a typhoid fever epidemic. The local lepers were blamed, and a few burned alive. Then in 1350 came the Black Death.

Amid the terrors of the next round of warfare, over religion this time, the duke of Sully recorded a story about Monpazier worthy of *Monty Python*: by sheer coincidence Monpazier decided to raid Villefranche-du-Périgord, the next *bastide* to the east, on the same night that Villefranche decided to do the same to Monpazier. By chance each militia took a different path; each was delighted to find their goal undefended and easy to plunder, and carried its booty back – to ransacked homes. An agreement was struck, and both sides gave back everything they stole.

Despite all the troubles, Monpazier has held itself together remarkably well, from its fortified church (still bearing its Revolutionary slogan, that 'The People of France believe in a Supreme Being and the Immortality of the Soul') to its 16th-century *halle*, complete with its original grain measures. Note that the regulation *cornières* around the square are irregular, and that narrow spaces were left between the houses – not to give the residents air or light so much as a place to throw their rubbish. In 1637 crowds stood under the arcades to watch Buffarot, the leader of the *Croquants*' revolt, broken on the wheel.

The Château de Biron and around

Château de Biron
t 05 53 63 13 39; open July and Aug daily 10–7; rest of year call for times; adm

From Monflanquin or Villeréal you may have already sighted the superb **Château de Biron**, largest of all Périgord's castles. The steep hill was a natural stronghold, and the first castle was built in the 11th century to command the northern approaches to the Agenais. In 1189 Gaston de Gontaut, chief of the four barons of Périgord (and an ancestor of Lord Byron) got his hands on it, and they were like glue – the Gontauts held on to the castle for 24 generations, until the early 20th century. Over the centuries the family created one of the most charmingly eclectic castles in France. The first Gaston built the square 12th-century keep, or Tour Anglaise, while Romanesque walls and the Tour du Concierge (with Renaissance dormers) date from after the 1212 siege of Biron by Simon de Montfort. Gaston de Gontaut was tainted with heresy after wedding his daughter to the Cathar captain, Martin Algaïs, England's seneschal of Gascony. Algaïs led a brave defence against the French crusaders, but de Montfort only agreed to go away when the young man was handed over for execution.

The next important building spree was initiated by Pons de Gontaut-Biron, who accompanied Charles VIII on his invasion of Italy in 1497. Pons returned to Biron determined to add some *quattrocento* grace to his muscular feudal domain with the delicate Pavillon de la Recette and a two-storey chapel – the ground floor built as a parish church for the villagers of Biron, and the upstairs reserved for the nabobs. This chapel long held two 14th-century masterpieces, a *Pietà* and *Mise au Tombeau*, which to the great outrage of many were sold by the Gontaut-Birons in the early 1900s to the Metropolitan Museum in New York; of the tombs, only two were priced too high for the New Yorkers, those of Pons de Gontaut-Biron, carved with the *Resurrection of Lazarus* and *Christ Appearing to his Disciples*, and his brother, Armand, bishop of Sarlat (d. 1531), with three dignified feminine *Virtues*.

A third round of building was begun by Baron Armand de Gontaut, a Maréchal de France (1524–92), who died fighting the Catholic League at the side of Henri IV. His hot-headed son Charles continued the fight, receiving 32 wounds in battle. Henri rewarded him by raising Biron to a duchy, and making Charles ambassador to England; but Charles found peace boring, and in 1602 he was un-duked and beheaded at the Bastille for conspiracy against the king (hence Biron's story of a headless ghost). The moat was filled in under Richelieu, who didn't like the great lords of France feeling safe or secure. Work was taken up again in the 18th century, but left incomplete at the time of the Revolution.

Parc de Loisirs P'Arc-en-Ciel
t 05 53 71 84 58; open April, May and Sept daily 1–6; June daily 1–7; July and Aug daily 9–8; adm

Musée B. Palissy
t 05 53 40 98 22; open May–Sept daily 2–6; April and Oct Sun and school hols 2–6; Nov–Mar 1st Sun of month 2–5

From the castle take the D150 south to **Lacapelle-Biron**, a village founded on the orders of Biron's baron to host the Monday market that used to take place under the château – the baron hated to be awakened by the noise. It's now home to the **Parc de Loisirs P'Arc-en-Ciel**, with animals, children's play area, picnic spot, gardens and walks. There's also a small museum where you can learn all about snails. In nearby **St-Avit** the little **Musée Bernard Palissy** covers the life and work of the great Renaissance potter and writer born here in 1510, who became famous for his superb enamels, before he was arrested for being a Protestant in 1589 and thrown into the Bastille, where he soon died. There is an annual exhibition of contemporary ceramics (see *www.ceramique.com/Palissy*).

Gavaudun and Around

Lacapelle-Biron and **St-Avit** are near the head of the sweet leafy valley and mini-gorge of the Lède, a little stream that not only sounds like the mythological river of oblivion, Lethe, but really does make the cares of the world seem far away – deceptively so: St-Avit, for instance, was razed by the retreating Germans in 1944. Troops marched through in the Middle Ages as well: a striking 12th-century six-storey donjon dominates the ruins of the **castle at Gavaudun**, set on a huge natural stone platform. The shelters in the cliffs around Gavaudun were densely populated from the Mousterian era to the Magdalenian.

Château de Gavaudun
t 05 53 95 62 04; open May, June, Sept and Oct Sat and Sun 10–1 and 2–6, July and Aug daily 10–6; adm

Just north of Gavaudun, **St-Sardos-de-Laurenque** has a pretty Romanesque church with fish carved on the portal.

Market Days in and around Monflanquin

Monflanquin: Thursday.
Villeréal: Saturday, plus farmers' market Wednesday in summer.
Castillonnès: Tuesday.
Lacapelle-Biron: Monday.
Issigeac: Sunday.

Where to Stay and Eat in and around Monflanquin

Monflanquin >
Place des Arcades, t 05 53 36 40 19, www.monflanquin.fr

Castillonnès >>
Place des Cornières, t 05 53 36 87 44

Villeréal >
Place de la Halle, t 05 53 36 09 65, www.aavie.com/villereal

Monflanquin ✉ 47150

****Moulin de la Boulède**, on road to Villeréal, **t** 05 53 36 16 49, *www.moulindeboulede.com* (€). A restored mill over a stream, with pleasant rooms and good food (€€€–€€).

Ferme du Bossu, 2.5km south of town off D253, **t** 05 53 36 40 61, *www.auberge-du-bossu.com* (€). A former *auberge* now offering four gîtes for 2–6 and 2–8 people.

Ferme-Auberge de Tabel, on Villeréal road 5km from Monflanquin, **t** 05 53 36 30 57 (€€). Lunches and dinners made using fresh local produce and home-reared meat. Booking is required. The British owners also offer three rooms (€) and a large gîte.

Villeréal ✉ 47210

Château de Scandaillac, St Eutrope de Born, **t** 05 53 36 65 40; *www.scandaillac.com* (€€). Eight beautifully furnished rooms, plus a heated pool, flowery terrace and magnificent Renaissance dining room (€€). *Restaurant closed Tues.*

Moulin de Labique, St-Vivien, on way to Born, **t** 05 53 01 63 90, *www.moulin-de-labique.fr* (€€). Colourful, pretty, traditional country rooms with wooden beams and heavy furniture, plus a pool. The restaurant (€€€), serving delicious regional fare, has the same cheerful feel and a lovely patio under a canopy of vines surrounded by flowers and butterflies. Book ahead. *Restaurant closed in winter.*

****Le Lac**, Route de Bergerac, **t** 05 53 36 01 39 (€). A fine un-gussied-up modern hotel in the trees by a little lake, popular with swimmers and fishermen, with a pool and restaurant (€€€–€€). *Closed Oct–Mar.*

***Europe**, Place Jean Moulin, **t** 05 53 36 00 35 (€). Simple rooms in the centre of the action. *Closed 2wks Oct.*

Castillonnès ✉ 47300

*****Hôtel des Remparts**, 26 Rue de la Paix, **t** 05 53 49 55 85 (€€). Ten handsome rooms in a 19th-century house overlooking the ramparts. The restaurant (€€€–€€) has a terrace with tables round a fountain. *Closed Sun eve and Mon outside high season, 2wks Nov and 2wks Jan.*

Ferme du Bois de Mercier, **t** 05 53 36 81 97, *www.fermedemercier.com* (€). An organic farm with lovely rooms, by a pond where you can swim, fish and go boating. There is also a gîte. *Closed Jan.*

ⓘ **Issigeac >**
t 05 53 58 79 62

ⓘ **Monpazier >**
t 05 53 22 68 59, www.monpazier-perigord.com

ⓘ **Lacapelle-Biron >>**
Mairie, *t 05 53 36 55 45 (summer only)*

★ **Le Prieuré >>**

Issigeac ✉ 24560

La Brucelière, Place de la Capelle, **t** 05 53 37 89 61, *www.bruceliere.com* (€). A 19th-century inn with simple doubles with free wi-fi access, serving some of the best seafood (€€€) in the Dordogne.

Monpazier ✉ 24540

*****Edward I**, 5 Rue St-Pierre, **t** 05 53 22 44 00, *www.hoteledward1er.com* (€€€–€€). A 19th-century mini-château with an attractive pool where the moat might have been. Rooms are fitted out with every comfort (including steam bath or Jacuzzi in some) and satellite TVs, and there's a restaurant for which you need to book in advance. Ask about packages with local golf clubs. *Closed mid-Nov–early Mar.*

Les Peyrouliers, along D660, **t** 05 53 22 66 10 (€€). Simple, well-prepared dishes such as *magret* and foie gras, plus southwest standards. *Closed Sun eve and Mon.*

La Bastide, 52 Rue St-Jacques, **t** 05 53 22 60 59 (€€€–€). A quirky old favourite serving up the likes of chicken in *verjus* (the juice of unripe wine grapes) and trout with almonds. Save room for the delectable walnut cake. *Closed Mon out of season.*

Lacapelle-Biron ✉ 24540

Le Prieuré, **t** 05 53 61 93 03, *www.fancyfrance.net* (€€€). A beautiful *chambres d'hôte* in the historic priory of the château, built in 1512 by Biron for his six priests. Guestrooms are large and sumptuous, and gourmet meals are available.

Gavaudun ✉ 47150

L'Auberge Le Donjon, **t** 05 53 40 82 32 (€€€–€). A popular place to come to enjoy local cuisine, with an outside play area for children and a shaded *pétanque* pitch. Note that you need to book ahead for evenings. *Closed late Aug–early Sept.*

Down the Lot: from Fumel to Villeneuve-sur-Lot

At **Fumel** the Lot moves into the 21st century, shedding its ringlets along with its pristine lack of industry, car parks and commercial sprawl as it meets flatter country en route to its confluence with the mighty Garonne at Aiguillon. From the valley road the scenery might seem unexciting, but take a short detour anywhere to the south and you'll find some of the most remarkable landscapes in the southwest: rank upon rank of flat-topped *mesas* cut out of the limestone by little streams over the past few million years – the northern extremity of the Agenais *Pays des Serres* (the viewpoint at the top of Penne is a good place to see the whole of them). However dramatic, it's still a green and pleasant land, especially in spring when its orchards burst into blossom.

Tournon-d'Agenais and Montaigu-de-Quercy

The hills here, at the crossroads of the *département* of the Lot-et-Garonne, the Lot, and the Tarn-et-Garonne, belong to the Haut Pays des Serres – the land of gentle undulations and valleys, a prelude to the Pays des Serres proper further downstream. Before leaving the Fumel area, there are two hill towns just to the south that merit a detour. **Tournon-d'Agenais**, the first, is a pretty *mesa*-top *bastide*, founded by the indefatigable Alphonse de Poitiers in 1270; there are several half-timbered houses, and arcades around the central

Getting to Villeneuve-sur-Lot

Trains run regularly each day between Villeneuve and Agen.

Place du Marché. The vineyards in the area produce red *vin de pays Thézac-Perricard*, which was served to Nicholas II of Russia. Won over, he ordered 1,000 bottles for a family party, and since then the wine's been known as the Vin du Tsar; try it at the **Vignerons de Thézac-Perricard** on the D151 between Tournon and Puy-l'Evêque.

Vignerons de Thézac-Perricard
t 05 53 40 72 76; open July and Aug daily 9.15–12 and 2–7; rest of year Mon–Sat 9.15–12 and 2–6

The second hilltown, **Montaigu-de-Quercy**, 'Mount Sharp', was the site of a 12th-century castle built by Count Raymond V of Toulouse. Montaigu manages to look more Italian than French from a distance but has a sufficiently large Brit contingent to support an English library. It also has a crystalline artificial lake, the **Plan d'Eau de Chênes**, with a white sandy beach. There's a pretty square with half-timbered houses, and some sharply steep streets in the centre. Ten minutes to the west, on an even higher hill, **Roquecor** is a sleepy, laidback place with a Sunday-morning market that attracts a jovial mix of twanging locals, squires in Rollers, bikers and expats. If you're continuing into the Tarn-et-Garonne, *see* Lauzerte, p.410.

Fermeraie du Jougla
t 05 63 94 41 42; open April–mid-June Sat, Sun and hols 10–7; mid-June–early Sept daily 10.30–7.30; rest of year call for times; adm

If you have small children, they're sure to love the **Fermeraie du Jougla** 8km away in **Belvèze** on the road to Lauzerte – a wooded park that's home to around 200 animals, from a llama to a Vietnamese pig, and lambs and kids they can bottlefeed, plus waterslides and games. Near Belvèze at **Pervillac**, on the D24, the **church** contains some charming 16th-century frescoes.

Penne-d'Agenais and Around

On the river itself, **Lustrac**, 9km west on the D911 from Fumel, is a charming spot marked by one of France's most impressive fortified mills, the **Moulin de Montnavés**, founded in 1296; the adjacent château was a glorified river tollbooth. Further downstream, rising high over the south bank, **Penne-d'Agenais** is a prettily restored artsy-craftsy *village perché* that has well earned its retirement from the affairs of this world. On a site inhabited since prehistoric times, by, among others, the Gauls (*penn* means hill crest in Celtic) and Romans, the medieval village grew up around a chapel of Our Lady of the Assumption first built around the year 1000 – one of the oldest churches in France dedicated to the Virgin. In 1182, Richard the Lionheart found the site inspirational in another way, and built a mighty castle here, making Penne 'the key of Guyenne'; he is locally recalled in the name of one of the three medieval gates, the Porte Ricarde, and in the nearby **Fontaine de Ricard**. Being chosen as the key of Guyenne was a mixed blessing at best: the town's other nickname was *Penne la Sanglante*. Many inhabitants were Cathars, and in 1212 they were besieged for 50 days by the Albigensian crusaders before they were captured and burned alive at the stake. In 1373, during the Hundred Years' War, the English set the town afire when Du Guesclin was at the point of capturing it; in 1562, Blaise de Monluc captured it from the Protestants, then put them all to the sword. Shortly after, Henri IV ordered the destruction of the castle, probably to the great relief of the people of Penne: today only two towers by the deep 'English ditch' remain, and the prison, in the cellar of the *mairie*.

The famous church, now known as **Notre-Dame-de-Peyragude** (from *pierre aiguë*, or sharp stone), was from the start an important stop along the road to Compostela; as it was outside the castle walls it took some hard knocks. It was rebuilt for the third time in 1653, in response to a vow, after floods from the Garonne set off a plague that killed half the population of the Agenais, then again in 1842 after the Revolution sold it off piecemeal for building stone. So many pilgrims kept turning up that in 1896 the local prelates built what you see today – a huge basilica in the kitschy neobyzantine taste of the time, but with a view in every direction.

Villeneuve-sur-Lot

The bustling market city of **Villeneuve** grew out of yet another *bastide*, founded by Alphonse de Poitiers, Count of Toulouse, in 1264. During a tour Alphonse had found the surrounding countryside in ruin and misery after the Albigensian crusade, and, hoping to stabilize the area, he acquired the land for a new town from the Benedictine abbey of Eysses – hence the city's first name, Villeneuve d'Eysses. Although the town now spreads every which way, it has retained its simple *bastide* heart, as well as a pretty medieval neighbour, Pujols. Villeneuve likes its *rugby à treize* so much that it needs three stadiums to contain all the action.

A Walk around the *Bastide*

Enter by way of the 13th-century Porte de Paris, crowned with a 30m tower, the bottom third made of stone, the top two-thirds brick. The central market square, Place Lafayette, is still framed in its *cornières*, rebuilt in the 17th century after the riots of the Fronde. Nearby, the elaborate brick Ste-Catherine was completed in the 1930s, replacing the original Gothic church which was in danger of collapse. The magnificent Gothic and early Renaissance stained glass of the latter (perhaps designed in part by Bernard Palissy) were incorporated in the modern church, depicting the *Life of Christ* and a bevy of saints associated with the city. St James the Greater appears three times, in honour of the many pilgrims who passed through en route to Compostela because Villeneuve was one of the few places on the Lot with a bridge, the Pont Vieux.

Musée d'Eysses
t 05 53 70 65 19; guided visits July and Aug daily 2–6; rest of year by appointment

Musée de Gajac
2 Rue des Jardins, t 05 53 40 48 00; open Mon–Fri 10–12 and 2–6, Sat and Sun 2–6

Haras National
open July and Aug Mon–Fri 2–5; guided visits with carriage rides Wed; call tourist office, see opposite, for more info

Villeneuve-sur-Lot Golf and Country Club
t 05 53 01 60 19; open daily 7.30am–10.30pm

This takes the Périgueux–Auch road, first tramped out in Neolithic times, and it made Villeneuve's fortune when the English built the bridge in 1282, with three fortified towers similar to those of Cahors's Pont Valentré. Unfortunately these tumbled down when the bridge partially collapsed in a flood – hence the asymmetrical wide arch. Further evil has since been averted thanks to a frilly, dolled-up statue of Our Lady of Joy in the chapel overhanging at the north end, rebuilt in 1642. Although the Benedictine abbey is gone, excavations have revealed bits of Eysses, originally the Roman *Excisum*, a pretty place with the remains of a tower and a villa 2km north on the Monflanquin road. The **Musée d'Eysses** displays the bits and pieces found, such as money and ceramics.

Not far from the bridge, the **Musée de Gajac** is in a 1264 building that was part of the original foundations of the walled town, then a flour mill in the 19th century. Today it houses an exhibition of local history and fine art, as well as various temporary shows and events. Horse-lovers can also walk around the **Haras National**.

North at **Castelnaud-de-Gratecambe** is a **golf complex** with 27 holes and a driving range, plus a swimming pool and tennis courts.

Pujols and Two Caves

The main attraction around Villeneuve is its own mother, medieval **Pujols**, up on a hill 2km from the Pont Vieux. This was a Celtic *oppidum* and Roman town named Podium, 'High Place', until its allegiance to the Cathars earned it near-total obliteration in the Albigensian crusade. It was rebuilt with the same stone by the Count of Toulouse, Alphonse de Poitiers, complete with a 14th-century castle that resembled a mini-Carcassonne (there's a model in the tourist office), and that was destroyed not by the enemy but by the town in 1880, when the town council sold off the stone for a mere 1800 francs to finance the prison at Eysses.

To enter Pujols's ancient square, pass under the arch of the tower of the 15th-century Flamboyant Gothic **St-Nicolas**, which has star vaulting and a chapel with bits discovered and moved here during various remodellings – Gothic tombstones and a Renaissance mausoleum, originally in the choir. A second church, **Ste-Foy la Jeune**, dates from the 1400s and contains some murals from the period, one showing St George, another of St Foy (Faith) of Agen – a 3rd-century maiden whom the Romans burned on a gridiron, just as they did St Lawrence. Although Foy's cult centre is up at Conques (Aveyron), some of her relics were taken to Glastonbury and a number of English churches were named after her.

Grottes de Fontirou
t 05 53 41 73 97; open Easter–June and 1st half Sept Mon–Sat, and Sun when weather allows, 2–5.30; July and Aug daily 10–12.30 and 2–6; adm

Grottes de Lestournelles
t 05 53 40 08 09; open July and Aug Mon–Sat 10–7, Sun 2–7; mid-June–end June and 1st half Sept daily 2–7; adm

Ten kilometres to the south of Pujols towards Agen are the **Grottes de Fontirou**, with extraordinary limestone formations. There's also mini-golf. About 7km northwest, in Ste-Colombe, the **Grottes de Lestournelles** are just as splendid.

(★) Le Beffroi >>

(i) Montaigu-de-Quercy >>
Place du Mercadiel, t 05 63 94 48 50

(i) Penne-d'Agenais >>
Rue du 14 Juillet, t 05 53 41 37 80, www.ville-pennedagenais.fr

(i) Villeneuve-sur-Lot >
3 Pl de la Libération, t 05 53 36 17 30, www.ville-villeneuve-sur-lot.fr/ www.cc-villeneuvois.fr

(i) Pujols >>
Place St-Nicolas, t 05 53 36 78 69, www.otpujols47.info (summer only)

(★) La Toque Blanche >>

Market Days in and around Villeneuve

Tournon-d'Agenais: Tuesday and Friday evenings July and August.

Montaigu-de-Quercy: Saturday.

Penne-d'Agenais: Sunday mornings, Port de Penne.

Villeneuve: Saturday, 2nd and 4th Tuesday of month, and Friday evening July–Aug, Place Lafayette; organic market Wednesday, Place d'Aquitaine.

Pujols: Sunday Mar–Nov, plus some other days in summer.

Activities in and around Villeneuve

You can hire electric **boats** or **canoes** from the Base Nautique de l'Aviron Villeneuvois in Villeneuve, **t** 05 53 49 18 27, which also runs canoeing lessons. For **horseriding holidays** in the area, contact the Ranch de Barulus (**t** 05 53 40 00 78, *www.ranchdebarulus.com*).

Ask at the respective tourist offices about summer **guided tours** of Montaigu-de-Quercy and Villeneuve.

Where to Stay and Eat in and around Villeneuve

Villeneuve-sur-Lot ✉ 47300

The hotels here are geared mostly to prune merchants.

****Le Terminus**, 2 Avenue Foch, **t** 05 53 70 94 36, *www.hotel-le-terminus.com* (€€). A well-preserved, charming hotel with a restaurant (€€–€).

****La Résidence**, 17 Av Lazare Carnot, **t** 05 53 40 17 03 (€€–€). A functional but pleasant choice.

***Les Remparts**, 1 Rue Etienne Marcel, **t** 05 53 70 71 63, *www.hoteldesremparts.fr* (€). Decent if unexciting rooms.

Hostellerie du Rooy, Chemin de Labourdette, just east on D661, **t** 05 53 70 48 48 (€€€–€€). A large, attractive inn with a garden terrace, serving flavourful seafood and mushroom dishes. *Closed Sun eve, Mon, and several wks throughout year.*

Chez Caline, **t** 05 53 70 42 08 (€€–€). Imaginative food and friendly service. *Closed Sun and Tues eve.*

L'Oustal, 24 Rue de la Convention, **t** 05 53 41 49 44 (€€–€). Basque cuisine and seafood. *Closed Sun and Tues eve.*

Tournon-d'Agenais ✉ 47370

****Le Beffroi**, **t** 05 53 01 20 59, *www.restaurant-lebeffroi.com* (€). Rooms in the centre of the medieval town, plus a bar and a good restaurant (€€€–€€). *Closed mid-Nov–mid-Dec.*

****Les Voyageurs**, **t** 05 53 40 70 28 (€). Comfy rooms plus a traditional restaurant (€€€–€). *Closed Sat exc July and Aug, plus mid-Oct–mid-Nov.*

Around Montaigu-de-Quercy ✉ 82150

****Château de l'Hoste**, 10km west of town at St-Beauzeil on D656, **t** 05 63 95 25 61, *www.chateaudelhoste.com* (€€€). An 18th-century *gentilhommière* with peaceful rooms and a library, in a large park with a pool. The restaurant (€€€–€€) specializes in southwest favourites, and offers a veggie menu.

Penne-d'Agenais and St-Sylvestre-sur-Lot ✉ 47140

******Château Lalande**, St-Sylvestre, **t** 05 53 36 15 15, *www.chateau-lalande.com* (€€€€€–€€€€). A 13th–18th-century château with heated pools cascading into one another and tennis courts. The restaurant (€€€€–€€€), one of the region's best, combines traditional ingredients with exotic flavours.

Le Moulin de Dausse, Dausse, **t** 05 53 41 26 00 (€€). Truly lovely food in an intimate atmosphere – try three mini-starters, a main course and a taster of three desserts. And sample the salmon; the chef smokes it himself. Advance booking is recommended. *Closed Jan–Mar, lunch, and Mon–Wed eve.*

Pujols ✉ 47300

*****Les Chênes**, Bel-Air, **t** 05 53 49 04 55, *www.hoteldeschenes.com* (€€). Charming, refined rooms, a warm family atmosphere and a heated pool.

La Toque Blanche, **t** 05 53 49 00 30, *www.la-toque-blanche.com* (€€€€–€€). An intimate, elegant restaurant amid the trees, attracting prune barons and gastronomes. Views to the medieval town are accompanied by delicious duck dishes, traditional and innovative. *Closed Sun eve, Mon and Tues lunch, mid-June–start of July, and mid-Nov.*

The Prune Kingdom: Villeneuve to Aiguillon

Some 65 per cent of French plums come from the Lot-et-Garonne and, dried as *pruneaux d'Agen*, are known around the world. As it happens, most of them do not come from Agen at all but from the rich lands of this last stage of the Lot valley. It isn't a touristy area but a businesslike, well-off agricultural paradise, packed tightly with not only plum orchards but strawberries, asparagus and all the other *primeurs* that decorate France's markets around the year.

Casseneuil to Granges

After Villeneuve, the first village on the Lot is picturesque medieval **Casseneuil**, on a peninsula formed by the confluence of the Lot and Lède. Charlemagne himself apparently had a summer house there in the 9th century. Since good stone was lacking in this part of the Lot valley, nearly everything is made of brick, including most of Casseneuil's houses and its church, containing good 15th-century frescoes. The same goes for **Ste-Livrade-sur-Lot**, where there is an odd brick fortification called the Tour du Roi, the *roi* in this case being its builder, Richard the Lionheart. The bricks of Ste-Livrade's church are half eroded away, giving the building a strangely outlandish air. This was the church of an important priory, although the ambitions of its founders far outran the resources of those who followed. Look inside for some fine carvings in the 'Romanesque Chapel', now housing the main altar: on the capitals, a mermaid and her baby, a satyr and a monster or two.

Roseraie Vicart
t 05 53 41 04 99; open May–Sept daily 9.30–12 and 2.30–7

Rose lovers may want to visit the **Roseraie Vicart** with its 300 types. Downriver, the humdrum church at **Fongrave** has an unexpected masterpiece: a beautifully sculpted wooden Baroque altarpiece.

Next down the river on the south bank, **Le-Temple-sur-Lot** was named for the Templar headquarters that oversaw all the order's holdings in the Agenais; the red brick commandery building survives along with its chapel, now the village church. Near the

Pruneaux d'Agen

If you recall the episode in *Le Tour de Gaule d'Astérix* in which a treacherous Agenais innkeeper tries to capture Astérix and Obélix by slipping a Mickey into their prunes, you'll be shocked to learn that this is a flagrant anachronism. The first plums in the area were brought over from Damascus by the crusaders in 1148; they took at once to the local soil and climate, and people soon learned to dry them out for the famous *pruneaux d'Agen*, the prunes of Agen. Most come from a fast-drying plum called *prune d'ente*.

Go to any local market to discover the extraordinary variety of prunes. The Lot-et-Garonne produces, on average, 30,000 tonnes a year. You'll see a considerable proportion prettily displayed in the purple shop windows of Agen: boxes of *pruneaux fourrés* (prunes stuffed with chocolate and so on), jars of prune cream, and prunes in armagnac. There are also some excellent prune liqueurs and *eaux de vie* made by small local producers, occasionally sold in pâtisseries. Local cooks bend over backwards to come up with new ways to use prunes; recipes combine them with quail, rabbit, pork and even fish.

Alose aux Pruneaux (Shad with Prunes)

Clean and cut into sections 1.5kg of shad. Soak 20 Agen prunes in warm water for five minutes, drain and stone them and then cook them for eight minutes on a low heat with a clove and orange peel in a cup of Côtes du Marmandais. Quickly brown the shad sections in a little oil in a large saucepan, sprinkle with armagnac, set alight and remove the fish. In the same pan sauté 150g chopped shallots, 50g thinly sliced carrots, 50g thinly sliced celery, and garlic, thyme, parsley and a bay leaf. Add the sauce from the prunes and two cups of red wine (minus a small glass), then, when it's a quarter boiled down, add a half-cup of *fumet de poisson* (or fish bouillon). Cook for another five minutes, then add the fish and prunes and cook for 20 minutes. When the fish is done, remove it and the prunes and strain the sauce and put back on the heat, add the glass of wine and season. Remove skin and bones of shad, arrange on a plate with the sauce ladled on top, sprinkle with chives, and then give it to the cat.

With thanks to the Marmande tourist office.

Latour-Marliac Etablissements Botaniques
*t 05 53 01 08 05; open May–Sept daily 10–5; **shop** open mid-Mar–Sept; adm*

village, the century-old **botanical gardens of the Latour-Marliac garden company** have more than 100 varieties of lotus, water lily and other water-loving plants, at their best May–September.

In the hills to the south, off the D13, is a delightful place called **St-Sardos** – a tiny, sleepy hamlet decked with flowers and sleeping dogs. The 12th-century church on the green has a lovely, well-preserved portal carved with beasts and floral designs. Where the D13 meets the river stands the unfortunately named **Castelmoron-sur-Lot**, where the Lot is backed up by a dam to make a little lake for swimming and boating; there's a beach along the river. The *mairie* occupies an Arabian Nights villa, built by the nostalgic wife of a former ambassador to Syria. The hills north of Castelmoron are quite pretty, though there is nothing to detain you there except another *bastide*, **Monclar d'Agenais**, built on a hill by Alphonse de Poitiers and enjoying lovely views in all directions.

Chaudron Magique
t 05 53 88 80 77; open daily 3–6; adm

West of here, at **Brugnac**'s **Chaudron Magique**, you can learn about raising angora goats, rabbits, other animals and natural plant dyes; there are baby goats for the kids to bottle-feed and a shop selling yarn, mohair pullovers and goat's cheese.

Musée du Pruneau et de la Prune
Domaine de Gabach, t 05 53 84 00 69; open Mon–Sat 9–12 and 2–6.30/7, Sun and hols 3–7, exc 2wks in Jan; adm

In **Granges-sur-Lot**, just downstream from Castelmoron, one of the largest plum farms in the valley created a **prune museum** for the curious and the constipated; a 35-minute prune video, old drying ovens, local costumes, a prune jammery and *chocolaterie*, free tastings, the plummiest shop in the hemisphere and a summer corn maze are only some of the attractions.

Clairac to Aiguillon

Clairac presents a beautiful panorama from the riverfront; from the inside, it is perhaps less beautiful, and has little to show from a busy history. Clairac once had a great abbey, where a roving monk brought back and planted the first *pétum* (tobacco) in France, beginning an important chapter in the local economy; the abbey itself was wrecked in the Wars of Religion, leaving only a bit called the Tour Ronde and bits restored from the ruins to become the

Abbaye des Automates
t 05 53 79 34 81; open April–Sept daily 10–6; Oct–Mar Wed, Sat and Sun 10–5; adm

Musée du Train
same hrs as Abbaye des Automates; adm

La Forêt Magique
same hrs as Abbaye des Automates; adm

Abbaye des Automates, where the clockwork monks work, pray and illuminate manuscripts, and dozens of other figures illustrate favourite fairytales. Little kids think it's a gas. Upstairs there are scenes of celebrated characters who spent some time at Clairac.

Nearby you can visit other models, this time of trains, at the **Musée du Train**, and – for the kids – at **La Forêt Magique**, with gnomes and elves, models of boats, monuments made out of matchsticks and Santa's house.

East of Clairac on the D911, follow the old blue historic marker signs and with luck you will find to one of the most remarkable monuments of the region: an ornate monumental **stone fountain** that is most likely the work of Jean Goujon, France's master sculptor of the Renaissance, standing at the edge of a broad lawn (it's on private property, so ask at the house to visit it).

The Lot meets the Garonne at **Aiguillon**, a town that began as a Roman encampment but knew its greatest fame as the residence of the wealthy Duc d'Aiguillon, a political figure of the last days of the *ancien régime*, whose little court and decadent parties made Aiguillon the hotspot of the Agenais in the summer, when lots of swells (including the duke's friend Madame du Barry) came down from Versailles. It is to him that the town owes its landmark **château** (1765), a stately work of early neoclassical architecture. There's also, in a 19th-century church in Rue de la République, the **Musée Raoul Dastrac**, with works by the post-Impressionist artist who was born in Aiguillon, and died there in 1969. There are also temporary exhibitions devoted to other artists, and other displays, usually of ceramics.

Musée Raoul Dastrac
contact tourist office for opening times

ⓘ Casseneuil >>
45 Les Promenades, t 05 53 41 13 33, www.mairie-de-casseneuil.com (summer only)

Market Days from Villeneuve to Aiguillon

Casseneuil: Wednesday and Sunday.
Ste-Livrade: Friday.
Monclar d'Agenais: Saturday.
Clairac: Thursday.
Castelmoron: Wednesday.
Aiguillon: Tuesday and Friday.

Activities from Villeneuve to Aiguillon

Both of the tourist offices in the area organize summer **guided tours**, and staff will provide details of summer river excursions.

Contact Connoisseur (**t** 05 53 79 58 17, *www.vacancesfluviales.com*) if you'd like to hire a **houseboat** for 4–8 people for a week.

Where to Stay and Eat from Villeneuve to Aiguillon

Casseneuil ✉ 47440

***Auberge La Résidence**, Route de Villeneuve, **t** 05 53 41 08 08 (€). A simple but sweet place with a restaurant (€€–€) with a shady terrace. *Closed Sat and Sun in winter.*

Ste-Livrade-sur-Lot ✉ 47110

****Le Midi**, 1 Rue Malfourat, **t** 05 53 01 00 32 (€). A Logis de France hotel in the village, with comfortable rooms and a restaurant (€€–€) serving local and Basque dishes. *Closed Sun eve, plus Mon in winter.*

Le Temple-sur-Lot ✉ 47110

*****Les Rives du Plantie**, Route de Castelmoron, **t** 05 53 79 86 86, www.rivesduplantie.com (€€€). A lovely 19th-century *maison de maître* beside the Lot, with a shady garden, a terrace, a pool and a restaurant (€€€–€). *Closed Jan.*

La Commanderie, **t** 05 53 01 30 66 (€€–€). A restored 12th-century building amidst fountains and water plants, serving tasty dishes with verve, including a duo of red mullet and foie gras. The menus change regularly. *Closed Sun eve and Mon.*

Tombebœuf ✉ 47380

****Hôtel du Nord**, north of Monclar, **t** 05 53 88 83 15 (€). A useful Logis de France hotel a bit outside the usual circuit, with a pool and a restaurant (€€–€). *Closed Fri and Sun eves out of season and several wks in Jan.*

Clairac ✉ 47320

Chambres d'Hôte Le Caussinat, between Clairac and Granges-sur-Lot, **t** 05 53 84 22 11 (€). A big rambling farmhouse overlooking fields, with decor reminiscent of a large Victorian parlour, a swimming pool and a large garden. In the evening you can have dinner (€€) with the family, who prepare dishes from fresh farm produce. *Open mid-Mar–Oct.*

Aiguillon ✉ 47190

****Le Jardin des Cygnes**, in countryside along Route de Villeneuve, **t** 05 53 79 60 02, *www.jardin-des-cygnes.com* (€). Simple rooms, a pool and a restaurant (€€) serving intriguing surprises such as *confit* of pork with prune chutney. *Closed Sat and Sun eves exc July and Aug, 1wk at end of summer, and mid-Dec–early Jan.*

****Terrasse de l'Etoile**, **t** 05 53 79 64 64, *www.laterrassedeletoile.com* (€). A central hotel with stylish Art Deco rooms, a little pool and terrace, and a restaurant (€€–€).

ⓘ **Aiguillon >>**
Place du 14 Juillet, **t** *05 53 79 62 58*

The *Pays des Serres*

A local geography teacher gets credit for naming the triangle between the Lot and Garonne the *Pays des Serres*. It is a fitting word: *serres* means an eagle's talons (the limestone looks as if it has been clawed by a huge bird, leaving gashes between its limestone 'tables'); coincidentally, the word also means greenhouses, and there are plenty of these too – or more likely plastic tunnels for fruit and vegetable *primeurs*, which farmers have added to supplement the income from their wheatfields.

Little *Bastides* and Foie Gras

Many of the villages in the *Pays des Serres* haven't changed much since the Middle Ages – places such as **Hautefage-la-Tour**, to the south of Villeneuve, with a Flamboyant Gothic church, hexagonal Renaissance belltower and a village *lavoir* in the centre. Nearby **Laroque-Timbaut** has a 12th-century *halle* and tiny medieval lanes, especially the Ruelle de Lô, entered under the clocktower. There is a permanent display of **modern sculpture by German artist Gertrude Schön**, who studied in Paris with Ossip Zadkine (*see* p.3336) and uses lots of metal. She came to live in Laroque in 1995.

Musee Gertrude Schön
Place de la Halle, **t** *05 53 87 62 79; open mid-May–mid-Sept Wed–Mon 4–7, or by appt*

According to legend, a church and fountain located in the nearby Vallon de St-Germain cured Roland's army of a contagious disease on their way to Spain. You can visit a living museum featuring more than 50 old breeds of poultry and various other animals at **Les Vallons de Marennes**.

Vallons de Marennes
t *05 53 95 97 32; open July and Aug daily 10–7; plus school hols 2–7; adm*

Musée du Foie Gras
t 05 53 41 23 24; open July and Aug daily 10–7; rest of year Mon–Sat 10–7, Sun exc Jan and hols 3–7; adm, includes tastings

To the northeast, **Frespech** is a delightful little hilltop hamlet where old gates and houses and an 11th-century church with a partial *lauze* roof still stand intact. Here you can learn all about the manna of the southwest at the **Musée du Foie Gras**, with an hour-long guided visit tracing the history of *gavage* and showcasing modern techniques on the farm.

Further east are two baby *bastides*: **Beauville**, clinging to its promontory, complete with its arcades, vestiges of its walls and Gothic church with a pyramidal belltower, and **Bourg-de-Visa**, near a sacred Gaulish spring now known as the Source de St-Quirin. Just southeast of Bourg at **Fauroux** (take the D43), is the fine Romanesque church of St-Romain and one of the prettiest places to swim in the region: the 'tropical' lagoon of Rikiki Plage, with a little waterfall and white sandy beach. South on the D7 bristles the moated, four-towered, military **Château de Brassac**, built in 1180 by Raymond V of Toulouse.

Château de Brassac
t 05 63 94 59 67; open Tues–Sun mid-June–mid-Sept 10–12 and 2–7; Easter–mid-June and mid-Sept–Oct Sun and public hols 2–6

In the same area you'll find **Castelsagrat**, another *bastide* (vintage 1270), with its old communal wells in the irregularly arcaded *place*, and a church of the Assumption with a wonderfully overripe 17th-century Baroque retable. Just west on its hill, half-timbered 13th-century **Montjoi**, with only two streets, could win a prize as the tiniest *bastide* of all. **St-Maurin**, further west, is a charming, half-timbered village near the ruins of an abbey founded in 1097 by the abbots of Moissac and destroyed in 1802. Bits that were salvaged, including the altar and a model of the abbey, may be seen in the church of St-Martin d'Anglars, as well as carved capitals telling the story of Maurin's martyrdom. St-Maurin's inhabitants have put together a small but intriguing **Musée de l'Abbaye de Saint Maurin** in the abbey cellars, where they found the 13th-century tombs of the monks. It recounts the daily life of the villagers at the start of the 20th century.

Musée de l'Abbaye de Saint Maurin
t 05 53 95 31 25; open July and Aug Wed–Mon 3–7; rest of year by appt

Approaching Agen: Puymirol and Prayssas

Towards Agen is the *bastide* of **Puymirol**, was built by Count Raymond VII of Toulouse in 1246. Located on a bluff, with a citadel and deep moat at its weakest point, Puymirol was believed to be impregnable until the Protestants shattered that illusion in 1574. Much of medieval Puymirol has survived – the counts' residence, the *cornières* and *halle* (now the village *salle des fêtes*), the 13th-century Gothic porch of the church, and the views from the Champs de Mars, site of the citadel before Richelieu had it razed.

The most interesting part of the western *Serres* is around **Prayssas**, a round *bastide*, market town and Chasselas grape grower. North of Prayssas, there once stood another *bastide* called St-Sardos, founded in 1323 by pro-French monks connected with Sarlat. This founding angered the pro-English contingent at nearby

Monpezat, who attacked and demolished the new town, put the monks to the sword and hanged the French seneschal from the maypole that had been set up to celebrate the founding of the *bastide*. Sorting out the incident caused the King of England to delay his homage to Charles IV for the Duchy of Aquitaine, giving Charles sufficient reason to send in an army to confiscate Aquitaine and ignite the Hundred Years' War.

South of Prayssas, medieval **Clermont-Dessous** is clustered under a handsome 11th-century fortified church and ruins of a castle, and offers superb views down the Garonne valley. In the 1950s the village was completely abandoned, but now it has been almost entirely restored. Catherine de' Medici and her daughter Marguerite de Valois spent time hiding out from the Protestants at **Port-Ste-Marie**, and met Henri of Navarre there – Marguerite's future husband. The 16th-century church of Notre-Dame was an important pilgrimage church for river men, who would pray here before braving the next particularly dangerous stretch of the Garonne. These days the village is known for its kiwis.

ⓘ **Puymirol >>**
*7 Rue Maréchal Leclerc, **t** 05 53 95 32 10, www.mairie-puymirol.fr (summer only)*

ⓘ **Laroque-Timbaut >**
*Place de l'Hôtel de Ville, **t** 05 53 95 79 50*

Market Days in the *Pays des Serres*

Beauville: Sunday June–Sept, farmers' market.

Puymirol: Sunday May–Dec, farmers' market; also Saturday 7pm early July–Aug.

Porte Ste-Marie: Saturday farmers' market.

Laroque-Timbaut: Sunday.

Where to Stay and Eat in the *Pays des Serres*

Laroque-Timbaut ✉ 47340

Le Roquentin, opposite church, **t** 05 53 95 78 78 (€€–€). Fine, mainly southwest food at reasonable prices, including a range of fish dishes and warm goats' cheese with honey. *Closed Mon, Wed, Thurs and Sun eves.*

Beauville ✉ 47470

***Hôtel du Midi**, **t** 05 53 95 41 18 (€). Simple rooms, good home-cooking (€€–€). *Closed 2wks in Jan and Sept.*

Bourg-de-Visa ✉ 82190

La Marquise, overlooking Château de Brassac, **t** 05 63 94 25 16 (€). A B&B serving fragrant specialities (€€) of fowl with fruit, plus cassoulet.

Ferme-Auberge de Lasbourdettes, 3km south of Château de Brassac on D7, **t** 05 63 94 26 75 (€€€–€). Delicious local duck, goose and rabbit. There are also two cosy rooms (€). *Closed Tues.*

Puymirol ✉ 47270

******L'Aubergade**, 52 Rue Royale, **t** 05 53 95 31 46, *www.aubergade.com* (€€€€€). A Relais et Châteaux hotel with 10 gorgeous rooms, in a one-horse *bastide* that once belonged to the counts of Toulouse. It has one of France's top-rated restaurants (€€€€), serving legendary desserts – try *larme de chocolat* ('chocolate teardrop') with tiny morello cherries. Booking is essential. *Closed Mon and Tues lunch, plus Sun eve in winter.*

Prayssas ✉ 47360

Terra Naturis, **t** 05 53 87 28 06, *www.terranaturis.fr* (€€). A 17th-century *gentilhommière* turned into a family naturist resort, with a pool. You can also hire horse-drawn caravans in high season. *Closed Oct–April.*

Clermont-Dessous ✉ 47130

Crêperie-Grill Le Troubadour, on main street, **t** 05 53 87 24 45 (€€). Grilled meats, galettes and crêpes served on a small terrace under fairylights with lovely views. *Closed Mon lunch July and Aug and Mon–Wed in winter.*

Agen

Agen

Caesar made the first known mention of the future prune capital, then the humble hilltop *oppidum* of Aginnum, in his *Gallic Wars*. In the *Pax Romana* that followed, Aginnum relocated down into the Garonne valley, where it suffered the usual barbarian and Norman invasions. In the 13th century Agen found itself smack on the front lines between French and English territory. It changed hands 11 times in the Hundred Years' War, but it could have been worse – each new ruler would try to make the Agenais happy to see him by granting the town new privileges.

Even after becoming a *commune* in the 13th century, Agen was under the influence of its noble bishops. During the Renaissance many of these were Italian, and they gave the little provincial town a jump-start in art appreciation and the humanities. A booming textile trade, begun in the 17th century when Agen grew by leaps and bounds, was snuffed out by the Continental Blockade. These days it owes much of its prosperity to its setting between Bordeaux and Toulouse; transport depots, fruit-packing, pharmaceuticals and bureaucracy are the things that keep the money coming in. Admittedly these aren't big tourist magnets, but this shapeless, rather staid but very regular departmental capital does have an ace up its sleeve: one of the finest provincial art museums in France.

Or come when the Agenais show their wild side, when their beloved rugby squad is thumping some hapless opponent. You'll know if they're doing well: all the shops in the centre have team photos and banners in their windows next to choc-filled prunes.

Musée Municipal des Beaux-Arts

Musée Municipal des Beaux-Arts
t 05 53 69 47 23, www.ville-agen.fr/musee; open May–Sept Wed–Mon 10–6; Oct–April Wed–Mon 10–12.30 and 1.30–6, exc some public hols; adm; themed guided tours by request

This, the one great reason to visit Agen, is in the centre of the city, at Place du Dr-Esquirol on the corner of Rue des Juifs, where its vast hoard occupies four beautifully restored 16th- and 17th-century *hôtels particuliers*. The collection begins with the Middle Ages – tombstones and effigies, goldwork, carved Romanesque and Gothic capitals and a 16th-century tapestry of the *Month of March*.

The star of the Gallo-Roman section is the *Vénus du Mas*, a 1st-century Greek marble dug up by a farmer at Mas d'Agenais in 1876, who, despite her lack of a head and part of an arm, is still a helluva tomato, a Venus de Milo in her early twenties; the special lighting perfectly shows off the exceptional cut of the drapery. Don't miss the fine small bronzes in the glass case – a Gaulish helmet, a Celtic horse head and a pawing horse.

The next room, with a Renaissance chimneypiece, is devoted to hunting and warfare, with another fine tapestry and a Renaissance dagger carved with an intricate *danse macabre*. Prehistoric finds are downstairs where Agen once keep its criminals – the dungeon.

Getting to and around Agen

Agen's **airport**, La Garenne (**t** 05 53 77 00 88, *www.aeroport-agen.com*) to the southwest of the city, has three flights a day from Paris with Aerocondor, **t** 08 92 68 87 77.

There are several **trains** a day from the station at Place Rabelais to Monsempron-Libos, Penne, Périgueux and Les Eyzies, plus TGVs to Bordeaux, Toulouse and Paris.

For a **taxi**, call **t** 05 53 98 28 31. In summer you can rent a houseboat to sail along the Canal Latéral, from Locaboat Plaisance, **t** 05 53 66 00 74.

A beautiful spiral stair leads up to the 16th- and 17th-century paintings: two striking Renaissance portraits by Corneille de Lyon, a *Portrait of a Man* by Philippe de Champaigne and a *Virgin and Child* by the school of Raphael. There's a reconstructed pharmacy, and ceramic works by philosopher Bernard Palissy, born in 1510 in St-Avit, who desperately sought the ancient secret of enamel, burning even his furniture to light his kilns. Here too are brightly coloured plates from the same period by the Italian masters, especially from Urbino.

Beyond minor works by Tiepolo and Greuze are five Goyas, left to the city by Chaudordy, French ambassador to Madrid, who got them from Goya's son; they form a complement to the more important collection of Goyas at Castres. There's a powerful *Self-portrait* painted by the artist in his 40s, and one of the *Caprichos*, with a donkey, elephant and bull flying over a crowd of people. Another crowd follows the ascent of the *Montgolfière*, recording the 1793 launch of a hot-air balloon in Madrid. The *Study for an Equestrian Portrait of Ferdinand VII* was a royal commission; and Goya painted *La Misada Parida*, a picture of the first Mass of a newly delivered young mother, on top of an old painting that is slowly but surely leaching through. There's also a copy of Goya's *La Promenade*, said to deplct Goya and the Duchess of Alba. Other works here include *Le conteur* by Watteau.

The last rooms move on to the 19th century, first with ceramics, including those of Agen's own Boudon de St-Amas (1774–1856), who introduced English glazed-ware techniques to France. There's a fine landscape by Corot, another by Sisley, and seascapes by proto-Impressionist Eugène Boudin, the master of Monet and one of the first French painters to paint out of doors. There is also a new permanent exhibition of around 1,600 pieces from the Middle East, principally from the Mediterranean and the Tigris-Euphrates and Oronte valleys, dating from the Bronze Age to the Crusades.

The Rest of Agen

Agen's cathedral, **St-Caprais** (north of the museum, a block from the station, in Rue Raspail), is named after a local boy who hid out during Diocletian's persecutions until he heard of the courageous martyrdom of Ste Foy, whereupon he outed himself as a Christian only to get his head chopped off. There isn't much to see inside

Jasmin, the 'Hero of the Occitan Renaissance'

Jacques Boé (1798–1864), son of a humble tailor of Agen, was a wig-maker who liked to recite the poems he wrote in his native Occitan to his customers. In 1830 he published the fruits of his labours, the *Papillotos*, under the name of his grandfather, Jacques Jasmin; by chance the book was picked up by Charles Nodier, author of *Trilby*, who made the verses the toast of Paris. The capital was then in the midst of a fervent, slightly retarded Romantic era, and the wig-maker poet of Agen caught its fancy. Fellow poet Lamartine dubbed Jasmin 'the Homer of the Proletariat'; the Académie Française honoured him; he was received by Louis Philippe and Napoleon III, and embarked on a lecture tour across France, reciting his poetry and donating the proceeds to charity.

Provençal poet Frédéric Mistral (who went on to become the only Nobel prizewinner in literature in a minority language) idolized Jasmin and in 1854 asked him to lead his Occitan literary movement, the *Félibrage*. But Jasmin preferred to devote the rest of his life to poetry and charity. Perhaps his finest lyrics were his love songs to Agen: *Me fas troubà, pel sero de ma bito/Sourel del mèl et cami del belour...* (You found for me in the evening of my life/A sun of honey and velvet way...)

(which is just as well, because it's often closed) other than the Romanesque tri-lobe apse with *modillons* sculpted with heads of humans and animals. In the northwest corner of Agen an impressive 23-arch aqueduct, the **Pont Canal** built in 1839, carries the Canal Latéral over the Garonne.

Musée de la Résistance et de la Déportation
t 05 53 66 04 26; open by appointment

Confiserie Pierre Boisson
t 05 53 66 20 61; open Mon–Sat 9–12 and 2–7.30

L&L Cognac House
t 05 53 77 44 77; open Mon–Fri 9–11 and 2–4 exc Aug; book in advance

Besides a stroll round Agen's prune-laden *pâtisseries* and *confiseries*, walk over to the banks of the Garonne and the city's favourite promenade, the Esplanade du Gravier, affording a fine view of the Pont Canal. Just up Avenue du Général de Gaulle, the **Monument à Jasmin** honours Agen's favourite poet (*see* above). At 40 Rue Montesquieu there's a **museum about the Resistance**, and at 20 Rue Grande Horloge you can visit **sweet-maker Pierre Boisson** and see staff preparing prune-based confectionery and the like.

Just south at Boé, **L&L** produces cocktails from cognac, passion fruit and cranberry juices – you can visit the factory and taste their delightful concoctions.

Around Agen: the Brulhois, a little corner of Gascony

Vines take over from plums between Agen and the Gers in the hills of the Brulhois. Hilltop **Layrac**, a short way south of Agen, is the main town here, one that grew up around a priory consecrated by Pope Urban II in 1096, itself built over a Roman villa. Don't miss the 17th-century *fontaine-lavoir*, or the roadside cross, carved with indecipherable symbols. Its 12th-century church, St-Martin, has capitals on its façade adorned with intertwined demons and a striking Roman-Byzantine apse; the dome was added in the 18th century, and there's a fine marble altarpiece and 12th-century mosaic on the triumph of Samson.

Dunes and round **Caudecoste** to the east are other picturesque *bastides* to visit; **Moirax** to the west has a delightful 11th-century Romanesque priory with a pretty façade and more than its share of fine carvings both outside and inside, some by 17th-century master

Côtes-de-Brulhois

South of the Garonne, on the borders of the Gers, AOC Côtes-de-Brulhois is perhaps the least-known wine from the Lot-et-Garonne. Grown on the alluvial pebbles atop a clay and limestone bed, this well-structured, dark-red wine is made from Malbec, Tannat and Le Fer Servadou, as well as Merlot and Cabernet Franc. A favourite tipple of the Templars, it can be aged up to 10 years and goes well with game, rich meat dishes and cheeses. Best of all, it's much cheaper than Madiran or Cahors.

You can try it at the **Cave Coopérative** at Goulens, **t** 05 53 87 01 65 (*open Mon–Sat 8–12 and 2–6, www.brulhois.com*), just south of Layrac by the N21. Or visit, on the east end of the *appellation*, the **Château La Bastide Orliac**, **t** 05 53 87 41 02 (call ahead), by the hilltop *bastide* Clermont-Soubiran, with lovely views as well as good bottles of Côtes-de-Brulhois.

Végétales Visions
t *05 53 67 07 77; open Mar–June and Sept Tues–Sun 9–12 and 2–6; July and Aug daily 9–12 and 2–6; Oct–mid-Jan and Feb Tues–Sat 9–12 and 2–6, Sun 9–12; adm*

Conservatoire Végétal Régional d'Aquitaine
t *05 53 47 29 14; open April–Oct Mon–Sat and sometimes Sun 9–12 and 1.30–5.30; Dec–Mar Mon 9–12, Tues–Fri 9–12 and 1.30–5.30, Sat 1.30–5.30; adm*

Jean Tournier. A French *bastide*, **Sérignac-sur-Garonne**, has an 11th-century church of Notre-Dame with a peculiar spiralling belltower, the *clocher hélicoïdal*, built in the 16th century, knocked down in 1922 and since rebuilt as it was.

Nearby are two attractions for plant-lovers: in **Colayrac-St-Cirq**, on the N113, **Végétales Visions**, with tropical greenhouses full of orchids, cacti and carnivorous plants; and in **Montesquieu** the **Conservatoire Végétal Régional d'Aquitaine**, with old varieties of fruit tree, exhibitions of regional fruit and tastings.

Estillac has a handsome 13th–16th-century château, one-time residence of Blaise de Montluc, *maréchal* of France and famous Protestant-crusher in the Wars of Religion. **Laplume** to the south was the old capital of the region and has a nice Renaissance church, with a *tour clocher*, but there's nothing feathery about it; *Penn* in Celtic means hill (the town stands on a steep one) and the Gallo-Romans called it Penna, eventually Latinized into Pluma.

Astaffort, further south, grew up as a stop on a Roman and medieval thoroughfare, and retains a scattering of half-timbered houses, as well as a fortified mill, and medieval churches.

Market Days in Agen

Wednesday and **Sunday**, on Place du Pin; and on **Saturday**, on Esplanade du Gravier and on Place des Laitiers (organic). There's also an annual **prune fair** mid-Sept, Place du 14 Juillet.

Activities in and around Agen

Parc Walibi (**t** 05 53 96 58 32; *open May, June, Sept and Oct Sat, Sun and hols 11–6, July and Aug daily 10–7, or until 8 mid-Aug*), at nearby Roquefort, is one of the biggest amusement parks in southwest France, with rides, entertainment and a waterpark. Agen also has pools at **Aquasud** (**t** 05 53 48 02 63; *open July and Aug daily 10–8*).

Learn to pilot a ULM or go karting at the **Base de Loisirs** (**t** 05 53 87 31 42; *open Wed–Mon 10–12.30 and 2–dusk or 9, plus Tues mornings in summer*) at Caudecoste, 15km east of Agen, or learn to water-ski at **Waterfun** (**t** 05 53 96 20 67) at Boé.

Bon-Encontre (**t** 05 53 96 95 78; *open daily 9–8*) is a local 9-hole golf course.

ⓘ Agen >>
107 Boulevard Carnot, **t** *05 53 47 36 09, www.ot-agen.org*

Where to Stay in and around Agen

Agen ✉ 47000

******Hôtel-Château des Jacobins**, Place des Jacobins, **t** 05 53 47 03 31, *www.chateau-des-jacobins.com* (€€€). A central, ivy-covered *hôtel particulier*, with a pretty garden and parking.

*****Le Provence**, 22 Cours du 14 Juillet, **t** 05 53 47 39 11, *www.hotel-leprovence.com* (€). A pleasant hotel in the centre, with spruce trees and soundproofing.

****Atlantic Hôtel**, 133 Av Jean Jaurès (N113 out to Toulouse), **t** 05 53 96 16 56, *www.agen-atlantic-hotel.fr* (€). Calm, spacious rooms despite busy road, plus a pool. *Closed end of Dec.*

***Les Ambans**, 59 Rue des Ambans, **t** 05 53 66 28 60 (€). A good budget option.

Outskirts of Agen

******Château St-Marcel**, Boé (✉ 47550), 3km south of town on N113 towards Toulouse, **t** 05 53 96 61 30, *www.chateau-saint-marcel.com* (€€€€–€€). A château owned by Montesquieu, who may have planted the majestic cedars. There are sumptuous suites with antiques in the 17th-century castle, or more modern (and far less pricey) rooms in the annexe, plus a pool and tennis courts. The restaurant (€€€–€€) serves imaginative combinations of local ingredients, and there's a grill. *Closed Sun eve and Mon.*

****Le Colombier du Touron**, 187 Route de Mont-de-Marsan, Brax (✉ 47310), **t** 05 53 87 87 91 (€€–€). A Logis de France hotel west of the city, with good regional food (€€€–€€). *Closed Mon and Sun eve.*

****La Corne d'Or**, Colayrac-St-Cirq (✉ 47450), on N113 towards Bordeaux, **t** 05 53 47 02 76, *http://lacornedor.free.fr* (€). A modern hotel soundproofed against the road, with superb views over the Garonne and an excellent restaurant (€€) serving regional favourites and seafood. *Restaurant closed Sun eve, Fri eve out of season, 1st wk Jan and mid-July–start of Aug.*

****La Table d'Antan**, 41 Rue de la République, Bon-Encontre (✉ 47240), **t** 05 53 77 97 00 (€). Ten cosy country rooms and a restaurant (€€€–€€). *Restaurant closed Sat lunch and Sun eve.*

Layrac ✉ 47390

La Terrasse, Place de la Mairie, **t** 05 53 87 01 69 (€). Five simple rooms and a restaurant (€€€–€€) with a panoramic terrace where you can dine extremely well on local river fish and more. *Closed Sat lunch, Sun eve and Mon.*

Sérignac-sur-Garonne ✉ 47310

*****Le Prince Noir**, **t** 05 53 68 74 30, *www.le-prince-noir.com* (€€–€). A 17th-century convent with comfy traditional rooms, a pool and tennis court, and a restaurant (€€€–€€) serving classic southwest dishes, including a speciality fresh duck liver with raisins. *Closed Fri and Sun eves.*

Laplume ✉ 47310

*****Château de Lassalle**, Brimont, **t** 05 53 95 10 58, *www.chateaudelassalle.com* (€€€€–€€€). The poshest place to stay hereabouts, with beautiful airy rooms, a pool, a billiards room and a terrace restaurant (€€€€–€€) serving southwest dishes produced from market produce with an imaginative touch. There's a mushroom month and a truffle week. *Closed Sun eve and Mon lunch out of season.*

Astaffort ✉ 47220

*****Le Square**, 5–7 Place de la Craste, **t** 05 53 47 20 40, *www.latrille.com* (€€€–€€). A large, amiable country house, with rooms with air-con, TVs and mini-bars, plus a restaurant serving regional dishes, including fish. *Closed Sun eve exc July and Aug, 3wks in Nov and 1wk in May.*

Eating Out in and around Agen

Agen ✉ 47000

★ Mariottat >>

Mariottat, 25 Rue Louis Vivent, **t** 05 53 77 99 77 (€€€€–€€). A handsome townhouse where the chef-owner works wonders with the best daily market produce. *Closed Sat lunch, Sun eve and Mon.*

Le Margoton, 52 Rue Richard Cœur de Lion, **t** 05 53 48 11 55 (€€€–€€). A very good restaurant where you can enjoy the likes of roast fillet of *maigre* (shadefish) with morels. *Closed Mon and Sat lunch, plus Sun lunch in summer and Sun eve in winter.*

L'Atelier, 14 Rue du Jeu de Paume, **t** 05 53 87 89 22 (€€). A charming, relaxed restaurant serving classic regional dishes with something extra. *Closed Sat and Sun.*

Le Cauquil, 9 Av du Général de Gaulle, **t** 05 53 48 02 34 (€€–€). A simple but good restaurant, with daily offerings chalked up on blackboards. It's known for its southwest favourites made from fresh market ingredients, but there are other options. *Closed Sat lunch and Sun.*

Buffet de la Gare, train station, **t** 05 53 66 09 40 (€). The top budget place to eat, serving the best *steak bordelaise* anywhere. At lunchtime it's packed.

Astaffort ✉ 47220

Une Auberge en Gascogne, 9 Faubourg Corné, **t** 05 53 67 10 27, *www.aubergeengascogne.com* (€€€€–€€). An inn that has won itself a good reputation among locals for its traditional regional recipes. In summer you can eat out on the tranquil terrace. There are also nine rooms (€€–€). *Closed Wed and Thurs lunch, Sun eve and Nov.*

The Néracais

This very pleasant *pays*, tucked between the Armagnac and the pine forests of the Landes, is also often called, along with parts of the neighbouring Landes, the 'Pays d'Albret'; its long history as the feudal domain of the D'Albrets (*see* p.26) has given it an identity that endures to this day.

Nérac

...an asylum sweeter than freedom
Clément Marot

A pretty little river, the Baïse, starts in the mountains near Lannemezan and bubbles down the Hautes-Pyrénées and Gers through rather unappreciative countryside; it doesn't pass anything particularly edifying until it gets to Nérac. This fat village counts scarcely more than 7,000 inhabitants, but its association with the D'Albret family in the 1500s has given it fine monuments and the air of a little capital, if you see it from the right angle.

The Château

On a height over the Baïse, this is quite the most elegant thing in Nérac – at least what's left of it. Vengeful demolitions ordered by Cardinal Richelieu in 1621 have left only one side of what was once a stout, old-fashioned castle, hiding inside it a magnificent Renaissance courtyard built by Henri d'Albret's grandfather Alain. The side that remains has a lovely loggia of twisted columns.

Musée Henri IV
t 05 53 65 21 11; open June–Sept 10–12 and 2–7, Oct–May 10–12 and 2–6, closed Mon; adm

Inside, the **Musée Henri IV** is largely devoted to explanatory exhibits of the town in its heyday, with models of the château as it originally looked; downstairs is the archaeology section, with everything from a mammoth's molar to scraps of Roman pottery with their manufacturers' trademarks.

A walk from here around the old centre of Nérac won't take you long. **Rue de l'Ecole** was the old main stem; on it you can see the 17th-century (former) town hall and a fine Renaissance palace, the **Maison des Conférences**. Nérac's **church of St-Nicolas**, like most

The Marguerite of Marguerites

It was no accident that the D'Albret family came into such spectacular prominence in the 15th and 16th centuries – they were the agents of the French Crown. Their loyalty assured Paris an important ally in a Gascony that had few natural ties to France, made up of regions accustomed to a large degree of independence under English sovereignty and the feudal anarchy that had preceded it. In return, the French kings showered every sort of prize on the family, not least advantageous marriages to increase the D'Albrets' wealth and influence. With their help Henri d'Albret became King of Navarre, at which point King François I found him a fitting match for his sister, Marguerite d'Angoulême (1492–1549).

Already a widow at 35, it was Marguerite's second go. Everyone at the time counted her the most eligible lady of France – not just for being the king's sister but for having a wit, charm and intelligence that stood out even in Renaissance courts. Henri d'Albret was no match for her, but he had sense enough to take care of political business and stay out of the way while Marguerite turned their favoured residence of Nérac into a brilliant court where poetry and the new humanistic learning were the order of the day. Though they never converted themselves, Henri and Marguerite welcomed many of the new Protestant thinkers to Nérac, including John Calvin; dissenters circulated Bibles and preached openly. Among the poets who enjoyed Marguerite's favour was Clément Marot of Cahors, who wrote some fulsome lines in her honour, describing her as *plus mère que maistresse*. Marguerite had literary ambitions of her own. Best known among her works, and widely popular throughout France, was the *Heptameron*, a collection of stories with a frame tale of travellers snowbound at Sarrance in the Pyrenees, inspired by Boccaccio's *Decameron*.

Marguerite and Henri had a cute daughter, known to the French as Mignonne, the nickname her uncle, King François, had given her. Sitting at her parents' table, Jeanne must have been more impressed with the fiery preachers than the poets. She grew up to be the redoubtable Jeanne d'Albret – 'nothing in her of a woman but the sex' – a dour, intolerant Protestant who enforced her theological opinions on most of her subjects, including the Néracais, and contributed as much as anyone in keeping the flames of the religious wars burning. As evidence for the idea that traits and qualities skip generations, consider her son, who was brought up a good Protestant and fought across France for the cause but finally found a way to use good sense and tolerance to put an end to the troubles – he was King Henri IV.

French churches of the 18th century, hardly rates a notice in most books, but this is a cut above the norm, with a restrained neoclassical 'Greek' façade that is probably the better off for never having been able to afford the statuary that was intended for it, and a clean, airy interior with 19th-century stained glass that impresses in the way such windows are supposed to impress: it tells the whole story, from Abel and Noah up to Jesus himself behind the altar.

Entering Nérac along the Allées d'Albret, you have probably already noticed the obligatory statue of 'Our Henry', Henri IV, with a twinkle in his bronze eye. Henri spent much of his time in Nérac after the St Bartholomew's Day Massacre until he became king; he especially enjoyed hunting boar in the pine forests of the Néracais. Even then the common people were fond of him, and it didn't bother Henri at all to learn that everybody in town called him 'Big Nose' (*Grand-nas*). The statue may not do it justice.

La Garenne

From the back of the château, an elegant stair descends to the Baïse, leading to the Pont Neuf and Nérac's cross-river *faubourg*, Petit Nérac. Henri's father, Antoine de Bourbon, laid out a royal park here for his family, called La Garenne, stretching for nearly 2km along the riverfront, which has survived to become the town's outstanding civic embellishment. Everyone in Nérac comes here in the afternoon, to stroll along the Baïse, to fish, or just to take the kids to the playground. Near the entrance on Avenue Georges Clemenceau, a small brick shelter covers a bit of Roman mosaic, excavated in an important villa that once stood nearby. Further on you'll come to the Fontaine de Fleurette. According to the local legend, Fleurette was the daughter of Antoine and Jeanne d'Albret's gardener, and Henri's first love – when he abandoned her, she drowned herself in the river. If you like, you may take La Garenne as the setting for *Love's Labour's Lost*; most of the action of the play takes place in 'the king's park at Navarre'.

Petit Nérac's streets are as old as the town centre; the best part is along the river, picturesque **Rue Sédérie**, site of the tanneries that were Nérac's main business in the old days. Now most of its houses have been restored (there's an art gallery). Around the corner on Rue Sully is the 16th-century **Vieux Pont**, and the **Maison de Sully**, a 16th-century house where Henri IV's great minister stayed when Henri was in Nérac.

Market Days in Nérac

The market takes place on **Saturday morning** in the Petites Allées.

Activities in and around Nérac

About 45km of the Baïse were reopened to navigation in 1993, making Nérac a lovely place to hop on a **boat** – you can take an excursion on a *gabare* or hire one from Croisières du Prince Henry (*www.croisieresduprincehenry.com*).

The **train touristique de l'Albret** makes leisurely 1hr trips between Nérac and Mézin (*see* p.372), with commentary (**t** 05 53 67 21 23; *June–Aug Tues–Sun, May and Sept Sat and Sun, rest of year by appointment*)

Where to Stay and Eat in Nérac

Nérac ✉ 47600

****Hôtel d'Albret**, 40 Allées d'Albret, **t** 05 53 97 41 10 (€€–€). A simple, clean hotel with a much-loved restaurant (€€) specializing in *poule au pot* and other traditional meals. There is an outside terrace. *Closed Fri and Sun eves and early Jan.*

****Hôtel du Château**, Av Mondenard, **t** 05 53 65 09 05 (€). An acceptable hotel for an unmemorable night, with a restaurant (€€€–€) that will fill you up royally with well-executed dishes. *Closed Fri eve, Sat lunch and Sun eve.*

***La Chaumière d'Albert**, Route de Nérac, Lavardac (✉ 47230), north of town, **t** 05 53 65 51 75 (€). A simple little ivy-covered Logis de France hotel with a restaurant (€€). *Closed Sun night and Mon, 1st half Mar and 1st half Oct.*

Aux Délices du Roy, 7 Rue du Château, **t** 05 53 65 81 12 (€€€€–€€). A fish-lover's paradise, with 15 or so kinds on the menu, plus shellfish and meat, served in a charmingly rustic dining room with a low, beamed ceiling. *Closed Wed and Sun eve in winter.*

Relais de la Hire, 11 Rue Porte-Neuve, Francescas, just off Baïse south of Nérac, **t** 05 53 65 41 59 (€€€–€€). An 18th-century country squire's house where the freshest ingredients appear in elegant creations such as artichoke soufflé with foie gras. Ask about armagnac tastings. *Closed Sun eve, Wed lunch, Mon and last wk Oct.*

ⓘ Nérac >
7 Av Mondenard, off Place de l'Hôtel de Ville, **t** *05 53 65 27 75, www.ville-nerac.fr and www.albret-tourisme.com*

Bastides, Castles and a Famous Mill

To the south of Nérac on the D656, where the road crosses the river Osse, there is a pretty medieval bridge called the Pont Romain. The next village, **Mézin**, was once the home of Armand Fallières, President of France 1906–13. Fallières's presidency caused no embarrassment to Mézin, and consequently the villagers have honoured him by naming their main square after him. The **Musée du Liège et du Bouchon** has been given some zip: you can learn about the fabrication of corks through lively exhibition areas and the history of a family involved in the business. Mézin grew up around an important Cluniac abbey, and it retains the church of St-Jean, Romanesque in the apse and the rest strong and graceful Gothic – though the builders may have botched it: currently there are cracks in the vault and iron girders holding up a tilted column. On the vault over the altar, note the whimsical carving of a grimacing giant and pot of flowers. The tympanum on the north door must have been destroyed in the Revolution; replacing it you can still (barely) make out some Revolutionary slogan about the 'Supreme Being'. These are common enough in French village churches; the radicals in Paris were telling the peasants that it was

Musée du Liège et du Bouchon
t 05 53 65 68 16; open April–June and Oct Tues–Sat 2–6 and Sun 3–5.30; July and Aug Tues–Sun 10–12 and 2–6.30; Sept Tues–Sat 10–12 and 2–6.30, Sun 3–5.30; adm

Armagnac

Although the main growing area of that most Gascon drink of all, armagnac, is just south in the Gers, all the growers owe a debt to Armand Fallières of Mézin, who just happened to be a vintner before he became president of France, and who, in 1909, decreed the current AOC armagnac area, which actually extends as far north as Agen and nearly as far south as the Pyrenees, although in practice only a strictly limited 20,000 hectares are under production.

Armagnac is the oldest known *eau-de-vie* distilled from grapes. The first written record of the process goes back to 1411 (arch-rival cognac dates only from the 17th century); it proved by far to be the best way to treat the weak, local white wine nicknamed *picquepoul*, 'tingle-lips', for its acidity. The Dutch provided the first market for the stuff; before setting out on a long voyage, they fitted their ships with a great barrel of *vin brûlé*, or brandy. In the late 19th century, when armagnac was the rage, 100,000 hectares were planted – in time to be devastated by phylloxera. Since then 10 varieties of resistant white grapes are allowed to be grown, the leading one bacco 22A, a hybrid of the original *picquepoul* and noah.

The essential technique for making armagnac hasn't changed since 1818, when the Marquis de Bonas patented an armagnac still that permitted a single-pass distillation process as opposed to the old two-step process still used in cognac. Sometime between December and April, when the wine has finished fermenting, it is distilled; two specialists, the *brûleurs*, watch the still day and night to maintain constant temperature. It is during distillation that the distinctive armagnac aromas are made in embryonic forms – violets, roses and plum flowers. Fresh from the still, the armagnac is a rough brandy with an alcohol content ranging from 58° to 63°; it is put in a 400-litre black oak cask and shut away in a dark storeroom. In the first decade of ageing, some 6% is lost a year through evaporation ('the angels' share') and is carefully replenished by distilled water; meanwhile the brandy receives its distinctive golden hue by dissolving the tannins of the wood.

The tannins make the brandy bitter, although after 10 years the bitterness gives way to the natural armagnac fragrance and the brandy is transferred into old tannin-less casks. The finest are aged for up to 40 years in oak barrels, demanding constant care and attention. When the *maître de chai* decides it has achieved its quintessence, further evolution is stopped by transferring it to glass vats or bottles.

all right to believe in God, although not necessarily in the god of the Christian Church – it's a mystery, however, that so many of these inscriptions survive.

The tourist office runs summer guided tours, and has leaflets with circuits of trees and chapels in the area. You could get lost for a long time in the lush countryside around Mézin and never mind it. On the stretch of the D656 along the valley of the Gélise, you'll pass a country chapel and a traditional Agenais *pigeonnier* on stilts, and farmers hang signs out to sell you asparagus and *cèpes*, foie gras, and *Floc de Gascogne*, the 'Flower of Gascony' – the sweet apéritif wine made since the 1500s and revived, uniquely for France, almost exclusively by women, the 'Dames du Floc de Gascogne'.

Poudenas, Moncrabeau and Around

Château de Poudenas
t 05 53 65 78 86; open for groups by appt; adm

Poudenas is famous for its old bridge and fine Italianate **château**, with period furniture and paintings. Built in the 13th century by the lords of Poudenas, vassals of Edward I, it was given its elegant Italian touches in the 17th century; the tour includes tastings of the château's *Floc de Gascogne*. There are Romanesque churches at **Sos** and **Gueyze**, and a fortified church with traces of frescoes from the 1200s at **Villeneuve-de-Mézin**, south of Mézin.

Meylan, just inside the pine forest of the Landes, is a tiny village that seems to consist of a swing set, a *mairie* in a shed, a picnic table and a war memorial, yet it contains so many curiosities that the Meylanais have drawn out a little itinerary for them, posted in front of the *mairie*. The circuit includes the château and unusual Romanesque church of St-Pau, a small cromlech hidden in the pine woods, called Las Naous Peyros, and the Lac Sans-fond. As the name implies, no one has yet found the bottom of this mysterious little lake. There are a number of legends: about the phantom that haunts it, and about the church that once stood on its bank – the lake swallowed it up one Sunday, parishioners and all.

East and south of Nérac, the landscapes are much the same. You can visit the attractive *bastide* of **Lamontjoie** (they've got St Louis' hand in a reliquary in the church), or else swap some lies with the experts at **Moncrabeau**. More than 200 years ago, a jolly, tale-telling monk founded the Académie des Menteurs here, and ever since its 40 members have met every first Sunday in August to throw the bull around and elect the King of Liars, consecrated in a solemn ceremony at the 'stone of truth'. Every three years this droll village also hosts the World Face-pulling Championship.

Barbaste and Vianne

37 Moulin de Henri IV
t 05 53 65 09 37; open July and Aug Thurs–Sun 10–12.30 and 2.30–6.30, rest of year by appt

North of Nérac, the D930 takes you to Barbaste, and one of the famous sights of the southwest, the **Moulin de Henri IV**. If it looks more like a castle, it is that too; fortified mills are not uncommon in France, built in feudal times when grain was precious and there were plenty of enemies ready to try to grab it. This one, along with the bridge in front of it, is from the 1200s. The story has it that the nobleman who built it had four daughters of different ages, and made the mill's four towers different heights in their honour. In later times the mill belonged to the d'Albrets, and it passed from them to Henri IV, who liked being called the 'Miller of Barbaste', at least, better than he liked being called 'Big Nose'.

Château Imaginaire
t 05 53 97 25 15; open July and Aug daily 10–12 and 2–7; April–June and Sept–Oct daily 2–6; night visits Tues 9pm July and Aug; adm

The huge mill house adjoining the towers has been transformed into a mini themepark; the **Château Imaginaire**, where you can take a magical journey into the land of elves and fairies. Live magicians and puppets along with holograms, film and light shows create a fantasy land of fairy stories throughout the castle, spilling into the river and surrounding forest. The owners proudly state: 'look further than you can see, your dreams will never be the same again after the quest for lost imagination.' To the west, on the D665, **Durance** is a 13th-century *bastide* surrounded by forests that were the hunting preserve of the D'Albrets and King Henri; the village has ruins of the castle they used for their hunting lodge.

Northeast of Barbaste is another *bastide*, **Vianne**, founded in 1284 by Jourdain de l'Isle, seneschal of King Edward I and named after his aunt, Vianne Gontaud-Biron – it's the only *bastide* named after a woman. Vianne still has most of its walls and gates, along with the church of Notre-Dame and its austere tower, and a pretty churchyard full of cypresses. It makes its living from faïence and crystal; there are lovely things for sale in the shops on the main street, and at Faïence des Remparts, built into the village's wall.

Musée de l'Ecole d'Autrefois
t 05 53 84 74 14; open July and Aug Tues–Sun 3–6

In the hills above Vianne is the **Château de Xaintrailles**, once the home of Maréchal Poton, a companion of Joan of Arc. North again, at St Pierre-de-Buzet, you can see the reconstruction of two **19th-century classrooms**, containing period furniture and rare books.

Market Days in and around Mézin

Mézin: Thursday and Sunday, farmers' market.

Barbaste: Monday and Friday.

Durance: Tuesday afternoon.

Vianne: Friday evening June–Aug.

Where to Stay and Eat around Mézin

ⓘ Mézin >
Pl Armand Fallières, t 05 53 65 77 46, www.mezin-tourisme.com

Mézin, Poudenas and Sos ✉ 47170

Le Postillon, Place Delbousquet, Sos, t 05 53 65 60 27 (€). A restored smithy with six simple rooms and a restaurant (€€–€) serving good fat *magrets* and *confits* with *cèpes*, among other things, outside on a terrace in good weather. *Closed Feb.*

Sept Princes, Avenue J.-Bertrand, Mézin, **t** 05 53 65 83 04 (€). Simple but satisfactory rooms (sharing showers on the landing) and a restaurant (€€–€) with a shady terrace.

Ferme du Boué, southwest of Poudenas in Ste-Maure-de-Peyriac, **t** 05 53 65 63 94 (€€). The place to come to enjoy excellent *rillettes*, foie gras and other delights. There is also a fishing lake, a swimming pool and five gîtes. Book ahead. *Closed Nov–Easter.*

ⓘ **Barbaste >**
Place de la Mairie,
t 05 53 65 84 85

ⓘ **Moncrabeau >>**
Mairie, *t 05 53 65 10 34*

Barbaste ✉ 47230

La Cascade aux Fées, La Riberotte, ✉ 47230 Barbaste, **t** 05 53 97 05 96, *www.cascade-aux-fees.com* (€€). Four cosy *chambres d'hôte* in a fine 18th-century house on the bank of the river. Relax in a hammock or take a dip in the pool in the surrounding park, or enjoy a drink at the riverside bar. You'll also find a boat for messing about on the river. Meals are available on Wednesday and Saturday by request.

Moncrabeau ✉ 47600

****Le Phare**, **t** 05 53 65 42 08, *www.lephare47.com* (€€–€). A traditional provincial hotel with a garden, and solid southwest cuisine (€€€–€€). *Closed Sun eve, Mon and Oct–Mar.*

Western Lot-et-Garonne

Down the Garonne Valley

In fact, it isn't just the Garonne: you can follow either the river or the 19th-century Canal Latéral à la Garonne paralleling the river, providing a complement to Languedoc's Canal du Midi and, for boats, a direct passage from the Med to the Atlantic.

From Aiguillon to Tonneins

Aquitaine Navigation
t 05 53 84 72 50

Nautic Aquitaine
t 05 53 79 59 39

Starting from Aiguillon (*see* p.360), across the river and the canal is **Buzet-sur-Baïse**, a village near the confluence of the Baïse and the Garonne, dominated by its castle, on a hill with tremendous views. There are two things to do here: take a ride along the Baïse or the canal in a modern houseboat or a traditional boat called a *capucine* with **Aquitaine Navigation**, or seek some of the local *vin*.

Damazan, another 13th-century *bastide*, has creaky, leaning half-timbered houses, *halles*, and some of its walls and towers intact. It's another main centre for canal tourism, with cruises and boats to rent in season: try **Nautic Aquitaine**.

Buzet

A cousin of Bordeaux, red Buzet is a mainly Merlot wine that owed its AOC status in 1973 to the tireless work of the Cave Coopérative de Buzet (now the Vignerons Réunis), created in 1955 in Buzet-sur-Baïse to bring back the wine-making traditions that made the wine important in the Middle Ages. Though the growing area stretches all the way down the Baïse beyond Nérac, the vineyards exist only in pockets among other crops, on the best-drained, pebbly land; many old mediocre family vineyards have been pulled up in the last 25 years in favour of the more popular modern varieties – Merlot, Cabernet Franc, Cabernet Sauvignon and Cot (Malbec). Dedication, discipline and a unique interest in just the right type of oak cask (the cooperative has a cooperage that makes 800–900 barrels a year, each with a five-year life span) have resulted in a fine, structured aromatic wine that goes beautifully with the region's rich dishes in prune sauces.

At the top of the list of reds is the superb Château de Gueyze, followed by Cuvée Baron d'Ardeuil, named by Napoleon after the Gascon soldier who offered him some from his gourd (he, too, was known henceforth as Baron). The whites have improved lately and are well worth a try. L'Excellence, light, fresh and fruity, is what it says; it can be bought at the Vignerons de Buzet, a union of 13 châteaux that markets more than 90% of the wine – 14 million-plus bottles a year – and offers tours of its vast cellars (**t** 05 53 84 17 16, *www.vignerons-buzet.fr; shop open July and Aug Mon–Sat exc hols 9–12.30 and 2–7, rest of year Mon–Sat exc hols 9–12 and 2–6*).

Espace Exposition A Garonna
t 05 53 79 22 79; open July and Aug by appt

Plaine aux Fleurs
t 05 53 83 47 90; open June–Sept Mon–Thurs 9–12 and 3–7

Maison de la Réserve Naturelle
t 05 53 88 02 57; open by appt

Down the Garonne, the large village of **Tonneins** has a wonderful panorama over the Garonne valley. It was once the capital of Gauloises and Gitanes – cigarettes only smokable by Frenchmen and masochists. The factory closed at the end of 2000, leaving a very bitter taste in the mouths of local residents – a taste that lingers on today. The old royal tobacco factory on the quay, the **Espace Exposition A Garonna**, tells tales of the river and its history.

North of Tonneins, at **Gontaud-de-Nogaret**, is a **garden** with 70 types of flower, a drying room, flower-arranging demonstrations, and an exhibition area. South of Tonneins, near Villeton, the **Maison de la Réserve Naturelle** has aquaria, photos, birds' nests and a film on the **Réserve Naturelle de l'Etang de la Mazière**.

Le Mas-d'Agenais

You reach this village by an elegant modern suspension bridge that crosses both the Garonne and the canal. The usual red-bordered sign, along with a floral arrangement of Mas's coat of arms (three gold hands on a red field), announces the village, but not a house is to be seen. Mas is up in the clouds, on a hill above the Garonne, a village closed into itself; it's special, and it knows it.

Velenum Pompeiacum in Roman times, Mas was still one of the most important centres of the area in the Middle Ages. It isn't a large village – just a few lovely streets and squares with restored houses, a brick medieval gateway, a wooden market *halle* from the 1600s, and a beautiful view over the Garonne from its little park on the cliff edge. It also has one of the region's most interesting churches, **St-Vincent**, begun in 1085, replacing an ancient church (*c.* 440) built on the site of a Roman temple. Tinkered and tampered with over the centuries, it isn't much to look at from outside; Viollet-le-Duc gave the main entrance its present appearance, and at about the same time the tall steeple over it was demolished. The interior, however, contains a wealth of excellent sculptural decoration, mostly on the capitals (nearby shops or the tourist office sell tokens for the lighting). In the south aisle, Old Testament scenes include *Samson, David and Goliath*, *The Sacrifice of Abraham* and *Daniel in the Lions' Den*. The capitals in the north aisle and choir are mostly New Testament vignettes, along with *St Michael and the Dragon* and the *Martyrdom of St Vincent*, while those high up in the nave itself have some surprising subjects: one is claimed to be the *Race of Atalanta* from Greek mythology and apparently the *Hunt of the Calydonian Boar* from the same story.

The church contains two ancient relics; one is an Early Christian sarcophagus said to be that of the obscure martyr St Vincent, which was on prominent display in Mas' original church. Hidden in the cemetery during the Norman invasions, it wasn't rediscovered until 1785. The other, a Roman *cippus* with a confusing inscription, may have originally been the base for the statue of a pagan god. Note also the beautifully carved choir stalls; these are believed to be a gift of Mary Stuart, originally intended for the church at La Réole. Mas' claim to fame, a painting by Rembrandt, was donated to the church in 1873 by a wealthy family from Mas who made it big in Dunkerque. Originally, this scene of *The Face of Christ on the Cross* was part of a series of seven on the Passion; all the rest are now together in Munich. For anyone who thinks Rembrandt only painted portraits, it will be a revelation (there are photographs of the others in the church); these are intense, remarkable paintings, in which Jesus goes up on the cross a man and comes down a god.

Towards Marmande

South of Mas, the D6 passes through the lovely forest of Mas-d'Agenais, another old hunting preserve, en route to **Casteljaloux**, a former possession of the D'Albrets and the gateway to the great piney Landes; the French immediately recall it as the base of the Cadets de Gascogne in Rostand's *Cyrano de Bergerac*. The name sounds as if means 'jealous' but comes from *gelos* ('perilous'), a reality confirmed by the state of the castle , now a ruin but once a favourite hunting and love retreat of Henri IV. There are a few 15th-century buildings around the centre, and the pretty sand-bordered Lac de Clarens just southwest. Just southeast down the D11, the striking multi-towered **Château du Sendat**, first built in the 12th century, is set amidst a tidy French garden. If you want to relax, try the **Bains de Casteljaloux** with their pools, sauna and hammam.

Bains de Casteljaloux
t 05 53 20 59 00

Among the Romanesque churches in the area, there's a good one at **Villefranche-du-Queyran** east on the D120, with a score of carved capitals; **Labastide-Castel-Amouroux** to the northwest has another one, with some good monsters on the capitals.

Northwest, **Romestaing** has the 12th-century **St-Christophe** with more mysterious capitals. **Cocumont**, a main centre of the Côtes-du-Marmandais growing area (*see* p.379), is just northwest of **Goutz** (or **Goux**), which has a remarkable 11th-century Romanesque church built on top of a 2,000-year-old tumulus; deep below is the circular tomb of a local chieftain, never excavated.

Marcellus is the site of a handsome 16th-century **château**, cradle of the count who bought the *Venus de Milo* from the Greek farmer who dug her up, and kept her from rival purchaser the Prince of Moldavia (the statue was on a Greek tender, ready to be placed aboard a ship for Romania just when the French vessel from Constantinople arrived; accounts say there was either some brisk bargaining, or a fight that the French sailors won – during which she may have lost her arms and pedestal). Downstream, **Meilhan-sur-Garonne** sits atop a natural balcony, overlooking the hills of the Entre-Deux-Mers and their famous vineyards.

ⓘ **Tonneins >>**
3 Boulevard Charles de Gaulle, **t** *05 53 79 22 79, www.tonneins.tourisme.com*

ⓘ **Le Mas-d'Agenais >>**
Place de la Halle, **t** *05 53 89 50 58 (summer only)*

ⓘ **Casteljaloux >>**
Maison du Roy, **t** *05 53 93 00 00, www.casteljaloux.com*

Market Days in and around Tonneins

Tonneins: Monday, Friday and Saturday.
Casteljaloux: Saturday and Tuesday.
Buzet: Friday.

Activities in and around Tonneins

You can tour the Canal Latéral by **houseboat** hired from Crown Blue Line (**t** 05 53 89 50 80, *www.vacancesfluviales.com)*; by the canal lock at Le Mas-d'Agenais; or from Aquitaine Navigation (**t** 05 53 84 72 50, *www.aquitaine-navigation.com)*, at Le Coustet in Buzet There are also **river trips** from Meilhan (**t** 05 53 94 36 82) and Fourques (**t** 05 53 89 25 59).

Ask at Casteljaloux tourist office about **guided tours** in summer.

Where to Stay and Eat in and around Tonneins

Buzet-sur-Baïse ✉ 47160

Le Goujon qui Frétille, Rue Gambetta, **t** 05 53 84 26 51 (€€). A cosy place that translates as 'The Wiggling Gudgeon', with a lovely terrace. The wonderful variations on old southwest themes and Provençale dishes come at very kind prices. *Closed Tues and Wed.*

Tonneins ✉ 47400

******Côté Garonne**, 36–38 Cours de l'Yser, **t** 05 53 84 34 34, *www.cotegaronne.com* (€€). Six exclusive rooms hanging over the Garonne, not far from the centre, with a superb restaurant with inventive seasonal cuisine (€€€–€€). *Closed Sun eve, Sat lunch and Tues lunch.*

Le Mas-d'Agenais ✉ 47430

Jean Champon, in centre by market stalls, **t** 05 53 89 50 06 (€). Good honest lunches: the €11 menu comprises four courses, with perhaps Bayonne ham as a starter and beef *daube* or chicken *confit* as a main. *Closed eves.*

Casteljaloux ✉ 47700

****Hôtel des Cordeliers**, 1 Rue des Cordeliers, **t** 05 53 93 02 19, *www.hotel-cordeliers.fr* (€€–€). A good central choice, with two rooms equipped for the disabled plus a restaurant. *Closed Sun eve and most of Jan.*

***Le Cassissier**, Place Jean Jaurès, **t** 05 53 93 03 38 (€). A simple family-run hotel with a decent restaurant (€€€–€€) serving traditional Gascon fare plus some generous fish dishes. *Closed Sat lunch, Sun eve and Mon.*

La Vieille Auberge, 11 Rue Posterne, old part of town, **t** 05 53 93 01 36 (€€€–€€). Delicious seasonal menus featuring duck and more. *Closed Sun eve and Tues lunch, and Wed in winter.*

Marmande

Marmande, the most important market town between Agen and Bordeaux, is currently on its third name. Originally it was Marmande-la-Royale, when it received its charter in 1182 from Richard the Lionheart. After being used as a kind of revolving door in the Hundred Years' War (when it changed hands eight times) and the Wars of Religion, it was Marmande-la-Sainte; now it's the more secular Marmande-la-Jolie, the queen of big red tomatoes.

A Walk around Marmande

Musée Municipal Albert Marzelles
t *05 53 64 42 04; open Tues–Fri 3–6, Sat 10–12 and 3–6, and some Sun afternoons*

The central Place Clemenceau is decorated with a bronze statue called *La Pomme d'Amour*, a kneeling nude clutching a *tomate de Marmande*, in reference to an old belief that tomatoes were an aphrodisiac. The tomato maiden overlooks the modern **fountain of Europa**; nearby is the **Musée Municipal Albert Marzelles** with a

Côtes-du-Marmandais (*www.origine-marmandais.fr*)

Rather unusually, Marmandais has two very distinct growing areas divided by the wide valley of the Garonne: the northern area has the same limestone-clay soil as Entre-Deux-Mers, while the south is an extension of the sandy, gravelly Graves region just to the west. In the 18th and 19th centuries the lusty red and dry white wines grown here were in great demand in the Netherlands, but the 20th century saw a decline only halted in the last few decades.

Like neighbouring Buzet, Marmandais owes its rise in status again to the cooperative efforts of its vintners, who after years of work achieved AOC status in 1990 for their bright, merry red wine that they promise 'will re-animate chagrined spirits and save an ordinary meal from insipidity'. One major change was the move from the somewhat obscure traditional grape varieties of the region (Boucalès, Abouriou, Ferservadou). The reds, by far the majority, are now made from Merlot, Cabernet Franc and Cabernet Sauvignon; the whites are mostly Sauvignon, with Sémillon and Muscadelle.

As in Buzet, most of the wine is produced in cooperatives such as that of **Beaupuy,** just to the north of Marmande (**t** 05 53 76 05 10; *open 9–12 and 2.30–6.30*), a village with grand views in every direction. You can also visit the **Cave de Cocumont** (**t** 05 53 94 50 21; *open daily 9–12 and 2.30–6.30*) at Cocumont, south of the Garonne and A62.

hotchpotch of local items, especially from the 19th century; don't miss the lavish firemen's helmets, which perhaps explain why pre-Impressionist French historical paintings were called *pompiers* (firemen). There are also temporary art exhibitions.

Rue Léopold Faye, lined with half-timbered houses, leads back towards the 13th-century **Notre-Dame**, with a pretty rose window, a Baroque *Mise en tombeau*, a 16th-century retable dedicated to St Benedict and a beautiful topiary garden in the cloister of 1545. From here Rue de la Libération leads up to the **Chapelle St-Benoît** with a fine 17th-century ceiling painted to imitate coffering.

Around Marmande

Down the Garonne, **Ste-Bazeille** was a Roman town, named after the daughter of a proconsul martyred for her faith; decapitated, her head bounced nine times, each bounce bringing forth a spring – now known as the nine fountains, *neuffonds*. There is a **Musée Archéologique** with more than 700 pieces from the Iron Age through Roman times to the Middle Ages.

Musée Archéologique
t *06 85 23 60 52; open July and Aug Wed–Mon 2.30–6.30; rest of year Sun 2.30–6; adm*

On the other side of the river, at Couthures-sur-Garonne, a new hi-tech attraction, **Gens de Garonne**, has films, audiovisual displays and more about life in this riverside village, including how locals have coped with floods. An on-site shop sells local produce.

Gens de Garonne
t *05 53 20 67 76; open July and Aug daily 10–7; June and Sept Tues–Sun 10–5; rest of year call for times; adm*

On the Gupie stream, **Mauvezin-sur-Gupie** has a 13th-century church covered by a remarkable roof shaped like a ship's keel. **Lagupie** has a 12th-century church with a sculpted tympanum; there's another, carved with Christ and the Elders of the Apocalypse, east of Marmande at **St-Pierre-de-Londres**, an English *bastide* project that never got further than this church. **Virazeil**, between Marmande and St-Pierre-de-Londres, has a neoclassical château built by Victor Louis, architect of Bordeaux's Grand Théâtre, in 1774.

Market Days in Marmande

There are general markets on **Tuesday** and **Saturday**, plus a fleamarket on the second **Sunday** of each month and some night markets in summer.

Activities in and around Marmande

Ask at Marmande tourist office about **guided tours**.

To the east of Marmande, south of Virazeil, there's a 10-hole **golf** course (**t** 05 53 20 87 60; *open daily April–Oct 9–6, rest of year 9–5*)

Where to Stay and Eat in and around Marmande

Marmande ✉ **47200**

****Le Capricorne**, just outside town on Route d'Agen, **t** 05 53 64 16 14, *www.lecapricorne-hotel.com* (€). A modern motel with a pool and a good restaurant (€€€–€€). *Closed Christmas and New Year; restaurant Sun, and Mon and Sat lunch.*

****Le Lion d'Or**, 1 Rue de la République, near Notre-Dame, **t** 05 53 64 21 30 (€). A hotel with adequate, modernized rooms and a decent if unexciting restaurant (€€€–€). *Closed Fri eve exc July and Aug.*

L'Escale, Pont-des-Sables, on banks of canal, **t** 05 53 93 60 11 (€€€–€€). Good honest food, including *magrets* with figs and Marmande tomatoes, served against a green backdrop. *Closed Sun eve and Mon.*

Auberge du Moulin d'Ané, Virazeil, 4km east of town by river Trec, **t** 05 53 20 18 25 (€€). A popular and romantic eatery offering delicate southwest and fish dishes made from good country ingredients. There's a terrace for good weather. *Closed Tues and Wed exc July and Aug.*

ⓘ **Marmande >** *Boulevard Gambetta,* **t** *05 53 64 44 44, www.mairie-marmande.fr*

Along the Dourdêze and Dropt, and the Pays du Duras

The low, rolling hills occupying this northwest corner of the Lot-et-Garonne *département* are home to some of its most unusual sights, and to some of its best wine. The French come here for *douceur de vie*, and the English, perhaps remembering Duras as one of the most pro-English corners of Aquitaine, have returned to buy large sections of it back.

Lauzun and Around

Il n'était pas permis de rêver comme il a vécu.

La Bruyère, on the Duc de Lauzun

Lauzun owes its fame to Antonin Nompar de Caumont, who was born the younger son of an impoverished local baron in 1633 but was so well endowed with natural talent, good looks and charm that he quickly become Louis XIV's favourite. The Sun King promoted him to marshal and duke; one of his missions was to help James II's queen, Mary of Modena, and her son flee from England to France during the Glorious Revolution. On another occasion Lauzun hid under the king's bed in order to hear what Louis and his mistress were saying about him.

Women adored him, most overwhelmingly the Big Miss herself, the *Grande Mademoiselle* – Louis' headstrong cousin. She fell head over heels for Lauzun, much to the astonishment of the court and to the fury of Louis, who sent Lauzun to the Bastille. Most accounts say that he secretly married the Grande Mademoiselle anyway, then proceeded to be terribly unfaithful to her. When she died, the spunky duke married a 15-year-old (he was 62), then to her horror went on to live to the ripe old age of 90. One thing that he did was add a domed pavilion to his golden half-medieval, half-Renaissance **château**; it also has magnificent fireplaces. The Gothic church, next to an 11th-century tower, has a retable by Tournié of Gourdon, an elaborately carved altar, and two statues of the Virgin dating from the 13th and 15th centuries.

Château de Lauzan
t 05 53 20 15 76; open July and Aug daily 2–6

Just to the northwest of Lauzun, and embraced by a meander of the Dropt, **Eymet** is another *bastide*, founded by Alphonse de Poitiers, with its arcades intact and a 13th-century donjon; Its 300-acre *plan d'eau* is a favourite retreat in the summer, and the place abounds with Brits. The tourist office (*see* p.383) runs tours.

Eymet's chief rival, **Miramont-de-Guyenne**, just to the south of here, was founded as a *bastide* by Edward I, but after sustaining grave damage in the Hundred Years' War and the Fronde it only retains some old houses (one once inhabited by Jeanne d'Albret) and a central arcaded square; the church is recent, with stained glass by modern master Emile Wachter.

Allemans-du-Dropt

Supposedly named after the barbaric German tribe who pushed and shoved their way through in the Dark Ages (and made such an impression on the French that they still call the whole country on the other bank of the Rhine *Allemagne*), Allemans-du-Dropt has an ancient **church** that was given a neogothic face-lift during the 19th century. The choir has a Mozarabic horseshoe arch, but best of all are the 15th-century frescoes in the nave, which were rediscovered in 1935 by the church bell-ringer. These are lively, colourful paintings – especially of the devils, one carrying off souls like a grape-picker in a basket on his back, another impaled by the armoured archangel in charge of separating baddies and goodies. All the damned appear to be either women or priests. You can learn more about them on a guided visit.

Eglise St-Eutrope
t 05 53 20 25 59; call for times of and bookings for guided tours

Nearby **La Sauvetat-du-Dropt** was yet another *bastide*, and one that saw a terrible blood-letting in 1637, when the Duc de la Valette brutally put down a peasant uprising by massacring 1,500 *Croquants*. From the 13th century there's **St-Gervais**, a church with an ornate portal and choir that survived a cyclone in 1242, and a charming bridge over the Dropt, near a picturesque *pigeonnier*. Don't miss the beautiful Renaissance house on the main street.

To the southwest, at little **Monteton**, the delightful Romanesque **Notre-Dame** sits high on a terrace where the keen of eye should be able to pick out 13 belltowers on the horizon. One of the few

Côtes-de-Duras (*www.cotesdeduras.com*)

Born during the Hundred Years' War, Côtes-de-Duras was one of France's first AOC wines, receiving the prized designation back in 1937. Of its gently rolling hills, only the sunniest slopes with the proper soil are under vines, and they produce a mere 100,000 hectolitres of wine – a drop in the bucket compared to the various Bordeaux wines next door.

Côtes-de-Duras reds are often made from either 100% Merlot or Cabernet Sauvignon; the whites are from Sauvignon, Mauzac or Sémillon. Domaine de Laulan in Duras (**t** 05 53 83 73 69; *open Mon–Sat 8–12 and 2–8, Sun by appointment*), offers an expressive white wine. Among the pride of the Vignerons de Landerrouat-Duras, the local *cave cooperative* comprising 200 producers are the Hauts de Berticot, Honoré de Berticot and Dagnet de Berticot (**t** 05 53 83 75 47; *open Mon–Sat 8–12 and 2–6*). Among the sweet *blancs moelleux*, the soft, rich Château La Moulière is usually outstanding,and forms the perfect accompaniment to foie gras. It now has a shop in Place du Marché, Duras (**t** 05 53 93 20 20).

churches to escape damage over the centuries, it has unusual interior buttresses, some fine vaults, and a triumphal arch complete with carved capitals.

Duras

Spread out along a spur overlooking the emerald valley of the Dropt, **Duras** is said to be the only town in France that never built a Catholic church; the current one began as a Protestant temple. Having the same name as a famous French novelist hasn't hurt it, nor has the renown of its excellent wines. It has some fine old houses and arcades along the high street, Rue Jauffret. On Place des Parcheminiers, the **Musée du Parchemin** demonstrates how parchment was made from sheepskin, bound into books and illustrated with goose quills in the time of St Louis. They also run courses, in case you want to learn.

Musée du Parchemin
t 05 53 20 75 55; open April–June and Sept daily 3–7; July and Aug daily 11–1 and 3–7; adm

But the main reason to stop here is to make a visit to the great prow-shaped **Château de Duras**, which was first constructed in the 1100s, only to be completely redone in 1310 by a cousin of Bertrand de Goth, Pope Clement V. His niece married a Durfort, and from 1325 the castle belonged to that powerful pro-English family; in 1389 it was captured by Du Guesclin. Henri IV's mother, Jeanne d'Albret, holed up here when Catholic Catherine de' Medici sent down the troops. In the late 17th century, its duke Jacques-Henri de Durfort served as a *maréchal* of France and helped capture the Franche-Comté for France, while his younger brother Louis went to England and became James II's top general. In 1794 the castle's surviving towers were cut down to size, and by the 20th century it was abandoned and falling to bits; the town purchased it in 1969.

Château de Duras
t 05 53 83 77 32; open June and Sept daily 10–12.30 and 2–7; July and Aug daily 10–7; Mar–May and Oct daily 10–12 and 2–6; Nov–Feb Sat, Sun and hols 10–12 and 2–6; guided visits in English mid-July–end Aug daily 3pm; adm

After a 20-year restoration, the castle has been brought back to life, not only in terms of its architecture – the grand halls, the kitchen, the 'room of secrets', the oratory, the prison and the moats, the tower with views that on a very clear day stretch as far as the Pyrenees – but also with regard to its troubadours, knights, ladies and music and boiling pots, thanks to lasers, video, sound and light and other hi-tech gimcracks by the same wizards who created Futuroscope near Poitiers. There are also concerts, festivals and events here throughout the year.

Around Duras

Domaine les Riquets
t 05 53 83 83 10; call for hrs

At **Domaine les Riquets** in **Baleyssagues** just to the north of Duras, some local wine producers have created a nature trail through their vines, woods and orchards, which are full of plum trees, orchids and wild plants.

Romanesque churches share the *pays de Duras* with the grapes, and one of the best examples is located to the north in **Esclottes**. Constructed during the 13th century, it has an unusually short nave, a false transept and some skilfully carved capitals, one with a fish. There are others worth seeking out at **Savignac-de-Duras**, **Lubersac** and **Loubès-Bernac**. This last church (situated to the northeast of St-Sernin-de-Duras) has two doors; the one on the north was known as the **Porte des Cagots**. Loubès-Bernac also boasts a 14th-century château that was completely redone in the course of the 17th century.

Domaine de Durand
t 05 53 89 02 23

Musée de l'Outil Ancien
t 05 53 93 85 46; open June–Aug Tues–Sun 3–7

For a bird's-eye view of the surrounds, go for a ride in a hot-air balloon from St-Jean-de-Duras in the company of organic wine-grower Michel Fonvielhe of the **Domaine de Durand**.

At nearby **Soumensac**, there's a **collection of more than 2000 tools** dating from the Stone Age onwards, organized, as far as is possible, according to profession.

ⓘ Eymet >
t 05 53 23 74 95, www.eymet-dordogne.fr

ⓘ Allemans-du-Dropt >
Place de la Liberté, t 05 53 20 25 59, and Place Mairie, t 05 53 94 13 09, www.valleedudropt.com

Market Days in and around Duras

Miramont-de-Guyenne: Monday, plus farmers' market Friday during summer months.

Lauzun: Saturday.

Duras: Monday and Saturday, plus Thursday in summer.

Eymet: Thursday, and Sunday in July and August.

Where to Stay and Eat in and around Duras

Allemans-du-Dropt ✉ 47800

L'Etape Gasconne, Place de la Mairie, **t 05 53 20 23 55 (€). Pleasant, well-priced rooms, a swimming pool and a good restaurant (€€–€). *Restaurant closed Fri and Sun eve out of high season.*

Monteton ✉ 47120

Château de Monteton, t 05 53 20 24 40, *www.chateaudemonteton.com* (€€). A popular 18th-century château offering *chambres d'hôte* (not all of them with baths) and delicious food (€€) based on fresh ingredients. In the winter months it often gets crammed to the gills with conference-goers. Book ahead.

Auberge des Treize Clochers, next to church, **t** 05 53 20 24 50 (€€). A good place for reasonably priced regional food, meat and fish, plus pizzas. *Closed Mon and Tues Sept–May.*

St-Pardoux-Issac ✉ 47800

Relais de Guyenne, Route de Paris, **t 05 53 93 20 76 (€). A simple place with eight soundproofed, comfortable enough rooms and a restaurant with a terrace for warm days. *Restaurant closed Sat out of season.*

ⓘ Miramont-de-Guyenne >
1 Rue Pasteur,
t *05 53 93 38 94*

ⓘ Duras >>
14 Bd Jean Brisseau,
t *05 53 83 63 06,*
www.paysdeduras.com

Miramont-de-Guyenne ✉ 47800

La Poste, 31 Place Martignac, **t** 05 53 93 20 03, *http://hotel.poste.miramont.free.fr* (€). Twelve Logis de France rooms occupying a former posthouse, plus the best restaurant (€€€–€) in town. *Closed Sat lunch and Sun eve out of season.*

Duras ✉ 47120

****Hostellerie des Ducs**, Bd Jean Brisseau, **t** 05 53 83 74 58, *www.hostellerieducs-duras.com* (€). A 19th-century convent amidst vines, with a pool and a great restaurant (€€€–€€) – try the sturgeon with leek fondue. *Closed Sun and Mon eves Oct–June, and Sat and Mon lunch July and Aug.*

Tarn-et-Garonne

South of the Lot lies Bas Quercy, the region's lost half. Although the Revolutionary bureaucrats in Paris left Quercy as a single département, *Montauban was mortified to find itself a mere spot on the map while rascally old Cahors got to be a capital. In 1808 the city saw its chance when Napoleon and Josephine happened to be passing through: the city fathers rolled out the red carpet, the mayor was ever so flattering, and Napoleon, his imperial ego aglow, promised to give the Montaubanais a* département *of their own. He sliced off the south end of the Lot, and gathered in the corners from other neighbouring* départements, *and No.82, the Tarn-et-Garonne, was born.*

15

Don't miss

1. **A crown jewel of French Romanesque**
   Moissac p.403
2. **Labyrinthine medieval lanes**
   St-Antonin-Noble-Val p.390
3. **World-class art by Ingres and co.**
   Montauban p.395
4. **Scenic winding walking paths**
   Aveyron Valley p.388
5. **Unique red-brick architecture**
   Auvillar p.412

See map overleaf

Tarn-et-Garonne

p.286

p.344–45

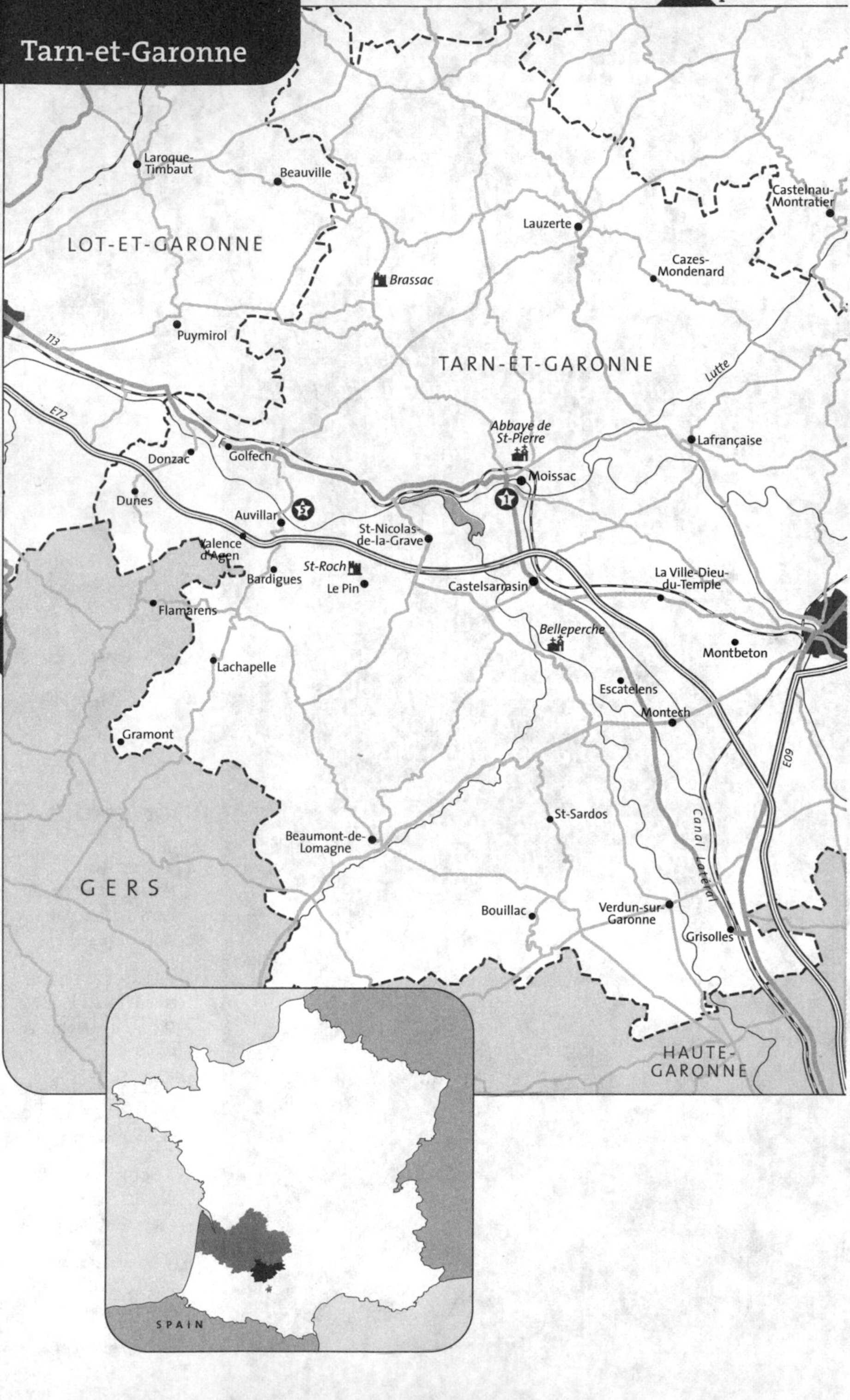

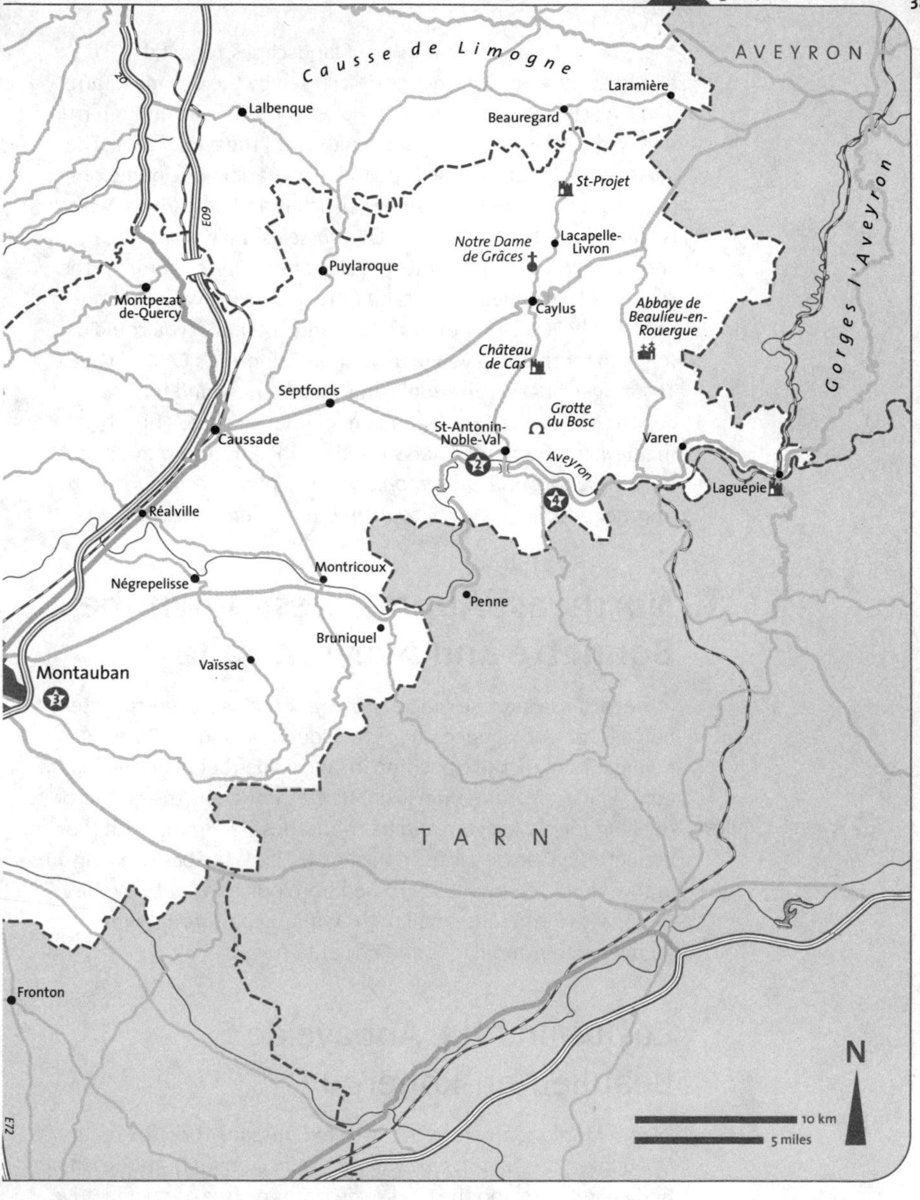

Don't miss

1. Moissac p.403
2. St-Antonin-Noble-Val p.390
3. Montauban p.395
4. Aveyron Valley p.388
5. Auvillar p.412

The Tarn-et-Garonne's mosaic of landscapes, regional architecture and allegiances, crisscrossed by the Garonne, Tarn and Aveyron rivers, contains a bit of everything, and enough fruit to have kept Carmen Miranda in hats until the end of time. The *département* is one of the top producers nationwide of melons (some of which are AOC), apples, peaches and nectarines. Moissac is particularly famous for its AOC *chasselas* table grapes. Pears, cherries, kiwis and hazelnuts are also grown. In the summer the main roads are lined with stands so overflowing with fruit and red wine (VDQS Lavilledieu, Quercy and St-Sardos) you could be forgiven for thinking you're driving up California's Central Valley. The gorges of Aveyron supply dramatic scenery, and the *département* can thank Napoleon for one of France's finest medieval monuments: Moissac Abbey. There is information at *www.cg82.com* and *www.montauban.cci.fr/cci/htm/tourisme.htm*. Another good site is *www.tourisme-tarn-et-garonne.com*.

Northeast Approaches: Down the Bonnette and Aveyron Valleys

④ Aveyron Valley

The Tarn-et-Garonne's most striking corner is the northeastern bulge Napoleon gouged out of the Rouergue and the Tarn. Its rolling hills mark the transition in landscapes between the Massif Central and the Aquitaine Basin, sliced through by the gorges of the languorous **Aveyron** and its tributaries, beginning with the Bonnette that descends from the north. This is the best walking area in the whole *département*, crossed from north to south by the GR46, with numerous small paths winding off through fine scenery, medieval villages and ancient abbeys.

Caylus and the Abbaye de Beaulieu-en-Rouergue

Château de St-Projet
t 05 63 65 74 85; guided tours July–Sept daily 2–7; Oct Sat and Sun 2–7; adm

From Montauban, the N20 north to Caussade then the main D926 take you straight to Caylus; if you're coming from the Lot, find Beauregard and the Causse de Limogne (*see* p.312) and drive south by way of the Renaissance **Château de St-Projet**, where Queen Margot once took refuge from the Protestants. There are sometimes exhibitions and entertainment in July and August, and you can stay in a two-bedroom apartment in the queen's donjon by the week or night.

Lacapelle-Livron, the next village south, has a Templar commandery (rebuilt in the 15th century) and a church so fortified that it looks more like a little castle. For a less bristling house of

Getting around the Bonnette and Aveyron Valleys

Public transport exists, on a limited scale. From Montauban there is one **bus** daily to Caylus, one to St-Antonin-Noble-Val and one a day to most of the other villages. For more details, call Montauban tourist office (*see* p.401).

God, continue south a kilometre to 15th-century Notre-Dame des Grâces, a miniature Flamboyant Gothic gem with a bird's-eye view across the *causse*; 4km south is another, built in 1302, called Notre-Dame de Livron, 'Our Lady of Liberation' in Occitan – a nearby cave was inhabited by a pesky dragon until a bold knight axed it and liberated the neighbourhood.

Caylus, the most important and certainly the prettiest town on the Bonnette, occupies an amphitheatre, most strikingly viewed from the west on the D926. The counts of Toulouse built a castle here in the 1200s, and its ruins still dominate the region. The medieval town, below the main road, is centred on the Place du Marché, with some arcades and a very sturdy *halle* with octagonal pillars. The church under the mighty stone steeple is St-Jean Baptiste, endowed with an elegant seven-sided choir of 1470 and the *Christ Monumental* by Zadkine, carved in 1954 from the trunk of an elm. Don't miss the 13th-century house nearby, the Maison des Loups – as if to get back at these terrors of the Middle Ages, the wolves were made to do duty as rainspouts. Thirteen kilometres west of Caylus, the beautiful 13th- and 14th-century hilltop *bastide* of **Puylaroque** is a miniature version of the famous hilltown of Cordes near Albi, with a 12th-century church of St-Jacques and fine views all around.

Beaulieu-en-Rouergue
t 05 63 24 50 10; open April–June, Sept and Oct Wed–Mon 10–12 and 2–6.30; July and Aug daily 10–6

Southeast of Caylus in Ginals, **Beaulieu-en-Rouergue**, like most Cistercian abbeys, is prettily isolated at the bottom of a wooded valley. It was founded in 1144 by 12 monks from Clairvaux, and the present buildings were begun in the late 1200s. In the Wars of Religion, the whole was stripped and the cloister devastated; the *parlement* of Toulouse had much of it rebuilt during the 17th century, and the last Italianate stuccoes and marble chimneypieces were put in place just in time to be wrecked in the Revolution. Viollet-le-Duc had the idea of taking the church apart piece by

Vin de Coteaux-de-Quercy

The vines that you see around here growing on the limestone terraces are destined for Vin de Coteaux-de-Quercy, which has VDQS status. Grown in microclimatic pockets between the AOC regions of Cahors and Gaillac (to the east), over an area of about 400 hectares, Coteaux-de-Quercy wines are made from five varieties of grape: Cabernet Franc, Merlot, Cot, Gamay and Tannat, in varying quantities. Some growers, especially the Meakins, are experimenting with more traditional varieties such as Jurançon, Abouriou and Syrah.

These are dark, well-structured and fruity wines that can be drunk young or aged – and with some of the escalating prices of Cahors, they're a bargain too. You can learn all about them in English at the Domaine du Merchien (t *05 63 64 97 21; open daily 11–7*) just west of Puylaroque.

piece and rebuilding it in St-Antonin-Noble-Val – a plan that fell through when St-Antonin couldn't come up with enough money for the job. Used as barns until 1960, the abbey was restored after 1974 and now houses a regional centre for contemporary art and music, with a permanent collection of late-20th-century works and annual summer art exhibitions. Although much rebuilt over the centuries, Beaulieu provides an excellent example of the development of Cistercian architecture (and of the monks' increasing concern for their physical comforts – a far cry from the original austerity of St Bernard of Clairvaux). The early-14th-century church is harmonious, with a beautiful portal and rose window. In the north crossing, a *porte des morts* survives – a door each monk went through but once in this vale of tears.

In the Gorges of the Aveyron: Laguépie to St-Antonin-Noble-Val

From the abbey of Beaulieu the D33/D20/D958 takes you down to Laguépie at the very corner of the Tarn-et-Garonne – a pretty village with a ruined castle at the junction of the Aveyron and Viaur rivers. Like **Varen**, the next village west, Laguépie is popular with riverside campers. But Varen has the added attraction of a well-preserved medieval core entered by a fortified gate called El-Faoure. The tiny lanes converge in the centre at a 10th-century Benedictine priory, St-Pierre – a barrel-vaulted, single-naved church from the late 1000s, which, unusually, has no door on its west front – originally the façade formed part of the town wall. The sculpted capitals on the north come from Varen's parish church, demolished in the 1700s, while the capitals in the choir, closed off by three mini-apses and two crypts, are among the most important from the early Middle Ages, decorated with sturdy knots, symmetrical face-to-face animals and biblical scenes. The adjacent 14th-century tower was the residence of the dean of the priory.

2 St-Antonin-Noble-Val

After Varen, the Aveyron flows below one of the oldest towns in the *département*, charming medieval **St-Antonin-Noble-Val** (maps with detailed walking tour available at tourist office). Its setting first delighted the Romans, who named it Nobilis Vallis; the St-Antonin was tacked on when the body of the apostle of this area floated downstream in a boat and a monastery was founded to hold the relics. In the Middle Ages St-Antonin was a Cathar stronghold; in the Hundred Years' War it was occupied by the English, who left their name behind in the tremendous cliffs of the Rocher d'Anglars that loom over the village. The monastery was wiped off the face of the earth by the Protestants, who were themselves clobbered in 1622 by Louis XIII; the king had failed to take Montauban after an 86-day siege, and in his pique came here to pick on someone smaller.

What it lacks in sacred architecture St-Antonin more than makes up for in the civic, beginning with the lovely Gothic Place des Halles and its **Maison des Consuls** of 1120, the latter Disneyfied by Viollet-le-Duc, who over-restored this rare example of Romanesque civic architecture and also added the incongruous Florentine belfry. On the first-floor gallery, note the pillar sculpted with Byzantine emperor Justinian holding his famous *Code* of laws. The hollowed-out spaces on the second floor originally held Hispano-Moorish ceramic plates. Bits of these are now in the building's **Musée Archéologique**, along with furniture and prehistoric items. The *halle* has a curious 15th-century *Crucifixion*, carved on a stone disc.

Musée Archéologique
t 05 63 68 23 52; open July and Aug Wed–Mon 10–1 and 3–6; rest of year by appointment

St-Antonin's labyrinthine lanes, many bearing pungent names, including Rue Bombecul (what an American would call 'Shelf-butt Street'), have such a rare assortment of medieval houses that the town has been called an outdoor museum of secular architecture, left untouched by any recent attempts at restoration. If you want to stock up on holiday reading here, visit the **English Bookshop**; St-Antonin is a popular town with British housebuyers.

English Bookshop
12 Rue Pelisserie, t 05 63 68 22 66

Down by the river along the Promenade des Moines are the remains of the tanneries that made St-Antonin's fortune, along with a working walnut-oil mill; you can walk around the former. Further along the river is a slate-roofed spa of 1913; the mineral spring here, the Fontaine de Saltet, rich in copper, has been a popular cure for urinary infections since the 18th century. Since 1990 it has been commercially bottled.

The well-marked paths around St-Antonin make for fine walking, especially along the Aveyron and up to the mighty 200m Rocher des Anglars with its belvedere over the gorge, offering stunning views over the town. The area is very popular with rock climbers, while stalactite spotters can aim for the **Grotte du Bosc**, 3km northeast, formed by a subterranean river; there are remarkable formations and a little museum of minerals and prehistoric finds.

Grotte du Bosc
t 05 63 30 60 03, open July and Aug daily 10–12 and 2–6; Easter–June and Sept Sun and hols 2–6; adm

Further north, the D19 leads to **Château de Cas**, an austere citadel that defended the Bonnette valley, with a Merovingian chapel. Once the seat of a Templar commandery, it was restored and refurnished after damage in the Revolution and the Second World War.

Château de Cas
t 05 63 67 07 40; call for times

Further down the Aveyron, to Caussade

Besides the kind of unspoiled beautiful scenery that makes this area a favourite with French film-makers, this section includes an excellent museum full of works by one of France's early-20th-century masters, who most people will never have heard of.

Bruniquel and Montricoux

After St-Antonin, the Aveyron cuts off a corner of the Tarn *département*, passing through a dramatic gorge; the best scenery and views are along the narrow corniche road, the D173, past the striking medieval village of **Penne** with its cadaver of a castle hanging with all the panache of an opera set over the cliffs. Next down the river is **Bruniquel**, a picturesque hilltown, Protestant stronghold and now an artists' colony, built under a large fortress overlooking the cliffs at the confluence of the Aveyron and Vère. This, according to Gregory of Tours, was founded by Queen Brunehaut (d. 613), a Visigoth, married to Siebert, grandson of Clovis. She was as fierce as a queen on a chessboard, fighting a relentless war with neighbouring queen Fredegunda, personally eliminating 10 members of Fredegunda's family, until her own nobles tired of her cruelty and handed her over to her son, who, with a decided lack of filial devotion, tied her by the hair to a wild horse.

Château de Bruniquel
t 05 63 67 27 67; open April–June and Sept–Nov school hols 10–12.30 and 2–6; July and Aug daily 10–7; adm

Maison des Comtes Payrol
t 05 63 67 26 42; open April–June, Sept and Nov school hols daily 10–6; July and Aug daily 10–7; Oct Sat and Sun 10–6; adm

Story or not, the **Château de Bruniquel**, rising 90m over the confluence of the Vère and the Aveyron, dates back only to the 12th century – the tour includes the keep, called the tower of Brunehaut, knights' room and chapel, and an elegant Renaissance gallery. The nearby **Maison des Comtes Payrol**, in Rue du Château, is a rare example of 13th-century civic architecture, with its original windows and a coffered ceiling. Two of Bruniquel's medieval gates are intact, including the picturesque Porte de l'Horloge, at the top of a winding lane. Ask at Bruniquel's tourist office about visits to the **Grotte de la Madeleine**, a cave in the cliffs decorated with prehistoric engravings.

Musée Lenoir
t 05 63 67 26 48; open April–mid-Oct daily 10–12.30 and 2.30–6; July and Aug daily 10–12.30 and 2.30–7

The gorge of the Aveyron begins (or peters out) at Montricoux, a town founded by the Templars. It has a 13th-century church, St-Eutrope, topped with a 16th-century Toulouse-style belltower; inside is a fresco from the 1920s by Marcel Lenoir. Marcel Lenoir? The name doesn't ring a bell? Then find out more in the **Musée Lenoir**, housed nearby in Montricoux's château, built around the Templar keep and given a Tuscan facelift in the 18th century. Briefly, Lenoir was born in Montauban in 1872 and died in Montricoux in 1931, although he spent most of his career in the artistic whirl of Paris, where his work was admired by Braque, Matisse and Rodin. Few artists have been more forgotten. Lenoir himself was partly to blame, through his own stubborn integrity: he refused to accept any honours or scratch anyone's back, whether they be critics, dealers or even his own peers, and the art world responded by boycotting his work. Another difficulty is that he refused to be pinned down with an easily recognizable (and marketable) style; like Picasso, he had an endless capacity and need to change, moving from the Symbolist influences of Gustave Moreau and Mucha to later experiments in Cubism, Surrealism and abstraction.

He approached each new change of style with religious intensity, sometimes in religious subjects, such as his *Descent from the Cross, with Orchestra*; the museum has examples from every period.

The largest town in these parts is **Caussade**, 'the city of hats', a pleasant, bustling place on the main Cahors–Montauban road, surrounded by small industries, including one that produced Maurice Chevalier's trademark boaters. Its landmark is a 15th-century brick belltower in the Toulouse style, and there are some good medieval buildings, including the *halle*, in the centre.

The D5 from St-Antonin leads west to **Septfonds**, home of a good set of dolmens (including a jauntily tilted proto-Baroque model) and an austere Spanish Republican cemetery of 1939, near a vast camp set up for refugees of the Civil War.

Ferme Malterie Brasserie de St-Martin
t 05 63 28 23 46

Just south of Cassaude, still on the N20, is a little *bastide* with the right name for our virtual times – **Réalville**. If you are desperate for a glass of beer after all that wine, visit to the **Ferme Malterie Brasserie de St-Martin**, towards Mirabel, for a taste of La Désirée.

ⓘ Caylus >>
*Rue Droit, **t** 05 63 67 00 28, www.caylus.com*

ⓘ Laguépie >>
*Place du Foirail, **t** 05 63 30 20 34*

Tourist Information in the Bonnette and Aveyron Valleys

Caylus has a tourist office, but info is also available at the **Maison du Patrimoine and museum**, in a park on the road to St-Antonin (*www.maisondupatrimoine-midiquercy.org*). There are also tourist offices at Laguépie and St-Antonin; the latter has a list of the many places where you can hire a **bike**, or **canoe**, in the town, including **Acti Eaux Vives**, Route de Marsac, **t** 06 12 51 83 23. Further down the Aveyron, there are tourist offices at Bruniquel and Caussade.

Market Days in the Bonnette and Aveyron Valleys

Caylus: Tuesday and Saturday; medieval market in August.

Laguépie: Wednesday; chestnut market Wednesday in October.

Varen: Saturday.

St-Antonin-Noble-Val: Sunday, food and flea market, and night markets in July and August.

Caussade: Monday farmers' market, plus Monday *marché au gras et aux truffes* in winter.

Montricoux: Friday.

Nègrepelisse: Tuesday.

Réalville: Saturday afternoon.

Where to Stay and Eat in the Bonnette and Aveyron Valleys

Caylus ✉ 82160

****La Renaissance**, Av Père Evariste Huc, **t** 05 63 67 07 26 (€). Simple, central lodgings and a restaurant (€€€–€). *Closed Sun eve and Mon in winter, 2wks Feb, 1wk early July and 2wks Oct.*

Ferme du Mas de Monille, north of town in Loze near St-Projet, **t** 05 63 65 76 85 (€€). A place to dine *à la Obélix* and see wild boar. Booking is required.

Laguépie ✉ 82250

****Les Deux Rivières**, Avenue Puech Mignon, **t** 05 63 31 41 41 (€). The best place to stay in the area, with pleasant, modern rooms and a restaurant (€€) serving well-prepared, sometimes local dishes. *Closed Fri, Sun and Mon eves, Sat lunch and 2wks Feb.*

Varen ✉ 82330

Le Moulin de Varen, on D958, **t** 05 63 65 45 10 (€€€–€€). A pretty old mill where you can enjoy simple but delicious meals based on seasonal produce. There are also apartments

(€), available for a minimum of three nights. *Closed mid-Dec–mid-Feb exc by reservation, and when river floods.*

ⓘ **St-Antonin-Noble-Val >**
Place de la Mairie, **t** *05 63 30 63 47, www.saint-antonin-noble-val.com*

St-Antonin-Noble-Val ✉ 82140

Le Lys Bleu de Payrols, 29 Place de la Halle, **t** 05 63 68 21 00 (€€€–€€). Rooms spread over several medieval houses in the heart of town, with antique furniture and mini-bars. The restaurant (€€€€–€€) serves refined regional cuisine, including good fish.

Bès de Quercy, on D926 towards Caylus, **t** 05 63 31 97 61 (€). Four comfortable B&B rooms, plus evening meals that may include chicken, duck or guinea fowl.

Féneyrols ✉ 82140

★ **Les Jardins des Thermes >**

Les Jardins des Thermes, east of St-Antonin-Noble-Val along D115, **t 05 63 30 65 49, *www.jardindesthermes.com* (€€–€). An attractive house and garden with trees beside the Aveyron river. Specialities in its restaurant (€€€–€) include wrapped slab of beef. *Closed Nov–Feb; restaurant also Wed and Thur Sept–June.*

ⓘ **Caussade >>**
9 Rue de la République, **t** *05 63 26 04 04*

Brousses ✉ 82140

La Corniche, just off D115 by St-Antonin-Noble-Val, **t** 05 63 68 26 95 (€€). A small restaurant with a terrace with a lovely view of a tree-covered cliff, where you can enjoy regional food and a few things besides to the relaxing sound of a stream. There are also rather rustic but airy apartments for two (€). *Closed Sun eve, Mon and Dec–Mar.*

ⓘ **Bruniquel >**
Promenade du Ravelin, **t** *05 63 67 29 84, http://bruniquel.org*

Bruniquel ✉ 82800

Chambres d'Hôte chez Marc de Bauduin, Promenade du Ravelin, **t** 05 63 67 26 16, *www.chambres-bruniquel.fr* (€). Four rooms with baths in a grand old house with fine views, plus evening meals (€€) by request.

Les Granges Tourondel, 3km from town, **t** 05 63 24 17 31, *www.tourondel.com* (€). An 19th-century farm and B&B oozing tranquil, rustic charm, with optional evening meals (€€).

Montricoux ✉ 82800

****Terrassier**, Vaïssac, southwest of town, **t** 05 63 30 94 60 (€€–€). A pleasant modern option with a pool and a good restaurant (€€€–€€). *Closed 2wks Jan and 1wk Nov; restaurant also Fri and Sun eves.*

Chambres d'Hôte Les Brunis, Brunis, 2km from Montricoux (signposted off D115), **t** 05 63 67 24 08, *www.chambres-aveyron.com* (€). A delightful place to stay, with five tastefully decorated rooms and a large swimming pool in a pleasant garden. Dinner (€€) is available.

Les Gorges de l'Aveyron, **t** 05 63 24 50 50 (€€€–€€). A chic modern restaurant in its own shady park along the banks of the Aveyron, serving gastronomic dishes. Book ahead. *Closed Tues, Wed and a few wks in winter.*

Caussade ✉ 82300

****Larroque**, Avenue de la Gare, **t** 05 63 65 11 77 (€€–€). A welcoming, cosy hotel in the heart of Caussade, with a pool and an excellent restaurant (€€€–€€) offering regional ingredients prepared with an imaginative touch. *Closed 2wks over Christmas and New Year; restaurant also closed Sun and 4wks throughout year.*

****Dupont**, 25 Rue des Récollets, **t** 05 63 65 05 00, *www.hotel-restaurant-dupont.com* (€). Comfortable rooms in a 14th-century building in the centre, plus a restaurant (€€–€). *Closed Sun eve, Fri and 2wks Jan.*

Réalville ✉ 82440

Eskualduna, Albias, on N20 just southwest of Réalville, **t** 05 63 31 01 58 (€€). A popular lunch venue offering Texas-size T-bones and other steaks, plus a selection of fish dishes. *Closed Mon out of season.*

Le St-Marcel, **t** 05 63 67 14 27 (€). Tasty *mélanges* of local ingredients with fruit, plus Catalan dishes, served in the castle's former stable. *Closed Sun eve and Mon out of season, plus several wks Oct–Nov and Feb–Mar.*

Nègrepelisse ✉ 82800

Ferme-Auberge de Belle Chasse, 2km from Nègrepelisse on D35 to Vaïssac, signposted on right, **t** 05 63 30 86 58 (€€). A rambling and relaxing place lost along narrow lanes, with lovely views from its terrace surrounded by wildflowers. The food is simple but generous and farm-fresh. Book in advance.

Montauban

Montauban

Originally covered with silvery willows, hence the name *Mons Albanus* ('white hill'), Montauban prefers to be known as 'the pinkest of the three pink cities' (pink as in brick; the other two are Toulouse and Albi). The capital of the Tarn-et-Garonne, Montauban was cast in an original mould from its foundation, a successful medieval experiment in city planning, a new possibility that caught and spawned dozens of baby Montaubans, the *bastides*, in the 13th and 14th centuries. Not many, though, have evolved into little cities with a prestigious art museum and a top summer jazz festival that counts Bob Dylan and James Brown among its alumnae.

History

Montauban owes its origins to a crew of oversexed monks. These were the brethren of the 'Golden Hill', Montauriol, a monastery founded in 820 by St Théobard, who claimed the *droit de cuissage* (the right to select their bedfellows from the local population). The monks abused their privilege to such an extent that the people of Montauriol asked Count Alphonse-Jourdain for a new town. He complied, and in 1144 laid out the grid plan of the first new town in the southwest, essentially a *bastide* 100 years before the others began sprouting like autumn mushrooms on the battle lines of the Hundred Years' War.

The counts allowed Montauban to elect its own consuls, and gave it so many privileges that it soon sucked up all the loose people in the area. In spite of being punished for loyalty to Toulouse during the Albigensian crusade, Montauban quickly rebounded; as a new town with a relatively free, new population it had something of the enterprising spirit of an American frontier town. By the mid 14th century Montauban was bustling with the import and export of textiles – just when the Treaty of Brétigny (1360) ceded it to England. John Chandos came in person to take it for the Black Prince, who spent many months here, plotting and fighting on the frontiers of French territory.

After the Hundred Years' War, Montauban's commerce quickly picked up again, and like other mercantile towns (Bergerac and Nîmes, for instance), it was very receptive to the new doctrines of Calvin. After a good deal of simmering the pot boiled over on 20 December 1561; the Montaubanais en masse broke down the cathedral door, pillaged the building and burnt it to the ground, then did the same to all the other churches and convents in town, except St-Jacques, which they converted into a Protestant *temple*. All the brick and stone of the churches immediately went into building walls, which were unusually efficient, twice repelling the concerted Catholic attacks.

Montauban

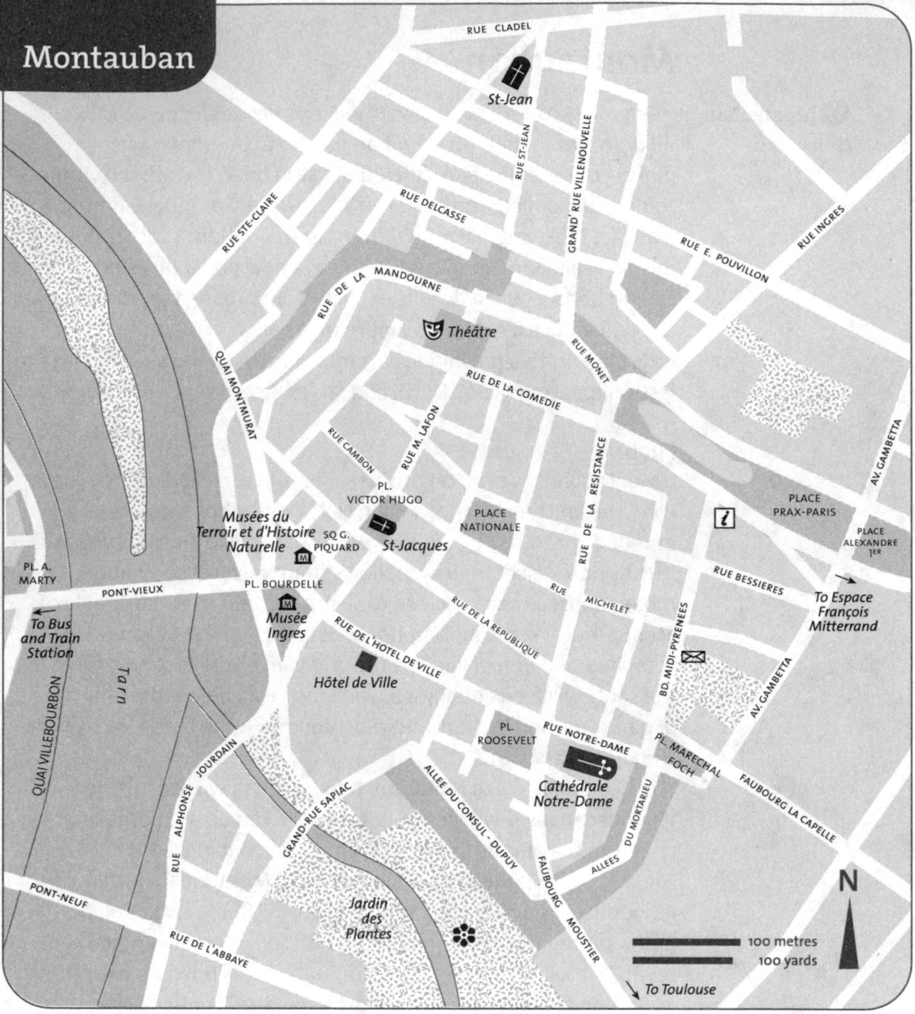

The future Henri IV spent much time here, and when he became King his Edict of Nantes made Montauban a Protestant place of safety. His less tolerant and less capable son Louis XIII marched down in 1621 with an army of 25,000 and besieged Montauban for weeks, setting the outskirts on fire, but he found the Protestants too tough for his taste and went home feeling sorry for himself. His grand vizier Richelieu, however, waited until the fall of La Rochelle in 1629, which left Montauban isolated as the last Protestant stronghold in France, and diplomatically convinced it to surrender.

No dummy, Richelieu's first act was to demolish Montauban's walls. His second was to cajole the inhabitants into not emigrating to Protestant countries, by offering them plums – money and job-generating bureaucracies, their own *intendants* and a regional bureau of finances. Richelieu may have been a cardinal but he

Getting to and away from Montauban

Montauban's station, off Avenue Mayenne at the west end of town over the Tarn, is well served by **trains** between Paris and Toulouse, which also stop at Angoulême and between Toulouse and Bordeaux (stopping at Moissac and Agen).

Autocars Barrière, 16 Rue du Châteauvieux, **t** 05 63 93 34 34, has **coaches** direct to Barcelona, Valencia, Morocco and elsewhere.

Getting around Montauban

Various **bus** companies combine to serve most of the *département* and the big towns beyond; call the tourist office (*see* p.401) to find out who goes where. The largest bus company with routes to local towns and villages is Transport Jardel, **t** 05 63 22 55 00.

For a **taxi**, call **t** 05 63 03 64 24 or **t** 05 63 66 99 99.

You can hire **bikes** at Guionnet Cyclosport, 87 Avenue d'Irlande (in the commercial centre south of town), **t** 05 63 66 32 32. There are cycle paths in town.

---

knew well enough that it was the mercantile Protestants who generated much of the nation's wealth. His plan worked so well that by the 18th century Montauban could proudly claim to be the third city in the southwest. Its weavers produced a thick wool fabric by the name of *cadis* that sold like hot cakes in France's American colonies. The *intendants* drew out new broad avenues and laid out the first parks.

Montauban's contribution to the Revolution was a woman about 200 years ahead of her time: Olympe de Gouges, born in 1748, daughter of the obscure poet-magistrate Lefranc de Pompignan. Defender of the rights of all people, even women, to live without oppression, Gouges wrote a brochure called *Les Droits de la femme et de la citoyenne*, declaring that 'if a woman has the right to mount the scaffold, she has the right to ascend to the seats of justice'. For trying to obtain political rights for women and 'forgetting the virtues of her sex' she was guillotined in 1793. But if the Revolution was blind to the need for women's rights, the Napoleonic code that followed a few years later really put half the population of France in its place by ending rights (especially the right to buy and sell property) that even medieval women had enjoyed. Only since the 1970s have French wives been able to open bank accounts in their own names.

Another setback was in store for Montauban – its invaluable *cadis* trade began to decline when France lost her colonies in Canada and Louisiana, then disappeared altogether when the new industrial mills in the north undersold the city's artisan weavers. Napoleon's intervention, making Montauban a departmental capital, assured at least a bureaucratic vocation that kept the town from complete economic decline in the 19th century, although it was a century burnished by the reflected glow of the international fame of its native sons Ingres and Bourdelle, Rodin's chief assistant. Since the last war, Montauban has typified the turnaround of a *ville moyenne* – the proximity of dynamic Toulouse and its key location on the southwest railways and highways have attracted numerous small enterprises and led to, among other things, the thorough restoration of its old brick charms.

Place Nationale

The finest gift bestowed by old Alphonse Jourdain on the new town of Montauban is its central square, Place Nationale. Although it was the prototype for the central *bastide* market square, none of the later squares can match its innovative, urbane sophistication. First off, it isn't even a square at all, but a more subtle, visually interesting irregular trapezoid with covered chamfered corners. The whole plan of the new town echoes this slight distortion of the plain, monotonous square grid. Its unique 'double cloister' arcades date from 1144 and were originally built in wood; after a fire in 1614 they were slowly rebuilt, exactly as they had been, in warm brick, even though the style of vaulting was considered archaic at the time (you can see the year when each bay was completed inscribed in the keystones of the vaults – the last reads 1708). The interior galleries functioned as covered lanes, the continuation of the streets that come into the angles of Place Nationale; the outer galleries were given over to displays of merchandise. In the central square the Montaubanais bought their food, hanged their thieves and issued their proclamations.

During the 17th-century fashion for homogenous squares, the city ordered that all the façades of the buildings facing Place Nationale should be rebuilt in the same style, with the attic storerooms lit by openings called *mirandes*. Note the sundial installed on the north side, with the legend *Una tibi* ('Your hour will come!'); the metal metre bar set vertically in the southwest corner of the square was put in place to instruct the locals when the Revolution standardized French measures.

St-Jacques and the Pont-Vieux

If you leave Place Nationale by the metre corner, you'll soon find yourself in Place Victor-Hugo, site of St-Jacques, a combination church, assembly and voting hall built by Montauban's consuls in the 13th century. During the repairs following the Hundred Years' War it was given an octagonal belltower that, like St-Sernin in Toulouse, has a curious change in design halfway up and still bears scars from Louis XIII's cannonballs. The neo-Roman portal with its coloured-tile decoration dates from the 19th century; the interior is typically southern Gothic, with a large single nave.

Down from St-Jacques, Place Bourdelle is named after Bourdelle's dramatic 1895 *Monument to the War Dead of 1870*, showing the influence of his master Rodin. Here the neoclassical Tribunal de

Musée d'Histoire Naturelle
t 05 63 22 13 85; open Tues–Sat 10–12 and 2–6, Sun 2–6, exc public hols

Commerce now houses two museums. Upstairs, the **Musée d'Histoire Naturelle** has an immense collection of birds and animals, fossils (starring some unique Quercy primates from 65 million years ago) and minerals, among them phosphorites from Quercy – one of the places on Earth where they are most abundant – and pieces of a meteorite that fell in the Tarn-et-Garonne in 1864, exciting much speculation about aliens from outer space. On the ground floor, the **Musée du Terroir** is devoted to country life in Bas-Quercy and southwest ethnography in general. Nearby is Square du Général Picquart, named after the army intelligence officer who went to prison for defending Dreyfus in 1898; Montauban is still a progressive town.

Musée du Terroir
t 05 63 66 46 34; same hrs

From Place Bourdelle the Tarn is spanned by the Pont-Vieux, a bridge planned from Montauban's foundation by Alphonse-Jourdain. However, financial and technical difficulties prevented its erection until King Philippe le Bel was passing through Montauban in 1303, and the town consuls (as they would later buttonhole Napoleon) got the king to promise his assistance in raising taxes and providing wood for the brick kilns for the construction of their long-awaited bridge, promising in turn to name its towers after him. Work on the 206m structure began in 1311 and was a technological *tour de force*; its seven uneven arches have stood up to the worst floods the unruly Tarn has sent down, including water so high in 1441 that it washed over the top of it. Originally the bridge resembled the Pont Valentré in Cahors, with Philippe le Bel's three fortified towers; these were demolished early in the 20th century to let more traffic through.

Musée Ingres

Musée Ingres
13 Rue de l'Hôtel de Ville, t 05 63 22 12 91; open July and Aug daily 9.30–12 and 1.30–6; Sept–mid-Oct and Easter–June daily 10–12 and 2–6; mid-Oct–Easter Mon and Wed–Sat 10–12 and 2–6, Sun 2–6

The Musée Ingres is housed in the pretty bishops' palace at the eastern end of the bridge, built over the foundations of an unfinished medieval castle that had been the local headquarters for English rule. The bishop's palace, begun in the 1640s – a decade after the King's troops marched in – was a symbol of the new political and religious order. After the Revolution the building became Montauban's *mairie*, though later the mayor moved elsewhere, leaving the palace to a role that seemed a more fitting: as a monument to the city's favourite son, Jean-Auguste-Dominique Ingres (1780–1867).

This painter, whose donations to his home town make up the core of the museum's collection, was tremendously popular in his time – a technical virtuoso whose icily perfect religious and mythological works fitted the mood of Napoleonic neoclassicism. In fact many of his first paintings were kitsch propaganda pieces commissioned by the Emperor. Ingres was an Academic artist from head to toe, the sort of dedicated conformist who believed in rules and precepts, and measured his success by the medals he won at competitions. His battles with the younger generation of Romantic painters, especially Delacroix, were legendary. The earlier paintings on display here were done when Ingres was still in the workshop of his master, the even more indigestible Jacques-Louis David.

The collection includes thousands of sketches and drawings, some displayed in a way that shows up the contrast between the Academic painter and the suppressed artist within, as in the *Jesus among the Doctors* (painted when Ingres was 82), in which a lovely, almost Pre-Raphaelite study is juxtaposed with the stiff and silly finished work. Ingres did much better at portraits, of which several are here, and also in mythological scenes such as the *Dream of Ossian*, a colossal canvas of ghostly figures in the sky, painted for Napoleon's bedroom (Ossian was the supposed medieval Scottish bard whose 'rediscovered' works, all fakes, nevertheless made a great impression on poets at the dawn of the Romantic era).

The Salle Ingres, the bishops' bedchamber, was partially decorated by Ingres' father, also an artist. It houses a little shrine to Ingres, with the great man's desk, his paints, a view of his studio in Rome, and his violin (he was an accomplished musician as well as a painter), all arranged the way Ingres planned it himself.

Not all the works present are by Ingres. From his collection there are archaeological items – an Etruscan burial urn and a black-figure Greek vase with the *Battle of Centaurs and Lapiths* that may be the best work in the museum – as well as a few Italian paintings (a Masolino predella panel and a *Nativity* by Carpaccio), and one from Spain, a striking *St Jerome* attributed to Ribera. A flatulent historical echo is supplied by Ingres' spiritual ancestor, Charles Lebrun, the first director of the Académie: *Louis XIV in the Chariot of State*. Montauban's other famous son, the sculptor Antoine Bourdelle (1861–1929), gets a room, with portrait busts of figures as diverse as Ingres himself and Krishnamurti; Bourdelle's most acclaimed work, however, stands out in front of the museum on the square, the *Last Centaur Dying*. There are other Bourdelle statues dotted about town; ask at the tourist office about the walk taking them all in.

Down below in the Salle du Prince Noir (all that remains of the English castle), the museum keeps a small archaeological collection, including a Roman mosaic, and some medieval items – among them a nasty torture contraption subtly called the *banc à question* ('questioning bench').

Cathédrale Notre-Dame

Cathédrale Notre-Dame
open Mon–Sat 9–12 and 2–6, Sun 9–12

From the Musée Ingres, Rue de l'Hôtel de Ville leads up to the cathedral, rebuilt between 1692 and 1739, when Louis XIV sent his own architects to build a church worthy of the Counter-Reformation, celebrating the victory over heresy and, as always, his own glory. In contrast to the warm red brick that epitomizes much of Montauban, the cathedral shows its foreign, Parisian origins in its white stone and frostily perfect classicism (not many cathedrals were built during this period in France; Versailles' is the most famous).

The vast interior is full of equally frigid 18th–19th-century furnishings, and one of Ingres' major works, the enormous *Vow of Louis XIII*, commissioned for the cathedral and painted in Florence between 1820 and 1824. He exhibited the painting in the 1824 Paris salon, where it hung next to the *Massacre of Chios*, the Romantic masterpiece of Delacroix. To the neoclassical heirs of Jacques-Louis David, Delacroix's work was 'the massacre of painting', and Ingres was declared the champion and upholder of Academic values; Delacroix sniffed that Ingres' painting was 'pure Italian', and a lifelong rivalry was born. It is certainly easy to see what Delacroix meant: the Virgin, Child and angels seem to have come straight out of Raphael's sketchbooks. Louis XIII is seen offering the Virgin his crown and sceptre, symbolizing the kingdom of France. The subject could only have been suggested by a rabid Catholic (or a Parisian), as Louis XIII certainly didn't do Montauban any favours.

ⓘ **Montauban >**
Ancien Collège, Place Prax-Paris, **t** *05 63 63 60 60, www.montauban-tourisme.com*

Tourist Information in Montauban

Montauban has a **tourist office** and is also home to the **Comité Départemental du Tourisme**, Boulevard Hubert Gouze, **t** 05 63 21 79 09, *www.cg82.com*, with information for the whole *département*.

Market Days in Montauban

Saturday mornings, Place Prax-Paris, farmers' market and fleamarket; **Wednesday** morning, Place Lalaque; **Wednesday and Saturday** mornings in winter, *marché au gras*, Place Nationale.

Activities in Montauban

There's a 9-hole **golf course** (**t** 05 63 31 35 40) 5km outside town on the D959.

Where to Stay in Montauban

Montauban ✉ 82000

******Hostellerie Les Coulandrières,*** Montbeton, on D958 3km west of city, **t** 05 63 67 47 47 (€€). One of the prettiest places to stay in Montauban – a modern inn under a superb cedar tree, with a pool, a park and bright rooms. The restaurant, specializing in duck and southwest classics, is one of the best in town too. *Restaurant closed Sun eve and Mon lunch.*

*****Mercure Montauban**, 12 Rue Notre-Dame, **t** 05 63 63 17 23 (€€). A chain hotel with a very central location. Its restaurant has a good reputation.

****Hôtel d'Orsay**, Rue Salengro, opposite station, **t** 05 63 66 06 66, *www.hotel-restaurant-orsay.com* (€€–€). Very comfortable rooms, several air-conditioned, and the best food in Montauban (*see* p.402). *Closed Christmas and New Year.*

****Lion d'Or**, 22 Av de Mayenne, **t** 05 63 20 04 04 (€). A good-value option in a 19th-century building by the station, with a restaurant (€€–€). *Closed Sun and over Christmas and New Year.*

Eating Out in Montauban

Look out for *montauriols* – chocolate truffles with a cherry marinated in armagnac – from the pastry shops.

Au Fil de l'Eau, 14 Quai du Dr Lafforgue, **t** 05 63 66 11 85 (€€€–€€). A pleasant spot on the banks of the Tarn, with a small play area opposite. There is a bias towards regional fare, and a good choice of wines from the southwest. *Closed Sun, Mon, and Wed eve.*

La Cuisine d'Alain >

La Cuisine d'Alain, Hôtel d'Orsay (*see* p.401) (€€€–€€). Local dishes with an original slant, including a local version of cassoulet. *Closed Sat and Mon lunch, Sun, and Christmas and New Year.*

Au Chapon Fin, Place St-Orens, just off roundabout across Pont-Neuf, **t** 05 63 63 12 10 (€€). A local favourite for traditional food and specialities such as foie gras with nectarines and fish. *Closed Sun eve, Sat and Aug.*

Le Ventadour, 23 Quai Villebourbon, **t** 05 63 63 34 58 (€€). Under the brick vaults of a restored 17th-century dyeworks, serving aromatic beef with morels and other delicacies. *Closed Sat lunch, Sun and Mon.*

Around Montauban

In 1679, Montauban's *intendant* Foucault initiated the greening of the pink city by planting thousands of elms on the banks of the Tarn, along the broad street that now bears his name, Cours Foucault. Enjoying a fine view of the historic centre, the *cours* has been the city's most popular promenade ever since. Its focal point, closing the view between the long alleys of trees, is Bourdelle's *La France veillant sur ses morts*, a First World War monument inspired by the temples and sculpture of ancient Greece, typical of the sculptor's later career, when he moved from Rodin's romanticism to a more classical style. Curiously enough, a small piece of the Cours Foucault belongs to the Osage of Oklahoma – in 1829, some members of the tribe showed up in Montauban, exhausted and demoralized from a two-year tramp across Europe; white trappers back home had told them they could escape discrimination in America and become French citizens. The people of Montauban couldn't grant their wish, but they raised money to pay for their passage home. Some 160 years later contact was renewed, and a symbolic patch of France was donated to the Osage; every other year cultural exchanges take place in summer. You can learn more from the **Association Oklahoma-Occitania**.

Association Oklahoma-Occitania
*18 Rue de Trapèze, **t** 05 63 95 87 61*

South of the centre, the **Jardin des Plantes**, created in 1860 and host to concerts during the town's popular jazz festival in July, has several rare species of tree. East of Place Prax-Paris (with the mushroom-roofed market) is the **Espace François Mitterrand** (formerly the Parc Chambord), created in 1972; here, in May and June, 12,000 roses from around the world (1100 varieties) burst into intoxicating bloom. At the end of the garden you'll find the municipal pool, Olympic-sized.

Lastly, north of Place Prax-Paris,there's a little **Musée de la Résistance et de la Déportation** with three permanent exhibitions on the period from the rise of Nazism to Liberation, internment camps in the region, and Free France. There are often temporary exhibitions as well.

Musée de la Résistance et de la Déportation
*33 Grand Rue Villenouvelle, **t** 05 63 66 03 11; open Tues–Sat 9–12 and 2–6 exc Aug*

Moissac

Moissac There's only one reason to go to Moissac, but it's a solid five-star reason: the Romanesque Abbaye de St-Pierre, a crown jewel of medieval French sculpture. The town of Moissac, washed clean of most of its character in a tragic flood in 1930 that killed more than 100 people and destroyed over 600 buildings, now busies itself growing aromatic pale golden *chasselas de Moissac*, France's finest dessert grapes, first cultivated in the Middle Ages in the abbey's vineyards and the first French fruit to attain AOC status in 1952.

The Abbaye St-Pierre

The first Benedictine monastery was founded here by Clovis in 506, commemorating his victory over the Visigoths. The battle had cost him 1,000 men, whom Clovis declared would be remembered by an abbey of 1,000 monks. Exactly marking the spot of such an important religious foundation being a very serious matter, Clovis, as the legend goes, climbed a hill and hurled his trusty javelin, telling God to guide it where he saw fit. Gshloop! went the javelin as it struck a marsh. Never questioning God's peculiar choice, Clovis ordered his builders to get on with it. He had to order them three times. In the end they had to sink deep piles to support the structure. No one knows if the story has a germ of truth in it, or if the monks made it up to explain their problems with rising damp.

One of Clovis's successors, King Dagobert, put the abbey under royal protection, thanks to the Bishop of Cahors, St Didier (AD 630–55), according to some accounts the true father of Moissac. Protection was promised into the 9th century, but the Merovingian and Carolingian kings were too far away to be of much help when the abbey was sacked by the Arabs in 721 and 732, then by the Normans in 850 and the Magyars in 864. Fed up with royal 'protection', the abbots placed themselves under the counts of Toulouse. After a roof collapsed in 1030 and a fire broke out in 1042, the monastery was in such spiritual and material disorder that the counts put it under the control of Cluny; they, noting its position along one of the main pilgrimage routes to Compostela (from Puy-en-Velay), sent money for its restoration and a new abbot, Durand de Bredon, also Bishop of Toulouse, who consecrated the new church in 1063.

Because of Moissac's close links with Toulouse, Simon de Montfort sacked it during the Albigensian crusade in 1212; though Raymond VII recaptured it in 1222, he was helpless to save the 210 Cathars burned by the Inquisition here in 1234. These human bonfires seem to mark a turning point in the abbey's popularity; in 1466 a papal bull stripped the abbey from Cluny's jurisdiction and put it under absentee *abbés commanditaires*, who sucked up most of the rents due to the abbey for their own pockets. By 1626 the monks had been

Getting to and around Moissac

Moissac is on the slow **train** line between Bordeaux, Agen, Montauban and Toulouse. For information about **buses**, ask at the tourist office (*see* p.409).

For a **taxi**, call **t** 05 63 04 03 88 or **t** 05 63 04 08 82.

replaced by a chapter of canons. Louis XIV's finance minster, Colbert, purchased Moissac's library and moved it to Paris, and many abbey buildings were demolished on the eve of the Revolution, which as usual could find no better use for the surviving monastery than as a saltpetre works, after taking care to surgically guillotine the carved figures of the greatest Romanesque cloister in France.

In 1847 Viollet-le-Duc was summoned by the then superintendent of historical monuments, Prosper Mérimée, to restore the majestic porch. He had hardly begun in 1850 when along came a cohort of philistines who made the sans-culottes look like schoolboys – the builders of the Bordeaux–Toulouse railway – who announced that the cloister was smack in the way of the line someone in Paris had drawn for the tracks. A huge battle ensued with the preservationists, and, although the tracks were realigned at the last moment, the railway men had their evil way with the splendid refectory and kitchens. A century and a half later, opinion has turned 180 degrees; now there are plans to cover up the railway tracks to enhance what remains of Moissac's medieval atmosphere.

The Porch

Given Moissac's record of trouble, the great abbot Ansquitil decided in 1115 to fortify the church's tower-porch. The tower is 12th century up to its first-floor chapel; Viollet-le-Duc restored the brick steeple and crenellations. Sheltered underneath is the sublime porch, one of the most powerful and beautiful works of the Middle Ages; the men who commissioned it are remembered in the two statues on pilasters off on either side, Abbot Ansquitil on the left (or, some say, St Benedict) and on the right Abbot Roger (1115–35), who completed the work after Ansquitil's death.

The tympanum, originally vividly painted, rests on a lintel recycled from a Gallo-Roman building, decorated with eight large thistle flowers and enclosed in a cable or vine, spat out and swallowed by a monster at each end. The main scene represents a key vision of the Apocalypse (Rev. 4: 2–8), of Christ sitting in the Judgement of Nations, with the Book of Life in his hand ('And he who sat there appeared like jasper and carnelian, and round the throne was a rainbow that looked like an emerald... and before the throne there is as it were a sea of glass, like crystal'). You might notice that this Christ has three arms, one on the book, one raised in blessing, and another on his heart (please don't ask for an explanation: no one's come up with a convincing one yet). The four symbols of the Evangelists twist to surround him, and two seraphim, carrying scrolls representing the Old and New Testaments, are squeezed under the rainbow. The rest of the tympanum is occupied by the 24 Elders, no two alike, each gazing up from their thrones at Christ, 'each holding a harp, and with golden bowls full of incense, which are the prayers of the saints'. Most writers describe the fear and awe in the Elders' eyes, but in fact they don't look frightened at all, and in place of harps they play the medieval proto-violin, the rebec. The whole wonderfully rhythmic composition could just as easily be an old-timers' band raising their glasses in an intermission toast to a stern but respected and beloved bandleader.

But that's not all. The central pillar of the door, the trumeau, is sculpted with three pairs of lions in the form of Xs, symbolically guarding the church (others prowl about the capitals of the tower). Note the scalloped edges of the doorway, a design picked up from Moorish Spain. On either side of the door are tall relief figures: St Peter with his keys, stepping on a dragon (left); Isaiah, whose scroll prophesies the coming Messiah (right); and, on the outer sides of the porch, a severe St Paul and a gentle, dreamy-eyed Jeremiah (also holding a scroll) – elongated, stylish, supple figures that sway and almost dance, probably from the same anonymous chisel that sculpted the wonderful Isaiah at Souillac. Right of the portal are scenes from the life of the Virgin – the *Annunciation*, *Visitation* and *Adoration of the Magi*; to the left, poor Lazarus' soul is taken into the bosom of Abraham while, below, the soul of the rich, feasting Dives is carried off in the other direction. Below him, you can make out a miser with demons on his shoulder as he refuses alms to a beggar, while to the left is Lust, serpents sucking at her breasts while an amused, very Chinese demon looks on. Up above the porch on the cornice – hiding, but in plain sight – is a large figure blowing a horn, perhaps Gabriel. Few visitors ever notice him.

The Church

Inside the porch, the vaulted square of the narthex has some excellent Romanesque capitals, carved with voluptuous vegetation playfully metamorphosed into animals; one shows Samson wrestling with a lion. Above it is the mysterious upper chapel, built of a dozen arches linked in a central oculus. This has been interpreted as a symbolic representation of heaven, or more specifically the New Jerusalem. As in other, similar constructions around Europe, whatever ceremonial or liturgical functions it might have had are lost. There are two ways to enter it, the broad door for the many, and a narrow one into the cloister for the monks.

The interior had to be rebuilt in 1430 and can't compete with the fireworks on the portal. You can see the foundations of the single-naved 1180 church (along the bottom of the Gothic nave), which like that at Cahors was crowned with Byzantine domes; they collapsed and were replaced with Flamboyant Gothic vaults in brick. Only one chapel has retained its 15th-century geometrical murals, which inspired the restoration on the other walls. Some of the church's excellent polychrome sculpture survives, especially a 12th-century *Christ* and, from the 15th century, the *Flight into Egypt* with a serious-minded burro, the beautiful *Entombment* and a *Pietà* (the figure with the swollen head is Gaussen de la Garrigue, consul of Moissac). Note the Baroque organ consul, bearing the arms of Cardinal Mazarin, *abbé commanditaire* from 1644 to 1661 and one of the most successful grafters of all time.

The Cloister

Abbey Cloister
t 05 63 04 01 85; open April–June, Sept and Oct Mon–Fri 10–12 and 2–6, Sat and Sun 2–6; July and Aug daily 9–7; Nov–Mar 10–12 and 2–5, Sat and Sun 2–5

Behind the church you'll find the abbey's serenely magnificent cloister, which was built by abbots Durand de Bredon and Ansquitil. After Simon de Montfort sacked Moissac, the arches had to be reconstructed, and were given a gentle hint of a Gothic point (1260), but all of the 76 magnificent capitals, set on alternating paired and single slender columns of various coloured marbles,

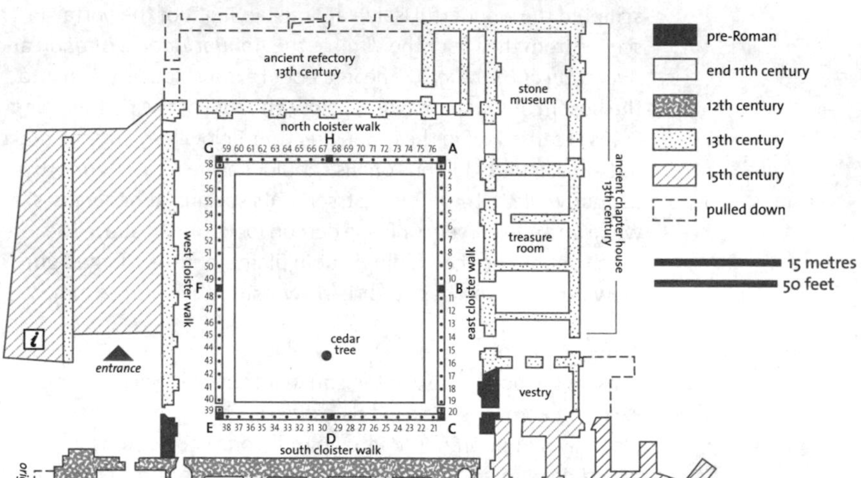

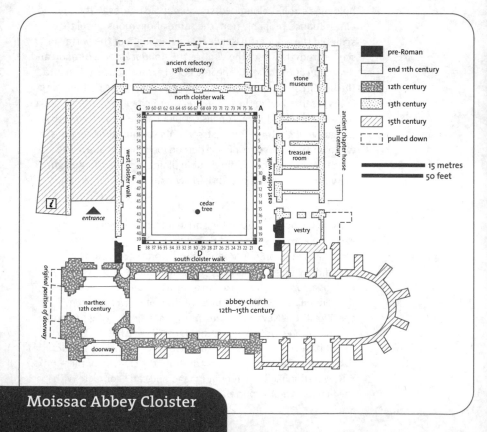

Moissac Abbey Cloister

Moissac Abbey Cloister

A Corner pillar: Sts John and James
1 Annunciation
2 Martyrdom of Sts Fructorosus, Eulogius and Augurius
3 Acanthus and vine decoration
4 Martyrdom of St Sernin
5 Acanthus decoration
6 Decoration, griffins and eagles
7 Adoration of the Magi; Massacre of the Innocents
8 Palm and vine decoration
9 Wedding at Cana
10 Decoration of eagles and human figures
B Central pillar: Abbot Durand of Bredon
11 Decoration of eagles and human figures
12 The rich man Dives and the beggar Lazarus (as on the portal)
13 Decoration of palms and birds
14 Jesus and the Apostles
15 Martyrdom of St Lawrence
16 Acanthus decoration
17 Adam and Eve
18 Decorations, alphabet and inscriptions
19 Martyrdom of Sts Peter and Paul, with Nero
20 Samson and the lion
C Corner pillar, Sts Peter and Paul
21 Baptism of Jesus
22 Liberation of St Peter
23 Transfiguration of Christ
24 Scenes from Revelations: the Reaper and the Four Horsemen
25 Temptations of Christ
26 Good Samaritan
27 Healing miracles of Jesus
28 The Four Evangelists
29 More Revelations: Michael defeats the Beast; Gog and Magog
D Central pillar: decorative
30 The New Jerusalem
31 David and his harp, and the other musicians
32 Lions and acanthus decoration
33 Martyrdom of St Stephen
34 Daniel and the punishment of Nebuchadnezzar
35 Eagles and floral decoration
36 Babylon (countertype to the New Jerusalem)
37 Dream of Nebuchadnezzar
38 Martyrdom of St John the Baptist
E Corner pillar: Apostles Matthew and Bartholemew
39 David and Goliath
40 Men and eagles with ropes
41 Vine decorations
42 Cain and Abel
43 Lions and figures
44 The Beatitudes (blessed are...)
45 Acanthus decorations
46 Lions and eagles
47 Decorations
48 Anointing of David
F Central pillar: dedicatory inscription of the cloister
49 Winged serpents
50 Acanthus decorations
51 The miracle of Lazarus
52 Musicians and archers
53 Acanthus and pomegranate decorations
54 Daniel in the lions' den; zodiacal sign of Capricorn
55 Birds and lions
56 Acanthus and floral decorations
57 The Cross
58 The sacrifice of Abraham
G Sts Philip and Andrew
59 Jesus and the Samaritan woman
60 Decorations
61 The story of St Martin
62 Shadrach, Meshach and Abednego in the furnace
63 Eagles and birds
64 The Four Evangelists
65 Arabesque decorations
66 The capture of Jerusalem on the First Crusade
67 Daniel in the lions' den
H Abstract designs
68 The Draught of Fishes, and Peter, John and James in the boat
69 Michael and Gabriel, seraphim and cherubim
70 Stags and horses
71 Miracles and Sts Peter and John
72 Birds and floral decoration
73 Miracles of St Benedict
74 Lions and griffins
75 Eagles and the sign of Pisces
76 St Michael and the dragon

come from the end of the 11th century; they are the oldest *in situ* in France. They also mark a major artistic turning point, away from the immobile, rather stiff, hieratical figures of the great Gilduin (as in Toulouse's St-Sernin) towards more fluid, stylized poses with a sense of movement, exquisite modelling, and a play of light and shadow that was hitherto unknown in Romanesque sculpture. The capitals are carved with foliage that was inspired by Corinthian capitals, but with luxuriant virtuosity; others have birds and animals intricately intertwined.

Some 46 capitals recount the lives of the saints – make sure that you don't miss the dynamic martyrdoms: St Lawrence burning on the grill while two Romans blow on the flames; St Martin dividing his cloak with the beggar; St John the Baptist and the feast of Herod; St Stephen being stoned; St Peter upside-down on his cross next to St Paul's beheading, a capital set near a little niche that once contained some of their relics. Other scenes are rare – the city of Jerusalem versus unholy Babylon, the story of Nebuchadnezzar, and Shadrach, Meshach and Abednego in the furnace. At the corners and in the centre of each gallery are some square pillars, covered with recycled tops of Roman sarcophaguses; the corners are carved with bas-reliefs of eight apostles, the 'pillars of the Church'; the central pillar in the east gallery has an effigy of Abbot Durand de Bredon, while on the west you can see the dedication inscription of the cloister: 'In the year of the Incarnation of the eternal Father 1100, this cloister was completed in the time of Lord Ansquitil, Abbot, Amen.'

Off the cloister, the 13th-century chapel of St-Ferréol boasts some faint frescoes depictings its eponymous saint curing the ill; it now contains a museum of other capitals and the original reliefs from the lower part of the portal, which were damaged by the damp and replaced by copies. Near the entrance, a narrow stair leads up to the Upper Chapel.

Other Sights

Musée M. Vidal
***t** 05 63 04 03 08; open April–June and Sept Mon–Sat 10–12 and 2–6, Sun 2–6; July and Aug Mon–Sat 10–1 and 3–7, Sun 3–7; Oct–Mar Mon–Sat 10–12 and 2–5, Sun 2–5*

Centre d'Art Roman Marcel Durliat
***t** 05 63 05 08 04; open Tues–Fri and Sun 10–12 and 2–6, Sat 9–12 and 2–6*

Just behind the church, in the old abbots' palace in Rue de l'Abbaye, you can visit the **Musée Marguerite Vidal**, which contains a bit of everything – from bonnets to bedwarmers – within old-fashioned settings. During the 11th and 12th centuries the monks of Moissac were famous for the colourful illuminated manuscripts that they produced; at the Association Pierres et Parchemins in Allées de Brienne, the **Centre d'Art Roman Marcel Durliat** hosts temporary exhibitions culled from its collection of photos of their works, nearly all of which have been carted off to the Bibliothèque Nationale in Paris.

To the south of the abbey you'll find Moissac's market square, Place des Récollets. From here Rue des Arts (turning into Rue Jean

Moura, which is lined with arts and crafts shops) leads to the deconsecrated church of St-Jacques. The Canal Latéral à la Garonne passes just to the south of here, and is spanned by the Pont St-Jacques, which is one of the very last of the revolving bridges that permitted canal barges to pass. Upstream, an impressive 356m Pont Canal, similar to that in Agen (*see* p.366), takes the canal over the Tarn river.

Pavillon de l'Uvarium
open in summer; hrs vary

Under this, in Place de l'Uvarium, is the charming **Pavillon de l'Uvarium**, decorated with Art Deco frescoes. This was constructed in 1933 for the benefit of health seekers who came here to take 'the grape cure' in order to improve their complexion, offering fresh fruit from Moissac's orchards, and glasses of *chasselas* grape juice in September. There are pretty views of the Tarn to be had from the pavilion, its various old mills and the wooded Ile de Beaucaire, which is the home of kingfishers and a number of other birds. There's a signposted walk around the island; the other island, Bidounet, has a campsite.

On the western outskirts of Moissac, the medieval church of St-Martin is unfortunately closed to visitors. A numbered plan from the tourist office will point you to the best spot for a fine view of the town; you may even see one of Moissac's herons.

Market Days in Moissac

Saturday and **Sunday** mornings, farmers' market.

Activities in Moissac

Canoes, kayaks and **electric boats** can be hired from Rand'Eau, **t** 05 63 02 85 10.

Where to Stay and Eat in and around Moissac

ⓘ **Moissac >**
6 Place Durand de Bredon, **t** *05 63 04 01 85, www.moissac.fr*

★ **Le Pont Napoléon >>**

Moissac ✉ 822000

Manoir Saint Jean, St Paul-d'Espis (✉ 82400), 9km from Moissac on D7 towards Bourg de Visa, **t** 05 63 05 02 34, *www.manoirsaintjean.com* (€€€). An elegant 19th-century, neoclassical house with spacious, bright bedrooms that have been furnished with attention to detail. The restaurant has a terrace overlooking the rolling countryside; in the summer months it's a fine setting for daily-changing dishes based on the freshest market produce. There is also a swimming pool. *Closed Mon, Sun eve, and Tues lunch out of season.*

*****Moulin de Moissac**, Esplanade du Moulin, **t** 05 63 32 88 88, *www.lemoulindemoissac.com* (€€). A beautiful old hotel situated on the banks of the Tarn, with classy, airy decor together with very good restaurant (€€€). *Restaurant closed at lunch and Sun.*

****Au Chapon Fin**, Place des Récollets, **t** 05 63 04 04 22, *www.lechaponfin-moissac.com* (€€–€). A pleasant, central provincial hotel with a restaurant (€€€–€€).

****Le Pont Napoléon**, 2 Allées Montebello, **t** 05 63 04 01 55, *www. le-pont-napoleon.com* (€). A delightful, old-fashioned hotel overlooking the Tarn, serving the best food (€€€€–€€) in Moissac. *Closed Sun eve and Mon.*

Au Bureau, across from market on Place des Récollets, **t** 05 63 04 00 61 (€€). A good place to come for pizzas and brasserie-style dishes.

North of Moissac

North of Moissac lies the realm of Quercy Blanc (*see* p.323), with its sunflowers, vineyards of *chasselas* grapes and striking dovecotes. The Tarn-et-Garonne is said to have more of these bird hotels than any other *département* in France; if rural architecture tends to follow traditional forms, when it came to building the dovecote, or *pigeonnier*, the farmer let his imagination stray – they come in all forms, all postdating the Revolution. Before then, only the nobility were allowed to have them, and there was nothing the peasants could do if the *seigneur*'s bird gobbled his corn. Pigeons or doves had several very practical purposes: they kept down insects on the vines, they provided food for the table, but, most of all, they made guano, considered the best of all fertilizers and so precious that many a girl was married off with a dowry of pigeon poop.

Lauzerte and Cazes-Mondenard

North of Moissac hovers the memorable site of the *bastide* of Lauzerte, founded by Raymond VI of Toulouse in the 12th century and nicknamed 'the Toledo of Quercy' for its proud profile on the hill. Charmingly irregular *cornières* surround its central square, but one corner of the cobblestoned pavement looks as if it's been turned up like the page of a book, with coloured tiles underneath. There's a fine selection of 14th- and 15th-century houses made from the white, sunbleached Quercy Blanc limestone.

Below Lauzerte, the **church of the Carmes** has an extraordinary high altarpiece of 1689. All Baroque is theatrical, but this action happens on a genuine stage, starring the Virgin handing rosaries to St Simon Stock and St Teresa of Avila, while prophet Elias and St John of the Cross stand by, under God stage-managing from above.

Musée des Corbillards
On D16, t 05 63 95 84 02; open daily 9–12 and 2–5 but call ahead

Even more surprising is the museum east in **Cazes-Mondenard** – the **Musée des Corbillards**, the only one in France dedicated to hearses. There are 80 of them, all horse-drawn, as well as old tractors and carriages. Tastings of local produce are available, and there's a restaurant (see opposite).

South of Cazes-Mondenard, and east of Moissac on the Tarn, is a French *bastide* of 1271. By then they'd run out of names for them and called this one **Lafrançaise**. It has a grand panoramic view over the Tarn, but food is the main reason to stop by (*see* opposite).

ⓘ Lauzerte >>
Place des Cornières, t 05 63 94 61 94, www.quercy-blanc.net

Market Days North of Moissac

Wednesday and Saturday mornings, Place des Cornières, **Lauzerte**. Make sure to try some of the town's speciality – **macaroons** that Raymond IV had delivered daily to his door.

Where to Stay and Eat North of Moissac

Lauzerte and Cazes-Mondenard ✉ 82110

Le Luzerta, Vignals, **t** 05 63 94 64 43, *www.hotel-quercy.com* (€). A cosy old mill with 20 rooms, two self-catering apartments, a swimming pool, and good southwest food (€€€–€€) with a nouvelle cuisine twist, such as roast eggs with foie gras. *Closed early Nov–early Feb.*

Restaurant Yvan Quercy, Cazes-Mondenard, **t** 05 63 95 84 02 (€€). A restaurant in the unlikely setting of the hearse museum (*see* opposite), with very good traditional and classic menus featuring the likes of crayfish tails with parsley and garlic sauce. Advance booking is required.

La Cassolette, Auléry (on main road), **t** 05 63 04 90 97 (€€–€). A modest-looking spot almost always filled with happy diners enjoying its tasty food and generous portions – try the *amuse-bouches* of spicy prawns and beef. *Closed Sun–Wed eves.*

Lafrançaise ✉ 82130

****Belvédère**, 16 Rue Mary Lafon, **t** 05 63 65 89 55 (€). A basic hotel with a good restaurant, **Au Fin Gourmet** (€€–€). *Restaurant closed Sat and Sun Oct–Mar.*

Ferme-Auberge des Trouilles, just north of town on D20, signposted, **t** 05 63 65 84 46, *http://lestrouilles.free.fr* (€). A huge farm with six delightful guestrooms, self-catering chalets, a pool and superb farm meals (€€€–€€), for which you must book ahead.

The Lomagne

West of Moissac, where the Tarn flows into the Garonne, is La Lomagne – the bit Napoleon nicked off the Gers. It was also known, after its hills, as *Gascogne bossue* – hunchbacked Gascony. Once part of the duchy of Gascony, it's a quiet corner of the *département* of fruit. Here, however, orchards give way to fields of little green sprouts – the Lomagne has the ideal climate and soil for garlic.

Heading West

St-Nicolas-de-la-Grave and Auvillar

St-Nicolas-de-la Grave uses the swollen confluence of the big rivers as a recreational lake – a favourite with small-scale sailors and migratory birds. There is also has a castle with four towers built by Richard the Lionheart, later inherited by the abbots of Moissac, and a church with a Toulouse-style belltower and porch. St-Nicolas was the birthplace of the founder of Detroit, Antoine de Lamothe-Cadillac (1658–1713; *see* p.245) – a debt that Motown acknowledged by turning his birthplace, near the village centre, into the **Musée Lamothe-Cadillac**, with displays on how Lamothe went to Canada to explore and seek his fortune, and fought on the frontlines against the English, and on how he founded Detroit as a French commercial base linking Louisiana to Canada. He borrowed the posh name 'Cadillac' from a château near Bordeaux (*see* pp.245–46), and General Motors also preferred it for its most prestigious tall-finned gas-hogs – 'Lamothe' sounds lightweight and fly-by-night to American car-buying ears.

Musée Lamothe-Cadillac
open July and Aug daily 10–12 and 3–6; rest of year ask at tourist office

In the same area, south of the motorway at **Le Pin**, there is an extraordinary 19th-century neo-Renaissance folly set in an English park. The Château St-Roch is a precursor of Disneyland's Sleeping

Beauty's Castle, built by a disciple of Viollet-le-Duc for an art lover who desperately wished he had inherited a château on the Loire and furnished it as if it really, really were. Sadly it can't be visited.

Auvillar

Aim for the lovely red-brick village of **Auvillar**, its name derived from the Latin *Alta Villa* – High House. Auvillar's strategic location on the Garonne saw it battered in the Hundred Years' and Religious wars, but it recovered well, and in the 18th century enjoyed a boom based on goose quills for pens and painted ceramics, which you can see in the **Musée d'Art et Traditions Populaires** in the fetching Place de la Halle. This, defying the usual *bastide* geometry with its triangular shape, goes a step further in its unique circular market, rebuilt in 1828, with Tuscan columns, a tile roof and medieval grain measures intact and ready for use. Back then, grain was measured by the *poignée* or fistful, the equivalent of 28.6lbs – some fists! By the *poignée* measure is a 19th-century one in metal.

Musée d'Art et Traditions Populaires
t 05 63 39 57 33; open May–Oct Wed–Mon 2.30–6.30; adm

Ask at the **tourist office** (**t** 05 63 94 82 81) about combined tours of the museum and town in July and August. In the Tour de l'Horloge, the **Musée de la Batellerie** tells the story of river life and transport. From the Promenade du Château, fine views down the Garonne sadly include the cooling towers of the nuclear plant at Golfech. War-scarred St-Pierre church hints at Auvillar's importance in the Middle Ages, when it produced Marcabru (*see* below).

Musée de la Batellerie
t 05 63 39 57 33; open May–Oct Wed–Mon 2.30–6.30; adm

Marcabru

The courts of love of Eleanor of Aquitaine in Poitiers had a role in changing European attitudes towards women, until then influenced by the Church's opinion that women, the daughters of Eve, were the source of Original Sin and deserved to be nothing but the property of men. With an astute mix of what we might call today 'politically correct' translations of Ovid, Arthurian legend and Occitan troubadour poetry, Eleanor and her daughters (especially Marie de Champagne, her firstborn with Louis VI) formulated a startling alternative: that men were the property of women. The queen and her ladies were the judges of the new chivalric standards of behaviour of a knight towards his lady.

Auvillar's troubadour Marcabru (active 1129–50) offered the opposing view, to put it mildly. A foundling raised by Aldric d'Auvillar, he fought the Moors in Spain and had for a patron Eleanor's father, Guilhem X of Aquitaine (son of the first known troubadour, the bawdy Guilhem IX). Marcabru was a great innovator in rhymes, rhythms and metrical schemes and used language in ways no one had done before, his vocabulary ranging from the most vulgar – even gross – realism to elegant, noble lyrics.

Of his 41 surviving poems, a few are in a tender mode, especially *A la fontana del vergier*, beautifully depicting a young girl's sorrow for her lover crusading in the Holy Land, but most lambast women as fickle adulterous whores in language unfit for travel guides. 'He was one of the first troubadours within memory... and he spoke ill of women and of love,' wrote one of his biographers, in amazement. Eleanor must have frowned to hear his songs – or perhaps she laughed. Marcabru's *Dirai vos senes duptansa*, at any rate, is the medieval version of Louis Jordan's classic *Brother, You Better Beware*:

...Don't you think I know
when Love's cross-eyed or blind?
His words are sweet and polished
Listen! –
and his bite is gentler than a fly's,
but the cure is far more painful.

Men who follow women's wisdom
Will surely come to ill,
as the Scripture tells us.
Listen! –
Misfortune will bear down on you,
all of you, if you don't beware.

Translated by Anthony Bonner, in *Songs of the Troubadours*

Valence-d'Agen and Further West

Visitors' Centre, Golfech
t 05 63 29 39 06; call for times

Conservatoire de la Ruralité
t 05 63 29 21 96; open July and Aug daily 3–7; Feb–June and Sept–Dec Tues–Sun 3–7

Oratoire des Templiers
open May, June, Sept and Oct daily 2–6, July and Aug daily 10–12 and 2–7; Nov–April Sun 2–5

Château de Gramont
t 05 63 94 05 26; open Mar, April, Oct and Nov daily 2–6; May–Sept 10–12 and 2–6; rest of year by appt

Musée du Miel
t 05 63 94 00 20; open June–Sept Thurs–Tues 10–12 and 2–7; rest of year by appt

Valence-d'Agen, a rather pretty town on the Garonne, started as an English *bastide* in 1283. Today it gets on as best it can in the shadow of the steaming concrete towers of the nuclear plant at **Golfech**. For years the EDF (the national electric monopoly) has been hoping to spin a web of high-tension lines across the northern Tarn-et-Garonne and Lot to sell Golfech's power elsewhere, but the project has become the local environmentalists' public enemy No.1. Meanwhile, on TV the EDF (which cleverly pays off residents when it wants to build a new nuke plant near the town) is trying to convince everyone to convert to expensive electric heating (while the government makes sure that all new public housing for the poor has it); at Golfech, they've opened a **visitors' centre**.

West of Valence on the D12, **Donzac** has a museum of the 'how we used to live' kind, the **Conservatoire de la Ruralité et des Métiers d'Autrefois**, with reconstructed workshops, old farm machinery, wine production equipment, regional pottery and minerals.

South of Auvillar and Valence d'Agen on the D11, in the middle of nowhere, **Lachapelle** is named after its **Oratoire des Templiers**, aka St-Pierre. The Templars originally built the oratory next to one of their castles, along the road to Compostela, and in the 15th century it became the parish church. Sometime in the 18th century, Lachapelle acquired money to lavish on the interior, creating a church with opera decor, complete with boxes in the arcades.

Further south, in the corner of the *département*, **Gramont** has a 12th-century military **château** turned into a Renaissance residence in the 16th century; it has a lovely 12th-century statue of the Virgin in the chapel, a 16th-century-style garden and other fine features. The **Musée du Miel** has displays on bees and honey, plus free tastings.

South towards Toulouse

Castelsarrasin and Belleperche

The Arabs never built a castle here in their 8th-century thrust into France, but Castelsarrasin, the *département*'s largest town after Montauban, had a six-towered 12th-century stronghold built by the counts of Toulouse, who picked up stylistic tips on journeys to the Middle East; hence *Castellum Sarracenum*. The castle's defenders were so terrified of Simon de Montfort in 1212, they gave up without a fight when his army appeared at the gate. They were more stalwart in the Wars of Religion against the Huguenots of Montauban, only to have their exotic castle razed in the 1600s.

Castelsarrasin has kept the grid plan laid out by the counts of Toulouse, and, more unusually, the virtuous Revolutionary names of its oldest streets, reinstated in 1876 by a mayor in the Third

Republic who had shared Victor Hugo's exile on Jersey: look for *rues* named Surveillance, Peace, Friendship, Reason, Wisdom and Equality, with Liberty Square in the centre. At 6 Place Lamothe-Cadillac lived the founder of Detroit, Antoine de Lamothe-Cadillac, who was so unimpressed with his new settlement in Michigan that he sold his title of *seigneur de Détroit* to buy the governorship of Castelsarrasin. The main sight here is **St-Sauveur** church, set up by the monks at Moissac in 961 and rebuilt in 1260 in the southern Gothic style, in brick, its heptagonal apse added in the 15th century. The magnificent Baroque woodwork, especially the elaborate organ console, crowned with wooden statues of angels and King David as conductor, the carved 17th-century choir stalls (only 39 of the original 80), the pulpit, and the pair of prayer stools, one carved with a Virgin and a unicorn, were originally at Belleperche.

Abbaye de Belleperche
t 05 63 95 62 75; open May and June Tues–Sun 2–6; July–Sept Tues–Sat 10–12 and 2–6, Sun 2–6; adm

The **Abbaye de Belleperche** is true to its name, prettily perched over the waters of the Garonne 5km south of Castelsarrasin. It was founded in 1143, when hermits in the area sent a request to the abbot of Clairvaux for permission to establish a branch; according to legend, when a group of Cistercians arrived to set things up, St Bernard himself came along to help the foundation. In its glory days the abbey had 200 monks; Pope Clement V and François Ier were among its guests. Nearly all was destroyed in the Wars of

Côtes-de-Frontonnais

This ancient district dates back to the 4th century BC, and was made AOC in 1975. An up-and-coming wine, Frontonnais owes its distinction and character to the predominant use of the local Negrette grape (50–70% of most vintages) brought back from Cyprus by the Crusaders. Grafted on to sturdier stock grown on tiered terraces between the Garonne and Tarn rivers, Negrette thrives on *boulbènes* – silty pre-glacial soil on top, red clay subsoil, and, 60–90cm under that, pebbles providing good drainage. A second factor is the local wind, the *autan* that usually assures fine weather in September and October. The resulting ruby-red wine, with a redcurrant fragrance, is drunk quite young or after a few years in the cellar, when it is the perfect accompaniment to cassoulet; the rosés are a fruity summer drink.

The two centres of the *appellation*, Fronton and Villaudric, have cooperatives. The **Cave de Fronton**, in Fronton, **t** 05 62 79 97 79, is home to the floral *Violette de Negret*, the red *Comte de Negrette* (always winning medals) and the *Exception du Comte de Negret* (always good, often very smooth), and several good rosés. The **Château de Joliet**, Route de Grisolles in Fronton, **t** 05 61 82 46 02, produces some of the more interesting Frontonnais, especially the 100% Negrette *Vin de Printemps* with a violet bouquet. Also in Fronton, **Château Bellevue-la-Forêt**, **t** 05 34 27 91 91, sells fine aromatic reds and a delightful rosé, and is among those using Cabernet Franc and Cabernet Sauvignon, Syrah, Gamay Noir à Jus Blanc with Negrette in some blends to get added complexity. Owner Patrick Germain was at the forefront of the Fronton revival. Those who like wine aged in oak barrels should try the *Prestige*. **Château Le Roc**, **t** 05 61 82 93 90, does a fine velvety wine; try the *Don Quichotte*. Also, don't miss the delectable Château Baudare red *Cuvée Prestige* or *Secret des Anges*. Father and son Claude and David Vigouroux were elected best Frontonnais vignerons in 2003 and 2004; call **t** 05 63 30 51 33 to visit the *cave* at Campsas.

On the south side of Toulouse itself, a very respectable red, rosé and white *vin de pays de la Haute-Garonne* comes from the **Domaine de Ribonnet** in Beaumont-sur-Lèze, **t** 05 61 08 71 02. This vineyard used to be air-pioneer Clément Ader's hobbyhorse, and has been revived by a Swiss owner. The *commune* of Toulouse, unique among the great cities of France, owns an 85-acre vineyard, the **Domaine de Candi**, that provides wine for its hospitals; you can also buy some at the Cave de Fronton.

Religion, except the vaulting in the library, the refectory entrance, and sections of the 13th-century painted tiled floor (partly removed to the Musée Ingres in Montauban; *see* p.399). The church was rebuilt at the end of the 16th century; and the last work was done in 1760, in time for it to be sold to speculators in the Revolution, who dismantled it (some of its furnishings may be seen in the churches at nearby Cordes-Tolosannes). The huge monastery, however, was used as a farm and survived. The *département* has made progress in restoring the building, and there's a summer programme of exhibitions, conferences and concerts . Plans are afoot to create a cultural centre dedicated to the arts of the table.

South of Castelsarrasin

The pleasant *bastide* of **Beaumont-de-Lomagne** was founded in 1276 by the French and has kept its fortified church, coiffed with an octagonal 14th-century Toulousain belltower, a handful of old houses, and an even rarer survivor – its huge wooden *halle* from the 14th century. Beaumont is famous for garlic; its garlic market, between July and October, claims to be the biggest in France, and there's a garlic festival in July. The statue here of a 17th-century gentleman represents native son Pierre de Fermat (*see* p.437).

Further south, the village of **Bouillac** has a striking church, 17th-century St-Sulpice, with an unusual arcaded *clocher-mur* – all that survived the Wars of Religion. Inside, however, in a glass case next to the choir, it has a rare treasure: the golden reliquaries from the 13th-century Cistercian abbey of Grand-Selve, secreted out before the abbey was smashed and burned in the Revolution – beautifully worked caskets and mini-churches of gold, filigree and precious stones from the 13th century.

St-Sardos Wine Cooperative
t 05 63 02 52 44; open Mon 2–6, Tues–Fri 9–12 and 2–6, plus Sat 9–6 in July and Aug and 9–12 in winter

Cave de Lavilledieu
t 05 63 31 60 05; open June–Aug Mon–Fri 2–6, Sat 9–12 and 3–6.30; Sept–May Mon 2–6, Tues–Fri 8–12 and 2–6, Sat 8–12

To the north begin the vineyards of **St-Sardos**, a pleasant *vin de pays*; there are tastings in the **cooperative** in the centre. On the other bank of the Garonne, a velvety red wine, the Ville-Dieu-du-Temple, has been produced ever since the Templars planted the first vines; there are tastings at the **Cave de Lavilledieu**.

Montech Navigation
t 05 63 26 31 15

On the Garonne, between the two wine-growing areas, **Montech** is in the centre of the Tarn-et-Garonne's only forest, the **Forêt d'Agre**. Donated by a wealthy couple to the abbey of Moissac in 680, this forest became the source of the abbey's prosperity; although now rather diminished in size and split by the railway and motorway, it has riding and walking paths. Montech was an old stronghold of the counts of Toulouse and has a fine 15th-century church with an enormous belltower. Montech is proudest these days of the world's first and only **Pente d'Eau** on its stretch of the Canal Latéral – a slope where barges are hauled up by a pair of engines, which replaces five canal locks. There are boat trips along the canal and through the Pente d'Eau with **Montech Navigation**.

ⓘ **Valence-d'Agen >**
27 bis Rue de la République,
t 05 63 39 61 67, www.valencedagen.f

ⓘ **Beaumont-de-Lomagne >>**
3 Rue Pierre de Fermat,
t 05 63 02 42 32, www.beaumont-de-lomagne.com or www.tourisme-en-lomagne.com

ⓘ **Auvillar >**
Place de la Halle,
t 05 63 39 89 82, www.auvillar.com

★ **Hôtel de l'Horloge >**

ⓘ **Castelsarrasin >**
Allée de Verdun-Capitainerie,
t 05 63 32 75 00, www.ville-castelsarrasin.fr

Market Days in the Lomagne

Valence-d'Agen: Tuesday and Saturday, farmers' market; *marché au gras* Tuesday morning in winter.

Castelsarrasin: All day Thursday.

Beaumont-de-Lomagne: Saturday; garlic market Tuesday and Saturday July–Jan; night markets July and Aug.

Where to Stay and Eat in the Lomagne

Auvillar ✉ 82340

****Hotel de l'Horloge**, Place de l'Horloge, **t** 05 63 39 91 61 (€€–€). A smart hotel for its price range, with modern rooms with shower or bath. The restaurant (€€) is considered the best in Auvillar, offering southwest favourites plus pigeon, beef, fish and more. At weekday lunchtimes you can eat on the terrace or in the bar. *Closed early Dec–early Jan, and Fri mid-Oct–mid-April; restaurant also Sat lunch.*

Bacchus, in countryside on road to Valence, **t** 05 63 29 12 20 (€€€–€). A neoclassical setting for traditional, good-value menus featuring excellent duck dishes, ostrich prepared in the old southwest French style, and more.

Bardigues ✉ 82340

Auberge de Bardigues, 3km from Auvillar, **t** 05 63 39 05 58 (€€€–€€). An inn in a pretty village, with a wide terrace with a view of the countryside. Try the smoked salmon and melon with ginger. *Closed Mon.*

Castelsarrasin ✉ 82100

*****Château des Vicomtes Terrides**, Labourgade, **t** 05 63 95 61 07, *www.chateau-de-terrides.com* (€€€–€€). A 16th-century castle with 53 quite upmarket rooms, a pool, golf practice and a restaurant (€€€€–€€€). *Closed Dec–April; restaurant also Mon, Sat lunch and Sun eve.*

****Marceillac**, 54 Rue de l'Egalité, **t** 05 63 32 30 10, *www.hotelmarceillac.com* (€). A delightful place in the centre, with 12 well-equipped, 1920s-style rooms overlooking a courtyard garden.

Les Dantous, 3km south of town on D958, off N113, **t** 05 63 32 26 95, *www.gite-les-dantous.com* (€). A charming old farm B&B right off the Canal Latéral, with a pool and *boules* court, plus a gîte. *Closed 2nd half Dec.*

Auberge du Moulin, Route de Toulouse (N113), **t** 05 63 32 20 37 (€€€–€). A good country inn serving regional food and dishes from further afield. *Closed Wed, Tues eve and Sat lunch.*

Beaumont-de-Lomagne ✉ 82500

L'Arbre d'Or, 16 Rue Despeyrous, **t** 05 63 65 32 34, *www.larbredor-hotel.com* (€€). A luxurious B&B in a 17th-century house, with dinner by reservation.

****Hôtel du Commerce**, 58 Avenue du Maréchal-Foch, **t** 05 63 02 31 02 (€). A reliable hotel in the centre, with a good restaurant (€€€–€€). *Closed Fri eve, Sun eve and Mon out of season.*

Auberge de la Gimone, Avenue du Lac, **t** 05 63 65 23 09 (€€). Decadent feasts of delicious duck dishes. Booking is required. *Closed Tues eve, plus Wed and Sun eve exc July and Aug.*

Montech ✉ 82700

****Notre-Dame**, Place Jean Jaurès, **t** 05 63 64 77 45 (€). Comfy rooms plus a pretty dining room (€€–€). *Closed Fri and Sun eve Oct–Mar.*

Grisolles ✉ 82170

****Relais des Garrigues**, Route de Fronton, **t** 05 63 67 31 59 (€). A modern hotel near the Canal du Midi, with a restaurant (€€–€) serving southwest standbys. *Closed Sun, Mon, and Christmas and New Year.*

Ancre Marine, Canals, on N20, **t** 05 63 02 84 00 (€€€–€). An old farm where you can enjoy superb Breton seafood dishes as well as foie gras and so on. It's set within shady grounds with a swimming pool and fish pond. *Closed Sun and Mon eves.*

Fronton ✉ 31620

Lou Grel, 49 Rue Jules-Bersac, **t** 05 61 82 03 00 (€). A hotel with modern rooms, a garden, a swimming pool and a great restaurant (€€€–€€). *Closed Sun and Sat eves, Mon lunch, 1wk Jan, 1wk Feb and 1wk Sept.*

Toulouse

Toulouse should have been the rosy capital of a nation called Languedoc, but it was knocked out of the big leagues in the 1220s by the popes and kings of France and their henchman Simon de Montfort. Seven and a half centuries later, the Toulousains are finally getting their rhythm back, and it's this big pink dynamo on the cutting edge of the 21st century that keeps southwest France from nodding off in its vats of goose fat and wine.

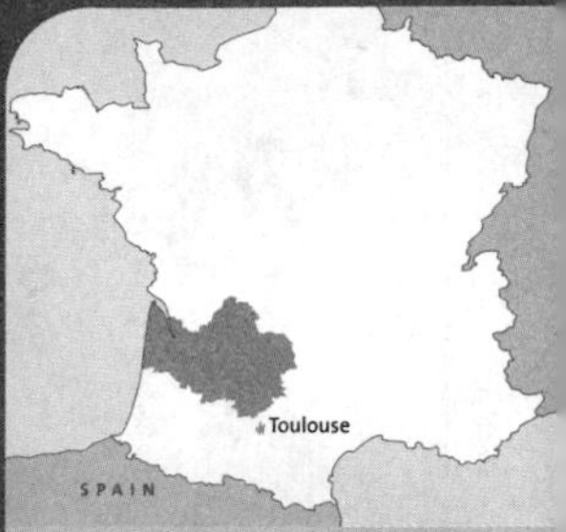

16

Don't miss

1. The biggest Romanesque church on Earth
St-Sernin Basilica **p.432**
2. A Gothic masterpiece
Les Jacobins **p.435**
3. Pastel palaces
Hôtels de Bernuy, d'Assézat, and de Pierre **pp.437–9**
4. Cutting-edge art in an old abattoir
Les Abattoirs **p.444**
5. Seeing Airbuses being built
Usine C. Adler **p.445**

See map overleaf

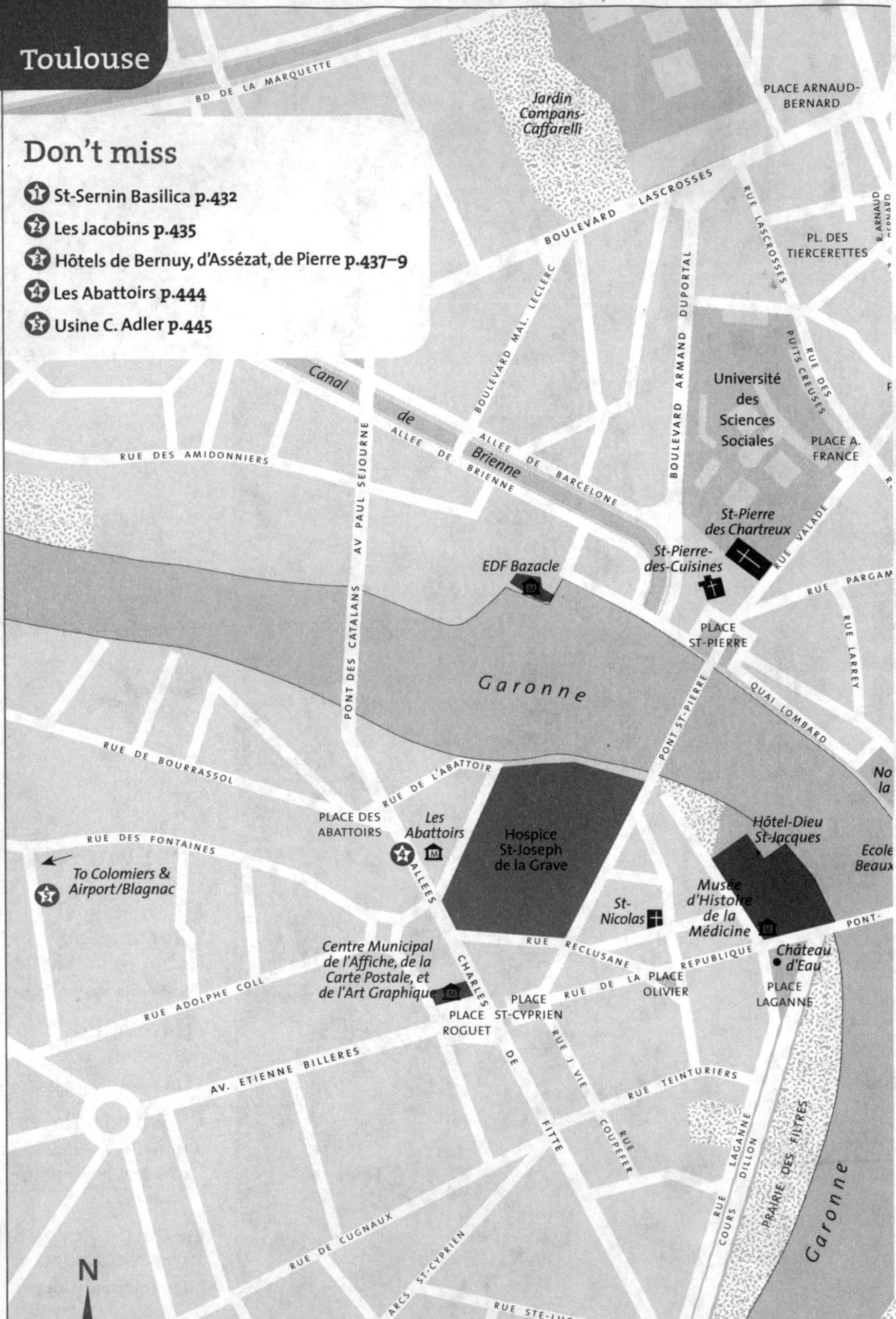
Don't miss
1 St-Sernin Basilica p.432
2 Les Jacobins p.435
3 Hôtels de Bernuy, d'Assézat, de Pierre p.437–9
4 Les Abattoirs p.444
5 Usine C. Adler p.445
BD DE LA MARQUETTE
Jardin Compans-Caffarelli
PLACE ARNAUD-BERNARD
BOULEVARD LASCROSSES
RUE LASCROSSES
PL. DES TIERCERETTES
BOULEVARD MAL. LECLERC
BOULEVARD ARMAND DUPORTAL
RUE DES PUITS CREUSES
Université des Sciences Sociales
PLACE A. FRANCE
Canal de Brienne
ALLEE DE BRIENNE
ALLEE DE BARCELONE
RUE DES AMIDONNIERS
AV PAUL SEJOURNE
St-Pierre des Chartreux
RUE VALADE
St-Pierre-des-Cuisines
EDF Bazacle
RUE PARGAMINIERES
PLACE ST-PIERRE
RUE LARREY
Garonne
PONT DES CATALANS
PONT ST-PIERRE
QUAI LOMBARD
RUE DE BOURRASSOL
RUE DE L'ABATTOIR
PLACE DES ABATTOIRS
Les Abattoirs
Hospice St-Joseph de la Grave
Hôtel-Dieu St-Jacques
RUE DES FONTAINES
To Colomiers & Airport/Blagnac
ALLEES CHARLES DE FITTE
St-Nicolas
Musée d'Histoire de la Médicine
RUE RECLUSANE
Château d'Eau
Centre Municipal de l'Affiche, de la Carte Postale, et de l'Art Graphique
RUE ADOLPHE COLL
RUE DE LA REPUBLIQUE
PLACE OLIVIER
PLACE LAGANNE
PLACE ROGUET
PLACE ST-CYPRIEN
RUE J VIE
AV. ETIENNE BILLERES
RUE TEINTURIERS
RUE COUPEFER
RUE LAGANNE
COURS DILLON
PRAIRIE DES FILTRES
Garonne
RUE DE CUGNAUX
RUE DES ARCS ST-CYPRIEN
RUE STE-LUCIE
PLACE DU FER-A-CHEVAL
PONT ST-MICHEL
N
250 metres
250 yards

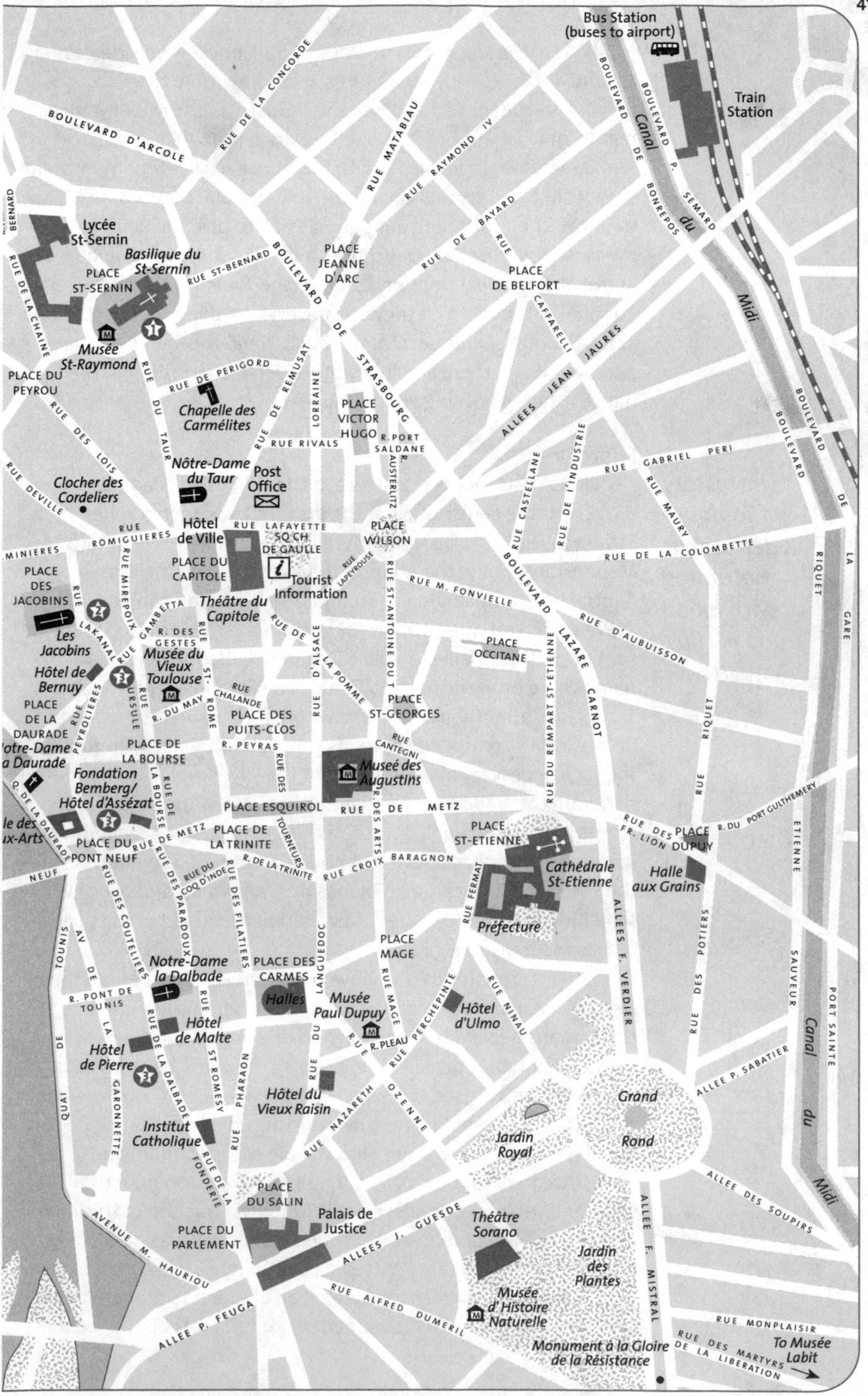
Bus Station
(buses to airport)
Train
Station
BOULEVARD D'ARCOLE
RUE DE LA CONCORDE
RUE MATABIAU
RUE RAYMOND IV
BOULEVARD DE BONREPOS
BOULEVARD P. SEMARD
Canal du Midi
Lycée
St-Sernin
Basilique du
St-Sernin
PLACE
ST-SERNIN
RUE ST-BERNARD
BOULEVARD DE STRASBOURG
PLACE
JEANNE
D'ARC
RUE DE BAYARD
PLACE
DE BELFORT
RUE CAFFARELLI
RUE DE LA CHAINE
Musée
St-Raymond
PLACE DU
PEYROU
RUE DE PERIGORD
RUE DU TAUR
Chapelle des
Carmélites
RUE DE REMUSAT
RUE LORRAINE
PLACE
VICTOR
HUGO
ALLEES JEAN JAURES
RUE RIVALS
R. PORT
SALDANE
R. AUSTERLITZ
RUE DE L'INDUSTRIE
RUE CASTELLANE
RUE GABRIEL PERI
RUE MAURY
BOULEVARD DE LA GARE
RUE DES LOIS
RUE DEVILLE
Clocher des
Cordeliers
Nôtre-Dame
du Taur
Post
Office
Hôtel
de Ville
RUE LAFAYETTE
SQ CH
DE GAULLE
PLACE
WILSON
RUE ROMIGUIERES
MINIERES
PLACE
DES
JACOBINS
RUE MIREPOIX
PLACE DU
CAPITOLE
RUE LAPEYROUSE
Tourist
Information
RUE ST-ANTOINE DU T
RUE DE LA COLOMBETTE
RUE M. FONVIELLE
RUE RIQUET
Les
Jacobins
RUE LAKANAL
RUE GAMBETTA
Théâtre du
Capitole
RUE DE LA POMME
R. DES
GESTES
Musée du
Vieux
Toulouse
BOULEVARD LAZARE CARNOT
RUE D'AUBUISSON
PLACE
OCCITANE
Hôtel de
Bernuy
RUE ST-ROME
RUE ST-URSULE
RUE CHALANDE
R. DU MAY
RUE D'ALSACE
PLACE
ST-GEORGES
PLACE
DE LA
DAURADE
RUE PEYROLIERES
PLACE DES
PUITS-CLOS
Notre-Dame
la Daurade
PLACE DE
LA BOURSE
R. PEYRAS
RUE CANTEGNI
Musée des
Augustins
RUE DU REMPART ST-ETIENNE
Fondation
Bemberg/
Hôtel d'Assézat
RUE DE LA BOURSE
RUE DES TOURNEURS
Q. DE LA DAURADE
PLACE ESQUIROL
RUE DE METZ
R. DES ARTS
PLACE
ST-ETIENNE
RUE DES FR. LION
PLACE
DUPUY
R. DU PORT GUILTHEMERY
PLACE DU
PONT NEUF
RUE DE METZ
PLACE DE
LA TRINITE
RUE DU COQ D'INDE
R. DE LA TRINITE
RUE CROIX BARAGNON
Cathédrale
St-Etienne
Halle
aux Grains
NEUF
RUE DES COUTELIERS
RUE DES PARADOUX
RUE DES FILATIERS
RUE FERMAT
Préfecture
ALLEES F. VERDIER
RUE ETIENNE SAUVEUR
PORT SAINTE
RUE DES POTIERS
PLACE
MAGE
QUAI DE TOUNIS
AV DE LA GARONNETTE
Notre-Dame
la Dalbade
PLACE DES
CARMES
RUE DU LANGUEDOC
RUE MAGE
RUE PERCHEPINTE
RUE NINAU
R. PONT DE
TOUNIS
Halles
Musée
Paul Dupuy
Hôtel
d'Ulmo
Hôtel
de Malte
RUE DE LA DALBADE
RUE ST ROMESY
RUE PHARAON
R. PLEAU
Hôtel
de Pierre
ALLEE P. SABATIER
Grand
Rond
Hôtel du
Vieux Raisin
RUE NAZARETH
RUE OZENNE
Institut
Catholique
RUE DE LA FONDERIE
Jardin
Royal
ALLEE DES SOUPIRS
PLACE
DU SALIN
PLACE DU
PARLEMENT
Palais de
Justice
ALLEES J. GUESDE
Théâtre
Sorano
Jardin
des
Plantes
ALLEE F. MISTRAL
AVENUE M. HAURIOU
RUE ALFRED DUMERIL
Musée
d' Histoire
Naturelle
RUE MONPLAISIR
ALLEE P. FEUGA
Monument à la Gloire
de la Résistance
RUE DES MARTYRS DE LA LIBERATION
To Musée
Labit

Called *La Ville Rose* for its millions of pink bricks, Toulouse has around 800,000 lively inhabitants, including more than 110,000 university students, and 70% of the industry in the Midi-Pyrénées region, much of it hi-tech and related to aeronautics and space. A massive 20,000 people flock to live here each year, many of them to work in these sectors. Spain, and in particular Barcelona, extend their cape here, distilling enough passion to give the heirs of medieval Toulouse's fat merchants a dose of madness. Toulouse is above all *une ville d'émotion*; listen to the *Toulousains* chant their national anthem, which they do at every possible occasion:'*O moun paiës, Toulouse, Toulouse! O moun paiës, Toulouse, Toulouse*!' over and over again. There aren't any other verses; according to the natives, there's nothing else to say.

History

The history of Toulouse is detestable, saturated with blood and perfidy.
Henry James

Toulouse was founded at a ford in the Garonne called the Bazacle, at the centre of what the ancient Greek geographer Strabo called the 'Gallic isthmus', the crossroads between the Mediterranean and the Atlantic, the Pyrenees and the Massif Central. Yet, confusingly, the original Toulouse (the name means 'elevated place') was on a hill, 10km from the modern city, at a spot now called Vieille Toulouse. The first *Toulousains* with a name came from the north: a Celtic tribe known as the Volcae Tectosages after their distinctive woollen cloaks (*tectus sago*). Because they controlled the roads through the Gallic isthmus, the Tectosages creamed profits from the silver mines to the south and from the trade in Italian wines. They mined the gold of the Ariège, but looked upon it as something too sacred to be minted into coins, and stored most of it at the bottom of a swamp. Despite their wealth, the insatiable *Toulousains* ranged far and wide ever searching for more; in 279 BC they even participated in the sack of the sacred treasuries of Delphi.

In 125 BC, Ligurian tribes in Provence asked Rome to defend them from the fearsome plunderers from Toulouse. This request was all the Romans needed to muscle in and do some plundering on their own account: they decreed the Tectosages were a 'new ally' and sent a Roman garrison to Toulouse to 'collaborate'. In 107 BC, when the Tectosages dared to give their unwanted new allies the boot, the Senate sent General Servilius Caepio to crush them and confiscate their fabulous swamp treasure – 110,000 pounds of silver and 100,000 pounds of gold. But only a fraction of this hoard ever made it to Rome. Caepio claimed his convoy was held up by Teutones near Massalia (Marseille); the Senate, suspecting another kind of highway robbery, confiscated all of Caepio's property, then sent him into exile and his womenfolk to the brothels. Hence the

Getting to and away from Toulouse

By Air

Toulouse's international **airport** at Blagnac, 10km from the centre, **t** 05 61 42 44 00, *www.toulouse.aeroport.fr*, is served by, among others, Air France, British Airways, BMI and 'no-frills' airlines Flybe and easyJet (*see* p.62).

The **airport bus**, **t** 05 34 60 64 00, departs from Toulouse's train station every 20mins 5am–8.20pm daily, and from the airport to central Toulouse every 20mins 7.35am–00.15. Tickets cost €4 one way. The ticket booth at the airport is outside Hall 1. For **taxis** (about €30 to the centre), *see* below.

By Train

The main **station** is Gare Matabiau. Trains run from Paris-Austerlitz through Gourdon, Souillac, Cahors and Montauban to Toulouse in 6hrs 30mins; **TGV**s from Paris-Montparnasse in around 5hrs, via Bordeaux. Slow trains to Bordeaux, stopping in Montauban, Castelsarrasin, Moissac, Agen and Aiguillon, take 2hrs 30mins. Other links include Albi (1hr), Castres (1hr 30mins), Lille (TGV, 7hrs), Auch, Carcassonne, Nice and Lyon.

By Bus

The **bus station**, **t** 05 61 61 67 67, is next to the train station; there are buses to Foix, Albi, Gaillac, Auch, Nogaro and Montauban. You can also travel by coach to London, Madrid and Barcelona (*www.eurolines.com*).

Getting around Toulouse

By Métro and City Bus

The *métro* and city buses are run by TISSEO, which has an info office at 7 Place Esquirol, **t** 05 61 41 70 70, *www.tisseo.fr*. A new métro line, running north to south, from Borderouge to Ramonville, should be operational by 2007. Bus and *métro* times coordinate.

Almost all sights are in the compact centre, so you'll hardly ever need to use either the *métro* or the bus, though the *métro* is useful for getting into the centre from the station. There's also a free shuttlebus (*navette*; Mon–Sat 9–7) around the historic quarters – you find a red line and stick your hand out when you see the bus coming. A tramway to the west of the city is scheduled to be up and running by 2009.

By Taxi

If you can't find one cruising around or at a taxi stand, try **t** 05 61 42 38 38, or **t** 05 34 25 02 50.

By Car

Toulouse's rapid growth and narrow streets have led to major traffic problems. Rush hour can be hell – it may be quicker to go around the **ringroad** (*rocade*) and come back into the centre where you need to be.

The most convenient pay **car parks** are at Place du Capitole, Allée J-Jaurès, Place V. Hugo and Place St-Etienne; they cost more than €1 an hour. The Jeanne d'Arc car park tends to be less crowded. Alternatively, battle to find a space in the free parking areas such as Place St-Sernin and Allées Jules Guesde (near the Grand Rond), trawl the streets for a free spot (easiest in summer when people leave for the coast) or park at Joliment or Gramont and take the *métro* in – the price of parking is included in the *métro* ticket (the car parks get full quickly, though, so you need to get there early).

There are quite a few **car hire** companies at the **airport**: ADA, **t** 05 61 30 00 33; Avis, **t** 05 34 60 46 50; Budget, **t** 05 61 71 85 80; Europcar, **t** 0825 825 514; Hertz, **t** 0825 801031.

By Bicycle and Motorcycle

Movimento, **t** 05 34 30 03 00, *www.movimento.coop*, has bike-hire kiosks at the bus station and near the tourist office. You can also be driven around on electric tricycles (**t** 06 67 71 17 22; *June–Sept*).

By Boat

In summer, Toulouse Croisières (**t** 05 61 25 72 57, *www.toulouse-croisieres.com*) offers **trips on the Garonne** from Quai de la Daurade (*Tues–Sun 10.30, 4.30 and 6, plus some other times*) and wonderful night cruises.

Other Means

A **tourist train** tours the main sites in 30mins or so (from in front of the post office on Rue Lafayette; **t** 05 62 71 08 51). You can also hire **tourist taxis** with driver-guides (**t** 05 34 25 02 50; about €40/75mins).

The tourist office has some bike and walking routes drawn up by the *mairie*.

Roman expression *habebat aurum tolosanum* ('to have the gold of Toulouse') – in other words, ill-gotten gains seldom prosper.

If Rome cleaned out Toulouse's sacred swamp, it also brought years of peace. The Tectosages felt safe enough to come down from Vieille Toulouse to the plain of the Garonne, and by all accounts they were soon doing well enough again as one of the most important cities in the province of Gallia Narbonensis, with a population of around 20,000. The city became known as *Palladia Tolosa* after its protectress, the goddess of wisdom Pallas Athena.

The Capital of the Visigoths

In 410 the Visigoths under Alaric captured Rome and took a valuable hostage – Galla Placidia, sister of Emperor Honorius. When Alaric died, Galla Placidia was inherited by his brother-in-law and new king Ataulf, who carried the young maiden off on his conquests in southwest France. Ataulf preferred Toulouse to Bordeaux, the Roman capital of Aquitaine, and made it the Visigothic capital. When his wife died, he married Galla Placidia. It was the love match of the Dark Ages, and her genteel Roman manners helped to tame his uncouth Visigothic temperament. Ataulf was later killed in a palace conspiracy and Galla Placidia returned to her brother in Ravenna, where she built herself a beautiful tomb of golden mosaics that can be seen to this day (she later remarried, gave birth to Emperor Valentinian III, and reigned for years as empress herself). Toulouse remained the elegant capital of the Visigoths until 507, when Clovis, the recently baptised king of the Franks, took it upon himself to wipe out the Arian heresy – the sect of the Visigoths. After Clovis defeated Alaric II in hand-to-hand combat, the Visigoths upped sticks over the Pyrenees for Toledo, which they made their capital until they were ousted in turn by the Arabs in 716.

Five years later these same Arab armies appeared at the gates of Toulouse. Although Clovis' successors, the Merovingian 'do-nothing kings' (*rois fainéants*), hadn't failed to neglect Toulouse, a brilliant resistance was organized by the city's Duke Eudes, who killed the emir and gave the Moors their first taste of defeat on 9 June 721. The Arabs' later defeat at Poitiers marked both their northernmost incursion into France and the triumph of Charles Martel, founding father of the Carolingian dynasty that replaced Duke Eudes and the Merovingians in the person of his son, Pepin the Short.

Pepin, recognizing the danger of a renewed Arab attack from over the Pyrenees, spent years hunting down Waiffre, the last Merovingian duke of Aquitaine, in order to establish his authority and guarantee the frontiers of the Franks' empire. Pepin's son Charlemagne continued this policy by pampering Toulouse. The most able and loyal counsellors of his sons and grandsons who inherited these marches became in 849 themselves the counts of Toulouse, responsible for Languedoc – a vast territory extending from the Rhône to the Garonne and the Pyrenees to the Dordogne.

The Counts of Toulouse

The counts of Toulouse are often called the Raymondine dynasty – because nearly all were named Raymond. The first to emerge from obscurity was Raymond St-Gilles, born in 1041, the younger brother of Count Guilhem. A mighty warrior, Raymond spent his youth battling the Moors in Spain with such audacity that the king of Castile married him to his daughter and put him under the wing of the great Cid himself. In 1090, Count Guilhem died without a male heir, and Raymond was summoned back to Toulouse, where he was so popular a ruler as Count Raymond IV that in 1095 Urban II asked him to lead the First Crusade. Before leaving Toulouse, Raymond IV oversaw the consecration of the great basilica of St-Sernin and, declaring he would never return, installed his son Bertrand as count. For his coat of arms in the Crusade, Raymond chose the 12-pointed red 'Cross of Languedoc', a symbol at least as old as the Visigoths and still used today by Toulouse and the Midi-Pyrénées region. As the leader of the Crusade, Raymond IV was offered the crown of Jerusalem in the Holy Land; to everyone's amazement he modestly refused and let the honour go to Godfrey of Bouillon. Before Raymond died in 1105, he saw the birth of a fourth son, Alphonse-Jourdain, and his baptism in the river Jordan.

Crusading quickly became a family pastime; little Alphonse-Jourdain was shipped home to Toulouse to take Bertrand's place as count when the latter succumbed to the itch. Alphonse-Jourdain remained on the job long enough to found, in 1152, one of Toulouse's most enduring and original institutions, the *domini de capitulo* (lords of the chapter), or *capitouls*. Each parish in Toulouse had its own *capitoul* – in 1438 the number was fixed at eight – who were appointed each November by the count from a list provided by the outgoing *capitouls*, who had to wait three years to be eligible again. At first the *capitouls* were in charge of administering justice; by the time of the Revolution they ran the whole city.

The next Count Raymond, the fifth in the series, took over at age 14, when his father Alphonse-Jourdain could no longer resist the call of the Crusades. Raymond V was a troubadour who presided over a golden age of poetry for Toulouse; and continued his father's administrative reforms by granting the city municipal autonomy. Another charter, in 1192, established the very first concern, anywhere, managed by shareholders, the Moulins du Bazacle, for centuries one of the largest mills in Europe; Rabelais wrote that 'they filled the ears with the infernal racket of their wheels that rotated ten heavy millstones'. Although Raymond V is known among non-

Toulousain historians as 'the weather vane', inconsistent and ambiguous in his diplomacy, his manœuvrings were all for the sake of his beloved Languedoc – a small but rich prize coveted by the most powerful rulers of Europe: France, England, Aquitaine and Barcelona all had tenuous claims and were ready to pounce. In 1190, the Duke of Aquitaine, Richard the Lionheart, did just that, capturing Cahors and 18 castles on the pretext of avenging alleged attacks on pilgrims passing through the lands of Toulouse. Raymond V quietly got his revenge by asking his Mediterranean allies to refuse a safe harbour for Richard's ship on his return from the Crusades, leading directly to his capture by Leopold of Austria.

To Lose Toulouse, through Love

When Raymond V died in 1195, his son Raymond VI had already been through three wives (the first died, the second and third were repudiated) and was ready to patch things up with the troublesome Plantagenets by wedding a fourth, Joanna, sister of Richard the Lionheart, who bore him an heir before she died. But the scandal of Raymond VI's private life was nothing compared to the reproach heaped on him for his ambiguous attitude towards the Cathars. In 1208, when one of his hot-headed Provençal vassals murdered the papal legate Pierre de Castelnau, Pope Innocent III demanded that the count, who knew nothing of the matter, do penance and let himself be stripped to the waist and beaten with rods. Even this humiliation, and the fact that he had undertaken the expense of constructing a new cathedral in Toulouse, failed to convince Innocent that he sufficiently hated the heretics. And he probably didn't. Raymond VI seems to have had quite a modern, tolerant attitude towards the Cathars: they lived honestly without harming anyone, and as their ruler he considered it his job to defend them. Such an attitude was so threatening to the Church that Innocent began recruiting in the north for what has come down in history as the Albigensian crusade. Raymond and his barons soon enough recognized what it really was – an excuse to grab the south of France.

With the Pope, the King of France and the crusaders' fanatical leader, Simon de Montfort, lined up against him, Raymond VI summoned his brother-in-law, Pere (Pedro) of Aragon, count of Barcelona, and offered to unite the counties of Barcelona and Toulouse into a kingdom of the south to defeat the northerners. Pedro was fresh from the great Catholic victory over the Moors at Las Navas de Tolosa, but he had no qualms about fighting against the pope's team – especially if he could combine war with a visit to his old flame, a certain Azalaïs de Boissezon. Simon de Montfort was near Toulouse at Muret when he intercepted the letter from Pedro, setting up a rendezvous with Azalaïs. 'How should I respect a king who, for a woman, marches against his God!' thundered de Montfort. Barcelona and Toulouse had 3,000 knights against de Montfort's 1,500, but what should have been an easy victory at Muret began ominously when King Pedro turned up for battle exhausted, barely able to sit in the saddle. One of his knights traded arms with him, hoping to conceal his identity, but from the beginning the Occitans were outmanœuvred by de Montfort. In the subsequent hand-to-hand combat, the king of Aragon, fearing to be labelled a coward, revealed himself and was quickly slain. The battle of Muret (12 September 1213) turned into a rout. It was the beginning of the end of the south's independence.

In 1215, with the king of France at his side, Simon de Montfort entered Toulouse, where he was made count in place of Raymond VI by the will of the pope. He ruled Toulouse with Bishop Folquet de Marseille, a former troubadour patronized by Raymond V who in 1195 got religion and became the most rabid bigot of them all (a contemporary wrote: 'And when he was elected Bishop of Toulouse he spread such fire throughout the land that no amount of water will ever suffice to extinguish it; he snuffed out, in body and in soul, the lives of more than fifteen hundred people... he is more an Antichrist than a messenger of Rome').

In 1217, when young Raymond, the son of the count, orchestrated an uprising in Provence in order to draw de Montfort out of Toulouse, the city welcomed back Raymond VI 'as if he were the Holy Spirit', and diligently prepared against de Montfort's return and inevitable siege. It was to be Raymond's last hurrah. A woman operating a kind of homemade mini-catapult recognized De Montfort from the walls, took aim and lobbed a large rock on his skull, dashing out his brains.

Raymond VI died soon afterwards (his body was stolen while awaiting burial in a monastery corridor, and never found), and he was succeeded by his son, Raymond VII. His reign was a troubled one. Simon de Montfort's heir waged war on Toulouse for 17 years before he gave up and ceded his claim to Louis VIII, who embarked on another 'crusade', a fancy name for a scorched-earth campaign to crush the south once and for all. In 1229 Raymond VII, seeing the distress of his subjects, sued for terms from the king, now Louis IX. As put down in the subsequent Treaty of Paris these terms were: first, the public submission of Count Raymond in front of Notre-Dame in Paris and his promise to round up all the remaining Cathars in his realm; then the division of booty, eastern Languedoc for the king of France and the Comtat-Venaissin for the pope (this later allowed the popes to install themselves in Avignon, and weighed in favour of Louis IX's canonization). Jeanne, Raymond's only child, was forced to wed Alphonse de Poitiers, the king's brother. In the spirit of the times, Jeanne and Alphonse also went crusading in the East, and died childless in 1271, and Toulouse reverted to the king of France as the chief city of his new province of Languedoc.

One spin-off of the Albigensian crusade was the founding of the Dominicans (*see* 'Les Jacobins', p.435–36). A second was the invention of the Inquisition. Raymond VII, in spite of his submission in Paris, had so little heart for persecuting the Cathars that in 1233 Pope Gregory IX came up with the idea of creating a spiritual police force and put the Dominicans in charge of it. This went down like a lead balloon in Toulouse; the *capitouls* themselves ordered an assault on the monastery and forced the Grand Inquisitors to flee. Raymond VII was ordered by Rome to take them back, and one night a band of Cathars descended from their mountain fastness in the Pyrenees and slit their throats – an act that tragically sealed the fate of Montségur, the Cathars' last refuge. Another side effect was the founding of the University of Toulouse: the 1229 Treaty of Paris ordered Raymond to support 14 masters of theology and canon law for a decade. They stuck around to form the second oldest university in France, one that was controlled for years by Parisians and papal appointees to enforce orthodoxy on the wayward, far too tolerant southerners.

Yet another effect of the Albigensian crusade was a boom in the slave trade: the French were not only buying up recalcitrant southerners, but they now found the path to Spain clear to capture Muslims to sell in the north. The *capitouls* found their behaviour revolting, and in 1226 they struck a precocious blow for human rights by granting the right of asylum to any slave, whatever his country of origin. Despite considerable pressure from Paris, the law remained on the books in Toulouse until the Revolution.

A Second Golden Age, in Pastel

Although the city got through the Hundred Years' War fairly intact, a fire that started in a bakery oven in 1463 destroyed around 7,000 buildings in the medieval centre. Toulouse rebounded from the disaster at once, thanks to a new cash crop – dyers' woad, locally called *pastel*. Cultivated in the hills of the Lauragais just southeast of Toulouse, pastel leaves were pulverized and squeezed into balls called *coques*. Left to dry, these were then crushed into paste, fermented for a year, and then mixed with urine to produce the deep blue dye so fashionable in the Renaissance; mixed with other ingredients it became bright green or violet. For a century so much *pastel* money poured into Toulouse that the Lauragais, the land of the *coques*, became the *païs de Cocanha* or Cockaigne, the carefree land of abundance and pleasure. Merchants from all around Europe speculated and dealt in *pastel* credits and futures, and in 1552 these activities were centralized with the founding of Toulouse's stock exchange – just before the *pastel* market collapsed in the 1560s with the import of a much cheaper substitute, indigo from South Carolina.

The 17th century brought Toulouse both deep economic depression and spiritual malaise. The clergy were openly corrupt, and many *Toulousains*, the Cathars of old, were receptive to the preachings of John Calvin. Although the *capitouls* tolerated the new religion (many of them were converts themselves), the *parlementaires* and *intendants* – representing royal power in Toulouse – stayed strictly in the Catholic camp, and conflicts were inevitable: a bloody riot broke out in 1562 when Catholic priests stole the body of a dead Protestant woman laid out in a *temple*, saying she had reconverted on her deathbed; by May it was open warfare in the streets. But the Catholics prevailed in the end, and Toulouse was one of the last cities to recognize Henri IV as king.

In 1632, with the dramatic execution of the governor of Languedoc, the Duke of Montmorency (*see* p.430), Toulouse saw its remaining independence and privileges slowly gobbled up by the absolute monarchy. One bright spot was the digging of the Canal du Midi, linking the Mediterranean and the Atlantic – a project according to legend first envisaged by Charlemagne and brilliantly planned, financed and achieved by Pierre-Paul Riquet, scion of a prominent Italian family in the region. Louis XVI was pleased to take credit for uniting two seas and two worlds in record time (1666–81), but the cost – 3,600,000 *livres* – was borne by Languedoc and the dedicated Riquet, who died ruined.

The new prosperity and agricultural trade (mostly in wheat) brought about by Riquet's ditch may have improved local morale if not local morals. The most popular entertainments in Toulouse were public executions, to the tune of three or four a month, which may be why the population grew only 10 per cent (to around 60,000) while the rest of France shot up 40% in the 1700s. The execution with the most repercussions was the 1761 *Affaire Calas*: the son of a fervently Protestant cloth merchant was found strangled. The family claimed they had tried to keep his suicide quiet, to prevent the dishonour of having the body put on trial (as suicide was a crime), but the neighbours had often overheard father and son quarrelling over religion, and were convinced from the beginning that Calas *père* had murdered Calas *fils* rather than see him convert to Catholicism. Found guilty by the *parlement* of Toulouse, Calas *père* was brutally tortured, then had all his limbs broken with iron bars, and survived another two hours, the whole time stalwartly maintaining his innocence. Voltaire wrote of the case, and soon enough even the king of Prussia and Catherine the Great were expressing their great indignation. Funds were raised on the streets of Holland and England for a retrial; the *parlement* of

Paris demanded the dossier, and three years later Calas was found innocent, his family rehabilitated. Encouraged by the result, Voltaire continued his sarcastic attacks on the inhumanity of French justice, until all the *parlements* in France were universally hated – adding another pile of kindling to the smouldering misery that ignited the Revolution.

Toulouse in the Sky with Diamonds

The mid-19th century found Toulouse a mere *départemental* capital, a sleepy provincial backwater where the elite invested in property and farms instead of joining the Industrial Revolution. In 1833 journalist Léon Faucher wrote: 'Life is too easy in Toulouse for the people there to feel pushed to be or do anything.' The arrival of the railway in 1856 shook things up a bit, or at least shook down branches of Paris's banks and department stores.

What proved to be the turning point for modern Toulouse literally fell from the sky. Clément Ader of Muret, born in 1841, gave a preview of coming events when one of his bat-winged, steam-powered *avions*, as he called them, hopped off the ground in 1873; in 1890 he flew a few dozen yards in the *Eole*, 13 years before Orville Wright's first flight at Kitty Hawk. In 1917, Latécoère founded the first aircraft factory in Toulouse – in honour of Ader, in part, but mainly because the city was far from the front lines of the First World War; at its peak it produced six combat aeroplanes a day.

After the Armistice, Latécoère continued production, for peaceful purposes, and on 12 March 1919 launched a Toulouse–Casablanca airmail route that soon extended to Dakar and eventually to South America. For this new airline, the now legendary Compagnie Générale Aéropostale, he recruited ace pilots – 'Archangel' Jean Mermoz, Daurat, Guillaumet and Antoine de St-Exupéry, the 'Lord of the Sands', who immortalized his comrades in his books. A second aircraft company, founded in 1920 by *Toulousain* Emile Dewoitine, was nationalized in 1937 and later became Aérospatiale, the birthplace of Ariane rockets and Hermès, the European space shuttle, as well as Caravelle, Concorde and Airbus jets.

In 1970 Aérospatiale became part of Airbus, itself now part of EADS. Airbus is assembling the major part of the A380-XXL, the largest civil aircraft in the world. Toulouse fought hard to be accepted as the assembly site and now looks forward to even greater prosperity as a result. A huge aeronautics industrial park, Aéroconstellation, has been built near the runways at Blagnac to accommodate the factory used to put together the giant aeroplane, and includes other aircraft-industry businesses. CNES, the French space agency, was transferred here in 1968 along with the French national weather service. Astrium, Europe's number one satellite manufacturer is also based here. The air and space industries have attracted scores of research centres, hi-tech firms and elite schools of engineering and aviation.

The population of Toulouse has since grown apace, but not only with engineers. It was the principal centre for refugees during and after the Spanish Civil War, and, of the 360,000 or so civilians and Republican soldiers who passed through the city, a quarter stayed and became French citizens (in the 1970s, when Franco executed the Catalan anti-fascist Puig Antich, 3,000 protestors set fire to the Spanish consulate in Toulouse). Thousands came to work in the new post-war industries; 25,000 *pieds-noirs* from Algeria settled here in the 1960s. Then in 1964, when France decided to ever so slowly reverse the centralizing policies of Richelieu and Louis XIV, Toulouse was made capital of the largest of France's new regions, the Midi-Pyrénées, encompassing the western half of its old province of Languedoc. By then Toulouse, after its slow start, had become the fourth largest city in France.

Although pink in its politics as well as its bricks for most of the 20th century, Toulouse from 1971 to 2001 was mayored by the centre-right Baudises, first the father, Pierre Baudis, then his son Dominique – a popular mayor with the majority of *Toulousains*, who thanked him for the city's economic and cultural achievements in recent years. The baton was passed to another relative right-winger, Philippe Douste-Blazy, formerly major of Lourdes, who probably owed his electoral success to Dominique Baudis's backing. In September 2001, when 29 people died and hundreds were injured in the A2F chemical factory explosion, he said he would prefer to remain mayor rather than accept a job at national level. Evidently he changed his mind – in 2004 he became minister of health and since 2005 he has been minister of foreign affairs. He was replaced in Toulouse by Jean-Luc Moudenc, a former Douste-Blazy ally out of the same stable. He continues to push Toulouse forward to higher and better things.

Another local bigwig who succeeded in making a bigger impact on the national stage was former socialist Prime Minister Lionel Jospin from L'Ile-Jourdain, just outside Toulouse. After a dismal showing in the presidential elections he retired, but he keeps popping up again, threatening, as all the old boys do, to return.

Place du Capitole

This dignified front parlour of Toulouse dates from 1850, when the 200-year-long tidying away of excess buildings was over and the edges rimmed with neoclassical brick façades. As a permanent memorial to the southern kingdom of nevermore, the centre of the pavement is marked by an enormous **Cross of Languedoc**. This

Capitole
t 05 61 22 29 22; historical rooms open Mon–Fri 9–5

same golden cross on a red background hangs proudly from Toulouse's city hall, the **Capitole**, or CAPITOLIUM as it reads, bowing to a 16th-century story claiming that ancient Rome got its Capitol idea from Toulouse's temple of Capitoline Jupiter.

Jupiter Poopiter! Everyone knows this Capitole is really named after the *capitouls*. In 1750, flush with money brought in by the Canal du Midi, these worthies decided to transform their higgledy-piggledy medieval buildings into a proper Hôtel de Ville. Parts of the original 12th–17th-century complex were saved, as much as could be masked by the neoclassical façade designed by Guillaume Cammas, who imported stone and marble to alternate with the homemade brick of Toulouse. Cammas's careful polychromatic effects were only briefly admired before the *capitouls* decided to order every building in the city to be whitewashed or covered with white stucco, the better to reflect the moonlight and make up for the lack of street lighting. The first building to get the treatment was the Capitole itself; the entire Place du Capitole lay under this dull make-up until 1946, when Toulouse decided to become the *Ville Rose* once more. Other critics have had trouble with the Capitole's height. '*C'est beau mais c'est bas*' was the only comment of Napoleon, an expert on the subject.

A Conspiracy's Martyr

Henri IV's companion-in-arms, Henri Duke of Montmorency, First Peer of the Realm and Governor of Languedoc, was succeeded in these titles by his son, Duke Henri II, a brave fighter and governor dedicated to the welfare of Languedoc. Richelieu, whose plans for creating an absolute centralized monarchy for Louis XIII necessitated tripping up the kingdom's mightiest barons, made it hot for Montmorency by choking Languedoc with taxes until it was at the point of insurrection. Montmorency hated Richelieu, and attracted the attention of 'Monsieur', who, in cahoots with his scheming mother, Marie de' Medici, was always ready to befriend an enemy of the cardinal. Monsieur offered to send down troops to liberate first Languedoc, then France, from the high-handed cardinal's policies. After much soul-searching, Montmorency cast his lot with Monsieur.

Richelieu must have rubbed his hands with glee. With the king in tow he led an army south to snuff out the revolt. The promised military aid from Monsieur failed to materialize, and Montmorency, realizing he'd made a terrible mistake, tried to surrender, hoping to avoid battle. Richelieu refused. The royal troops surprised the hapless duke while he was reconnoitring the lines. Montmorency, fighting singlehandedly, was wounded 17 times; he might even have escaped, it was said, had he had his proper warhorse. Richelieu was careful to keep Montmorency alive, knowing he could make a much more memorable example *pour encourager les autres* by persuading the king to sentence the duke to death.

Montmorency's fate quickly became a *cause célèbre* across Europe – Charles I of England, the Pope, the Republic of Venice and most nobles of France pleaded for mercy. Louis XIII turned a deaf ear, but on the appointed day of execution, 30 October 1632, popular feeling in Toulouse ran so high the authorities decided to hold the execution privately in this courtyard of the Capitole rather than in public. In spite of his wounds, Montmorency walked alone to the chopping block (a slab in the pavement marks the spot), his eyes falling on the statue of Henri IV. 'He was a great and generous prince, and I had the honour to be his godson,' were Montmorency's last words. His blood splattered over the statue; the guard dipped their swords in the red pool; a throng of grieving *Toulousains* were allowed in to touch and kiss the sticky pavement. He was buried in St-Sernin, the basilica's first non-saint to receive such a high honour.

The portal on the right belongs to the **Théâtre du Capitole**, while over the central door pink marble columns represent the eight *capitouls*; the extravagant, pompous **historical rooms** upstairs were decorated in the 1800s with busts of famous Toulousains. In Salle Henri Martin is Toulouse's contribution to the Impressionist movement, a painting of the pre-First World War Socialist leader from nearby Castres, *Jean Jaurès on the banks of the Garonne*.

Pedestrians cut through the **Cour Henri IV**, with a statue of said king, who in 1602 gave his permission for the construction of the courtyard. He might not have said yes had he known what was going to happen here 30 years later, thanks to the jealous rivalries and schemes of his two neurotic sons, Louis XIII and Gaston d'Orléans ('*Monsieur*' for short), and the prime minister and arch-puppeteer Cardinal Richelieu. One back door of the Cour Henri IV gives on to Square Charles de Gaulle, defended by the **Donjon** of 1525, where the *capitouls* kept the city archives. The building, well restored by Viollet-le-Duc, houses the city tourist office (*see* p.446).

From Place du Capitole to the Basilica of St-Sernin

Running north from Place du Capitole, narrow **Rue du Taur** was the road to Cahors in Roman times. The Taur in its name means 'bull', which features in the life of the city's first saint, Sernin, who died here in the 240s. Sernin (a corruption of Saturnin) was a missionary from Rome who preached in Pamplona and Toulouse. One day, runs the legend, he happened by the temple of Capitoline Jupiter, where preparations were under way for the sacrifice of a bull to Mithras. The priests ordered him to kneel before the pagan idol, and, when Sernin refused, a sudden gust of wind blew over the statue of Mithras, breaking it to bits. In fury the crowd demanded the sacrifice of Sernin instead, and he was tied under the bull, which, maddened by the extra weight, dragged his body through the city streets. Curiously, an identical martyrdom awaited Sernin's disciple Fermin in Pamplona, where he became the patron saint of matadors and is honoured each year by the famous running of the bulls, even though the official hagiography claims that Fermin died peacefully in bed as bishop of Amiens. One wonders: could Fermin really be Sernin, transformed long ago by a slip of a monastic quill?

After turning Sernin to pulp, the bull left his body where the 14th-century **Notre-Dame-du-Taur** now stands, replacing an oratory built over Sernin's tomb in 360. Its 41m *clocher-mur* looks like a false front in a Wild West town; the nave is surprisingly wide, and has a faded fresco of the Tree of Jesse along the right wall.

Sernin's tomb attracted so many pilgrims and Christians who desired to be buried near him that in 403 a *martyrium* was built just under 300m to the north. An imperial decree permitted the removal of the saint's relics to this spot, and over the centuries tombs lined Rue de Taur, as in the Alyscamps in Arles. In 1075, just as the pilgrimage to Compostela was getting underway, Count Guilhem decided Sernin deserved something more grand.

The Basilica of St-Sernin

Basilique St-Sernin
t 05 61 21 80 45; open June Mon–Sat 8.30–12.30 and 2–6.15, Sun 8.30–12.15 and 2–7; July–Sept Mon–Sat 8.30–6.15, Sun 8.30–7.30; Oct–May Mon–Sat 8.30–11.45 and 2–5.45, Sun 8.30–12.30 and 2–7; ***ambulatory*** *July–Sept Mon–Sat 10–6, Sun 10–11.30; rest of year Mon–Sat 10–11.30 and 2–5.30, Sun 10–11.30; adm (ambulatory)*

The construction of the Basilique St-Sernin was continued by Guilhem's famous brother Raymond IV, and the building was of such importance that in 1096 Pope Urban II, on tour that year preaching the First Crusade, came to consecrate its marble altar. The whole wasn't finished, however, until 1220.

At 116m, this the largest surviving Romanesque church in the world (only the great abbey church of Cluny, destroyed in the Revolution, was bigger). It was begun at the same time, and has the exact same plan, as the basilica of St James at Compostela: a cross, ending in a semicircular apse with five radiating chapels. In the 19th century the abbey and cloister were demolished, and in 1860 Viollet-le-Duc was summoned to restore the basilica. He spent 20 years on the project – and botched the roof so badly that rainwater seeped directly into the stone and brick. A century later the church was found to be in danger of collapse – hence a 22-million-franc 'de-restoration' project to undo Viollet-le-Duc's mischief. Off came his neogothic ornamentation and heavy stone, to be replaced with tiles handcrafted in the 13th-century manner.

The Exterior

The apse of St-Sernin (seen from Rue St-Bernard) is a fascinating play of white stone and red brick, a crescendo culminating in the octagonal belltower that is Toulouse's most striking landmark. New York had its war of skyscrapers in the 1930s; 13th-century Toulouse had its war of bell towers: St-Sernin's original three storeys of arcades were increased to five for the sole purpose of upstaging the bell tower of the Jacobins. The most elaborate of the basilica's portals is an odd, asymmetrical one on the south side, the **Porte Miège-ville**. It faces Rue du Taur; apparently this street, called Miège-ville or 'mid-city' in medieval times, ran right through the spot before the basilica was built. Devotees of medieval *Toulousain* arcana – a bottomless subject – say that this portal is the real cornerstone of the kingdom of Languedoc that the 11th-century counts were trying to create; books have been written about its proportions and the symbolism of its decoration, even claiming that it is the centre of a geomantic construction, with 12 lines radiating from here across the counts' territories, connecting various chapels and villages and forming – what else? – Raymond IV's Cross of Languedoc. The tympanum was carved by the 11th-century master Bernard Gilduin, showing the *Ascension of Christ*, a rare scene in medieval art, and one of the most choreographic: Christ surrounded by dancing angels, watched by the Apostles on the lintel. On the brackets are figures of David and others riding on lions; the magnificent capitals tell the story of the Redemption (*Original Sin*, *Massacre of the Innocents*, *Annunciation*), all from the expressive chisel of Gilduin.

The north transept door, now walled up, was the royal door; the south transept door, the **Porte des Comtes**, is named after the several 11th-century counts of Toulouse who are buried in palaeo-Christian sarcophagi in the deep *enfeu* nearby. The eight capitals here, also by Gilduin (*c.* 1080), are the oldest Romanesque works to show the torments of hell, most alarmingly a man having his testicles crushed and a woman whose breasts are being devoured by serpents, both paying the price for Lust.

The Interior

Begun in 1969, the 'de-restoration' of the barrel-vaulted interior stripped the majestic brick and stone of Viollet-le-Duc's ham-handed murals and fiddly neogothic bits. In the process, some fine 12th-century frescoes have been found, especially the serene angel of the Resurrection in the third bay of the north transept, which also has some of the best capitals. In the south transept, the shrine of St Jude, the patron saint of lost causes, blazes with candlelight in July – when French students take their exams.

For a small fee you can enter the **ambulatory** and make what the Middle Agers called 'the Circuit of Holy Bodies', for the wide array of saintly anatomies stashed in the five radiating chapels. In the 17th century, bas-reliefs and wood panels on the lives of the saints were added to bring the relics to life, and although these were removed in the 1800s they were restored and replaced in 1980. Opposite the central chapel are seven magnificent marble bas-reliefs of 1096, carved and signed by Bernard Gilduin. The *Christ in Majesty* set in a mandorla is as serene, pot-bellied and beardless as a Buddha, surrounded by the four Evangelists; the others show a seraph, a cherub, two apostles and a pair of hierarchic, extremely well-coiffed angels – scholars guess these were perhaps modelled after a Roman statue of Orpheus.

The Holy Bodies circuit continues down into the upper crypt, with the silver shrine of St Honoratus (1517) and the 13th-century reliquaries of the Holy Cross and of St Sernin, the latter showing the saint under the hooves of the bull. The dark, dank lower crypt contains, more bodily, two Holy Thorns (a present from St Louis), 13th-century gloves and mitres, and a set of six 16th-century painted wooden statues of apostles. In the choir an 18th-century baldachin shelters St Sernin's tomb, remade in 1746 and supported by a pair of bronze bulls. In the south transept, note the big feet sticking out of a pillar, all that remains of a shallow relief of St Christopher effaced by the hands of centuries of pilgrims.

Around Place St-Sernin and the Quartier Arnaud-Bernard

At No.3, the Lycée St-Sernin occupies the **Hôtel du Barry**, built by Louis XV's pimp, the Roué du Barry. Du Barry married his charming lover, Jeanne de Bécu, to his brother and then in 1759 introduced her to the king. His pandering earned him the money to build this mansion in 1777; it would later earn the Comtesse du Barry the guillotine in the Terror. (The word *roué*, incidentally, was first used in the 1720s, to describe the bawdy companions of the regent, the Duke of Orléans; it was invented by some disapproving soul who thought they should have been broken on the wheel.)

On the south side of the square stood a pilgrims' hostel, founded in the 1070s by a chanter of St-Sernin named Raymond Gayard, who was canonized for his charity to the poor. His hostel was succeeded by the *collège* of St Raymond (1505) for poor university students, and now by the rich archaeological collections of the **Musée St-Raymond**. This is the antiquities museum of Toulouse, with some exceptional pieces. The top floors concentrate on finds from the Roman region of Narbonnaise and one of its biggest towns, Tolosa, ancient Toulouse. One of the most interesting exhibits is the section of a relief depicting two Amazons in combat, one clearly with the upper hand over a man: this would have formed part of a temple or major monument. The collection of outstanding busts is small compared to the avenue of heads of emperors, men, women and children on the floor below: all found, with the other exhibits here, at Chiragan in Martres-Tolosane, 60km to the south of Toulouse. Don't miss the splendid marbles depicting the *Labours of Hercules*. Digs in the basement of the museum have revealed the presence of a Christian necropolis dating from the 4th century which grew up around the tomb of St Sernin. Several of the tombs have been left not far from where they were found, close to a large, circular 5th-century lime kiln. Ornate sarcophagi from southwest France and other funerary objects are also on display. There are also vestiges of walls from an 11th-century hospital and 13th-century college. Temporary exhibitions allow the public to see other artefacts from the Iron Age to the Middle Ages. The museum's specialist **library** at 11 Rue des Trois Renards can be used by the public.

Musée St-Raymond
t *05 61 22 31 44; open June–Aug daily 10–7; rest of year daily 10–6;* ***library*** *Mon–Fri 10–6, Sun 10–1 and 2–6*

Just south of St-Sernin in Rue du Périgord, the atavistic southern Gothic **Chapelle des Carmélites** (1643) owes its existence to Anne of Austria, wife of Louis XIII, who laid the foundation stone on the day that she learned of the canonization of St Theresa. The walls are covered with paintings, and vaulting has been restored to bring out its lavish ceiling, covered with an unusual allegory on the *Glory of Carmel* by Jean-Baptiste Despax.

This northernmost medieval neighbourhood, the lively **Quartier Arnaud-Bernard**, has been the city's Latin Quarter ever since 1229, when the **University of Toulouse** was founded in Rue des Lois (part of it now occupies the old seminary of St-Pierre-des-Chartreux to the west). Although forced down Toulouse's throat by Paris (*see* History, p.426), the university enjoyed a certain prestige in the Middle Ages; among its alumni were three popes and Michel de Montaigne. Rabelais started to study here, where he 'well learned to dance and to play at swords with two hands', but he quickly got out because its regents still had a certain problem when it came to freethinkers; several were burned alive at the stake. 'It didn't please God that I linger,' Rabelais continued, 'me with my nature already rather parched, and not in need of any more heat.'

The three principal squares of the quarter – Place du Peyrou, Place des Tiercerettes and Place Arnaud Bernard – became the centre of immigrant life in the last century; today they are quickly being gentrified but remain quite lively after dark.

Jardin Compans-Caffarelli
open daily 7.45–6

To the north of Boulevard Lascrosses, the neighbourhood's 'lung', the **Jardin Compans-Caffarelli**, was laid out in 1982 and has exotic plants, a Japanese garden and a tearoom.

Les Jacobins

27 Les Jacobins
t 05 61 22 23 82; open 9–7 daily; adm (cloister)

Just west of Place du Capitole stands the great Dominican mother church, Les Jacobins, the prototype for Dominican foundations across Europe and one of the masterpieces of southern French Gothic. The Spanish priest Domingo de Guzmán had tried hard to convert the Cathars before the Albigensian crusade, although the persuasive powers of one man, even a saint, proved negligible in the face of an intellectual revolt against the openly corrupt, materialistic clergy. In 1206 Domingo had re-converted enough women to found a convent, which became the germ of his Order of Preaching Friars, established in Toulouse in 1215. Promoted by Folquet, the bishop of Toulouse, and confirmed by the pope in 1216, the new Dominican order quickly found adherents across Europe. In 1230, the Dominicans erected this, their third convent in Toulouse, which took the name of the Jacobins from the Dominicans' Paris address, in Rue St-Jacques (the very same convent where the fanatical party of Robespierre would later meet, hence the *Jacobins* of the French Revolution – a fitting name in light of the Dominicans' role as Inquisitors). The magnificent Jacobins in Toulouse so impressed the popes that they made it the last resting place of the relics of the greatest Dominican of them all, St Thomas Aquinas (d. 1274).

Confiscated in the Revolution, the church and convent were requisitioned by Napoleon as a barracks for his artillery, which built an upper floor in the nave. When Prosper Mérimée, inspector of historic monuments, visited Toulouse in 1845, he found the mutilated complex occupied by 500 horses and cannoneers, with a pig-ignorant military administration bent on demolishing the whole thing. In 1865 the military was finally convinced to leave the Jacobins to the city, and Toulouse spent 100 years on its restoration.

The church is the perfect expression of the 13th-century reaction to Rome's love of luxury, which made the great preaching orders, the Dominicans and Franciscans, so popular in their day. Gargoyles are the only exterior sculpture in this immense but harmonious brick pile of buttresses, alternating with Flamboyant windows; its octagonal belltower of brick and stone crowned with baby towers is one of the landmarks of the city skyline. The interior is breathtakingly light and spacious, consisting of twin naves divided by seven huge columns, crisscrossed by a fantastic interweaving of ribs in the vault, reaching an epiphany in the massive Flamboyant *palmier* in the apse. The painted decoration dates from the 13th to the 16th century, but only the glass of the rose windows on the west side is original. The 19th-century gilded reliquary shrine of St Thomas Aquinas was returned to the high altar in 1974.

A small door leads out into the lovely garden **cloister** (1309), with brick arcades and twinned columns in grey marble, used in summer for the concert series *Piano aux Jacobins*. The east gallery gives on to the **chapterhouse**, supported by a pair of slender marble columns. The walls of the **Chapelle St-Antonin**, the funerary chapel, were painted in the early 1300s with scenes from the life of St Antonin, while the ceiling is decorated with southwest France's favourite vision from the Apocalypse: the 24 Elders and angels glorifying Christ. In Rue Pargaminières, the **Refectory**, more than 60m long, houses temporary historical and cultural exhibitions.

West of Les Jacobins

St-Pierre-des-Cuisines
t 05 61 22 31 44; open July Mon 10–1, with guided tour at 11; Aug daily 10–12 and 2–7, with guided tour at 4

Near the Garonne's hog-backed Pont St-Pierre are Toulouse's two churches dedicated to St Peter. **St-Pierre-des-Cuisines**, a little Romanesque priory associated with Moissac, is named after its kitchens, where a person's bread could be baked at cheaper rates than at the counts' ovens. It was used as a warehouse from the Revolution until 1965. Excavations have revealed that it was built on a 4th-century Gallo-Roman necropolis, and some sarcophagi can be seen in the crypt. The auditorium is also used as a concert venue. **St-Pierre-des-Chartreux**, to the north in Rue Valade, was founded in the 17th century by monks fleeing the Huguenots of Castres. If it's open, you can admire fine works from the 17th and 18th century – the grand organ (1686; originally in Les Jacobins), elaborate sculpted wood panels, stuccoes and 1680s murals.

Le Bazacle
t 05 62 30 16 01; open Tues–Fri 2–7, plus Sat and Sun during exhibitions, exc public hols and Aug

Just west, along the **Canal de Brienne** that links the Garonne to the Canal du Midi, runs one of Toulouse's favourite leafy promenades. Just beyond that, **Le Bazacle** was where the grumbling of the massive 12th-century mills so annoyed Rabelais. It is now a hydroelectric works; you can visit its guts, its fish passages and its special exhibitions, and enjoy a fine view of Toulouse .

Pastel Palaces and Violets of Gold

Hôtel de Bernuy

Just south of Les Jacobins, towards the south end of Rue Gambetta, is one of the city's most splendid residences, the **Hôtel de Bernuy**, built in 1504 by a *pastel* merchant from Burgos, Don Juan de Bernuy, a Spanish Jew who fled Ferdinand and Isabella's Inquisition and became a citizen – and *capitoul* – of Toulouse. Although Gothic on the outside, inside his master mason Loys Privat designed an eclectic fantasy courtyard, a mix of Gothic, Plateresque and Loire château, topped by a lofty tower rivalling those of all the other *pastel* nabobs. De Bernuy had a chance to repay France for the fortune he made when King François I was captured at the battle of Pavia by Emperor Charles V and imprisoned in Madrid; the king fell gravely ill, but no one could afford the ransom of 1,200,000 gold écus demanded by the emperor – until De Bernuy bailed him out. In his distress the king had promised an *ex voto* to St Sernin if he survived, and in the ambulatory you can still see the black marble statue he donated when he came in 1533 to thank the saint and de Bernuy for his generosity. Not long after de Bernuy's time the Jesuits converted his *hôtel particulier* into a college, now the prestigious **Lycée Pierre de Fermat**, named after its star pupil, the brilliant mathematician (1595–1665) who left his last theorem as a challenge to subsequent generations of mathematicians (there's a statue of him one of the Capitol's public rooms).

Musée du Vieux Toulouse
t 05 62 27 11 50; open mid-May–mid-Oct Mon–Sat 2–6; guided tours Wed and Fri at 3

Just east, the 16th-century *hôtel particulier* at 7 Rue du May houses the **Musée du Vieux Toulouse**, with a fascinating collection from the city's history and its former porcelain industry, as well as paintings and etchings. Rue du May gives on to Rue St-Rome, decorated with 16th-century mansions built by the *capitouls* and wealthy merchants. At its south end don't miss triangular **Place de la Trinité**, with a 19th-century fountain supported by bronze mermaids. Near here, you can examine the popular artistic pulse of Toulouse in the ever-changing murals along Rue Coq-d'Inde.

13 Hôtel d'Assézat

One of the finest private residences constructed in Toulouse, the **Hôtel d'Assézat**, is just west, off Rue de Metz. The *hôtel particulier* was begun in 1555 by another *pastel* magnate, Pierre d'Assézat, who had a near monopoly on the dye in northern Europe. Designed by Nicolas Bachelier, Toulouse's master architect-sculptor-engineer, it consists of two buildings around a large square court, and a curious tower crowned with an octagonal lantern and dome that served the merchant as an observation post over the Garonne, enabling him to keep an eye on his fleet. The decoration, a rhythmic composition of Ionic, Doric and Corinthian columns, is so similar to that on the old Louvre that for a long time Bachelier was thought to have copied the idea, although the records prove that both buildings went up at the same time. Facing the street, an Italianate loggia has seven brackets decorated with pastel pods.

Fondation Bemberg
t 05 61 12 06 89, www.fondation-bemberg.fr; open Tues–Sun 10–12.30 and 1.30–6; night visits Thurs 9pm; themed visits Thurs 7pm; adm

Inside the *hôtel particulier*, the **Fondation Bemberg** has a fine collection of art, particularly Renaissance works – with some paintings by François Clouet and Lucas Cranach – and modern French paintings, including 35 canvases by Pierre Bonnard, and work by Manet, Monet, Picasso, Dufy, Picasso, Modigliani and various others. Since the 19th century, the *hôtel* has also been home to the **Palais des Académies**, seat of the Académie des Jeux Floraux poetry society (*see* below). Over the portico there's a statue of Dame Clémence Isaure, legendary patroness of the Floral Games.

The Eisteddfod of France

In November 1323, seven burghers of Toulouse met together in a monastery garden. Although not poets, these 'Seven Troubadours' were connoisseurs who regretted that good poetry in their town had died out with the counts of Toulouse. To inspire some new verse, the seven decided to invite all the bards of Languedoc to gather in the monastery garden to recite on 3 May; the poem the seven judged best would receive a violet made of gold. A big crowd showed up, and ever since then 3 May in Toulouse has hosted what has become known as the *Jeux Floraux*. The Seven Troubadours were soon succeeded by the 'Maintainers' of the Collège du Gay Scavoir, the world's oldest literary society, renamed the Académie des Jeux Floraux by Louis XIV.

Early on, the Seven Troubadours added two other prizes, an eglantine and a marigold in silver. To cope with the bewildering disorder of entries in the competition, they commissioned a code from one of Toulouse's top jurists and humanists, Guilhem Molinier; the resulting *Las Leys d'Amors* in 1356 was widely read, and soon copied in Barcelona, which in 1388 started its own *Jocs Florals*. There the first prize was not a gold rose but a real rose, because, like the greatest poetry, a rose can never be imitated. Although any true blue *Toulousain* would deny it, Barcelona's Floral Games actually produced the better poetry; so great was the fear of heresy or challenging accepted moral norms in the hometown of the Inquisition that nearly all of Toulouse's entries were safe, bloodless praises of the Virgin Mary that hold little interest today. (Chaucer, a contemporary of the Seven Troubadours, would have told them the poetry might have been better had they chosen a different date for the contest: 3 May is the Invention of the Cross, traditionally the unluckiest day in the year.)

Along the Garonne

Rue de Metz continues to Toulouse's oldest bridge, which, as in Paris, is confusingly known as the new, or **Pont Neuf**. This Pont Neuf, with its seven unequal arches of brick and stone and curious holes (*oculi*), took from 1544 to 1632 to build, and links Gascony – the Left Bank – with the medieval province of Languedoc. Just down the quay is the **Ecole des Beaux-Arts**, its façade larded with allegorical figures (1895). Hidden under the icing is a 17th-century U-shaped monastery connected to **Notre-Dame-la-Daurade**. Only the name recalls what was for centuries one of the wonders of Toulouse, the 10-sided, domed, 5th-century palatine chapel of the Visigothic kings, known as the Daurade ('the golden one') after its shimmering mosaics. Similar to the churches of Ravenna, it was destroyed in 1761, when the nitwitted monks who owned it decided to replace it with a reproduction of the Vatican. Plans for the new church collided with the Revolution and the building was only completed in the mid 19th century. The paintings in the choir are by Ingres's master, Roques. Don't miss the pretty **Place de la Daurade** just north of the church; it overlooked the Garonne until the rebuilding of the quays in the 19th century.

One of the finest views of the Pont Neuf and riverfront is south along the **Quai de Tounis**. Rue du Pont de Tounis, built in 1515 as a bridge over the Garonnette (a now covered tributary of the Garonne), leads back to the original riverbank and **Notre-Dame-la-Dalbade** (Our Lady the Whitened, after its medieval whitewash, in contrast to the Golden One). This church too has taken some hard knocks. It was rebuilt in the Renaissance with a 85m spire, to show up St-Sernin's belltower; this was chopped down in the Revolution,and rebuilt in the 1880s, using such cheap materials it fell through the roof in 1926. It has a rich Renaissance door, under the tympanum's ceramic reproduction of Fra Angelico's *Coronation of the Virgin* (1874).

Hôtel de Pierre

Rue de la Dalbade was the favourite address for the nobility; among its *hôtels particuliers*, the standout is the sooty **Hôtel de Pierre** (No.25), which, extravagantly for the *ville rose*, is made of stone. In 1538 Nicolas Bachelier designed the façades around the courtyard, the doorway, framed by two bearded old men, and the monumental chimney. In the early 17th century, the next owner, a president of the *parlement*, married a *pastel* heiress and added the grandiose Baroque façade in imitation of one in Italy. Opposite is the grand **Hôtel de Malte** (1680), headquarters of the Knights of St John in Toulouse since 1115; after 1315, they took over the wealth and duties of the Templars (who before their suppression were at No.13).

Musée Archéologique de l'Institut Catholique
t 05 61 36 81 00; open one Sun a month, call for details

At 31 Rue de la Fonderie, the Catholic Institute includes an **archaeology museum** that includes some Gallo-Roman fragments and a number of funerary artefacts.

The Quartier du Jardin

At the south end of Rue de la Dalbade/Rue de la Fonderie in Place du Salin stood the fortified residence of the counts of Toulouse, the celebrated Château Narbonnais; it was also the site of the *parlement*, established in Toulouse in 1443. The whole complex was demolished in the 19th century for the **Palais de Justice**, with only the square brick tower, the 14th-century royal treasury (converted into a Protestant church), as a memory. In the adjacent Place du Parlement is an old house built on the Roman wall, donated to Domingo Guzmán for his new preaching order, and later converted to the use inscribed over the door: 'Maison de l'Inquisition'.

Musée d'Histoire Naturelle
closed for renovation at time of writing, with reopening scheduled for Oct 2007; ask at tourist office (see p.446) for details

Monument à la Gloire de la Résistance
open Mon–Fri 10–12 and 2–5 exc hols

Musée Départemental de la Résistance et de la Déportation
*52 Allées des Demoiselles, **t** 05 61 14 80 40; call for times*

Musée G. Labit
*43 Rue des Martyrs-de-la-Libération, **t** 05 61 22 21 84; open summer Wed–Mon 10–6, rest of year Wed–Mon 10–5, exc hols*

South of Place du Parlement, Allées Jules Guesde replaces the walls torn down in 1752. Here, by the Théâtre Sorano, a plaque marks the spot where the hated Simon de Montfort was brained; nearby, at No.35, is Toulouse's fascinating **Musée d'Histoire Naturelle**. The **Jardin Royal** was planted outside the walls and, in the 19th century, Toulouse's prettiest park, the **Jardin des Plantes**, was added. The garden's grand 16th–17th-century portal on Allée Frédéric-Mistral was salvaged from the original Capitole. Just south of this is the **Monument à la Gloire de la Résistance**, with a crypt aligned to be illuminated by the sun's rays on 19 August, the anniversary of the Liberation of Toulouse. It is near the old Gestapo quarter. There's a **museum** about the Resistance and deportation at 52 Allées des Demoiselles.

There is one last museum in this quarter, and it's not to be missed if you're fond of Egyptian, Coptic, Indian and Far Eastern Art – the **Musée Georges Labit**, housed in a neo-Moorish villa off the Allée Frédéric-Mistral. Labit was a 19th-century traveller with plenty of money and a good eye who accumulated a choice Oriental collection, considered the best in France after the Guimet Museum in Paris.

From Place du Salin to the Musée des Augustins

Musée Paul Dupuy
*13 Rue de la Pleau, **t** 05 61 14 65 50; open summer Wed–Mon 10–6; rest of year Wed–Mon 10–5, exc hols*

The parliamentarians liked to build themselves distinguished houses in the unified quarter between the old *parlement* and the cathedral: all pink brick, with light grey shutters and black wrought-iron balconies. In this mesh of quiet lanes, there are a few to pick out during a stroll, such as the sumptuously ornate **Hôtel du Vieux Raisin** (1515) at 36 Rue du Languedoc, built by another *capitoul* in love with Italy. Another *hôtel* houses the **Musée Paul Dupuy**, named after the obsessed collector – every city seems to have one – who left to Toulouse his hoard of watches, automata, guns, coins, fans, faïence, pharmaceutical jars and gems such as the 11th-century 'horn of Roland' and other exquisite medieval ivories, as well as a silver marigold from the Jeux Floraux of 1762. Some of the exhibits can only be seen by appointment.

In Rue Ninau the 16th-century **Hôtel d'Ulmo** (with the marble baldachin in the courtyard) was built by Jean de Ulmo, president of the Toulouse *parlement*, whose motto *Durum patientia frango* ('my constancy breaks adversity') hid a scoundrel to the core; caught selling every favour his office had to dispense, he was flogged, stripped of his possessions and sent off to prison, where he was given the task of keeping the accounts of the prison governor – which he falsified to his own advantage before he was hanged.

Rue Perchepinte and Rue Fermat, lined with antique shops, lead up to Place St-Etienne, with Toulouse's oldest fountain (1546) and the massive archbishop's palace (1713), now used as the Préfecture. All are overpowered by the **cathedral of St-Etienne**, begun in the 11th century by Raymond IV but completed only in the 17th century. Fashions and finances rose and fell in the three major building campaigns, resulting in a church that seems a bit drunk. Have a good look at the façade: in the centre rises a massive brick belltower with a clock, over the Romanesque base. To the right is a worn, asymmetrical stone Gothic façade, where the portal and rose window are off-centre; to the left extends the bulge of the chapel of Notre-Dame, a small church in itself stuck on the north end. It's even tipsier inside. In 1211, Raymond VI inserted the oldest known representation of the Cross of Languedoc as the key in one of the vaults, just before 1215, when Bishop Folquet rebuilt most of Raymond IV's church in the form of a single nave 19m high and 19m wide, with ogival crossings – a style that went on to become the model for southern Gothic.

In 1275, Bishop Bertrand de l'Isle-Jourdaine decided that Bishop Folquet's bit of the cathedral was hardly grandiose enough for Toulouse's dignity and came up with a plan based on northern French Gothic that involved realigning the axis of the church. The choir was built, a fine example of Flamboyant Gothic, with beautiful 14th-century glass on the west side, but the vaults, designed to be 40m high, were cut short at 27m due to limited funds. Money and energy ran out completely when Bishop Bertrand died, leaving a curious dogleg where his choir meets Raymond IV and Bishop Folquet's nave, marked by the massive Pilier d'Orléans, one of four intended to support the transept; it bears a plaque marking the tomb of Pierre-Paul Riquet, father of the Canal du Midi. Although many of the cathedral's best decorations are now stowed away in the Musée des Augustins, there are tapestries, faded into negatives of themselves, from the 15th and 16th centuries, and some interesting grotesques in the choir. The organ, a remarkable instrument from the early 1600s, was at the point of collapsing in the 1970s then restored and bolted high on its wall bracket like an elephant in a flower vase.

Rue Croix Baragnon, opposite the cathedral, has two beautiful Gothic houses, especially No.15, decorated with a band of stone carvings. But the greatest medieval art in this part of town is in the Musée des Augustins, a block north.

Musée des Augustins

Musée des Augustins
corner Rue de Metz and Rue d'Alsace-Lorraine, ***t*** *05 61 22 21 82, www.augustins.org; open Thurs–Mon 10–6, Weds 10–9, exc hols*

This museum, one of the oldest in France, is in a beautifully restored 14th-century Augustinian convent. During the Revolution, the *ville rose* gaily smashed up its fabulous architectural heritage, as ordered in 1790 by the Convention, 'to leave standing no monument that hinted of slavery'. Enter Alexandre Dumège, self-taught son of a Dutch actor, who had such a passion for antiquities he singlehandedly rescued most of the contents of this museum and opened its doors in 1794. Gothic sculptures occupy the Augustinians' Flamboyant chapterhouse: the beautiful 14th-century *Virgin and Child* from Avignon, *Notre-Dame de Grasse* from the Jacobins, scenes from a 14th-century retable, the *Group of Three Persons, One of Whom is Strangled by a Monster*, and effigies from tombstones. A crooning choir of gargoyles from Toulouse's demolished Franciscan convent keep company with the sarcophaguses around the cloister; one is said to belong to the Visigothic Queen Ranachilde – *la reine Pédauque*, the goose-foot (*see* p.41), maybe because of the web-footed bird carved in the side.

The nave of the convent church is devoted to religious paintings (Van Dyck's *Christ aux anges* and *Miracle de la mule*, Rubens's *Christ entre deux larrons*, and *San Diego en extase* by Murillo) and reliefs by Nicolas Bachelier. Best of all are the Romanesque works, most rescued from demolished cloisters: from St-Sernin, there's a capital sculpted with the *War of Angels* and an enigmatic bas-relief from the Porte des Comtes showing two women looking at one another, one holding a lion in her arms, the other a ram, an image that also appears on the main portal at Compostela. Other capitals stylistically related to those of Moissac are from the Romanesque cloister of the Daurade; the most beautiful are from Raymond IV's 11th-century cloister of St-Etienne – note the delicate, almost fluid scene of the dance of Salome and the beheading of John the Baptist. From the Romanesque portal of St-Etienne's chapterhouse are statue-columns of the Apostles that look ahead to Chartres.

The first floor of the convent is devoted to paintings, including two portraits of *capitouls*; one of their oldest prerogatives was the *droit d'image* – the right to have their portraits painted. In the 13th and 14th centuries this was exceptional: kings, emperors, the doge of Venice and the pope were among the few allowed to leave their likenesses for posterity. Other paintings include a 15th-century Florentine hunt scene, a highly unpleasant *Apollo flaying Marsyas* by the 'Divine' Guido Reni, a typical froufrou portrait by Hyacinthe Rigaud, and works by Simon Vouet, Philippe de Champaigne, Van Dyck, Rubens (in the Augustins' church), the two Guardis, Delacroix, Ingres, Manet, Morisot, Vuillard, Maurice Denis and Count Henri de Toulouse-Lautrec. There's also a medieval garden here.

North of the Musée des Augustins

From the museum, Rue des Arts leads up to **Place St-Georges**, once the main venue for Toulouse's favourite, pre-rugby spectator sport, executions – including that of Jean Calas – because it could hold the biggest crowds (this was before Place du Capitole was enlarged). Nowadays the many spectators dawdling in the cafés mainly look at one another. The square lent its name to an inner-city development completed in 1982, the Nouveau St-Georges, which stretches off to Place Occitane. Here, in Rue Lapeyrouse, the Nouvelles Galeries department store has a splendid view over Toulouse from its rooftop tearoom.

Rue St-Antoine-de-T (named after the *tau* symbol on the robes of the monks of St Anthony) leads from Place St-Georges to an early, cosier experiment in urban renewal, the elliptical **Place Président Wilson**, laid out by municipal architect Jean-Paul Virebent in the early 19th century, with a centrepiece monument to one of the last troubadours, Pierre Godolin (1580–1649).

Toulouse's Left Bank

Although the Left, or Gascon, bank of the Garonne has been settled since the early Middle Ages, the periodic rampages of the river dampened property values until the end of the 19th century, when flood control projects were completed.

The main reason for visiting the area lies just over the Pont Neuf – the round brick lighthouse-shaped tower of a pumping and filtering station, which was constructed in 1817 to provide pure drinking water for the city. In 1974 this found a new role as the **Galerie Municipale du Château-d'Eau**. The hydraulic machinery is still intact on the bottom level, while upstairs you can visit one of Europe's foremost photographic galleries – over and over again, since exhibitions change 15 times a year. An annexe has been installed in a dry arch of the Pont Neuf. There is also a reference **library** on the history of photography .

Galerie Municipale du Château-d'Eau
t 05 61 77 09 40; open Tues–Sat 1–7 exc hols; ***library*** *Mon–Fri 1.30–6 and 1st Sat of month; adm*

Facing the watertower is the **Hôtel-Dieu St-Jacques**, a medieval pilgrimage hospital rebuilt in the 17th century. The grand Salle

Musée d'Histoire de la Médecine
t 05 61 77 84 25; open Wed–Sun 1–6

Musée des Instruments de Médecine des Hôpitaux de Toulouse
t 05 61 77 82 72; open Thurs and Fri 1–5

St-Jacques and Salle St-Lazare have magnificent ceilings, while down on the ground floor are the **Musée d'Histoire de la Médecine** and a **museum of medical instruments** from the city's hospitals, dating from the second half of the 19th century to today.

Nearby, a single arch survives of a 17th-century covered bridge over the Garonne, the Pont de la Daurade. Each of France's four great rivers has a nickname, and the Garonne is 'the Laughing'. Often enough, the joke has been on Toulouse. St Cyprien, the original dedicatee of the Left Bank's parish church (behind the Hôtel-Dieu), proved to wield so little celestial influence over the water that when his church was rebuilt in 1300 he was sacked in favour of St Nicolas, patron of sailors and protector of the flooded. **St Nicolas church** is a small southern Gothic version of Les Jacobins and boasts a grand 18th-century altar painted by Despax.

Centre Municipal de l'Affiche, de la Carte Postale et de l'Art Graphique
58 Allées Charles de Fitte, t 05 61 59 24 64, St-Cyprien métro; open Mon–Fri 9–12 and 2–6; library open to public by appt; adm

More visual arts, this time in the form of graphics, posters, ads and postcards from the 17th century to the present, are the subject of the changing exhibits at the **Centre Municipal de l'Affiche, de la Carte Postale et de l'Art Graphique**; there's an extensive library of books, films and records, and, most popular of all, French commercials – those that used to be shown in the cinemas – dating from 1904 to 1968, on video cassettes.

Les Abattoirs
76 Allées Charles de Fitte, t 05 34 51 10 60; open Tues–Sun 11–7

Just up the road is **Les Abattoirs**, dedicated to art at its most contemporary, with all the main movements from the second half of the 20th century into the 21st represented. Some of it is quite disturbing stuff, such as Alberto Burri's *Sacco IV* with patched and tattered heavy sacking, holes in places resembling sores. The prize exhibit, displayed on and off throughout the year, was created just outside the timeframe for most of the work: a stage curtain for the play *14 Juillet* by Romain Rolland, painted by Luis Fernandez in 1936 on the request of Pablo Picasso, and copied from the great man's gouache of the corpse of a Minotaur dressed in the costume of a Harlequin. Massive, it mirrors themes in Picasso's other works displayed around the room. There is also a changing programme of temporary exhibitions. You would never guess the building's original purpose as the city's abattoir (of course): it is now large and airy with a sense of space throughout. You can take a turn about the landscaped grounds, which look on to the Garonne.

Le Mirail, Toulouse's Shadow Utopia

In 1993, when Toulouse's *métro* was inaugurated, it was with dire warnings of invasions from Le Mirail, now within a 10-minute ride of the Capitole. Le Mirail is home to the last-off-the-boat in Toulouse: different nationalities living together as part of an experiment in integration yet in the face of high unemployment. It's a far cry from the experiment originally planned for Le Mirail. The housing development also suffered when the AZF chemical factory exploded in 2001, shattering windows and destroying buildings.

Le Mirail ZUP (*zone à urbaniser en priorité*) was envisaged in 1960 as a *Toulouse bis* near the university, a futurist self-contained white-collar utopia for 100,000 people. This, of course, was back in the days when planners believed that architecture could modify behaviour, and they were the great doctors who knew what was good for everyone else. Toulouse's Socialist government chose as its master-builder George Chandalis, who had worked with Le Corbusier on the Cité Radieuse project in Marseille. Chandalis planned a star-shaped city of five separate neighbourhoods of 20,000 inhabitants, each with its own shopping, social and cultural services, with a communal centre in the middle. Cars and pedestrians were to be kept strictly apart, so that children could play without danger: vehicles were banished to vast underground car parks under the large central squares of each neighbourhood. Each apartment was designed to have a view over the square, the ideal centre of urban life, and a view over the gardens at the back. Chandalis meant his 13-storey blocks or 'tripods' to be residential cooperatives, linked one to the other by long concourses (the *coursives*) or suspended streets with shops and other services that people would stroll past daily en route to the centralized lifts.

Two of Chandalis' five neighbourhoods, Bellefontaine and La Reynerie, were built as planned by 1971, when Pierre Baudis became mayor and radically changed the next stage of building to fit into a more traditional idea of a French *faubourg*. No one complained too vehemently; Le Mirail was already going awry. Toulouse's white-collar workers didn't care to be convivial and live in cooperatives, but instead bought bungalows in suburban dreamland, with their own little gardens and gates. Le Mirail's idealistic vision was altered: walls went up in the *coursives* to keep people in their own buildings, and new entrances and elevators have gone up to lower the amount of forced public interaction. In recent years the tenants' frustration with their lot has sometimes spilt over into violence, most recently in spring 2006, alongside riots in other French cities.

Usine C. Ader
10 avenue Georges-Guynemer, 31770 Colomier, **t** *05 34 39 42 00; open Mon–Sat by appt 5 days in advance*

Aérothèque
t *05 61 93 93 57; open Wed 2–5*

On the Outskirts of Toulouse

You see what makes Toulouse tick by watching Airbus build its planes at Colomiers' **Usine Clément Ader**, or taking a trip to see the assembly site of the A380. You can learn about Toulouse's aviation history at the **Aérothèque** on Rue Montmorency.

Cité de l'Espace
Avenue Jean-Gonord off Rocade Est, between Bordeaux and Montpellier autoroute *exit 18,* **t** *08 20 37 72 23, www.cite-espace.com; bus 37 from Joliment métro, or from Place Marengo near train station; open generally 9.30–5/7 exc Sun and hols, but see website for variations; adm*

Then there's the **Cité de l'Espace**, which showcases the city's role as Europe's leader in the space race. It has a life-size model of *Ariane 5*, the *Mir* space station, the Terradome (where you float in orbit and witness the earth's evolution), interactive exhibits, planetariums, simulations, 3D films and more.

Near the airport, **Blagnac** (buses 66 or 70) has the tomb-oratory of 5th-century bishop St Exupère, friend of St Jerome, who once dispersed a besieging army of Vandals by sprinkling them with holy water, and who sold all the goods of his church to buy food for Palestine and Egypt in a famine. When the *Toulousains* proved impious ingrates in spite of his best efforts, Exupère stomped off to his father's farm in the Pyrenees. A Toulouse delegation was sent to bring him back but he said he'd return only if the ox goad in his hand burst into bloom. It did, and back he went; hence the naïve 16th-century frescoes on the walls with inscriptions in Occitan.

Sanctuaire Rural d'Ancely-Purpan
t *05 61 22 31 44; open June and Sept Sat and Sun 2–6, with guided tour at 4; July and Aug Sat and Sun 2–7, with guided tour at 4.30*

Also out this way, at **Purpan**, are the remains of a 1st-century Roman amphitheatre where gladiators fought. It doesn't approach the splendour of Nîmes amphitheatre, but there are enough piles of stones and reconstructed bits and bobs to let your imagination fill in the rest. A guided tour gives access to the remains of Roman baths. Both formed part of a **rural sanctuary** linked to a water cult.

ⓘ Toulouse >
Donjon du Capitole, Rue Lafayette, behind Capitole, **t** *05 61 11 02 22, www.toulouse-tourisme.com and www.toulouse.fr.*

Tourist Information in Toulouse

Ask at the **tourist office** about the **themed tours**, some in English (about €9/hr). If you're around for a while, buy an *En Liberté* card (€10 or €13) with discounts on tours, entrance fees, activities, hotels and eating out.

For information on the whole of the Midi-Pyrénées region, go to (call ahead) the **Comité Régional du Tourisme Midi-Pyrénées**, 54 Bd de l'Embouchure, **t** 05 61 13 55 55, *www.tourisme-midi-pyrenees.com*, or the **Maison Midi-Pyrénées**, 1 Rue Rémusat, near Place Capitole (*Mon–Fri 10–7*).

Central post office: 9 Rue Lafayette, **t** 05 34 45 70 85.

Night pharmacy (*8pm–8am*): 70–76 Allées Jean Jaurès, **t** 05 61 62 38 05.

Doctors on Duty (SOS Médecins de Garde): **t** 05 61 49 66 66 (for instructions about where to go when ill/injured).

Purpan hospital: Rond-Point de Purpan, **t** 05 61 77 22 33 (interpreters available).

Rangueil hospital: Avenue Professeur Jean Poulhes, **t** 05 61 32 25 33.

Markets and Shopping in Toulouse

There are **covered markets** Tues–Sun at Place des Carmes and Les Halles in Bd Victor Hugo. On Tuesday and Saturday mornings Place du Capitole has a lively **organic market**. There is a good **fruit and veg market** (Tues–Sun) along Bd de Strasbourg, starting near Place Jeanne d'Arc. Sunday (and to a lesser extent Saturday) mornings see a huge **fleamarket** around St-Sernin and along the boulevards. For the many other markets, specializing in books, flowers, duck and more, ask at the tourist office.

Toulouse is home to various major **department stores**. Local products are mostly violet-based – scented soaps, eau-de-cologne, and candied-violet *confits*; visit the **violet barge** on the Canal du Midi near the station.

The delightful **Boutique des Saveurs** at 1 Rue Ozenne, **t** 05 61 53 75 21, has fine **preserves and French classics**, and tasting evenings in summer. At No.2, **Maison Pillon**, produces delicious handmade **chocolates**, voted France's best in 1996. But the ultimate taste

Hôtel des Beaux Arts >>

treat is an aniseed or mint **Cachou** pellet, invented by pharmacist Lajaunie at 64 Av de Larrieu and sold all over France in little metal tins.

Betty, 2 Place Victor Hugo, has 200 types of cheese from all over the country, some quite special, such as the Vieux Salers, made in one village in the Cantal. There are also local goats' cheeses and even some Stilton, plus a good selection of southwest wines. The shop also has a stall in Marché Victor Hugo opposite.

The Bookshop, 17 Rue Lakanal, **t** 05 61 22 99 92, has **books in English**.

Sports and Activities in Toulouse

Whatever sport is your bag, you'll find it here; ask at the tourist office.

The **Toulouse Football Club** (TFC, pronounced 'tayfessay') plays in France's first division, but the city's heart lies with its **rugby team**, the Stade (*www.stadetoulousain.fr*), frequent champions of France (and of Europe in 1996, 2003 and 2005). The stadium is at Sept Deniers; you can buy tickets online. Local teams are divided into Rugby à XV and Rugby à XIII (heretical 'Cathar rugby').

Where to Stay in and around Toulouse

Toulouse ✉ 31000

Toulouse has chain hotels galore for business visitors and a few reliable independents in the historic centre. Book early, and check hotel websites for special offers, especially at weekends and in summer.

****__Grand Hôtel de l'Opéra__, 1 Place du Capitole, **t** 05 61 21 82 66, *www.grand-hotel-opera.com* (€€€€€–€€€€). The city's most beautiful hotel, with 50 sumptuous rooms and three suites in an old convent, an indoor pool and a magnificent restaurant (*see* p.448).

***__Holiday Inn__, 13 Place Wilson, **t** 05 61 10 70 70, *www.hotel-capoul.com* (€€€€–€€€). A swish member of the chain, with large, light rooms and an excellent brasserie. Adjoining it, **Le Capoul** is a *hôtel-résidence* with quite chic apartments and studios.

***__Hôtel des Beaux Arts__, 1 Place Pont-Neuf, **t** 05 34 45 42 42, *www.hoteldesbeauxarts.com* (€€€€–€€). An 18th-century *hôtel particulier* with pleasant, cosy, soundproofed rooms overlooking the Garonne.

***__Mermoz__, 50 Rue Matabiau, **t** 05 61 63 04 04, *www.hotel-mermoz.com* (€€€). The best hotel near the station, with delightful air-conditioned rooms overlooking inner courtyards.

***__Brienne__, 20 Bd du Maréchal Leclerc, **t** 05 61 23 60 60, *www.hoteldebrienne.com* (€€). An ultra-modern, good-value choice with well-equipped rooms.

***__Parthénon__, 86 Allées J-Jaurès, **t** 05 61 10 24 00, *www.mercure.com* (€€). A decent *hôtel-résidence* for longer stays.

__Albert Ier__, 8 Rue Rivals, **t 05 61 21 17 91, *www.hotel-albert1.com* (€€). A charming central option with parking.

__Arnaud-Bernard__, 33 Place des Tiercerettes, **t 05 61 21 37 64 (€€). Good rooms in the centre of the lively popular quarter near St-Sernin.

__Castellane__, 17 Rue Castellane, **t 05 61 62 18 82, *www.castellanehotel.com* (€€). Light, spacious rooms on a quiet sidestreet, with private parking (for a fee) and a pleasant breakfast area.

__Hôtel Ours Blanc__, 25 Pl Victor Hugo, **t 05 61 23 14 55, and 2 Rue Victor Hugo, **t** 05 61 21 62 40, *www.hotel-oursblanc.fr* (€€). Sister hotels on opposite sides of the Victor Hugo car park, with small but neat rooms with televisions, soundproofing and air-conditioning.

__Grand Hôtel d'Orléans__, 72 Rue de Bayard, **t 05 61 62 98 47, *www.grand-hotel-orleans.fr* (€€–€). A characterful choice near the station, with interior galleries, a garden and satellite TV.

__Hôtel de France__, 5 Rue d'Austerlitz, **t 05 61 21 88 24, *www.hotel-france-toulouse.com* (€€–€). Traditional rooms and a vaguely funky lounge.

__St-Sernin__, 2 Rue St-Bernard, **t 05 61 21 73 08, *www.hotel-saint-sernin.new.fr* (€€–€). Good rooms with baths, mini-bars and TVs, opposite the basilica.

*__Anatole France__, 46 Place A. France, **t** 05 61 23 19 96 (€). Some of the best low-priced rooms in Toulouse, with showers, near the Capitole.

*__Croix-Baragnon__, 17 Rue Croix-Baragnon, **t** 05 61 52 60 10 (€). Rooms with bath and shower, by St-Etienne.

***Hôtel des Arts**, 1 bis Rue Cantegril, **t** 05 61 23 36 21 (€). Friendly place near lively Place St-Georges, with good rooms with showers but shared WCs.

Foyer des Jeunes Travailleurs, Résidence San Francisco, 92 Route d'Espagne, **t** 05 61 43 23 00, *www.ucjg-monnier.org* (€). A popular youth hostel; book ahead.

Outskirts of Toulouse

*****La Flânerie**, Route de Lacroix-Falgarde, Vieille-Toulouse (✉ 31320), 8km south on D4, **t** 05 61 73 39 12, *www.hotellaflanerie.com* (€€€–€€). A pretty country house where the Tectosages once roamed, with grand views over the Garonne. There's a pool, and tennis and golf nearby. *Closed Sun, Dec, 1 weekend Jan, and 1wk end of Aug.*

****Relais Blanhac (Atrium)**, by airport, **t** 05 61 71 93 93 (€€–€). Motel-like rooms sleeping up to 4, and an acceptable restaurant (€€). Book ahead for Mon–Fri. *Restaurant closed Sat lunch and Sun.*

★ Guest House Joséphine >

★ Michael Sarran >>

Guest House Joséphine, 1 Rue des Ecoles, Villenouvelle (along N113, direction Villefranche-de-Lauragais), **t** 05 34 66 20 13, *http://maison.josephine.free.fr* (€). A sensitively restored 18th-century house run by a welcoming Franco-Irish couple, with airy bedrooms with marble fireplaces, some ideal for those with young kids, a pool and dinner (€€) by request.

Where to Eat in and around Toulouse

Toulouse's restaurant revolution has trickled down from *les grandes tables* to corner bistros. But the city hasn't forgotten its place in the southwest bean belt, and claims to make a cassoulet that walks all over those of rivals Carcassonne and Castelnaudry. To the base recipe (white beans, garlic, herbs, goose fat, salt bacon, fat pork and *confits* of goose or duck), they chuck in a foot or two of their famed sausage (*saucisse de Toulouse*), shoulder of mutton, and perhaps ham. This is sprinkled with breadcrumbs and baked. To aid digestion, locals advise a game of rugby, or a tipple of *eau de noix Benoît Serres*, the local walnut *digestif*, or of armagnac.

The first floor of the **Marché Victor Hugo** (Tues–Sun) has a number of cheaper places popular for lunch.

Note that many of the city's restaurants close for all of August.

Toulouse ✉ 31000

Cosi Fan Tutte, 8 Rue Mage, **t** 05 61 53 07 24 (€€€€–€€€). Top Italian food in an operatic setting. *Closed Sun and Mon.*

Les Jardins de l'Opéra, Grand Hôtel de l'Opéra (*see* p.447), **t** 05 61 23 07 76 (€€€€–€€€). Toulouse's finest gastronomic experience, and one of the southwest's most beautiful restaurants. The food matches the hushed, sophicated setting – it includes aromatic mushroom dishes, seafood cooked to perfection, flavourful regional specialities, and delicate desserts. *Closed Sun and Mon, Aug and 1st wk Jan.*

Le Pastel, 237 Rue de St-Simon, Mirail, **t** 05 62 87 84 30 (€€€€–€€€). Some of the finest, most imaginative gourmet food in Toulouse, at some of the kindest prices. Book at lunchtimes. *Closed Sun, Mon, and 2wks in Aug.*

Michel Sarran, 21 Bd Armand Duportal, **t** 05 61 12 32 32 (€€€€–€€€). A superb synthesis of sun-soaked southwest and Provençal cuisines served in an elegant townhouse. *Closed Wed lunch, Sat, Sun, Aug and Christmas.*

La Belle Chaurienne, Allée de Barcelone, Canal de Brienne, **t** 05 61 21 23 85 (€€€–€€) . A barge (*péniche*) in a pretty canal location, serving good regional dishes. *Closed Sat lunch, Sun, Mon lunch and Aug.*

Le Bon Vivre, 15 Place Wilson, **t** 05 61 23 07 17 (€€€–€€). A place popular for its authentic southwestern cooking.

Le Bouchon Lyonnais, 13 Rue de l'Industrie (off Rue de la Colombette), **t** 05 61 62 97 43 (€€€–€€). Delicious dishes from Provence and Lyon, served in an Art Deco setting. *Closed Sat lunch and Sun.*

Les Caves de la Maréchale, 3 Rue Jules Chalande, **t** 05 61 23 89 88 (€€€–€€). Sophisticated regional dishes served in the vast cellar of a 13th-century priory off Rue St-Rome. *Closed Sat lunch, Sun, and Mon lunch.*

Chez Emile, 13 Place St-Georges, **t** 05 61 21 05 56 (€€€–€€). An institution, serving some of the finest seafood in

Toulouse, duck *confit* and other meats. *Closed Sun and Mon lunch, plus Mon eve out of high season.*

Le Colombier >

Le Colombier, 14 Rue Bayard, **t** 05 61 62 40 05 (€€€–€€). Some of the finest cassoulet in Toulouse (the owner's recipe is safeguarded by his lawyer) and other southwest treats. *Closed Sat lunch, Sun, Aug and Christmas.*

Les Ombrages, 48 bis Route de St-Simon, **t** 05 61 07 61 28 (€€€–€€). Fresh, sunny cuisine: try minced duck with berries and foie gras. It's a bit hard to find – take a taxi. *Closed Sun and Mon eves and 2wks Aug.*

Sept Place St-Sernin, 7 Place St-Sernin, **t** 05 62 30 05 30 (€€€–€€). A large ivy-covered house opposite the cathedral, with delightful menus featuring the likes of foie gras with figs and herb salad. *Closed Sat lunch and Sun.*

La Bascule, 14 Av Maurice-Hauriou, **t** 05 61 52 09 51 (€€). A popular brasserie a short way from the centre, with good seafood, traditional meat and game, and a few adventurous offerings. *Closed Sat lunch, Sun and Mon.*

Les Beaux-Arts-Flo, 1 Quai Daurade, **t** 05 61 21 12 12 (€€). A handsome *belle époque* brasserie on the Garonne, offering well-prepared favourites.

Le Bibent, 5 Place du Capitole, **t** 05 61 23 89 03 (€€). One of the most beautiful brasseries in Toulouse, with an excellent shellfish selection and southwest favourites.

Grand Café de l'Opéra, 1 Place du Capitole, **t** 05 61 21 37 03 (€€). A cosy, elegant brasserie with excellent classics, with the emphasis on seafood. *Closed Sun and Aug.*

La Grillothèque, 16 Bd Strasbourg, **t** 05 61 62 87 31 (€€). Great grilled meat, including an excellent beef with *sauce maison* (gravy to you and me).

Benjamin, 7 Rue des Gestes (off Rue St-Rome), **t** 05 61 22 92 66 (€€–€). The likes of fennel and courgette terrine and steak with *cèpes*, in the heart of old Toulouse at friendly prices.

New Delhi, 9 Rue de l'Industrie, **t** 05 61 62 20 64 (€€–€). Simple, authentic Indian food (which you can also enjoy in the nearby Frog and Rosbif English pub). *Closed Sun and Aug.*

La Tantina de Burgos, 27 Avenue de la Garonnette, **t** 05 61 55 59 29 (€€–€). A zesty tapas bar/restaurant with tasty *zarzuela* (Catalan fish soup) and more. *Closed Sun and Mon.*

A la Truffe du Quercy, 17 Rue Croix-Baragnon, **t** 05 61 53 34 24 (€€–€). Southwestern home cooking and some Spanish dishes too. *Closed Sun, Mon eve and Aug.*

Le Gout en Train, 5 bis Rue Caussette, **t** 05 62 30 08 08 (€). A salad stop featuring regional specialities plus a few hot dishes.

Outskirts of Toulouse

L'Amphitryon, Chemin de Gramont, ✉ 31770 Colomiers (exit 3 off *rocade*), **t** 05 61 15 55 55 (€€€€–€€€). Delicate southwestern cuisine, including lamb fillet with mint and citrus fruits, served in a leafy park a short drive out of the city. Desserts are sumptuous.

O Saveurs, 8 Place Ormeaux, Rouffiac Tolosan, on N88 to Albi, **t** 05 34 27 10 11 (€€€€–€€). A charming restaurant in a delightful, calm square, with very light and fish and meat dishes such as roast scampi with seasonal fruits and mango vinaigrette. *Closed Sat lunch, Sun eve, Mon and 3wks Aug.*

Au Pois Gourmand, 3 Rue E Heybrard, Casselardit (just off *rocade*), **t** 05 34 36 42 00 (€€€€–€€). A handsome old manor with wooden galleries, serving refined, original cuisine such as red mullet grilled in fig leaves with thyme and lemon. *Closed Sat and Mon lunch, Sun, and several wks Aug.*

Le Cantou, 98 Rue Vélasquez, St-Martin-du-Touch, **t** 05 61 49 20 21 (€€€). A lovely ivy-covered house in a beautiful garden in the suburbs, offering some of Toulouse's best regional cuisine and a huge southwest wine list. *Closed Sat, Sun, and 2wks in Aug.*

Le Manoir du Petit Prince, Château de Vincasses, Route de Seysses, ✉ 31120 Portet sur Garonne, **t** 05 61 31 14 14 (€€€–€€). A lovely château serving neglected regional fare such as roast beef with thyme and mushroom cream. *Closed Sat lunch, Sun eve and Mon.*

Les 3 Dynasties, 21 Av du Compans, Blagnac, **t** 05 61 15 70 00 (€€–€). Excellent Thai/Cambodian food and friendly service in a pretty *maison de maître* near the airport. It's often packed out with Airbus employees, so book. *Closed Mon.*

Cafés, Bars and Wine Bars in Toulouse

Gay bars are clustered round Rue de la Colombette, east of Place Wilson.

L'Ancienne Belgique, 16 Rue de la Trinité. A wide selection of beer.

Bar Florida, Place du Capitole, **t** 05 61 23 94 61. *The* place in central Toulouse to sit and watch the world go by on a warm day, attracting tourists but plenty of *Toulousains* too, with an Art Deco interior. Choose from local wine, champagne, cocktails, spirits, beer and coffee. It's open daily from first thing in the morning to the early hours.

Dubliners, 46 Av Marcel Langer, **t** 05 61 25 91 13. Toulouse's chief Irish pub, south of the centre and very popular with the French. There's live music thrice-weekly.

Le Mangevins, 46 Rue Pharaon, **t** 05 61 52 79 16. Wines accompanied by fancy snacks and local menus.

Mon Caf', Place du Capitole, **t** 05 61 23 14 07. A discreet venue where locals lounge on big maroon seats to enjoy beers, spirits, hot drinks and snacks.

Le Père Louis, 45 Place des Tourneurs, between Rue Peyras and Rue de Metz, **t** 05 61 21 33 45. A fiercely traditional bar (it's a historical landmark) and magnet for *quinquina* drinkers.

Texxas Café, 26 Rue Castellane, **t** 05 61 99 14 15. Toulouse's oldest Tex Mex bar.

Entertainment and Nightlife in Toulouse

Thanks to Toulouse's students, its Spanish blood and the do-re-mi provided by its hi-tech jobs, there's plenty to do. There's a weekly listings mag *Flash*, available at newsstands, or pick up the free *Toulouse Cultures*, published by the *mairie*.

Since the Second World War, the *Toulousains* have discovered **classical music** in a big way, with the *gonfalon* held high by the **Orchestre Nationale du Capitole** (*www.onct.mairie-toulouse.fr*), one of France's top symphony orchestras, who often play in the acoustically excellent **Halle aux Grains**, Place Dupuy (just east of St-Etienne cathedral), **t** 05 61 63 13 13. In July and August, the city **music festival** hosts performances by the fine **Orchestre National de Chambre de Toulouse** (*www.orchestredechambredetoulouse.fr*). In September, **Les Jacobins cloister** hosts the **Festival International Piano aux Jacobins, t** 05 61 22 40 05, *www.pianojacobins.com* (early booking advised). There is also a prestigious **organ festival**, Toulouse Les Orgues, **t** 05 61 22 20 44, in October, and from October to June the **Théâtre du Capitole**, Place du Capitole, **t** 05 61 22 31 31, hosts an **opera and dance** season.

Concerts and exhibitions of dance are also given in the renovated auditorium of the church of **St-Pierre-des-Cuisines, t** 05 61 22 31 44.

The **Sorano Théâtre National**, 35 Allées Jules-Guesde, **t** 05 34 31 67 16, puts on some of the finest **plays** in Toulouse. For modern French **poetry, *chanson* and theatre**, try **La Cave Poésie**, 71 Rue du Taur, **t** 05 61 23 62 00.

Zénith, Av Raymond Badiou, **t** 05 62 74 49 49, is one of France's largest performance venues; events range from displays of Basque sport to pop concerts, ice-skating competitions to musicals. The nearest *métro* stations are Patte d'Oie and Arènes.

Toulouse goes for **cinema** in a big way as well; the **Cinémathèque**, 69 Rue du Taur, **t** 05 62 30 30 10, is the second biggest in France, and often shows films in V.O. (*version originale* – their original language), as does **ABC**, 13 Rue St-Bernard, **t** 05 61 29 81 00.

Toulouse stays up later than other cities in this book, but places open and close like flowers in the night, so check posters and flyers for current venues. Popular **music bars** include:

L'Aposia, 9 bis Rue Jean Rodier, **t** 05 05 71 84 11. A huge club, playing groove, techno, disco and more to a young mixed crowd.

Chez Tonton, 16 Place St-Pierre, **t** 05 61 21 89 54. A trendy *pastis* hangout.

El Barrio Latino, 144 Av de Muret, **t** 05 61 59 00 58. A good Latin venue with a restaurant. *Closed Mon–Wed*.

Havana Café, Av des Crêtes, Ramonville, **t** 05 62 88 34 94. A happening place with regular live music.

La Maison, 9 Rue G. Péri, **t** 05 61 62 87 22. Fun cocktails and a homely ambiance.

Puerto Habana, 12 Port St-Etienne, **t** 05 61 54 45 61. Distinctly lively nights out *à la cubana*, with live salsa.

Glossary

abbaye abbey
arrondissement city district
auberge inn
aven natural well
bastide fortified new town founded in the Middle Ages, usually rectangular, with a grid of streets and an arcaded central square, or sometimes circular in plan
cardo a north–south street in a Roman *castrum*; a street running east–west was called a *decumanus*
caryatid column or pillar carved in the figure of a woman
castelnau village, often planned, that grew up around a *seigneur*'s castle (often the parish church will be on the edge of a *castelnau* instead of at its centre)
castrum rectangular Roman army camp, which often grew into a permanent settlement (like Bordeaux and many others); in Quercy, the word was often used in the same sense as *castelnau*
cave cellar
chai wine and spirit storehouse
château mansion, manor house or castle. A strictly military castle is a *château fort*
château des Anglais cave fortress along the cliffs of the Lot or Dordogne, first built by the English in the Hundred Years' War
chemin path
chevet eastern end of a church, including the apse
cingles oxbow bends in a meandering river, such as the Dordogne and Lot
clocher-mur west front of a church that rises high above the roofline for its entire width to make a belltower; a common feature in medieval architecture in many parts of southwest France
cloître cloister
commanderie local headquarters of a knightly order (such as the Templars or Knights Hospitallers), usually to look after the order's lands and properties in an area
commune in the Middle Ages, the government of a free town or city; today, the smallest unit of local government, encompassing a town or village
cornière arched portico surrounding the main square of a *bastide*
cour d'honneur principal courtyard of a palace or large *hôtel*
couvent convent or monastery
Croquant 'teeth grinder', a peasant guerrilla, especially from the Dordogne, in the anti-French revolts of the 17th and 18th centuries
écluse canal lock
église church
enfeu niche in a church's exterior or interior wall for a tomb
gare station
gariotte small dry-stone building with a corbelled dome or vault for a roof; many were built as shepherds' huts, others as refuges for villagers in plague times; also called *bories*, *caselles* or *cabanes* in different parts of the Midi
gentilhommière small country château, especially popular in Périgord in the 18th century
gisant sculpted prone effigy on a tomb
halle covered market
hôtel originally the town residence of the nobility; by the 18th century the word became more generally used for any large, private residence
lauze heavy grey stones used for making steep roofs in the Dordogne, now mostly replaced by machine-made tiles; the rare *lauze* roofer these days manages to do about a square metre a day
lavoir communal fountain, usually covered, for the washing of clothes

mairie town hall
marché market
mas (from Latin *mansio*) large farmhouse, or manor, or hamlet
mascaron ornamental mask, usually carved on the keystone of an arch
modillon stone projecting from the cornice of a church, carved with a face or an animal figure
Mozarabic elements in art and architecture derived from Muslim Spain in the Middle Ages
oppidum Roman town
Parlement French juridical body, with members appointed by the king; by the late *ancien régime*, *parlements* exercised a great deal of influence over political affairs
pays region, or village
pech hill
plan d'eau artificial lake
Ponts et Chaussées France's national public works office
puy hill
retable carved or painted altarpiece, often consisting of a number of scenes or sculptural ensembles
rez-de-chaussée (RC) ground floor (US first)
routiers English mercenaries in the Hundred Years' War.
sauveterre village or town founded under a guarantee against violence in wartime, agreed to by the Church and local barons; *sauveterres*' boundaries are often marked by crosses on all the roads leading in to them
soleiho top storey of a Quercy townhouse with an open loggia, especially in Figeac and Cahors
tour tower
transi in a tomb, a relief of the decomposing cadaver
trumeau column between twin doors of a church portal, often carved with reliefs
tympanum semicircular panel over a church door; often the occasion for the most ambitious ensembles of medieval sculpture

Language

Even if your French is brilliant, the soupy twang that grows more pronounced the further south you travel may throw you. In particular, note that any word with a nasal *in* or *en* becomes something like *aing* (*vaing* for *vin*).

What remains the same as anywhere else in France is the level of politeness expected: use *monsieur*, *madame* or *mademoiselle* when speaking to everyone (and never *garçon* in restaurants!), from your first *bonjour* to your last *au revoir*.

See pp. xxx–xxx for a menu vocabulary.

Pronunciation

Vowels

a, à, â between *a* in 'bat' and 'part'
é, er, ez at end of word as *a* in 'plate' but a bit shorter
e, è, ê as *e* in bet
e at end of word not pronounced
e at end of syllable or in one-syllable word pronounced weakly, like *er* in 'mother'
i as *ee* in 'bee'
o as *o* in 'pot'
ô as *o* in 'go'
u, û between *oo* in 'boot' and *ee* in 'bee'

Vowel Combinations

ai as *a* in 'plate'
aî as *e* in 'bet'
ail as *i* in 'kite'
au, eau as *o* in 'go'
ei as *e* in 'bet'
eu, œu as *er* in 'mother'
oi between *wa* in 'swam' and *u* in 'swum'
oy as 'why'
ui as *wee* in 'twee'

Nasal Vowels

Vowels followed by an n or an m have a nasel sound.

an, en as *o* in 'pot' + nasal sound
ain, ein, as *a* in 'bat' + nasal sound
on as *aw* in 'paw' + nasal sound
un as *u* in 'nut' + nasal sound

Consonants

Many French consonants are pronounced as in English, but there are some exceptions:
c followed by e, i or y and ç as *s* in 'sit'
c followed by a, o or u as *c* in 'cat'
g followed by e, i or y as *s* in 'pleasure'
g followed by a, o or u as *g* in 'good'
gn as *ni* in 'opinion'
j as *s* in 'pleasure'
ll as *y* in 'yes'
qu as *k* in 'kite'
s between vowels as *z* in 'zebra'
s otherwise as *s* in 'sit'
w except in English words as *v* in 'vest'
x at end of word as *s* in 'sit'
x otherwise as *x* in 'six'

Stress

The stress usually falls on the last syllable except when the word ends with an unaccented **e**.

Useful Words and Phrases

General

hello *bonjour*
good evening *bonsoir*
good night *bonne nuit*
goodbye *au revoir*
please *s'il vous plaît*
thank you (very much) *merci (beaucoup)*
yes *oui*
no *non*
good *bon (bonne)*
bad *mauvais(e)*
excuse me *pardon, excusez-moi*

Can you help me? *Pourriez-vous m'aider?*
My name is... *Je m'appelle...*
What is your name? *Comment t'appelles-tu?* (informal), *Comment vous appelez-vous?* (formal)
How are you? *Comment allez-vous?*
Fine *Ça va bien*
I don't understand *Je ne comprends pas*
I don't know *Je ne sais pas*
Speak more slowly *Pourriez-vous parler plus lentement?*
How do you say ... in French? *Comment dit-on ... en français?*
Help! *Au secours!*

Where is (the railway station)? *Où se trouve (la gare)?*
Is it far? *C'est loin?*
left *à gauche*
right *à droite*
straight on *tout droit*

entrance *l'entrée*
exit *la sortie*
open *ouvert*
closed *fermé*
WC *les toilettes*
men *hommes*
ladies *dames* or *femmes*

doctor *le médecin*
hospital *un hôpital*
emergency room *la salle des urgences*
police station *le commissariat de police*
tourist information office *l'office de tourisme*

How much is it? *C'est combien?*
Do you have...? *Est-ce que vous avez...?*
It's too expensive *C'est trop cher*
bank *une banque*
money *l'argent*
change *la monnaie*
traveller's cheque *un chèque de voyage*
post office *la poste*
stamp *un timbre*
postcard *une carte postale*
public phone *une cabine téléphonique*
shop *un magasin*
central food market *les halles*
tobacconist *un tabac*
pharmacy *la pharmacie*
aspirin *l'aspirine*
condoms *les préservatifs*
insect repellent *l'anti-insecte*
sun cream *la crème solaire*
tampons *les tampons hygiéniques*

Transport

airport *l'aéroport*
aeroplane *l'avion*
go on foot *aller à pied*
bicycle *la bicyclette/le vélo*
mountainbike *vélo tout terrain, VTT*
bus *l'autobus*
bus stop *l'arrêt d'autobus*
coach station *la gare routière*
railway station *la gare*
train *le train*
platform *le quai*
date-stamp machine *le composteur*
timetable *l'horaire*
left-luggage locker *une consigne automatique*
car *la voiture*
taxi *le taxi*
subway *le métro*
ticket office *le guichet*
ticket *le billet*
single to... *un aller* (or *aller simple*) *pour...*
return to... *un aller et retour pour...*
What time does the ... leave? *A quelle heure part...?*
delayed *en retard*
on time *à l'heure*

Accommodation

single room *une chambre pour une personne*
twin room *une chambre à deux lits*
double room *une chambre pour deux personnes*
bed *un lit*
blanket *une couverture*
cot (child's bed) *lit d'enfant*
pillow *un oreiller*
soap *du savon*
towel *une serviette*
booking *une réservation*
I would like to book a room *Je voudrais réserver une chambre*

Months

January *janvier*
February *février*
March *mars*
April *avril*
May *mai*
June *juin*
July *juillet*
August *août*
September *septembre*
October *octobre*
November *novembre*
December *décembre*

Days

Monday *lundi*
Tuesday *mardi*
Wednesday *mercredi*
Thursday *jeudi*
Friday *vendredi*
Saturday *samedi*
Sunday *dimanche*

Time

What time is it? *Quelle heure est-il?*
month *un mois*
week *une semaine*
day *un jour/une journée*
morning *le matin*
afternoon *l'après-midi*
evening *le soir*
night *la nuit*
today *aujourd'hui*
yesterday *hier*
tomorrow *demain*
day before yesterday *avant-hier*
day after tomorrow *après-demain*

Numbers

one *un*
two *deux*
three *trois*
four *quatre*
five *cinq*
six *six*
seven *sept*
eight *huit*
nine *neuf*
ten *dix*
eleven *onze*
twelve *douze*
thirteen *treize*
fourteen *quatorze*
fifteen *quinze*
sixteen *seize*
seventeen *dix-sept*
eighteen *dix-huit*
nineteen *dix-neuf*
twenty *vingt*
twenty-one *vingt et un*
twenty-two *vingt-deux*
thirty *trente*
forty *quarante*
fifty *cinquante*
sixty *soixante*
seventy *soixante-dix*
seventy-one *soixante-onze*
eighty *quatre-vingts*
eighty-one *quatre-vingt-un*
ninety *quatre-vingt-dix*
hundred *cent*
two hundred *deux cents*
thousand *mille*

Index

Main page references are in **bold**. Page references to maps are in *italics*.

Abadie, Paul 43, 100
Abri du Cap Blanc 128
Abri du Moustier 124
Abri Pataud 127
Abri des Poissons 128–9
accommodation 67–70
see also under individual places
Ader, Clément 428
Agen 345–6, **364–6**, 367–8
Agen prunes 358–9
Aiguille de Lissac 300
Aiguille du Pressoir 300
Aiguillon **360**, 361, 375
air travel 62–3, 64–5
Albas **330**, 331
Albigensian crusade 24, 355, 403, 424–4, 426
Allemans 106
Allemans-du-Dropt 381
L'Amélie-sur-Mer 270
Andernos-les-Bains **281**, 282, 283–4
Anglars 293
Anglars-Juillac 331
Angoulême 79
Animalier de Gramat 290
Antonne-de-Trigonant 93
Aquarium du Périgord Noir 131
Aquitaine, duchy of 23
Aquitanii people 21
Arcachon **276–7**, 282, 283, 284
Arcambal 310
Archambault, count of Périgord 117–18
architecture 41–4
Arcins-en-Médoc 268
Ardennes, Château 255
Arès **281**, 284
Argentat **136**, 140
Armagnac 372
Arsac 261
Assier **294–5**, 296
Astaffort **367**, 368, 369
Atur 103
Aubas 116
Auberoche 91
Aubeterre-sur-Dronne 42, 107–8
Aubrade, Château 243
Aubusson tapestries 138
Audenge 281
Aujols 312
Ausone, Château 50
Ausonius, Decimus Magnus 225
Autoire 139
Auvillar **412**, 416
Aveyron Valley 388–93
Aynac 293

Bach 312
Baker, Josephine 173
Baleyssagues 383
banks 74
Bannes, Château 178
Bara-Bahau caves 130
Barbaste **373–4**, 375
Barbe, Château 204
Bardigues 416
Barsac 251–3
Bassin d'Arcachon 255, 269, **275–84**, *275*
bastides 25, *348*, 349, 361–2
Bastor-Lamontagne, Château 254
Bazas **257–8**, 259–60
bear cults 36–8, 119, 305
Beaulieu 136
Beaulieu-en-Rouergue 389–90
Beaumont-de-Lomagne **415**, 416
Beaumont-du-Périgord **178**, 179
Beauregard 312
Beauregard-Ducasse, Château 255
Beauville **362**, 363
bed and breakfast 68
beer 49
Bélaye 330–1
Belin-Béliet 255, **280–1**
Belleperche 414–15
Bellevue caves 304
Bellevue-la-Forêt, Château 414
Belloc, Château 239
Belmontet 325
Belvès **175–6**, 179
Belvèze 354
Berbiguières 175
Bergerac **183–6**, **184**, 189
west of *190*, 190–3
wine 50, 187–8
Bernard, Roger 96, 117
Bernifal caves 128
Bertran de Born **33–5**, 89, 90, 117, 144
Besse 167–8
Beychevelle, Château 264
Beynac-et-Cazenac **172–3**, 174–5
bicycles 66–7, 75
Biganos **281**, 283
Biron, Château 350–1
Blaignan 268
Blars 292
Blasimon 242–3
Blaye 205–6
Bommes 253
Bonaguil, Château 340, **347**
Bonnet, Château 243
Bonnette Valley **388–90**, 393–4
Bordeaux **207–36**, *208–9*
Base Sous-Marine 231
Basilique St-Seurin 224–5
Bordeaux Monumental 226
Bourse du Travail 220
Cap Sciences 231
Cathédrale St-André 220–1
Centre André-Malraux 218
Centre National Jean Moulin 221
Chartrons 230–1
Cité Frugès 232
Cité Mondiale du Vin 230
Colonnes Rostrales 229
Croiseur Colbert 231
eating out 235–6
entertainment and nightlife 236
Entrepôt Lainé 230
Esplanade des Quinconces 228–9
Galerie des Beaux-Arts 223
getting around 211
getting to 211
Golden Triangle 226–8
Grand Théâtre 227–8
Grande Cloche 219
Grande Façade project 225
history 210–17, 241
Jardin Botanique 231
Jardin Public 229
Loi Malraux 216
Maison des Bordeaux et Bordeaux Supérieur 241
Maison des Vins de Bordeaux 228
Marché des Grands-Hommes 227
Monument aux Girondins 228
museums
d'Aquitaine **219–20**, 242
d'Art Contemporain 230–1

Bordeaux (*cont'd*)
museums (*cont'd*)
des Arts Décoratifs 223
des Beaux-Arts 221–3
des Chartrons 231
Domaine de la Grave 241
des Douanes 226
Goupil 220
d'Histoire Naturelle 229
Vinorama 231
Notre-Dame 227
Nouveau Quartier Mériadeck 223
Palais de la Bourse 226
Palais Gallien 229
Palais Rohan 221–2
Pessec 232
Planète Bordeaux 241
Pont de Pierre 219
Quartier du Lac 231
Quartier St-Pierre 225–6
Right Bank 231
Ste-Croix 218
St-Eloi 219
St-Michel 218–19
shopping 233
Site Paléochrétien 225
slave trade 214, 215
sports and activities 233–4
Théâtre National de Bordeaux en Aquitaine 218
Tour Pey-Berland 221
tourist information 233
Village des Antiquaries 231
where to stay 234–5
wine 50, 217, 228, 241
Bories, Château des 92, 92
Bosc caves 391
Boschaud 85
Boudeilles 85–6
Bouilh, Château 203
Bouillac 415
Bourdeilles, Château 85–6
Bourdelle, Antoine 398–9, 400, 402
Bourg-du-Bost 106
Bourg-sur-Gironde **204**, 206
Bourg-des-Maisons 106
Bourg-de-Visa **362**, 363
Bouriane *326*, 335–42
Bourideys 256
Boussac 306
Bouziès **310**, 311
Bouziès-Bas 310
Branda, Château 202
Brantôme **83–5**, 86–7
Brassac, Château 362
Brengues 303
Bretenoux **137**, 140
Breuil, Henri 39
Brion 267
Brousses 394
Brugnac 359
Bruniquel **392**, 394
Budos, Château 253
buses and coaches 64, 66
Bussière-Badil 82
Butte de Cazevert, Château 243
Buzet-sur-Baïse **375**, 378

Cabanac 333
Cabouy 147
Cabrerets **304**, 306
Cadillac **245–6**, 249–50
Cadouin 175, **176–7**, 179
cafés 49
Cagots 41
Cahors 306, **313–23**, *314*, 326
Caillac **327**, 331
Caïx **327**, 331
Cajarc **307–8**, 311
Calès 143
Calon-Ségur, Château 266
Cambes 245
Cambes, Château 204
Camboulit 302
Campagne **130**, 131
camping 69
Canal de Brienne 437
Canal Latéral Garonne 375
Canal du Midi 375, 427, 430, 437
Caniac-du-Causse 292
canoeing 75
Canon-Fronsac, wine 201
Cap Ferret 281–2
Capdenac-le-Haut 300–1, 306
car travel 64, 66
Carcans-Maubuisson 273
Cardaillac **295**, 296
Carennac **148–50**, 152–3
Carlucet 143
Carlux 157
Carolingian dynasty 23
Carsac 158
Cas, Château 391
Cascade de la Cogne 308
Casseneuil **358**, 360
Castelfranc 330
Casteljaloux **377**, 378
Castelmoron d'Albret 243
Castelmoron-sur-Lot 359
Castelnau, Château 136–7
Castelnau-de-Médoc 268
Castelnau-Montratier 324–5
Castelnaud, Château 173
Castelnaud-la-Chapelle **173–4**, 175
Castelsagrat 362
Castelsarrasin **413–15**, 416
Castillon-la-Bataille **190**, 191, 192, 193
Castillonnès **349**, 352
Cathars 24, 355, 403, 426, 427
Catus 335
Caudecoste 366
Caussade **393**, 394
Causse de Gramat 288–96, *289*
Causse de Limogne 312
Cavagnac 152
cave art 38–9, **118–19**, 121
cave-churches 42
Caylus 388, **389**, 393
Cayrou, Château 329
Cazals **339**, 341
Cazaux, lake 278
Cazeneuve, Château 256
Cazes-Mondenard 410–11
Cèdre, Château 329
Ceint d'Eau, Château 302
Célé Valley 302–6
Cénevières, Château 308
Centre d'Art Préhistorique du Thot 121
Centre de Cynophilie 290
Centre François Mauriac 247
Centre Hélio-marin 272
Cercles 106
Chaban-Delmas, Jacques 216
Chai de Moncalou 167
Chambert, Château 329
Champollion, Jean François 299
Champs Romain 83
Chancelade **102**, 103
Chandalis, Georges 445
Chantegrive, Château 255
Charlemagne 23, 38, 422–3, 427
Chasse-Spleen, Château 263
Chaudron Magique 359
Chavagnac 115
Chemin de Fer de Guitres 200–1
Cherval 106
Cherveix-Cubas 90, 92–3
Chourgnac d'Ans 91
Christ's Turban **176**, 177
Cieurac 312
Circuit Eco-Archéologique du Camp de César 176
Cirque de Montvalent 152
Clairac **359–60**, 361
Claouey 281
Clarke, Château 264
Clement V, Pope 212–13, 255–7, 414
Clermont 336
Clermont-Dessous 363
climate 58
Climens, Château 253
Cloître des Cordeliers (St-Emilion) 195–6
Cloître des Récollets (Bergerac) **185–6**, 187
Clos de Gamot 329
Clos Triguedina 329
Clos d'Un Jour 329
coaches and buses 64, 66
Cocumont 377
Colayrac-St-Cirq 367
Collégiale St-Martin (Montpezat-de-Quercy) 323–4

Coly 121
Combarelles caves 39, 128
Commarque, Château 128
Concorès 336
Condat-sur-Vézère **116**, 120
confits 40, 47
consulates 60
Corn 302
Cos d'Estournel, Château 266
Côte d'Argent 269–74
Côteaux-de-Glanes 137
Côteaux-de-Quercy 389
Côtes-de-Blaye 204
Côtes-de-Bourg 204
Côtes-de-Brulhois 367
Côtes-de-Duras 50, **382**
Côtes-de-Frontonnais 414
Côtes-du-Marmandais 379
Côtes-de-Quercy 50
Cougnac caves 338
Cougnaguet, Moulin de 143
Coulaures 89–90
Courpiac 245
Court-les-Muts, Château 187
Coutellerie Nontronnaise 81
Coutet, Château 253
Coutras 200
Coux-et-Bigaroque 179
Couze-et-St-Front 181
Cras 292
Crayssac 327
credit cards 61
Créon **239–40**, 244
Creysse **152**, 153, 181–2
crime 73
Cro-Magnon man 20, 38, **115**, 126
Croquants 27–8, 97, 250
Cubzac-les-Ponts 203
Curzorn 347
Cussac 264
customs 60
Cuzals 304
cycling 66–7, 75

Daglan 167
D'Albret family 26, 370, 374
Damazan 375
Daniel, Arnaut 105
Daumesnil, General Pierre **99**, 101
Dépée 272
Désert de la Braunhie 292
Diable, Château 304
disabled travellers 60–1
Distillerie la Salamandre 165
Doissant 176
Doisy, Château 253
Domaine de Candi 414
Domaine de Chantelle 328
Domaine de Durand 383
Domaine Le Garinet 329
Domaine de Paillas 329
Domaine de Ribonnet 414
Domaine les Riquets 383
Domme 117, **165–7**, 168
Donjon de Piégut 82
Donzac 413
Dordogne Quercynois *134–5*, **136–41**
Douelle **327**, 331
Douzains 349
drink *see* food and drink; wine
Dronne, river 104
drugs 73
Ducru-Beaucaillou, Château 265
Dune du Pilat 278
Dunes 366
Durance 374
Duras, Château (Gironde) 243
Duras, Château
(Lot-et-Garonne) 382–3
Duras (Gironde) 243
Duras (Lot-et-Garonne)
382–3, 383, 384
Duravel **332–3**, 334

Echourgnac 110
Eleanor of Aquitaine
24, 212, 280–1, 328, 412
electricity 73
embassies 60
emergencies 61, 73
Entre-Deux-Mers **239–45**, *240*
l'Ermitage caves 197
Escamps 312
Esclottes 383
Espagnac-Ste-Eulalie 303
Espédaillac 292
Espère 327
Estillac 367
Etang de Cousseau 273
Etron de Garguantua 290
European Health Insurance Card
(EHIC) 61
Eurotunnel 64
Excideuil **89**, 92
Eymet 381

Fallières, Armand 372
Fanlac 122
farms, camping on 69
Fauroux 362
Faye, Château 116
Fénelon, Château 157
Fénelon, François 150
Féneyrols 394
Ferme de Découverte des
Causses du Quercy 147
Ferme Equestre de la Mouthe 188
Ferme aux Oiseaux 201
Ferme du Parcot 110
Ferme de Siran 140
Ferme de la Vielcroze 174
ferme-auberges 46, 47, 52, 68
Fermeraie du Jougla 354
ferries 64
festivals 58–9
Figeac 293, **297–300**, 301–2
Filhot, Château 253
First World War 29
fishing 75
Flaugnac 325
foie gras 40–1, 46
Fongrave 358
Font-de-Gaume 39, **127–8**
Fontet 249
Fontirou caves 356
food and drink 45–9
  breakfast 49, 68
  cassoulet 47, 448
  cèpes 48
  confits 40, 47
  desserts 47–8
  drinks 49 *see also* wine
  ferme-auberges 46, 47, 52
  foie gras 40–1, 46, 362
  lampreys 48, 217
  markets 35–6, 48–9
  menu reader 52–6
  oysters 48, **279**
  picnic food and snacks 48–9
  prunes 358–9
  restaurants 52, 73
    see also under individual places
  truffles 46, **92**, 312
  vegetarians 52
footpaths 67
Fôret d-Agre 415
Forêt de la Double 109–10
Fôret des Ecureuils 165
Forêt des Singes 146
Fort Médoc 264
Fort Troglodytique 171
Frayssinet-le-Gélat **339–40**, 341
Frédignac, Château 204
French Revolution **28–9**, 97,
214–15, 223–4, 397
Frespech 362
Fronsac 202
Fronton 416
Fumel **346**, 348, 353

Galiot de Genouillac 294–5, 308
Galla Placidia 422
Gambetta, Léon 317
Garonne Valley 375–8
Gaul 21–2
Gauriac 205
Gavaudun **352**, 353
Gayard, Raymond 434
Génis 90
Gensac 192
Gironde **237–84**, *238*
  Estuary 261, 262
Girondists 28
Giscours, Château 261
Gisement Laugerie Basse 129
Gisement Laugerie Haute 129

Gisement du Regourdou 119
gîtes **68–9**
gîtes d'étape 69
Glanes 137
Gluges **152**, 153
golf 75
Golfech nuclear plant 413
Gontaud-de-Nogaret 376
Gouffre de Cabouy 147
Gouffre de Lantouy 308
Gouffre de Padirac
136, **141–3**, 147, 289
Gouffre de Planegrèze 292
Gouffre de Proumeyssac 130–1
Gouffre de St-Saveur 147
Gouges, Olympe de 397
Goujounac **340**, 341–2
Gourdon **336–8**, 341
Goutz (Goux) 377
Goya, Francisco 227
Gramat **290**, 296
Gramont 413
Grand Brassac 105
Grand Launay, Château 204
Grand Roc caves 129
Grande Filolie, Château 119–20
Granges-sur-Lot 359
Graules 338
Graves, wine 232, 241, 250, 251, **254–5**
Gravette Samonac, Château 204
Graveyron 281
Grézels **332**, 334
Grisolles 416
Groléjac 157
grottes see caves
Grugnac, Château 140
Guillaume IX, duke of Aquitaine 24
Gujan-Mestras **279–80**, 282,
283, 284

hanggliding 74
Haut-Bertinerie, Château 204
Haut-Brion, Château 232
Haut-Médoc 260–4
Haute-Gironde 203–6
Haute-Serre, Château 328
Hautefage-la-Tour 361
Hautefort 90–1
health and emergencies 61, 73
Henry of Navarre (Henry IV of
France) 27, 297, 316, 345, 355,
370, 374, 396, 431
Henry Plantagenet (Henry II
of England) 24, 34, 144, 212
Herm, Château 123
history 19–30
horse-riding 75
hot-air balloons 74–5
hotels 67–8
Hourtin-Carcans, lake 273
Hourtin-Plage 273
houseboats 69

Hundred Years' War **25–6**, 30,
190–1, 213, 239, 309, 316, 320,
339, 350, 355, 364, 378

Igue de la Vierge 291
Ile aux Oiseaux 282
Ile de Patiras 265
Indian Forest Périgord 158
Ingres 399–400
Inquisition 24
Insectorama (Groléjac) 157
Institut de Tabac 187
insurance 61, 73
Internet access 73–4
Issan, Château 262
Issigeac **350**, 353

Jacobins 28
Jasmin, Jacques 366
Javerlhac 82
Joan of Arc 26
John XXII, Pope 315, 317, 320, 328
Joliet, Château 414
Jumilhac-le-Grand 89

kayaking 75

La Bachellerie 116
La Bastide Orliac, Château 367
La Brède, Château 251
La Chapelle St Robert 82
La Chapelle-Aubareil 121
La Chapelle-Faucher 87
La Fôret Magique 360
La Garenne 370–1
La Gonterie 83
La Grézette, Château 327, 328
La Haye, Château 266
La Hume 278–9
La Lande-de-Fronsac 202
La Madeleine 125
La Masse 335
La Mission-Haut-Brion, Château 232
La Mouthe caves 39, 115, 127
La Pannonie 290
La Pescalerie 304
La Prade, lake 258
La Réole **248–9**, 250
La Rivière 202
La Roque-Gageac **170–2**, 174
La Sauve 242
La Teste de Buch **278**, 282
La Tour-Blanche 106
La Truffière 175
Labarde 261
Labastide-Castel-Amouroux 377
Labastide-Murat **291**, 296
Labastide-du-Vert 335
Lacanau-Océan 273–4
Lacapelle-Biron **351**, 353
Lacapelle-Livron 388–9
Lacapelle-Marival **293**, 296

Lacave **152**, 153
Lachapelle 413
Lafaurie-Peyraguey, Château 253
Lafite-Rothschild, Château 50, 266
Lafrançaise **410**, 411
Laguépie **379**, 393
lakes
Cazaux 278
Etang de Cousseau 273
Hourtin-Carcans 273
La Prade 258
Lacanau 273
Laromet 246
Marais du Logit 271
Lalbenque **312**, 313
Lalinde **181**, 182
Lamagdelaine 311
Lamarque, Château 264
Lamontjoie 373
Lamonzie Monstratruc 182
Lamothe-Cadillac, Antoine de
245–6, 411, 414
Lamothe-Montravel 190
lamprey 48
Lanessan, Château 264
Langoa-Barton, Château 265
Langoiran **245**, 249
Langon 255, 259
language 453–5
Lanquais, Château 181
Lanton 281
Lantouy 308
Laplume **367**, 368
Laramière 312
Laromet, lake 246
Laroque-des-Arcs 310
Laroque-Timbaut **361**, 363
Larroque-Toirac 307
Lascaux 20, 37, 115, **118–19**, 121
Lassalle, Château 253
Lastournelles caves 356
Lasvaux 152
Latouille-Lentillac 141
Latour, Château 50, 265
Latour-Marliac 359
Lauzan, Château 381
Lauzerte 410–11
Lauzun **380–1**, 383
Lavergne 290
Layrac **366**, 368
Le Bastit 290–1
Le Bourg 293
Le Bugue-sur-Vézère 130–1
Le Buisson-de-Cadouin **177**, 179
Le Change **91**, 93
Le Conquil 124
Le Gurp 272
Le Lardin-St-Lazare 116
Le Mas-d'Agenais **376–7**, 378
Le Moulleau 278
Le Pen, Jean-Marie 79
Le Pian-Médoc 267

Le Pin 411–12
Le Porge 274
Le Roc, Château 414
Le Roy, Eugène 118
Le Sauvetat-du-Dropt 381
Le Teich 280
Le Verdon-sur-Mer 270–1
Le Vigan **338**, 341
Le-Temple-sur-Lot **358–9**, 360–1
Lège-Cap-Ferret **281**, 284
Lenoir, Marcel 392–3
Les Arques **336**, 341
Les Bouysses, Château 327
Les Combarelles 39, 128
Les Domaines de Certes 281
Les Etains Maigne 290
Les Eyzies-de-Tayac **126–8**, 129–30
Les Junies **335**, 340
Les Mai 166
Les Milandes, Château 173–4
Les Sentiers du Quercy 312
Lesparre-Médoc 267, 268
L'Herbe 281
Lherm 336
L'Hospital 293
L'Hospitalet **143**, 146, 325
Libourne **199–200**, 202
Lignan 239
Limargue 293
Limeuil **180**, 182
Limoges 79
Limogne-en-Quercy **312**, 313
Listrac **264**, 268
Livernon 292–3
Loisirs Préhistorique Le Conquil 124
Lomagne **411–13**, 416
Lorient-Sadirac 244
Losse, Château 121–2
Lot **285–342**, *286–7*, *326*
Lot-et-Garonne **344–84**, *344–5*
  tourist office 346
  Western **375–84**
Loubens, Château 247
Loubès-Bernac 383
Loubressac **140**, 141
Loudenne, Château 267
Loumède, Château 204
Loupiac 246
Lubersac 383
Lurçat, Jean 138
Lusignac 106
Lustrac 354
Luzech **329–30**, 331
Luzette 140

Macau 261
Magdalenian culture 114–15, 119, 121
Maison Forte de Reignac 125
Malagar 247
Malartrie, Château 171
Malle, Château 254
Malromé, Château 248
Manoir d'Eyrignac 165
Manzac-sur-Vern 111–12
maps 32–3
Marais du Conseiller 271
Marais du Logit 271
Marcabru 412
Marcamps 203
Marcayrac 328
Marcellus 377
Marcilhac-sur-Célé 206, **303–4**
Mareuil–sur-Belle 80–1
Margaux **261**, 267–8
  wine 50
Margaux, Château 261
markets 35–6, 48–9, 74, 446
Marmande 378–80
Marot, Clément 317
Marquay 128, 130
Marqueyssac, Château 172
Martel **151–2**, 153
Martignac 332
Mascaret, Association du 202
Masclat 338
Maucaillou, Château 263
Mauroux **333**, 334
Mauvezin-sur-Gupie 379
Maxange caves 177
Mazères 255
Medici, Catherine de' 180, 183
Médoc 241, 261, 263–4
Meilhan-sur-Garonne 377
Mellet, Château 110
Mendoce, Château 204
Menota, Château 253
Mercier, Château 204
Mercuès **321**, 327
Merlande 102
Merovingian dynasty 22–3, 422
Merveilles caves 143
Mesolithic cultures 20
Meylan 373
Meyronne 153
Mézin **372–3**, 374
Middle Ages 23–6, 212–14, 239
Milhac 338
Miramont-de-Guyenne **381**, 383, 384
Mistral, Frédéric 366
mobile phones 76
Moirax 366–7
Moissac 42, 388, **403–8**, **403–9**
Molières 178
Monbazillac 50, **187–8**, 189
Monbazillac, Château 187–8
Monbos 188
Moncalouc, Chai de 167
Monclar d'Agenais 359
Moncrabeau **373**, 375
Monestier 192
Monflanquin 253, **349**
Mongenan, Château 251
Monpazier **350**, 353
Monsec 82–3
Monségur **244**, 245
Monsempron-Libos **346**, 348
Mont-Real 111
Montagne 198
Montagrier 104–5
Montaigne, Château 192
Montaigne, Michel de **191**, 192, 435
Montaigu-de-Quercy **354**, 357
Montal, Château 138–9
Montalivet-les-Bains 272
Montauban 25, 385, **395–402**, *396*
Montayral 346
Montbrun **307**, 310
Montcabrier **340**, 342, 347
Montcaret 191–2
Montcléra 339
Montcuq 325–6
Montech 416
Montesquieu 367
Montesquieu, Baron de 251
Monteton **381–2**, 383
Montfaucon 291
Montferrand-du-Périgord 178
Montfort, Château 158
Montgesty 335
Montignac **117–18**, 120–1
Montjoi 362
Montmorency, Henri duke of 430
Montpezat-de-Quercy 323–4
Montpon-Ménestérol **111**, 112
Montricoux **392**, 393, 394
Moulis-en-Médoc 263
Mouton-Rothschild, Château 265–6
Murat, Joachim 291
Mussidan **110–11**, 112

Nairac, Château 253
Nantes, Edict of (1598) 27, 28
Nanthiat 89
Napoleon museum (Cendrieux) 132
national holidays 74
Naturel Régional du
    Périgord-Limousin 79
naturist resorts/beaches 272, 278
Neanderthals 20, 119
Nègrepelisse 394
Neolithic culture 20–1
Nérac 369–71
Néracais 369–71
Neuvic-sur-l'Isle 110
Nontron **81**, 83
Notre-Dame de
    Bonne-Espérance 110
Nozières, Château 329
Nuzéjouls 331

Occitan language 24, 26
Oppidum de Mursens 292
oysters 48, 269

Padirac 136, **141–3**, 147, 289
Pain-de-Sucre 205

Pair-non-Pair caves 203–4
Palmer, Château 263
Pape-Clément, Château 232
Papeterie de Vaux 90
parachuting 74
Parc Aquatique La Saule 150
Parc Archéologique de Beynac 173
Parc des Artigues 280
Parc de Causseyre 280
Parc Claude Quancard 280
Parc de Loisirs P'Arc-en-Ciel 351
Parc de la Moulette 280
Parc Naturel Régional des
Landes de Gascogne 280
Parc Ornithologique du Teich 280
Parnac 328
passports 60, 73
Pauillac 50, **265**, 267, 268
Pauliac 312
Payrac **338**, 341
Pays des Serres 361–3
Pech-Farrat 290
Pech-Merle 39, **304–5**
Pellegrue 244
Penne 392
Penne-d'Agenais 354–5
Périgord **77–112**, *78*
Noir 117, **165**
Northeast **87–93**, *88*
Périgord Vert **79–87**, *80*
where to stay and eat 82–3
Périgueux 79, **93–102**, *94–5*, 104
Pervillac 354
Pescadoires 330
Pessac-Léognan, wine 232
Pessec 232
Pestilhac 340
pétanque 75
Petit-Bersac 106–7
Petit-Palais-et-Cornemps 191
petrol stations 66
Peyrelevade dolmen 85
Peyzac-le-Moustier 124
Phare du Cap Ferret 282
Phare de Cordouan 271
Phare de Grave 271
pharmacies 73
phylloxera epidemic 29
Pic, Château 247
Pichon-Longueville, Château 265
Pierrefite 198
pigeonniers 32, 82, 410
Planegrèze 292
Plassac 205
Plassan, Château 245
Plazac 122
Podensac 251
Pointe de Grave 269–72
police 73
Polminhac, Château 310
Pomerol, wine 60, 197
Pompidou, Georges 307
Pons de Gontaut-Biron 351
Pontcirq 341
Port Bloc 271
Port de Gagnac 140
Port-Ste-Foy 193
Port-Ste-Marie 363
Portets 251
post offices 74
Pouchaud-Larquey, Château 243
Poudenas **373**, 374
Pradines 322, **327**
Prats-du-Périgord 167
Prayssac **330**, 331
Prayssas 362–3
Préchac 256
Preignac 254
Première Côtes de Bordeaux 247
Presque caves 139
Prieuré des Bénédictins
(La Réole) 248
Prieuré St-Pierre (Carennac) 148–9
Prignac-et-Marchamps 203–4
Protestantism 26–7, 395–6
Proumeyssac 130–1
Prudhomat-Castelnau 137
Pujols **356**, 357
Puy de Beaumont 106
Puy l'Evèque 327, **332**, 333, 334
Puy-d'Issolud 150–1, 288
Puy-Bardens, Château 247
Puyguilhem, Château 85
Puylaroque 389
Puymartin, Château 165
Puymirol **362**, 363
Pyla-Plage 278
Pyla-sur-Mer **278**, 283, 284

Quat'Sos, Château 249
Quercy **285–342**, *286*–7
Bas Quercy 385
Dordogne Quercynois
134–5, **136–41**
history 288
Quercy Blanc 323–6, *324*, 410
Quercyland 156
Queyrac 269
Quinsac 245
Quissac 292

Rabaud-Prommis, Château 253
Rabelais, François 435, 437
Rahoul, Château 255
rail travel 63–4, 65
Rampoux 339
Rastignac, Château 116
Rauzan 243
Razac-sur-l'Isle 103
Réalville **393**, 394
refuges 69
Résistance 30
restaurants 52, 73
menu reader 52–6
see also under individual places;
food and drink
Ribérac **105**, 111
Ricaud, Château 247
Richard the Lionheart 24, 33–4, 89,
172, 249, 281, 336–7, 354, 378, 424
Richemont, Château 85
Rieussec, Château 253–4
Rimons 245
Rions 245
Robillard, Château 203
Roc Branlant (Nontron) 81–2
Roc de Cazelle 128
Rocamadour 136, 142, **143–8**
Roland caves 325
Roland, lord of Blaye 206, 335
Romanesque architecture 41–4
Romans **21–2**, 79, 210, 225, 288, 313,
328, 364, 420–2
Romestaing 377
Roque St-Christophe 124
Roquecor 354
Roquetaillade, Château 258–9
Rosetta Stone 299
Rouffignac , 125
Rouilhac 325
roulottes 67
Roussillon, Château 321
Rudel, Jaufre 205
rugby 76

Sadillac 188
Sadirac 239
St-Amand-de-Coly **120**, 121
St-André-de-Cubzac **203–4**, 206
St-Antonin-Noble-Val
390–1, 393, 394
St-Astier 110
St-Aulaye 109
St-Avit **351**, 352
St-Avit Sénier 178
Ste-Bazeille 379
St-Céré **137–8**, 140, 141
St Chamarand 338
St-Christoly Médoc 268
St-Ciers-d'Abzac 201
St-Cirq-Lapopie **309–10**, 311
Ste-Croix-du-Mont 246
St-Cybranet 168
St-Cyprien **175**, 179
St-Denis-de-Pile 200
St-Emilion 42, **193–9**
wine 50, 195
St-Estèphe 266
St-Ferme 243–4
Ste-Foy-la-Grande 190
St Genès-de-Lombaud 240
St-Georges, Château 198
St Germain d'Esteuil 267
St-Germain-du-Bel-Air 336
St-Jean-de-Côle **87–8**, 92
St-Jean-Lespinasse 139

St-Julien (Domme) 167
St-Julien-Beychevelle 268
St-Julien-de-Lampon 157
St-Just 105
St-Laurent-et-Front 178
St-Léger de Balson 256
St-Léon-sur-Vézère **123–4**, 125
Ste-Livrade-sur-Lot **358**, 360
St-Loubès 202
St-Macaire **247**, 250
St-Martial-d'Artenset 111
St-Martial-Viveyrol **106**, 111
St-Martin-de-Mazeret 198
St-Martin-de-Sescas 248
St-Martin-de-Vers 292
St-Martin-le-Redon 333
St-Maurin 362
St-Médard **335**, 340
St-Mesmin 90
St-Michel-de-Montaigne **192**, 193
Ste-Mondane 157
St-Pierre-des-Liens 245
St-Pierre-de-Londres 379
St-Pierre-Toirac 306–7
St-Pompont 167
St-Privat-des-Prés 107
St-Projet 338, 388
Ste-Radegonde 193
St-Roch, Château 411–12
St-Sardos (Lot-et-Garonne) 359
St-Sardos (Tarn-et-Garonne) 415
St-Sardos-de-Laurenque 352
St-Sauveur 247

Ste-Nathalène 165
St-Nicolas (Blasimon) 242–3
St-Nicolas-de-la-Grave 411
St Pardon 201–2
St-Pardoux-de-Mareuil 81
St-Pardoux-Issac 383
St-Paul-de-Loubressac 325
St-Paul-Lizonne 106
St-Philippe d'Aiguille 191
St-Pierre-d'Aurillac 248
St-Pierre-Lafeuille 322
St-Saveur 147
St-Sernin 23–4
St-Seurin-de-Cardourne 267
St-Sulpice 303
St-Vincent Rive d'Olt 328
St-Yzans-de-Médoc 267
Salignac-Eyvignes 165
Salles, Géraud de 176
Sals 335
Salviac 339
Sanxet, Château 188
Sarlat-la-Canéda 158, **159–64**
Sauliac-sur-Célé 304
Saut de la Mounine 307
Sauteranne 109
Sauternes 60, 250, 252, **253–4**, 259
Sauve-Majeure 240–2
Sauveboeuf, Château 116
Sauveterre-de-Guyenne **242**, 244
Sauveterre-la-Lémance **347**, 348
Sauzet **330**, 331
Savignac-de-Duras 383
Savignac-Lédrier 90
Second World War 29–30
Ségala dolmen 290
Ségala region 140
Seigneurs de Pommiers 243
self-catering accommodation 68–9, 70
Sendat, Château 377
Séniergues 291
Septfonds 393
Sergeac **124**, 125
Sérignac-sur-Garonne 367
Sernin, St 431–2
Servat lavender distillery 325
Seurin, St 211–12
Simon de Montfort 24, 158, 172, 173, 351, 403, 413, 424–5
Siorac-en-Périgord **175**, 179
Siorac-de-Ribérac 110
Siran, Château 261
Site de Castel-Merle 124
Sorges **92**, 93
Souillac 42, 136, **154–6**
Soulac-sur-Mer **269**, 272
Soulomès 291
Soumensac 383
Sousceyrac **140**, 141
sports and activities 74–6
Suduiraut, Château 254

Talbot, Château 265
Tarn-et-Garonne **385–416**, *386–7*
Tauriac 150, 203
Taussat 283, 284
telephones 76
Terrasson-la-Villedieu **115–16**, 120
Teyjat 82
Thégra **290**, 296
Thémines 293
Thiviers 88
Thonac **122**, 125
time 76
tipping 76
Tiregand, Château 188
Tocane-St-Apre 104
toilets 76
Tombeboeuf 361
Tonneins **376**, 378
Toulouse 30, **417–50**, *418–19*
- Aérothèque 445
- bars and cafés 450
- Basilica of St-Sernin 432–4
- Blagnac 446
- Canal de Brienne 437
- cathedral of St-Etienne 441–2
- Chapelle des Carmélites 435
- Cité de l'Espace 446
- Cour Henri IV 431
- Cross of Languedoc 429–30
- Ecole des Beaux-Arts 439
- entertainment and nightlife 450
- Fondation Bemberg 438
- Galerie Municipale du Château-d'Eau 443
- gay bars 450
- getting around 421
- getting to and away from 421
- history 420–9
- Jardin Compans-Caffarelli 435
- Jardin des Plantes 440
- Jardin Royal 440
- Le Bazacle 437
- Le Mirail 444–5
- Left Bank 443–4
- Les Abbatoirs 444
- Les Jacobins 435–6
- markets and shopping 446–7
- museums
  - Archéologique 439
  - Augustins 442–3
  - Centre Municipal d'Affiche 444
  - Georges Labit 440
  - Histoire de la Médecine 444
  - Histoire Naturelle 440
  - Paul Dupuy 440–2
  - Resistance 440
  - St-Raymond 434
  - Vieux Toulouse 437–8
- Notre-Dame-du-Taur 431
- Notre-Dame-la-Dalbrade 439
- Notre-Dame-la-Daurade 439
- Palais des Académies 438
- Palais de Justice 440
- Pont Neuf 439
- Purpan 446
- Quai de Tounis 439
- Quartier Arnaud-Bernard 435
- Quartier du Jardin 440
- St Nicholas church 444
- St-Pierre-des-Cuisines 436–7
- St-Sernin 43
- sports and activities 447
- Théâtre du Capitole 431
- tourist information 446
- University 426, **435**
- Usine Clément Ader 445
- where to stay and eat 447–9
- wine bars 450

Toulouse, Counts of 423–4
Toulouse-Lautrec 258, 277
tour operators 70
Tour-de-Faure 311
Tour-des-Gendres, Château 187
tourist information 59–60
Tournon-d'Agenais **353–4**, 357
Tourtoirac 91
Touzac **333**, 334
trains 63–4, 65
travel 62–7

traveller's cheques 61
Trémolat **180**, 182
troglodyte villages 125
troubadours 412
truffles 46
Turcaud, Château 243

Upper Palaeolithic cultures
20, 38–9, 119
Uzeste 256–7

Vaillac 291
Valence-d'Agen 413
Vallons de Marennes 361
Valojouix 125
Vandals 22
Vanxains 109
Varaignes **82**, 83
Varen **390**, 393–4
Vayrac 150
Vayres **201**, 202
vegetarians 52
Vendoire 106
Verdelais 258
Verdus, Château 267
Vergt 103
Vers **310**, 311
Vertheuil 266
Vézac **172**, 174
Vézère valley 113–32, *114*
where to stay and eat 120–1
Vianne 374
Vieux-Mareuil **81**, 82
Villa et Thermes Gallo-Romains 246
Village du Bourant 132
Villandraut 212–13, **255–6**, 260
Villars 85
Villefranche-du-Périgord 168
Villefranche-du-Queyran 377
Villeneuve-de-Mézin 373
Villeneuve-sur-Lot 346, **355–6**,
357, 360
Villeréal 253, **349**
Villesèque 325
Virazeil, Château 379
visas 60
Vitrac 158

walking 67
Wars of Religion 27, 97, 337, 346,
378, 414–15
when to go 58
where to stay 67–70
see also under individual places
wine 21–2, 50–1
Barsac 251–3
Bergerac 50, 187–8
Bordeaux 50, 217, 241
Buzet 50, 375
Cahors 50, 328–9
Canon-Fronsac 201
classification system 50
Côteaux-de-Glanes 137
Côteaux-de-Quercy 389
Côtes-de-Blaye 204
Côtes-de-Bourg 204
wine (*cont'd*)
Côtes-de-Brulhois 367
Côtes-de-Duras 50, **382**
Côtes-de-Frontonnais 414
Côtes-du-Marmandais 379
Côtes-de-Quercy 50
Entre-Deux-Mers 241, **243**
fête du vin 50
Fronsac 201
Graves 232, 241, 250, 251, **254–5**
Haut-Médoc 263–4
Margaux 50
Médoc 241, 263–4
Monbazillac 50
Pauillac 50
Pessac-Léognan 232
Pomerol 60, 197
Première Côtes de Bordeaux 247
revolution 51
St-Emilion 50, 195
St-Sardos 415
Sauternes 60, 250, 252,
253–4, 259
Vin du Tsar 50

Xaintrailles, Château 374

youth hostels 69
Yquem, Château 50, 254

Zoo de La Teste 278

Authors' Acknowledgements

The authors would like to express their thanks to Bob, Carole, Nigel, Michele, Steve, Tessa, Michel, Jane, Jock, Sandie, Gordon, Chris, Carolyn, Pippa, Gerald, Lily, Bill, Morgan, Trish, Dany, Ken and Daniel for all their help and suggestions.

About the updater

Linda Rano has lived near Toulouse for nearly nine years with her husband and two children. She writes regularly for a number of publications, mainly on tourism and the property market in southwest France.

Cadogan Guides
2nd Floor, 233 High Holborn,
London WC1V 7DN
info@cadoganguides.co.uk
www.cadoganguides.com

The Globe Pequot Press
246 Goose Lane, PO Box 480, Guilford,
Connecticut 06437–0480

Cover and introduction photographs: Tim Mitchell
Maps © Cadogan Guides, drawn by
Maidenhead Cartographic Services Ltd

Art Director: Sarah Gardner
Managing Editor: Antonia Cunningham
Editor: Rhonda Carrier
Assistant Editor: Nicola Jessop
Proofreading: Elspeth Anderson
Indexing: Isobel McLean

Printed in Italy by Legoprint
A catalogue record for this book is available from the British Library
ISBN: 978-1-86011-354-3

Please help us to keep this guide up to date. We have done our best to ensure that the information in this guide is correct at the time of going to press. But places and facilities are constantly changing, and standards and prices in hotels and restaurants fluctuate. We would be delighted to receive any comments concerning existing entries or omissions. Authors of the best letters will receive a Cadogan Guide of their choice.

The Dordogne, Lot & Bordeaux touring atlas

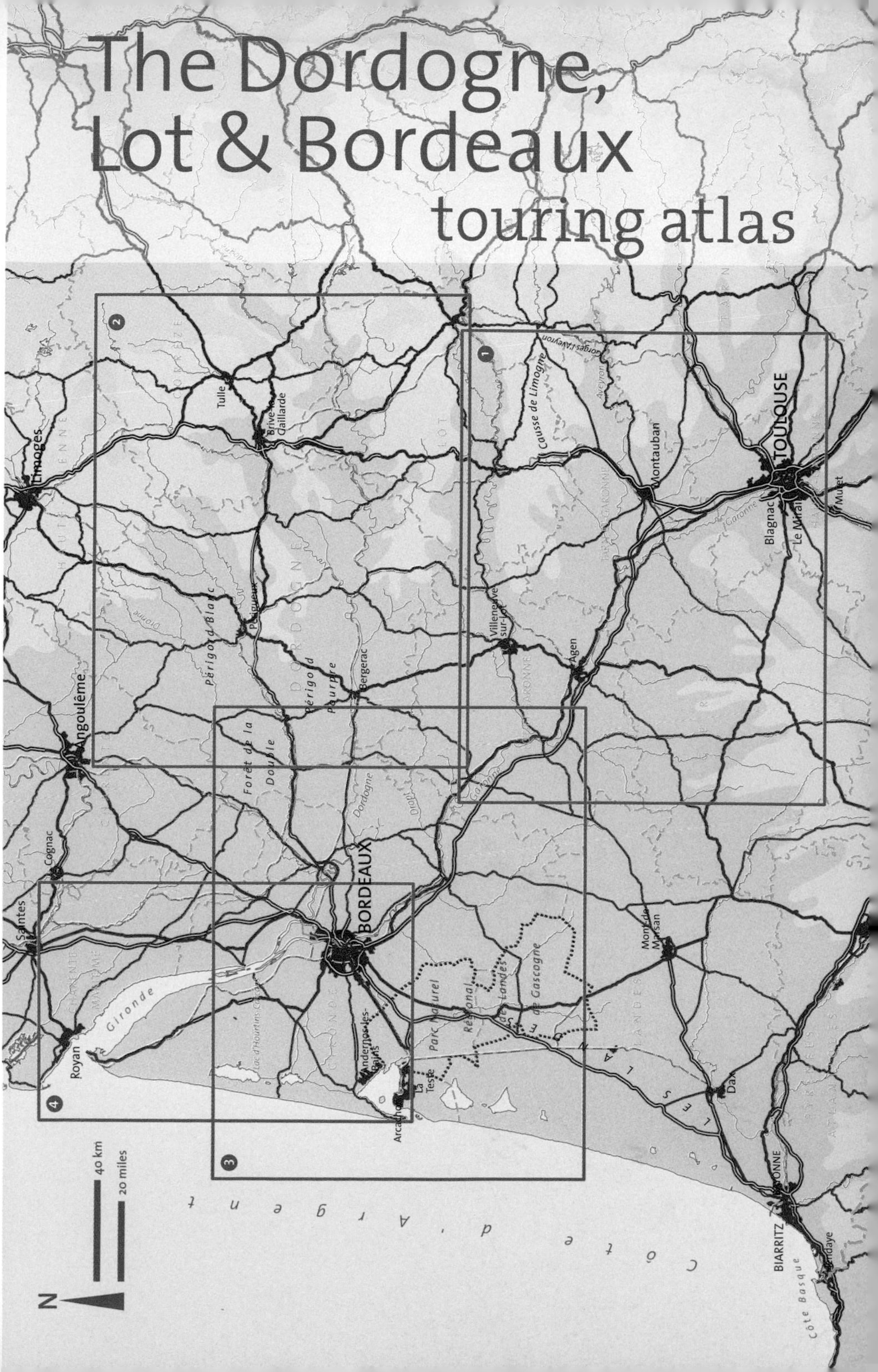

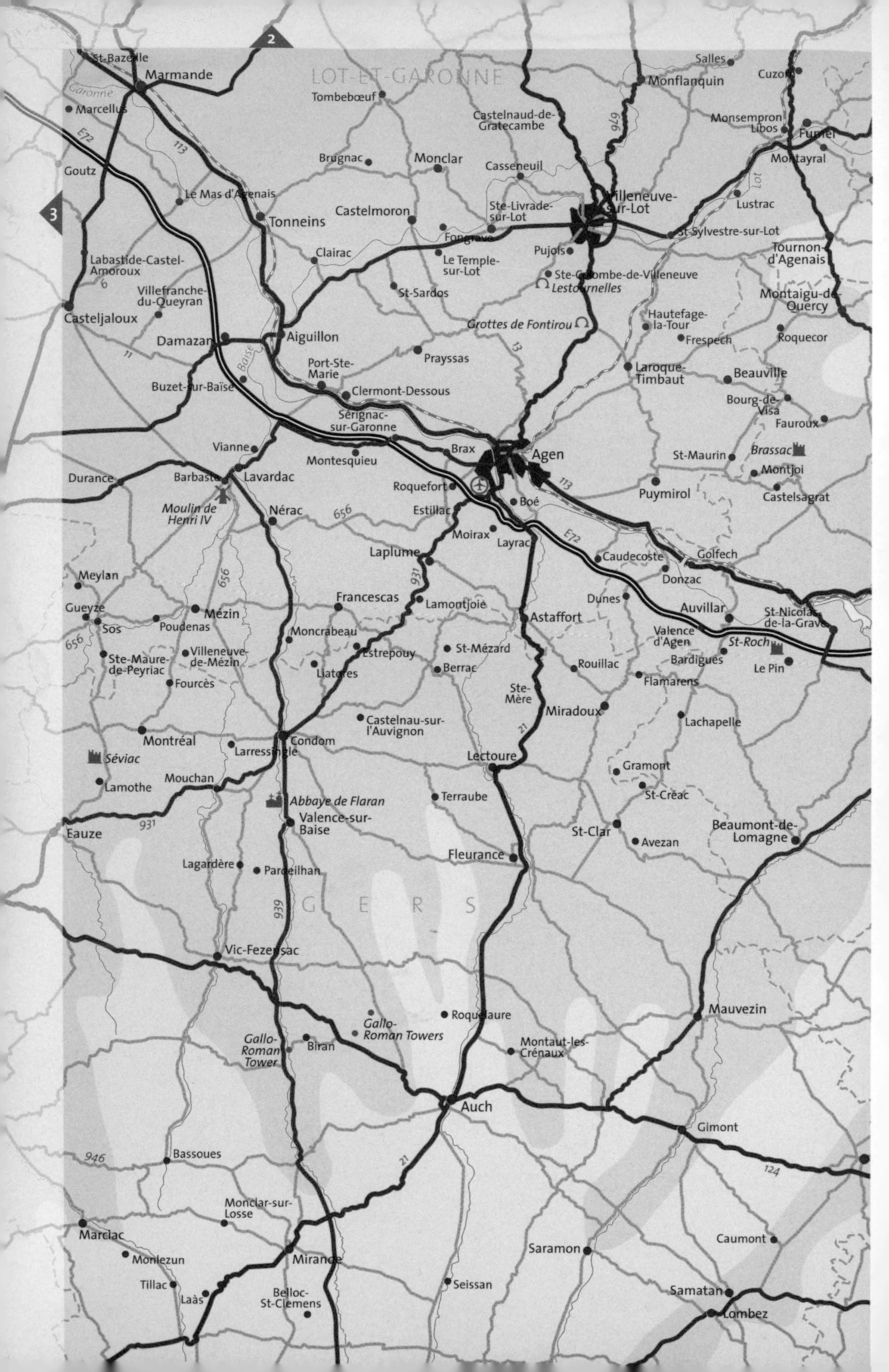

2
3
LOT-ET-GARONNE
GERS
St-Bazeille
Marmande
Garonne
Marcellus
E72
113
Goutz
Le Mas d'Agenais
Tonneins
Labastide-Castel-Amoroux
6
Villefranche-du-Queyran
Casteljaloux
Damazan
11
Baïse
Buzet-sur-Baïse
Tombebœuf
Brugnac
Monclar
Castelmoron
Clairac
Aiguillon
Port-Ste-Marie
Clermont-Dessous
Prayssas
St-Sardos
Le Temple-sur-Lot
Fongrave
Ste-Livrade-sur-Lot
Casseneuil
Castelnaud-de-Gratecambe
Monflanquin
976
Villeneuve-sur-Lot
Pujols
Ste-Colombe-de-Villeneuve
Lestournelles
Grottes de Fontirou
13
Salles
Cuzorn
Monsempron Libos
Fumel
Montayral
Lot
Lustrac
St-Sylvestre-sur-Lot
Tournon-d'Agenais
Montaigu-de-Quercy
Hautefage-la-Tour
Frespech
Roquecor
Laroque-Timbaut
Beauville
Bourg-de-Visa
Fauroux
Sérignac-sur-Garonne
Vianne
Montesquieu
Brax
Agen
Roquefort
Estillac
Boé
Moirax
Layrac
St-Maurin
Brassac
Montjoi
Puymirol
Castelsagrat
Durance
Barbaste
Lavardac
Moulin de Henri IV
Nérac
656
Laplume
931
Caudecoste
Golfech
Donzac
Dunes
Auvillar
St-Nicolas-de-la-Grave
Valence d'Agen
St-Roch
Bardigues
Le Pin
Meylan
Gueyze
Sos
Mézin
Poudenas
Ste-Maure-de-Peyriac
Villeneuve-de-Mézin
Fourcès
Francescas
Lamontjoie
Moncrabeau
Estrepouy
Liatores
St-Mézard
Berrac
Astaffort
Ste-Mère
Rouillac
Flamarens
Miradoux
Lachapelle
Castelnau-sur-l'Auvignon
Montréal
Séviac
Larressingle
Condom
Lamothe
Mouchan
Abbaye de Flaran
Valence-sur-Baise
Lectoure
21
Terraube
Gramont
St-Créac
St-Clar
Avezan
Beaumont-de-Lomagne
Eauze
Lagardère
Pardeilhan
Fleurance
939
Vic-Fezensac
Roquelaure
Gallo-Roman Towers
Gallo-Roman Tower
Biran
Montaut-les-Crénaux
Mauvezin
Auch
Gimont
124
946
Bassoues
Monclar-sur-Losse
Marciac
Monlezun
Mirande
Tillac
Laàs
Belloc-St-Clemens
Seissan
Saramon
Caumont
Samatan
Lombez

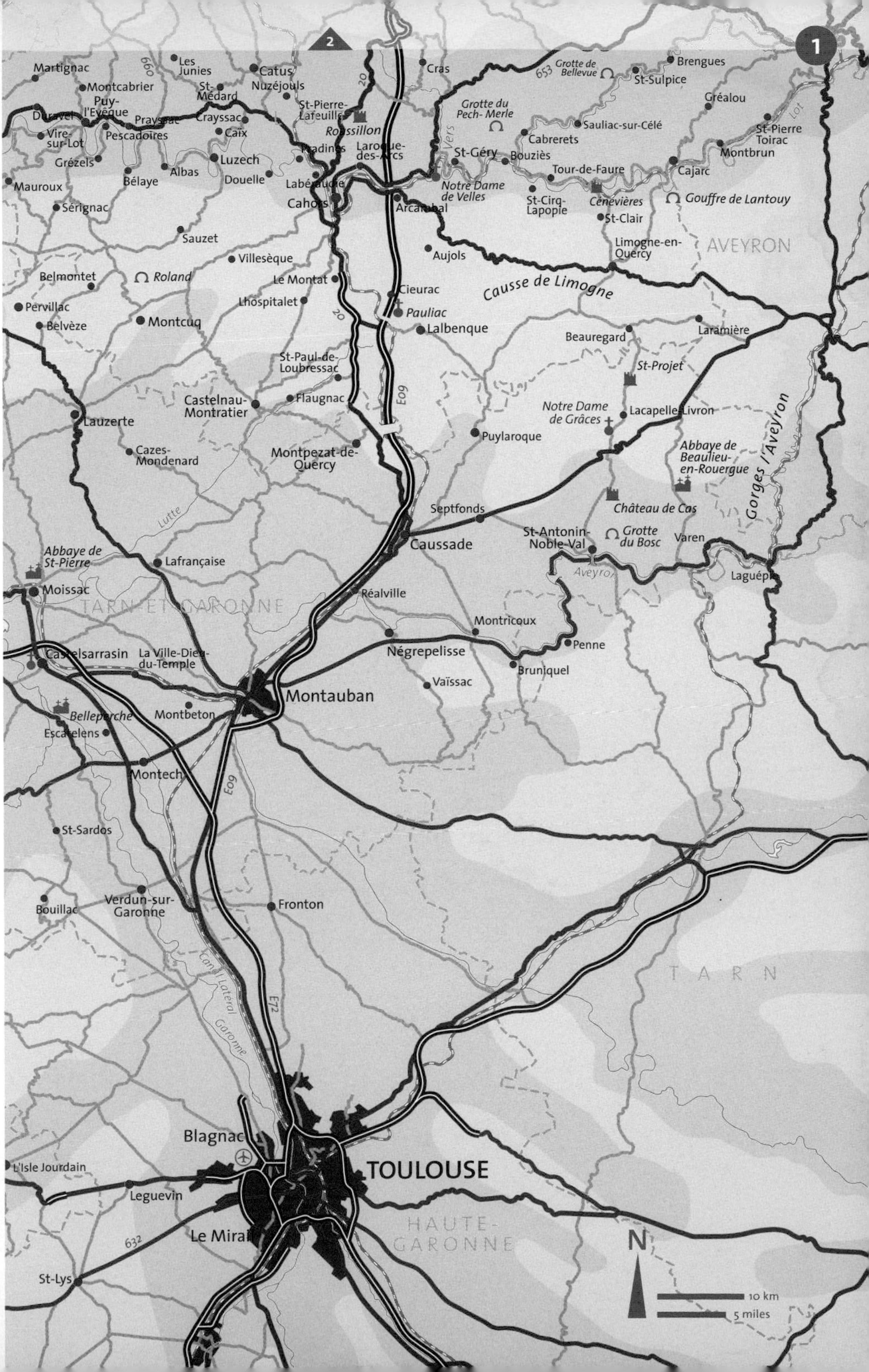

2
1
Martignac
Les Junies
Catus
Cras
Grotte de Bellevue
Brengues
St-Sulpice
Montcabrier
St-Médard
Nuzéjouls
Puy-l'Evêque
Duravel
Prayssac
Crayssac
St-Pierre-Lafeuille
Grotte du Pech-Merle
Gréalou
Vire-sur-Lot
Pescadoires
Caïx
Roussillon
Sauliac-sur-Célé
St-Pierre Toirac
Cabrerets
Lot
Grézels
Luzech
Pradines
Laroque-des-Arcs
Vers
St-Géry
Bouziès
Montbrun
Albas
Bélaye
Douelle
Tour-de-Faure
Cajarc
Mauroux
Labéraudie
Notre Dame de Velles
St-Cirq-Lapopie
Cénevières
Gouffre de Lantouy
Cahors
Arcambal
Sérignac
St-Clair
Sauzet
Limogne-en-Quercy
AVEYRON
Villesèque
Aujols
Belmontet
Roland
Le Montat
Causse de Limogne
Cieurac
Pervillac
Lhospitalet
Pauliac
Belvèze
Montcuq
Lalbenque
Beauregard
Laramière
St-Projet
St-Paul-de-Loubressac
Flaugnac
Castelnau-Montratier
Notre Dame de Grâces
Lacapelle-Livron
Lauzerte
Puylaroque
Abbaye de Beaulieu-en-Rouergue
Cazes-Mondenard
Montpezat-de-Quercy
Gorges l'Aveyron
Château de Cas
Septfonds
Lutte
St-Antonin-Noble-Val
Grotte du Bosc
Varen
Abbaye de St-Pierre
Caussade
Lafrançaise
Aveyron
Laguépie
Moissac
Réalville
TARN-ET-GARONNE
Montricoux
Castelsarrasin
La Ville-Dieu-du-Temple
Penne
Négrepelisse
Bruniquel
Vaïssac
Montauban
Belleperche
Montbeton
Escatelens
Montech
St-Sardos
Bouillac
Verdun-sur-Garonne
Fronton
Canal Lateral Garonne
TARN
Blagnac
L'Isle Jourdain
TOULOUSE
Leguevin
HAUTE-GARONNE
Le Mirail
St-Lys
N
10 km
5 miles

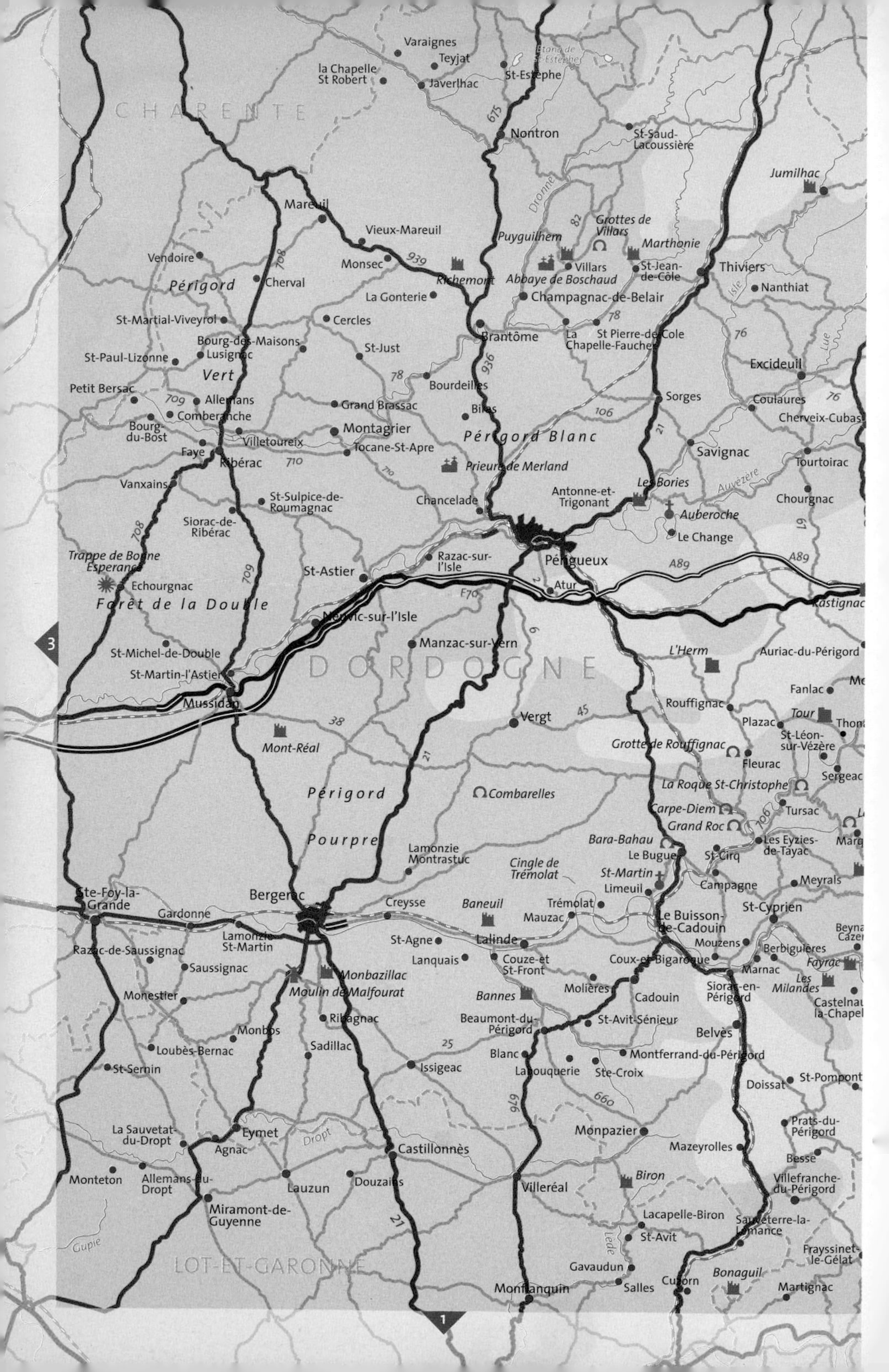

Varaignes
Teyjat
la Chapelle St Robert
Javerlhac
Etang de St-Estèphe
St-Estèphe
CHARENTE
675
Nontron
St-Saud-Lacoussière
Jumilhac
Dronne
Mareuil
Vieux-Mareuil
82
Grottes de Villars
Puyguilhem
Marthonie
Vendoire
708
Monsec
939
Villars
St-Jean-de-Côle
Thiviers
Périgord
Cherval
Richemont
Abbaye de Boschaud
Nanthiat
Isle
La Gonterie
Champagnac-de-Belair
St-Martial-Viveyrol
Cercles
78
Brantôme
La Chapelle-Faucher
St Pierre-de-Cole
76
Lue
Bourg-des-Maisons
St-Just
Lusignac
St-Paul-Lizonne
936
Excideuil
Vert
78
Bourdeilles
Petit Bersac
709
Allemans
Grand Brassac
Sorges
Coulaures
76
Comberanche
Bilas
106
Cherveix-Cubas
Bourg-du-Bost
Montagrier
21
Villetoureix
Périgord Blanc
Savignac
Faye
Tocane-St-Apre
Ribérac
710
Prieuré de Merland
Tourtoirac
Vanxains
710
Les Bories
Auvézère
Antonne-et-Trigonant
Chourgnac
St-Sulpice-de-Roumagnac
Chancelade
Auberoche
Siorac-de-Ribérac
19
708
Le Change
Trappe de Bonne Esperance
Razac-sur-l'Isle
Périgueux
A89
A89
St-Astier
709
Echourgnac
2
Atur
Forêt de la Double
F70
Rastignac
Neuvic-sur-l'Isle
6
3
Manzac-sur-Vern
L'Herm
Auriac-du-Périgord
St-Michel-de-Double
DORDOGNE
St-Martin-l'Astier
Fanlac
Mussidan
Rouffignac
Tour
Plazac
38
Vergt
45
St-Léon-sur-Vézère
Mont-Réal
Grotte de Rouffignac
Fleurac
Sergeac
21
La Roque St-Christophe
Périgord
Combarelles
Carpe-Diem
Tursac
706
Grand Roc
Pourpre
Bara-Bahau
Les Eyzies-de-Tayac
Lamonzie Montrastuc
Le Bugue
St-Cirq
Cingle de Trémolat
St-Martin
Meyrals
Limeuil
Campagne
Ste-Foy-la-Grande
Bergerac
Creysse
Baneuil
Trémolat
St-Cyprien
Gardonne
Mauzac
Le Buisson-de-Cadouin
Lamonzie St-Martin
St-Agne
Lalinde
Mouzens
Berbiguières
Razac-de-Saussignac
Lanquais
Couze-et St-Front
Coux-et-Bigaroque
Fayrac
Saussignac
Monbazillac
Marnac
Les Milandes
Moulin de Malfourat
Bannes
Molières
Siorac-en-Périgord
Monestier
Cadouin
Castelnau-la-Chapelle
Ribagnac
Beaumont-du-Périgord
St-Avit-Sénieur
Monbos
Belvès
Loubès-Bernac
Sadillac
25
Blanc
Montferrand-du-Périgord
St-Sernin
Issigeac
Labouquerie
Ste-Croix
Doissat
St-Pompont
676
660
La Sauvetat-du-Dropt
Eymet
Dropt
Monpazier
Prats-du-Périgord
Agnac
Castillonnès
Mazeyrolles
Besse
Monteton
Allemans-du-Dropt
Lauzun
Douzains
Biron
Villeréal
Villefranche-du-Périgord
Miramont-de-Guyenne
21
Lacapelle-Biron
Sauveterre-la-Lémance
Lède
St-Avit
Gupie
Frayssinet-le-Gélat
LOT-ET-GARONNE
Gavaudun
Bonaguil
Monflanquin
Salles
Cuzorn
Martignac
1